TAKING SIDES

Clashing Views in

Drugs  y

Selected, Edited, and with Introductions by

Raymond Goldberg
Vance-Granville Community College

Mc Graw Hill

Connect Learn Succeed™

TAKING SIDES: CLASHING VIEWS IN DRUGS AND SOCIETY, TENTH EDITION

Published by McGraw-Hill, a business unit of The McGraw-Hill Companies, Inc., 1221 Avenue
of the Americas, New York, NY 10020. Copyright © 2012 by The McGraw-Hill Companies, Inc.
All rights reserved. Previous edition(s) © 2010, 2008, and 2006. Printed in the United States
of America. No part of this publication may be reproduced or distributed in any form or by any
means, or stored in a database or retrieval system, without the prior written consent of The
McGraw-Hill Companies, Inc., including, but not limited to, in any network or other electronic
storage or transmission, or broadcast for distance learning.

Some ancillaries, including electronic and print components, may not be available to customers
outside the United States.

Taking Sides® is a registered trademark of the McGraw-Hill Companies, Inc.
Taking Sides is published by the **Contemporary Learning Series** group within the McGraw-Hill
Higher Education division.

This book is printed on acid-free paper.

1 2 3 4 5 6 7 8 9 0 DOC/DOC 1 0 9 8 7 6 5 4 3 2 1

MHID: 0-07-805022-7
ISBN: 978-0-07-805022-0
ISSN: 1094-7566

Managing Editor: *Larry Loeppke*
Senior Developmental Editor: *Jill Meloy*
Senior Permissions Coordinator: *Lenny J. Behnke*
Marketing Specialist: *Alice Link*
Lead Project Manager: *Jane Mohr*
Design Coordinator: *Brenda A. Rolwes*
Cover Graphics: *Rick D. Noel*
Buyer: *Nicole Baumgartner*
Media Project Manager: *Sridevi Palani*

Compositor: MPS Limited, a Macmillan Company
Cover Image: © Brand X Pictures RF

www.mhhe.com

Editors/Academic Advisory Board

Members of the Academic Advisory Board are instrumental in the final selection of articles for each edition of TAKING SIDES. Their review of articles for content, level, and appropriateness provides critical direction to the editors and staff. We think that you will find their careful consideration well reflected in this volume.

TAKING SIDES: Clashing Views in DRUGS AND SOCIETY

Tenth Edition

EDITORS

Raymond Goldberg
Vance-Granville Community College

ACADEMIC ADVISORY BOARD MEMBERS

Preface

One of the hallmarks of a democratic society is the freedom of its citizens to disagree. This is no more evident than on the topic of drugs. The purpose of this tenth edition *of Taking Sides: Clashing Views in Drugs and Society* is to introduce drug-related issues that (1) are pertinent to the reader and (2) have no clear resolution. In the area of drug abuse, there is much difference of opinion regarding prevention, causation, and treatment. For example, should drug abuse be prevented by increasing enforcement of drug laws or by making young people more aware of the potential dangers of drugs? Is drug abuse caused by heredity, personality characteristics, or environment? Is drug abuse a medical, legal, or social problem? Are the dangers of some drugs such as caffeine, salvia, and steroids overexaggerated? Should there be more stringent enforcement of marijuana use and underage drinking?

There are many implications to how the preceding questions are answered. If addiction to drugs is viewed as hereditary rather than as the result of flaws in one's character or personality, then a biological rather than a psychosocial approach to treatment may be pursued. If the consensus is that the prevention of drug abuse can be achieved by eliminating the availability of drugs, then more money and effort will be allocated for interdiction and law enforcement than education. If drug abuse is viewed as a legal problem, then prosecution and incarceration will be the goal. If drug abuse is identified as a medical problem, then abusers will be given treatment. However, if drug abuse is deemed a social problem, then energy will be directed at underlying social factors, such as poverty, unemployment, health care, and education. Not all of the issues have clear answers. One may favor increasing penalties for drug violations *and* improving treatment services. And, it is possible to view drug abuse as a medical *and* social *and* legal problem.

The issues debated in this volume deal with both legal and illegal drugs. Although society seems most interested in illegal drugs, it is quite pertinent to address issues related to legal drugs because they cause more deaths and disabilities. No one is untouched by drugs, and everybody is affected by drug use and abuse. Billions of tax dollars are channeled into the war on drugs. Thousands of people are treated for drug abuse, often at public expense. The drug trade spawns crime and violence. Medical treatment for illnesses and injuries resulting from drug use and abuse creates additional burdens to an already extended health care system. Babies born to mothers who used drugs while pregnant are entering schools, and teachers are expected to meet the educational needs of these children. Ritalin and other stimulants are prescribed to several million students to deal with their lack of attention in the classroom. Drug use by secondary students is rampant. The issues debated here are not whether drug abuse is a problem, but what should be done to rectify this problem.

Many of these issues have an immediate impact on the reader. For example, Issue 3, *Should the United States Drinking Age Remain at 21?* has an impact on anyone under age 21 who imbibes alcohol. Issue 14, *Should Smokeless Tobacco Be Promoted as an Alternative to Cigarette Smoking?* is relevant to individuals considering alternatives to cigarette smoking. Issue 10, *Should Drug Addicts Be Given Access to Free Needles?* is important because contaminated needles increase the risk of human immunodeficiency virus (HIV) syndrome. And the question *Should Laws Prohibiting Marijuana Use Be Relaxed?* (Issue 9) is relevant to the millions of people who smoke marijuana.

Organization of the book   In this tenth edition of *Taking Sides: Clashing Views in Drugs and Society*, there are 38 selections dealing with 19 issues. Each issue is preceded by an introduction and followed by a postscript. The purpose of the introduction is to provide some background information and to set the stage for the debate as it is argued in the YES and NO selections. The postscript summarizes the debate and challenges some of the ideas brought out in the two selections, which can enable the reader to see the issue in other ways. Included in the postscripts are additional suggested readings on the issue. Also, Internet site addresses (URLs) have been provided at the beginning of each unit, which should prove useful as starting points for further research. The issues, introductions, and postscripts are designed to stimulate readers to think about and achieve an informed view of some of the critical issues facing society today. At the back of the book is a list of all the contributors to this volume, which gives information on the physicians, lawyers, professors, pharmacists, authors, and policymakers whose views are debated here.

Taking Sides: Clashing Views in Drugs and Society is a tool to encourage critical thinking. In reading an issue and forming your own opinion, you should not feel confined to adopt one or the other of the positions presented. Some readers may see important points on both sides of an issue and may construct for themselves a new and creative approach. Such an approach might incorporate the best of both sides, or it might provide an entirely new vantage point for understanding.

Changes to this edition   This tenth edition represents a significant revision. Six of the 19 issues are new: *Should Salvia Be Banned?* (Issue 4); *Should Women Who Use Drugs Lose Custody of Their Children?* (Issue 5); *Should There Be More Regulation of Performance-Enhancing Drugs?* (Issue 7); *Are the Risks of Secondhand Smoke Overstated?* (Issue 8); *Should Laws Prohibiting Marijuana Use Be Relaxed?* (Issue 9); and *Should Drug Addicts Be Given Access to Free Needles?* (Issue 10). For 10 of the remaining 13 issues from the previous edition, one or both selections were replaced to reflect more current points of view.

A word to the instructor   To facilitate the use of Taking Sides, an *Instructor's Manual With Test Questions* (multiple-choice and essay) and a general guidebook called *Using Taking Sides in the Classroom*, which discusses methods and techniques for implementing the pro-con approach into any classroom setting, can be obtained from the publisher. An online version of *Using Taking Sides in the Classroom* and a correspondence service for Taking Sides adopters can be found at http://www.mhhe.com/cls. For students, we offer a field guide to analyzing argumentative essays called *Analyzing Controversy: An Introductory Guide*, with exercises and techniques to help them decipher genuine controversies.

Taking Sides: Clashing Views in Drugs and Society is only one title in the Taking Sides series. If you are interested in seeing the table of contents for any of the other titles, please visit the Taking Sides Web site at http://www.mhhe.com/cls.

Acknowledgments I am grateful to my students and colleagues, who did not hesitate to share their perceptions and to let me know what they liked and disliked about the ninth edition. Without the editorial staff at McGraw-Hill Contemporary Learning Series, this book would not exist. The insight and professional contributions have been most valuable. Their thoughtful perceptions and encouragement are most appreciated. In no small way can my family be thanked. I am grateful for their patience and support.

Raymond Goldberg
Dean
Health Sciences
Vance-Granville Community College
Henderson, NC

Contents In Brief

Contents

Herbert Kleber, the executive vice president of the Center on Addiction and Substance Abuse (CASA), and Joseph Califano, founder of CASA, maintain that drug laws should remain restrictive because legalization would result in increased use, especially by children, and legalization would not eliminate drug-related violence. The report from the U.S. Department of Health and Human Services points out that a number of factors affect drug use by young people. One of the most important factors is perception of risk. If young people perceive that drugs are harmful, they are less likely to engage in drug use. Other relevant factors include the perception of drug use by peers, religious beliefs, and parental involvement. Legal sanctions are not noted as a deterrent to drug use.

Because the trafficking of drugs represents a direct threat to national security, the U.S. State Department maintains that more effort is needed to interdict drugs coming into the United States. Better cooperation with countries in Latin America, the Caribbean, Africa, and Asia, where drugs are grown and exported, is essential. Ethan Nadelmann, the executive director of the Drug Policy Alliance, contends that attempts to stem the flow of drugs are futile and that it is unrealistic to believe that the world can be made free of drugs. Nadelmann points out that global production is about the same as it was ten years earlier and that cocaine and heroin are purer and cheaper because producers have become more efficient.

Carla Main contends that the drinking age should remain at 21. Underage drinking has been linked to sexual assaults, violent behavior, unprotected consensual sex, and numerous automobile accidents. Although one can serve in the military before age 21, alcohol use among that age group contributes to poor morale and productivity according to Main. Rather than tolerating underage drinking, more effort should be placed on enforcing underage drinking laws. Judith McMullen, a law professor at Marquette University, argues that laws prohibiting underage drinking have been ineffective. Young adults between the ages of 18 and 21 who do not live at home have opportunities to drink alcohol without parental interference. In addition, this same age group has other legal rights, such as the right to marry, drive a car, or join the military. Enforcement of underage drinking laws, says McMullen, is destined for failure.

Pharmacists Pearl Nyi and others maintain that *Salvia divinorum* is a potentially abusive drug that is banned in more than a dozen states. Often described as the next "marijuana," salvia is widely promoted on the Internet despite the fact that its adverse effects have not been thoroughly studied. In their research, Nyi and others found that salvia produces hallucinogenic effects. Author Jacob Sullum contends that salvia has been unfairly demonized although it has been used for centuries for healing and spiritual reasons. One factor contributing to salvia's appeal, states Sullum, is the negative press attributed to it. Historically, many drugs become more popular when they are highly criticized in the press. Salvia can result in adverse effects but that the drug has been unfairly demonized. The stories of the horrific effects of salvia have been difficult to substantiate, says Sullum.

Mark Testa, a professor of social work at the University of North Carolina, and Brenda Smith, a professor in the School of Social Work at the University of Alabama maintain that drug treatment to prevent child maltreatment is not especially effective. They argue that it is in the best interest of children to remove them from environments where drugs are used. Mark Testa and Brenda Smith indicate that the threat of losing custody of children acts as a deterrent to drug use. Fordham University professor Jeanne Flavin and attorney Lynn Paltrow of the National Advocates for Pregnant Women argue that the stigma of drug use may result in the avoidance of treatment and prenatal care. They assert that the prosecution of drug users is unfair because poor women are more likely to be the targets of such prosecution. To enable pregnant women who use drugs to receive perinatal care, it is necessary to define their drug use as a health problem rather than as a legal problem.

Because there are biological and chemical changes in the brain following drug abuse, the National Institute on Drug Abuse (NIDA) claims that drug addiction is a disease of the brain. One may initially use drugs voluntarily, but addiction occurs after repeated drug use. NIDA acknowledges that environment plays a role in the development of drug addiction, but one's genes play a major role as well. Writer Gene M. Heyman maintains that drug addiction, including alcoholism, runs in families. There is no doubt that genes are hereditary. However, Heyman argues that behaviors are not hereditary. Whether an individual engages in drug use or abuse is a choice made by the individual. Claiming that drug addiction is a disease removes the stigma of drug addiction because one can assert that it is the disease that causes one's addiction, not one's behavior.

University of Texas kinesiology professors Jan Todd and Terry Todd, who were competitive powerlifters, are concerned about the impact of performance-enhancing drugs. One of their biggest concerns is that competitors who do not use performance-enhancing drugs will feel compelled to use them to keep up with other competitors. They advocate for more drug testing because of the safety issues related to performance-enhancing drugs and to ensure that competition is fair. In her book, author Laura Egendorf cites individuals who feel that athletes are aware of the risks of taking steroids and other performance-enhancing drugs. Competition and the desire to succeed drive individuals to improve their athletic performance. Allowing steroid use would essentially level the playing field for all athletes. In addition, some experts believe that the negative consequences are exaggerated.

that the number of syringe exchange programs will continue to proliferate. The group Drug Free Australia, which opposes syringe exchange programs, believes that providing free syringes gives the wrong message. Drugs like heroin and cocaine are illegal and drug abusers should not be allowed to continue their abuse by being provided with free syringes. Drug Free Australia also questions the validity of those statements supporting the value of syringe exchange programs.

Paul Antony, the chief medical officer for the Pharmaceutical Research and Manufacturers of America (PhRMA) contends that the direct advertising of prescription drugs to consumers results in better communication between patients and their doctors. Furthermore, patients take a more proactive role in their own health care. Advertising prescription drugs fills an educational purpose, says Paul Antony. Peter Lurie, a physician who is the deputy director of the Health Research Group at Public Citizen in Washington, D.C., argues that the direct advertising of prescription drugs leads to more patients asking for drugs that are unnecessary or inappropriate. In addition, many prescription drug advertisements are misleading and a means for drug manufacturers to encourage and pressure physicians to prescribe drugs.

UNIT 3   DRUG PREVENTION AND TREATMENT   305

Professors John Britton and Richard Edwards advocate the use of smokeless tobacco as an alternative to tobacco smoking because the harm from tobacco is rooted more in the act of smoking than from nicotine. They recognize that smokeless tobacco carries certain risks, although they note that nicotine is neither a known carcinogen nor does it reduce birthweight as much as tobacco smoking. Adrienne Mejia and Pamela Ling maintain that tobacco manufacturers are marketing smokeless tobacco products as a way to counter smoke-free laws at the workplace and in bars and restaurants. They feel that smokeless products are especially targeted toward younger smokers. Mejia and Ling argue that smokeless tobacco is not a healthy alternative to smoked tobacco.

Markus Heilig, Clinical Director of the National Institute on Alcohol Abuse and Alcoholism, argues that molecular changes in the brain result in positive reinforcement from alcohol. Heilig notes that alcoholism has a behavioral component, but certain genes may be responsible for individuals who abuse alcohol despite its adverse consequences. Grazyna Zajdow, a lecturer in sociology at Deakin University, maintains that the concept of alcoholism results from a social construct of what it means to be alcoholic. Because alcoholism is a social stigma, it is viewed as a disease rather than as a condition caused by personal and existential pain. Environmental conditions, especially consumerism, says Zajdow, are the root cause of alcoholism.

Peter Cohen argues that the federal argument has thwarted attempts to study the medicinal benefits of marijuana. Cohen refers to scientific studies in which marijuana has shown to be safe and effective in controlling nausea, relieving spasticity caused by multiple sclerosis, ameliorating certain types of pain, and reducing weight loss associated with AIDS. The Drug Enforcement Administration (DEA) states that marijuana has not been proven to have medical utility. The DEA cites the positions of the American Medical Association, the American Cancer Society, the American Academy of Pediatrics, and the National Multiple Sclerosis Society to support its position. The DEA feels that any benefits of medicinal marijuana are outweighed by its drawbacks.

Susanne James-Burdumy of Mathematica Policy Research and her colleagues report that schools which implemented mandatory random drug testing had less substance use. Moreover, random drug testing did not have a negative impact on the number of students engaging in school activities. Likewise, drug testing did not affect how students feel about their schools. Jennifer Kern and associates maintain that drug testing is ineffective and that the threat of drug testing may dissuade students from participating in extracurricular activities. Moreover, drug testing is costly, it may make schools susceptible to litigation, and it undermines relationships of trust between students and teachers. Drug testing, according to Jennifer Kern, does not effectively identify students who may have serious drug problems.

The National Institute on Drug Abuse report acknowledges that drug addiction is difficult to overcome but that treatment can be effective and works best when individuals are committed to remain in treatment for an extended time. Drug treatment experts Robert Hubbard, D. Dwayne Simpson, and George Woody indicate that there is a need to establish scientific evidence for treatment to achieve desirable outcomes, and there is no clear consensus on what constitutes substance abuse treatment.

Issue 19.   Should Schools Enforce a Zero Tolerance Drug Policy?   419

Tracy J. Evans-Whipp, of the Murdoch Children's Research Institute in Melbourne, Australia, and her colleagues maintain that an abstinence message coupled with harsh penalties is more effective at reducing drug use than a message aimed at minimizing the harms of drugs. They contend that an abstinence message is clear and that a harm reduction message may give a mixed message. Rodney Skager, formerly a professor at UCLA, argues that a zero tolerance drug policy does not change drug-taking behavior among young people. Instead of merely punishing drug offenders, Skager suggests that effective drug education is needed. Instances in which drug use presents a significant problem for the user may require intervention and treatment. Again, zero tolerance does very little to rectify behavior.

Correlation Guide

The *Taking Sides* series presents current issues in a debate-style format designed to stimulate student interest and develop critical-thinking skills. Each issue is thoughtfully framed with an issue summary, an issue introduction, and a postscript. The pro and con essays—selected for their liveliness and substance—represent the arguments of leading scholars and commentators in their fields.

Taking Sides: Clashing Views in Drugs and Society, 10/e is an easy-to-use reader that presents issues on important topics such as *the drinking age, drug addiction, secondhand smoke in the workplace,* and *caffeine and health.* For more information on *Taking Sides* and other *McGraw-Hill Contemporary Learning Series titles,* visit http://www.mhhe.com/cls.

This convenient guide matches the issues in **Taking Sides: Clashing Views in Drugs and Society, 10/e** with the corresponding chapters in three of our best-selling McGraw-Hill Health textbooks by Hart et al., Fields, and Goode.

Taking Sides: Clashing Views in Drugs and Society, 10/e	Drugs, Society, and Human Behavior, 14/e by Hart et al.	Drugs in Perspective, 7/e by Fields	Drugs in American Society, 8/e by Goode
Issue 1: Should Laws Against Drug Use Remain Restrictive?	**Chapter 2:** Drug Use as a Social Problem **Chapter 3:** Drug Products and Their Regulations **Chapter 17:** Preventing Substance Abuse	**Chapter 1:** Putting Drugs in Perspective **Chapter 8:** Prevention of Substance-Abuse Problems **Chapter 11:** Alcohol/Drug Recovery Treatment and Relapse Prevention	**Chapter 3:** Drugs in the News Media **Chapter 12:** Controlling Drug Use: The Historical Context **Chapter 15:** Law Enforcement, Drug Courts, Drug Treatment **Chapter 16:** Legalization, Decriminalization, and Harm Reduction
Issue 2: Should the United States Put More Emphasis on Stopping the Importation of Drugs?	**Chapter 3:** Drug Products and Their Regulations	**Chapter 1:** Putting Drugs in Perspective	**Chapter 14:** The Illicit Drug Industry **Chapter 15:** Law Enforcement, Drug Courts, Drug Treatment **Chapter 16:** Legalization, Decriminalization, and Harm Reduction
Issue 3: Should the United States Drinking Age Remain at 21?	**Chapter 9:** Alcohol **Chapter 17:** Preventing Substance Abuse	**Chapter 1:** Putting Drugs in Perspective **Chapter 8:** Prevention of Substance-Abuse Problems **Chapter 12:** Alcohol/Drug Recovery Treatment and Relapse Prevention	**Chapter 7:** Alcohol and Tobacco **Chapter 12:** Controlling Drug Use: The Historical Context **Chapter 16:** Legalization, Decriminalization, and Harm Reduction

Taking Sides: Clashing Views in Drugs and Society, 10/e	Drugs, Society, and Human Behavior, 14/e by Hart et al.	Drugs in Perspective, 7/e by Fields	Drugs in American Society, 8/e by Goode
Issue 4: Should Salvia Be Banned?	**Chapter 14:** Hallucinogens		
Issue 5: Should Women Who Use Drugs Lose Custody of Their Children?	**Chapter 2:** Drug Use as a Social Problem **Chapter 9:** Alcohol **Chapter 10:** Tobacco **Chapter 17:** Preventing Substance Abuse	**Chapter 3:** Drug-Specific Information **Chapter 9:** Change, Motivation, and Intervention for Substance-Abuse Problems	**Chapter 1:** Drug Use: A Sociological Perspective **Chapter 12:** Controlling Drug Use: The Historical Context **Chapter 15:** Law Enforcement, Drug Courts, Drug Treatment
Issue 6: Is Drug Addiction a Brain Disease?	**Chapter 2:** Drug Use as a Social Problem **Chapter 4:** The Nervous System **Chapter 5:** The Actions of Drugs **Chapter 9:** Alcohol **Chapter 18:** Treating Substance Abuse and Dependence	**Chapter 2:** Why Do People Abuse Drugs? **Chapter 7:** Growing Up in an Alcoholic Family System **Chapter 12:** Alcohol/Drug Recovery Treatment and Relapse Prevention	**Chapter 2:** Drug Use: A Pharmacological Perspective **Chapter 6:** Theories of Drug Use
Issue 7: Should There Be More Regulation of Performance-Enhancing Drugs?	**Chapter 3:** Drug Products and Their Regulations **Chapter 16:** Performance-Enhancing Drugs	**Chapter 3:** Drug-Specific Information **Chapter 9:** Change, Motivation, and Intervention for Substance-Abuse Problems	**Chapter 12:** Controlling Drug Use: The Historical Context **Chapter 16:** Legalization, Decriminalization, and Harm Reduction
Issue 8: Are the Risks of Secondhand Smoke Overstated?	**Chapter 3:** Drug Products and Their Regulations **Chapter 10:** Tobacco	**Chapter 1:** Putting Drugs in Perspective **Chapter 3:** Drug-Specific Information	**Chapter 7:** Alcohol and Tobacco
Issue 9: Should Laws Prohibiting Marijuana Use Be Relaxed?	**Chapter 3:** Drug Products and Their Regulations **Chapter 5:** The Actions of Drugs **Chapter 15:** Marijuana	**Chapter 1:** Putting Drugs in Perspective **Chapter 3:** Drug-Specific Information **Chapter 11:** Alcohol/Drug Recovery Treatment and Relapse Prevention	**Chapter 1:** Drug Use: A Sociological Perspective **Chapter 8:** Marijuana, LSD, and Club Drugs **Chapter 12:** Controlling Drug Use: The Historical Context **Chapter 15:** Law Enforcement, Drug Courts, Drug Treatment **Chapter 16:** Legalization, Decriminalization, and Harm Reduction
Issue 10: Should Drug Addicts Be Given Access to Free Needles?	**Chapter 2:** Drug Use as a Social Problem **Chapter 5:** The Actions of Drugs **Chapter 13:** Opioids	**Chapter 11:** Alcohol/Drug Recovery Treatment and Relapse Prevention	**Chapter 10:** Heroin and the Narcotics **Chapter 16:** Legalization, Decriminalization, and Harm Reduction

(Continued)

Taking Sides: Clashing Views in Drugs and Society, 10/e	Drugs, Society, and Human Behavior, 14/e by Hart et al.	Drugs in Perspective, 7/e by Fields	Drugs in American Society, 8/e by Goode
Issue 11: Is Caffeine a Health Risk?	**Chapter 11:** Caffeine		**Chapter 4:** How Do We Know It's True? Methods of Research
Issue 12: Should School-Age Children with Attention Deficit/Hyperactivity Disorder (ADHD) Be Treated with Ritalin and Other Stimulants?	**Chapter 5:** The Actions of Drugs **Chapter 6:** Stimulants **Chapter 8:** Medication for Mental Disorders	**Chapter 4:** Definitions of Substance Abuse, Dependence, and Addiction **Chapter 10:** Disorders Co-occurring with Substance Abuse	**Chapter 9:** Stimulants: Amphetamine, Methamphetamine, Cocaine, and Crack
Issue 13: Do Consumers Benefit When Prescription Drugs Are Advertised?	**Chapter 3:** Drug Products and Their Regulations **Chapter 7:** Depressants and Inhalants		
Issue 14: Should Smokeless Tobacco Be Promoted as an Alternative to Cigarette Smoking?	**Chapter 5:** The Actions of Drugs **Chapter 10:** Tobacco	**Chapter 3:** Drug-Specific Information	**Chapter 7:** Alcohol and Tobacco
Issue 15: Is Alcoholism Hereditary?	**Chapter 2:** Drug Use as a Social Problem **Chapter 9:** Alcohol	**Chapter 5:** Substance Abuse and Family Systems **Chapter 7:** Growing Up in an Alcoholic Family System	**Chapter 6:** Theories of Drug Use **Chapter 7:** Alcohol and Tobacco
Issue 16: Should Marijuana Be Approved For Medical Use?	**Chapter 5:** The Actions of Drugs **Chapter 8:** Medication for Mental Disorders **Chapter 15:** Marijuana	**Chapter 1:** Putting Drugs in Perspective **Chapter 3:** Drug-Specific Information **Chapter 12:** Alcohol/Drug Recovery Treatment and Relapse Prevention	**Chapter 1:** Drug Use: A Sociological Perspective **Chapter 8:** Marijuana, LSD, and Club Drugs **Chapter 12:** Controlling Drug Use: The Historical Context **Chapter 15:** Law Enforcement, Drug Courts, Drug Treatment
Issue 17: Should Schools Drug Test Students?	**Chapter 17:** Preventing Substance Abuse	**Chapter 8:** Prevention of Substance Abuse Problems	
Issue 18: Does Drug Abuse Treatment Work?	**Chapter 17:** Preventing Substance Abuse	**Chapter 8:** Prevention of Substance Abuse Problems	**Chapter 15:** Law Enforcement, Drug Courts, Drug Treatment
Issue 19: Should Schools Enforce a Zero Tolerance Drug Policy?	**Chapter 17:** Preventing Substance Abuse	**Chapter 8:** Prevention of Substance Abuse Problems	**Chapter 12:** Controlling Drug Use: The Historical Context

Topic Guide

This topic guide suggests how the selections in this book relate to the subjects covered in your course. You may want to use the topics listed on these pages to search the Web more easily.

On the following pages, a number of Web sites have been gathered specifically for this book. They are arranged to reflect the units of this Taking Sides edition. You can link to these sites by going to http://www.mhhe.com/cls.

All the articles that relate to each topic are listed below the bold-faced term.

(Continued)

Introduction

Drugs: Divergent Views

An Overview of the Problem

The topic of drugs remains controversial in today's society. Very few topics generate as much debate and concern as drugs. Drug use, either directly or indirectly, affects everyone. Drugs and issues related to drugs are evident in every aspect of life. There is much dismay that drug use and abuse cause many of the problems that plague society. Individuals, families, and communities are adversely affected by drug abuse, and many people wonder if the very fabric of society will continue to experience decay because of drugs. The news media are replete with horrific stories about people under the influence of drugs committing crimes or perpetrating violence against others, of people who die senselessly, of men and women who compromise themselves for drugs, and of women who deliver babies that are addicted or impaired by drugs. In some countries, drug cartels have a major impact on government. One does not need to be a drug user to experience its effects.

From conception until death, almost everyone is touched by drug use. Some college students take stimulants so that they can stay up late to write a term paper or lose a few pounds. In many instances, stimulants such as Ritalin and others are prescribed for children so that they can learn or behave better in school. Many teenagers take drugs because they want to be accepted by their friends or use drugs to cope with daily stresses and increasing responsibilities. For many people, young and old, the elixir for relaxation may be sipped, swallowed, smoked, or sniffed. Some people who live in poverty-stricken conditions anesthetize themselves with drugs as a way to escape consciously from their unpleasant environment. On the other hand, some individuals who seem to have everything immerse themselves in drugs, possibly out of boredom, emptiness in their lives, or simply to find the next thrill. To contend with the ailments that accompany getting older, the elderly often rely on drugs. Many people use drugs to confront their pains, problems, frustrations, and disappointments. Others take drugs simply because they like their effects or they take drugs due to curiosity. Some people just want to experience more happiness in their lives.

Background on Drugs

Despite one's feelings about drug use, legal and illegal drugs are an integral part of society. The popularity of various drugs rises and falls with the times. For example, according to annual surveys of 8th-, 10th-, and 12th-grade students in the United States, the use of LSD, marijuana, cocaine, and methamphetamines declined during the first decade in 2000 (Johnston, O'Malley, Bachman, and Schulenberg, 2009). During the same period, alcohol consumption, drunkenness, and tobacco use also showed declines. The illegal use of prescription drugs have increased in recent years. Ecstasy and other "club drugs" such as ketamine (Special K) and GHB remain popular with many young people. Another drug that has appeared in recent years is *Salvia divinorum*. Issue 4 looks at the issue of whether or not salvia should be banned.

Understanding the history and role of drugs in society is critical to our ability to address drug-related problems. Drugs have been used throughout human history. Alcohol played a significant role in the early history of the United States. According to Lee (1963), for example, the Pilgrims landed at Plymouth Rock because they ran out of beer. Marijuana use dates back nearly 5000 years, when the Chinese Emperor Shen Nung prescribed it for medical ailments like malaria, gout, rheumatism, and gas pains. Ironically, 5000 years after marijuana was first used medicinally, its medical benefits remain a matter of contention. Some issues simply refuse to go away. Hallucinogens have existed since the beginning of humankind and have been used for a variety of reasons. For example, hallucinogens were used to enhance beauty or to cast spells on enemies. About 150 of the estimated 500,000 different plant species have been used for hallucinogenic purposes (Schultes and Hofmann, 1979).

Opium, from which narcotics are derived, was written about extensively by the ancient Greeks and Romans; opium is even referred to in Homer's *Odyssey* (circa 1000 B.C.). In the Arab world, opium and hashish were widely used (primarily because alcohol was forbidden). The Arabs were introduced to opium through their trading in India and China. Arab physician Avicenna (A.D. 1000) wrote an extremely complete medical textbook in which he describes the benefits of opium. Ironically, Avicenna died from an overdose of opium and wine. Eventually, opium played a central role in a war between China and the British government.

Caffeine remains the most commonly consumed drug throughout the world. It is estimated that more than 9 out of every 10 Americans drink beverages that include caffeine. Coffee dates back to A.D. 900, when, to stay awake during lengthy religious vigils, Muslims in Arabia consumed coffee. However, coffee was later condemned because the Koran, the holy book of Islam, described coffee as an intoxicant (Brecher, 1972). Drinking coffee became a popular activity in Europe, although it was banned for a short time. In the mid-1600s, coffeehouses were prime locations for men to converse, relax, and conduct business. Medical benefits were associated with coffee, although England's King Charles II and English physicians tried to prohibit its use. Many claims have been made regarding the safety of caffeine. A Swedish study found that three to five cups of coffee daily may reduce the development of dementia (Kesner, 2009) while another study reported erratic behavior following caffeine use (Lam, Mites, and von Nyssen, 2009). Issue 11 discusses whether or not caffeine consumption is a health risk.

Coffeehouses served as places of learning. For a one-cent cup of coffee, one could listen to well-known literary and political leaders (Meyer, 1954). Lloyd's of London, the famous insurance company, started around 1700 from Edward Lloyd's coffeehouse. However, not everyone was pleased with these "penny universities," as they were called. In 1674, in response to the countless hours men spent at the coffeehouses, a group of women published a pamphlet titled *The Women's Petition Against Coffee*, which criticized coffee use. Despite the protestations against coffee, its use proliferated. Today, more than 325 years later, coffeehouses are still flourishing as centers for relaxation and conversation.

Coca leaves, from which cocaine is derived, have been chewed since before recorded history. Drawings found on South American pottery illustrate that coca chewing was practiced before the rise of the Incan Empire. The coca plant was held in high regard: considered a present from the gods, it was used in religious rituals and burial ceremonies. When the Spaniards arrived in South America, they tried to regulate coca chewing by the natives but were unsuccessful. Cocaine was later included in the popular soft drink Coca-Cola. Another stimulant, amphetamine, was developed in the 1920s and was originally used to treat narcolepsy. It was later prescribed for treating asthma and for weight loss. Today, the stimulant Ritalin and similar variations are given to approximately six million school-age children annually to address attention-deficit disorders. Some people claim that too many children are receiving Ritalin and other stimulants, while others assert that not enough students are receiving these drugs. This raises the question of whether or not Ritalin and other drugs should be used for treating attention disorder is debated in Issue 12.

Minor tranquilizers, also called "antianxiety drugs," were first marketed in the early 1950s. The sales of these drugs were astronomical. Drugs to reduce anxiety were in high demand. Another group of antianxiety drugs are benzodiazepines. Two well-known benzodiazepines are Librium and Valium; the latter ranks as the most widely prescribed drug in the history of American medicine. Xanax, which has replaced Valium as the minor tranquilizer of choice, is one of the five most prescribed drugs in the United States today. Minor tranquilizers are noteworthy because they are legally prescribed to alter one's consciousness. Mind-altering drugs existed prior to minor tranquilizers, but they were not prescribed for that purpose. In many instances, consumers request prescribed drugs from their physicians after seeing them advertised in the media. It is estimated that one-third of all prescription drugs are written at the request of the patient. Pharmaceutical companies spend nearly $5 billion on advertising in magazines and on television (Frosch, Grande, Tarn, and Kravitz, 2010). Is it a good practice for patients to encourage their physicians to prescribe drugs that they saw advertised? Whether there should be more regulation on advertising prescription drugs directly to consumers is examined in Issue 13.

Combating Drug Problems

The debates in *Taking Sides: Clashing Views in Drugs and Society* confront many important drug-related issues. For example, what is the most effective way to reduce drug abuse? Should laws preventing drug use and abuse be more strongly enforced, or should drug laws be less punitive? How can the needs of individuals be met while serving the greater good of society? Should drug abuse be seen as a public health problem or a legal problem? Are drugs an American problem or an international problem? The debate whether the drug problem should be fought nationally or internationally is addressed in Issue 2. Many people argue that America would benefit most by focusing its attention on stopping the proliferation of drugs in other countries. Others feel that reducing the demand for drugs should be the primary focus. If federal funding is limited, should those funds focus on reducing the demand for drugs or stopping their importation?

One of the oldest debates concerns whether drug use should be decriminalized. In recent years, this debate has become more intense because well-known individuals such as former New Mexico governor Gary Johnson and politician Ron Paul have come out in support of changing drug laws. For many people, the issue is not whether drug use is good or bad, but whether people should be punished for taking drugs. Is it worth the time and expense for law enforcement officials to arrest nonviolent drug offenders? One question that is basic to this debate is whether drug decriminalization causes more or less damage than keeping drugs illegal. Issue 1 addresses the question of whether restrictive drug laws are effective at reducing drug use and abuse.

In a related matter, should potentially harmful drugs be restricted even if they may be of medical benefit? Some people are concerned that drugs used for medical reasons may be illegally diverted. Yet, most people agree that patients should have access to the best medicine available. In referenda in numerous states, U.S. voters have approved the medical use of marijuana. Is the federal government consistent in allowing potentially harmful drugs to be used for medical purposes? For example, narcotics are often prescribed for pain relief. Is there a chance that patients who are given narcotics will become addicted? Issue 16 debates whether or not marijuana should be approved for medical use. In California, there are about 1000 medical marijuana dispensaries (Harkinson, 2011). Issue 10 addresses whether drug addicts should be given access to free hypodermic needles as a means for reducing harm associated with injecting drugs.

Addiction to drugs is a major problem in society. Yet, most people who stop their addiction do so on their own. Others maintain that addiction is connected to one's biochemical makeup and that stopping volitionally is not likely to occur (Lemonick, 2007). Issue 6 looks at the issue of drug addiction and whether addiction is based on heredity or it is a choice that people make. In other words, is drug abuse a disease or is it a matter of poor decisions?

A major emphasis in society today is on competition, especially athletic competition. With a win-at-all-cost mentality, many athletes try to get the upper edge. One way to achieve this is through the use of performance-enhancing drugs. Yet, as stated by Murray (2010), "is it not unfair to put the athletes who want to compete without drugs at a competitive disadvantage by permitting everything—to tilt the playing field in favor of the drug users?" The issue is whether or not the federal government should play a larger role in regulating steroids and other performance-enhancing drugs is discussed in Issue 7.

Many of the issues discussed in this book deal with drug prevention. As with most controversial issues, there is a lack of consensus on how to prevent drug-related problems. For example, Issue 5 debates whether or not women who use drugs should retain custody of their children. On the other hand, will drug-using women avoid drug treatment for fear of losing their children? Are children better served if they are taken away from their mothers? Are these laws discriminatory, because most cases that are prosecuted involve poor women?

Some contend that drug laws discriminate not only according to social class, but also according to age and ethnicity. Many drug laws in the United States were initiated because of their association with different ethnic groups: Opium smoking was made illegal after it was associated with Chinese immigrants. Cocaine became illegal after it was linked with blacks. And marijuana was outlawed after it was linked with Hispanics.

Drug-related issues are not limited to illegal drugs. Tobacco and alcohol are two pervasive legal drugs that generate much debate. For example, should employers limit secondhand smoke (Issue 8)? Should nonsmokers look to smokeless tobacco as a safer alternative to cigarette smoking (Issue 14)? At a congressional hearing, executives at the largest tobacco companies swore tobacco is not addictive (Godrej, 2004). With regard to alcoholism, a debate is whether alcoholism is caused by one's heredity or whether it is caused by environmental factors (Issue 15). A fourth issue relating to legal drugs deal with whether or not the legal drinking age should remain at 21 (Issue 3).

Gateway Drugs

Drugs like inhalants, tobacco, and alcohol are considered "gateway" drugs. These are drugs that are often used as a prelude to other, usually illegal, drugs. This does not mean necessarily that young people who use these drugs will use other drugs. For many individuals, drug use begins in middle school and high school. This raises the question as to the role of schools. Some schools try to help students who engage in drug use while others take a sterner approach and will not tolerate any drug use. Will a zero tolerance policy stop students from using drugs or will they simply learn better ways of concealing their drug use? Whether or not schools should enforce a zero tolerance drug policy is the focus of Issue 19.

One factor that may influence whether young people use drugs is the media. Advertisements are an integral part of the media, and their influence can be seen in the growing popularity of cigarette smoking among adolescents. In the 1880s, cigarette smoking escalated in the United States. One of the most important factors contributing to cigarettes' popularity at that time was the development of the cigarette-rolling machine (previously, cigarettes could be rolled at a rate of only four per minute). Also, cigarette smoking, which was considered an activity reserved for men, began to be seen as an option for women. As cigarettes began to be marketed toward women, cigarette smoking became more widespread. As one can see from this introduction, numerous factors affect drug use. Young people need to be educated on the role of media in drug use.

Drug Prevention and Treatment

Some people maintain that educating young people about drugs is one way to prevent drug use and abuse. Studies show that by delaying the onset of drug use, the likelihood of drug abuse is reduced. In the past, however, drug education had little impact on drug-taking behavior (Goldberg, 2010). Another strategy being adopted in many schools is to drug test students. The belief is that the threat of drug testing will reduce drug use. One needs to balance the possible benefits against the costs. Also, what should be the consequences for students who test positive for drug use? Moreover, if schools conduct drug tests, who should be tested? Should it include all students, student athletes, or student government leaders? Whether or not schools *should* drug test students is debated in Issue 17.

Another way to reduce drug abuse that has been heavily promoted is drug abuse treatment. However, is drug abuse treatment effective? Does it prevent recurring drug abuse, reduce criminal activity and violence, and halt the spread of drug-related disease? Issue 18 examines whether or not drug abuse treatment affects these outcomes. The results of drug abuse treatment are contradictory. A European study found that the majority of people in drug treatment drop out (*The Economist*, 2004). Other studies show that drug abuse treatment may have some benefits. But do those benefits outweigh the costs of the treatment? If society feels that treatment is a better alternative to incarceration, it is imperative to know if treatment works.

Some people maintain that illegal drug use, especially marijuana, should be regulated rather than prohibited. Moreover, it is contended that if drugs remain illegal, it is more difficult to control its distribution and use. Others argue that if a drug is illegal, then tougher enforcement would be a better control mechanism. By legalizing drugs such as marijuana, the gates are open to greater abuse. In Issue 9, the debate centers on whether or not marijuana laws should be relaxed.

Distinguishing Between Drug Use, Misuse, and Abuse

Although the terms *drug*, *drug misuse*, and *drug abuse* are commonly used, they have different meanings to different people. Defining these terms may seem simple at first, but many factors affect how they are defined. Should a definition for a drug be based on its behavioral effects, its effects on society, its pharmacological properties, or its chemical composition? One simple, concise definition of a drug is "any substance that produces an effect on the mind, body, or both." One could also define a drug by how it is used. For example, if watching television and listening to music are forms of escape from daily problems, then they may be considered drugs.

Legal drugs cause far more death and disability than illegal drugs, but society appears to be most concerned with the use of illegal drugs. The potential harms of legal drugs tend to be minimized. By viewing drugs as illicit substances only, people fail to recognize that commonly used substances such as caffeine, tobacco, alcohol, and over-the-counter preparations are drugs. If these substances are not perceived as drugs, then people might not acknowledge that they can be misused or abused.

Definitions for misuse and abuse are not affected by a drug's legal status. Drug misuse refers to the inappropriate or unintentional use of drugs. Someone who smokes marijuana to improve his or her study skills is misusing marijuana because the drug impairs short-term memory. Drug abuse alludes to physical, emotional, financial, intellectual, or social consequences arising from chronic drug use. Under this definition, can a person abuse food, aspirin, soft drinks, or chocolate? Also, should a person be free to make potentially unhealthy choices?

The Cost of the War on Drugs

The United States government spends billions of dollars each year to curb the rise in drug use. A major portion of that money goes toward law enforcement. Vast sums of money are used by the military to intercept drug shipments, while foreign governments are given money to help them with their own wars on drugs. A smaller portion of the funds is used for treating and preventing drug abuse.

The expense of drug abuse to industries is staggering: Experts estimate that more than 8 percent of full-time workers in the United States used an illegal drug during the past 30 days. The number of full-time employees who binge drink and drink heavily is 34.5 million and 9.8 million, respectively (Substance Abuse and Mental Health Services Administration, 2010). The cost of drug abuse to employers is approximately $171 billion each year (Kesselring and Pittman, 2002). Compared to nonaddicted employees, drug-dependent employees are absent from their jobs more often, and drug users are less likely to maintain stable job histories than nonusers. In its report *America's Habit: Drug Abuse, Drug Trafficking and Organized Crime*, the President's Commission on Organized Crime supported testing all federal workers for drugs. It further recommended that federal contracts be withheld from private employers who do not implement drug-testing procedures.

A prerequisite to being hired by many companies is passing a drug test. Drug testing may be having a positive effect. The percentage of employees testing positive for marijuana and amphetamines have declined (Davidson, 2007). Still, between 10 and 20 percent of employees who are killed on the job test positive for either alcohol or other drugs (Stanley, 2009). An important question is, "What is the purpose of drug testing?" Drug testing raises three other important questions: (1) Does drug testing prevent drug use? (2) Is the point of drug testing to help employees with drug problems or to get rid of employees who use drugs? (3) How can the civil rights of employees be balanced against the rights of companies?

How serious is the drug problem? Is it real, or is there simply an unreasonable hysteria regarding drugs? In the United States, there has been a growing intolerance toward drug use. Drugs are a problem for many people. Drugs can affect one's physical, social, intellectual, and emotional health. Ironically, some people take drugs because they produce these effects. Individuals who take drugs receive some kind of reward from the drug; the reward may come from being associated with others who use drugs or from the feelings derived from the drug. Many people use illegal drugs or legal drugs like tobacco and alcohol as forms of self-medication. If people did not receive rewards from their use of drugs, then they would likely cease using drugs.

The disadvantages of drugs are numerous: They interfere with career aspirations, educational achievement, athletic performance, and individual maturation. Drugs have also been associated with violent behavior; addiction; discord among siblings, children, parents, spouses, and friends; work-related problems; financial troubles; problems in school; legal predicaments; accidents; injuries; and death. Yet, are drugs the cause or the symptom of the problems that people have? Perhaps drugs are one aspect of a larger scenario in which society is experiencing much change and in which drug use is merely another thread in the social fabric.

References

E. M. Brecher, *Licit and Illicit Drugs* (Little, Brown, 1972).

M. A. Davidson, "Drug Use and Testing in the Workplace," *Security Management* (vol. 35, July 2007), p. 24.

D. L. Frosch, D. Grande, D. M. Tarn, and R. L. Kravitz, "A Decade of Controversy: Balancing Policy with Evidence in the Regulation of Prescription Drug Advertising," *American Journal of Public Health* (January 2010), pp. 24–32.

R. Goldberg, *Drugs Across the Spectrum* (Cengage Publishing, 2010).

J. Harkinson, "Joint Ventures," *Mother Jones* (January/February 2011).

L. D. Johnston, P. O. O'Malley, J. G. Bachman, and J. E. Schulenberg, *Monitoring the Future* (National Institute on Drug Abuse, 2009).

J. Kesner, "Wake Up to a Better Brain," *Prevention* (vol. 61, June 2009).

T. Lam, J. Mites, and L. von Nyssen, "Jittery," *Current Events* (vol. 108, January 12, 2009), pp. 4–5.

H. Lee, *How Dry We Were: Prohibition Revisited* (Prentice Hall, 1963).

M. D. Lemonick and A. Park, "The Science of Addiction," *Time* (July 16, 2007).

H. Meyer, *Old English Coffee Houses* (Rodale Press, 1954).

T. Murray, "Making Sense of Fairness in Sports," *Hastings Center Report* (March 1, 2010), pp. 13–14.

R. E. Schultes and A. Hofmann, *Plants of the Gods: Origins of Hallucinogenic Use* (McGraw-Hill, 1979).

T. L. Stanley, "Workplace Substance Abuse: A Grave Problem," *SuperVision* (vol. 70, June 2009), pp. 18–21.

Substance Abuse and Mental Health Services Administration. *Results from the 2009 National Survey on Drug Use and Health: Volume I. Summary of National Findings* (Office of Applied Studies, Rockville, MD, 2010).

Internet References . . .

Drug Policy Alliance

Formerly the Drug Policy Foundation, this site is an excellent source of information dealing with legal issues as they relate to drugs.

http://www.drugpolicyfoundation.org

Office of National Drug Control Policy (ONDCP)

This site provides information regarding the government's position on many drug-related topics. Funding allocations by the federal government to deal with drug problems is also included.

http://www.whitehousedrugpolicy.gov

National Institute on Drug Abuse

Current information regarding numerous drugs such as *Salvia divinorum* and anabolic steroids can be accessed through this site.

http://www.nida.nih.gov

World Health Organization

Information regarding worldwide trends in drug use and abuse can be found at this site.

http://www.who.int

Drugs and Public Policy

*D*rug abuse causes a myriad of problems for society: The psychological and physical effects of drug abuse can be devastating; many drugs are addictive; drug abuse wreaks havoc on families; disability and death result from drug overdoses; and drugs frequently are implicated in crimes, especially violent crimes. Identifying drug-related problems is not difficult. What is unclear is the best course of action to take when dealing with these problems.

Three scenarios exist for dealing with drugs: Policies can be made more restrictive, they can be made less restrictive, or they can remain the same. The position one takes depends on whether drug use and abuse are seen as legal, social, or medical problems. Perhaps the issue is not whether drugs are good or bad, but how to minimize the harm of drugs. The debates in this section explore these issues.

- Should Laws Against Drug Use Remain Restrictive?

- Should the United States Put More Emphasis on Stopping the Importation of Drugs?

- Should the United States Drinking Age Remain at 21?

- Should Salvia Be Banned?

- Should Women Who Use Drugs Lose Custody of Their Children?

- Is Drug Addiction a Brain Disease?

- Should There Be More Regulation of Performance-Enhancing Drugs?

ISSUE 1

Should Laws Against Drug Use Remain Restrictive?

YES: Herbert Kleber and Joseph A. Califano Jr., from "Legalization: Panacea or Pandora's Box?" *The World & I Online* (January 2006)

NO: U.S. Department of Health and Human Services, from "Youth Prevention-Related Measures," *Results from the National Survey on Drug Use and Health: Volume 1. Summary of National Findings* (2010)

ISSUE SUMMARY

YES: Herbert Kleber, the executive vice president of the Center on Addiction and Substance Abuse (CASA), and Joseph Califano, founder of CASA, maintain that drug laws should remain restrictive because legalization would result in increased use, especially by children, and legalization would not eliminate drug-related violence.

NO: The report from the U.S. Department of Health and Human Services points out that a number of factors affect drug use by young people. One of the most important factors is perception of risk. If young people perceive that drugs are harmful, they are less likely to engage in drug use. Other relevant factors include the perception of drug use by peers, religious beliefs, and parental involvement. Legal sanctions are not noted as a deterrent to drug use.

In 2010, the federal government allocated $15.5 billion to control drug use and to enforce laws that are designed to protect society from the perils created by drug use. Some people believe that the government's war on drugs could be more effective if governmental agencies and communities fought hard enough to stop drug use. They also hold that laws to halt drug use are too few and too lenient. Others contend that the war against drugs is unnecessary; that, in fact, society has already lost the war on drugs. These individuals feel that the best way to remedy drug problems is to end the fight altogether by ending the current restrictive policies regarding drug use.

There are conflicting views among both liberals and conservatives on whether legislation has had the intended result of curtailing the problems of drug use. Many argue that legislation and the criminalization of drugs have been counterproductive in controlling drug problems. Some suggest that the criminalization of drugs have actually contributed to the social ills associated with drugs. Proponents of drug legalization maintain that the war on drugs, not drugs themselves, is damaging to society. They do not advocate drug use; they argue only that laws against drugs exacerbate problems related to drugs.

Proponents of drug decriminalization argue that the strict enforcement of drug laws damages society because it drives people to violence and crime and that the drug laws have a racist element associated with them. People arrested for drug offenses overburden the court system, thus rendering it ineffective. Moreover, proponents contend that the criminalization of drugs fuels organized crime, allows children to be pulled into the drug business, and makes illegal drugs themselves more dangerous because they are manufactured without government standards or regulations. Decriminalization advocates also argue that decriminalization would take the profits out of drug sales, thereby decreasing the value of and demand for drugs.

Some decriminalization advocates argue that the federal government's prohibition stance on drugs is an immoral and impossible objective. To achieve a "drug-free society" is self-defeating and a misnomer because drugs have always been a part of human culture. Furthermore, prohibition efforts disregard the private freedom of individuals—assuming that individuals are incapable of making their own choices. Drug proponents assert that their personal sovereignty should be respected over any government agenda.

People who favor reducing the restrictive nature of drug laws feel that such a measure would give the government more control over the purity and potency of drugs and that the international drug trade would be regulated more effectively. Less restrictive laws, they argue, would take the emphasis off law enforcement policies and allow more effort to be put toward education, prevention, and treatment.

Opponents of this view maintain that less restrictive drug laws are not the solution to drug problems and that it is a very dangerous idea. Less restrictive laws, they assert, will drastically increase drug use. This upsurge in drug use will come at an incredibly high price: society will be overrun with drug-related accidents, loss in worker productivity, and hospitals filled with drug-related emergencies. Drug treatment efforts would be futile because users would have no legal incentive to stop taking drugs. Also, users may prefer drugs rather than rehabilitation, and education programs may be ineffective in dissuading children from using drugs.

Advocates of less restrictive laws maintain that drug abuse is a "victimless crime" in which the only person being hurt is the drug user. Opponents argue that this notion is ludicrous and dangerous because drug use has dire repercussions for all of society. Also, regulations to control drug use have a legitimate social aim to protect society and its citizens from the harm of drugs. Individuals who favor restrictive laws maintain that such laws are not immoral or a violation of personal freedoms. Rather, they allow a standard of control to be established in order to preserve human character and society as a whole.

In the YES selection, Kleber and Califano Jr. explain why they feel drugs should remain illegal, whereas in the NO selection, the report from the Department of Health and Human Services describes those factors that affect drug use, and point out that restrictive drug laws did not serve as a deterrent.

YES

Herbert Kleber and
Joseph A. Califano Jr.

Legalization:
Panacea or Pandora's Box

Introduction

Legalization of drugs has recently received some attention as a policy option for the United States. Proponents of such a radical change in policy argue that the "war on drugs" has been lost; drug prohibition, as opposed to illegal drugs themselves, spawns increasing violence and crime; drugs are available to anyone who wants them, even under present restrictions; drug abuse and addiction would not increase after legalization; individuals have a right to use whatever drugs they wish; and foreign experiments with legalization work and should be adopted in the United States.

In this, its first White Paper, the Center on Addiction and Substance Abuse at Columbia University (CASA) examines these propositions; recent trends in drug use; the probable consequences of legalization for children and drug-related violence; lessons to be learned from America's legal drugs, alcohol and tobacco; the question of civil liberties; and the experiences of foreign countries. On the basis of its review, CASA concludes that while legalization might temporarily take some burden off the criminal justice system, such a policy would impose heavy additional costs on the health care system, schools, and workplace, severely impair the ability of millions of young Americans to develop their talents, and in the long term overburden the criminal justice system.

Drugs like heroin and cocaine are not dangerous because they are illegal; they are illegal because they are dangerous. Such drugs are not a threat to American society because they are illegal; they are illegal because they are a threat to American society.

Any relaxation in standards of illegality poses a clear and present danger to the nation's children and their ability to learn and grow into productive citizens. Individuals who reach age 21 without using illegal drugs are virtually certain never to do so. Viewed from this perspective, substance abuse and addiction is a disease acquired during childhood and adolescence. Thus, legalization of drugs such as heroin, cocaine, and marijuana would threaten a pediatric pandemic in the United States.

While current prohibitions on the import, manufacture, distribution, and possession of marijuana, cocaine, heroin, and other drugs should remain,

As seen in *The World & I Online*, January 2006, from a report of The National Center on Addiction and Substance Abuse at Columbia University, September 1995. Copyright © 2006 by The National Center on Addiction and Substance Abuse (CASA) at Columbia University. Reprinted by permission.

America's drug policies do need a fix. More resources and energy should be devoted to prevention and treatment, and each citizen and institution should take responsibility to combat drug abuse and addiction in America. . . .

Legalization, Decriminalization, Medicalization, Harm Reduction: What's the Difference?

The term "legalization" encompasses a wide variety of policy options from the legal use of marijuana in private to free markets for all drugs. Four terms are commonly used: legalization, decriminalization, medicalization, and harm reduction—with much variation in each.

Legalization usually implies the most radical departure from current policy. Legalization proposals vary from making marijuana cigarettes as available as tobacco cigarettes to establishing an open and free market for drugs. Variations on legalization include: making drugs legal for the adult population, but illegal for minors; having only the government produce and sell drugs; and/or allowing a private market in drugs, but with restrictions on advertising, dosage, and place of consumption. Few proponents put forth detailed visions of a legalized market.

Decriminalization proposals retain most drug laws that forbid manufacture, importation, and sale of illegal drugs, but remove criminal sanctions for possession of small amounts of drugs for personal use. Such proposals suggest that possession of drugs for personal use be legal or subject only to civil penalties such as fines. Decriminalization is most commonly advocated for marijuana.

Medicalization refers to the prescription of currently illegal drugs by physicians to addicts already dependent on such drugs. The most frequently mentioned variation is heroin maintenance. Proponents argue that providing addicts with drugs prevents them from having to commit crimes to finance their habit and insures that drugs they ingest are pure.

Harm reduction generally implies that government policies should concentrate on lowering the harm associated with drugs both for users and society, rather than on eradicating drug use and imprisoning users. Beginning with the proposition that drug use is inevitable, harm reduction proposals can include the prescription of heroin and other drugs to addicts; removal of penalties for personal use of marijuana; needle-exchange programs for injection drug users to prevent the spread of AIDS and other diseases that result from needle sharing among addicts; and making drugs available at low or no cost to eliminate the harm caused by users who commit crimes to support a drug habit.

Variations on these options are infinite. Some do not require any change in the illegal status of drugs. The government could, for instance, allow needle exchanges while maintaining current laws banning heroin, the most commonly injected drug. Others, however, represent a major shift from the current role of government and the goal of its policies with regard to drug use and availability. Some advocates use the term "harm reduction" as a politically attractive cover for legalization.

Where We Are

Most arguments for legalization in all its different forms start with the contention that the "war on drugs" has been lost and that prevailing criminal justice and social policies with respect to drug use have been a failure. To support the claim that current drug policies have failed, legalization advocates point to the 80 million Americans who have tried drugs during their lifetime. Since so many individuals have broken drug laws, these advocates argue, the laws are futile and lead to widespread disrespect for the law. A liberal democracy, they contend, should not ban what so many people do.[1]

The 80 million Americans include everyone who has ever smoked even a single joint. The majority of these individuals have used only marijuana, and for many their use was brief experimentation. In fact, the size of this number reflects the large number of young people who tried marijuana and hallucinogenic drugs during the late 1960s and the 1970s when drug use was widely tolerated. During this time, drug use was so commonly accepted that the 1972 Shafer Commission, established during the Nixon Administration, and later, President Jimmy Carter called for decriminalization of marijuana.[2]

Since then, concerned public health and government leaders have mounted energetic efforts to de-normalize drug use, including First Lady Nancy Reagan's "Just Say No" campaign. As a result, current* users of any illicit drugs, as measured by the National Household Survey on Drug Abuse, decreased from 24.8 million in 1979 to 13 million in 1994, a nearly 50 percent drop. Over the same time period, current marijuana users dropped from 23 million to 10 million and cocaine users from 4.4 million to 1.4 million.[3] The drug-using segment of the population is also aging. In 1979, 10 percent of current drug users were older than 34; today almost 30 percent are.[4]

With these results and only 6 percent of the population over age 12 currently using drugs,[5] it is difficult to say that drug reduction efforts have failed. This sharp decline in drug use occurred during a period of strict drug laws, societal disapproval, and increasing knowledge and awareness of the dangers and costs of illegal drug use.

Several factors, however, lead many to conclude that we have not made progress against drugs. This feeling of despair stems from the uneven nature of the success. While casual drug use and experimentation have declined substantially, certain neighborhoods and areas of the country remain infested with drugs and drug-related crime, and these continuing trouble spots draw media attention. At the same time, the number of drug addicts has not dropped significantly and the spread of HIV among addicts has added a deadly new dimension to the problem. The number of hardcore** cocaine users (as estimated by the Office of National Drug Control Policy based on a number of surveys including the Household Survey, Drug Use Forecasting, and Drug Abuse Warning Network) has remained steady at roughly 2 million.[6] The overall number

---

*Throughout this paper, "current" drug users refers to individuals who have used drugs within the past month, the definition used in most drug use surveys.

**Throughout this paper, "hardcore" users refers to individuals who use drugs at least weekly.

of illicit drug addicts has hovered around 6 million, a situation that many experts attribute both to a lack of treatment facilities[7] and the large numbers of drug-using individuals already in the pipeline to addiction, even though overall casual use has dropped.

Teenage drug use has been creeping up in the past three years. In the face of the enormous decline in the number of users, however, it is difficult to conclude that current policies have so failed that a change as radical as legalization is warranted. While strict drug laws and criminal sanctions are not likely to deter hardcore addicts, increased resources can be dedicated to treatment without legalizing drugs. Indeed, the criminal justice system can be used to place addicted offenders into treatment. In short, though substantial problems remain, we have made significant progress in our struggle against drug abuse.

Will Legalization Increase Drug Use?

Proponents of drug legalization claim that making drugs legally available would not increase the number of addicts. They argue that drugs are already available to those who want them and that a policy of legalization could be combined with education and prevention programs to discourage drug use.[8] Some contend that legalization might even reduce the number of users, arguing that there would be no pushers to lure new users and drugs would lose the "forbidden fruit" allure of illegality, which can be seductive to children.[9] Proponents of legalization also play down the consequences of drug use, saying that most drug users can function normally.[10] Some legalization advocates assert that a certain level of drug addiction is inevitable and will not vary, regardless of government policies; thus, they claim, even if legalization increased the number of users, it would have little effect on the numbers of users who become addicts.[11]

The effects of legalization on the numbers of users and addicts is an important question because the answer in large part determines whether legalization will reduce crime, improve public health, and lower economic, social, and health care costs. The presumed benefits of legalization evaporate if the number of users and addicts, particularly among children, increases significantly.

Availability

An examination of this question begins with the issue of availability, which has three components:

- **Physical,** how convenient is access to drugs.
- **Psychological,** the moral and social acceptability and perceived consequences of drug use.
- **Economic,** the affordability of drugs.

Physical
Despite assertions to the contrary, the evidence indicates that presently drugs are not accessible to all. Fewer than 50 percent of high school seniors and young adults under 22 believed they could obtain cocaine "fairly easily" or "very easily."[12] Only 39 percent of the adult population reported they could

get cocaine; and only 25 percent reported that they could obtain heroin, PCP, and LSD.[13] Thus, only one-quarter to one-half of people can easily get illegal drugs (other than marijuana). After legalization, drugs would be more widely and easily available. Currently, only 11 percent of individuals reported seeing drugs available in the area where they lived;[14] after legalization, there could be a place to purchase drugs in every neighborhood. Under such circumstances, it is logical to conclude that more individuals would use drugs.

Psychological

In arguing that legalization would not result in increased use, proponents of legalization often cite public opinion polls which indicate that the vast majority of Americans would not try drugs even if they were legally available.[15] They fail to take into account, however, that this strong public antagonism towards drugs has been formed during a period of strict prohibition when government and institutions at every level have made clear the health and criminal justice consequences of drug use. Furthermore, even if only 15 percent of population would use drugs after legalization, this would be triple the current level of 5.6 percent.

Laws define what is acceptable conduct in a society, express the will of its citizens, and represent a commitment on the part of the Congress, the President, state legislatures, and governors. Drug laws not only create a criminal sanction, they also serve as educational and normative statements that shape public attitudes.[16] Criminal laws constitute a far stronger statement than civil laws, but even the latter can discourage individual consumption. Laws regulating smoking in public and workplaces, prohibiting certain types of tobacco advertising, and mandating warning labels are in part responsible for the decline in smoking prevalence among adults.

The challenge of reducing drug abuse and addiction would be decidedly more difficult if society passed laws indicating that these substances are not sufficiently harmful to prohibit their use. Any move toward legalization would decrease the perception of risks and costs of drug use, which would lead to wider use.[17] During the late 1960s and the 1970s, as society, laws, and law enforcement became more permissive about drug use, the number of individuals smoking marijuana and using heroin, hallucinogens, and other drugs rose sharply. During the 1980s, as society's attitude became more restrictive and anti-drug laws stricter and more vigorously enforced, the perceived harmfulness of marijuana and other illicit drugs increased and use decreased.

Some legalization advocates point to the campaign against smoking as proof that reducing use is possible while substances are legally available.[18] But it has taken smoking more than 30 years to decline as much as illegal drug use did in 10.[19] Moreover, reducing use of legal drugs among the young has proven especially difficult. While use of illegal drugs by high school seniors dropped 50 percent from 1979 to 1993, tobacco use remained virtually constant.[20]

Economic

By all of the laws of economics, reducing the price of drugs will increase consumption.[21] Though interdiction and law enforcement have had limited success in reducing supply (seizing only 25 percent to 30 percent of cocaine imports, for example)[22] the illegality of drugs has increased their price.[23] Prices of illegal drugs are roughly 10 times what they would cost to produce legally. Cocaine, for example, sells at $80 a gram today, but would cost only $10 a gram legally to produce and distribute. That would set the price of a dose at 50 cents, well within the reach of a school child's lunch money.[24]

Until the mid-1980s, cocaine was the drug of the middle and upper classes. Regular use was limited to those who had the money to purchase it or got the money through white collar crime or selling such assets as their car, house, or children's college funds. In the mid-1980s, the $5 crack cocaine vial made the drug inexpensive and available to all regardless of income. Use spread. Cocaine-exposed babies began to fill hospital neonatal wards, cocaine-related emergency room visits increased sharply, and cocaine-related crime and violence jumped.[25]

Efforts to increase the price of legal drugs by taxing them heavily in order to discourage consumption, if successful, would encourage the black market, crime, violence, and corruption associated with the illegal drug trade. Heroin addicts, who gradually build a tolerance to the drug, and cocaine addicts, who crave more of the drug as soon as its effects subside, would turn to a black market if an afford-able and rising level of drugs were not made available to them legally.

Children

Drug use among children is of particular concern since almost all individuals who use drugs begin before they are 21. Furthermore, adolescents rate drugs as the number one problem they face.[26] Since we have been unable to keep legal drugs, like tobacco and alcohol, out of the hands of children, legalization of illegal drugs could cause a pediatric pandemic of drug abuse and addiction.

Most advocates of legalization support a regulated system in which access to presently illicit drugs would be illegal for minors.[27] Such regulations would retain for children the "forbidden fruit" allure that many argue legalization would elim-inate. Furthermore any such distinction between adults and minors could make drugs, like beer and cigarettes today, an attractive badge of adulthood.

The American experience with laws restricting access by children and adolescents to tobacco and alcohol makes it clear that keeping legal drugs away from minors would be a formidable, probably impossible, task. Today, 62 per-cent of high school seniors have smoked, 30 percent in the past month.[28] Three million adolescents smoke cigarettes, an average of one-half a pack per day, a $1 billion a year market.[29] Twelve million underage Americans drink beer and other alcohol, a market approaching $10 billion a year. Although alcohol use is illegal for all those under the age of 21, 87 percent of high school seniors report using alcohol, more than half in the past month.[30] These rates of use persist despite school, community, and media activities that inform youths about the dangers of smoking and drinking and despite increasing public awareness of these risks. This record indicates that efforts to ban drug use among minors while allowing it for adults would face enormous difficulty.

Moreover, in contrast to these high rates of alcohol and tobacco use, only 18 percent of seniors use illicit drugs, which are illegal for the entire society.[31] It is no accident that those substances which are mostly easily obtainable—alcohol, tobacco, and inhalants such as those found in household cleaning fluids—are those most widely used by the youngest students.[32]

Supporters and opponents of legalization generally agree that education and prevention programs are an integral part of efforts to reduce drug use by children and adolescents. School programs, media campaigns such as those of the Partnership for a Drug-Free America (PDFA), and news reports on the dangers of illegal drugs have helped reduce use by changing attitudes towards drugs. In 1992, New York City school children were surveyed on their perceptions of illegal drugs before and after a PDFA campaign of anti-drug messages on television, in newspapers, and on billboards. The second survey showed that the percentage of children who said they might want to try drugs fell 29 points and those who said drugs would make them "cool" fell 17 points.[33] Another study found that 75 percent of students who saw anti-drug advertisements reported that the ads had a deterrent effect on their own actual or intended use.[34]

Along with such educational programs, however, the stigma of illegality is especially important in preventing use among adolescents. From 1978 to 1993, current marijuana use among high school seniors dropped twice as fast as alcohol use.[35] California started a $600 million anti-smoking campaign in 1989, and by 1995, the overall smoking rate had dropped 30 percent. But among teenagers, the smoking rate remained constant—even though almost one-quarter of the campaign targeted them.[36]

In separate studies, 60 to 70 percent of New Jersey and California students reported that fear of getting in trouble with the authorities was a major reason why they did not use drugs.[37] Another study found that the greater the perceived likelihood of apprehension and swift punishment for using marijuana, the less likely adolescents are to smoke it.[38] Because a legalized system would remove much, if not all of this deterrent, drug use among teenagers could be expected to rise. Since most teens begin using drugs because their peers do[39]—not because of pressure from pushers[40]—and most drugs users initially exhibit few ill effects, more teenagers would be likely to try drugs.[41]

As a result, legalization of marijuana, cocaine, and heroin for adults would mean that increased numbers of teenagers would smoke, snort, and inject these substances at a time when habits are formed and the social, academic, and physical skills needed for a satisfying and independent life are acquired.

Hardcore Addiction

A review of addiction in the past shows that the number of alcohol, heroin, and cocaine addicts, even when adjusted for changes in population, fluctuates widely over time, in response to changes in access, price, societal attitudes, and legal consequences. The fact that alcohol and tobacco, the most accepted and available legal drugs, are the most widely abused, demonstrates that behavior is influenced by opportunity, stigma, and price. Many soldiers who were regular heroin users in Vietnam stopped once they returned to the United States where heroin was much more difficult and dangerous to get.[42] Studies have shown that even among chronic alcoholics, alcohol taxes lower consumption.[43]

Dr. Jack Homer of the University of Southern California and a founding member of the International System Dynamics Society estimates that without retail-level drug arrests and seizures—which reduce availability, increase the danger of arrest for the drug user, and stigmatize use—the number of compulsive cocaine users would rise to between 10 and 32 million, a level 5 to 16 times the present one.[44]

Not all new users become addicts. But few individuals foresee their addiction when they start using; most think they can control their consumption.[45] Among the new users created by legalization, many, including children, would find themselves unable to live without the drug, no longer able to work, go to school, or maintain personal relationships. In fact, as University of California at Los Angeles criminologist James Q. Wilson points out with regard to cocaine,[46] the percentage of drug triers who become abusers when the drugs are illegal, socially unacceptable, and generally hard to get, may be only a fraction of the users who become addicts when drugs are legal and easily available—physically, psychologically, and economically.

Harming Thy Neighbor and Thyself: Addiction and Casual Drug Use

To offset any increased use as a result of legalization, many proponents contend that money presently spent on criminal justice and law enforcement could be used for treatment of addicts and prevention.[47] In 1995, the federal government is spending $13.2 billion to fight drug abuse, nearly two-thirds of that amount on law enforcement; state and local governments are spending at least another $16 billion on drug control efforts, largely on law enforcement.[48] Legalization proponents argue that most of this money could be used to fund treatment on demand for all addicts who want it and extensive public health campaigns to discourage new use.

With legalization, the number of prisoners would initially decrease because many are currently there for drug law violations. But to the extent that legalization increases drug use, we can expect to see more of its familiar consequences. Costs would quickly rise in health care, schools, and businesses. In the long term, wider use and addiction would increase criminal activity related to the psychological and physical effects of drug use and criminal justice costs would rise again. The higher number of casual users and addicts would reduce worker productivity and students' ability and motivation to learn, cause more highway accidents and fatalities, and fill hospital beds with individuals suffering from ailments and injuries caused or aggravated by drug abuse.

Costs

It is doubtful whether legalization would produce any cost savings, over time even in the area of law enforcement. Indeed, the legal availability of alcohol has not eliminated law enforcement costs due to alcohol-related violence. A third of state prison inmates committed their crimes while under the influence of alcohol.[49] Despite intense educational campaigns, the highest number of arrests in 1993—1.5 million—was for driving while intoxicated.[50] Even if, as some legalization proponents propose, drug sales were taxed, revenues raised would be more than offset by erosion of the general tax base as abuse and addiction limited the ability of individuals to work.

Like advocates of legalization today, opponents of alcohol prohibition claimed that taxes on the legal sale of alcohol would dramatically increase revenues and even help erase the federal deficit.[51] The real-world result has been quite different. The approximately $20 billion in state and federal revenues from alcohol taxes in 1995[52] pay for only half the $40 billion that alcohol abuse imposes in direct health care costs,[53] much less the costs laid on federal entitlement programs and the legal and criminal justice systems, to say nothing of lost economic productivity. The nearly $13 billion in federal and state cigarette tax revenue[54] is one-sixth of the $75 billion in direct health care costs attributable to tobacco,[55] to say nothing of the other costs such as the $4.6 billion in social security disability payments to individuals disabled by cancer, heart disease, and respiratory ailments caused by smoking.[56]

Health care costs directly attributable to illegal drugs exceed $30 billion,[57] an amount that would increase significantly if use spread after legalization. Experience renders it unrealistic to expect that taxes could be imposed on newly legalized drugs sufficient to cover the costs of increased use and abuse.

Public Health

Legalization proponents contend that prohibition has negative public health consequences such as the spread of HIV from addicts who share dirty needles, accidental poisoning, and overdoses from impure drugs of variable potency. In 1994, more than one-third of new AIDS cases were among injection drug users who shared needles, cookers, cottons, rinse water, and other paraphernalia; many other individuals contracted AIDS by having sex, often while high, with infected injection drug users.[58]

Advocates of medicalization argue that while illicit drugs should not be freely available to all, doctors should be allowed to prescribe them (particularly heroin, but also cocaine) to addicts. They contend that giving addicts drugs assures purity and eliminates the need for addicts to steal in order to buy them.[59]

Giving addicts drugs like heroin, however, poses many problems. Providing them by prescription raises the danger of diversion for sale on the black market. The alternative—insisting that addicts take drugs on the prescriber's premises—entails at least two visits a day, thus interfering with the stated goal of many maintenance programs to enable addicts to hold jobs.

Heroin addicts require two to four shots each day in increasing doses as they build tolerance to its euphoric effect. On the other hand, methadone can be given at a constant dose since euphoria is not the objective. Addicts maintained on methadone need only a single dose each day and take it orally, eliminating the need for injection.[60] Because cocaine produces an intense, but short euphoria and an immediate desire for more,[61] addicts would have to be given the drug even more often than heroin in order to satisfy their craving sufficiently to prevent them from seeking additional cocaine on the street.

Other less radical harm reduction proposals also have serious flaws. Distributing free needles, for example, does not guarantee that addicts desperate for a high would refuse to share them. But to the extent that needle exchange programs are effective in reducing the spread of the AIDS virus and other diseases without increasing drug use, they can be adopted without legalizing drugs. Studies of whether needle exchange programs increase drug use have generally focused on periods of no longer than 12 months.[62] While use does not seem to increase in this period, data is lacking on the long-term effects of such programs and whether they prompt attitude shifts that in turn lead to increased drug use.

Some individuals do die as a result of drug impurities. But while drug purity could be assured in a government-regulated system (though not for those drugs sold on the black market), careful use could not. The increased numbers of users would probably produce a rising number of overdose deaths, similar to those caused by alcohol poisoning today.

The deaths and costs due to unregulated drug quality pale in comparison to the negative impact that legalization would have on drug users, their families, and society. Casual drug use is dangerous, not simply because it can lead to addiction or accidental overdoses, but because it is harmful per se, producing worker accidents, highway fatalities, and children born with physical and mental handicaps. Each year, roughly 500,000 newborns are exposed to illegal drugs in the womb; many others are never born because of drug-induced spontaneous abortions.[63] Newborns already exposed to drugs are far more likely to need intensive care and suffer the physical and mental consequences of low birth weight and premature birth, including early death.[64] The additional costs just to raise drug-exposed babies would outweigh any potential savings of legalization in criminal justice expenditures.[65]

Substance abuse aggravates medical conditions. Medicaid patients with a secondary diagnosis of substance abuse remain in hospitals twice as long as patients with the same primary diagnosis but with no substance abuse problems. Girls and boys under age 15 remain in the hospital three and four times as long, respectively, when they have a secondary diagnosis of substance abuse.[66] One-third to one-half of individuals with psychiatric problems are also substance abusers.[67] Young people who use drugs are at higher risk of mental health problems including depression, suicide, and personality disorders.[68] Teenagers who use illegal drugs are more likely to have sex[69] and are less likely to use a condom than those who do not use drugs.[70] Such sexual behavior exposes these teens to increased risk of pregnancy as well as AIDS and other sexually transmitted diseases.

In schools and families, drug abuse is devastating. Students who use drugs not only limit their own ability to learn, they also disrupt classrooms, interfering with the education of other students. Drug users tear apart families by failing to provide economic support, spending money on drugs, neglecting the emotional support of the spouse and guidance of children, and putting their children at greater risk of becoming substance abusers themselves.[71] With the advent of crack cocaine in the mid-1980s, foster care cases soared over 50 percent nationwide in five years; more than 70 percent of these cases involved families in which at least one parent abused drugs.[72]

Decreased coordination and impaired motor skills that result from drug use are dangerous. A recent study in Tennessee found that 59 percent of reckless drivers who, having been stopped by the police, test negative for alcohol on the breathalyzer, test positive for marijuana and/or cocaine.[73] Twenty percent of New York City drivers who die in automobile accidents test positive for cocaine use.[74] The extent of driving while high on marijuana and other illegal drugs is still not well known because usually the police do not have the same capability for roadside drug testing as they do for alcohol testing. . . .

Crime and Violence

Legalization advocates contend that *drug-related* violence is really *drug-trade-related* violence. They argue that what we have today is not a drug problem but a drug prohibition problem, that anti-drug laws spawn more violence and crime than the drugs themselves. Because illegality creates high prices for drugs and huge profits for dealers, advocates of legalization point out that users commit crimes to support their habit; drug pushers fight over turf; gangs and organized crime thrive; and users become criminals by coming into contact with the underworld.[75]

Legalization proponents argue that repeal of current laws, which criminalize drug use and sales, and wider availability of drugs at lower prices will end this black market and thus reduce the violence, crime, and incarceration associated with drugs.

Researchers divide drug-related violence into three types: systemic, economically compulsive, and psychopharmacological:[76]

- **Systemic violence** is that intrinsic to involvement with illegal drugs, including murders over drug turf, retribution for selling "bad" drugs, and fighting among users over drugs or drug paraphernalia.
- **Economically compulsive violence** results from addicts who engage in violent crime in order to support their addiction.
- **Psychopharmacological violence** is caused by the short or long-term use of certain drugs which lead to excitability, irrationality and violence, such as a brutal murder committed under the influence of cocaine.

Legalization of the drug trade and lower prices might decrease the first two types of violence, but higher use and abuse would increase the third. Dr. Mitchell Rosenthal, President of the Phoenix House treatment centers, warns, "What I and many other treatment professionals would expect to see in a drug-legalized America is a sharp rise in the amount of drug-related crime that is *not* committed for gain—homicide, assault, rape, and child abuse. Along with this, an increase in social disorder, due to rising levels of drug consumption and a growing number of drug abusers."[77]

In a study of 130 drug-related homicides, 60 percent resulted from the psychopharmacological effects of the drug; only 20 percent were found to be related to the drug trade; 3.1 percent were committed for economic reasons. (The remaining 17 percent either fell into more than one of these categories or were categorized as "other.")[78] U.S. Department of Justice statistics reveal that six times as many homicides, four times as many assaults, and almost one and a half times as many robberies are committed under the influence of drugs as are committed in order to get money to buy drugs.[79] Given these facts, any decreases in violent acts committed because of the current high cost of drugs would be more than offset by increases in psychopharmacological violence, such as that caused by cocaine psychosis.

The threat of rising violence is particularly serious in the case of cocaine, crack, methamphetamine, and PCP—drugs closely associated with violent behavior. Unlike marijuana or heroin, which depress activity, these drugs cause irritability and physical aggression. For instance, past increases in the New York City homicide rate have been tied to increases in cocaine use.[80]

Repeal of drug laws would not affect all addicts in the same way. Addicts engage in criminal behavior for different reasons. A small proportion of addicts is responsible for a disproportionately high number of drug-related crimes and arrests. Virtually all of these addicts committed crimes before abusing drugs and use crime to support themselves as well as their habits. Their criminal activity and drug use are symptomatic of chronic antisocial behavior and attitudes. Legally available drugs at lower prices would do little to discourage crime by this group. For a second group, criminal activity is associated with the high cost of illegal drugs. For these addicts, lower prices would decrease drug-related crimes. For a third group, legally available drugs would mean an opportunity to create illegal diversion markets, as some addicts currently do with methadone.[81]

Legalization advocates point to the exploding prison population and the failure of strict drug laws to lower crime rates.[82] Arrests for drug offenses doubled from 470,000 in 1980 to 1 million in 1993.[83] Some 60 percent of the 95,000 federal inmates are incarcerated for drug-law violations.[84]

Rising prison populations are generated in large part by stricter laws, tough enforcement, and mandatory minimum sentencing laws—policy choices of the public and Congress. But the growing number of prisoners is also a product of the high rate of recidivism—a phenomenon tied in good measure to the lack of treatment facilities, particularly in prison. Eighty percent of prisoners have prior convictions and 60 percent have served time before.[85] Despite the fact that more than 60 percent of all state inmates have used illegal drugs regularly and 30 percent were under the influence of drugs at the time they committed the crime for which they were incarcerated,[86] fewer than 20 percent of inmates with drug problems receive any treatment.[87] Many of these inmates also abuse alcohol, but there is little alcoholism treatment either for them or for those prisoners dependent only on alcohol.[88]

While strict laws and enforcement do not deter addicts from using drugs, the criminal justice system can be used to get them in treatment. Because of the nature of addiction, most drug abusers do not seek treatment voluntarily, but many respond to outside pressures including the threat of incarceration.[89]

Where the criminal justice system is used to encourage participation in treatment, addicts are more likely to complete treatment and stay off drugs. . . .[90]

Notes

1. Kurt Schmoke, "Decriminalizing Drugs: It Just Might Work—And Nothing Else Does," in *Drug Legalization: For and Against,* ed. Rod Evans and Irwin Berent (Lasalle: Open Court Press, 1992), p. 216; Merrill Smith, "The Drug Problem: Is There an Answer?" in Evans and Berent, eds., p. 84; Steven Wisotsky, "Statement Before the Select Committee on Narcotics Abuse and Control," in Evans and Berent, eds., p. 189.

2. National Commission on Marijuana and Drug Abuse, *Marijuana: Signal of Misunderstanding* (Washington, DC: GPO, 1972); Musto, p. 267.

3. U.S. Department of Health and Human Services, *Preliminary Estimates from the 1994 National Household Survey on Drug Abuse* (September 1995), pp. 2, 58.

4. Dept. of Health and Human Services (1995), p. 11.

5. Dept. of Health and Human Services (1995), p. 2.

6. Office of National Drug Control Policy (ONDCP), *National Drug Control Strategy: Strengthening Communities' Response to Drugs and Crime* (February 1995), p. 139.

7. ONDCP, *Breaking the Cycle of Drug Abuse* (September 1993), pp. 6–9.

8. Todd Austin Brenner, "The Legalization of Drugs: Why Prolong the Inevitable," in Evans and Berent, eds., p. 173; Schmoke, in Evans and Berent, eds., p. 218; Smith, in Evans and Berent, eds., p. 85.

9. Smith, in Evans and Berent, eds., pp. 83–86; Kevin Zeese, "Drug War Forever?" in *Searching for Alternatives: Drug-Control Policy in the United States,* eds. Melvyn Krauss and Edward Lazear (Stanford: Hoover Institute Press, 1992), p. 265.

10. Ethan Nadelmann, "The Case for Legalization," in *The Drug Legalization Debate,* ed. James Inciardi (Newbury Park: Sage Publications, 1991), pp. 39–40.

11. Michael Gazzaniga, "The Opium of the People: Crack in Perspective," in Evans and Berent, eds., p. 236.

12. Lloyd Johnston, Patrick O'Malley, and Jerald Bachman, *National Survey Results on Drug Use from The Monitoring the Future Study, 1975–1993* (Rockville: 1994), Vol. 1, p. 191 and Vol. 2, p. 144; Center on Addiction and Substance Abuse at Columbia University, *National Survey of American Attitudes on Substance Abuse* (July 1995).

13. Dept. of Health and Human Services *Preliminary Estimates from the 1993 National Household Survey: Press Release* (July 1994), p. 4.

14. Dept. of Health and Human Services (July 1994), p. 4.

15. See for example, Lester Grinspoon and James Bakalar, "The War on Drugs—A Peace Proposal," *The New England Journal of Medicine,* 330(5) 1994, pp. 357–60; Arnold Trebach, "For Legalization of Drugs" in *Legalize It? Debating American Drug Policy,* Arnold Trebach and James Inciardi, eds., (Washington: American University Press, 1993), p. 108.

16. Mark Moore, "Drugs: Getting a Fix on the Problem and the Solution," in Evans and Berent, eds., p. 152.

17. Johnston, O'Malley and Bachman, Vol. 1, p. 206.

18. Schmoke, in Evans and Berent, eds., p. 218; Brenner, in Evans and Berent, eds., p. 171; Wisotsky in Evans and Berent, eds., p. 210.

19. ONDCP (1995), p. 139; Centers for Disease Control, *Morbidity and Mortality Weekly Report,* 34(SS-3) 1994, p. 8.

20. Johnston, O'Malley and Bachman, Vol. 1, p. 79.

21. Moore in Evans and Berent, eds., p. 148; and Mark Moore, "Supply Reduction and Law Enforcement" in *Drugs and Crime,* Michael Tonry and James Wilson, eds., *Crime and Justice: A Review of Research,* Volume 13 (Chicago: University of Chicago Press, 1990), pp. 109–158; Michael Grossman, Gary Becker and Kevin Murphy, "Rational Addiction and the Effect of Price on Consumption," in Krauss and Lazear, eds., p. 83.

22. ONDCP (1995), p. 146.

23. Michael Farrell, John Strang and Peter Reuter, "The Non-Case for Legalization" in *Winning the War on Drugs: To Legalize or Not* (Institute of Economic Affairs: London, 1994).

24. Herbert Kleber, "Our Current Approach to Drug Abuse—Progress, Problems, Proposals," *The New England Journal of Medicine* 330(5), 1994, pp. 362–363; for higher estimates of the differences between illegal and legal costs see Moore, in Evans and Berent, eds., p. 148 and Wisotsky, in Evans and Berent, eds., p. 190.

25. Moore, in Evans and Berent, eds., pp. 129–130.

26. Center on Addiction and Substance Abuse at Columbia University, *National Survey of American Attitudes on Substance Abuse* (July 1995).

27. See for example, Wisotsky, in Evans and Berent, eds. p. 204.

28. Johnston, O'Malley and Bachman, Vol. 1, pp. 76–79.

29. K. Michael Cummings, Terry Pechacek and Donald Shopland, "The Illegal Sale of Cigarettes to US Minors: Estimates by State," *American Journal of Public Health,* 84(2) 1994, pp. 300–302.

30. Johnston, O'Malley and Bachman, Vol. 1, pp. 76–79.

31. Johnston, O'Malley and Bachman, Vol. 1, p. 79.

32. Lloyd Johnston, "A Synopsis of the Key Points in the 1994 Monitoring the Future Results" (December 1994), Table 1; Johnston, O'Malley and Bachman, Vol. 1, pp. 136–137.

33. Drug Strategies, *Keeping Score* (Washington, DC: 1995), p. 11.

34. Evelyn Cohen Reis et al, "The Impact of Anti-Drug Advertising: Perceptions of Middle and High School Students," *Archives of Pediatric and Adolescent Medicine,* 148, December 1994, pp. 1262–1268.

35. Johnston, O'Malley and Bachman, Vol. 1, p. 79.

36. "Hooked on Tobacco: The Teen Epidemic," *Consumer Reports,* March 1995, pp. 142–148.

37. Rodney Skager and Gregory Austin, *Fourth Biennial Statewide Survey of Drug and Alcohol Use Among California Students in Grades 7, 9, and 11,* Office

of the Attorney General, June 1993; Wayne Fisher, *Drug and Alcohol Use Among New Jersey High School Students,* New Jersey Department of Law and Public Safety, 1993.

38. David Peck, "Legal and Social Factors in the Deterrence of Adolescent Marijuana Use," *Journal of Alcohol and Drug Education,* 28(3) 1983, pp. 58–74.

39. Diedre Dupre, "Initiation and Progression of Alcohol, Marijuana and Cocaine Use Among Adolescent Abusers," *The American Journal on Addiction,* 4, 1995, pp. 43–48.

40. Ronald Simmons, Rand Conger and Leslie Whitbeck, "A Multistage Learning Model of the Influences of Family and Peers Upon Adolescent Substance Abuse," *Journal of Drug Issues* 18(3) 1988, pp. 293–315.

41. Simmons, Conger and Whitbeck, p. 304; Mark Moore, "Drugs: Getting a Fix on the Problem and the Solution," in Evans and Berent, eds., p. 143.

42. Musto, pp. 258–259.

43. Philip Cook, "The Effect of Liquor Taxes on Drinking, Cirrhosis, and Auto Accidents" in *Alcohol and Public Policy: Beyond the Shadow of Prohibition,* Mark Moore and Dean Gerstein, eds. (Washington, DC: National Academy Press, 1981), p. 256.

44. Jack Homer, "Projecting the Impact of Law Enforcement on Cocaine Prevalence: A System Dynamics Approach," *Journal of Drug Issues* 23(2) 1993, pp. 281–295.

45. Kleber, p. 361.

46. James Q. Wilson, "Against the Legalization of Drugs," *Commentary* (February 1990), pp. 21–28.

47. See for example, Schmoke in Evans and Berent, eds., p. 218.

48. ONDCP (1995), p. 138.

49. Bureau of Justice Statistics, *Survey of State Prison Inmates, 1991* (Washington, DC: 1993), p. 26.

50. Bureau of Justice Statistics, *Prisoners in 1994* (Washington, DC: 1995), p. 13.

51. Paul Aaron and David Musto, "Temperance and Prohibition in America: A Historical Overview," in Moore and Gerstein, eds., p. 172.

52. Drug Enforcement Administration (DEA), *How to Hold Your Own in a Drug Legalization Debate* (Washington, DC, 1994), p. 26, adjusted to 1995.

53. Center on Addiction and Substance Abuse at Columbia University (CASA), *The Cost of Substance Abuse to America's Health Care System, Final Report* (To be issued, 1995).

54. The Tobacco Institute (1994), adjusted to 1995.

55. CASA (To be issued, 1995).

56. Center on Addiction and Substance Abuse at Columbia University, *Substance Abuse and Federal Entitlement Programs* (February 1995).

57. CASA (To be issued, 1995).

58. Centers for Disease Control, National AIDS Clearinghouse (1994).

59. See for example, "Prescribing to Addicts Appears to Work in Britain: Interview with Dr. John Marks," *Psychiatric News,* December 17, 1993, pp. 8, 14.

60. Joyce Lowinson et al, "Methadone Maintenance," pp. 550–561; Jerome Jaffe, "Opiates: Clinical Aspects," pp. 186–194; and Eric Simon, "Opiates: Neurobiology," pp. 195–204 in *Substance Abuse: A Comprehensive Textbook,* 2nd ed., Joyce Lowinson, Pedro Ruiz and Robert Millman, eds. (Baltimore: Williams and Wilkins, 1992).

61. Mark Gold, "Cocaine (and Crack): Clinical Aspects," in Lowinson, Ruiz and Millman, eds., pp. 205–221.

62. Peter Lurie, Arthur Reingold et al, *The Public Health Impact of Needle Exchange Programs in the United States and Abroad,* 2 vols., (University of California, 1993).

63. Dept. of Justice (1992), p. 12; Paul Taubman, "Externalities and Decriminalization of Drugs," in Krauss and Lazear, eds., p. 99.

64. Dept. of Justice (1992), p. 12; Joel Hay, "The Harm They Do to Others," in Krauss and Lazear, eds., pp. 204–213.

65. Hay, in Krauss and Lazear, eds., p. 208.

66. Center on Addiction and Substance Abuse at Columbia University (CASA), *The Cost of Substance Abuse to America's Health Care System, Report 1: Medicaid Hospital Costs,* (July 1993), pp. 38–46.

67. Ronald Kessler et al, "Lifetime and 12-month prevalence of DSM-III-R psychiatric disorders in the United States: Results from the National Comorbidity Study," *Archives of General Psychiatry,* 51(1) 1994, pp. 8–19.

68. Dept. of Justice (1992), p. 11.

69. Centers for Disease Control, "Youth Risk Behavior Survey, 1991."

70. M. Lynne Cooper, Robert Pierce, and Rebecca Farmer Huselid, "Substance Abuse and Sexual Risk Taking Among Black Adolescents and White Adolescents," *Health Psychology* 13(3) 1994, pp. 251–262.

71. Dept. of Justice (1992), p. 9.

72. General Accounting Office, *Foster Care: Parental Drug Abuse Has Alarming Impact on Young Children* (Washington, DC: 1994).

73. Daniel Brookoff et al, "Testing Reckless Drivers for Cocaine and Marijuana" *The New England Journal of Medicine* 331(8) 1994, pp. 518–522.

74. Peter Marzuk, Kenneth Tardiff, et al, "Prevalence of Recent Cocaine Use among Motor Vehicle Fatalities in New York City," *Journal of the American Medical Association* 1990; 263, pp. 250–256.

75. See for example, Nadelmann, in Inciardi (1991), ed., pp. 31–32; Brenner, in Evans and Berent, eds., p. 174; Ira Glasser, "Drug Prohibition: An Engine for Crime," in Krauss and Lazear, eds., pp. 271–283; Milton Friedman, "The War We are Losing," in Krauss and Lazear, eds., pp. 53–57.

76. Paul J. Goldstein, "The Drugs/Violence Nexus: A Tripartite Conceptual Framework," *Journal of Drug Issues* (Fall 1985) pp. 493–516.

77. Mitchell Rosenthal, "Panacea or Chaos: The Legalization of Drugs in America," *Journal of Substance Abuse Treatment* 11(1) 1994, pp. 3–7.

78. Henry Brownstein and Paul J. Goldstein, "A Typology of Drug-Related Homicides" in *Drugs, Crime and the Criminal Justice System,* Ralph Weisheit, ed., (Cincinnati, OH: Anderson Publishing Co., 1990), pp. 171–191.

79. Bureau of Justice Statistics (1993), p. 22.

80. Kenneth Tardiff et al, "Homicide in New York City: Cocaine Use and Firearms," *Journal of the American Medical Association,* 272(1) 1994, pp. 43–46.

81. Jon Chaiken and Marcia Chaiken, "Varieties of Criminal Behavior," (Santa Monica: Rand, 1982); HK Wexler and George De Leon, "Criminals as Drug Abusers and Drug Abusers Who Are Criminals" Paper presented to the Annual Convention of the American Psychological Association, Washington, DC, 1980; cited in George De Leon, "Some Problems with the Anti-Prohibitionist Position on Legalization of Drugs," *Journal of Addictive Diseases,* 13(2) 1994, p. 38.

82. See for example, New York City Bar Association, "A Wiser Course: Ending Drug Prohibition," *The Record* 49(5) 1994, pp. 525–534.

83. Bureau of Justice Statistics (1995), p. 13.

84. Bureau of Justice Statistics (1995), pp. 1, 10.

85. Bureau of Justice Statistics (1993), p. 11.

86. Bureau of Justice Statistics (1993), p. 21.

87. General Accounting Office, *Drug Treatment: State Prisons Face Challenges in Providing Services* (Washington, DC: 1991).

88. Bureau of Justice Statistics (1993), p. 26.

89. De Leon, p. 38.

90. M. Douglas Anglin. "The Efficacy of Civil Commitment in Treating Narcotic Addiction" in *Compulsory Treatment of Drug Abuse: Research and Clinical Practice,* NIDA Research Monograph 86, 1988, pp. 8–34; Robert Hubbard et al, *Drug Abuse Treatment: A National Study of Effectiveness* (Chapel Hill: University of North Carolina Press, 1989).

 **NO**

Youth Prevention-Related Measures

The National Survey on Drug Use and Health (NSDUH) includes questions for youths aged 12 to 17 about a number of risk and protective factors that may affect the likelihood that they will engage in substance use. Risk factors are individual characteristics and environmental influences associated with an increased vulnerability to the initiation, continuation, or escalation of substance use. Protective factors include individual resilience and other circumstances that are associated with a reduction in the likelihood of substance use. Risk and protective factors include variables that operate at different stages of development and reflect different domains of influence, including the individual, family, peer, school, community, and societal levels (Hawkins, Catalano, & Miller, 1992; Robertson, David, & Rao, 2003). Interventions to prevent substance use generally are designed to ameliorate the influence of risk factors and enhance the effectiveness of protective factors.

This chapter presents findings for youth prevention-related measures collected in the 2009 NSDUH and compares these with findings from previous years. Included are measures of perceived risk from substance use (cigarettes, alcohol, and illicit drugs), perceived availability of substances, being approached by someone selling drugs, perceived parental disapproval of youth substance use, feelings about peer substance use, involvement in fighting and delinquent behavior, participation in religious and other activities, exposure to substance use prevention messages and programs, and parental involvement.

In this chapter, rates of substance use are compared for persons responding differently to questions reflecting risk or protective factors, such as the perceived risk of harm from using a substance. Because the NSDUH data for an individual are collected at only one point in time, it is not possible to determine causal connections from these data. However, a number of research studies of youths have shown that reducing risk factors and increasing protective factors can reduce rates of substance use (Botvin, Botvin, & Ruchlin, 1998). This report shows that marijuana, cigarette, and alcohol past month use among youths aged 12 to 17 decreased between 2002 and 2009, yet corresponding changes in individual risk and protective factors for the same period may or may not have occurred. There can be many reasons for this, such as the lack of or a weak causal connection, a lagged relationship between the occurrence of a risk factor and the change in drug use behavior, or that individual

From *Results from the 2009 National Survey on Drug Use and Health: Volume 1*, U.S. Department of Health and Human Services, 2010.

use is typically the result of multiple simultaneous risk factors rather than a single factor (Newcomb, Maddahian, & Bentler, 1986).

Perceptions of Risk

One factor that can influence whether youths will use tobacco, alcohol, or illicit drugs is the extent to which youths believe these substances might cause them harm. NSDUH respondents were asked how much they thought people risk harming themselves physically and in other ways when they use various substances in certain amounts or frequencies. Response choices for these items were "great risk," "moderate risk," "slight risk," or "no risk."

- The percentages of youths reporting binge alcohol use and use of cigarettes and marijuana in the past month were lower among those who perceived great risk in using these substances than among those who did not perceive great risk. For example, in 2009, 5.1 percent of youths aged 12 to 17 who perceived great risk from "having five or more drinks of an alcoholic beverage once or twice a week" reported binge drinking in the past month (consumption of five or more drinks of an alcoholic beverage on a single occasion on at least 1 day in the past 30 days); by contrast, past month binge drinking was reported by 11.4 percent of youths who saw moderate, slight, or no risk from having five or more drinks of an alcoholic beverage once or twice a week (Figure 1). Past month marijuana use was reported by 1.3 percent of youths who

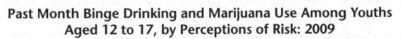

Figure 1

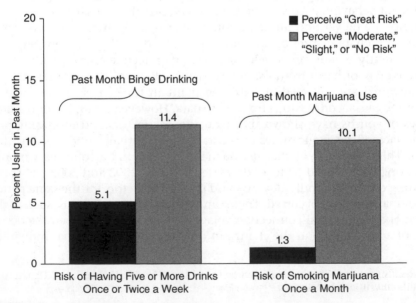

Past Month Binge Drinking and Marijuana Use Among Youths Aged 12 to 17, by Perceptions of Risk: 2009

saw great risk in smoking marijuana once a month compared with 10.1 percent of youths who saw moderate, slight, or no risk.

- Decreases in the rate of current use of a substance often occur when there are increases in the level of perceived risk of using that substance. Looking over the 8-year period, the proportion of youths aged 12 to 17 who reported perceiving great risk from smoking one or more packs of cigarettes per day increased from 63.1 percent in 2002 to 69.7 percent in 2008, but it declined between 2008 and 2009 (65.8 percent) (Figure 2). During the same period, the rate of past month cigarette smoking among youths aged 12 to 17 dropped from 13.0 percent in 2002 to 9.1 percent in 2008, but it remained statistically unchanged between 2008 and 2009 (8.9 percent).

- The percentage of youths aged 12 to 17 indicating great risk in having four or five drinks of an alcoholic beverage nearly every day increased from 62.2 percent in 2002 to 65.9 percent in 2008, but it decreased between 2008 and 2009 (64.3 percent) (Figure 2). The rate of past month heavy alcohol use among youths aged 12 to 17 decreased from 2.5 percent in 2002 to 2.0 percent in 2008, but it remained stable between 2008 and 2009 (2.1 percent).

- The percentage of youths aged 12 to 17 perceiving great risk in having five or more drinks of an alcoholic beverage once or twice a week increased from 38.2 percent in 2002 to 39.9 percent in 2009 (Figure 2). The rate of past month binge alcohol use among youths decreased from 10.7 percent in 2002 to 8.8 percent in 2009.

Figure 2

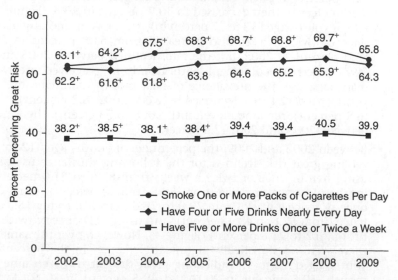

Perceived Great Risk of Cigarette and Alcohol Use Among Youths Aged 12 to 17: 2002–2009

†Difference between this estimate and the 2009 estimate is statistically significant at the .05 level.

Figure 3

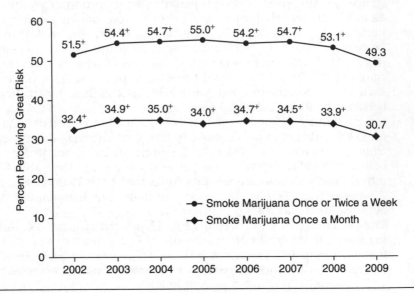

Perceived Great Risk of Marijuana Use Among Youths Aged 12 to 17: 2002–2009

⁺Difference between this estimate and the 2009 estimate is statistically significant at the .05 level.

- The percentage of youths aged 12 to 17 indicating great risk in smoking marijuana once a month increased from 32.4 percent in 2002 to 34.9 percent in 2003, remained unchanged between 2003 and 2008 (33.9 percent), then decreased to 30.7 percent in 2009 (Figure 3). The rate of youths aged 12 to 17 perceiving great risk in smoking marijuana once or twice a week also increased from 51.5 percent in 2002 to 55.0 percent in 2005, but the rate declined between 2005 and 2009 (49.3 percent). Coincident with trends in perceived great risk of marijuana use, the prevalence of past month marijuana use among youths aged 12 to 17 decreased between 2002 (8.2 percent) and 2005 (6.8 percent), remained level until 2008 (6.7 percent), then increased between 2008 and 2009 (7.3 percent).

- Between 2002 and 2009, the percentage of youths aged 12 to 17 perceiving great risk declined for the following substance use patterns: using heroin once or twice a week (from 82.5 to 81.0 percent), trying heroin once or twice (from 58.5 to 57.0 percent), using cocaine once or twice a week (from 79.8 to 78.5 percent), trying LSD once or twice (from 52.6 to 48.4 percent), and using LSD once or twice a week (from 76.2 to 71.8 percent) (Figure 4). However, over the same period there were no statistically significant changes in the percentages of youths aged 12 to 17 indicating great risk for using cocaine once a month (50.5 percent in 2002 and 49.5 percent in 2009). Moreover, percentages for the two heroin and the two cocaine perceptions of risk

Figure 4

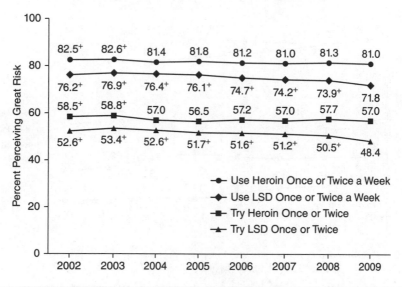

**Perceived Great Risk of Use of Selected Illicit Drugs
Among Youths Aged 12 to 17: 2002–2009**

†Difference between this estimate and the 2009 estimate is statistically significant at the .05 level.

measures remained stable between 2008 and 2009, while the two LSD measures declined during this time period.

Perceived Availability

- In 2009, about half (49.9 percent) of the youths aged 12 to 17 reported that it would be "fairly easy" or "very easy" for them to obtain marijuana if they wanted some (Figure 5). One in eight (12.9 percent) indicated that heroin would be "fairly" or "very" easily available, and 13.5 percent reported so for LSD. Between 2002 and 2009, there were decreases in the perceived availability of marijuana (from 55.0 to 49.9 percent), cocaine (from 25.0 to 20.9 percent), crack (from 26.5 to 22.1 percent), LSD (from 19.4 to 13.5 percent), and heroin (from 15.8 to 12.9 percent). The perceived availability of cocaine declined from 22.1 percent in 2008 to 20.9 percent in 2009. However, the perceived availability of marijuana, crack, LSD, and heroin did not change significantly during this 2-year period.
- The percentage of youths who reported that marijuana, cocaine, and LSD would be easy to obtain increased with age in 2009. For example, 19.8 percent of those aged 12 or 13 said it would be fairly or very easy to obtain marijuana compared with 52.9 percent of those aged 14 or 15 and 72.2 percent of those aged 16 or 17.
- In 2009, 14.3 percent of youths aged 12 to 17 indicated that they had been approached by someone selling drugs in the past month, which was down from the 16.7 percent reported in 2002 (Figure 6). The rate remained stable between 2008 (13.7 percent) and 2009.

Figure 5

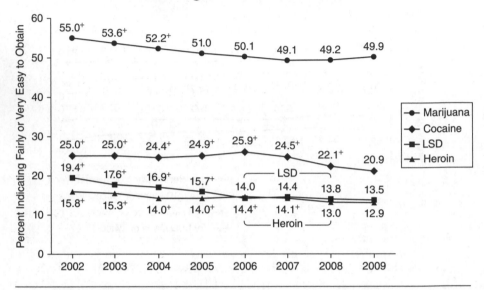

Perceived Availability of Selected Illicit Drugs Among Youths Aged 12 to 17: 2002–2009

+Difference between this estimate and the 2009 estimate is statistically significant at the .05 level.

Figure 6

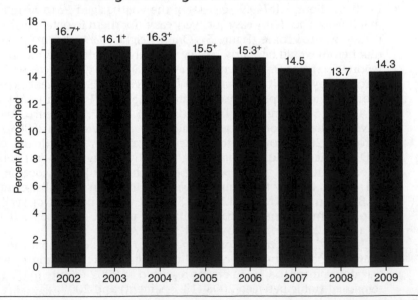

Approached in the Past Month by Someone Selling Drugs Among Youths Aged 12 to 17: 2002–2009

+Difference between this estimate and the 2009 estimate is statistically significant at the .05 level.

Perceived Parental Disapproval of Substance Use

- Most youths aged 12 to 17 believed their parents would "strongly disapprove" of their using substances. In 2009, 90.5 percent of youths reported that their parents would strongly disapprove of their trying marijuana or hashish once or twice; this was similar to the 90.8 percent reported in 2008, but was higher than the 89.1 percent reported in 2002. Most (90.3 percent) reported that their parents would strongly disapprove of their having one or two drinks of an alcoholic beverage nearly every day, which was similar to the rate in 2008 (89.7 percent) and was higher than the rate in 2002 (89.0 percent). In 2009, 92.6 percent of youths reported that their parents would strongly disapprove of their smoking one or more packs of cigarettes per day, which was similar to the 92.4 percent reported in 2008, but was higher than the 89.5 percent reported in 2002.
- Youths aged 12 to 17 who believed their parents would strongly disapprove of their using substances were less likely to use that substance than were youths who believed their parents would somewhat disapprove or neither approve nor disapprove. For example, in 2009, past month cigarette use was reported by 6.5 percent of youths who perceived strong parental disapproval of their smoking one or more packs of cigarettes per day compared with 40.5 percent of youths who believed their parents would not strongly disapprove. Past month marijuana use also was much less prevalent among youths who perceived strong parental disapproval for trying marijuana or hashish once or twice than among those who did not (4.8 vs. 31.3 percent, respectively).

Feelings About Peer Substance Use

- A majority of youths aged 12 to 17 reported that they disapprove of their peers using substances. In 2009, 90.1 percent of youths "strongly" or "somewhat" disapproved of their peers smoking one or more packs of cigarettes per day, which was similar to the rate of 89.6 percent in 2008, but higher than the 87.1 percent in 2002. Also in 2009, 82.0 percent strongly or somewhat disapproved of peers using marijuana or hashish once a month or more, which was similar to the 82.7 percent reported in 2008, but was an increase from the 80.4 percent reported in 2002. In addition, 87.4 percent of youths strongly or somewhat disapproved of peers having one or two drinks of an alcoholic beverage nearly every day in 2009, which was similar to the 87.0 percent reported in 2008, but was higher than the 84.7 percent reported in 2002.
- In 2009, past month marijuana use was reported by 2.6 percent among youths aged 12 to 17 who strongly or somewhat disapproved of their peers using marijuana once a month or more, lower than the 28.7 percent among youths who reported that they neither approve nor disapprove of such behavior from their peers.

Fighting and Delinquent Behavior

- In 2009, 21.1 percent of youths aged 12 to 17 reported that, in the past year, they had gotten into a serious fight at school or at work; this was similar to the rates in 2008 (21.4 percent) and 2002 (20.6 percent).

Approximately one in seven youths (14.4 percent) in 2009 had taken part in a group-against-group fight, which was similar to the rate in 2008 (14.5 percent) and lower than the rate in 2002 (15.9 percent). About 1 in 30 (3.2 percent) had carried a handgun at least once in 2009, which was the same as the rate in 2008 (3.2 percent) and was similar to the rate in 2002 (3.3 percent). An estimated 7.2 percent had, in at least one instance, attacked others with the intent to harm or seriously hurt them in 2009, which was the similar to the rate in 2008 (7.3 percent) and was similar to the 7.8 percent reported in 2002. An estimated 3.2 percent had sold illegal drugs in 2009, which was similar to the rate of 3.0 percent in 2008, but was lower than the 4.4 percent rate in 2002. In 2009, 4.4 percent had, at least once, stolen or tried to steal something worth more than $50; this was similar to the rate of 4.6 percent in 2008, but was lower than the rate of 4.9 percent in 2002.

- Youths aged 12 to 17 who had engaged in fighting or other delinquent behaviors were more likely than other youths to have used illicit drugs in the past month. For example, in 2009, past month illicit drug use was reported by 18.8 percent of youths who had gotten into a serious fight at school or work in the past year compared with 7.7 percent of those who had not engaged in fighting, and by 38.3 percent of those who had stolen or tried to steal something worth over $50 in the past year compared with 8.7 percent of those who had not attempted or engaged in such theft.

Religious Beliefs and Participation in Activities

- In 2009, 31.4 percent of youths aged 12 to 17 reported that they had attended religious services 25 or more times in the past year, which was similar to the rate in 2008 (31.7 percent), but was lower than the rate in 2002 (33.0 percent). Also, 74.7 percent agreed or strongly agreed with the statement that religious beliefs are a very important part of their lives, which was similar to the 75.0 percent reported in 2008, but was lower than the 78.2 percent reported in 2002. In 2009, 34.0 percent agreed or strongly agreed with the statement that it is important for their friends to share their religious beliefs, which was similar to the rate in 2008 (33.8 percent) and was lower than the rate in 2002 (35.8 percent).
- The rates of past month use of illicit drugs, cigarettes, and alcohol (including binge alcohol) were lower among youths aged 12 to 17 who agreed with these statements about religious beliefs than among those who disagreed. For example, in 2009, past month illicit drug use was reported by 7.4 percent of those who agreed that religious beliefs are a very important part of life compared with 17.6 percent of those who disagreed with that statement.

Exposure to Substance Use Prevention Messages and Programs

- In 2009, approximately one in eight youths aged 12 to 17 (12.0 percent) reported that they had participated in drug, tobacco, or alcohol prevention programs outside of school in the past year. This rate was higher than the 11.1 percent reported in 2008, but was similar to the rate reported in 2002 (12.7 percent) and lower than the rate reported in 2003 (13.9 percent). In 2009, the prevalence of past month use of illicit drugs, marijuana, or cigarettes or past month binge alcohol use among those who participated in these prevention programs outside of school was not significantly different (10.5, 6.9, 8.9, or 8.1 percent, respectively) from the prevalence among those who did not (10.0, 7.4, 8.9, or 8.9 percent, respectively).

- In 2009, 77.0 percent of youths aged 12 to 17 reported having seen or heard drug or alcohol prevention messages in the past year from sources outside of school, which was similar to the 78.0 percent reported in 2008, but was lower than the 83.2 percent reported in 2002 (Figure 7). In 2009, the prevalence of past month use of illicit drugs was lower among those who reported having such exposure (9.7 percent) than among those who reported having no such exposure (11.3 percent).

- In 2009, 74.9 percent of youths aged 12 to 17 enrolled in school in the past year reported having seen or heard drug or alcohol prevention messages at school, which was similar to the 75.9 percent reported in 2008, but was lower than the 78.8 percent reported in 2002 (Figure 7). In 2009, the prevalence of past month use of illicit drugs or marijuana was lower among those who reported having such exposure (9.2 and 6.7 percent for illicit drugs and marijuana, respectively) than among those who reported having no such exposure (12.7 and 9.7 percent, respectively).

Figure 7

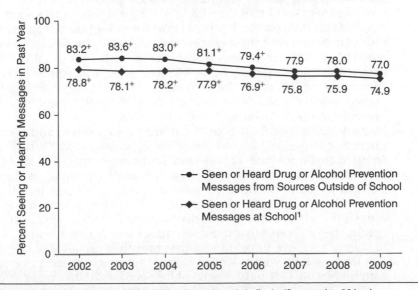

Exposure to Substance Use Prevention Messages and Programs Among Youths Aged 12 to 17: 2002–2009

†Difference between this estimate and the 2009 estimate is statistically significant at the .05 level.
[1]Estimates are from youths aged 12 to 17 who were enrolled in school in the past year.

- In 2009, 58.2 percent of youths aged 12 to 17 reported that in the past year they had talked at least once with at least one of their parents about the dangers of drug, tobacco, or alcohol use, which was similar to rates reported in 2008 (58.7 percent) and 2002 (58.1 percent). The prevalence of past month use of illicit drugs, marijuana, or cigarettes or past month binge alcohol use among those who reported having had such conversations with their parents (9.8, 7.3, 8.6, and 8.7 percent, respectively) was not significantly different from that among those who reported having no such conversations (10.4, 7.4, 9.4, and 9.1 percent, respectively).

Parental Involvement

- Youths aged 12 to 17 were asked a number of questions related to the extent of support, oversight, and control that they perceived their parents exercised over them in the year prior to the survey. In 2009, among youths aged 12 to 17 enrolled in school in the past year, 79.8 percent reported that in the past year their parents always or sometimes checked on whether or not they had completed their homework, and 70.6 percent reported that their parents limited the amount of time that they spent out with friends on school nights. Both of these rates reported in 2009 were similar to those reported in 2008 and remained statistically unchanged from the rates reported in 2002. However, in 2009, 79.9 percent reported that their parents always or sometimes provided help with their homework, which was similar to the rate in 2008 (80.0 percent), but was lower than the rate in 2002 (81.4 percent).

- In 2009, 87.4 percent of youths aged 12 to 17 reported that in the past year their parents made them always or sometimes do chores around the house, 85.7 percent reported that their parents always or sometimes let them know that they had done a good job, and 85.4 percent reported that their parents let them know they were proud of something they had done. All of these percentages in 2009 were similar to those reported in 2008 and remained statistically unchanged from the rates reported in 2002. In 2009, however, 40.1 percent of youths reported that their parents limited the amount of time that they watched television, which was similar to the rate in 2008 (39.9 percent), but was higher than the 36.9 percent reported in 2002.

- In 2009, past month use of illicit drugs, cigarettes, and alcohol (including binge alcohol) was lower among youths aged 12 to 17 who reported that their parents always or sometimes engaged in monitoring behaviors than among youths whose parents "seldom" or "never" engaged in such behaviors. For example, the rate of past month use of any illicit drug was 8.2 percent for youths whose parents always or sometimes helped with homework compared with 17.5 percent among youths who indicated that their parents seldom or never helped. Rates of current cigarette smoking and past month binge alcohol use were also lower among youths whose parents always or sometimes helped with homework (7.5 and 7.4 percent, respectively) than among youths whose parents did not (15.7 and 15.6 percent, respectively).

POSTSCRIPT

Should Laws Against Drug Use Remain Restrictive?

Kleber and Califano assert that utilizing the criminal justice system to maintain the illegal nature of drugs is necessary to keep society free of the detrimental effects of drugs. Loosening drug laws is unwise and dangerous. They argue that international control efforts, interdiction, and domestic law enforcement are effective and that many problems associated with drug use are mitigated by drug regulation policies. They maintain that restrictive drug laws are a feasible and desirable means of dealing with the drug crisis.

It has been charged that restrictive drug laws are highly destructive and discriminatory and that if drug laws remain stringent, the result would be more drug users in prison and that drug abusers and addicts would engage in more criminal activity. Also, there is the possibility that more drug-related social problems would occur. One could conclude that society cannot afford to retain its intransigent position on drug legalization. The potential risks of the current federal policies on drug criminalization outweigh any potential benefits. Society suffers from harsh drug laws by losing many of its civil liberties.

Proponents for less restrictive drug laws argue that such laws have not worked and that the drug battle has been lost. They believe that drug-related problems would diminish if more tolerant policies were implemented. Citing the legal drugs alcohol and tobacco as examples, legalization opponents argue that less restrictive drug laws would not decrease profits from the sale of drugs (the profits from cigarettes and alcohol are incredibly high). Moreover, opponents argue, relaxing drug laws does not make problems associated with drugs disappear (alcohol and tobacco have extremely high addiction rates as well as a myriad of other problems associated with their use). To reduce drug use, according to the report from the Department of Health and Human Services, attention needs to focus on perception of risk and drug use by peers.

Many European countries, such as the Netherlands and Switzerland, have a system of legalized drugs, and most have far fewer addiction rates and lower incidences of drug-related violence and crime than the United States. These countries make a distinction between soft drugs (those identified as less harmful) and hard drugs (those with serious consequences). However, would the outcomes of less restrictive laws in the United States be the same as in Europe? Relaxed drug laws in the United States could still be a tremendous risk because its drug problems could escalate and reimposing strict drug laws would be difficult. This was the case with Prohibition in the 1920s, which, in changing the status of alcohol from legal to illegal, produced numerous crime- and alcohol-related problems.

Many good articles debate the pros and cons of this issue. These include "Perceptions of Risk from Substance Use Among Adolescents," by the Substance Abuse and Mental Health Services Administration (2009); "Who's Using and Who's Doing Time: Incarceration, the War on Drugs, and Public Health," by Lisa Moore and Amy Elkavich, *American Journal of Public Health* (September 2008); "Too Dangerous Not to Regulate," by Peter Moskos, *U.S. News and World Report* (August 4, 2008); "Reorienting U.S. Drug Policy," by Jonathon Caulkins and Peter Reuter, *Issues in Science and Technology* (Fall 2006); "Lighting Up in Amsterdam," by John Tierney, *New York Times* (August 26, 2006); and "What Drug Policies Cost: Estimating Government Drug Policy Expenditures," by Peter Reuter, *Addiction* (March 2006).

ISSUE 2

Should the United States Put More Emphasis on Stopping the Importation of Drugs?

YES: Bureau of International Narcotics and Law Enforcement Affairs, from *2009 INCSR: Policy and Program Developments* (U.S. Department of State, 2009)

NO: Ethan Nadelmann, from "The Global War on Drugs Can Be Won," *Foreign Policy* (October 2007)

ISSUE SUMMARY

YES: Because the trafficking of drugs represents a direct threat to national security, the U.S. State Department maintains that more effort is needed to interdict drugs coming into the United States. Better cooperation with countries in Latin America, the Caribbean, Africa, and Asia, where drugs are grown and exported, is essential.

NO: Ethan Nadelmann, the executive director of the Drug Policy Alliance, contends that attempts to stem the flow of drugs are futile and that it is unrealistic to believe that the world can be made free of drugs. Nadelmann points out that global production is about the same as it was ten years earlier and that cocaine and heroin are purer and cheaper because producers have become more efficient.

Since the beginning of the 1990s, overall drug use in the United States has increased. Up to now, interdiction has not proven to be successful in slowing the flow of drugs into the United States. Drugs continue to cross U.S. borders at record levels. This may signal a need for stepped-up international efforts to stop the production and trafficking of drugs. Conversely, it may illustrate the inadequacy of the current strategy. Should the position of the U.S. government be to improve and strengthen current measures or to try an entirely new approach?

Some people contend that rather than attempting to limit illegal drugs from coming into the United States, more effort should be directed at reducing the demand for drugs and improving treatment for drug abusers. Foreign countries would not produce and transport drugs like heroin and cocaine into the United States if there was no market for them. Drug policies, some people maintain, should be aimed at the social and economic conditions underlying domestic drug problems, not at interfering with foreign governments.

Many U.S. government officials believe that other countries should assist in stopping the flow of drugs across their borders. Diminishing the supply of drugs by intercepting them before they reach the user is another way to eliminate or curtail drug use. Critical elements in the lucrative drug trade are multinational crime syndicates. One premise is that if the drug production, transportation, distribution, and processing functions as well as the money laundering operations of these criminal organizations can be interrupted and eventually crippled, then the drug problem would abate.

In South American countries such as Peru, Colombia, and Bolivia, where coca—from which cocaine is processed—is cultivated, economic aid has been made available to help the governments of these countries fight the cocaine kingpins. An alleged problem is that a number of government officials in these countries are corrupt or fearful of the cocaine cartel leaders. One proposed solution is to go directly to the farmers and offer them money to plant crops other than coca. This tactic, however, failed in the mid-1970s, when the U.S. government gave money to farmers in Turkey to stop growing opium poppy crops. After one year the program was discontinued due to the enormous expense, and opium poppy crops were once again planted.

Drug problems are not limited to the Americas. Since the breakup of the Soviet Union, for example, there has been a tremendous increase in opium production in many of the former republics. These republics are in dire need of money, and one source of income is opium production. Moreover, there is lax enforcement by police officials in these republics.

There are many reasons why people are dissatisfied with the current state of the war on drugs. For example, in the war on drugs, the casual user is generally the primary focus of drug use deterrence. This is viewed by many people as a form of discrimination because the vast majority of drug users and sellers who are arrested and prosecuted are poor, members of minorities, homeless, unemployed, and/or disenfranchised. Also, international drug dealers who are arrested are usually not the drug bosses but lower-level people working for them. Finally, some argue that the war on drugs should be redirected away from interdiction and enforcement because they feel that the worst drug problems in society today are caused by legal drugs, primarily alcohol and tobacco.

The following selections address the issue of whether or not the war on drugs should be fought on an international level. The U.S. Department of State takes the view that international cooperation is absolutely necessary if we are to stem the flow of drugs and reduce drug-related problems in the United States. Ethan Nadelmann argues that an international approach to dealing with drugs has been ineffective because the production of drugs has not been curtailed.

YES ⤾ Bureau of International Narcotics and Law Enforcement Affairs

2009 INCSR: Policy and Program Developments

Overview for 2008

International narcotics trafficking directly threatens the national security of the United States. Drugs sold on U.S. streets lead to overdose deaths and ruined lives, erode families, and foster criminality and violence. Trafficking organizations, looking to build their customer base, sometimes pay in drugs instead of cash, promoting drug abuse and its social consequences in source and transit countries in Latin America, the Caribbean, Africa, and Asia. Many of these same countries are besieged by narcotics criminals who corrupt and financially undermine legitimate law enforcement and government institutions. The environment is equally threatened, as drug producers hack down forests and dump toxic chemicals in fragile ecosystems.

The United States Government (USG) confronts the threat of international narcotics trafficking through a combination of law enforcement investigation, interdiction, diplomatic initiatives, targeted economic sanctions, financial programs and investigations, and institutional development initiatives focused on disrupting all segments of the illicit drug market, from the fields and clandestine laboratories where drugs are produced, through the transit zones, to our ports and borders. In 2008, U.S. federal law enforcement officials worked cooperatively with the police of partner nations to conduct international investigations that successfully apprehended, among others, Zhenli Ye Gon, Eduardo Arellano Felix, and Haji Juma Khan. Another international law enforcement operation involving the DEA, the Royal Thai Police, the Romanian Border Police, the Korps Politie Curacao of the Netherlands Antilles, and the Danish National Police Security Services led to the arrest of Victor Bout on charges of attempting to provide sophisticated weapons to the narco-terrorist organization the Fuerzas Armadas Revolucionarias de Colombia.[1]

The USG continued to provide partner nations with essential training assistance to strengthen their law enforcement and judicial systems and helped them improve their capacity to investigate, prosecute, and punish transnational criminal activity. Closer international cooperation among governments and financial institutions continues to close the loopholes that allow

From *2009 INCSR Report: Policy and Program Developments,* 2009. Published by Bureau of International Narcotics and Law Enforcement Affairs, U.S. Department of State.

narcotrafficking organizations to legitimize their enormous profits through sophisticated money laundering schemes.

Much of our cooperation with partner nations occurred under bilateral arrangements for mutual legal assistance, extraditions, and training programs. Multilateral efforts also continued to be a key component of the overall U.S. counternarcotics strategy. Through multilateral organizations, the United States has the opportunity to encourage contributions from other donors so that we can undertake counternarcotics assistance programs, jointly sharing costs and expertise. U.S. participation in multilateral programs also supports indigenous capabilities in regions where the United States is unable to operate bilaterally for political or logistical reasons. Counternarcotics assistance through international organizations promotes awareness that drug producing and transit countries inevitably become consuming nations; today it is clearly understood that drugs are not a U.S. problem, but a global challenge.

One example of working with partner donors is the Good Performers Initiative (GPI) in Afghanistan, a U.S.-UK-funded initiative launched in 2006 to reward provinces for successful counternarcotics performance. Based on the results of the UN Office on Drugs and Crime's annual Afghanistan Opium Cultivation Survey, this incentive program provides funds for development projects to provinces that were poppy-free or reduced their poppy cultivation by more than 10 percent from the previous year. In 2008, 29 of Afghanistan's 34 provinces qualified for over $39 million in GPI development assistance projects. To date, the U.S. government has contributed over $69 million to GPI and its predecessor the Good Performer's Fund, while the UK has provided approximately $12 million. In Nangarhar province, for example, four micro-hydro projects that generate electricity for rural villages have been completed with these funds and 20 more are scheduled to be built in 2009.

International treaties are another key tool in the fight against international narcotics trafficking. Three mutually reinforcing UN conventions are particularly important:

- The Single Convention on Narcotic Drugs—1961
- The Convention on Psychotropic Substances—1971, and
- The United Nations Convention against Illicit Traffic in Narcotic Drugs and Psychotropic Substances (the "1988 UN Drug Convention")

The 1988 UN Drug Convention is nearly universally accepted and serves as one of the bases for this report (For a full explanation, see the chapter titled "Legislative Basis for the INCSR"). A list of the countries that are parties to the 1988 UN Drug Convention is included in this report (source: UNODC). In 2008, there were no additional parties to the 1988 UN Drug Convention. Although the Convention does not contain a list of goals and objectives, it does set forth a number of obligations that the parties agree to undertake. Generally speaking, it requires the parties to take legal measures to outlaw and punish all forms of illicit drug production, trafficking, and drug money laundering; to control chemicals that can be used to process illicit drugs; and to cooperate in international efforts to these ends.

In addition to the UN conventions that are focused exclusively on drugs, newer international instruments, such as the United Nations Convention against Transnational Organized Crime and the United Nations Convention against Corruption, have helped in the fight against the international narcotics trade by making law enforcement cooperation, extraditions, border security, and tracking of illicit funds more efficient among the parties to the treaties.

While most countries are parties to the UN conventions, the ultimate success of international drug control efforts does not hinge completely on whether countries are parties to them. The vast majority of countries also have their own domestic laws and policies to support their obligations under the conventions. Success in international drug control depends on international political will to meet the commitments made when countries joined the UN conventions. Sustainable progress also requires sufficient capacities to enforce the rule of law and implementing the objectives of committed governments. To assist this process, the United States is committed to enhancing the capacity of partner governments to uphold their international commitments.

Controlling Supply

Cocaine, amphetamine-type stimulants (ATS), marijuana and heroin are the internationally trafficked drugs that most threaten the United States and our international allies. The United States is a producer of two of these drugs, marijuana and ATS. The USG is committed to confronting the illicit cultivation and manufacture of these drugs. In 2007, the DEA-initiated Domestic Cannabis Eradication/Suppression Program was responsible for the eradication of 6,600,000 cultivated outdoor cannabis plants and 430,000 indoor plants. In 2008, California alone eradicated 5,250,000 plants. Pharmaceutical preparations containing ephedrine and pseudoephedrine are the primary chemicals necessary for methamphetamine production. The Combat Methamphetamine Epidemic Act (CMEA), passed in 2005, established regulations for the sale of such products in the United States and became effective at the national level for the first time in late 2006. In 2008, the Methamphetamine Production Prevention Act was passed allowing states to institute computerized log books of purchases of methamphetamine precursor preparations. According to the National Clandestine Laboratory Database, methamphetamine lab incidents reported by all law enforcement agencies nationwide declined from more than 17,000 in 2005 to 5,900 in 2007 (2007 is the last complete year for which there are statistics, preliminary 2008 statistics are discussed later in this chapter, but the number in 2008 is expected to remain well below 50% of the 2005 figure). This dramatic decline is due to increased enforcement, the controls authorized by the two recent methamphetamine acts, and public and private demand reduction efforts.

In addition to eradicating marijuana crops found within the United States as part of our drug control strategy, the USG has provided assistance to countries that have made a policy decision to eradicate illicit crops as part of their own comprehensive drug control strategies. Crops in the ground are one of the critical nodes of production. Coca and poppy crops require adequate growing conditions, ample land, and time to reach maturity, all of which make them vulnerable to detection and eradication.

Perhaps the most acute and crucial challenge of achieving sustainable development in territories where drug cultivation takes place is the need to integrate otherwise marginalized regions into the economic and political mainstream of their country. The term that is most often used for this by the United States, the United Nations, and other international actors is "alternative development." Alternative development goes far beyond crop substitution, the usual assumed meaning. In some situations, crop substitution is neither feasible nor desirable. In some areas, the same soil that supports illicit drug crop cultivation does not have adequate nutrients to support licit crops. Licit crops rarely produce the same income as drug crops, and in some cases, farmers will need inducement to pursue non-agricultural pursuits. Anecdotal evidence suggests that in 2008 economic and environmental inducements caused many farmers in Afghanistan to plant wheat instead of poppy. One factor that possibly influenced this shift was the rise in global food prices, making wheat a more viable economic alternative to poppy. Other powerful inducements could include access to credit, improved security, and the provision of government services such as the building of roads, schools, and health centers, and a reliable supplying of basic services like electricity and water, and the threat of losing an investment in illicit crops to eradication or asset forfeiture. These programs are vulnerable to disruption from crime, corruption and non-state actors, such as the FARC in Colombia or the Taliban in Afghanistan. Establishing them on the ground is a lengthy, sometimes frustrating process; however, if implemented correctly, alternative development is an effective policy. Without it, crop eradication alone will never amount to more than a temporary palliative, and will not achieve sustainable reduction of illicit narcotic crops. However, without security and government control of outlaw areas, neither program can succeed.

For synthetic drugs, such as ATS, physical eradication is impossible. Instead, the United States and our allies must create a legal regime of chemical controls and law enforcement efforts aimed at thwarting those who divert key chemicals, and destroying the laboratories needed to create ATS. As with our domestic enforcement efforts, our international programs focus on all the links in the supply-to-consumer chain: processing, distribution, and transportation, as well as the money trail left by this illegal trade.

Cocaine

The rate of U.S. cocaine consumption has generally declined over the past decade. From 2002 to 2007, rates of past-year use among youths aged 12 to 17 declined significantly for cocaine as well as for illicit drugs overall (Source: SAMHSA, Office of Applied Studies, National Survey on Drug Use and Health). Despite the declines, cocaine continues to be a major domestic concern. Internationally, cocaine continues to pose considerable risk to societies in the Americas, and increasingly to fragile transit states in West Africa. The 2008 World Drug Report by the UN Office of Drugs and Crime noted, as it has in previous years, that the decline in cocaine consumption and demand in North America has been replaced by demand in Europe. The UN report is hopeful that demand in Europe is leveling off, but notes that, "the growth in markets which are either close to source (South America) or on emerging trafficking routes (Africa) indicate that further containment is still a challenge."

Since all cocaine originates in the Andean countries of Colombia, Peru, and Bolivia, the U.S. Government provides assistance to help these countries develop and implement comprehensive strategies to reduce the growing of coca, processing coca into cocaine, abuse of cocaine within their borders, and illegal transport of cocaine to other countries.

Coca Eradication/Alternative Development: The 2008 Interagency Assessment of Cocaine Movement (IACM) estimates that between 500 and 700 metric tons (MT) of cocaine departed South America toward the United States in 2007, slightly less than the previous year's estimate of 510 to 730 metric tons. We support efforts by these governments to eliminate illegal coca. Alternative development programs offer farmers opportunities to abandon illegal activities and join the legitimate economy, a key tool for countries seeking to free their agricultural sector from reliance on the drug trade. In the Andean countries, such programs play a vital role in providing funds and technical assistance to strengthen public and private institutions, expand rural infrastructure, improve natural resources management, introduce alternative legal crops, and develop local and international markets for these products.

In Colombia, USG alternative development (AD) initiatives supported the cultivation of over 238,000 hectares of legal crops and completed 1,212 social and productive infrastructure projects in the last seven years. More than 291,000 families in 18 departments have benefited from these programs, and the USG has worked with Colombia's private sector to create an additional 273,000 full-time equivalent jobs.

At the close of the sixth year of the Peru alternative development program, more than 756 communities have renounced coca cultivation and over 49,000 family farmers have received technical assistance on 61,000 hectares of licit crops (cacao, coffee, African palm oil, etc.). With many of these long-term crops now entering their most productive years, the alternative development program has expanded business development activities to link AD producers to local and world markets at optimum prices. The direct link between AD and eradication is successfully reducing coca cultivation and is a model for further progress against illicit cultivation.

In 2008, the annual value of USAID-promoted exports reached almost $35 million in Bolivia, assistance to farm communities and businesses helped generate 5,459 new jobs, new sales of AD products of nearly $28 million, and approximately 717 kilometers of roads were improved and 16 bridges constructed. However, these cooperative efforts were overshadowed by the Government of Bolivia's (GOB) ousting of USAID from the Chapare region.

The government of Colombia dedicates significant resources to reduce coca growing and cocaine production; however, its large territory and ideal climate conditions make Colombia the source of roughly 60 percent of the cocaine produced in the region and around 90 percent of the cocaine destined for the United States, with Peru and Bolivia a distant second and third respectively.

In 2008, the Colombian National Police (CNP) Anti-Narcotics Directorate reported aerial spraying of over 130,000 hectares of coca and manually eradicating over 96,000 hectares despite entrenched armed resistance by the FARC, a drug-trafficking organization that is also a designated Foreign Terrorist Organization. If harvested and refined, this eradicated coca could have yielded hundreds of metric tons of cocaine worth billions of dollars on U.S. streets.

In 2008, Peru exceeded its eradication goals for the second year in a row by eradicating more than 10,000 hectares. This success was achieved despite the continued targeting of eradication teams by the Shining Path, a designated Foreign Terrorist Organization (FTO). The Shining Path, which is reliant on drug trafficking for its funding, was reportedly responsible for attacks on police and military personnel in the Upper Huallaga Valley (UHV) and the Apurimac and Ene River Valleys and threatened eradication workers and other government authorities and alternative development teams. Coca growers in the UHV engaged in violent acts to resist eradication.

Bolivian President Evo Morales continued to promote his policy of "zero cocaine but not zero coca" and to push for legitimization of coca. His administration continues to pursue policies that would increase government-allowed coca cultivation from 12,000 to 20,000 hectares—a change that would violate current Bolivian law and contravene the 1988 UN Drug Convention, to which Bolivia is a party. On September 11, 2008, President Morales expelled the U.S. Ambassador to Bolivia. During 2008, President Morales also expelled the Drug Enforcement Administration (DEA) from Bolivia and the U.S. Agency for International Development from the coca-growing Chapare region. Coupled with continued increases in coca cultivation, cocaine production, and the Government of Bolivia's (GOB) unwillingness to regulate "licit" coca markets, President Bush determined on September 15 that Bolivia had "failed demonstrably" in meeting its international counterdrug obligations. For greater detail see the memorandum of justification in this report.

Cocaine Seizures: Colombian authorities reported seizing over 223 metric tons of cocaine in 2008, an all-time record, and destroyed 301 cocaine HCl labs and 3,238 cocaine base labs. Peru reported seizing over 22 metric tons of cocaine. In Bolivia, USG-supported counternarcotics units reported seizing 26 metric tons of cocaine base and cocaine hydrochloride (HCl) and destroying 6,535 cocaine labs and maceration pits.

Collectively, the eradication of coca and seizures of cocaine within the Andean source countries prevented hundreds of metric tons of cocaine from reaching U.S. streets and deprived international drug syndicates of billions of dollars in profits.

Interdiction in the Cocaine Transit Zone: The cocaine transit zone drug flow is of double importance for the United States: it threatens our borders, and it leaves a trail of corruption and addiction in its wake that undermines the social framework of societies in Central America, Mexico and the Caribbean. Helping our neighbors police transit zones has required a well-coordinated effort among the governments of the transit zone countries and the USG. With high levels of post-seizure intelligence collection, and cooperation with allied nations, we now have more actionable intelligence within the transit zone.

The U.S. Joint Inter-Agency Task Force—South (JIATF-S), working closely with international partners from throughout the Caribbean Basin, has focused its and regional partners' intelligence gathering efforts to detect, monitor, and seize maritime drug shipments. The USG's bilateral agreements with Caribbean and Latin American countries have eased the burden on these countries by allowing the United States to conduct boardings and search for contraband on their behalf. They also allow the USG to gain jurisdiction over cases, removing the coercive pressure from large drug trafficking organizations on some foreign governments.

Mexican law enforcement reported seizing 19 metric tons (MT) of cocaine in 2008.

Venezuela reported seizures of over 54 metric tons of cocaine in 2008. However, the Government of Venezuela does not allow the USG to confirm its seizures, and these figures include seizures made by other countries in international waters that were subsequently returned to Venezuela, the country of origin. According to the U.S. government's Consolidated Counterdrug Database, 239 non-commercial cocaine flights departed Venezuela in 2008, some bound for Caribbean islands in route to major markets.

Dominican authorities seized approximately 2.4 metric tons of cocaine. There was a fifteen percent increase in drug smuggling flights to Haiti in 2008. While Haitian law enforcement units worked to improve their response to air smuggling of cocaine, the seizure and arrest results were limited.

West Africa has become a hub for cocaine trafficking from South America to Europe. Although according the UNODC's 2008 *World Drug Report,* Africa accounts for less than 2 percent of global cocaine seizures, this number is expected to rise in future years. Seizures of cocaine in Africa reached 15 MT in 2006, but were below 1 MT between 1998 and 2002. Out of the total number of cocaine seizures made in Europe in 2007 (where the 'origin' had been identified), 22% were smuggled via Africa, up from 12% in 2006 and 5% in 2004. This onslaught is due to more effective interdiction along traditional trafficking routes, and the convenient location of West Africa between Andean cocaine suppliers and European consumers. It also reflects the vulnerability of West African countries to transnational organized crime.

Synthetic Drugs

Amphetamine-Type Stimulants (ATS): Abuse and trafficking in highly addictive amphetamine-type stimulants (ATS) remain among the more serious challenges in the drug-control arena. The 2008 edition of the UN Office of Drugs and Crime's World Drug Report notes that a stabilization in the ATS market over the past three years appears to have occurred in parallel with the implementation of precursor control programs and prevention programs. The report states that ATS abuse has decreased in the United States and increases in consumption have slowed in some other markets, such as Europe and Asia. Consumption, however, has increased in the Middle East and Africa.

Methamphetamine production and distribution are undergoing significant changes in the United States. The number of reported methamphetamine laboratory seizures in the United States decreased each year from 2004 through 2007; however, preliminary 2008 data and reporting indicate that domestic methamphetamine production, while still well below its peak, is increasing in some areas, and laboratory seizures for 2008 outpaced seizures in 2007. The pattern of decreased lab presence from 2004–2007 was probably due in part to increasingly effective domestic controls over the retail sale of licit pharmaceutical preparations containing ephedrine and pseudoephedrine, the primary chemicals necessary for methamphetamine. Regulations for the sale of such products in the United States became effective at the national level for the first time in late 2006 under the Combat Methamphetamine Epidemic Act (CMEA). To capitalize on these gains and prevent production from merely shifting ground, the U.S. Government enhanced the scale and pace of its law enforcement cooperation with the Government of Mexico to target the production and trafficking of methamphetamine. For its part, according to the National Drug Intelligence Center's 2009 National Drug Threat Assessment, ephedrine and pseudoephedrine import restrictions in Mexico contributed to a decrease in methamphetamine production in Mexico and reduced the flow of the drug from Mexico to the United States in 2007 and 2008. Methamphetamine shortages were reported in some drug markets in the Pacific, Southwest, and West Central Regions during much of 2007. In some drug markets, methamphetamine shortages continued through early 2008. In 2008, however, small-scale domestic methamphetamine production increased in many areas, and some Mexican drug trafficking organizations shifted their production operations from Mexico to the United States, particularly to California.

The United States is keenly aware that drug traffickers are adaptable, well-informed, and flexible. New precursor chemical trans-shipment routes may be emerging in Southeast Asia and Africa, and there is also ample evidence that organized criminal groups ship currently uncontrolled chemical analogues of ephedrine and pseudoephedrine for use in manufacturing illicit methamphetamine-type drugs. Some methamphetamine produced in Canada is distributed in U.S. drug markets and Canada is a source country for MDMA to U.S. markets as well as a transit or diversion point for precursor chemicals used to produce illicit synthetic drugs (notably MDMA, or ecstasy), according to the NDIC 2009 National Drug Threat Assessment.

The Netherlands remains an important producer of ecstasy as well, although the amount of this drug reaching the United States seems to have declined substantially in recent years, following new enforcement measures by the Dutch government. Labs in Poland and elsewhere in Eastern Europe are major suppliers of amphetamines to the European market, with the United Kingdom and the Nordic countries among the heaviest European consumers of ATS.

Pharmaceutical Abuse and the Internet: According to the National Drug Intelligence Center's December 2008 *National Drug Threat Assessment,* the number of Internet sites offering sales of controlled prescription drugs decreased in 2008, for the first time after several years of increase. It is not known what percentage of this abuse involves international sources. In the United States, the Ryan Haight Online Pharmacy Consumer Protection Act of 2008 was enacted in October 2008. The new federal law amends the Controlled Substances Act and prohibits the delivery, distribution, or dispensing of controlled prescription drugs over the Internet without a prescription written by a doctor who has conducted at least one in-person examination of the patient.

Cannabis (Marijuana)

Cannabis production and marijuana consumption continue to appear in nearly every world region, including in the United States. Marijuana still remains the most widely used of all of the illicit drugs. According to the December 2008 "Monitoring the Future" study, marijuana use among 8th, 10th, and 12th graders was not statistically different from the year before. However, since the peak years of the mid-1990s, annual use has fallen by over 40 percent among 8th graders, 30 percent among 10th graders, and nearly 20 percent among 12th graders. The prevalence rates for marijuana use in the prior year now stand at 11 percent, 24 percent, and 32 percent for grades 8, 10, and 12, respectively.

Drug organizations in Mexico produced more than 15,000 metric tons of marijuana in 2008, much of which was marketed to the more than 20 million users in the United States. Overall, Canada supplies a small proportion of the overall amount of marijuana consumed in the United States; however, large-scale cultivation of high potency marijuana is a thriving illicit industry in Canada. Other source countries for marijuana include Colombia, Jamaica, and possibly Nigeria. Production of marijuana within the United States may exceed that of foreign sources.

According to the U.S. Drug Enforcement Administration (DEA), marijuana potency has increased sharply. Of great concern is the high potency, indoor-grown cannabis produced on a large scale in Canada and the United States in laboratory conditions using specialized timers, ventilation, moveable lights on tracks, nutrients sprayed on exposed roots and special fertilizer that maximize THC levels. The result is a particularly powerful and dangerous drug.

Opium and Heroin

Opium poppy, the source of heroin, is cultivated mainly in Afghanistan, Southeast Asia, and on a smaller scale in Colombia and Mexico. In contrast to coca, a perennial which takes at least a year to mature into usable leaf, opium poppy is an easily planted annual crop. Opium gum can take less than 6 months from planting to harvest.

In Afghanistan, a combination of factors led to a reduction in the cultivation and production of opium for the first time in several years. Among these factors were: including Afghan government and international donor programs that rewarded entire provinces for decreasing or eliminating opium cultivation; increased prices for other commodities such as wheat; decreased prices for opium; and bad weather. Nangarhar province alone shifted from having the second highest area of poppy cultivation in 2007 to achieving poppy-free status in 2008. This was due in large part to the high-profile law enforcement and incentives campaign implemented by the provincial governor. Even with this limited progress, Afghanistan continues to be the source of more than 90% of the world's illicit opiates. This glut of narcotics has fueled increasing addiction rates in Afghanistan, Pakistan, and Iran. The narcotics trade thrives in the conditions created by insurgents and warlords, who exact a portion of the profits for protection of crops, labs, trucks, and drug markets. Exact figures for the black market economy are impossible to obtain, but the UN estimates that the Taliban and other anti-government forces have extorted $50 million to $70 million in protection payments from opium farmers and an additional $200 to $400 million of income in forced levies on the more-lucrative drug processing and trafficking in 2008.

Most of the heroin used in the United States comes from poppies grown in Colombia and Mexico, although both countries are minor producers in global terms. Mexico supplies most of the heroin found in the western United States while Colombia supplies most of the heroin east of the Mississippi. Long-standing joint eradication programs in both countries continue with our support. Colombian law enforcement reported eradicating 381 hectares of opium poppy in 2008. We estimate that poppy cultivation decreased 25 percent from 2006 to 2007 in directly comparable areas of Colombia. This led to a 27 percent drop in potential production of heroin and a 19 percent decrease in purity of Colombian heroin seized in the United States, according to the DEA. The Government of Mexico (GOM) reported eradicating 12,035 hectares of opium poppy.

Controlling Drug-Processing Chemicals

Cocaine and heroin are manufactured with certain critical chemicals, some of which also have licit uses but are diverted by criminals. The most commonly used chemicals in the manufacture of these illegal drugs are potassium permanganate (for cocaine) and acetic anhydride (for heroin). Government controls strive to differentiate between licit commercial use for these chemicals and illicit diversion to criminals. Governments must have efficient legal and regulatory regimes to control such chemicals, without placing undue burdens on legitimate commerce. Extensive international law enforcement cooperation is also required to prevent their diversion from licit commercial channels, and to investigate, arrest and dismantle the illegal networks engaged in their procurement. This topic is addressed in greater detail in the Chemical Control Chapter of this report.

Drugs and the Environment

Impact of Drug Cultivation and Processing: Illegal drug production usually takes place in remote areas far removed from the authority of central governments. Not surprisingly, drug criminals practice none of the environmental safeguards that are required for licit industry, and the toxic chemicals used to process raw organic materials into finished drugs are invariably dumped into sensitive ecosystems without regard for human health or the costs to the environment. Coca growers routinely slash and burn remote, virgin forestland in the Amazon to make way for their illegal crops; coca growers typically cut down up to 4 hectares of forest for every hectare of coca planted. Tropical rains quickly erode the thin topsoil of the fields, increasing soil runoff and depleting soil nutrients. By destroying timber and other resources, illicit coca cultivation decreases biological diversity in one of the most sensitive ecological areas in the world. In Colombia and elsewhere, traffickers also destroy jungle forests to build clandestine landing strips and laboratories for processing raw coca and poppy into cocaine and heroin.

Illicit coca growers use large quantities of highly toxic herbicides and fertilizers on their crops. These chemicals qualify under the U.S. Environmental Protection Agency's highest classification for toxicity (Category I) and are legally restricted for sale within Colombia and the United States. Production of the drugs requires large quantities of dangerous solvents and chemicals. One kilogram of cocaine base requires the use of three liters of concentrated sulfuric acid, 10 kilograms of lime, 60 to 80 liters of kerosene, 200 grams of potassium permanganate, and one liter of concentrated ammonia. These toxic pesticides, fertilizers, and processing chemicals are then dumped into the nearest waterway or on the ground. They saturate the soil and contaminate waterways and poison water systems upon which local human and animal populations rely. In the United States, marijuana-processing operations take place in national parks, especially in California and Texas near the border with Mexico. These marijuana growing operations leave behind tons of garbage, biohazard refuse, and toxic waste. They also contribute to erosion as land is compacted and small streams and other water sources are diverted for irrigating the illegal marijuana fields.

Methamphetamine is also alarming in its environmental impact. For each pound of methamphetamine produced in clandestine methamphetamine laboratories, five to six pounds of toxic, hazardous waste are generated, posing immediate and long-term environmental health risks, not only to individual homes but to neighborhoods. Poisonous vapors produced during synthesis permeate the walls and carpets of houses and buildings, often making them uninhabitable. Cleaning up these sites in the United States and Mexico requires specialized training and costs thousands of dollars per site.

Impact of Spray Eradication: Colombia is currently the only country that conducts regular aerial spraying of coca, although countries throughout the world regularly spray other crops with herbicides. The only active ingredient in the herbicide used in the aerial eradication program is glyphosate, which has been thoroughly tested in the United States, Colombia, and elsewhere. The U.S. Environmental Protection Agency (EPA) approved glyphosate for general use in 1974 and re-registered it in September 1993. EPA has approved its use on food croplands, forests, residential areas, and around aquatic areas. It is one of the most widely used herbicides in the world. Colombia's spray program represents a small fraction of total glyphosate use in the country. Biannual verification missions continue to show that aerial eradication causes no significant damage to the environment or human health. The eradication program follows strict environmental safeguards, monitored permanently by several Colombian government agencies, and adheres to all laws and regulations, including the Colombian Environmental Management Plan. In addition to the biannual verification missions, soil and water samples are taken before and after spray for analysis. The residues in these samples have never reached a level outside the established regulatory norms. The OAS, which published a study in 2005 positively assessing the chemicals and methodologies used in the aerial spray program, is currently conducting further investigations expected to be completed in early 2009 regarding spray drift and other issues.

Attacking Trafficking Organizations

Law enforcement tactics have grown more sophisticated over the past two decades to counter the ever-evolving tactics used by trafficking networks to transport large volumes of drugs internationally. Rather than measuring progress purely by seizures and numbers of arrests, international law enforcement authorities have increasingly targeted resources against the highest levels of drug trafficking organizations. Increasingly, international law enforcement authorities are learning the art of conspiracy investigations, using mutual legal assistance mechanisms and other advanced investigative techniques to follow the evidence to higher and higher levels of leadership within the syndicates, and cooperating on extradition so that the kingpins have no place to hide. These sophisticated law enforcement and legal tools are endorsed as recommended practices within both the 1988 UN Drug Control Convention and the UN Convention against Transnational Organized Crime.

The drug trade depends upon reliable and efficient distribution systems to get its product to market. While most illicit distribution systems have short-term back-up channels to compensate for temporary law enforcement disruptions, a network under intense enforcement pressure cannot function for long. In cooperation with law enforcement officials in other nations, our goal is to disrupt and dismantle these organizations, to remove the leadership and the facilitators who launder money and provide the chemicals needed for the production of illicit drugs, and to destroy their networks. By capturing the leaders of trafficking organizations, we demonstrate both to the criminals and to the governments fighting them that even the most powerful drug syndicates are vulnerable to concerted action by international law enforcement authorities.

Mexican drug syndicates continue to oversee much of the drug trafficking into the United States, with a strong presence in most of the primary U.S. distribution centers. President Calderon's counternarcotics programs seek to address some of the most basic institutional issues that have traditionally confounded Mexico's success against the cartels. The Government of Mexico is using the military to reestablish sovereign authority and counter the cartels' firepower, moving to establish integrity within the ranks of the police, and giving law enforcement officials and judicial authorities the resources and the legal underpinning they need to succeed.

   To help Mexico achieve these goals, the United States Congress appropriated $465 million in June 2008 to provide inspection equipment to interdict trafficked drugs, arms, cash and persons; secure communications systems for law enforcement agencies; and technical advice and training to strengthen judicial institutions. Similarly, Congress has provided support to Central American countries, including the continued implementation of the USG's anti-gang strategy, support for specialized vetted units and judicial reforms, and enhanced land and maritime drug interdiction.

   This appropriation will complement existing and planned initiatives of U.S. domestic law enforcement agencies engaged with counterparts in each participating country. On December 3, 2008, a Letter of Agreement (LOA) was signed with the Government of Mexico obligating $197 million of the funding for counternarcotics programs. On December 19, the governments of the United States and Mexico met to coordinate the implementation of the Mérida Initiative through a cabinet-level High Level Group, which underscored the urgency and importance of the Initiative. A working level inter-agency implementation meeting was held February 3 in Mexico City with the aim of accelerating the rollout of the 39 projects for Mexico under the Initiative. In addition, LOAs were signed with Honduras on January 9, El Salvador on January 12, Guatemala on February 5 and Belize on February 9.

Extradition

There are few legal sanctions that international criminals fear as much as extradition to the United States, where they can no longer use bribes and intimidation to manipulate the local judicial process. Governments willing to risk domestic political repercussions to extradite drug kingpins to the United States are finding that public acceptance of this measure has steadily increased.

   Mexican authorities extradited 95 persons to the United States in 2008. Colombia has an outstanding record of extradition of drug criminals to the United States, and the numbers have increased even more in recent years. The Government of Colombia extradited a record 208 defendants in 2008. Since President Uribe assumed office in 2002, 789 individuals have been extradited.

Institutional Reform

Fighting Corruption: Among all criminal enterprises, the drug trade is best positioned to spread corruption and undermine the integrity and effectiveness of legitimate governments. Drugs generate illegal revenues on a scale without historical precedent. No commodity is so widely available, so cheap to produce, and as easily renewable as illegal drugs. A kilogram of cocaine can be sold in the United States for more than 15 times its value in Colombia, a return that dwarfs regular commodities and distorts the licit economy.

   No government is completely safe from the threat of drug-related corruption, but fragile democracies in post-conflict situations are particularly vulnerable. The weakening of government institutions through bribery and intimidation ultimately poses just as great a danger to democratic governments as the challenge of armed insurgents. Drug syndicates seek to subvert governments in order to guarantee themselves a secure operating environment. Unchecked, the drug cartels have the wherewithal to buy their way into power. By keeping a focus on fighting corruption, we can help avoid the threat of a drug lord–controlled state.

Improving Criminal Justice Systems: A pivotal element of USG international drug control policy is to help strengthen enforcement, judicial, and financial institutions worldwide. Strong institutions limit the opportunities for infiltration and corruption by the drug trade. Corruption within a criminal justice system has an enormously detrimental impact; law enforcement agencies in drug source and transit countries may arrest influential drug criminals only to see them released following a questionable or inexplicable decision by a single judge, or a prosecutor may obtain an arrest warrant but be unable to find police who will execute it. Efforts by governments to enact basic reforms involving transparency, efficiency, and better pay for police and judges helps to build societies based on the rule of law.

Strengthening Border Security: Drug trafficking organizations must move their products across international borders. A key element in stopping the flow of narcotics is to help countries strengthen their border controls. Through training and technical assistance we improve the capability of countries to control the movement of people and goods across their borders. Effective border security can disrupt narcotics smuggling operations, forcing traffickers to adjust their methods and making them vulnerable to further detection and law enforcement action.

Note

1. The focus of this report is on the international aspects of drug trafficking, but we want also to acknowledge the hard work of law enforcement, drug prevention, and drug treatment professionals within the United States who work every day to reduce the demand for illicit drugs and to reduce the misery they bring to our own citizens. Federal, state, local, and tribal law enforcement agencies within the United States dedicate significant resources to confronting drug criminals. The United States has substantial public and private sector programs focused on drug prevention and treatment and has invested in cutting-edge medical and social research on how to decrease demand. We are proud of the results and have worked with the Organization of American States, the United Nations, and countries all over the world to share programs such as drug courts, early intervention, school and work-place drug testing coupled with counseling and other interventions, and medically sound treatment options that help addicted persons reclaim their lives. For more information about domestic drug control efforts, please see the National Drug Control Strategy of the White House Office of National Drug Control Policy, available on the . . . website.

Ethan Nadelmann

 **NO**

The Global War on Drugs
Can Be Won

No, it can't. A "drug-free world," which the United Nations describes as a realistic goal, is no more attainable than an "alcohol-free world"—and no one has talked about that with a straight face since the repeal of Prohibition in the United States in 1933. Yet futile rhetoric about winning a "war on drugs" persists, despite mountains of evidence documenting its moral and ideological bankruptcy. When the U.N. General Assembly Special Session on drugs convened in 1998, it committed to "eliminating or significantly reducing the illicit cultivation of the coca bush, the cannabis plant and the opium poppy by the year 2008" and to "achieving significant and measurable results in the field of demand reduction." But today, global production and consumption of those drugs are roughly the same as they were a decade ago; meanwhile, many producers have become more efficient, and cocaine and heroin have become purer and cheaper.

It's always dangerous when rhetoric drives policy—and especially so when "war on drugs" rhetoric leads the public to accept collateral casualties that would never be permissible in civilian law enforcement, much less public health. Politicians still talk of eliminating drugs from the Earth as though their use is a plague on humanity. But drug control is not like disease control, for the simple reason that there's no popular demand for smallpox or polio. Cannabis and opium have been grown throughout much of the world for millennia. The same is true for coca in Latin America. Methamphetamine and other synthetic drugs can be produced anywhere. Demand for particular illicit drugs waxes and wanes, depending not just on availability but also fads, fashion, culture, and competition from alternative means of stimulation and distraction. The relative harshness of drug laws and the intensity of enforcement matter surprisingly little, except in totalitarian states. After all, rates of illegal drug use in the United States are the same as, or higher than, Europe, despite America's much more punitive policies.

We Can Reduce the Demand for Drugs

Good luck. Reducing the demand for illegal drugs seems to make sense. But the desire to alter one's state of consciousness, and to use psychoactive drugs to do so, is nearly universal—and mostly not a problem. There's virtually never been a drug-free society, and more drugs are discovered and devised every year.

Reprinted in entirety by McGraw-Hill with permission from *Foreign Policy*, September/ October 2007, pp. 24–26, 28–29. www.foreignpolicy.com. © 2007 Washingtonpost.Newsweek Interactive, LLC.

Demand-reduction efforts that rely on honest education and positive alterna-tives to drug use are helpful, but not when they devolve into unrealistic, "zero tolerance" policies.

As with sex, abstinence from drugs is the best way to avoid trouble, but one always needs a fallback strategy for those who can't or won't refrain. "Zero tolerance" policies deter some people, but they also dramatically increase the harms and costs for those who don't resist. Drugs become more potent, drug use becomes more hazardous, and people who use drugs are marginalized in ways that serve no one.

The better approach is not demand reduction but "harm reduction." Reducing drug use is fine, but it's not nearly as important as reducing the death, disease, crime, and suffering associated with both drug misuse and failed pro-hibitionist policies. With respect to legal drugs, such as alcohol and cigarettes, harm reduction means promoting responsible drinking and designated driv-ers, or persuading people to switch to nicotine patches, chewing gums, and smokeless tobacco. With respect to illegal drugs, it means reducing the trans-mission of infectious disease through syringe-exchange programs, reducing overdose fatalities by making antidotes readily available, and allowing people addicted to heroin and other illegal opiates to obtain methadone from doctors and even pharmaceutical heroin from clinics. Britain, Canada, Germany, the Netherlands, and Switzerland have already embraced this last option. There's no longer any question that these strategies decrease drug-related harms with-out increasing drug use. What blocks expansion of such programs is not cost; they typically save taxpayers' money that would otherwise go to criminal jus-tice and healthcare. No, the roadblocks are abstinence-only ideologues and a cruel indifference to the lives and well-being of people who use drugs.

Reducing the Supply of Drugs Is the Answer

Not if history is any guide. Reducing supply makes as much sense as reduc-ing demand; after all, if no one were planting cannabis, coca, and opium, there wouldn't be any heroin, cocaine, or marijuana to sell or consume. But the carrot and stick of crop eradication and substitution have been tried and failed, with rare exceptions, for half a century. These methods may succeed in targeted locales, but they usually simply shift production from one region to another: Opium production moves from Pakistan to Afghanistan; coca from Peru to Colombia; and cannabis from Mexico to the United States, while over-all global production remains relatively constant or even increases.

The carrot, in the form of economic development and assistance in switching to legal crops, is typically both late and inadequate. The stick, often in the form of forced eradication, including aerial spraying, wipes out illegal and legal crops alike and can be hazardous to both people and local environ-ments. The best thing to be said for emphasizing supply reduction is that it provides a rationale for wealthier nations to spend a little money on economic development in poorer countries. But, for the most part, crop eradication and substitution wreak havoc among impoverished farmers without diminishing overall global supply.

The global markets in cannabis, coca, and opium products operate essentially the same way that other global commodity markets do: If one source is compromised due to bad weather, rising production costs, or political difficulties, another emerges. If international drug control circles wanted to think strategically, the key question would no longer be how to reduce global supply, but rather: Where does illicit production cause the fewest problems (and the greatest benefits)? Think of it as a global vice control challenge. No one expects to eradicate vice, but it must be effectively zoned and regulated—even if it's illegal.

U.S. Drug Policy Is the World's Drug Policy

Sad, but true. Looking to the United States as a role model for drug control is like looking to apartheid-era South Africa for how to deal with race. The United States ranks first in the world in per capita incarceration—with less than 5 percent of the world's population, but almost 25 percent of the world's prisoners. The number of people locked up for U.S. drug-law violations has increased from roughly 50,000 in 1980 to almost 500,000 today; that's more than the number of people Western Europe locks up for everything. Even more deadly is U.S. resistance to syringe-exchange programs to reduce HIV/AIDS both at home and abroad. Who knows how many people might not have contracted HIV if the United States had implemented at home, and supported abroad, the sorts of syringe-exchange and other harm-reduction programs that have kept HIV/AIDS rates so low in Australia, Britain, the Netherlands, and elsewhere. Perhaps millions.

And yet, despite this dismal record, the United States has succeeded in constructing an international drug prohibition regime modeled after its own highly punitive and moralistic approach. It has dominated the drug control agencies of the United Nations and other international organizations, and its federal drug enforcement agency was the first national police organization to go global. Rarely has one nation so successfully promoted its own failed policies to the rest of the world.

But now, for the first time, U.S. hegemony in drug control is being challenged. The European Union is demanding rigorous assessment of drug control strategies. Exhausted by decades of service to the U.S.-led war on drugs, Latin Americans are far less inclined to collaborate closely with U.S. drug enforcement efforts. Finally waking up to the deadly threat of HIV/AIDS, China, Indonesia, Vietnam, and even Malaysia and Iran are increasingly accepting of syringe-exchange and other harm-reduction programs. In 2005, the ayatollah in charge of Iran's Ministry of Justice issued a *fatwa* declaring methadone maintenance and syringe-exchange programs compatible with *sharia* (Islamic) law. One only wishes his American counterpart were comparably enlightened.

Afghan Opium Production Must Be Curbed

Be careful what you wish for. It's easy to believe that eliminating record-high opium production in Afghanistan—which today accounts for roughly 90 percent of global supply, up from 50 percent 10 years ago—would solve everything from heroin abuse in Europe and Asia to the resurgence of the Taliban.

But assume for a moment that the United States, NATO, and Hamid Karzai's government were somehow able to cut opium production in Afghanistan. Who would benefit? Only the Taliban, warlords, and other black-market entrepreneurs whose stockpiles of opium would skyrocket in value. Hundreds of thousands of Afghan peasants would flock to cities, ill-prepared to find work. And many Afghans would return to their farms the following year to plant another illegal harvest, utilizing guerrilla farming methods to escape intensified eradication efforts. Except now, they'd soon be competing with poor farmers elsewhere in Central Asia, Latin America, or even Africa. This is, after all, a global commodities market.

And outside Afghanistan? Higher heroin prices typically translate into higher crime rates by addicts. They also invite cheaper but more dangerous means of consumption, such as switching from smoking to injecting heroin, which results in higher HIV and hepatitis C rates. All things considered, wiping out opium in Afghanistan would yield far fewer benefits than is commonly assumed.

So what's the solution? Some recommend buying up all the opium in Afghanistan, which would cost a lot less than is now being spent trying to eradicate it. But, given that farmers somewhere will produce opium so long as the demand for heroin persists, maybe the world is better off, all things considered, with 90 percent of it coming from just one country. And if that heresy becomes the new gospel, it opens up all sorts of possibilities for pursuing a new policy in Afghanistan that reconciles the interests of the United States, NATO, and millions of Afghan citizens.

Legalization Is the Best Approach

It might be. Global drug prohibition is clearly a costly disaster. The United Nations has estimated the value of the global market in illicit drugs at $400 billion, or 6 percent of global trade. The extraordinary profits available to those willing to assume the risks enrich criminals, terrorists, violent political insurgents, and corrupt politicians and governments. Many cities, states, and even countries in Latin America, the Caribbean, and Asia are reminiscent of Chicago under Al Capone—times 50. By bringing the market for drugs out into the open, legalization would radically change all that for the better.

More importantly, legalization would strip addiction down to what it really is: a health issue. Most people who use drugs are like the responsible alcohol consumer, causing no harm to themselves or anyone else. They would no longer be the state's business. But legalization would also benefit those who struggle with drugs by reducing the risks of overdose and disease associated with unregulated products, eliminating the need to obtain drugs from dangerous criminal markets, and allowing addiction problems to be treated as medical rather than criminal problems.

No one knows how much governments spend collectively on failing drug war policies, but it's probably at least $100 billion a year, with federal, state, and local governments in the United States accounting for almost half the total. Add to that the tens of billions of dollars to be gained annually in tax revenues from the sale of legalized drugs. Now imagine if just a third of that total were committed to reducing drug-related disease and addiction. Virtually everyone, except those who profit or gain politically from the current system, would benefit.

Some say legalization is immoral. That's nonsense, unless one believes there is some principled basis for discriminating against people based solely on what they put into their bodies, absent harm to others. Others say legalization would open the floodgates to huge increases in drug abuse. They forget that we already live in a world in which psychoactive drugs of all sorts are readily available—and in which people too poor to buy drugs resort to sniffing gasoline, glue, and other industrial products, which can be more harmful than any drug. No, the greatest downside to legalization may well be the fact that the legal markets would fall into the hands of the powerful alcohol, tobacco, and pharmaceutical companies. Still, legalization is a far more pragmatic option than living with the corruption, violence, and organized crime of the current system.

Legalization Will Never Happen

Never say never. Wholesale legalization may be a long way off—but partial legalization is not. If any drug stands a chance of being legalized, it's cannabis. Hundreds of millions of people have used it, the vast majority without suffering any harm or going on to use "harder" drugs. In Switzerland, for example, cannabis legalization was twice approved by one chamber of its parliament, but narrowly rejected by the other.

Elsewhere in Europe, support for the criminalization of cannabis is waning. In the United States, where roughly 40 percent of the country's 1.8 million annual drug arrests are for cannabis possession, typically of tiny amounts, 40 percent of Americans say that the drug should be taxed, controlled, and regulated like alcohol. Encouraged by Bolivian President Evo Morales, support is also growing in Latin America and Europe for removing coca from international antidrug conventions, given the absence of any credible health reason for keeping it there. Traditional growers would benefit economically, and there's some possibility that such products might compete favorably with more problematic substances, including alcohol.

The global war on drugs persists in part because so many people fail to distinguish between the harms of drug abuse and the harms of prohibition. Legalization forces that distinction to the forefront. The opium problem in Afghanistan is primarily a prohibition problem, not a drug problem. The same is true of the narcoviolence and corruption that has afflicted Latin America and the Caribbean for almost three decades—and that now threatens Africa. Governments can arrest and kill drug lord after drug lord, but the ultimate solution is a structural one, not a prosecutorial one. Few people doubt any longer that the war on drugs is lost, but courage and vision are needed to transcend the ignorance, fear, and vested interests that sustain it.

POSTSCRIPT

Should the United States Put More Emphasis on Stopping the Importation of Drugs?

The drug trade spawns violence: people die from using drugs or by dealing with people in the drug trade; families are ruined by the effects of drugs on family members; prisons are filled with tens of thousands of people who were and probably still are involved with illegal drugs; and drugs can devastate aspirations and careers. The adverse consequences of drugs can be seen everywhere in society. How should the government determine the best course of action to follow in remedying the negative effects of drugs? Would more people be helped by reducing the availability of drugs, or would more people benefit if they could be persuaded that drugs are harmful to them?

Two paths that are traditionally followed involve reducing either the supply of drugs or the demand for drugs. Four major agencies involved in the fight against drugs in the United States—the Drug Enforcement Administration (DEA), the Federal Bureau of Investigation (FBI), the U.S. Customs Service, and the U.S. Coast Guard—have seized thousands of pounds of marijuana, cocaine, and heroin during the past few years. Drug interdiction appears to be reducing the availability of drugs. But what effect does drug availability have on use? If a particular drug is not available, would other drugs be used in its place? Would the cost of drugs increase if there were a shortage of drugs? If costs increase, would violence due to drugs go up as well?

Annual surveys of 8th-, 10th-, and 12th-grade students indicate that availability is not a major factor in drug use. Throughout the 1980s drug use declined dramatically even though marijuana and cocaine could be easily obtained. According to the surveys, the perceived harm of these drugs, not their availability, is what affects students' drug use. As individuals' perceptions of drugs as harmful increase, usage decreases; as perceptions of harm decrease, usage increases. Generally, availability of drugs is a weak predictor of drug use.

Efforts to prevent drug use may prove fruitless if people have a natural desire to alter their consciousness. In his 1989 book *Intoxication: Life in the Pursuit of Artificial Paradise* (E. P. Dutton), Ronald Siegel contends that the urge to alter consciousness is as universal as the craving for food and sex.

A publication that examines trends in world drug markets is *Understanding Illicit Drug Markets, Supply-Reduction Efforts, and Drug-Related Crime in the European Union* by Beau Kilmer and Stijn Hoorens (Cambridge, UK: Rand Europe, 2010). Another publication that critically views current drug policies is *How Goes the War on Drugs? An Assessment of U.S. Drug Problems and Policy* by

Jonathon Caulkins and associates (RAND Drug Policy Research Center, 2005). Articles that examine international efforts to deal with the issue of drugs include "Latin America's Drug Problem," by Michael Shifter (*Current History*, February 2007) and "End the Demand, End the Supply," by Lee P. Brown (*U.S. News and World Report*, August 4, 2008).

ISSUE 3

Should the United States Drinking Age Remain at 21?

YES: **Carla T. Main**, from "Underage Drinking and the Drinking Age," *Policy Review* (2009)

NO: **Judith G. McMullen,** from "Underage Drinking: Does Current Policy Make Sense?" *Lewis & Clark Law Review* (Summer 2006)

ISSUE SUMMARY

YES: Carla Main contends that the drinking age should remain at 21. Underage drinking has been linked to sexual assaults, violent behavior, unprotected consensual sex, and numerous automobile accidents. Although one can serve in the military before age 21, alcohol use among that age group contributes to poor morale and productivity according to Main. Rather than tolerating underage drinking, more effort should be placed on enforcing underage drinking laws.

NO: Judith McMullen, a law professor at Marquette University, argues that laws prohibiting underage drinking have been ineffective. Young adults between the ages of 18 and 21 who do not live at home have opportunities to drink alcohol without parental interference. In addition, this same age group has other legal rights, such as the right to marry, drive a car, or join the military. Enforcement of underage drinking laws, says McMullen, is destined for failure.

More than 90 percent of high school seniors consume alcohol and a significant percentage of these students engage in binge drinking. There is little doubt that many students drink to excess and that many young people drink alcohol irresponsibly. Regardless of the message that many underage drinkers receive, it is unhealthy, unlawful, and potentially dangerous for young people to drink alcohol, especially in excess. The question revolves around the best way to reduce the harms associated with alcohol use. Will reducing the drinking age make it easier to teach young people to drink responsibly? Or, is reducing the drinking age simply capitulating to the realities that young people drink?

One important question is whether or not young people will respond to a message of responsible alcohol consumption if they are legally allowed to drink. Because it is a recognized fact that the vast majority of people under age 21 drink alcohol, simply telling young people to not drink does not stop that behavior. However, does it make more sense to teach young people how to drink alcohol responsibly so they do not endanger themselves, their friends, or innocent bystanders? The current message that one should wait until age 21 to drink is not being heard by the majority of people under that age. On the other hand, will someone be more amenable to being responsible if they are allowed to drink? Will reducing the drinking age result in very young people driving while under the influence? Will young people engage in less binge drinking?

Another relevant question deals with whether or not drinking laws discriminate against people under age 21. For example, one does not need to be age 21 to enter the military service. Obviously, being in the military can result in putting one's life in danger. Sixteen-year-olds are allowed to drive a car if they pass certain requirements. Driving a car safely requires one to be very responsible. However, should one be allowed to consume alcohol at age 16 simply because one can drive a car at age 16? Many young people become parents before age 21. Marriage is permitted before age 21. Again, if one can marry and have children, then should one not have the right to drink alcohol?

Whether or not young people under age 21 will drink responsibly if they are allowed legally to drink remains unclear. If the law is changed and the drinking age was lowered, and if the drinking rates increased or other problems surfaced, then would it be easy to change the law back to 21? Perhaps, whether or not young people drink responsibly has nothing to do with the current drinking age? Some people are responsible regardless of the drinking age. There are many older people who drink irresponsibly. One might be able to argue that one should pass certain requirements, besides age, before being allowed to drink. Maybe, individuals with a history of substance abuse or some other type of unlawful or inappropriate behavior should not be allowed to drink.

In 2007, the United States Surgeon General published a paper with suggestions to reduce underage drinking. In this paper, the Surgeon General outlined numerous goals. One goal focused on societal changes that would reduce underage drinking. Another goal attempted to get parents, caregivers, schools, communities, and all social systems to work together to address this problem. The Surgeon General recommended improving surveillance of underage drinking as well as additional research on adolescent alcohol use.

In the YES selection, Carla Main believes that the risk of lowering the drinking age has too many potential problems and that it would be a grievous mistake to change the drinking age from 21. To reduce drinking-related problems, better enforcement of current laws is needed. In the NO selection, Judith McMullen believes the law is hypocritical. Setting the drinking age at 21 is arbitrary and inconsistent. There are many activities one can engage in before age 21 and she cites numerous examples.

Underage Drinking and the Drinking Age

The problem of underage drinking on college campuses has been brewing for many years to the continued vexation of higher education administrators. In 2008, John McCardell, president emeritus of Middlebury College, began to circulate for signature a public statement among colleagues titled "The Amethyst Initiative,"[1] which calls for elected officials to reexamine underage drinking laws. The project grew out of outreach efforts of a nonprofit [organization] he founded in 2007 called Choose Responsibility. The nonprofit [organization] advocates lowering the drinking age to 18 and licensing alcohol use for young people in much the same manner as driving—following coursework and an exam. Choose Responsibility also favors the repeal of the laws that set 21 as the mandatory minimum age for drinking (known as the "21 laws") and encourages states at the least to adopt exceptions to the 21 laws that would allow minors to drink at home and in private clubs. It also favors social changes that shift the focus on alcohol use among youth to the home, family, and individual.

The Amethyst Initiative's statement has been signed by 135 college presidents and chancellors at schools from Duke to Bennington. The majority is private; most are in the Northeast. The statement takes no formal position, unlike Choose Responsibility. It does, however, drop heavy hints as to where the debate ought to come out. The statement says "21 is not working" and asks "How many times must we relearn the lessons of Prohibition?" It draws comparisons to other age-of-majority rights conferred on 18-year-olds, such as voting and serving in the military, and calls upon elected officials to consider "whether current public policies are in line with current realities."

It seems that the presidents of 135 colleges, including elite schools, large universities, and small state schools find themselves so exasperated with the amount of alcohol guzzled by undergraduates—or more to the point, the trouble the undergraduates get into while inebriated—that they now beseech lawmakers to "rethink 21," an elegant and rather roundabout way of saying: Let undergrads drink with the sanction of the law.

The primary argument made in the Initiative's statement in favor of repealing the 21 laws is that the 21 laws make alcohol taboo, thus driving underage drinking underground and causing more binge drinking to take place than otherwise would, due to the allure of forbidden fruit and the need for secrecy. Hence, by lowering the drinking age, youth consumption would come out in the open and binge drinking would be largely reduced or even eliminated. The second salutary effect of lowering the drinking age, the Initiative argues, would be educational: Colleges would be allowed to have open, frank discussions about responsible drinking. In other words, institutions of higher education could teach young people how to drink responsibly. The Initiative makes vague references to the "unintended consequences" of 21 "posing increasing risks to young people," and says that the original impetus for the 21 laws—reduction of highway fatalities by young drivers—has outlived its usefulness.

Since its launch, the Initiative has created a public dialog about the drinking age, resulting in media coverage and a hearing before the New Jersey state legislature in November 2008. Despite its gravity as a public health problem, even among children younger than 18, the topic of underage alcohol abuse has been underaddressed in the popular media and in public funding compared to illicit drug abuse. The Initiative is a welcome development insofar as it challenges us to examine whether 21 "is working." The answer: It is not, as currently enforced. So should 21 be scrapped or salvaged? First, a look at how we got here, and why the 21 laws are broken.

The 21 Laws

Americans generally have not allowed young people to drink. Older teens were allowed to drink legally during part of the 1970s and early 1980s—a blip on the American-history radar screen. Here is how it happened.

During the 19th century, cultural and social norms prevented young people from drinking. The expense and limited availability of liquor also helped keep it out of youthful hands. After Prohibition, it was left up to the states to regulate alcohol, and most states made the legal drinking age 21, the same as the age for voting and other adult rights. The issue remained largely untouched until the late 1960s when protests over the Vietnam War raised the question of the national voting age. For the first time, the question of the draft age and the voting age were linked in the popular imagination, at least among the left. "If a boy is old enough to fight and die for his country, why isn't he old enough to vote?" was the popular refrain.

The legal drinking age got swept up in the political upheaval of the era, as states generally reexamined their age-of-majority laws. Between 1970 and 1976, 29 states lowered their age for drinking alcohol. The results were catastrophic. Highway deaths among teenagers and young adults skyrocketed. Almost immediately, states began raising the minimum drinking age again— years before Congress in 1982 and 1984 dangled the carrot of federal highway monies as an incentive. Between 1976 and 1984, 24 of the 29 states raised the age back up again. By 1984, only three states allowed 18-year-olds to drink. Five states and the District of Columbia regulated various degrees of alcohol consumption among those 18 and over. The remaining states had a patchwork of minimum ages ranging from 19 to 21.[2]

While states experimented with age-of-majority laws, a cultural shift was taking place in how society regarded drunk driving. In 1980, a 13-year-old California girl named Cari Lightner was walking to a carnival when she was struck by a hit-and-run drunk driver and killed instantly. Her mother became enraged when she learned that drunk driving was not treated seriously in the American judicial system. What followed was one of the great stories of American grassroots activism. Together with a friend, Candace Lightner founded Mothers Against Drunk Driving (MADD), which quickly garnered local and later national support in a campaign that focused on putting a human face on the damage done by drunk drivers. By 1982, with MADD 100-chapters strong, President Reagan created a presidential commission to study drunk driving and Congress authorized highway funds to states that passed stiffer drunk driving laws. In 1984, Congress passed the Uniform Drinking Age Act, which required states to have a minimum drinking age of 21 for all types of alcohol consumption if they wanted to receive federal highway monies. The legal drinking age has stayed at 21 since then.

In most of the television debates about the Amethyst Initiative, the success or failure of 21 has been primarily linked to the issue of highway deaths, with the debaters arguing fatality statistics to prove whether the 21 laws should be shelved because of the advent of safer cars. But that suggests, wrongly, that the debate largely begins and ends with the question of teenage bodies splattered across the interstates. While drunk driving among underage drinkers remains a problem, unfortunately it is only one of several ways that underage drinking threatens young people. Time has not stood still since 1984. American campuses and drinking patterns have changed, and not for the better.

Binge Drinking

The logic of the Initiative is that if we take away the allure of illegality, American youth will stop binging. That conclusion is wrong. Alcohol should be forbidden to 18- to 20-year-olds precisely because *they have a propensity* to binge drink whether the stuff is illegal or not—especially males.

Henry Wechsler and Toben F. Nelson, in the landmark Harvard School of Public Health College Alcohol Study, or CAS, which tracked college student drinking patterns from 1992 to 2001, explained that binge drinking is five or more drinks on one occasion. Binge drinking brings the blood alcohol concentration to 0.08 gram percent or above (typically five drinks for a man or four for a woman within two hours). To understand just how drunk that makes a person, consider that it violates criminal laws to drive with a blood alcohol level of 0.08 gram percent or above.

To call alcohol taboo implies that drinking is done in secret and rarely. Yet college drinking is so common as to have lost all tinge of intrigue. Drinking greases the social wheels, and college life for many is saturated with popular drinking games that no doubt seem brilliant to the late-adolescent: Beerchesi, Beergammon, BeerSoftball, coin games like Psycho, Quarters, and BeerBattleship, and card and dice games linked to beer.

When undergraduates binge drink, they get into trouble—a lot of it. They endanger and sometimes kill their fellow students by setting fires.[3] They sexually assault their female companions (approximately 100,000 incidents annually). They get into fights with other young undergrads (some 700,000 assaults annually). On average 1,100 a year die from alcohol-related traffic crashes and another 300 die in nontraffic alcohol-related deaths. According to the CAS, among the 8 million college students in the United States surveyed in one study year, more than 2 million drove under the influence of alcohol and more than 3 million rode in cars with drivers who had been drinking. Eight percent of students—474,000—have unprotected consensual sex each year because they have been drinking.[4] In short, college students do stupid, illegal, dangerous, and sometimes deadly things when they drink.

Moreover, the drinking doesn't begin in college. More kids drink alcohol than smoke pot, which is the most commonly used illicit drug. A third of our youth taste their first drink before the age of 13 and have drinking patterns as early as 8th to 10th grade. In a pattern that continues in college, boys fall into binge drinking patterns in greater numbers than girls by 12th grade.[5] The Pacific Institute for Research and Evaluation has estimated the social cost of underage drinking (for all youth) at some $53 billion. That includes only highway deaths and injuries and does not factor in brain damage associated with early adolescent drinking, or the array of other injuries and social problems such as opportunity costs that crop up when children drink.

The majority of those who binge drink in college started down that road long before they matriculated—they simply continue their drinking habits once they arrive on campus. Brett Sokolow, president of the consulting firm National Center for Higher Education Risk Management (NCHERM), which counsels colleges on reducing "risk" through educational programs and institutional policies, said in an interview that based on his anecdotal experience, 60 to 70 percent of the students attending his on-campus alcohol seminars have had drinking experiences prior to attending college and about 40 percent have "deeply engrained drinking habits" by the time they get to college.

Consider the scope of college drinking. Among the general population in America, 15 percent of 18- to 25-year-olds binge drink, according to the Centers for Disease Control [and Prevention]. Among college students, 80 percent reported drinking and of those, 40 percent binge drink once a month— that is more than twice the rate of their peers in the general population.[6] About one fourth drank in this way frequently—three or more times in a two week period.[7]

If college life, with its basic structure and lack of privacy, forces drinking underground as the Amethyst Initiative posits, then one should see far less binge drinking among youth who are not in college. A study drawn on data from the National Household Survey on Drug Abuse, which looked at heavy episodic drinking among all 18- to 24-year-olds, comparing those in college to those outside the ivy-covered walls, does not bear out the Initiative's theory. While 41 percent of those in college binge drank at least once a month, according to that study, so did 36 percent of other youth. And as we shall see, in the military and in countries where they may drink legally, the young guzzle apace.

U.S. Military

The initiative, as well as students arguing in favor of the right to go to keggers, invoke the plight of the parched soldier—old enough to die for his country but not allowed to have a beer. The cascading images on Choose Responsibility's Web site even include the wordless image of a young soldier.

Reality check: The U.S. Department of Defense takes substance abuse among military personnel very seriously and has been addressing drug and alcohol issues for many years. While it has made great progress against illicit drugs, it has found alcohol more intractable. DOD devotes substantial resources to counseling and prevention programs. Heavy alcohol use is regarded as a drain on morale and productivity and a potential threat to unit readiness. DOD in 2005 undertook a comprehensive study of health-related behaviors among active-duty military personnel that compared alcohol use among men and women in the four branches of the service and the civilian population.

It found high rates of binge drinking among young service members, especially men aged 18 to 25. Binge drinking was especially high in the Army and the Marines, where binge drinking rates of young men were similar to those of male college students. The consequences of heavy alcohol use in the military can be severe, including being passed over for promotion and punishment under the Uniform Code of Military Justice.

Not all military drinking by young men and women is illegal, depending on where soldiers and sailors are stationed. Under federal law, military personnel must comply with the law of the jurisdiction in which their installation is located. Contrary to the lure-of-the-illicit theory, the DOD study showed that soldiers drink *more* when it is *legal*. Among the entire military (all ages), 15 percent are heavy users of alcohol in the continental United States, while outside the United States, 25 percent are heavy users. The study found that one of the factors that made binge drinking less likely was being located in the United States.

This throws into doubt two fundamental assumptions of the Initiative: that young people drink because of the allure of forbidden fruit and that enforcement does not work. Young men in the military, who clearly have a very strong propensity to drink, do less of it when stationed in the United States. While one can surmise that some of the decrease could be due to lower levels of stress, it is a comparison that bears further inquiry. There is something about young males being grouped together in bonding experiences, whether in college or in the military, that seems to lend itself to heavy drinking.

The military experience of lower drinking levels in the U.S. could also mean that factors such as enforcement, fear of consequences, and difficulty in obtaining alcohol influences the amount of binge drinking. The Air Force has the lowest rate of binge drinking among the service branches and the Navy has made an effort to change the culture of sailors on liberty engaging in binge drinking. Clearly, drinking is influenced by organizational culture. The CAS study came to similar conclusions: It found that drinking cultures differ among schools and states, sometimes depending on the level of binge drinking among *adults* and the type of enforcement in the state. The environment in which young people are placed and the adult support systems and level of enforcement count.

Other settings bear comparison. American students studying abroad in France or Italy notice that college students there don't drink like fish, and assume that is the case among young people everywhere in Europe. While many Americans cling to the belief that Europeans are better than us, studies of drinking habits across all of Europe show that their binge drinking problems are worse than ours in many countries, start at younger ages, and continue into adulthood.

The legal drinking ages in Europe generally range from 16 to 18 with varying rules as to when youth may purchase and consume alcohol. Serious binge drinking begins *at age 15* in countries across the European Union. The highest rates are seen in the Nordic countries, Slovenia, Latvia, the UK, and Ireland.[8] Young teenagers, 15- to 16-year-olds, are drinking six drinks at a clip when they go out (even more in the UK and Ireland), and 18 percent of that age group is binge drinking three times a month. Things aren't much better south of the equator. When New Zealand lowered its drinking age to 18 it experienced a "sharp increase in binge drinking among teenagers and young adults."[9]

The Alcohol–Sex Cocktail

Man does not live by drink alone. There is something else college students, far from the confines of home, like to do: have sex. And when we consider that the vast majority of binge drinkers are male and then factor in their role as the initiator in sexual adventures, the role of sex drive in campus alcohol abuse becomes clearer.

One of the results of the fall of *in loco parentis* in the early 1970s was the rise of the ivory-towered Sodom and Gomorrah. Mind you, today we are not talking about dating as the Baby Boomer generation understands it. We are talking about "hooking up." That means young people go out in groups and then pair off, have casual sex, and quite possibly never get together again. Alcohol, sadly, is directly linked to the hookup culture. It fuels casual and often dangerous sexual encounters on campuses. (The danger lies in unprotected sex and date rape.)

It's important to think about the hookup culture as we weigh whether lowering the drinking age, coupled with education and licensing, would work. Picture this: A 19-year-old male has heard the lectures and has an alcohol license in his hip pocket. Yet he knows that plying himself and his female companions with beer will vastly increase his chances that the evening will end with a hookup. Oh, and he's at a bar selling 25-cent beer pitchers. Care to wager how that night will turn out?

Brett Sokolow of NCHERM said in an interview that the alcohol-related campus workshops he conducts grew out of sexual assault presentations he has done. In speaking with students and exploring how assault situations arose, he found that alcohol played an integral role. His anecdotal observations of the connection between alcohol and problematic sexual encounters on campus are reflected in research in the field. In 2001, 474,000 college students had unprotected sexual intercourse as a result of their drinking. In the same year, more than 696,000 reported being assaulted or hit by another drinking student and of those episodes, 97,000 were alcohol-related sexual assault or date rape victims.[10]

Sexual misconduct hearings are now "no longer rare occurrences on many college campuses," Sokolow wrote in a white paper. The paper (available on the NCHERM website) provides painstaking guidelines for college administrators to follow in conducting disciplinary hearings to determine if the victim of an alleged assault was truly "incapacitated" or just plain "drunk," "under the influence," "intoxicated," or "inebriated." Parsing such terms is a job skill for today's college administrator, since only "incapacitation" renders a victim unable to give consent to a sexual encounter.

Just Another Privilege?

The initiative takes pains to refer to college students as "adults," and argues that the 21 laws should be brought "into sync" with age-of-majority rights such as voting, military service, or contract. These are not apt comparisons because the basis of those rights is the doctrine of emancipation. Given the grave consequences of underage alcohol consumption, the legal test for emancipation is helpful in thinking about whether the typical American 18-year-old is mature enough for the rights and responsibilities of legal drinking.

When a minor enters the military (with parental permission), he or she *automatically* becomes emancipated in the eyes of the law. The law assumes that the military will only accept someone who demonstrates the necessary level of maturity for duty. In the event the military is wrong, it has an excellent system for weeding out mistakes: basic training. The military can discharge those not up to the challenge. For a minor to become emancipated under other circumstances, it's a tougher process. He must show a court that he is self-supporting, can handle his own personal affairs, and understands what emancipation means.

Although a typical 18-year-old is technically emancipated, it is the rare college student who could pass such a test. Rather than living a life of real emancipation like his married or enlisted counterparts, the college student exists in a strange netherworld suspended between adolescence and real adulthood. While college students demonstrate a good deal of independence in the sense that they live away from home, make friends, study, and do their own laundry, they are nonetheless dependent on their parents financially and demonstrate varying degrees of autonomy and good sense. They are often busy having the time of their lives. Indeed, a common suggestion for reigning in campus drinking is to hold classes on Friday mornings, thus preventing the weekend revelry from beginning on Thursday nights.

Alcohol consumption is unique among the rights conferred by age-of-majority laws because it alters brain chemistry, and the risk of conferring it on the wrong person can be immediate and violent. Bear in mind that under various provisions of state and federal law, even minors emancipated at an early age through marriage or military service see no change in their right to drink.

In addition, colleges are not the bastions of the hale and hearty they were for most of the 20th century. Today, students attend college while managing chronic illnesses such as arthritis, diabetes, multiple sclerosis, asthma, depression and other psychiatric maladies, endocrine disorders, and attention deficit disorder. College populations even include cancer survivors in various stages of remission. "Two generations ago [ill students] would not have been mainstreamed," said Patricia Fennell, head of Albany Health Management Associates and an expert on managing chronic health conditions. Now they are coping with chronic illnesses far from the watchful eyes of their parents—which means taking medicines and dealing with the temptations of college life—including alcohol.

Emancipation is not always desirable. Indeed, there is a tradition in the law to that effect. Many states have an express, statutory exception to age-of-majority emancipation rules. Exceptions usually relate to special rights conferred on the disabled, who are entitled to certain protections beyond the age of 18. Many state and federal child poverty programs cover children through age 21. Given the rates of binge drinking on campus and the number of deaths, injuries, and social costs associated with underage alcohol use, the emancipation-exception doctrines provide a useful perspective from which to think about the 21 laws. By delaying legal drinking, the 21 laws provide a valuable, *partial* exception to emancipation for 18-, 19- and 20-year-olds on the grounds that when it comes to alcohol, they can benefit from society's protection.

The question is not whether we should protect youth from alcohol, but why has society done such a lousy job of it by largely failing to enforce the 21 laws? The Initiative, in its rhetorical question about "repeating the lessons of Prohibition," intimates that laws proscribing alcohol are simply doomed to failure. Are they? . . .

Why Not Just Educate?

Choose Responsibility would replace the 21 laws with alcohol education at home and on campus. But colleges already educate college students about drinking. Even though schools are required to have anti-underage drinking policies under federal law, there is nothing to prevent them from teaching moderation or techniques to prevent alcohol poisoning. Indeed, college students get alcohol education from numerous sources: official school policy and abstinence programs and alcohol moderation programs provided by colleges; moderation programs provided by outside consulting groups; an online program called AlcoholEdu that has reached almost a quarter of a million students on over 400 college campuses; and normative marketing programs. Sokolow estimates that 10 to 20 percent of colleges now have outside consultants come to campus to provide alcohol moderation programs.

A large role is also played by social-norms marketing programs in which "latent healthy norms" about college drinking are made known to students through posters, flyers, and other forms of high-profile communication on campus. In other words, messages on billboards and flyers all over campus model the way grown-ups drink. A program may present the idea that a typical young drinker consumes *five or fewer* drinks when he parties with friends. Such marketing programs carry a positive message and do *not* discuss the dangers of drinking. About half of all four-year residential colleges have conducted social-norms marketing programs for alcohol.[11]

They are not necessarily a good idea. A study of alcohol-related social-norms marketing was done based on the data gathered in the Harvard CAS that compared the 118 schools in the survey. The social-norms study included the schools that had experienced social-norms marketing programs and those that didn't. The study showed that social-norms marketing did not reduce college drinking. In fact, in the schools that had the programs, drinking increased. In the schools without the programs, no change in drinking rates occurred.

The study did not show why drinking increased at schools with the programs, but it is a cautionary tale. The college drinking scene is a battleground with two fronts: coping with those who already are binge drinkers and fighting for the hearts and souls of the others. We know that about half of freshman classes enter with no history of alcohol use and can be lured into drinking. Hearing a message sanctioned by the college that some drinking is all right could tip the balance.

We do know that many environmental factors influence the likelihood of a nondrinking student continuing on that course, including diversity of the student body, the number of female students, the risk and cost of obtaining alcohol and the presence of "zero-tolerance" dorms. Much depends on the state and its culture of enforcement. Measures such as increasing prices, imposing excise taxes, and local laws that regulate the density of liquor-selling establishments close to campus can have a strong impact on underage drinking.[12]

The Institute of Alcohol Studies in London looked at individual as well as meta-analyses of European, Australian, and American youth alcohol education efforts. It found that although there were "individual examples of the beneficial impacts of school-based education," there was not enough evidence to conclude that education has an impact on binge drinking among young people. The Institute said it was not implying that education should not be done, but it "should not be seen as the answer to reduce the harm done by binge drinking." Education, the Institute concluded, plays only a supportive role.[13]

The Amethyst Initiative says, in essence, that the phenomenon of underage drinking is a tidal wave that society cannot stop. Our only hope is to ride the wave along with our children, give them an oar, and hope they don't drown. That relies on the very big—and untested—assumption that their young minds have the capacity to listen when it comes to alcohol, no matter how badly they want to party, hook up, fit in.

Given the stakes, America should not throw in the towel on the 21 laws until we have actually enforced them as they were meant to be enforced—though it will require a clear dedication of political will. It can be done; a similar revolution occurred during the 1980s with respect to driving under the influence laws. Disparities in enforcement do not mean that the laws are impossible to enforce. It signals that we have not gotten serious as a nation about using the laws we have—and improving them where needed.

Notes

1. The use of the word "amethyst" alludes to an ancient myth associating the stone with the ability to ward off drunkenness.

2. Richard J. Bonnie and Mary Ellen O'Connell, eds., *Reducing Underage Drinking: A Collective Responsibility, Committee on Developing A Strategy to Reduce and Prevent Underage Drinking* (National Academies Press, 2004), 25–26.

3. Robert Davis and Anthony DeBarros, "Alcohol and Fire a Deadly Mix," *USA Today*, Dec. 18, 2008.

4. Ralph W. Hingson et al., "Magnitude and Morbidity Among U.S. College Students Ages 18–24," *Journal of Studies on Alcohol* (March 2002); Ralph W. Hingson, et al., "Magnitude and Morbidity Among U.S. College Students Ages 18–24: Changes from 1998 to 2001, Ages 18–24," *Annual Review of Public Health* (2005); and "The Surgeon General's Call to Action to Prevent and Reduce Underage Drinking" (Office of the Surgeon General, 2007), available at http://www.surgeongeneral.gov/topics/underagedrinking/calltoaction.pdf (accessed May 4, 2009).

5. J.A. Grunbaum, et al., "Youth risk behavior surveillance—United States, 2003," *Morbidity and Mortality Weekly Report Summary* 53:2 (May 21, 2004), and L.D. Johnston, et al., "Teen Drug Use Continues Down in 2006, Particularly Among Older Teens; but Use of Prescription-Type Drugs Remains High," University of Michigan News and Information Services (2006).

6. "The Surgeon General's Call to Action to Prevent and Reduce Underage Drinking."

7. "Magnitude and Morbidity Among U.S. College Students Ages 18–24."

8. Bjorn Hibell., et al., "The ESPAD Report 2003: Alcohol and Other Drug Use Among Students in 35 European Countries" (2004).

9. Institute of Alcohol Studies, "Binge Drinking—Nature, prevalence and causes, IAS Fact Sheet" (2006).

10. "Magnitude and Morbidity Among U.S. College Students Ages 18–24: Changes from 1998 to 2001, Ages 18–24."

11. Henry Wechsler and Toben F. Nelson, "What We Have Learned From the Harvard School of Public Health College Alcohol Study: Focusing Attention on College Student Alcohol Consumption and the Environmental Conditions That Promote It," *Journal of Studies on Alcohol and Drugs* (July 2008).

12. Robert Zimmerman and William DeJong, "Safe Lanes on Campus: A Guide for Preventing Impaired Driving and Underage Drinking" (Higher Education Center for Alcohol and Other Drug Prevention, 2003).

13. Peter Anderson, "Binge Drinking and Europe," (Institute of Alcohol Studies, 2008).

Judith G. McMullen  **NO**

Underage Drinking: Does Current Policy Make Sense?

This Article examines the history of laws and policies regulating consumption of alcoholic beverages by young people in the United States, and examines youth drinking patterns that have emerged over time. Currently, all 50 states have a minimum drinking age of 21. Various rationales are offered for the 21 drinking age, such as the claim that earlier drinking hinders cognitive functions and the claim that earlier drinking increases the lifetime risk of becoming an alcoholic. While there is sufficient evidence to support the claim that it would be better for adolescents and young adults if they did not drink prior to age 21, research shows that vast numbers of underage persons consume alcoholic beverages, often in large quantities. The Article discusses the question of why underage drinking laws have not been able to effectively stop underage drinking.

Normally, discussions of underage drinking focus on persons under age 21 as one group. This Article breaks underage drinkers into two groups: minors (drinkers under the age of 18) and young adults (drinkers between the ages of 18 and 21). The Article goes on to separately analyze the two groups' drinking patterns and reasons for drinking. The Article concludes that prohibitions on drinking by minors could be made more effective because restrictions on activities by minors are expected and normally honored by parents, law, and society. The Article also concludes, however, that the enforcement of a drinking prohibition for young adults between the ages of 18 and 21 is doomed to remain largely ineffective because the drinking ban is wholly inconsistent with other legal policies aimed at that age group. The Article discusses three areas (health care decisions, educational decisions, and smoking) where persons over the age of 18 have virtually unfettered personal discretion, and applies the reasoning of those situations to the decision about whether to consume alcoholic beverages. The Article also compares the total drinking ban for young adults with the graduated privilege policies applied to drivers' licensing. The Article concludes that the total prohibition of alcohol consumption for young adults is inconsistent with other policies affecting young adults, and this inconsistency, coupled with harms that may come from the 21 drinking age, make the current policies ineffective and ill-advised for young adults between the age of 18 and 21.

Introduction

On the surface, youth alcohol policy is simple and straightforward: the legal age for alcohol consumption is 21 in all states, and drinking before then is illegal. As it happens, though, these laws are not terribly effective. Huge numbers of youngsters age 12 and up (and probably younger) consume alcoholic beverages, despite the law.[1] The numbers of underage drinkers skyrocket once kids are over 18, and college campuses are known hotbeds of underage consumption.[2] According to researchers, large numbers of young people drink alcohol, many heavily, before they attain the legal drinking age.[3]

This Article addresses the question of why underage drinking laws have not been able to effectively stop underage drinking. It examines some of the classic reasons: ambivalence among adults as to the law, feelings of entitlement by young people, and glorification of alcohol consumption by society as a whole. The Article argues that alcohol consumption by adolescents under the age of 18 could be reduced by stricter and more consistent enforcement. However, the Article goes on to conclude that the prohibition of alcohol consumption cannot ever be effective for the 18 to 21-year-old cohort, because it is wholly inconsistent with other legal policies aimed at that age group. Further, the Article argues that outlawing alcohol consumption for young adults[4] may cause harm because the policy may encourage unhealthy alcohol consumption patterns in young adults, and it carries the risk of engendering a lack of respect for the law in general.

Underage drinking laws need to be assessed in two parts. One policy is the prohibition of alcohol consumption for minors, i.e., persons under the age of 18. The second policy is prohibition of alcohol consumption for persons between the ages of 18 and 21. While similar justifications are offered for the restrictions on each of these groups, in fact, as we shall see, there are very different factors at play in terms of parental control, societal expectations, and overall consistency with other situations where the law asserts control over individual behaviors. Most articles on youth alcohol policy address whether the current policy is a good thing. This Article concedes that it might indeed be a good thing if persons under age 21 abstained from alcohol. However, the Article goes on to discuss how the youth alcohol policy fits—or does not fit—into the patchwork of laws and policies concerning state intervention into the lives of parents and their children.

This Article argues that banning alcohol consumption for the under-18 crowd is consistent with other child protective policies advanced by state laws, largely because the law does not accord many rights of self-determination to minors. Thus, the ban could be reasonably effective if enforcement were increased—perhaps with such measures as holding parents and other adults accountable for behaviors that facilitate illegal underage drinking. However, the Article also concludes that current alcohol policy for persons over age 18 is *not* consistent with analogous policies for persons who are legally adults: e.g., the right to refuse medical treatment or the right to smoke cigarettes. In fact, the alcohol laws governing young adults seem to substitute state policies for both parental judgment and the young person's self-determination on this single issue. Thus, the Article concludes that the policy cannot ever be widely effective with this group, and creates as many problems as it solves. This is despite the inarguable fact that alcohol consumption may well be harmful to persons in this disputed age group.

First, the Article gives an overview of drinking policies in the United States, from colonial times to the present.[5] Second, the Article discusses the current laws and the justifications offered for them.[6] Next, the Article examines the effectiveness of the laws and the drinking patterns among younger underage youths (up to age 18),[7] and older underage youths (ages 18 to 21).[8] The Article compares youth drinking policies with other policies affecting young adults and argues that the practical and philosophical differences between the drinking ban for 18- to 21-year-olds and other legal policies affecting that age group make the alcohol ban for young adults largely unenforceable.[9] The Article also discusses problems arguably caused by the prohibition of alcohol use by young adults and examines whether the drinking age law might have significant value despite its unenforceability.[10] Finally, the Article suggests that alcohol use by 18- to 21-year-olds might be more appropriately addressed in a manner analogous to drivers' licensing policies for young drivers: by providing a combination of alcohol education and supervision to young adults who choose to drink.

Assessing Current Policies and Patterns

A. Structure of Current Laws

Currently, all fifty states have a minimum legal drinking age of 21.[11] Enforcement is aimed at both underage drinkers and their suppliers. Underage drinkers may be penalized with municipal or state citations or drivers' license suspensions.[12] Parents or other individual adults who supply alcohol to underage persons may be held criminally responsible, which might result in assessment of a fine or a jail sentence, although several states do not impose these penalties on parents who are serving alcoholic beverages to their *own* children.[13] Adults who provide alcohol to minors may also be exposed to civil liability in the event of harm caused by the underage drinker.[14] Bar owners or storeowners may be hit with fines or may lose their liquor licenses.[15] Penalties for underage driving while under the influence are effectively more severe for young adults than for adults over the age of 21, because the offense is typically committed if the young driver has *any* detectable alcohol in her blood.[16]

B. Policy Objectives

There are two stated justifications for enforcing a minimum drinking age: protection of young people, and protection of society. Numerous studies and statistics are offered to support each justification.

The first argument, that a 21 drinking age protects young people from harm, is supported by recent research that suggests alcohol can have an especially detrimental effect on the developing brain. The American Medical Association released a report in 2002 stating that drinking by adolescents and young adults could result in long-term brain damage, including diminishment of memory, reasoning, and learning abilities.[17] Experts think that memory and learning impairment is worse in adolescents, who may experience adverse effects after consuming only half as much alcohol as adults.[18] Human research at the University of Pittsburgh showed that heavy-drinking girls between the ages of 14 and 21 had smaller hippocampi than girls of the same age who were non-drinkers.[19] Admittedly, this research does not prove whether it is the heavy drinking that causes changes in the hippocampus, or the reduced size of the hippocampus that causes the urge to engage in heavy drinking.[20] Moreover, teenage hormonal changes, eating habits, or abuse of other substances like marijuana could also be causes of learning and memory impairment.[21] However, research with rats has shown similar bad effects from alcohol consumption on the rodents' learning and memory, even extending into adulthood.[22]

In addition, some researchers contend that alcohol abuse in the teenage years is more likely to lead to alcohol dependence later in life than if the drinking had begun at a later age. A study released in 1998 by the National Institute of Alcohol Abuse and Alcoholism concluded that "[c]hildren who begin drinking regularly by age 13 are more than four times as likely to become alcoholics as those who delay consuming alcohol until age 21 or older. . . ."[23] The study found that children who started drinking regularly at age 13 faced a 47% lifetime risk of becoming an alcoholic, compared with a 25% risk for youth who began drinking at age 17, and a 10% risk for people who began drinking at age 21.[24] However, it is not clear why some children are prone to such early and heavy drinking and others are not. It may be, for example, that children who begin drinking heavily at age 13 do so because of some biological characteristic that also causes them to have more of a lifetime risk for alcoholism.[25] In other words, rather than the early drinking causing the later alcoholism, it may be a symptom of the existing vulnerability to alcoholism.

It is also claimed that withholding drinking privileges until a later age protects young people by reducing the number of fatal automobile accidents involving teenagers. Indeed, "[t]he National Highway Traffic Safety Administration estimates that since the '70s, the age-21 policy has saved 20,970 teenage lives from serious car crashes alone."[26] For example, "[i]n 1982, a study by the National Highway Traffic Safety Administration found that 5,380 persons between the ages of 15 and 20 had died in drunken driving accidents that year. . . . [By 1995] the number had been reduced to 2,206 nationwide. . . .[27] However, drunk driving enforcement in general has been taken more seriously since the drinking age was changed, and this might also account for some of the improvement.[28]

The second argument, that a 21 drinking age protects society from the bad effects of underage drinking, is partly supported by data on traffic fatalities that could be caused by young drunk drivers.[29] In addition, there is another claimed benefit to society in banning underage drinking: the possible reduction of crime perpetrated by persons under age 21. Alcohol has been shown to be a major contributing factor in teen deaths from accidents, homicide, and suicide, and it has also been shown to increase the chances of juvenile delinquency and crime.[30] Alcohol abuse appears to increase the likelihood that young people will engage in unprotected sex or acquaintance rape, suicide, and other violent behavior.[31] Of course, alcohol is a known inhibition-reducer and is implicated in crimes for all age groups.[32] Moreover, both the drinking and other problem behaviors may be caused by the general turmoil of adolescence, which is characterized by impulsiveness, sensation seeking, and unconventionality.[33]

There is no doubt that a significant number of young people consume alcohol in violation of the minimum age laws. While state laws outlaw alcohol purchase and consumption for all persons under age 21, there are in fact two distinct groups of underage drinkers who present different issues. First of all are the minors (high school and younger drinkers), and second are the young adults or college age drinkers.[34]

C. Underage Drinking by Minors

Studies show that a significant minority of high school students consume alcohol on a regular basis: "According to 2002 Monitoring the Future (MTF) data, almost half (48.6 percent) of twelfth graders reported recent (within the past 30 days) alcohol use."[35] Although younger teens report lower incidences of alcohol use, "NHSDA[36] data indicate that the average age of self-reported first use of alcohol among individuals of all ages reporting any alcohol use decreased from 17.6 years to 15.9 years between 1965 and 1999."[37] Moreover, underage drinkers are more likely than adults to be heavy drinkers.[38]

Even for those minors who are not regular drinkers, certain rites of passage such as school dances, proms, and graduation can be the occasion of much alcoholic excess. A notorious incident that occurred in Scarsdale, New York in 2002 provides an excellent example of the dynamics. In the fall of 2002, *The New York Times* reported that the prestigious Scarsdale High School homecoming dance and pre-dance parties included widespread binge drinking "which left scores of students falling-down drunk, 27 with three-day school suspensions and five hospitalized with acute alcohol poisoning. . . ."[39] When the principal arrived at the dance shortly after its 8 pm start, he "found perhaps a third of the 600 students there in a stupor from drinking screwdrivers they had mixed at various homes. They had used vodka sneaked from their parents['] liquor cabinets and disguised in Poland Spring water bottles."[40]

While major high school events have precipitated underage drinking for generations, *The New York Times* cited differences noted by education and mental health experts. First, "[t]he drinking starts younger. . . . The quantity and speed of alcohol consumption are dangerously high and the goal seems to be total oblivion."[41] Second, certain psychological factors are different: baby boomer parents are less likely to be seen as authority figures by their children, and the children in upscale communities are in a super-competitive atmosphere with "enormous pressure to succeed."[42] If they don't meet parental expectations, they may drown their sorrows in drugs or alcohol. Finally, "[e]ducators and mental health professionals also say that affluence breeds a sense of entitlement in children. They're told from the time they're young that they're the prize of the community. . . . The conclusion an adolescent may draw is: 'I'm special. I get to do what I want.'"[43]

The Scarsdale incident also illustrates another phenomenon that has become common: placing much of the blame for underage drinking on adults, especially parents. According to Geraldine Greene, executive director of the Scarsdale Family Counseling Service, underage drinking is "an adult failure. In every case, an adult has let a child down. Somewhere along the way they haven't exercised due care."[44] Although Greene's comments could be directed at a large variety of adults, including parents, vendors, and teachers, she is most critical of affluent parents who she feels do not take enough time to raise their teenagers properly.[45] Adolescent psychologist Dr. Alan Tepp said that while parents hold their adolescents to ever-higher achievement standards, "at the same time, we're putting less restraint on them, watching them less. We push them, and then allow them out."[46]

Studies provide some support for these opinions. Large amounts of time free from adult supervision, including after-school time without parent contact, has been related to higher alcohol consumption among teens.[47] "'Hanging out' with friends in unstructured, unsupervised contexts is generally related to negative outcomes, while spending time with others in adult-sanctioned, structured contexts is generally related to positive outcomes."[48]

There is, of course, a more direct way in which parents can be responsible for youth drinking: they may provide the liquor consumed by high school–aged children. Some parents take the position that kids will drink anyway, and if the parents allow supervised drinking at home parties, this will reduce more dangerous binge drinking or drinking in cars, followed by driving while intoxicated.[49] For example, a 17-year-old graduate of Scarsdale High School said, "I know one of my friend's parents said, 'If you're staying in the house, then I don't have a problem with you drinking.' That's kind of promoting it. . . ."[50] Indeed, "having parents who sanction alcohol use (even in 'controlled' settings) is related to heavier drinking among adolescents."[51] A Westchester County District Attorney commented that the "number of kids getting drunk at home is on the increase, as is the frequency of alcohol being provided by an adult or older sibling. . . ."[52]

Herein lies part of the enforcement problem: some parents think drinking is a normal rite of passage for teenagers; others believe in zero-tolerance. A Scarsdale police detective, firmly in the latter camp, said, "Parents should send a clear message to their kids that this behavior will not be condoned. . . ."[53]

Yet even parents who might be willing to crack down are not always convinced that it will work. A principal in Chappaqua, New York quoted a parent who told him that "setting earlier curfews just makes the kids drink faster."[54] He added that since many parents feel powerless to stop their kids from drinking, they have adopted the view that "until society solves the problem, I want my kids alive."[55]

There are a number of different issues jumbled together here. First, we must consider whether it is reasonable for the state to prevent children under the age of 18 from consuming alcohol. Second, we must address whether we have consensus on this issue in this society. Finally, we must assess the reasonableness of the notion that parents can in large degree control the drinking behavior of their offspring.

Ever since *Prince v. Massachusetts*[56] upheld the state's right to protect a young Jehovah's Witness from the dangers of street preaching, it has been clear that a state can adopt reasonable policies to protect children, even over the heartfelt objections of their parents.[57] Unlike *Prince*, challenges to a state's protective alcohol policy do not rest on First Amendment free exercise claims; at best they depend upon arguments that reasonable parents might exercise their prerogative in favor of allowing their children to engage in moderate social drinking. A state's purposes of preventing traffic accidents, crime, and potential damage to a young imbiber's health or cognitive function would clearly survive any constitutional claim of infringement on parental authority. This is especially true in those few states that allow parents to serve alcohol to their own minor children while those children are in the parent's presence.[58] Even the most inconclusive of the scientific studies cited in Part III.B signals enough risk of harm that a state could reasonably prohibit alcohol consumption by minors.[59]

As to whether we have consensus about whether the absolute ban on consumption is a good thing, the answer is that we clearly do not. While a majority may favor the ban, a significant minority either thinks that it is counterproductive, or simply ineffective. These are the folks that may either look the other way or actually provide alcohol, on the theory that kids will drink anyway, and "I would rather know where they are."[60] In some national surveys, many parents admit to purchasing alcohol for their teenagers, in the hopes of providing a safe place for their kids to drink.[61] Ironically, these parents contribute to the fact that the ban is ineffective, and they make it ineffective not only for their own children, but for other people's children as well.

In fact, the combination of typical adolescent rebellion and readily available alcohol supplied by dissenting or indifferent adults makes it impossible for individual parents to completely control whether or not their children consume alcohol, unless the parents achieve round-the-clock supervision, amounting to lockdown, of their children.[62] Thus, penalizing parents for facilitating consumption, but not holding them accountable for the behavior of sneaky adolescent drinkers, makes good sense.

There are a myriad of situations where parents or the state effectively control situations involving persons under age 18. Parents are held responsible for the support and education of their minor children.[63] The law is generally structured to help parents in these endeavors, and to regulate parents who fall short. Thus, fit parents are generally entitled to custody of their minor children,[64] and deference is given to parental decisions about the incidents of that custody.[65] Laws that regulate minors' activities, such as truancy or curfew laws that may penalize errant children, are widely viewed as reinforcements to judicious parental controls.[66] Parents who stray from societal norms, such as parents who abuse their children or parents who are complicit in the truancy of their children, can be subjected to various penalties.[67]

Statutes and cases have attempted to strike a balance between parental prerogatives, children's rights, and societal interests in regulating minors' activities.[68] Where underage drinking is concerned, parents have an important role in restricting minors' access to alcohol.[69] Due to the fact that most minors live with at least one adult, greater adult consensus on the value of banning alcohol consumption by minors, as well as greater adult compliance with the laws, could combine to significantly reduce alcohol consumption by persons under age 18. Moreover, even if adolescent consumption is not reduced to zero, it could be reduced from current epidemic proportions, and abstinence from underage alcohol consumption could be internalized by minors as an important social norm.

D. Underage Drinking by Young Adults

Regulation of underage drinking becomes more problematic after a young person reaches the age of majority—usually 18—or moves away from home into a dorm or apartment. However imperfect parental supervision may have been before, it becomes nearly impossible at that time. Persons over the age of 18 are legally adults for any purpose *except* consuming alcohol. Even parents of economically dependent college students may not know whether their children are drinking, since schools have no obligation to notify parents when a young person violates underage drinking laws or school rules.[70]

Drinking in the 18 to 21 age group, however, is rampant. Young people in this age group who do not attend college drink less than those that do attend, but they are not teetotalers as a group.[71] And although not every child goes to college, these are the prime college age years for those that do, and college campuses are notorious for widespread alcohol consumption. According to one source, 44% of college students report binge drinking in the past two weeks, and 23% report frequent binge drinking.[72] Apparently, membership in fraternities and sororities greatly increases the likelihood of excessive drinking: a 2001 survey "showed that three-quarters of fraternity or sorority house residents (80 percent and 69 percent, respectively) are binge drinkers," an improvement over the 1993 figure of 83%.[73] Although binge drinking is typically defined as five or more drinks per occasion, the bingeing at many Greek organizations is reportedly far more extreme. One consultant stated:

> Our organization has worked extensively with Greek groups over the past twenty years and has found some chapters to report that more than 70 percent of their members consume thirteen or more drinks per occasion. We frequently hear from other professionals on campuses that fifteen to twenty drinks per occasion, though not the norm, is not uncommon among some groups of students.[74]

Theories abound as to why drinking is so extreme on college campuses. Researchers Wechsler and Wuethrich think one reason is that students "developed a sense of entitlement to alcohol" after the drinking age was lowered to 18 during the 1970s and then re-raised to 21.[75] They also point to the relaxation of dormitory supervision, the increasingly cultivated party images of fraternities and even schools themselves, and the rising importance of college sports as big business, with attendant alcohol industry sponsorships.[76] They also acknowledge alcohol's role in larger society as a factor.[77]

I believe that there is another important reason for widespread drinking among young adults: with the exception of alcohol, parental control over the young person's activities grinds to a halt after age 18, if not before then. Moreover, with the exception of alcohol, and to some extent drivers' licenses, state control of the activities of a person over 18 is no different for the 18 to 21 age group than for an adult of any age. Once a person attains age 18, he or she can legally marry without parental permission, join the military, enter contracts, smoke, make decisions concerning medical care, or drop out of school. These newfound freedoms occur at age 18, despite the fact that the young person may be immature or financially dependent on his parents, and despite the fact that he may have parents who disapprove of his decisions. It is this legal autonomy in other areas, I think, that makes enforcement of a 21 drinking age impossible.

For the sake of discussion, I will compare the 21 drinking age policy with policies aimed at the 18 to 21 age group in the areas of medical decision-making, decisions to forgo education, decisions about smoking, and regulations concerning driving. All of these represent adult privileges that can have serious consequences for the young person, and potentially for others around him. All also represent situations where a mistake in judgment, perhaps due to immaturity, can have dire consequences. Yet, unlike current alcohol policy, the policies in these areas defer to the judgment of the young person, for good or ill. If the main reason for forbidding alcohol consumption for persons under the age of 21 is protection from the adverse physical effects of youth drinking, such as greater likelihood of later alcoholism or greater damage to the brain, then the policy is entirely consistent with other policies for children under the age of 18. It is, however, completely unprecedented compared with other policies for young people in the 18 to 21 age group.

Problems Caused by the Prohibition of Alcohol Use by Young Adults

There are two potential problems that may result from the prohibition of alcohol use by young adults. The first problem is that the impossibility of enforcing the law will engender a lack of respect for the law in general among young adults. The second problem is that, for those who choose to violate the law, the necessity of sneaking around to drink may lead to more dangerous drinking patterns and may preclude access to avenues that might imbue healthier drinking habits.

A. The Difficulty of an Unenforceable Law

Laws that are difficult or impossible to enforce have always been problematic. Of course, no law is one hundred percent enforceable: history is replete with unsolved crimes and unpunished offenders of every sort.[78] However, laws may serve a useful symbolic or deterrent function despite sporadic enforcement. Indeed, "the effectiveness of symbolic laws depends on public affirmation rather than legal enforcement. 'People obey symbolic laws not for fear of legal sanction, but because they are backed by the consensus of society and the force of major social institutions.'"[79] As Lawrence Friedman has pointed out, even laws that are imperfectly enforced may reduce a given behavior by making it more costly: "[P]olicy choices are essentially selections among various techniques and means of encouraging or discouraging behavior, by making that behavior safer, cheaper, and more pleasant; or more expensive, more aversive."[80]

When we examine the 21 drinking age in this context, it can be argued that the current law reduces drinking by young adults and conveys important social values to all young adults, even those who violate the law. Advocates of the 21 drinking age claim that the law has resulted in more college-age students who abstain from alcohol use (and are willing to admit it), which thereby reduces alcohol-related problems of all sorts.[81] Not everyone credits the 21 drinking age with this progress, however. Richard Keeling, a physician and former director of health services at the University of Wisconsin-Madison, believes that enforcement methods such as crackdowns on house parties and increased fines for alcohol-related offenses are more likely reasons for changes in young adult behavior.[82]

The argument that a 21 drinking age conveys important societal values to teenagers and young adults is less persuasive in light of the fact, already discussed,[83] that the drinking ban for young adults does not seem to be backed by a broad consensus of society. As we have seen, many parents and other adults disagree with the law in principle.[84] These adults may view drinking as a rite of passage, or may believe that an earlier drinking age would be conducive to more moderate drinking habits later. Such adults may not only ignore violations of the drinking ban by young adults, but they may enable the young adults to commit the violations by supplying alcohol or hosting drinking parties.[85] In these circumstances, where the social consensus on youth drinking is divided at best, it is harder to claim that a strong moral message is being delivered to underage drinkers.

In addition, alcohol continues to be glorified in sports sponsorships and advertising, making it unclear exactly what social message teenagers and young adults are getting about alcohol. Research has shown that adolescents who are exposed to alcohol advertising are more likely to consume alcohol and to consume it in greater amounts.[86] It is clear that vast numbers of adolescents are in fact exposed to alcohol advertising. Voluntary conduct codes adopted in the late 1990s by the Distilled Spirits Council of the United States suggest that ads should only run in media outlets having no more than 30% of their audience under the age of 21.[87] However, 30% of a broadcast such as a sporting event can be a substantial number of underage viewers.

Sporting events often have alcohol companies as sponsors, such as the sponsorship of NASCAR driver Dale Earnhardt by Budweiser beer and the Busch beer sponsorship of the NASCAR Busch series.[88] Stadiums such as Miller Park in Wisconsin and Coors Field in Colorado associate their corporate sponsors with sports. College sports are no exception, with the NCAA allowing one minute per hour of alcohol ads during broadcast of NCAA events.[89] In a recent report, the Center for Science in the Public Interest argued that because the

NCAA has many underage followers (including kids as young as 9 or 10), the NCAA is effectively helping brewers to recruit kids to beer drinking in general, as well as to particular brands of beer.[90] The American Medical Association recently joined the Center for Science in the Public Interest in urging the NCAA to ban alcohol advertising during events,[91] but the NCAA decided to retain its existing policy.[92]

B. Potential Harmful Effects of a 21-Year-Old Drinking Age

Mixed messages sent to young drinkers are only part of the problem. In addition, it is possible that the drinking ban for young adults may have harmful effects.[93] We have seen that even during Prohibition, commentators bemoaned the lack of respect for the law that came from the widely flaunted ban.[94] Some argue that Prohibition may have exacerbated alcohol abuse, at least for some consumers:

> It's the same pattern observed during Prohibition, when illicit stills would blow up, and there was a rise in deaths from alcohol poisoning. Far from instilling virtue in Americans, Prohibition caused them to switch from beer and wine to hard liquor. Overall consumption of alcohol might even have increased.[95]

In modern times, many parents and adults fear that banning alcohol outright leads rebellious young adults to drink in more dangerous ways: "The pattern for underage students is more dangerous. . . . Afraid of being caught, they drink a lot in a short period of time. They do it less often but more intensely."[96]

The legal ban on drinking before age 21 also eliminates the possibility of teaching responsible drinking behaviors to young adults who, because of relative economic dependence, are often accessible to parents, college administrators, and others. The president of Middlebury College in Vermont, John McCardell, believes that the lack of supervised drinking experience for young adults causes much of the problem.[97] He argues that colleges should play an active role in teaching students how to drink responsibly.[98] Says McCardell: "You have to give them some exposure. . . . That doesn't mean sending everybody out to get drunk. But if you're serious about teaching somebody biology, you're going to include a laboratory. College campuses could be little laboratories of progressiveness."[99]

Nor is McCardell alone in his views. A recent article in the student newspaper at Tufts University quoted several University administrators who expressed similar concerns. "It's very complicated when you're living in a country where the legal drinking age forces you to bury your head in the sand," said Margot Abels, Director of Drug and Alcohol Education Services.[100] Tufts Dean of Students, Bruce Reitman, regrets that the 21 drinking age makes it impossible for faculty members to "model responsible drinking," as they did when an 18 drinking age allowed Friday afternoon student-faculty sherry hours where alcohol was used in a civilized, non-abusive manner.[101] Nowadays, Reitman notes, it is "naive" to tell freshmen that he expects them to never touch alcohol, especially in light of a recent survey of Tufts freshmen that indicated that more than 80% of respondents had tried alcohol before arriving at the University.[102]

The notion of allowing young adults to drink, at least in supervised settings such as college-sponsored parties, has some parallels with the grant of driving privileges to young drivers. Combining education and supervision with probationary privileges allows young drivers to acquire necessary skills. If they proceed through their probationary period without incident, they may obtain regular drivers' licenses. If they have violations, they may face delays or lose their licenses altogether.[103] Likewise, college campuses could sponsor parties where adult supervision is provided. Alcohol education could be incorporated into the mandatory curriculum. Nor are colleges the only institutions that could institute this approach. Churches, community centers, or other organizations frequented by young people could also provide much needed education and supervision to young adults who choose to drink. Otherwise, the furtive, excessive drinking patterns exhibited by a significant percentage of young adults may cause far greater problems than would come from lowering the drinking age.

Conclusion

This Article has attempted to show that prohibiting alcohol consumption by young adults aged 18 to 21 is a policy that is neither currently effective, nor likely to be effective in the future. This failure is partly due to the fact that parents, who are key players in the control of minors, no longer have legally enforceable control over offspring who have attained the age of majority. The failure of policy is also due to the fact that an outright ban on drinking by young adults is philosophically different from policies governing analogous decisions that may be made by adults in our society. Whereas adults may make questionable decisions in areas such as education, health, or smoking, decisions about alcohol are uniquely restricted. Due to this dichotomy, I believe that prohibition of alcohol use by young adults will never be widely effective, no matter how desirable a teetotaler young adult population might be.

Notes

1. *See, e.g.*, NAT'L RES. COUNCIL INST. OF MED., REDUCING UNDERAGE DRINKING: A COLLECTIVE RESPONSIBILITY 35–57 (Richard J. Bonnie & Mary Ellen O'Connel eds., 2004).

2. *Id.* at 43–48.

3. *Id.* at 40–42.

4. Throughout the Article, I will use the term "young adults" to denote persons in the 18- to 21-year-old age group.

5. *See infra* Part II.

6. *See infra* Part III.A–B.

7. *See infra* Part III.C.

8. *See infra* Part III.D.

9. *See infra* Part IV.

10. *See infra* Part V.

11. Shelley, *supra* note 19, at 709.

12. *See, e.g.,* MNOOKIN & WEISBERG, *supra* note 29, at 663; WIS. STAT. § 125.07(4) (2004).

13. One Maryland father was charged with maintaining a disorderly house, "a misdemeanor subject to a fine of up to $300 or a maximum jail sentence of six months." Other possible charges include "contributing to the delinquency of a minor" and "drinking in prohibited places." Veronica T. Jennings, *Md. Parents Cited in Teen Drinking Crackdown*, WASH. POST, June 14, 1988, at B1. Some states impose criminal liability on persons who provide alcohol to minors, where the minor later dies or suffers bodily harm as a consequence of the drinking. *See, e.g.,* WIS. STAT. § 125.075 (2004). However, some states, such as Wisconsin and Texas, allow drinking in the presence of a minor's own parent. MNOOKIN & WEISBERG, *supra* note 29, at 664.

14. *See, e.g.,* WIS. STAT. § 125.035 (2004); Congini v. Portersville Valve Co., 470 A.2d 515 (Pa. 1983) (holding that guardian had a cause of action against the minor ward's employer where the employer served alcohol at a party, minor became drunk, drove away from the party with the knowledge of employer's agent, and the minor was subsequently injured in an automobile accident.). *But see* Charles v. Seigfried, 651 N.E.2d 154, 165 (Ill.1995) (holding that there is no common law right of action against social hosts who serve alcohol to minors).

15. *See, e.g.,* MNOOKIN & WEISBERG, *supra* note 29, at 663–64; WIS. STAT. § 125.07.

16. *See* JAMES H. HEDLUND & ANNE T. MCCARTT, DRUNK DRIVING: SEEKING ADDITIONAL SOLUTIONS 8 (2002). . . .

17. Michael Stroh, *Younger Drinkers Risk Damaging Brain Cells*, BALTIMORE SUN, Dec. 10, 2002, at 1A.

18. Joseph A. Califano, Jr., Editorial, *Don't Make Teen Drinking Easier*, WASH. POST, May 11, 2003, at B7.

19. Stroh, *supra* note 51. The hippocampus is a part of the brain involved in memory and learning.

20. *Id.*

21. *Id.*

22. *Id.*; Kathleen Fackelmann, *Teen Drinking, Thinking Don't Mix; Alcohol Appears to Damage Young Brains, Early Research Finds*, USA TODAY, Oct. 18, 2000, at 1D (citing Aaron M. White et al., *Binge Pattern Ethanol Exposure in Adolescent and Adult Rats: Differential Impact on Subsequent Responsiveness to Ethanol*, 24 ALCOHOLISM: CLINICAL & EXPERIMENTAL RES. 1251 (2000)).

23. Sally Squires, *Early Drinking Said to Increase Alcoholism Risk*, WASH. POST, Jan. 20, 1998, at Z7 (These findings "are drawn from the National Longitudinal Alcohol Epidemiologic Survey, a national sample that

included face-to-face interviews with nearly 28,000 current and former drinkers aged 18 years and older.").

24. *Id.* However, there were some gender and racial variations in these risk statistics: "Early drinking is especially risky for boys. Those who began drinking by age 13 had a 50 percent lifetime risk of alcoholism. For girls, the risk was 43 percent for those who began drinking at age 13. Among blacks, those who were drinking alcohol at age 13 had a 44 percent lifetime risk of alcoholism, while nonblack children the same age had a 48 percent lifetime risk." Id.

25. *Id.*

26. Alexander Wagenaar, Letter to the Editor, *Teenage Drinking: Rites and Wrongs*, WASH. POST, May 9, 2003, at A34.

27. Kevin Cullen & Karen Avenoso, *Deaths Show Backsliding on Alcohol; Teenage Drinking May Undo Progress*, BOSTON GLOBE, Aug. 6, 1996, at B1.

28. *See* HEDLUND & MCCARTT, *supra* note 50, at 7–9 (citing several examples of improved public awareness and enforcement of drunk driving laws throughout the 1980s and 1990s, including mandatory driver's license suspension, mandatory jail time, administrative license revocation, widely used breath test equipment, training in field sobriety testing, sobriety checkpoints, special drunk driving saturation patrols, zero tolerance for youth, and lowering of BAC limits to 0.08 by many states). See also Glen Martin, *Holiday Sees Rise in DUI Arrests; 3,000 Officers Join Effort to Prevent Highway Deaths*, S.F. CHRON., May 31, 2005, at B1 (California Highway Patrol Officer Mike Wright said, "Each year we've been able to throw more and more resources at the problem, so we're getting more and more arrests. . . . Bigger is better. We have more people looking for drunks, so we're catching more drunks.").

29. Cullen & Avenoso, *supra* note 61.

30. Califano, Jr., *supra* note 52.

31. Cullen & Avenoso, *supra* note 61.

32. Nat'l Council on Alcoholism and Drug Dependence, FYI: Alcohol & Crime. . . .

33. Nat'l Inst. on Alcohol Abuse and Alcoholism, *Youth Drinking: Risk Factors and Consequences*, ALCOHOL ALERT NO. 37, July 1997. . . .

34. I am using the terms "college age" and "young adult" to refer to persons between the ages of 18 and 21. Of course, some kids are only 17 when they enter college, many young people in that age group do not attend college, and many people attending colleges and universities are over age 21. However, many studies and discussions of underage drinking concern college students and refer to drinking patterns among persons of "college age," perhaps because there is a significant drinking culture on many college campuses.

35. NAT'L RES. COUNCIL INST. OF MED., *supra* note 1, at 35.

36. *See id.* at 36 (now called the National Survey on Drug Use and Health).

37. *Id.* at 38.

38. *Id.* at 39 (This was true even among the 7% of 12–14–year-olds who reported drinking at all. "With increasing age, more youth drink and more drinkers are heavy drinkers.").

39. Jane Gross, *Teenagers' Binge Leads Scarsdale to Painful Self-Reflection,* N.Y. TIMES, Oct. 8, 2002, at B1.

40. *Id.*

41. *Id.*

42. *Id.*

43. *Id.*

44. *Id.*

45. *Id.*

46. *Scarsdale School Suspends 28 Students for Drunkenness,* N.Y. TIMES, Sept. 27, 2002, at B6.

47. NAT'L RES. COUNCIL INST. OF MED., *supra* note 1, at 82.

48. *Id.*

49. *Id.*

50. Elizabeth Nesoff, *A Prim Suburb Rallies to Curb Teen Drinking,* CHRISTIAN SCI. MONITOR, July 22, 2003, at 2.

51. NAT'L RES. COUNCIL INST. OF MED., *supra* note 1, at 82.

52. Corey Kilgannon, *Drinking Young,* N.Y. TIMES, Oct. 27, 2002, at WE1.

53. Nesoff, *supra* note 84.

54. Kilgannon, *supra* note 86.

55. *Id.*

56. 321 U.S. 158 (1944).

57. *Prince v. Massachusetts* was an appeal from convictions for violation of Massachusetts' child labor laws by Sarah Prince, who had allowed her 9-year-old niece to offer Jehovah's Witness literature for sale one evening, shortly before 9 pm. Mrs. Prince argued that her right to religious freedom coupled with her right to raise her children as she saw fit made the enforcement of the statute unconstitutional. However, the U.S. Supreme Court upheld the statute and the convictions, stating that the State's power to protect children from the dangers of street preaching was not foreclosed by the presence of parents, who could reduce, but not eliminate, the possible dangers. The Court famously proclaimed: "Parents may be free to become martyrs themselves. But it does not follow they are free, in identical circumstances, to make martyrs of their children before they have reached the age of full and legal discretion when they can make that choice for themselves." *Id.* at 170.

58. Several states allow parents to supply alcoholic beverages to their own children. *See* MNOOKIN & WEISBERG, *supra* note 29, at 664; WIS. STAT. § 125.07 (2004).

59. *See* NAT'L RES. COUNCIL INST. OF MED., *supra* note 1, at 64–65; Stroh, *supra* note 51; Fackelmann, *supra* note 56.

60. *See* NAT'L RES. COUNCIL INST. OF MED., *supra* note 1, at 82; Kilgannon, *supra* note 86.

61. Karina Bland, *Crackdown on Teen Keggers; Don't Buy Liquor, Parents Warned*, ARIZ. REPUBLIC, May 26, 2004, at A1.

62. In another context, I have noted that advocates of such an extreme form of parental supervision are few. *See* Judith G. McMullen, *"You Can't Make Me!": How Expectations of Parental Control over Adolescents Influence the Law*, 35 LOY. U. CHI. L.J. 603 (2003) [hereinafter McMullen, *"You Can't Make Me!"*]. In his 1995 book, *Parent in Control*, author Gregory Bodenhamer advises close monitoring of difficult children and teens, including following them, accompanying them on every outing, and physically forcing or restraining actions. GREGORY BODENHAMER, PARENT IN CONTROL 102–07 (1995). I could find no other authors who advocate such an extreme hands-on approach, although most parenting experts advocate discipline, persuasion, and communication.

63. *See* MNOOKIN & WEISBERG, *supra* note 29, at 144–46 (quoting WILLIAM BLACKSTONE, 2 COMMENTARIES *446, *446–51).

64. *See* MICHAEL GROSSBERG, GOVERNING THE HEARTH: LAW AND THE FAMILY IN NINETEENTH-CENTURY AMERICA 234–59 (1985) (discussing the historical evolution of parental fitness as the basis of custody).

65. Troxel v. Granville, 530 U.S. 57, 65–66 (2000).

66. *See* Ginsberg v. New York, 390 U.S. 629, 639 (1968) (stating that the "legislature could properly conclude that parents and others, teachers for example, who have this primary responsibility for children's well-being are entitled to the support of laws designed to aid discharge of that responsibility"). *Ginsberg* upheld a New York statute that restricted access of minors to sexually suggestive publications, in this case "girlie magazines." *Id.* at 631–33.

67. McMullen, *"You Can't Make Me!"*, supra note 96, at 622–25.

68. *See Ginsberg*, 390 U.S. at 639 (The Court balanced parental prerogatives in allowing children access to pornographic literature with the State's interest in limiting such access. The Court concluded that the State had an interest in restricting minor's access to sexually suggestive publications, but noted that the New York statute, which forbade the *sale* of such literature to persons under the age of 17, did not preclude a parent from allowing his own child to view such literature purchased by the parent.). *See also* Wisconsin v. Yoder, 406 U.S. 205, 214, 234 (1972) (The Court balanced the social interest in an educated citizenry with the right of parents to bring up children according to the parents' own religious beliefs. Here, the Court found that the state interest did not justify enforcing compulsory education rules requiring formal education until 16 against Amish parents whose religious convictions required them to remove their children from school after the eighth grade.).

69. *See* NAT'L RES. COUNCIL INST. OF MED., *supra* note 1, at 82 (stating that "both agesegregation and lack of adult supervision have been related to . . . greater alcohol consumption").

70. *Id.* at 204 (In the Higher Education Amendments of 1998, "Section 952 clarified that institutions of higher education are allowed (but not required) to notify parents if a student under the age of 21 at the time of notification commits a disciplinary violation involving alcohol or a controlled substance.").

71. *Id.* at 45 (The 2000 National Household Survey of Drug Abuse (NHSDA) reported that "41 percent of full-time college students aged 18 to 22 engaged in heavy drinking, compared with 36 percent of young adults who were attending college part time or not at all.").

72. *Providing Substance Abuse Prevention and Treatment Services to Adolescents: Hearing Before the Subcomm. on Substance Abuse and Mental Health Services of the Comm. on Health Education, Labor, and Pensions*, 108th Cong. 19 (2004) (prepared statement of Sandra A. Brown, Professor of Psychology and Psychiatry, Univ. of Cal.-San Diego).

73. WECHSLER & WUETHRICH, *supra* note 26, at 35.

74. *Id.* at 38 (quoting Mark Nason, prevention consultant with Prevention Research Institute, "a nonprofit organization that develops curricula to reduce the risk of alcohol and drug problems").

75. *Id.* at 30.

76. *Id.* at 30–31.

77. *Id.* at 31–32.

78. "Small" crimes, such as purse-snatching or low-level speeding while driving are examples of laws that often go unpunished because of the difficulty of apprehending every suspect. However, serious crimes sometimes go unpunished as well. The infamous and unsolved case of Jack the Ripper is but one example. L. PERRY CURTIS, JR., JACK THE RIPPER & THE LONDON PRESS 1 (2001).

79. Elizabeth A. Heaney, *Pennsylvania's Doctrine of Necessities: An Anachronism Demanding Abolishment*, 101 DICK. L. REV. 233, 259 (1996) (quoting Note, *The Unnecessary Doctrine of Necessaries*, 82 MICH. L. REV. 1767, 1798 (1984)).

80. Lawrence M. Friedman, *Two Faces of Law*, 1984 WIS. L. REV. 13, 14 (1984).

81. *See* Rutledge, *supra* note 158 (citing comments of Susan Crowley, director of PACE (Policy, Alternatives, Community and Education), a "10-year, $1.2 million program aimed at curtailing underage drinking" funded by the Robert Wood Johnson Foundation).

82. Id.

83. *See supra* Part III.C.

84. *See id.*

85. *See id.*

86. CTR. FOR SCI. IN THE PUBLIC INTEREST, TAKE A KID TO A BEER: HOW THE NCAA RECRUITS KIDS FOR THE BEER MARKET 10 (2005) . . . Alan W. Stacy et al., *Exposure to Televised Alcohol Ads and Subsequent Adolescent Alcohol Use*, 28 AM. J. OF HEALTH BEHAV. 498, 507–08 (2004); Susan E. Martin et al., *Alcohol Advertising and Youth*, 26 ALCOHOLISM: CLINICAL & EXPERIMENTAL RES. 900, 905 (2002).

87. Melanie Warner, *A Liquor Maker Keeps a Close Watch on Its Ads*, N.Y. TIMES, July 27, 2005, at C10.

88. *Id.*

89. CTR. FOR SCI. IN THE PUBLIC INTEREST, *supra* note 198, at 1.

90. *See generally id.* (The title of the report is a play on the NCAA's campaign to "Take a Kid to a Game.").

91. *NCAA Board OKs 12th Game; Decision Could Revive WVU-Herd Series,* CHARLESTON GAZETTE, Apr. 29, 2005, at P1B.

92. Jeff Miller, *NCAA Extends Brand's Deal; Board Also Approves Start of Academic Performance Guidelines,* DALLAS MORNING NEWS, Aug. 6, 2005, at 11C.

93. "Of course, many laws also produce side-effects and may do more harm than good. Policy choices should take these costs into account." Friedman, *supra* note 192, at 14.

94. *See* John Tierney, *Debunking the Drug War,* N.Y. TIMES, Aug. 9, 2005, at A19.

95. *Id.* (arguing that media exaggeration and law enforcement over-reaction to amphetamine use makes the problem worse, not better).

96. Rutledge, *supra* note 158 (quoting Richard Keeling, physician and former director of health services at the University of Wisconsin-Madison).

97. *Id.*

98. *Id.*

99. *Id.*

100. Keith Barry, *Survey Offers Insight Into Freshman Substance Use,* TUFTS DAILY, Mar. 11, 2005. . . .

101. *Id.*

102. *Id.* (The administrators were commenting in light of an online questionnaire sent to freshmen. 600 students, or 47.1% of the Class of 2008, responded to the October, 2004 survey.)

103. MNOOKIN & WEISBERG, *supra* note 29, at 649.

POSTSCRIPT

Should the United States Drinking Age Remain at 21?

In view of the fact that the majority of youths consume alcohol, is it a worthwhile endeavor to try to teach young people how to drink responsibly? Are young people capable of drinking responsibly? Can young people learn to moderate their behavior, especially behaviors that apply to alcohol consumption? Will lowering the drinking age produce positive results? In some areas, young people have shown that they are capable of being responsible. Despite the fact that many young people get into accidents when operating motor vehicles, most do not have accidents. Many parents trust their children with babysitters. Putting the care of our children into the hands of young people shows much trust. Many young people hold jobs and are very responsible in that regard. Young people are allowed to own firearms and most understand the importance of handling firearms responsibly.

In many ways young people are treated as adults. For example, one can join the military before age 21. Many young people are sent to war where they are placed in jeopardy. Eighteen-year-olds are allowed, and encouraged, to vote. One can marry and bear children long before age 21. If one can be legally allowed to go to war, get married, and produce children, one could ask the question whether it is hypocritical to prohibit those under age 21 from drinking alcohol.

Of course, there is a major difference between an 18- 19- or 20-year-old and one who is age 14 or 15 drinking alcohol. An important question is if the drinking age is lowered to age 18, what effect would that have on teenagers aged 15, 16, and 17? Would there be an increase in this age group consuming alcohol? Would 18-year-olds provide alcohol to younger teens? If older teens are given the message that they can drink, younger teens may interpret that it is more permissible for them to drink. It has been shown that the younger the person is when drinking is initiated, the greater the likelihood that dependency may develop. Besides the obvious physical problems associated with heavy alcohol abuse, such as those of the liver and endocrine system, young people who drink also have behavioral problems like being disruptive, aggressive, and rebellious. Anxiety and depression are associated with youth drinking also. According to statistics from the federal government, there are 1.4 million youth who meet the criteria for alcohol abuse or dependency.

In the YES selection, Carla Main recommends that there should be stricter enforcement of laws to prevent youth drinking. It is suggested that there should be zero-tolerance for underage drinking and for those individuals and establishments that sell alcohol. Among those under age 21, several thousand die annually from motor vehicle crashes, homicide, and suicide. These statistics substantiate the need for preventing underage drinking. In the NO selection, Judith McMullen points out the inconsistency in a policy that forbids alcohol consumption before age 21. Young people between ages 18 and 21 have discretion when it comes to health care decisions, educational decisions, and smoking.

The federal government's position on underage drinking is noted in *The Surgeon General's Call to Action to Prevent and Reduce Underage Drinking* by Kenneth Moritsugu (2007). Articles that address some of the problems and issues of underage drinking include "For MADD, the Legal Drinking Age Is Not Up for Debate," by Eric Hoover, *Chronicle of Higher Education* (November 11, 2008); "Taking on 21," by Paula Wasley, *Chronicle of Higher Education* (April 4, 2007); and "Binge Drinking and Associated Health Risk Behaviors Among High School Students" by Jacqueline Miller and others, *Pediatrics* (January 2007).

ISSUE 4

Should Salvia Be Banned?

YES: Pearl P. Nyi, Emily P. Lai, Diana Y. Lee, Shannon A. Biglete, Gilsky I. Torrecer, and Ilene B. Anderson, from "Influence of Age on *Salvia divinorum* Use: Results of an Internet Survey," *Journal of Psychoactive Drugs* (September 2010)

NO: Jacob Sullum, from "The Salvia Ban Wagon," *Reason* (December 2009)

ISSUE SUMMARY

YES: Pharmacists Pearl Nyi and others maintain that *Salvia divinorum* is a potentially abusive drug that is banned in more than a dozen states. Often described as the next "marijuana," salvia is widely promoted on the Internet despite the fact that its adverse effects have not been thoroughly studied. In their research, Nyi and others found that salvia produces hallucinogenic effects.

NO: Author Jacob Sullum contends that salvia has been unfairly demonized although it has been used for centuries for healing and spiritual reasons. One factor contributing to salvia's appeal, states Sullum, is the negative press attributed to it. Historically, many drugs become more popular when they are highly criticized in the press. Salvia can result in adverse effects but that the drug has been unfairly demonized. The stories of the horrific effects of salvia have been difficult to substantiate, says Sullum.

*S*alvia *divinorum*, a plant related to sage and mint, was originally grown by Native American religious leaders for spiritual purposes. It is imported from Mexico and Central and South America. Salvia is also referred to by many names such as diviners' sage, Magic Mint, Maria Pastora, etc. It is believed to have hallucinogenic properties although in one study salvia users compared its effects more to marijuana than to potent hallucinogens. Although it has been available for a relatively short period of time, its popularity is growing. According to data published by the federal government, nearly 2 million Americans aged 12 and older have tried salvia. Because it has a small but significant following, the question arises as to whether it should be banned or not.

One could argue that enforcing laws that would prohibit salvia use increases the likelihood that adverse effects will occur because there would be no oversight on the purity of the drugs. This raises the question whether it would be better to educate individuals about the potential harm of salvia or simply be more vigilant in preventing its use. Another problem associated with banning salvia is that individuals would have to purchase it from unregulated sources. This may result in dealing with disreputable sellers. By keeping salvia legal, there is better regulation of the drug. Opponents to the ban on salvia argue that the drug may have medicinal value but that further study is needed. They also point out that salvia is not addicting.

A possible unintended consequence of banning salvia is that a ban may lead to more interest and, therefore, greater use of the drug. There have been historical examples in which banning a drug increased its popularity. When glue sniffing first occurred, the media and government officials issued numerous reports of the dangers of glue sniffing. Consequently, thousands of young people sniffed glue who had not been familiar with the practice.

Although the federal government has not legally restricted salvia, more than a dozen states have banned it. Some states list salvia as a Schedule A drug. This means that the drug has a high potential for abuse, is not recognized as safe, and has no proven medicinal value. The ban on salvia extends to other countries such as Australia, Denmark, and Finland. Reasons for the ban on salvia can be based on several reasons. Because the substance has not been extensively studied, the ban can be viewed as a public safety measure. Should people be using a drug if the long-term effects are unclear? Moreover, there are instances in which individuals have had adverse reactions to salvia. There is also the question whether people using salvia represent a danger to others. Will salvia use lead to reckless behavior?

Salvia is relatively inexpensive and it is not difficult to obtain seeds for growing it. Most users do not grow salvia but purchase it from sites on the Internet or from tobacco shops or local head shops. According to the United States Department of Justice, salvia produces visual and auditory hallucinations. Other effects of salvia include altered perceptions of lights, colors, and shapes, and loss of physical coordination, dizziness, slurred speech, chills, nausea, decreased heart rate, uncontrolled laughter, and a sense of floating. When smoked, the effects occur within 30 seconds and last for approximately one and a half hour. When chewed, the effects take about 5 to 10 minutes before appearing.

The YES and NO selections debate whether or not salvia should be banned. Some opponents fear that the effects of salvia represent a serious threat to the physical and emotional well-being of young people and that the dangers may escalate in the absence of a ban. Pearl Nyi and her associates discuss the availability of salvia and the ease to obtain it. Jacob Sullum notes that the hype over salvia is overblown. He cautions that the warnings associated with drugs are unwarranted and that the dangers of salvia have not been conclusively proven.

YES

Pearl P. Nyi et al.

Influence of Age on *Salvia divinorum* Use: Results of an Internet Survey

Salvia divinorum is a perennial herb in the mint family native to Mexico and Central and South America (NIDA 2007; Vortherms & Roth 2006). It was traditionally used for its hallucinogenic properties by the Mazatec Indians of Oaxaca, Mexico for shamanistic purposes (NIDA 2007; Vortherms & Roth 2006). In addition, *Salvia divinorum* has also been used for various healing purposes including pain relief, diarrhea, and for the treatment of neurologic diseases (Weissner 2009). In the modern world, *Salvia divinorum* has been increasingly recognized for its abuse potential by sources that range from the general media to federal authorities. An Internet search using the term "salvia" results in hundreds of thousands of website resources providing information on its history, instructions regarding recreational use, as well as how to purchase *Salvia divinorum*. According to the Substance Abuse and Mental Health Services Administration's (SAMHSA) report on hallucinogen use, about 1.8 million people aged 15 years or greater used *Salvia divinorum* at least once in their lifetime (SAMHSA 2008). It is important to note that hundreds of salvia species exist that do not contain any psychoactive substances. Although the term "salvia" is commonly used as a colloquial term for *Salvia divinorum*, the hundreds of nonpsychoactive salvia species should not be confused with *Salvia divinorum*, the specific species that is psychoactive and the only species that is addressed in this study. To minimize repetition, the term "salvia" will refer specifically to the *Salvia divinorum* species throughout this article.

Interestingly, *Salvia divinorum* is structurally different from the prototypical psychoactive substances, LSD and mescaline, which act at serotonin receptors (Roth 2002). Salvia's active component is thought to be salvinorin A, a neoclerodane diterpene (Roth 2002). Salvinorin A has been shown to be a potent kappa opioid receptor agonist (Vortherms & Roth 2006; Roth 2002). Binding at kappa opioid receptors is known to result in neurologic effects including sedation, analgesia, and perceptual disturbances (Hooker et al. 2008; Roth 2002). Its agonistic activity at kappa opioid receptors likely plays a role in the hallucinogenic effects of salvia (Roth 2002).

Due to its potential for abuse and possible addiction, 13 states have instituted legal restrictions on salvia use as of November 2008 (Office of Diversion Control 2008). Delaware, Florida, Illinois, Kansas, Mississippi, Missouri, North

Dakota, Oklahoma, and Virginia have all named *Salvia divinorum* or salvinorin A as a Schedule I substance, indicating that it has potential for abuse, has no proven medicinal use, and is not recognized as safe (Office of Diversion Control 2008; US DEA 2002). Worldwide, Finland, Denmark, and Australia have prohibited the use, cultivation, and selling of *Salvia divinorum* (Office of Diversion Control 2008). In California, however, salvia remains legal. In addition, it is easily cultivated and its purchase remains readily accessible in all states and around the world via Internet websites. We identified 23 "social networking Internet websites" (e.g. Facebook, LiveJournal) through which to identify individuals who were likely to be knowledgeable regarding salvia use. This information was based on testimonials, videos, or membership in salvia use groups. Over 1,211 self-identified salvia users were identified in this search. These numbers suggest that our research would likely affect a broad spectrum of people across the United States.

While numerous Internet websites cite testimonials describing the effects of salvia when used for recreational purposes, it is vastly understudied and little information regarding toxicity or adverse effects is available. A 2004 survey of salvia users found that about 25% experienced positive antidepressant-like effects for approximately 24 hours following use (Baggott & Erowid 2004). However, about 5% of users experienced lingering negative effects, including anxiety, dizziness, and lack of coordination (Baggott & Erowid 2004). Although salvia appears to have little potential for physical dependence, there still remains a great possibility for negative effects related to use.

As salvia is currently legal in most U.S. states and non-U.S. countries, and sold without age restrictions, we dichotomized our subjects by age at first use (21 years of age or less vs. 22 or more years of age) to explore potential differences in the source, frequency, method, and reasons related to salvia use. Through this investigation, we hoped to identify associated motivations, circumstances, demographics, and adverse effects. Also, it was hoped that this study would identify key findings that could be useful to health care practitioners as well as policy makers.

Methods

Overview

In order to determine the use and/or abuse patterns among *Salvia divinorum* users, we developed an anonymous, Internet-based, self-completed, structured survey instrument to collect data among knowledgeable salvia users and ex-users. An innovative recruiting method was utilized in which self-identified users were systematically and specifically targeted within social networking websites (e.g. Facebook, LiveJournal). Notices were posted to selected groups indicating interest or experience in the recreational use of salvia and key data points were then collected. This innovative recruitment method allowed the study to successfully target the specific population that we wished to survey. This study was approved by the Committee on Human Research at the University of California, San Francisco.

Survey Development and Content

We created a 33 question survey instrument designed to address the following characteristics surrounding recreational use of salvia: age at first use, frequency and method of use, health literacy concerning *Salvia divinorum*, reasons or beliefs for use, concurrent use with other legal and/or illegal substances, sources used in gaining information about and physically obtaining salvia, and experiences associated with salvia use including behavioral changes and adverse effects. Participant demographics collected included education, socioeconomic status, and ethnicity. Pilot testing revealed an average completion time of seven minutes.

Identification of Target Populations

Internet websites were utilized as the sole vehicle for subject recruitment in this study. In order to ensure a robust sample size for the purposes of this study, we chose to post our survey on networking sites that would yield a high frequency of responses. Recruitment consisted of inclusion from social networking websites likely to be visited by individuals knowledgeable of salvia or illicit drug use. We used the *Wikipedia* List of Social Networking Websites (Wikipedia 2008) posted on September 14, 2008 to formulate an initial list of sites (n = 77) which we systematically evaluated to identify those likely to be visited by salvia-knowledgeable individuals (n = 23). Networking sites met inclusion criteria if the search term "salvia" or "*Salvia divinorum*" yielded groups with any interest in or discussion of salvia. Reasons for exclusion of certain websites on the *Wikipedia* list are detailed in Table 1.

Table 1

Recruitment by Internet Website: Inclusion and Exclusion Criteria

Internet Websites by Inclusion & Exclusion Criteria	N	%
Total Potential Internet Websites*	77	100%
Excluded Websites		
Foreign/Non-English Predominant Language	28	
Unable to Search Website for Search Term	11	
Invitation Only	6	
Teens Only	1	
Unable to Contact Individual/No Group	1	
Closed/Scheduled to Close	4	
Mobile Community	3	
Total Excluded Websites	54	70%
Total Included Websites used in Subject Recruitment	23	30%

*Websites were comprised of Wikipedia's list of social networking sites (Wikipedia 2008)

Survey Subject Recruitment

Participants were recruited from selected websites as described above. The survey was advertised by posting a study recruitment announcement, including the study's direct URL hyperlink, on all message boards or forums for groups (n = 69) meeting the inclusion criteria. In some cases, the advertisement was sent via group email. For certain websites, posting the survey required the investigators to join the respective group of interest as a member prior to advertisement. Of note, subjects had an opportunity to submit questions or concerns regarding the contents of the survey via voicemail (a phone number was also provided). Investigators fielded all questions on a daily basis.

It is also noteworthy to mention that this innovative recruitment method was time-consuming, faced various restrictions, and presented several limitations. Certain websites allowed only a limited number of postings per day (e.g., Yelp) prior to being "locked out," "warned," or "banned" to prevent users from "spamming." To circumvent further losses from our sample size, survey postings were on occasion reduced to two or three times weekly. In addition, other websites held content restrictions for posting to the discussion boards. Therefore, although posting to communities or groups that required administrator review or approval was systematically attempted, publication of the recruitment announcement was left to the discretion of the administrator (e.g. LiveJournal). Those groups that listed salvia as an interest but had not been updated in over six months were screened for content to determine if recreational use was discussed. Only communities with relevant salvia discussions were then targeted.

Survey Administration

This self-administered study was conducted solely via the Internet over a 10-week period (November 20, 2008 through January 31, 2009). The survey was posted using a unique URL (https://ihrc.ucsf.edu/Collector/Survey.ashx?Name=Salvia_FINAL) created by DatStat, the UCSF-affiliated survey software company under the auspices of the UCSF Internet World Health Research Center (IWHRC). Collection and processing of data met the Committee on Human Research standards and was Health Insurance Portability and Accountability Act (HIPAA)-compliant. No personal identifying information, electronic or otherwise, was collected. All data was stored in a secure, password-protected customized database accessible only by study investigators. There was no financial or other incentive provided for participation.

Subject inclusion criteria included: (1) self-stated age was 18 years or older; (2) self-reported current or past salvia use; (3) access to the Internet; (4) ability to read and understand English; and (5) voluntarily consented and initiated survey participation. Only subjects meeting study eligibility requirements were allowed access to the study information screen containing the actual survey content. Participants could refuse to answer any question or end the survey at any time.

Summary Data for Survey Internet Site Inquiries

A total of 349 individuals visited the survey site. Of these individuals, 126 (36.1%) declined to answer at least 40% of the survey questions and were excluded from this analysis. Importantly, 87% (109 of the 126 excluded) answered less than 15% of the survey questions. An additional four individuals (1.2%) did not provide a response for age at time of first salvia use and were therefore excluded. Ultimately, 219 completed surveys were included in this statistical analysis. . . .

Results

Subject Location and Demographics

We analyzed data from 219 survey respondents who reported both lifetime use of salvia as well as age at first-time salvia use. [A]ll survey respondents were at least 18 years of age during the time of survey participation. Survey participants had a median age of 23 years at time of survey response, with a range of 18 to 62 years. Respondents first used salvia predominantly as young adults (61%), defined as less than or equal to 21 years. The young adult sample included 133 survey participants, while the adult sample included 86. Overall, most participants identified with the male gender (61%); however, when divided by age, there is a shift in female presence. There was a greater proportion of female users in the young adult group as compared to the adult group (44% vs. 28%). The young adult group was almost three times as likely to identify with United States (U.S.) residence compared to non-U.S. residence (71% vs 29%). Countries of origin for non-U.S. survey respondents, in order of frequency, included: Russia (41), Canada (17), United Kingdom (9), Poland (4), Ukraine (4), Czech Republic (2), and Netherlands (2), with the remaining countries represented by just one respondent per country (Australia, Moldova, France, Germany, New Zealand, and Spain). Demographic characteristics of the young adult compared to the adult groups were similar in regard to race/ethnicity and sexual orientation. Although data regarding education level, marital status, and employment status were collected, these demographics are likely to be strongly linked to age. Since we expected a large difference between the samples for this reason, we did not analyze this data.

Characteristics of Salvia Use and Acquisition

We compared the characteristics of salvia use and acquisition between young adult and adult survey participants (Table 2). There was no significant difference regarding reason for salvia use between the two groups in terms of frequency of salvia use, source of initial salvia knowledge, or source of salvia purchase. Any reduction or cessation of salvia use in the last 12 months, or interest in trying other hallucinogens, also did not differ between the two groups. Both groups commonly reported purchasing salvia from a retail store and the Internet. Although the younger adult group more commonly purchased salvia from a retail store, the difference in source of salvia purchase (retail store vs. Internet) between the two groups was marginal: retail store.

Table 2

Characteristics of Salvia Use and Acquisition Among 219 Survey Respondents

	Age ≤ 21 Young Adult N = 133	Age ≥ 22 Adult n = 86	P Value
Frequency of Use			0.41
1-2 Times	31 (23%)	24 (28%)	
3-5 Times	58 (44%)	27 (31%)	
6-20 Times	28 (21%)	22 (26%)	
More than 20 Times	12 (9%)	8 (9%)	
Source of Initial Salvia Knowledge			0.14
Friend	78 (59%)	37 (43%)	
Family	45 (34%)	35 (41%)	
Other	10 (7%)	10 (12%)	
Purchase at a Retail Store			0.04
Yes	90 (68%)	41 (48%)	
No	42 (32%)	35 (41%)	
Purchase on the Internet			0.07
Yes	79 (59%)	56 (65%)	
No	54 (41%)	22 (26%)	
Reduction or Cessation of Salvia Use in the Last 12 Months			0.10
Yes	75 (56%)	39 (45%)	
No	56 (42%)	46 (53%)	
Interest in Trying Other Hallucinogens			0.71
Yes	98 (74%)	57 (66%)	
No	32 (24%)	21 (24%)	

Frequency of Salvia use was not reported by four young adult and five adult respondents. Source of recreational potential was not reported by four adult respondents. Purchase at a retail store not reported by one young adult and 10 adult respondents. Purchase on the Internet not reported by eight adult respondents. Reduction or cessation of Salvia use in the last 12 months was not reported by two young adult and one adult respondent. Interest in trying other hallucinogens was not reported by three young adult and eight adult respondents.

Reasons for Salvia Use

Table 3 summarizes the reasons for salvia use. These include: to enhance creativity, for fun, for spiritual effects, and to relieve boredom. There was no difference between the two groups in regards to using salvia to enhance creativity. However, participants who first used salvia as young adults favored using salvia for fun or to relieve boredom while participants who first used salvia as adults favored use for spiritual effects.

Table 3

Reasons for Salvia Use Among 219 Survey Respondents

	Age ≤ 21 Young Adult N = 133	Age ≥ 22 Adult n = 86
Enhance Creativity		
Yes	80 (61%)	48 (63%)
No	52 (39%)	28 (37%)
Fun		
Yes	83 (65%)	36 (49%)
No	44 (35%)	37 (51%)
Spiritual Effects		
Yes	108 (82%)	71 (92%)
No	24 (18%)	6 (8%)
Relieve Boredom		
Yes	52 (40%)	18 (25%)
No	77 (60%)	55 (75%)

*OR in favor of adults; young adults less likely to use for spiritual reasons OR = 0.38, (0.15–0.98)
Use to enhance creativity was not reported by one young adult and 10 adult respondents. Use for fun was
not reported by six young adults and 13 adult respondents. Use for spiritual effects was not reported by
one young adult and nine adult respondents. Use to relieve boredom was not reported by four young adult
and 13 adult respondents. Note that the % listed is calculated based on the number of respondents who
answered each particular question.

Concurrent Substance Use with Salvia

Survey respondents were asked about concurrent substance use with salvia. Using salvia for the first time as an adult was associated with almost three times higher odds of concurrently using marijuana with salvia. In addition, first time use as an adult was also associated with a two-fold odds of using tobacco in conjunction with salvia. There was no difference in concurrent alcohol and salvia use between young adult and adult groups.

Effects and Other Substance Use

We collected and analyzed data from 219 survey participants who completed the survey. Since salvia is a hallucinogen, expectedly, the most common effects reported were visual effects, including hallucinations (77.6%), distorted images (66.8%), merging of objects (59.2%), and color changes (57.4%). Other common effects were consistent with the herb's strong dissociative effects including sensation of entering or perceiving other dimensions or realities (75.8%), confusion (64.6%), and loss of coordination/inability to control muscles/maintain balance (63.7%). Less common effects included depersonalization (57.4%), uncontrolled laughter (55.2%), feeling happy (55.2%), and experiencing past memories (27.4%). Physical changes experienced by users included slowed or

Table 4

Stated Reason for Reduction or Cessation of Salvia Use Among 114 Respondents

Reason for Reduction or Cessation of Salvia Use	N	%
Any Health and Safety Concerns	43	37.7
Didn't Like the High	38	33.3
Health Risks	5	4.4
Any Legal or Other Non-Health Risks	57	50.0
Lost Interest	33	28.9
Difficult to Acquire	2	1.8
Legal Risks	6	5.3
Too Expensive	9	7.9
Other	7	6.1
Declined to State a Reason	14	12.3

slurred speech (51.1%), dizziness (39.9%), and changes in body temperature (39.4%). Some undesirable side effects included fear/panic (38.6%), paranoia (23.8%), feeling sad (13.9%), nausea (9.0%), and irritability (9.0%).

In addition to concurrent substance use in the same sitting as salvia, survey respondents were also asked about general use of other substances. The most common agents reported also being used were marijuana (50.2%), tobacco (32.7%), and alcohol (30.0%). Other substances reported include psychedelics (LSD [lysergic acid diethylamide], PCP [phencyclidine], ketamine, or shrooms [psilocybin]) in 8.1% of total respondents, uppers (amphetamines, speed, cocaine, crank, crack) in 5.4%, downers (Valium™, heroin, Soma™, GHB [gamma hydroxybutyrate], Vicodin™) in 4.0%, Ecstasy (MDMA [methylene dioxymethamphetamine], E) in 4.0%, and dextromethorphan (e.g.: DXM, Triple C, Coricidin™, Robitussin DM™) in 3.1%.

Reduction or Cessation of Salvia Use

Although there was no significant difference between the young adult and adult groups, over half of all survey respondents reported reduction or cessation of salvia use in the last 12 months (114 of 219, 52%). Of these, 100 participants provided a reason for reduction or cessation (Table 4). The top reasons were: not liking the high achieved from salvia (33.3%) and simply losing interest in salvia (28.9%).

Discussion

One observation that can be made from this survey is the prevalence of young salvia users, which may demonstrate a shift in the reasons for, and characteristics of, salvia use. The National Survey on Drug Use and Health (NSDUH) estimated that 1.8 million persons aged 12 or older had used *Salvia divinorum* in their lifetime (SAMHSA 2008). We surveyed a relatively small number of salvia users to capture sociodemographic factors that could be used to identify important correlates regarding salvia use. The overall age of salvia users appears to be consistent with previous studies (SAMHSA 2008). Likewise, salvia use among young adults (18 to 21 years) was more common than among adults (22 years or older). Salvia use is more common among males than females. The NSDUH reports that among individuals 18 to 25 years old, salvia use was up to four times more common in males than in females (SAMHSA 2008). A previous study of college students also suggested males were a subpopulation more likely to use salvia (Lange et al 2008). Interestingly, our data shows a shift in the population of salvia users: among young adults 21 years of age or younger, the male to female ratio is closer to 1:1. While our definition of young adults differed from that of the NSDUH, this finding still raises an important consideration that warrants further exploration: there may be increased interest in salvia use among younger females.

Because salvia is legal in most U.S. states and non-U.S. countries and sold without age restrictions, it is not surprising that there is high accessibility through both Internet and retail purchase, and that no significant difference was seen across age at first use.

Salvia has gained widespread popularity in the media targeting young audiences including television, YouTube, and Ebay. For this reason, there is growing concern that an increasing number of individuals, especially adolescents and young adults, may turn to salvia for recreational use and abuse. Salvia has been coined "the next marijuana" by many concerned individuals, including parents, religious groups, and political activists (Mueller 2008). However, findings from the present study may contradict this claim. Most of our respondents reported only using salvia five times or less in their lifetime. In fact, about half of these participants reported a reduction in or cessation of salvia use, listing unpleasant highs and loss of interest as the top reasons for the change in use. Therefore, it is not surprising that salvia sellers report having few repeat customers because "most users don't enjoy the experience" (Wincele 2008).

Additionally, the results of this survey indicate that the reasons for salvia use differ between young adults and adults. Participants who used salvia for the first time as young adults were more likely to use it for fun or to relieve boredom. Such reasons may translate to curiosity or experimentation. On the other hand, participants who used salvia for the first time as adults were more likely to use it for spiritual effects. An explanation for the different reasons for use between the two samples may be maturity. Sagewisdom.org states those who are most attracted to salvia are mature and philosophically minded (Sagewisdom 2009). The adult group claimed to use salvia for a focused reason or spiritual effects, much like the Mazatec shamans did to facilitate visions during healing.

Based on the reported predominance of younger salvia users in this study, and their respective interest for use being for fun and to relieve boredom, a potential observation can be made. Perhaps a large component of the increased salvia use among young adults can be attributed to curiosity and experimentation rather than continued recreational use and abuse. This is further supported by reasons for cessation, as well as previously reported low numbers of repeat salvia customers as described above.

Limitations

Certain limitations are undoubtedly evident both in the methodology and design of this salvia research survey. As noted in the methodology, Internet access, age, and language were requirements for initial participation, thus limiting the overall pool of salvia users. It is unknown whether visitors to Internet-based social networking websites are representative of the larger population of recreational salvia users, or of a younger population with higher levels of education or greater financial resources. Respondents to the salvia survey were additionally limited to those who filtered in through the sources described in detail above. Namely, these limitations include membership or access to the websites selected as target recruitment venues, subsequent logging on to such websites within the time window in which the advertisement remained easily visible, and participation in the actual salvia survey during the period of active enrollment. The pool of salvia users responding to the survey could thus be subject to seasonal, vocational, or other factors unknown to the researchers.

Recruitment was also highly variable between websites, as well as the number of salvia users which can be potentially drawn from each website. While we utilized a systematic Internet-based recruiting approach, this recruitment strategy could still have introduced sampling bias. The sample size of this survey is also relatively small compared to the identified salvia users in our search.

Since this was an anonymous survey, we were unable to rule out the possibility of survey resubmission from any one individual without compromising respondent anonymity. No financial or other incentive for participation was offered to reduce any motivation for multiple responses, although this does not guarantee exclusively single submissions. Surveys with less than 60% of questions answered were also excluded in this analysis to decrease resubmission bias from incomplete entries. Despite this limitation, the anonymous survey design may have produced more reliable responses considering the sensitive subject of substance abuse. In addition, this survey relied on subject self-report and independent confirmation of responses was not possible.

The survey itself was primarily developed using a closed-ended format given the multiple-choice nature of its design. While qualitative data was allowed in responses to certain questions and outlying answers were being captured, analysis of such data is limited by consistency and power. Answers relating graded experiences (extremely likely, likely, somewhat likely, etc.) are also subjective in nature and limited by variability between respondents. Informal piloting of the survey was done, although not extensively, and likely did not provide ideal circumstances in which to pretest. However, previously validated question formats were used whenever possible in designing the survey.

Conclusion

Utilizing an innovative Internet-based targeted survey strategy, these findings capture sociodemographic factors that predict characteristics and trends of salvia use based on age at first use. A predominance of younger salvia users may demonstrate a shift toward using salvia for fun and to relieve boredom rather than for targeted spiritual reasons. However, reports on cessation trends also suggest salvia use may be more attributed to curiosity than abuse.

References

Baggott, M. & Erowid, E. 2004. A survey of salvia divinorum users. *Erowid Extracts* 6: 12-15. Available at www.erowid.org/general/newsletter/erowid_newsletter6.pdf.

Hooker, J.M.; Xu, Y.; Schiffer, W.; Shea, C.; Carter, P. & Fowler, J. S. 2008. Pharmacokinetics of the potent hallucinogen, salvinorin A in primates parallels the rapid onset and short duration of effects in humans. *Neuroimage* 41 (3): 1044–50.

Lange, J.E.; Reed, M.B.; Croff, J.M. & Clapp, J.D. 2008. College student use of *Salvia divinorum. Drug and Alcohol Dependence* 94 (1-3): 263–66.

Mueller, W. 2008. Center for Parent Youth Understanding Trend Alert: Salvia A New and Dangerous Drug. *Center for Parent Youth Understanding.* Available at https://www.cpyu.org/Page.aspx?id=308434.

National Institute on Drug Abuse (NIDA). 2007. *NIDA InfoFacts: Salvia.* Available at http://www.nida.nih.gov/Infofacts/salvia.html.

Office of Diversion Control. 2008. *Salvia Divinorum and Salvinorin A.* Available at http://www.deadiversion.usdoj.gov/drugs_concern/ salvia_d/salvia_d.htm.

Roth, B. 2002. Salvinorin A: A potent naturally occurring nonnitrogenous k opioid selective agonist. *Proceedings of the National Academy of Sciences* 99 (18): 11934–39.

Sagewisdom. 2009. *The Salvia Divinorum Research and Information Center.* Available at http://www.sagewisdom.org.

Substance Abuse and Mental Health Services Administration, Office of Applied Studies (SAMHSA). 2008. *The NSDUH Report: Use of Specific Hallucinogens: 2006.* Available at http://www.oas.samhsa. gov/2k8/hallucinogens/hallucinogens.htm.

US Drug Enforcement Administration (US DEA). 2002. *Schedules of Controlled Substances.* Available at http://www.usdoj.gov/dea/pubs/csa/812.htm.

Vortherms, T.A. & Roth, B.L. 2006. Salvinorin A: From natural product to human therapeutics. *Molecular Interventions* 6 (5): 257–65.

Weissner, W. 2009. Salvia Divinorum: Professional Monograph. Natural Standard. Available at http://www.naturalstandard.org.

Wikipedia. 2008. List of social networking websites. Available at http://en.wikipedia. org/wiki/List_of_social_networking_websites.

Wincele, T. 2008. Salvia isn't close to the new marijuana. *CBS News.* Available at http://www.cbs.com/story/2008/05/05/politics/uwire/main4073275.shtml.

 **NO**

The Salvia Ban Wagon

How Does Terrible Drug Policy Get Made?
The Mad Rush to Criminalize a Psychedelic
Herb Provides a Textbook Case

A couple of years ago, John Bulloch watched an alarming report on an Atlanta TV station about an exotic-sounding drug called Salvia divinorum. Bulloch had never heard of the plant, a psychoactive relative of sage that the Mazatec Indians of Oaxaca, Mexico, have used for centuries in healing and divination rituals. But according to the news report, salvia was becoming increasingly popular among American college students, who sometimes called it "Sally D" or "magic mint" (since salvia, like sage, is a member of the mint family).

The most horrifying fact of all: Salvia was perfectly legal. In their far-reaching crackdowns on drugs that people enjoy, state and federal legislators somehow had missed a plant that contains the most powerful naturally occurring psychedelic known to man.

Bulloch—a Republican state senator who represents the area around Ochlocknee, Georgia, a tiny town near the Florida border—was astounded. "I thought, 'Why hasn't somebody already jumped on this?'" he told the Florida Times-Union in March 2007. "I hurriedly got legislative counsel to draft the bill"—legislation making it a misdemeanor to grow, sell, or possess salvia. "Since then," the Times-Union reported, "Bulloch has been scouring the Internet to find information about salvia. None of what he has learned has dissuaded him from trying to make it illegal."

Bulloch's approach to salvia—ban first, ask questions later—epitomizes how drug policy is made in America. Although his bill has not yet passed, 15 states have banned salvia since 2005, and many others are considering similar legislation. Their precipitous action makes the U.S. Drug Enforcement Administration, which has been monitoring salvia as "a drug of concern" since 2003 but still has no definite plans to classify it as a prohibited substance, look rational and reticent by comparison.

The penalties for violating state salvia laws vary from modest fines to decades in prison. Kenneth Rau, a North Dakota bottling plant employee who has the dubious distinction of being the first American arrested for salvia possession, bought eight ounces of leaves on eBay for $32 in December 2007. He says he did not realize a state ban on the plant had taken effect the previous

From *Reason Magazine*, December 2009. Copyright © 2009 by Reason Foundation, 3415 S. Sepulveda Blvd., Suite 400, Los Angeles, CA 90034. www.reason.com

August—a plausible claim, especially since the plant matter that police discovered in his home was clearly labeled "salvia." Last spring Rau received three years of probation for simple possession. But he originally was charged as a dealer and could have received a prison sentence of up to 20 years, all for a bag of leaves that was legal in North Dakota four months before he bought it and remains legal in most of the country.

To drug policy historians, the reasons for the rush to ban salvia are familiar. Sensationalistic press coverage, in this case supplemented by salvia users' documentation of their own trips on YouTube, has attracted the attention of legislators eager to grandstand as guardians of vulnerable and impressionable "young people." Few politicians can resist the allure of a drug described as "cheaper than marijuana, stronger than LSD, as fast-acting as crack cocaine, and legally available to minors" (as The Ithaca Journal put it in 2004). The endless repetition of a few anecdotes that supposedly demonstrate salvia's dangers—most conspicuously, the story of a Delaware teenager's 2006 suicide—has found a receptive audience among politicians who automatically assume that an unfamiliar psychoactive substance must be a menace. And since these lawmakers bridle at the notion that anything good could possibly come from altering your consciousness, they see no downside to banning salvia before it becomes a problem.

The idea that salvia "could become the next marijuana" (as the Associated Press warned last year) is mostly misbegotten. The salvia experience is so unpredictable, so incompatible with social interaction, and so frequently boring or unpleasant that it's safe to assume the herb will never be as popular as pot. But the comparison rings true in several other respects: Both salvia and marijuana are psychoactive plants linked in the public mind to Mexico, both appear to be nontoxic for all practical purposes, and both have intriguing medical potential. Salvia's detractors, like marijuana's in the 1920s and '30s, claim it causes insanity and violence. In both cases prohibition occurred at the state level first. If salvia continues to follow the pattern set by marijuana, it will ultimately be banned throughout the country, despite a dearth of evidence that it poses a serious threat to individual health or to public safety.

Something About Mary

Salvia's ritual use in Mexico goes back hundreds of years, but outsiders paid little attention to it until the mid-20th century. Starting in 1938, anthropologists and naturalists visiting Oaxaca mentioned a visionary tea made from a plant variously called hierba Maria (herb of Mary), hoja de adivinación (leaf of prophecy), or ska Maria Pastora (leaves of Mary the Shepherdess). They reported that the local healers known as curanderos used the potion, traditionally linked to the Virgin Mary, to diagnose illness and locate lost objects, finding clues in what their patients/clients said under its influence.

The self-taught American mycologist and ethnobotanist R. Gordon Wasson, best known for his research on hallucinogenic mushrooms, was the first visitor to describe his own experiences with ska Maria Pastora. In a 1962 leaflet published by Harvard University's Botanical Museum, Wasson announced "a new Mexican psychotropic drug from the mint family" that he and his colleagues dubbed Salvia divinorum (diviner's sage). He said it was "a psychotropic plant that the Mazatecs consume when mushrooms are not available," a "less desirable substitute" for psilocybin-containing fungi.

In a 1961 salvia ceremony, Wasson drank a foul-tasting mixture of leaf juice and water under the guidance of a curandera. "The effect of the leaves came sooner than would have been the case with the mushrooms, was less sweeping, and lasted a shorter time," he reported. "There was not the slightest doubt about the effect, but it did not go beyond the initial effect of the mushrooms—dancing colors in elaborate, three-dimensional designs." The second time around, about a year later, Wasson was joined by his friend Albert Hofmann, the Swiss chemist who first synthesized LSD. They experienced similar effects.

Given Wasson's lack of enthusiasm for salvia, it's not surprising that the plant remained obscure for decades, with nothing like the fame or following attracted by LSD, psilocybin, or peyote. That began to change in the 1990s, thanks largely to the efforts of another amateur ethnobotanist.

Daniel Siebert first came across salvia in the late 1970s while researching medicinal plants. Later someone gave him a cutting, which he used to grow a plant that he added to his collection of interesting herbs. About a year later he accidentally broke off part of the plant and decided to try it, chewing up a wad of 26 large leaves. "It was that initial experience that really piqued my interest," he says. "I found the effects really intriguing, and it was very comfortable and easy to handle—piqued much more manageable than most other psychedelic drugs I had tried." Today Siebert, who lives in Malibu, runs the Salvia Divinorum Research and Information Center (sagewisdom.org), the most comprehensive online repository of information about the plant.

The website, which also sells the herb, includes a link to a 1994 article Siebert published in the Journal of Ethnopharmacology that helped explain why ska Maria had disappointed so many psychonauts. Siebert's research confirmed that salvinorin A, first isolated a decade before, was the plant's main psychoactive ingredient. It turned out to be highly potent, producing noticeable effects at a dose of half a milligram, compared to about 10 milligrams for psilocybin and 250 milligrams for mescaline. (Contrary to some overheated press reports about salvia, LSD, a synthetic psychedelic, is far more powerful than any of these, effective at doses as low as 50 micrograms, or five-hundredths of a milligram.) Siebert's experiments with volunteers who tried different routes of administration revealed that swallowing salvia was the worst way to absorb salvinorin A, which is "deactivated by the gastrointestinal system." Two other routes were much more successful: through the oral mucous membrane (by holding masticated leaves or leaf juice in the mouth) and through the lungs (by inhaling the vapor).

This information, combined with the realization that salvinorin A is highly stable and remains in salvia leaves even when they're dried, set the stage for the plant's commercialization. Soon it was available from head shops and online vendors in the form of liquid extracts and smokable dried leaves, often fortified with extract. Holding the liquid in the mouth more closely resembles the traditional method of consuming salvia, with the effects felt in five to 10 minutes and lasting an hour or two. But the alcohol-based extract tastes terrible and produces relatively subtle effects. (See "Salvia and Salivation," page 42.) The smoked form produces faster, more intense, and shorter effects, appearing within 30 seconds and subsiding after five to 10 minutes. It sells much better.

According to the latest data from the federal government's National Survey on Drug Use and Health, 1 million Americans used salvia in 2007, up from 750,000 in 2006, the first year the survey asked about the drug. Those numbers make salvia currently more popular than LSD, used by 620,000 Americans in 2007. (In terms of lifetime use, however, acid droppers outnumber salvia smokers by nearly 10 to 1.) Salvia, like other psychedelics, is most popular among 18-to-25-year-olds, 2 percent of whom report past-year use.

As is often the case with drug fads, interest in salvia has been driven partly by the same press coverage that has encouraged legislators to crack down on it. Salvia distributors say they see spikes in sales after anti-salvia articles appear. "Every time there's a news story on it," says John Boyd, CEO of Arena Ethnobotanicals in Encinitas, California, "it brings it to people's attention."

Still, salvia is much less popular than marijuana, used by 25 million Americans in 2007. It is also less likely to be used more than once. Tiffin University psychologist Jonathan Appel, who co-authored a 2007 article on the rising popularity of salvia in the International Journal of Mental Health and Addiction, says, "We're talking about a small percentage of people who are using it and an even smaller percentage of people who go back and use it again."

'The Worst Substance of This Earth'

Siebert says the prevalence of smoking, which produces quick, intense effects, helps explain why many users report overwhelming experiences they are not eager to repeat. High doses are another factor, since vendors compete based on the potency of their fortified leaves, bragging that they are anywhere from five to 100 times as powerful as the untreated plant. "When you smoke," Siebert says, "the effects come on almost instantly, and it's disorienting. Suddenly you have this dramatic shift of consciousness, especially if you're taking a high dose, and it can be frightening and uncomfortable. That starts everything off on the wrong foot."

Last year a commenter on reason's blog, Hit & Run, called salvia "THE WORST substance of this Earth," adding, "If you want kids to stay off of drugs, give them some Salvia and tell them this is what cannabis, hash, and LSD are all like." Erowid.org, a website that provides information on a wide variety of psychoactive substances for an audience that is more Leary than leery, is less vehement, but it notes that salvia's effects "are considered unpleasant by many people." Bryan Roth, a psychiatrist and pharmacologist at the University of North Carolina, led the research that showed how salvinorin A binds to the brain. "Most people will say they don't like it," he says. "It's just too intense. If it has any effect at all, I would say it would be to diminish the tendency for drug abuse."

Users are apt to be especially disappointed if they are expecting a fun party drug similar to marijuana. "I smoked with a friend last week who became the leg of a table," says Rick Doblin, president of the Multidisciplinary Association for Psychedelic Studies. In his 1994 paper, Siebert listed commonly reported themes of salvia experiences, including "becoming objects," "visions of various two-dimensional surfaces," "revisiting places from the past," "loss of the body and/or identity," "various sensations of motion," "uncontrollable hysterical laughter," and "overlapping realities." Such experiences might be interesting, rewarding, or revealing, but they are not exactly conducive to social activities.

"Salvia is not a recreational substance," says Jeffrey Bottoms, who works at Mazatec Garden, a salvia importer and distributor in Houston. "It isn't pleasant. It doesn't make you feel good. It's not a mood elevator. If you're depressed, it's not going to make you feel a little better. In fact, it will make you feel a lot worse." Ready to try it yet?

First you may want to check out the videos. Search for "salvia" on YouTube, and you'll find hundreds of videos of teenagers and young adults staring into space, laughing hysterically, falling over, crawling on the floor, and speaking in tongues while their friends alternately giggle and reassure them that it will all be over soon. These videos, widely credited with helping to popularize salvia, do not make it seem very appealing. Nor are they all that alarming, except perhaps as a sign that a disturbingly large number of people want the world to see their displays of drug-induced idiocy. In some of the videos, the salvia smoker freaks out a little, but these "bad trips" (breathlessly advertised as such) look pretty mild, consisting mainly of restlessness and a repeatedly expressed wish for an end to the ride, which arrives soon enough.

Yet the YouTube videos come up frequently in newspaper stories about salvia and in the comments of politicians who want to ban it. In January, explaining his motive for sponsoring a prohibition bill, Maryland state Sen. Richard Colburn (R-Dorchester County) told the Baltimore Examiner that the YouTube footage is "pretty disturbing," adding, "Just imagine if that was your child." Colburn's YouTube-inspired bill would classify salvia as a Schedule I substance, making people who sell it subject to prison terms of up to 20 years. According to the Santa Fe Reporter, New Mexico state Rep. Keith Gardner (R-Chavez), sponsor of a similar bill, "says all the evidence he needs of the drug's dangerous potential is available on YouTube." He told the paper the videos are "dramatic as hell—you gotta watch'em. At first I thought, 'This is just somebody pretending.' It's amazing how powerful this drug is."

Texas state Rep. Armando Martinez (D-Weslaco) says he introduced a bill that would ban salvia sales to minors based on "what we've seen on YouTube and what a friend of mine's nephew had mentioned about all this." He settled on age restrictions, as opposed to a complete ban, because it seemed easier to accomplish. "Any way we could stop this from getting into the hands of our children or adolescents," he says, "I think that it's something we need to do. If that means a complete ban, then I would support a complete ban."

Texas state Rep. Charles "Doc" Anderson (R-Waco) already does, arguing that age restrictions could "do more harm than good," making salvia use a mark of adulthood. The New York Times reports that Anderson has tried to stir up support for a ban among his colleagues by citing a YouTube video that shows a salvia smoker behind the wheel of a car. The video in question, "Driving on Salvia," is part of a humorous series called "Being Productive on Salvia" featuring a Los Angeles production assistant named Erik Hoffstad. Other episodes include "Gardening on Salvia" and "Writing a Letter to Congress on Salvia." The running gag is that Hoffstad can't manage to do much of anything after taking a salvia hit. In "Driving on Salvia," he never actually tries to start the car, and the scariest moment occurs when a cat unexpectedly jumps on the hood.

'Beyond Anything We Have Seen Before'

Martinez and Anderson both raise the specter of salvia-im-paired driving, but neither can cite any real-life examples of it, in Texas or elsewhere. That's not surprising, since (as Hoffstad's video illustrates) someone tripping on salvia, unlike someone who has had a few drinks, is in no condition to get into a car, start it up, and drive away. It seems the only way this hazard could materialize is if someone brought a bongful of salvia with him on a drive and lit it up while stopped at a light. Although the driving scenario seems implausible, salvia prohibitionists are right that there is a potential for accidents under the drug's influence, which is why vendors warn their customers to put away hazardous objects and enlist a "sober sitter" to keep an eye on them during their trip.

When I press Martinez and Anderson for examples of actual harm caused by salvia use, as opposed to hypothetical risks, the best they can do is cite bad but brief trips. Anderson also claims "we are seeing the flashback scenario." But as Siebert notes, "Any kind of intense or traumatic experience," including war, car crashes, and near-death experiences, "can produce flashbacks. . . . Intense psychedelic experiences can be extremely frightening, and it may be that there's some internal psychological mechanism of revisiting that kind of material later. But it doesn't appear that there's any organic, direct reason for this. It's not like the drug hangs around the system and suddenly pops up in your brain one day. It seems to be more like the way the brain deals with very intense or confusing experiences."

Last fall Anderson told the Waco Tribune-Herald that "with a single use [salvia smokers] can cause some serious, serious damage to their brain." Roth, the salvia researcher, says "there's no evidence for that statement." In fact, says Siebert, animal studies of salvia give "no indication of it having any significant toxic effects, even at doses that are hundreds of times more than what humans would ordinarily use." Even salvia's detractors concede that addiction does not seem to be an issue, since few people who try the drug want to use it on a regular basis. Despite a dramatic increase in use during the last few years, emergency rooms are not seeing a flood, or even a trickle, of salvia users, probably because a hospital trip usually takes longer than a salvia trip.

The lack of alarming statistics helps explain why the Drug Enforcement Administration (DEA), which has the power to ban psychoactive substances without new legislation, is still waiting and watching six years after declaring salvia a "drug of concern." DEA spokesman Rusty Payne says, "I don't think we have enough information yet." And there's no telling when they will. "It's going to take a while," Payne says. "If we decide to schedule [salvia], we'll publish a notice [in the Federal Register]. If we don't, we won't." Although Payne says the delay should not be read as a judgment on salvia's dangers, the DEA can act much more quickly when it wants to, as when it banned MDMA on an emergency basis in 1985. "When they say they've been looking at it for years," says Rick Doblin, "it means it's not much of a problem."

Nor is salvia a high priority at the Food and Drug Administration (FDA). Officially, the FDA says herbal products like salvia are "unapproved new drugs" and "misbranded drugs" if they are "marketed with claims implying that these products mimic the effects of controlled substances." Products are deemed to be "illegal street drug alternatives" when they are "intended to be used for recreational purposes to effect psychological states (e.g., to get high, to promote euphoria, or to induce hallucinations)."

"I am aware of that law," says Arena Eth-nobotanicals CEO John Boyd, "and that's why if you check our website there are no references to anything like that." Many salvia vendors do tout the psychoactive effects of their products, promising "psychedelic," "visionary," "enlightening," and "enjoyable" experiences. Yet except for two warning letters it sent in 2002, the FDA does not seem to have taken any enforcement actions against companies that sell salvia. While FDA spokesman Christopher Kelly says "we do not discuss potential, pending, or ongoing actions," none of the distributors I interviewed was aware of any recent warnings or seizures.

As for Congress, Rep. Joe Baca (D-Calif.) introduced a bill to ban salvia in 2002, declaring, "We know very little about the drug, but what we do know is frightening. This drug's power is beyond anything we have seen before." But the bill died in committee, and Baca never reintroduced it. I contacted his office a couple of times to find out why but did not get an answer.

'Our Existence in General Is Pointless'

By contrast, there's been a flurry of anti-salvia activity at the state level in the last few years. With so little evidence that salvia is hazardous, prohibitionists lean heavily on anecdotes. Ohio state Rep. Thom Collier (R-Mount Vernon), who introduced a salvia ban that took effect in April, said he was motivated by the death of a Loudon-ville boy who was shot by a friend. But according to the Cleveland Plain Dealer, "it isn't clear whether the friend was on the drug when he shot and killed the 12-year-old." The Columbus Dispatch notes "there was no direct evidence . . . that the shooting was drug-related."

Similarly, when Rep. Baca proposed a federal salvia ban in 2002, he cited the case of Daniel Moffa, a 15-year-old Rhode Island boy who smoked salvia one morning and stabbed his pot dealer on the way to school. Moffa later told WPRI, the Fox affiliate in Providence, that he was "paranoid" and "hallucinating," thinking the dealer looked "evil" and "horrible." The story sounded fishy to Daniel Siebert, since he didn't think a salvia user on a trip that intense would be able to coordinate his movements well enough to meet someone and repeatedly stab him. Still, Moffa's parents initially blamed salvia for the assault because "we had no other plausible explanation," the boy's father explained in a 2007 email message to Siebert. Since then, the father said, "we have found out that Dan suffers from bipolar affective disorder with psychosis." While "the salvia may have contributed to an episode," he added, it "was not the real cause."

The most influential salvia horror story involves Brett Chidester, a Wilmington, Delaware, 17-year-old who in January 2006 pitched a tent in his parents' garage, went inside it with a burning charcoal grill, and stayed there until he was dead from carbon monoxide poisoning. Brett had been experimenting with salvia and claimed it had given him profound insights. "Salvia allows us to give up our senses and wander in the interdimensional time and space," he wrote in an essay discovered after his death. "Also, and this is probably hard for most to accept, our existence in general is pointless. Final point: Us earthly humans are nothing."

A month after Brett's death, his mother, Kathy Chidester, told the Wilmington News-Journal: "We just won't have any answers, and we have to learn to accept that. But my gut feeling is it was the salvia. It's the only thing that can explain it." A month later, the state legislature had approved Brett's Law, which made salvia a Schedule I drug. The same week the ban took effect, Delaware's deputy chief medical examiner, Adrienne Sekula-Perlman, changed Brett's death certificate, adding "salvia divinorum use" as a contributing cause.

Since then Kathy Chidester has campaigned for similar laws across the country, and 15 more states have either banned salvia or (in the case of California and Maine) prohibited sales to minors. The laws all passed by overwhelming margins, in some cases unanimously. Anti-salvia bills have been introduced in at least 22 other states. "My hope and goal is to have salvia regulated across the U.S.," Chidester wrote in testimony supporting the proposed salvia ban in Maryland last January. "It's my son's legacy and I will not end my fight until this happens."

Appel, the Tiffin University psychologist, does not think salvia should be legal for general use, but he is reluctant to draw any firm conclusions about Brett Chidester's death. "I wouldn't feel comfortable saying it caused him to commit suicide," he says. Such explanations, he adds, are "a way to try to make sense of something that's pretty senseless. We're always looking for rationalizations and reasons, particularly when there aren't any."

Roth, the University of North Carolina psychiatrist, is also opposed to using salvia recreationally, partly because of the psychological risks. But he says it's difficult to say what role the drug might have played in Brett Chidester's suicide. Although "it's tragic that this young guy killed himself," he says, "there's no way of knowing if salvia had anything to do with it. . . . There have been a couple of reports of people having long-term psychotic episodes after smoking it that have appeared in the literature. It would seem, given the apparent widespread use of salvia, that if these are side effects, they don't occur at very high prevalence. Otherwise, the ERs would be filled with people having bad salvia reactions."

Siebert concedes that salvia "might have influenced [Brett Chidester's] thinking in some way" but adds: "He must have already had some thoughts about suicide. I don't think salvia's just going to put thoughts into peoples' heads. Mentally healthy people don't decide to take such a drastic action based on [an idea] they had during a drug state. Psy-chedelics basically amplify a lot of your own internal stuff. If you're already having some kind of dark thoughts, a psychedelic experience could amplify that, and it could lead to a problem for some people."

Notably, there is no indication that Brett Chidester was under the influence of salvia when he killed himself. The idea seems to be that using the drug encouraged him to reach conclusions about the nature of life that were conducive to suicide. That theory, notes Richard Glen Boire, a senior fellow at the Center for Cognitive Liberty & Ethics, "could apply to some of the greatest pieces of art in the history of the world. It would make Nietzsche a controlled substance. There is a lot of cultural production out there that shows a way of looking at the world that isn't all sunny and rosy."

'One Life Lost Is One Too Many'

If Brett Chidester's suicide looms large in the thinking of anti-salvia legislators in other states, that's partly because they rarely have evidence of harm caused by the drug closer to home. According to local press coverage in one state after another, police are not reporting salvia-related problems. Neither are schools, hospitals, or drag treatment centers. Legislators want to ban it anyway.

Their reasoning is simple: Why wait for a problem? Martinez, the Texas legislator, says he favors "a proactive approach." Over the course of my 10-minute interview with him, he says "one life lost is one too many" four times and "you can't put a price on life" three times. To his colleague Anderson, who utters the phrase "it's a hallucinogen" eight times during a 30-minute conversation, it's self-evident that any drug falling into that category should be banned.

Georgia state Sen. Don Thomas (R-Dalton) has a similar attitude. In 2007 he candidly told the Florida Times-Union he knew nothing about the benefits of salvia use. "I just know about the publicity of the dangers of it," he said, "so my first impression is to ban anything of that nature." That same year, defending legislation that would ban the sale of salvia to adults, Wisconsin state Rep. Sheldon Wasserman (D-Milwaukee) told the Wisconsin State Journal, "This bill is all about protecting our children."

Salvia prohibitionists say a complete ban is necessary to protect children because, as Wisconsin state Sen. Julie Lassa (D-Stevens Point) told the Wausau Daily Herald in 2007, "many people believe that because it is legal there are no risks associated with using salvia." Last year Massachusetts state Rep. Vinny deMacedo (R-Plymouth) told the Plymouth News, "I believe by not making this drug illegal we are sending a message to our youth that it is OK." Appel, the psychologist, agrees that salvia users "make the assumption that because it's legal it'll be safe."

But people do not assume that tobacco and alcohol are safe simply because they are legal. Furthermore, anyone researching salvia online would come across myriad warnings from vendors and users about the drug's risks, along with the YouTube videos, which highlight the potential for bad trips. "I don't buy this idea that people think because it's legal it must be good," says Doblin, "because the corollary is not true." Especially when it comes to marijuana, he says, "People don't think, 'It's illegal, so it must be bad.'" People inclined to experiment with salvia, he says, generally don't believe that "the drug laws make sense."

To the extent that people do believe that, says Richard Glen Boire of the Center for Cognitive Liberty & Ethics, it's a dangerous misconception. "In a mature society," he says, "you would laugh at the idea that if something is available it is therefore stamped 'approved' and 'safe.' I don't think we should be creating a society that's safety proofed in a way that [ignores] the reality of living."

Yet the war on drugs has conditioned people to expect that, with a few grandfathered exceptions, psychoactive substances that are not classified as pharmaceuticals will be banned. You hear it from salvia smokers on YouTube as well as salvia scaremongers in state legislatures: I can't believe this stuff is legal. Ultimately, that is the crux of the prohibitionist argument. Salvia must be banned because it's legal.

Once a few legislatures act on that premise, public officials in other states start to worry they will look irresponsible if they don't follow suit. Last year Van Ingram, compliance branch manager with the Kentucky Office of Drug Control Policy, told the Owensboro Messenger-Inquirer, "Our neighbors in Tennessee and Missouri felt it was important enough, so it is important for us to look at it as well." A month later, after the Florida legislature approved a salvia ban, state Sen. Evelyn Lynn (R-Daytona Beach) told the Associated Press, "I'd rather be at the front edge of preventing the dangers of the drug than waiting until we are the 40th or more."

'A Philosopher's Tool'

Since there is no political upside to resisting prohibitionism, it's surprising when legislators decline to panic. Two states—Maine and California—have prohibited salvia sales to minors instead of banning the drug completely. This year Maryland's House of Delegates likewise ended up rejecting a ban and endorsing age restrictions, but the state Senate did not act on the bill before the end of the legislative session. The Drug Policy Alliance, which testified against the Maryland ban, also helped change a New Mexico prohibition bill into a ban on sales to minors, although the legislation has not passed yet.

One respectable antiprohibitionist argument is that banning salvia could impede valuable medical research. Salvinorin has intriguing properties that have made its derivatives the focus of research aimed at finding better treatments for pain, drug addiction, depression, and various neurological conditions. "For those of us who study this sort of thing," says Bryan Roth, "the fact that salvinorin binds to just one [brain receptor] is pretty amazing. It opens up the possibility that if we can find drugs that block the effects of salvinorin at that receptor, they might be effective in treating a number of diseases."

Roth worries that placing salvinorin on Schedule I of the federal Controlled Substances Act, the most restrictive category, will "make it more difficult to do research on it and investigate the potential therapeutic utility of derivatives. By definition, a Schedule I drug is devoid of any medical benefit. That makes it next to impossible to demonstrate any medical benefit. They made LSD Schedule I in the '60s, and they're only now getting around to looking at potential medical benefits. It really slows things down."

While some salvia prohibitionists say they don't want to interfere with scientific research, they do not recognize any legitimate nonmedical use for the plant. They see teenagers getting wasted on YouTube, and they see medical applications that might one day be approved by the FDA, but nothing in between. Siebert, who thinks thrill-seeking salvia smokers do not understand what the plant is all about, recently told the German magazine Hanfblatt, "Salvia is not an escapist drug. Quite the contrary: It is a philosopher's tool." He says, "It produces a very internal state where you go into yourself. You're more aware of your subconscious feelings, and often you gain insight into problems in your life that you're trying to tackle." Last year he told Newsweek, "I realized I wanted to marry my wife as a result of the salvia experience."

In a 2003 Erowid survey of 500 salvia users who filled out an online questionnaire, 47 percent reported "increased insight," while 40 percent said they felt an "increased sense of connection with the universe or nature." Other commonly reported effects were improved mood (45 percent), calmness (42 percent), weird thoughts (36 percent), a feeling of unreality (32 percent), and a feeling of floating (32 percent). About 26 percent reported "persisting positive effects," compared to 4 percent who reported "persisting negative effects" (typically anxiety). The sample was self-selected, so the responses are not necessarily representative, but they give a better sense than the YouTube videos do of why some people might find value in the salvia experience.

"It makes things that are bothering you become clear," says Mazatec Garden's Jeffrey Bottoms. Some users report that salvia relieved their depression or helped them break bad habits. A 2001 case report in the Journal of Clinical Psychopharmacology described a 26-year-old woman whose chronic depression disappeared after she started taking small doses of salvia three times a week. Arena Ethnobotanicals CEO John Boyd says he tried to give up cigarettes many times over the years and finally quit the week after his first salvia experience. Doblin notes that Canadian Quakers who have used salvia during meetings "felt that it deepened the silence and made people speak more from the heart."

Although Siebert does not put much stock in spiritualism, he recognizes that other salvia users see their experiences in religious terms. "It seems so real that people often interpret it at face value and think they have actually had some kind of spiritual journey," he says. "I don't personally believe that's what is really going on. But that doesn't mean it's not meaningful for people."

By contrast, Worcester County, Maryland, Commissioner Linda Busick is sure a salvia experience cannot possibly be meaningful, at least not in a good way. "It's supposed to be inducing spiritual growth," Busick scoffed in a 2008 interview with the Salisbury Daily Times. "It's certainly detrimental to anyone who uses it. I don't know of any beneficial effects that it has." Van Ingram, the Kentucky drug control official, is on the same page. "Anything that makes you see visions or things that are not there," he told the Owensboro Messenger-Inquirer last year, "is hardly harmless."

Anything? As Boire notes, "The visionary state goes back millennia, and it cannot be prohibited. Every night we enter into a visionary state. Every book you read, everything that goes through your sensory apparatus, creates a type of vision." Doblin adds: "Seeing visions is the core of a lot of different religions, and whether that's harmful or not depends on the context, the support, how people interpret the visions. Seeing things that are not there is not necessarily harmful. This whole idea that different is bad, that a change in consciousness is in itself harmful, is really one of the fundamental problems inherent in the drug war."

Few politicians can resist the allure of a drug described as "cheaper than marijuana, stronger than LSD, as fast-acting as crack cocaine, and legally available to minors.' YouTube videos of salvia trips have made the plant even more appealing as a legislative target.

According to local press coverage in one state after another, police are not reporting salvia-related problems. Neither are schools, hospitals, or drug treatment centers. Legislators want to ban it anyway. Their reasoning is simple: Why wait for a problem?

Users are apt to be especially disappointed if they are expecting a fun party drug similar to marijuana. "l smoked with a friend last week who became the leg of a table," says Rick Doblin, president of the Multidisciplinary Association for Psychedelic Studies.

You hear it from salvia smokers on YouTube as well as salvia scaremongers in state legislatures: I can't believe this stutf is legal. Ultimately, that is the crux of the prohibitionist argument. Salvia must be banned because it's legal.

POSTSCRIPT

Should Salvia Be Banned?

There is little argument that mind-altering drugs can cause physical and emotional havoc for the user. People may become less inhibited and become involved in behaviors they would not typically do if they were not on drugs. It is not uncommon for salvia users to experience changes in perception as well as psychological and physical effects. However, is one's use of salvia likely to increase unwanted and undesirable behaviors? Perhaps individuals who use salvia are the types of people who would engage in reckless behavior regardless. In other words, does salvia produce certain behaviors or is salvia an excuse to engage in certain behaviors?

According to Pearl Nyi and her associates, most salvia users maintain that the drug enhances creativity, is fun, and produces spiritual effects. To a lesser degree, salvia is consumed to relieve boredom. Whether salvia is banned may not be a major reason for stopping salvia use. Nyi reported that one-third of the users ceased use because they did not like the high they got from the drug. Slightly more than one-fourth stopped because they lost interest in the drug. Nonetheless, nearly 2 million people have tried salvia.

Some people argue that history shows that bringing attention to certain drugs results in their increased use. Young people would not know to alter their consciousness with certain drugs unless they were alerted to their effects. For example, how would one know that salvia produces hallucinogenic-like effects unless that fact was established? However, if young people participate in an activity that is potentially harmful, one could argue that it is the government's responsibility to step in. At what point is too much information counterproductive? Balancing one's right to know about drugs with the publicity generated by informing the public about certain drugs is difficult.

The issue of whether or not we should prohibit salvia raises a number of interesting questions. For example, how much danger must a drug represent before it is considered too dangerous? Are exaggerating the effects of drugs like salvia providing a disservice because other information about drugs that are especially harmful may be ignored? Should the government's focus be on prohibiting the use of salvia at all costs or should the government try to educate people about its potential adverse effects?

Some people feel that salvia may have medicinal value. If the drug is banned, then research into its potential benefits is not likely to be pursued. If salvia has the potential of being beneficial, can the drug be as bad as it is purported to be?

There are a number of articles that look at the effects, benefits, and dangers of salvia. In "Subjective Effects of *Salvia divinorum*: LSD- or Marijuana-like?" by Dawn Albertson and Laura Grubbs (*Journal of Psychoactive Drugs*,

September 2009), most users likened salvia's effects to that of marijuana. The potential medicinal value of salvia is discussed in "Salvia on Schedule," by David jay Brown (*Scientific American*, August 2009). In *Drug Alert Watch Salvia Divinorum* (March 2, 2010), the United States Department of Justice describes the adverse effects of salvia. An article that examines the legal ramifications regarding salvia is "Legally High? Legal Considerations of *Salvia divinorum*," by O. Hayden Griffin, Bryan Lee Miller, and David N. Khey (*Journal of Psychoactive Drugs*, June 2008). One group that sponsors research into the therapeutic benefits of hallucinogenic drugs is the Multidisciplinary Association for Psychedelic Studies (MAPS). Its Web site is http://www.maps.org.

ISSUE 5

Should Women Who Use Drugs Lose Custody of Their Children?

YES: Mark F. Testa and Brenda Smith, from "Prevention and Drug Treatment," *The Future of Children* (Fall 2009)

NO: Jeanne Flavin and Lynn M. Paltrow, from "Punishing Pregnant Drug-Using Women: Defying Law, Medicine, and Common Sense," *Journal of Addictive Diseases* (2010)

ISSUE SUMMARY

YES: Mark Testa, a professor of social work at the University of North Carolina, and Brenda Smith, a professor in the School of Social Work at the University of Alabama maintain that drug treatment to prevent child maltreatment is not especially effective. They argue that it is in the best interest of children to remove them from environments where drugs are used. Mark Testa and Brenda Smith indicate that the threat of losing custody of children acts as a deterrent to drug use.

NO: Fordham University professor Jeanne Flavin and attorney Lynn Paltrow of the National Advocates for Pregnant Women argue that the stigma of drug use may result in the avoidance of treatment and prenatal care. They assert that the prosecution of drug users is unfair because poor women are more likely to be the targets of such prosecution. To enable pregnant women who use drugs to receive perinatal care, it is necessary to define their drug use as a health problem rather than as a legal problem.

The effects that drugs have on a fetus can be mild and temporary or severe and permanent, depending on the extent of drug use by the mother, the type of substance used, and the stage of fetal development at the time the drug crosses the placental barrier and enters the bloodstream of the fetus. Both illegal and legal drugs, such as cocaine, crack, marijuana, alcohol, and nicotine, are increasingly found to be responsible for incidents of premature births, congenital abnormalities, fetal alcohol syndrome, mental retardation, and other serious birth defects. The exposure of the fetus to these substances and the long-term involuntary physical, intellectual, and emotional effects are disturbing. In addition, the medical, social, and economic costs to treat and care for babies who are exposed to or become addicted to drugs while in utero (in the uterus) warrant serious concern.

An important consideration regarding the prosecution of pregnant drug users is whether this is a legal problem or a medical problem. In recent years, attempts have been made to establish laws that would allow the incarceration of drug-using pregnant women on the basis of "fetal abuse." Some cases have been successfully prosecuted: Mothers have been denied custody of their infants until they enter appropriate treatment programs, and criminal charges have been brought against mothers whose children were born with drug-related complications. The underlying presumption is that the unborn fetus should be afforded protection against the harmful actions of another person, specifically the use of harmful drugs by the mother.

Those who profess that prosecuting pregnant women who use drugs is necessary insist that the health and welfare of the unborn child is the highest priority. They contend that the possibility that these women will avoid obtaining health care for themselves or their babies because they fear punishment does not absolve the state from the responsibility of protecting the babies. They also argue that criminalizing these acts is imperative to protect fetuses and newborns who cannot protect themselves. It is the duty of the legal system to deter pregnant women from engaging in future criminal drug use and to protect the best interests of infants.

Others maintain that drug use and dependency by pregnant women is a medical problem, not a criminal one. Many pregnant women seek treatment, but they often find that rehabilitation programs are limited or unavailable. Shortages of openings in chemical dependency programs may keep a prospective client waiting for months, during which time she will most likely continue to use the drugs to which she is addicted and prolong her fetus's drug exposure. Many low-income women do not receive drug treatment and adequate prenatal care due to financial constraints. Women who fear criminal prosecution because of their drug use may simply avoid prenatal care altogether.

Some suggest that medical intervention, drug prevention, and education—not prosecution—are needed for pregnant drug users. Prosecution, they contend, drives women who need medical attention away from the very help they and their babies need. Others respond that prosecuting pregnant women who use drugs will help identify those who need attention, at which point adequate medical and social welfare services can be provided to treat and protect the mother and child.

In the YES selection, Mark Testa and Brenda Smith argue that it is in the best interest of children to remove them from environments where drugs are used. They feel that drug treatment is ineffective. The threat of having children taken away serves as a deterrent to drug use. In the NO selection, Jeanne Flavin and Lynn Paltrow contend that prosecuting pregnant drug users may be counterproductive to improving the quality of infant and maternal health. Women may avoid prenatal care if they believe they may have their children removed. To help women who use drugs during pregnancy, it would be more helpful to identify the problem as a medical problem and not as a legal problem.

YES ⬅

Mark F. Testa and
Brenda Smith

Prevention and Drug Treatment

For much of the past century of U.S. public involvement in the protection and care of abused and neglected children, the problem of parental alcohol and other drug abuse (AODA) was hidden, at least from the public's eye. Even though insobriety, alcoholism, and drug addiction have long been recognized as serious family problems by front-line workers and duly noted in case records and service plans, it was only after these afflictions manifested themselves tangibly in physical battery, sexual abuse, lack of supervision, and child abandonment that officials would invoke their authority to intervene in the private affairs of the family. It was this tangible evidence of child maltreatment that was usually recorded and reported as the reason for investigations, court petitions, and child removals. The scale of the underlying AODA problem remained largely hidden in the shadows from public sight.

Several trends during the mid-1980s and 1990s helped to bring about greater public awareness of the AODA connection to child maltreatment and foster care. The first was the change in the gender profile of users from disproportionately males and fathers to increasingly females and mothers. Public officials may have been able to turn a blind eye when it was mostly fathers who returned home drunk or stoned; it was quite another matter when female caregivers increasingly numbered among the users.

Second, the spread of illicit drugs, particularly "crack" cocaine in inner-city neighborhoods, alarmed public officials, who predicted dire consequences for crime, welfare dependency, and public health. Even though the detrimental effect of fetal alcohol syndrome had been well established, the uncertain effects of intrauterine exposure of infants to cocaine, heroin, and other hard drugs prompted hospital officials to increase the number of toxicology screenings at birth. In some states, a positive finding from such a test provided sufficient grounds for filing a child abuse report.

Finally, the shift from a "rights" to a "norms" perspective in federal and state income assistance and child welfare programs helped to enlarge the scope of public interest beyond a narrow focus on child safety to a more diffuse concern with parental responsibility and child well-being in general. Although it is arguable whether parental substance abuse provides a legitimate basis in its own right for protective intervention and child removal, the greater acceptance of government's role in enforcing mainstream parental fitness standards has enlarged the scope of public interest in AODA as a child welfare concern.

These changes in gender profile, hospital surveillance practices, and scope of public interest affect the ways in which researchers classify, make connections, and speculate about cause and effect in the prevention, treatment, and control of parental substance abuse. In this article we examine the magnitude of the AODA problem under different definitions of drug use and at various stages of child protective services (CPS) action, from maltreatment investigation and family case opening to child removal and placement into foster care. We first address the association between parental substance abuse and child maltreatment and the strength of any causal connection between the two. That is, we address the extent to which substance abuse, per se, elevates the risk for child maltreatment and how a link between the two may reflect other causal influences. We review empirical evidence on the extent to which prevention and intervention programs successfully reduce drug abuse, on whether family services help addicted parents control substance use and improve their parenting, and on how well drug treatment programs reinforce sobriety so that foster children can safely be returned to parental custody. For two reasons, we focus our discussion on experiences in the state of Illinois. First, in 1989 Illinois became one of the first states in the nation to approve legislation making intrauterine exposure to illicit substances, by itself, evidence of child abuse and neglect. And, second, in 1999 the state secured permission from the federal government to mount a randomized controlled experiment of the efficacy of "recovery coach" services in promoting drug treatment and family reunification.

Reflecting on the research findings, we address the extent to which social policy should be broadly concerned with AODA as a child well-being matter beyond narrow safety and permanency concerns. We discuss whether the weight of the evidence refutes or supports the notion of maintaining children in parental custody or, if removed, returning them home while parents are still in the process of recovery from drug addiction. Finally, we consider how long children should wait while parents struggle to manage their drug dependency before caseworkers initiate termination-of-parental-rights (TPR) proceedings or put into action other permanency plans, such as kinship custody and legal guardianship.

Children's Exposure to Parental AODA

The prevalence of children's exposure to parental AODA refers to the proportion of abused and neglected children who are affected by parental alcohol and other drug use at a given time. Estimates vary depending on the definition of AODA used to classify cases, the segment of the child population examined, and the method of data collection used to count the cases. Prevalence estimates are best generated through carefully conducted studies using uniform definitions that rely on samples of cases drawn at random or using some other statistically valid method of selection to generate an estimate within some margin of error, for example, plus or minus a few percentage points.

Because "substance abuse" is defined differently and measured more precisely by drug professionals than by ordinary folks, an important element of the estimation process is the definition of substance abuse that is used for classifying and counting. AODA is variously measured in terms of current use, lifetime use, abuse, or dependence. Current or lifetime use of illicit substances or large amounts of alcohol (often defined as four or more drinks in one day) is best measured using uniform screening questions such as those in the Composite International Diagnostic Interview-Short Form (CIDI-SF). In such diagnostic interviews, respondents are asked a series of questions such as, "In the past 12 months did you ever use . . . [insert name of substance]"?

Substance abuse and dependence are distinct concepts and refer to detrimental or debilitating use. They can be systematically measured with criteria specified in the *Diagnostic and Statistical Manual of Mental Disorders* (DSM-IV). The manual lists seven potential dependency symptoms and suggests that dependence is indicated when at least three of the seven are present. The DSM-IV defines substance abuse in narrower terms, as a pattern of substance use that is "maladaptive" without meeting the criteria for dependence. The manual specifies four characteristic symptoms of substance abuse and specifies that at least one must be present to indicate a diagnosis of substance abuse.

The National Survey of Drug Use and Health (NSDUH; formerly known as the National Household Survey of Drug Abuse) conducts in-home surveys with probability samples of the population to estimate prevalence rates of alcohol and drug use within the past year. It uses DSM-based criteria to assess substance abuse and dependency. In 2002, the NSDUH found that among married women aged twenty-one to forty-nine living with children under the age of eighteen, 14.5 percent engaged in binge drinking and 4 percent used illicit drugs in the past month. The 2003 NSDUH found that among women aged eighteen to forty-nine, 5.5 percent abused or were dependent on alcohol or any illicit drug.

These prevalence estimates suggest that between 6 million and 9 million children live in households in which a caregiver abuses alcohol or drugs. These numbers far exceed the number of children who become involved in the child welfare system for any reason. Of the approximately 900,000 children with substantiated maltreatment allegations of any kind in 2005, about 300,000 (33 percent) were placed in foster care, leaving about 600,000 children with substantiated allegations at home with their parents. Even if all of these substantiated cases with children in the home involved parental substance abuse, the number would conservatively reflect only about 10 percent of the estimated number of children living with a parent who abuses substances.

It is equally challenging to identify the prevalence of AODA among families already involved with the child welfare system. Just as substance abuse can be measured differently in general population studies, so can exposure to parental AODA in the child welfare population be defined and counted in a variety of ways. In the child welfare research literature, measures of AODA range from the impressions of state administrators elicited in phone surveys, to references in case files, to caregivers' scores on standardized measures such as the CIDI-SF. As described below, when substance abuse is measured with standardized and validated measures, the resulting prevalence estimates tend to be lower than those of phone surveys and case records.

An added complication is that the child welfare population can also be defined in a variety of ways. The definitions range from the total number of children involved in CPS investigations to the fraction having a substantiated maltreatment report to the smaller number who are removed and placed into foster care. Prevalence rates vary not only across these different population groupings but also by geographical location and time period. Child welfare jurisdictions have different policies and norms regarding when substance abuse triggers child welfare involvement, and those policies and norms change over time. Hence, even if the same child welfare subpopulations are assessed using the same substance abuse measures, prevalence rate estimates may vary depending on the specific location and time period examined.

In light of the range of possibilities, it is easy to see how specific choices of substance abuse definitions and child welfare subpopulations can affect prevalence estimates. The most reliable prevalence estimates come from studies that meet generally accepted criteria of sampling rigor and measurement precision. Studies with unspecified response rates, response rates of less than 50 percent, or those that use only impressions as an indicator of substance abuse tend to produce unreliable estimates. The best estimates derive from studies with well-defined indicators of substance abuse and clearly specified samples. The best studies will also differentiate between samples that focus on the smaller foster care subpopulation and those that focus on the larger population of abused and neglected children.

Evidence meeting the above criteria suggests that caseworkers and investigators report substance abuse in about 11 to 14 percent of investigated cases and in 18 to 24 percent of cases with substantiated maltreatment. Of the cases that are opened for in-home services following a maltreatment investigation, 24 percent screen positive for alcohol abuse or illicit drug use in the past year. This figure is a nationwide average. In an urban sample with no specification about timing, 56 percent of such caregivers had a notation of illicit drug or alcohol abuse in their case files or self-reported as having engaged in drug or alcohol abuse.

The prevalence of substance abuse runs higher for children taken into foster care, with estimates meeting the above criteria ranging from 50 to 79 percent among young children removed from parental custody. Although few studies meeting the specified criteria have assessed the prevalence of DSM-defined substance abuse or dependency in child welfare populations, those that do suggest that 4 percent of families having contact with the child welfare system and 16 percent of families having a child in foster care meet DSM criteria for substance abuse or dependence. Comparing reports of prevalence of substance abuse or current use to more standardized measures of drug abuse and dependency suggests that approximately one-fourth of users of alcohol and other drugs who come to the attention of CPS authorities present serious enough problems to warrant a DSM designation.

Two key generalizations may be drawn from the research about the prevalence of children's exposure to parental AODA. First, when detection methods and measures of substance abuse are more precise, prevalence estimates tend to be lower. Prevalence rates generated from impressions (from administrators, state liaisons, or caseworkers) or from wide-ranging references in case files (such as reports of past substance abuse or a past referral to substance abuse treatment) are substantially higher than are estimates generated through individual parent assessments or professional diagnosis. A clearer picture of links between substance abuse and child maltreatment will require greater attention to definitions of substance abuse and the timing and method of assessment. Second, the prevalence of parental substance abuse is lower among children who are subjects of a CPS investigation than among those who are indicated for maltreatment and substantially lower than among those placed into foster care. These distinctions are important because, as noted, only about one-third of substantiated maltreatment allegations result in out-of-home care. Prevalence estimates derived from a foster care subpopulation should not be generalized to the larger child welfare populations of abused and neglected children.

Does Parental AODA Place Children at Increased Risk of Maltreatment?

Selective prevention, as distinct from universal prevention, refers to interventions that target groups that exhibit above-average risks, such as children exposed to parental AODA. Several studies document a link between parental AODA and child maltreatment, particularly neglect. However, establishing a causal relationship between parental substance abuse and child maltreatment is difficult. Most investigations of the link between substance abuse and child maltreatment start with a sample of parents involved with either child welfare or substance abuse services. For example, a sample of parents who have been found to abuse substances might be assessed for child maltreatment reports and the report rate may be compared with that of the general population or a matched comparison group without substance abuse problems. Sometimes such studies factor in other potential influences on child maltreatment, such as parental mental health or education. Such studies often find higher child maltreatment rates among parents in a substance abuse group than in the comparison group or, conversely, higher substance abuse rates among parents in a child welfare services group than in a comparison group.

Using similar methods, researchers have identified an association between parental substance abuse and child maltreatment as measured by scores on a child abuse potential index, parental self-reports, CPS reports, and incidents of maltreatment noted in medical records. In a rigorous study that is among the few prospective studies to assess the risk of child maltreatment among parents who abuse substances, Mark Chaffin and several colleagues followed for one year parents from a community sample. The researchers compared parents identified as having a substance use disorder and parents without a substance use disorder in self-reports of child maltreatment. Parents with a substance use disorder were three times more likely than those without one to report the onset of child abuse or neglect within the one-year follow-up period. About 3 percent of parents with a substance abuse problem reported child abuse or neglect within the year compared with 1 percent of parents without a substance abuse problem. The researchers found that the influence of substance abuse on maltreatment was maintained even when the parents being compared were similar with respect to such characteristics as parental depression, obsessive-compulsive disorder, household size, age, race, marital status, and socioeconomic status.

The Chaffin study is rigorous and convincing. It offers the best type of evidence for demonstrating a link between substance abuse and child maltreatment. And similar patterns are found in repeated studies that control for other co-existing risk factors. Such studies, however, cannot rule out the possibility that other co-factors associated with substance abuse, such as parental depression, social isolation, or domestic violence, are more directly responsible for higher maltreatment rates. Targeting interventions on a "spurious" association between drug use and maltreatment without attending to the underlying direct causes of both will be ineffectual. For example, researchers studying the effects of crack cocaine use during pregnancy found that the deleterious consequences originally attributed to substance abuse were actually related to the environments and associated hazards in drug users' lives.

In the Illinois experiment on "recovery coach" services in promoting drug treatment and family reunification, among parents who were identified as having a substance abuse problem and having a child placed out of the home, substance abuse was the sole problem for only 8 percent. The vast majority of the parents experienced co-existing problems with mental health, housing, or domestic violence. The best studies attempt to control for these other risk factors, but even multiple-regression and matched-sample studies are challenged to control adequately for the myriad of social, environmental, and other variables that can "confound" the association between parental substance abuse and threats to child safety. Differences attributed to substance use can also arise from other unobserved factors that affect the detection or identification of substance use, maltreatment reporting (including self-reports), and the likelihood of child welfare involvement.

The role of substance abuse in increasing risks for child maltreatment will become clearer as researchers succeed in identifying exactly what it is that explains the link between parental substance abuse and child maltreatment. Researchers have proposed a range of potential explanations. For example, substance abuse may strain social support relationships, leading to social isolation and heightening the risks that family, friends, and neighbors will refrain from lending a hand or stepping in when child-rearing problems arise. Substance abuse may promote impulsivity or reduce parental capacity to control anger under stressful situations. Substance abuse may also distract parents from meeting children's needs or impair their ability to supervise them. The links between parental substance abuse and child maltreatment surely warrant further study because different causal mechanisms call for different ways to conceptualize the problem and determine how to intervene. As one example, different substances may have different consequences for parenting and child safety. The ways in which a sedative, such as alcohol, impairs parenting or threatens child safety could be quite different from the ways in which a stimulant, such as methamphetamine, impairs parenting and threatens child safety. Perhaps child safety will be promoted most effectively by specifically targeted interventions for different types of substance abuse. Likewise, different mechanisms may explain different pathways to child neglect and physical abuse, or mechanisms may differ in different social or economic contexts.

Is It Possible to Target AODA Families for Treatment?

Indicated prevention involves screening abuse and neglect cases for signs of parental substance abuse to promote sobriety and prevent the recurrence of maltreatment. To date, usual caseworker practices have not proved effective in identifying AODA problems among families in the child welfare system or in preventing subsequent maltreatment allegations once families are investigated for child maltreatment. An analysis using data collected on families reported for child maltreatment as part of the National Survey of Child and Adolescent Well-Being (NSCAW) found that among at-home caregivers who screened positive for past-year alcohol abuse or illicit drug use, only 18 percent were identified by caseworkers as having a substance abuse problem. Among at-home caregivers meeting criteria for alcohol or drug dependency, caseworkers identified a substance abuse problem for only 39 percent. Such findings are consistent with other research indicating that child welfare caseworkers are ill-equipped to identify substance abuse problems.

When substance abuse is indicated, evidence also casts doubt that CPS is effective in linking parents to substance abuse services and treatment. A study focusing on parents with substance abuse problems involved with child welfare services found that about half received substance abuse treatment; 23 percent were offered treatment but did not receive it; and 23 percent were not offered treatment.

Shares of parents completing treatment are similarly low. An Oregon-based study found that both before and after implementation of the Adoption and Safe Families Act of 1997, about one-third of mothers involved with the child welfare system who entered substance abuse treatment completed their first treatment episode; about half completed any treatment episode within a three-year observation window. A more recent study found that among parents with substance abuse problems and children in foster care, only 22 percent completed treatment.

To upgrade identification of substance abuse problems and improve treatment access for parents in the child welfare system, service organizations in both child welfare and substance abuse treatment have increasingly adopted programs or policies that encourage or mandate inter-agency collaboration. For example, child welfare caseworkers are sometimes required to involve substance abuse treatment providers in service planning, or substance abuse treatment counselors may be required to enlist child welfare caseworkers in client engagement. Nevertheless, inter-agency collaboration in child welfare and substance abuse treatment has proven difficult to achieve. Organizational policies promoting collaboration have not always been sufficient to establish widespread changes in staff collaborative practices. . . .

How Effective Is Substance Abuse Treatment in Preventing Maltreatment Recurrence?

Concerted efforts to link clients with treatment sometimes fall short of the goal of preventing subsequent maltreatment, either because of problems with program attendance or because of the nature of the services provided. Barbara Rittner and Cheryl Davenport Dozier studied a sample of children with maltreatment allegations who either remained at home under court supervision or were placed with relatives. In about half the cases, a caregiver was mandated by the courts to attend substance abuse treatment. After rating the caregivers for treatment compliance and tracking the cases for eighteen months, the researchers found no correlation between caregivers' treatment compliance and subsequent child maltreatment. In the researchers' view, the findings raise questions about whether mandated treatment can prevent subsequent maltreatment and whether the treatment is of sufficient quality to help parents. Reflecting on the study findings, the researchers speculate that child welfare caseworkers may rely too heavily on indications of caregiver treatment compliance and give too little attention to family functioning and other indicators of child safety.

In an investigation with related findings, researchers studied an urban sample of children following an initial CPS report of maltreatment. All the children in the sample were living in families that received public assistance. Those in families that also received Medicaid-funded substance abuse or mental health services before the first CPS report were about 50 percent more likely to have a subsequent maltreatment report within seven years than were children in families that had not received the services. The study findings suggest an increased risk of maltreatment among families with substance abuse or mental health problems even when compared with other families involved with child welfare services. The findings also raise questions about the effectiveness of substance abuse and mental health services in preventing child maltreatment.

An evaluation of a treatment service program for women who used drugs during pregnancy lends support to the argument that treatment compliance, per se, may not be enough to promote child safety. The evaluation found that program attendance was not related to subsequent maltreatment reports—mothers who attended more sessions were about as likely to have subsequent maltreatment reports as mothers who attended fewer sessions—but completion of treatment goals reduced chances of a subsequent report. That is, mothers who attained treatment goals were less likely than those who simply attended treatment sessions to have a subsequent maltreatment report. The authors argue that full and "genuine" engagement in treatment may be associated with child safety.

Uncertainties about whether substance abuse treatment services can prevent subsequent maltreatment are also reinforced by a series of studies using data from the National Study of Child and Adolescent Well-Being (NSCAW) involving children reported to CPS who remained at home. Aware that the apparent benefits of treatment can often reflect the characteristics of the clients who access, enter, and attend treatment rather than the net effects of the services received, researchers matched caregivers according to characteristics that indicated a need for substance abuse treatment using propensity score methods. Among in-home caregivers matched on need for treatment, those who received treatment services were more likely than those who did not to incur a subsequent maltreatment report within the next eighteen months. In addition, children of the in-home caregivers who received treatment had lower well-being scores than children of caregivers who did not receive treatment. Questions raised by such perplexing findings are further discussed below.

Do Substance Abuse Interventions Promote Family Reunification?

Failure to engage parents in drug recovery services or to prevent the recurrence of maltreatment will usually precipitate the children's removal from parental custody and placement into foster care. In these circumstances, attention turns to encouraging or compelling parents to attain sobriety or total abstinence so that the children can safely be restored to their care. The shock of child removal is thought to provide a sufficient incentive for parents to engage in treatment to avoid permanent separation from their children through continued state custody or termination of parental rights.

A statewide long-term study of substance-abusing mothers in Oregon found that the more quickly mothers entered treatment and the more time they spent in treatment, the fewer days their children spent in foster care. Also, children of mothers who completed at least one treatment episode were more likely to be reunified with their parents than were children whose mothers did not complete treatment.

In an effort to boost reunification rates among children taken from substance-involved parents, the Illinois Department of Children and Family Services secured federal permission to fund a randomized controlled trial of a state-funded enhanced services program that previous quasi-experimental findings suggested showed promise. The Illinois demonstration was initially implemented in Cook County (which includes the city of Chicago) in April 2000. The demonstration randomly assigned Illinois Performance-Based Contracting agencies to treatment and comparison conditions. Parents were referred on a rotational basis to these agencies and subsequently screened for drug abuse problems. Eligible parents assigned to the comparison condition received the standard substance abuse services. Those assigned to the treatment condition received the standard services plus a package of enhanced services coordinated by a "recovery coach." The recovery coach worked with the parents, child welfare caseworker, and AODA treatment agency to remove barriers to drug treatment, engage the parents in services, provide outreach to re-engage the parent if necessary, and provide ongoing support to the parent and family throughout the permanency planning process.

The final results from the independent evaluation showed that assignment of a recovery coach only marginally increased parental participation in drug treatment (84 percent versus 77 percent, not significant) but that 43 percent of the treatment group managed to complete at least one level of treatment compared with 23 percent of caregivers in the comparison group. The higher rate of completion in the treatment group helped to boost the difference in reunification rates between the treatment and comparison groups by a small but statistically significant difference of 3.9 percentage points (15.5 percent versus 11.6 percent). Although this difference was compelling enough for federal officials to grant Illinois a five-year extension to expand the demonstration to downstate regions, the failure of the sizable difference in treatment completion rates to carry over to a larger difference in reunification rates prompted a closer look at some possible explanations for the shortfall.

An investigation by Jeanne Marsh and several colleagues found that although completing at least one level of treatment helped to boost reunification rates, only 18 percent of participants in the Illinois demonstration completed all levels of treatment. Furthermore, besides substance abuse, participants faced other serious problems, such as domestic violence, housing, and mental illness. Only 8 percent of participants had no other problem besides substance abuse; 30 percent had at least one other problem; 35 percent had two other problems; and 27 percent had three or more. Parents whose only problem was substance abuse achieved a 21 percent reunification rate, while parents with one or more other problems achieved only an 11 percent rate. Reunification rates were highest among the 5 percent of participants who completed mental health treatment (41 percent) and next highest among the 10 percent of participants who solved their housing problems (12 percent). Of the 18 percent of participants who completed all levels of drug treatment, only 25 percent regained custody of their children. The authors concluded that a service integration model designed to increase access to substance abuse treatment will not successfully promote reunification unless outreach and retention services can ensure client progress in the three co-occurring problem areas as well as in completing substance abuse treatment.

In another area, preventing subsequent substance-exposed infant (SEI) reports, assignment of a recovery coach was linked with a reduced likelihood of recurrence. At baseline, 69 percent of parents randomly assigned to the treatment group had previously delivered an infant reported for intrauterine substance exposure compared with 70 percent in the comparison group. After at least eighteen months of follow-up, 21 percent of parents assigned to the comparison group experienced a subsequent SEI report compared with 15 percent in the treatment group. Prior SEI reports were most strongly associated with the hazards of subsequent SEI reports. Parents with prior SEI reports were seven times more likely than those without reports to experience the birth of a child reported for intrauterine substance exposure. Parents randomly assigned to the comparison group were 1.4 times more likely than those assigned to the recovery coach treatment to have a subsequent SEI report. Despite the lowered risk in the treatment group, the fact that 15 percent of mothers assigned a recovery coach experienced a subsequent SEI report further compounds the permanency planning dilemma—whether to continue investing in the uncertain outcomes of drug recovery and family reunification or to cut the process short by terminating parental rights and proceeding with adoption or other

Figure 1

Birth Cohorts of Substance-Exposed Infant (SEI) Reports, Indicated Reports, Protective Custody Taken, and Foster Care Placements per Thousand Births in Illinois, Fiscal Years 1985–2007

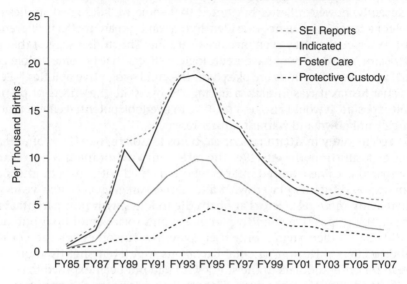

planned permanency arrangements such as legal guardianship and long-term placement with extended kin. . . .

Might Other Interventions Better Address the Risk of Child Maltreatment?

In the spring of 2008, the *Chicago Tribune* ran a story about a recent graduate of Morehouse College under the headline: "Proof Positive of Flawed Data." It told the story of a Rhodes Scholarship finalist who was born substance-exposed at the start of the SEI epidemic in Chicago in 1986, "among a wave of inner-city babies exposed to crack in their mother's womb, children written off by much of society as a lost generation doomed to failure." The article asserted that the drug panic was fueled by flawed data that warned of neurologically damaged and socially handicapped children that would soon flood the nation's schools and, later on, its prisons.

More recent opinion has backed away from such dire predictions. Much of the earlier work failed to consider the myriad of adverse social, environmental, and other factors that confound the association between parental substance use and impaired childhood growth and development. Barry Lester was among the first researchers to note that early studies of substance-exposed infants over-estimated the effects of cocaine exposure by attributing to cocaine adverse effects that were probably related to other influences such as multiple-drug use, poverty, or cigarette smoking. The challenges associated with identifying specific effects of prenatal cocaine exposure, along with the wide-ranging findings of research on the topic, led a group of leading researchers, including Lester, to argue publicly that no particular set of symptoms supports the popular notion of a "crack baby" syndrome. They asked the media to stop using the stigmatizing term.

Recently, however, Lester has noted that some well-designed studies that control for a range of influences are identifying some apparent effects of prenatal cocaine exposure that may even increase over time. The studies suggest that prenatal cocaine exposure may have neurological effects that become visible only when "higher level demands are placed on the child's cognitive abilities." Lester argues that just as it was initially a mistake to overstate the effects of prenatal cocaine exposure, it would also be a mistake to overlook potential effects that are still largely unknown and warrant further research.

A recent study in Atlanta, Georgia, helps to isolate the effects of prenatal cocaine exposure from the effects of the caregiving environment. The researchers compared cocaine-exposed infants who remained with their mothers and cocaine-exposed infants placed with alternative caregivers. At two years old, despite having more risk factors at birth, the toddlers with non-parental caregivers had more positive cognitive-language and social-emotional outcomes than did the toddlers living with their parents. Outcomes for the cocaine-exposed toddlers with non-parental caregivers were even slightly more positive than for other toddlers in the study who had not been exposed to cocaine and remained with their mothers. The results underscore the importance of a nurturing caregiving environment for children's well-being and illustrate that efforts to identify and isolate effects of prenatal cocaine exposure must account for the caregiving context.

In the absence of a definitive link between intrauterine substance exposure and developmental harm, it is difficult to justify categorizing such exposure as a form of child abuse and neglect in its own right. At the same time, it would be imprudent to back off entirely from drug screening at birth. Although some of the higher association of intrauterine substance exposure with subsequent maltreatment is clearly self-referential—that is, drug addicts are more likely to be indicated for future child maltreatment than non-addicts simply because ingestion of illicit substances during pregnancy is itself a reportable allegation—an indicated SEI report is still a useful marker of future risk. SEI reports are correlated with mental illness, domestic violence, poverty, homelessness, and other disadvantages that may be more directly associated with child maltreatment. The major inadequacy with existing hospital surveillance practices is that screening is done selectively in such a way that puts African American infants at disproportionate risk of CPS detection and involvement.

Universal screening of all births for substance exposure may be one way to address the inequities in the current process, but targeting illicit substances for special attention may serve only to reify the belief that drug treatment, recovery, and abstinence mark out the best route for ensuring child safety and justifying family reunification. Attending to this one visible manifestation of an underlying complex of family and personal problems can give the false impression that complying with treatment regimes and demonstrating prolonged abstinence are sufficient for deciding when to move forward with reunification plans. But the best evidence to date suggests that successful completion of drug treatment is no better a predictor of future maltreatment risk than non-completion. Caseworkers and judges seem to have learned this lesson from their own experience because only one-quarter of participants who successfully completed drug treatment in the Illinois AODA demonstration were eventually reunified with their children.

Conversely, parental failures to comply with treatment plans and to demonstrate abstinence may be imperfect indicators of their capacity to parent their children at a minimally adequate level. The best evidence to date suggests that parents of substance-exposed infants pose no greater risk to the safety of their children than parents of other children taken into child protective custody. Caseworkers and judges may thus want to consider implementing reunification plans some time after parents engage successfully in treatment but before they demonstrate total abstinence from future drug use. Perhaps the best course of action is to take the spotlight off of parental drug abuse and treatment completion and shine it instead on other co-factors, such as mental illness, domestic violence, and homelessness, that may be more directly implicated in causing harm to a child. A shift of attention from substance abuse to other risk factors could have the additional benefit of reducing stigma and the conflict parents may face if they fear that admitting substance abuse or asking for help with an addiction will lead to loss of child custody.

Although clearly more can be done to improve the integration of services to address the myriad of family and personal problems, such as mental illness, domestic violence, and homelessness, that, along with substance abuse, impair parenting, at some point in the intervention process attention needs to turn to the permanency needs and well-being of the child. Even though the young man profiled in the *Chicago Tribune* story was one of the 50 percent of substance-exposed infants who were never taken into foster care, by his own account life was not easy for him: "Mom would get drunk and hit me. I had to call the cops and send her to the drunk tank a couple of times." Things finally turned around when his aunt, a Chicago Public Schools administrator, took him into her home at age fourteen: "My aunt's house was a place of peace. She gave me a place that allowed me to grow. She had books everywhere, even in the bathroom."

Both personal accounts and the best research evidence indicate that finding a safe and lasting home for children born substance-exposed is critical to their healthy development and well-being. As of December 2007, however, only 39 percent of children assigned to the treatment group under the Illinois AODA demonstration had exited from foster care, compared with 36 percent in the comparison group. Not only does this small, albeit statistically significant, difference raise concerns about the advisability of heavily investing in recovery coach services, it raises additional questions about the permanency needs of the remaining 61 to 64 percent of drug-involved children who are still in foster care. Because the average age of children born substance-exposed who are removed from parental custody is less than three, it should not be too challenging to find them permanent homes with relatives either as guardians or as adoptive parents or with foster parents who are willing to become their adoptive parents. Although it is unwise to set too firm guidelines, it strikes us as sensible to set a six-month timetable for parents to engage in treatment and twelve to eighteen months to show sufficient progress in all identified problem areas (presuming that both engagement and progress are determined with fair and valid measures). Thereafter, permanency plans should be expedited to place the child under the permanent guardianship of a relative caregiver or in the adoptive home of a relative, foster parent, or other suitable family. As regards the birth of another substance-exposed infant, it seems reasonable, assuming the availability of services, to initiate alternative permanency plans for all of the children unless the parent demonstrates sufficient progress in all problem areas within six months of the latest child's birth.

In light of the difficulty of isolating the direct effects of prenatal substance abuse and the most recent evidence that some detrimental effects of intrauterine substance exposure on child development may increase over time, the newest empirical findings on the efficacy of Illinois' recovery coach model in decreasing births of substance-exposed infants helps to bolster the case for improved treatment and service coordination regardless of whether intrauterine substance exposure is considered a form of child maltreatment in its own right. Preventing another potential risk to future child well-being, even if parental substance abuse and intrauterine substance exposure prove not to be determinative of child maltreatment directly, seems well worth the cost of investing in parental recovery from substance abuse and dependence. Such efforts, however, should not substitute for a comprehensive approach that addresses the myriad of social and economic risks to child well-being beyond the harms associated with parental substance abuse.

Jeanne Flavin and
Lynn M. Paltrow

Punishing Pregnant Drug-Using Women: Defying Law, Medicine, and Common Sense

Introduction

No human being, not even a parent or a twin, is required to sacrifice his or her life or health for the benefit of another individual. Although the state may require sacrifices for the benefit of the community at large (e.g., vaccinations), U.S. courts have steadfastly refused to use state power to weigh the value of two individual lives and require one person to sacrifice his or her life, health, or liberty for another. Nonetheless, claims made on behalf of individual fetuses have been used to justify deprivations of women's liberty, bodily integrity, and even their lives. Such actions reflect increasing and highly contested claims that not only does a fetus have "rights" that must be protected, but that these rights are superior to those of pregnant women and, for that matter, all human beings.

Significantly, these claims of fetal rights are often coupled with and strengthened by drug war propaganda which makes grossly exaggerated claims about the risks posed by prenatal exposure to certain substances. Indeed, the vast majority of punitive interventions based on claims of fetal rights involve the arrest and detention of pregnant women alleged to have used an illegal drug or alcohol. These cases assert that pregnant women are obliged to subordinate themselves to state claims of fetal rights. In addition, these cases reinforce false and misleading ideas about addiction and its treatment and the availability of appropriate health services.

The arrests and other punitive measures levied against pregnant drug-using women also serve a larger political purpose: they distract attention from significant social problems, such as our lack of universal health care, the dearth of policies to support pregnant and parenting women, the absence of social supports for children, and the overall failure of the drug war. Relying on punitive approaches undermines efforts to develop effective responses to the problematic aspects of drug use and pregnancy. In this article, we draw on information from hundreds of cases that National Advocates for Pregnant Women has compiled. We seek to expose some of the flawed premises on which these arrests, detentions, and prosecutions are based. In so doing, we highlight the injustice of expecting low-income and drug-dependent pregnant women to provide their fetuses with the health care and safety to which women themselves are not deemed to be entitled.

The Panic Over Drug-Dependent Women and Their Pregnancies

The fear-mongering tenor of discourse surrounding women's drug use cannot be justified by women's rates of illicit drug use, drinking, and smoking. Most women in the United States use some type of drug on a regular basis. We use prescription and over-the-counter drugs to help us sleep, stay awake, alleviate pain, lose weight, cope with depression and anxiety, and so forth. We drink coffee and tea and eat chocolate, all substances that contain caffeine. We consume alcoholic beverages, and we smoke cigarettes. However, when we think of "women and drugs" what comes to mind are users of illegal drugs even though fewer than 1 in 10 women and only approximately 4 in 100 pregnant women use illicit drugs and even fewer are dependent on them.

The drug war of the 1980s and 1990s included women who used illicit drugs among its targets. A national panic ensued over "crack mothers" giving birth to "crack babies." Women who used illicit drugs (including marijuana, heroin, and methamphetamine, but particularly cocaine) were portrayed as hypersexual, out-of-control women who would "do anything" for drugs. They were characterized as being completely indifferent to any harm they might cause to themselves or others, especially the children they would give birth to. At a time when evidence existed that there was no such thing as "crack babies" and that poverty explained many of the health problems that some children were experiencing, *Time* magazine, the *New York Times,* and other leading news outlets continued to describe cocaine use during pregnancy as an epidemic destroying a generation of young people. Even respected organizations such as Columbia University's Center on Addiction and Substance Abuse discussed the exposure of newborns to alcohol and cocaine in extraordinarily exaggerated and unjustified terms, describing it as "a slaughter of innocents of biblical proportions."

As a consequence of this moral panic surrounding women using drugs, thousands of women were and continue to be ensnared in the criminal justice system for non-violent offenses related to their use of illegal drugs; hundreds more have been singled out specifically for being pregnant and using an illegal drug or alcohol.

Consider the case of Cornelia Whitner. On April 7, 1992, Cornelia Whitner was indicted for violating South Carolina's criminal child neglect statute for her alleged unlawful neglect of a "child." Ms. Whitner, an African American woman, was born and raised in South Carolina. At the age of 14, her mother suddenly died, an event which Ms. Whitner described as the worst thing that ever happened to her. After her mother's death, Ms. Whitner dropped out of school and started smoking pot and drinking. By age 15, she was pregnant with the first of her three children. Her youngest child, Tevin, was born in good health on February 2, 1992. When a test indicated that Tevin had been exposed prenatally to cocaine, Ms. Whitner was arrested and charged with criminal child neglect, even though she was not accused of actually abusing or endangering Tevin. Instead, the prosecutors introduced a new interpretation of an existing child neglect statute, asserting that the statute also criminalized a woman's failure "to provide proper medical care for her unborn child."

Like virtually all women who have been prosecuted under similar circumstances, Ms. Whitner could not afford private counsel. Instead, she was represented by a court-appointed attorney who did not meet with her until the day of her scheduled court hearing. Her defense attorney had recently worked in the prosecutor's office, where she had previously prosecuted pregnant addicted women.

Ms. Whitner was never counseled about her substance abuse problem nor was she offered drug treatment as a way of avoiding arrest. When she was indicted, there was not a single residential drug treatment program in the entire state designed to treat pregnant drug users. Believing that an admission of guilt would help her get access to inpatient treatment, Ms. Whitner pled guilty to the charge of child abuse. At her sentencing hearing, she admitted that she was chemically dependent and requested assistance from the court, stating in part "I need some help, Your Honor." She stressed her need and desire for inpatient treatment. The judge responded, "I think I'll just let her go to jail." The court then sentenced Ms. Whitner to 8 years in prison. Although another court later ruled that there was no basis for the conviction, the South Carolina Supreme reversed that decision, effectively rewriting state law to make the word "child" in the state's child endangerment statute include a viable fetus.

The panic over women's use of cocaine abated somewhat in the late 1990s. Today, leading federal government agencies confirm that "the phenomena of 'crack babies'. . . is essentially a myth."As the National Institute for Drug Abuse has reported, "Many recall that 'crack babies,' or babies born to mothers who used crack cocaine while pregnant, were at one time written off by many as a lost generation. . . . It was later found that this was a gross exaggeration." The U.S. Sentencing Commission concluded: "[t]he negative effects of prenatal cocaine exposure are significantly less severe than previously believed" and those negative effects "do not differ from the effects of prenatal exposure to other drugs, both legal and illegal."

Nevertheless, in recent years, we have witnessed the reanimation of deeply rooted prejudice against women who use drugs, again targeting those who are pregnant and continue to term. National Advocates for Pregnant Women has and documented hundreds of known cases in at least 40 states where pregnant women who are identified as drug users have been arrested; dozens of known arrests came to light in 2005 and 2006 alone. Our analysis shows that the brunt of the criminal justice system's intrusions into women's pregnancies has been borne by low-income minority women.

White, Black, and Hispanic women have comparable rates of drug use and substance dependence; the percent of White, Black, and Hispanic women in metropolitan areas who have used an illicit drug in the past month is 8.6%, 8.4%, and 5.6%, respectively. However, a 1992 survey of arrests and prosecutions of pregnant women found overwhelming evidence that low-income Black and Hispanic women were singled out. An analysis of more recent cases is underway; the evidence so far suggests ongoing racial bias and an undeniable focus on low-income women.

In addition to racial and class bias, the uncritical acceptance of medical misinformation about drugs and the stereotyping of the people who use them are being revisited today in the metham-phetamine scare. Concern about metham-phetamine has jumped to the fore much like concern about crack cocaine did in the 1980s. For example, in April 2004 Theresa Lee Hernandez of Oklahoma was charged with first degree murder despite community opposition to her prosecution. The state claimed that the stillbirth that Ms. Hernandez had suffered was caused by her use of methamphetamine, even though research has not found an association between methamphetamine use and stillbirths. In 2007, Ms. Hernandez plead guilty to second degree murder rather than risk a trial by jury and a life sentence. Ms. Hernandez was sentenced to 15 years in prison. In an apparent response to extensive community education and opposition to the arrest and prosecution, Ms. Hernandez was released a year after being sentenced.

Is current media coverage of women's illicit drug use and drug dependency as sensational as it was in the late 1980s and 1990s? On one hand, leading researchers and medical professionals themselves have insisted that media coverage about drugs and pregnancy be grounded in science, not sensation, asking that experts (rather than the local pediatrician or the local sheriff) are given the opportunity to address what, if any, risks have been linked to prenatal exposure to cocaine, methamphetamine and other drugs. On the other hand, the public is still fed a regular diet of accounts that distort and misrepresent the effects of illicit drug use (including presenting the effects of drug use on populations of mice as if they are applicable to humans), rely on non-experts, and demonize the people who use illicit drugs. Popular media accounts continue to falsely decry an "epidemic" and a "scourge" of drug use despite evidence that rates of methamphetamine use have stabilized since 1999 and have been declining since 2002. Many reports play on exaggerated fears about the impact and addictiveness of methamphetamine and wrongly assert that we lack any effective treatments for methamphetamine addiction.

The front page story of the July 11, 2005, *New York Times*, "A Drug Scourge Creates its Own Form of Orphan," typifies the problematic ways in which women who use illicit drugs are presented to the public, as well as the biases found among workers in the helping professions. As with earlier media coverage of the crack epidemic, the story discussed methamphetamine's "highly sexualized" users and depicted the "children of methamphetamine" as lost causes "with so many behavioral problems." The article twice mentioned that some of the children had lice. The article's sources were harried social workers, a lawyer for a department of human services, a pediatrician involved in a state program that was run in conjunction with the Department of Justice, and other professionals with a stake in convincing the public of the gravity of the methamphetamine "scourge." Not one parent was quoted nor were any researchers actually qualified to express an opinion about the effects of prenatal exposure or trends in methamphetamine use, as distinct from trends in child welfare system intervention. The article's sources provided opinions that fell outside their areas of expertise (i.e., a pediatrician's "professional" opinion that "The parents are basically worthless"). A state attorney general urged an audience of hundreds to become foster parents, "Because we're just seeing so many kids being taken from these homes." The article never questioned whether taking so many children away from their parents and their homes was justified or even in the best interests of the children. The National Coalition for Child Protection Reform and others convincingly conclude that it is not.

The Problems with Punishment

The misinformed public, of course, includes not only journalists, but also police and prosecutors. Operating under false assumptions that a woman's drug dependency is inevitably and irreversibly harming her future child, police and prosecutors have persisted in arresting and pursuing charges against pregnant women. They typically claim that prosecution (or the threat of prosecution) is an effective tool in deterring pregnant women from using drugs, and that it is a useful device for forcing women to get treatment they would otherwise avoid. In reality, these measures are more likely to deter women from seeking prenatal care or from being completely forthcoming with their health care providers.

Achieving total abstinence from drugs when one is addicted to them is generally a difficult and long-term process that is unlikely to occur in the relatively short term of a pregnancy. If a woman who is already addicted to drugs becomes pregnant and is not able to completely abstain from using drugs, the only way she can be assured of avoiding criminal charges for such crimes as child abuse, drug delivery to minors, and homicide is to get an abortion. Even though proponents of arrests and prosecution articulate the problem as one of a woman who uses drugs while she is pregnant, their perspective is more accurately characterized as an objection to a woman becoming and remaining pregnant.

In another South Carolina case, a woman was charged with and convicted of homicide by child abuse based on the claim that she suffered an unintentional stillbirth as a result of her cocaine use. Despite the medical evidence that Regina McKnight's pregnancy loss was the result of an infection and research studies finding no link between cocaine use and an increased incidence of stillbirths, Ms. McKnight was convicted and given a 20-year sentence that was reduced to 12-years incarceration. If she had had an early abortion, there would have been no crime. Even if she had intentionally ended her pregnancy through an illegal third-trimester abortion she would have received, at most, a 3-year sentence.

After having served almost 8 years, Ms. McKnight's conviction was finally overturned. As a result of ongoing post-conviction relief efforts, the court was finally persuaded that the conviction was based on inaccurate science. The Court ruled that Ms. McKnight had not received a fair trial and that her trial counsel was "ineffective in her preparation of McKnight's defense through expert testimony and cross-examination." Specifically, the court noted that the research the state relied on was "outdated" and that trial counsel failed to call experts who would have testified about "recent studies showing that cocaine is no more harmful to a fetus than nicotine use, poor nutrition, lack of prenatal care, or other conditions commonly associated with the urban poor." However, to avoid a re-trial and a lengthy legal battle, Ms. McKnight plead guilty to manslaughter, permitting her release from prison and removing the threat of reincarceration.

In our ongoing review of this and similar cases, we find that women are often charged with felonies, including murder or manslaughter, child abuse or neglect, and drug delivery (through the umbilical cord) and drug possession, based on evidence of pregnancy and drug use. Women have been sentenced to incarceration or given probation with numerous and sometimes impossible conditions imposed for many years.

Brenda Vaughan, a 30-year-old African American woman from Temple Hills, Maryland, pleaded guilty to felony charges for forging $721.98 in checks. The prosecutor recommended that Ms. Vaughan receive probation instead of jail time. During her sentencing hearing, Ms. Vaughan told the judge she was pregnant. The judge then ordered a drug test. When Ms. Vaughan tested positive, allegedly for cocaine, the judge ordered her to jail for 30 days, pending a decision on whether to admit her to a special intensive probation program. When it turned out that she was not eligible for the intensified probation program because she was not a District of Columbia resident, the judge sentenced her to 6 more months in jail, subject to a motion to reduce the sentence after the baby was born. At her sentencing hearing, the judge explained: "I'm going to keep her locked up until the baby is born because she's tested positive for cocaine when she came before me. . . . She's apparently an addictive personality and I'll be darned if I'm going to have a baby born that way." The judge added, "I can't trust you, Ms. Vaughan, and that's a hell of a thing to say". There was no trial or conviction on any charge relating to possession or use of an illegal drug. As noted previously, in many cases women have pleaded guilty or accepted plea bargains rather than risk a protracted legal challenge that could result in an even longer period of incarceration.

When the arrests, detentions, and prosecutions of women have been challenged, they are nearly always found, eventually, to be without legal basis or to be unconstitutional. There has been near unanimity among the country's appellate courts; all but one have dismissed charges or overturned convictions of women who used drugs or experienced an addiction and sought to continue their pregnancies to term. Courts faced with challenges to such prosecutions have routinely ruled that a plain reading of the applicable criminal statute and the absence of legislative intent to address the issue of drug using pregnant women through the criminal justice system require that the charges be dropped. Many of these courts have recognized that the application of existing criminal laws (such as those prohibiting child abuse, drug delivery, and homicide) to pregnant women in relationship to the fetuses they carry raises significant constitutional issues, including due process principles of notice, vagueness, and overbreadth, as well as privacy and sex discrimination. Numerous courts have also acknowledged the extraordinary consensus among medical groups condemning these prosecutions as counterproductive and dangerous. That is why the Supreme Court of Florida, in overturning Jennifer Johnson's conviction for drug delivery, declared: "The Court declines the State's invitation to walk down a path that the law, public policy, reason and common sense forbid it to tread."

In addition to state appellate courts, in 2001 the U.S. Supreme Court, in a landmark decision, held that health care providers who secretly search pregnant women for evidence of drug use and turn that information over to the police are violating the 4th Amendment's prohibition on illegal searches and seizures and may be held personally liable for such actions. In reaching this conclusion, the Court observed that the numerous *amici* in the case pointed to "a near consensus in the medical community that programs of the sort at issue, by discouraging women who use drugs from seeking prenatal care, harm, rather than advance, the cause of prenatal health."

In the remainder of this article, we propose three principles that should guide our responses to pregnant drug-using women: (1) rely on the best available research and the principles of evidence-based medicine and social science rather than flawed assumptions about drug use by pregnant women and its effects; (2) distinguish, as we do with alcohol, between use and addiction and recognize that drug addiction is a chronic, relapsing health condition rather than a crime; and (3) provide support for low-income pregnant women rather than rely on policing and punishment.

Rely on Science Rather Than Sensation About Maternal Drug Use

If a child is born prematurely or has a low birthweight or if a woman miscarries or delivers a stillborn baby, many hospital staff, medical examiners, social workers, and other officials blame the woman for the outcome. This is especially true if a woman has ingested any amount of an illegal drug, used too much alcohol, or in some way, such as by her race, class, or personality, offended the hospital or agency staff or officials. Also, some health care providers see drug testing as part of defensive medicine. That is, if something has gone wrong with the birth raising the specter of a lawsuit, a positive drug test provides staff with a powerful defense regardless of what actually caused the bad birth outcome.

The use of methamphetamine, cocaine, and other illicit drugs certainly presents a valid public health concern. But medical and scientific evidence suggests that the harms associated with illicit drug use have been greatly overstated. In contrast, not only are alcohol and tobacco more widely used, but the evidence of potential harm to fetuses and children from tobacco use and heavy alcohol use are far better established as a matter of scientific research. However, our harshest responses have been reserved for those women who consume illicit drugs.

The relationship between using a substance and fetal or infant health is not straightforward. Although a correlation may exist between the use of some substances (and some medical conditions) and some pregnancy outcomes, a causal relationship does not necessarily exist. For example, two well-constructed, independent studies tried to determine whether cocaine could be linked to an increased risk of stillbirths. The authors found that it could not. A recent article published in the peer-reviewed *American Journal of Obstetrics and Gynecology* concluded that "despite widespread reports linking methamphetamine use during pregnancy with preterm birth and growth restriction, *evidence confirming its association with an increased risk of stillbirth remains lacking."* Most pregnant women who use substances such as cocaine, methamphetamine, nicotine, caffeine, or alcohol will give birth to healthy babies. Additionally, most pregnancy losses and other negative birth outcomes cannot be traced solely, or even mainly, to the use of an illicit substance, especially when it is likely that substance use is accompanied by other risk factors such as violence, heavy alcohol consumption, cigarette smoking, the use of prescription drugs, poverty, and environmental risks.

The best available medical evidence indicates that the use of illicit drugs and other substances is but one of many other factors which may affect pregnancy outcome. Recognizing this, a wide spectrum of respected medical and public health organizations, including the American Medical Association, the American Society of Addiction Medicine, the American Public Health Association, the American College of Physicians, the American College of Obstetricians and Gynecologists, the American Academy of Pediatrics, the March of Dimes, and the National Council on Alcoholism and Drug Dependence, have voiced their opposition to the arrests and prosecutions of pregnant women who use illicit drugs.

Treat Addiction as a Public Health Concern, Not a Crime

Being pregnant is not a crime, nor is being addicted to an illicit substance, as the Supreme Court held in the 1962 case, *Robinson v. California.* Because of the very nature of addiction and dependency, not every person who uses a substance "chooses" or "intends" to continue to use it or can even be said to be indifferent to its consequences. Prolonged drug use can cause dramatic changes in brain function, making it difficult for people to overcome drug dependence on their own without treatment. The National Institute on Drug Abuse (which, in 2007, began to consider a name change to "The National Institute of Diseases of Addiction") defines addiction as "a chronic, relapsing brain disease that is characterized by compulsive drug seeking and use, despite harmful consequences." The American Psychiatric Association's *Diagnostic and Statistical Manual of Mental Disorders* (DSM-IV) recognizes that an "inability to control drug use" is often a key feature of chemical dependency.

Women's attempts to cease using drugs completely during pregnancy are common. Indeed, pregnancy and motherhood have been identified as catalysts for change among women who use drugs. Although many women can and do stop or reduce their consumption and tolerance of potentially harmful substances while they are pregnant, permanent abstinence is no more attainable for low-income pregnant women than it is for other people, including affluent White men, such as conservative shock jock Rush

Limbaugh. Wanting or intending to stop is an important element of recovery, but the physical, behavioral, and social aspects of dependence are such that it is rarely sufficient.

A woman's continued drug use should not be assumed to reflect a lack of desire to quit using drugs. Along similar lines, women who do not receive treatment for drug dependence cannot be assumed to have rejected treatment. In a country where 47 million people have no health insurance coverage, where most private insurance programs offer limited coverage for the expenses of mental health and drug treatment services, where state and federal funding for such programs is exceedingly limited, and where the most successful treatment modalities (such as methadone treatment) are deliberately limited, it is simply wrong to assume that lack of treatment is a question of personal intention or desire. Many pregnant women do not enter drug treatment because they cannot afford to, there are no spaces available, or the programs do not provide childcare or account for the fact that most women have family responsibilities. A 1993 study of 294 drug treatment programs in five major cities showed that, although most programs accepted pregnant women on some basis, the method of payment accepted and the availability of child care significantly limited access. Only 55% of residential/detoxification programs accepted pregnant women on Medicaid or for free. Only one-fifth of all programs accepted pregnant women *and* provided child care, even though past research has found that lack of child care precludes addicted women's participation in treatment. A survey conducted in 2007 found that only 19 states have created drug treatment programs specifically for pregnant women, and only seven states give pregnant women priority access to state-funded drug treatment programs. Even in these states, the demand exceeds the number of available spaces in treatment programs. Moreover, programs touted as allowing women to bring their children typically limit the number and age of the children. This means that many women must separate from their family to get help. Also, while there is strong evidence that treatment for drug addiction is as effective, if not more effective, than treatment for other chronic relapsing conditions such as diabetes mellitus, asthma, and high blood pressure, treatment often fails patients. As a result, it is inappropriate to assume that simply entering treatment will be sufficient to "cure" a woman of her dependency on drugs.

Women who *do* enter treatment are not necessarily insulated from inappropriate or punitive state responses. For example, women already in treatment became the subject of a South Carolina prosecutor's decision to seek out and punish pregnant drug-using women. National Advocates for Pregnant Women also has documented several cases in which women who were in successful methadone treatment programs became targets of child welfare interventions to remove the child at birth because of a belief that the methadone treatment proved that they had once been drug users and therefore posed a threat to their children.

Incarcerating pregnant women to "protect the fetus" is based on similarly false assumptions that jails and prisons consistently offer high-quality prenatal care programs, nutritional diets, and reproductive health care. Although pregnancy receives more attention than most other health concerns of incarcerated women, the quality of incarcerated women's care before, during, and after delivery typically leaves much to be desired. Incarcerated women routinely receive little to no education about prenatal care and nutrition, do not receive regular pelvic exams or sonograms, and cannot alter their diets to meet their changing caloric needs. Prison medical staff and administrators may ignore orders from outside OB/GYNs. In most states, pregnant women, even those who pose no security risk, may be shackled or otherwise restrained during transport to the hospital and during labor and delivery.

As we should have learned from the crack panic, the distrust that stigma and prejudice engender among drug-using women may pose greater dangers to maternal and fetal health than the use of an illicit drug itself. Reporting pregnant women to child protection agencies and the police or locking them up in the name of "protecting the fetus" can be expected to have a chilling impact on women's willingness to seek care and on physicians' relationships with their patients. Health care workers and hospital social workers, in particular, should play important roles in finding out from the women what services and support they need and, when appropriate, securing drug treatment for women who are addicted to drugs. Frequently, however, a hospital worker's report of a pregnant woman's drug use leads, directly or indirectly, to the mobilization of the criminal justice system and highly intrusive interventions by child welfare authorities.

Pregnant women's fears of being judged by those who are assigned with helping them are not without foundation. Survey results suggest a sizable proportion of hospital medical staff and social workers already support defining illicit drug use as "child abuse" and coercive approaches to addressing a woman's drug use (e.g., incarceration or threatening women with loss of custody of their children to "encourage" them to complete drug treatment). At the same time, some health care providers may refrain from asking women in their care about drug use for fear they will have to turn their patients over to punitive state authorities.

As the AMA notes: "punishing a person who abuses drugs or alcohol is not generally an effective way of curing their dependency or preventing future abuse." Furthermore, intimidation and punitive measures are far more likely to deter women from seeking help than from using the drugs upon which they have become dependent. On a strictly pragmatic level, by the time a pregnant woman has experienced a stillbirth or a baby is born testing positive for an illicit substance, valuable opportunities have been missed to provide a woman with support and access to good quality health care, including drug treatment.

Support Low-Income Pregnant Women Rather Than Infringe Upon Their Civil and Human Rights

Mobilizing the criminal justice system to address a health concern creates a precedent for the supervision and punishment of pregnant women with regard to all aspects of their lives. In Maryland, two women were convicted of reckless endangerment and sentenced to several years in prison for continuing their pregnancies to term and using cocaine during pregnancy, and three other women faced similar charges. The Maryland Court of Appeals ruled, however, that prosecution of such cases might open the way for pregnant women to be prosecuted for any number of injury-prone activities that might endanger the well-being of an unborn child, such as driving without a seatbelt, skiing, or horseback riding. This ruling, like others before it, is a strong and important recognition of the larger issues of pregnant women's civil and human rights beyond the issue of drug use and addiction. Indeed, the fact that the same legal arguments used to justify the prosecution of pregnant drug and alcohol using women have been used to justify court ordered interventions and arrests of women who do not accede to doctor's advice regarding childbirth makes clear that concerns about the application of fetal homicide laws to drug-dependent pregnant women are not speculative.

Court decisions and statutes creating the crime of feticide and unborn victims of violence laws have directly and indirectly become grounds for arresting pregnant drug-using women. In the *Whitner* case mentioned earlier in this article, the state argued that there was precedent for prosecuting Cornelia Whitner for child abuse. That precedent was a case where a man, Home, brutally stabbed his pregnant wife, causing her to lose the pregnancy. The South Carolina Supreme Court created the crime of feticide in response. *Whitner* argued that experiencing an addiction as a pregnant woman is not the same as a third party attacking a pregnant woman. The court disagreed, stating that if they ruled that way "there would be no basis for prosecuting a mother who kills her viable fetus by stabbing it, by shooting it, or by other such means, yet a third party could be prosecuted for the very same acts. We decline to read *Home* in a way that insulates the mother from all culpability for harm to her viable child."

The court's reasoning ignores the bald reality that in order to shoot or stab her fetus, the pregnant woman would first have to cut through her own flesh, her own body. The court's rationale requires treating a pregnant woman as if on becoming pregnant she loses her humanity, her capacity to become psychologically and physically addicted like other human beings, her identity as a unique individual whose actions (including stabbing or shooting herself) have obviously different meanings and implications than when another person commits those actions against her.

This distinction has been ignored in states like Texas, where the Prenatal Protection Act (SB 319) was passed in 2003. This law established that for the purposes of murder and aggravated assault, a fetus is considered "an unborn child at every stage of gestation from conception to birth." The bill was ostensibly written to ensure criminal liability in the event of a crime against a pregnant woman that harmed or killed her fetus (e.g., a drunk-driving accident or an incident of domestic violence). The immediate and primary effect of that law, however, was the arrest and prosecution of more than 40 pregnant women and new mothers who were believed to have had drug problems while pregnant. Three weeks after the governor signed the bill into law, 47th District Attorney Rebecca King sent a letter to Potter County physicians informing them that under the Act, "it is now a legal requirement for anyone to report a pregnant woman who is using or has used illegal narcotics during her pregnancy." King reasoned that the new definition of "individual" directly affected the Controlled Substances Act, since the Penal Code provides punishment for "delivery" of narcotics to children, and now to fetuses. Although defense counsel and civil rights organizations were eventually able to overturn the convictions, women were imprisoned for years while a key case worked its way through the court system.

While court decisions overwhelmingly reject the expansion of criminal law as a tool for policing pregnant women and it is still true that, as of this writing, no state legislature has passed a law explicitly criminalizing pregnancy for drug users, many other kinds of laws and policies are being used to police and punish drug-using pregnant women. Take, for example, the Child Abuse Prevention and Treatment Act (CAPTA). In 2003, CAPTA was amended so that states could only receive federal funding under the act if they passed laws to require health care providers involved in the delivery and care of infants to report to child protective services infants "affected" by illegal substance use. The act excludes from consideration fetal alcohol effect or fetal alcohol syndrome.

Neither CAPTA nor any of the civil state reporting laws that pre-dated it mandate universal drug testing. In other words, who gets tested and identified as a drug user, and therefore, who gets reported to authorities is highly discretionary. Nor does CAPTA clearly define what is meant by "drug-affected," leaving states to decide for themselves the criteria health care providers will use to identify infants to be reported to child protective services. Some states require only an unconfirmed positive toxicology screen at birth, others require physical signs of addiction or dependence, and still others mandate an actual assessment of the newborn's imminent risk of harm or need for protection.

Although such reporting laws do not mandate that the information be turned over to the police, these laws typically do not prohibit it. As mentioned earlier, hospital workers (including medical staff and social workers) and child welfare workers, who are potentially best situated to provide important care and services to drug-dependent women, are often the very ones who contact law enforcement or who contact child welfare workers, who in turn notify the police. The result has been that many women who used illicit drugs while they were pregnant are being arrested, interrogated, detained, prosecuted, and punished rather than receiving the services and care they need. Punitive state authorities are willing to mobilize resources to punish and separate families but not to treat and support them.

Conclusion

That punitive measures taken under the auspices of protecting the fetus continue to appeal to the public is not surprising. People are genuinely and understandably concerned about the possibility of poor pregnancy outcomes, including sick babies and pregnancy loss. They are sincerely and justifiably interested in ensuring that pregnancies result in healthy babies. Opposing the punishment of pregnant women and the recognition of fetal rights distinct from the rights of pregnant women does not contradict any of these legitimate concerns nor does it deny the value of potential life as matter of religious belief, emotional conviction, or personal experience. Rather, it is to recognize that punitive approaches do not advance either maternal or fetal health, and that on becoming pregnant, women (including those who use drugs and alcohol) do not lose their civil and human rights.

Singling out pregnant women not only for arrest and prosecution, but also for court orders (through family courts and drug treatment courts) and civil commitments, contributes to a climate where pregnant women are increasingly seen as adversaries of the fetuses they carry rather than people who have a stake in a healthy pregnancy and a favorable outcome. There is no question that some people's drug use has become so chaotic and out of control that it can affect their parenting ability. No one is suggesting that such situations be ignored. Too often, however, a single, unconfirmed positive drug test is accepted as incontrovertible evidence of a woman's criminality or unfitness to parent. Rather than a thoughtful evaluation of whether drug use or any other factor has rendered someone incapable of parenting, a single positive drug test result becomes the basis for massive and often highly punitive state intrusions on family life.

Punitive actions against drug-using pregnant women persist even though they remain inconsistent with legal, medical, and public health standards of acceptable practice and even though they do not, in fact, advance maternal, fetal, or child health interests. Our knowledge of existing cases suggests that at some of the points at which a woman is most amenable to help or may benefit most from support (e.g., when she becomes pregnant or gives birth or when she is locked up), our official responses are the harshest and least effective.

This speaks to the need to overcome a national tendency to ignore evidence-based medicine and research and to pursue costly and counterproductive punitive state interventions. The harms to both health and human rights posed by institutionalizing coercive forms of state power are significant. Rather than continue to vilify pregnant women and exaggerate the harms of their drug use, research and experience support the provision of respectful, supportive services to all pregnant women and families who need it as the most effective way to encourage healthy pregnancies and birth outcomes.

POSTSCRIPT

Should Women Who Use Drugs Lose Custody of Their Children?

Babies born with health problems as a result of their mothers' drug use is a tragedy that needs to be rectified. The issue is not whether this problem needs to be addressed but what course of action is best. The need for medical intervention and specialized treatment programs serving pregnant women with drug problems has been recognized. The groundwork has been set for funding and developing such programs. The Office of Substance Abuse Prevention is funding chemical dependency programs specifically for pregnant women in several states.

It has been argued that drug use by pregnant women is a problem that requires medical, not criminal, attention. One can contend the notion that pregnant drug users and their drug-exposed infants are victims of drug abuse. Critics contend that there is an element of discrimination in the practice of prosecuting women who use drugs during pregnancy because these women are primarily low-income, single, members of minorities, and recipients of public assistance. Possible factors leading to their drug use—poverty, unemployment, poor education, and lack of vocational training—are not addressed when the solution to drug use during pregnancy is incarceration. Moreover, many pregnant women are denied access to treatment programs.

Prosecution proponents contend that medical intervention is not adequate in preventing pregnant women from using drugs and that criminal prosecution is necessary. Logli argues that "eliminating the pain, suffering and death resulting from drug exposure in newborns must be a prosecutor's priority." He maintains that the criminal justice system should protect newborns and, if legal cause does exist for prosecution, then statutes should provide protection for the fetus. However, will prosecution result in more protection or less protection for the fetus? If a mother stops using drugs for fear of prosecution, then the fetus benefits. If the mother avoids prenatal care because of potential legal punishment, then the fetus suffers.

If women can be prosecuted for using illegal drugs such as cocaine and narcotics during pregnancy because they harm the fetus, then should women who smoke cigarettes and drink alcohol during pregnancy also be prosecuted? The evidence is clear that tobacco and alcohol place the fetus at great risk; however, most discussions of prosecuting pregnant drug users overlook women who use these drugs. Also, the adverse health effects from secondhand smoke are well documented. Should people be prosecuted if they smoke around pregnant women?

"The Legality of Drug-Testing Procedures for Pregnant Women" by Kristin Pulatie, *Virtual Mentor* (January 2008), provides a good review of the legal aspects of drug testing on pregnant women. The extent of alcohol use by pregnant women is highlighted in "Alcohol Use Among Women and Recent Mothers: 2002 to 2007," *The NSDUH Report* (September 11, 2008). Two older but excellent articles that address this issue are Paul Logli's "Drugs in the Womb: The Newest Battlefield in the War on Drugs," *Criminal Justice Ethics* (Winter/Spring 2009) and Carolyn Carter's "Perinatal Care for Women Who Are Addicted: Implications for Empowerment," *Health and Social Work* (August 2002). The adverse effects of drug use during pregnancy are described in "Effects of Substance Abuse During Pregnancy," by Anne Greenough and Zainab Kassim, *The Journal of the Royal Society for the Promotion of Health* (September 2005).

ISSUE 6

Is Drug Addiction a Brain Disease?

YES: National Institute on Drug Abuse, from *The Science of Addiction* (April 2007)

NO: Gene M. Heyman, from *Addiction: A Disorder of Choice* (Harvard University Press, 2009)

ISSUE SUMMARY

YES: Because there are biological and chemical changes in the brain following drug abuse, the National Institute on Drug Abuse (NIDA) claims that drug addiction is a disease of the brain. One may initially use drugs voluntarily, but addiction occurs after repeated drug use. NIDA acknowledges that environment plays a role in the development of drug addiction, but one's genes play a major role as well.

NO: Writer Gene M. Heyman maintains that drug addiction, including alcoholism, runs in families. There is no doubt that genes are hereditary. However, Heyman argues that behaviors are not hereditary. Whether an individual engages in drug use or abuse is a choice made by the individual. Claiming that drug addiction is a disease removes the stigma of drug addiction because one can assert that it is the disease that causes one's addiction, not one's behavior.

Is drug addiction caused by a brain disease, or is it caused by inappropriate behavioral patterns? This distinction is important because it has both legal and medical implications. Should people be held accountable for behaviors that stem from a brain disease over which they have no control? For example, if a person cannot help being an alcoholic and hurts or kills someone as a result of being drunk, should that person be treated or incarcerated? Likewise, if an individual's addiction is due to lack of self-control, rather than due to a disease, should taxpayers' money go toward paying for that person's treatment?

It can be argued that the disease concept of drug addiction legitimizes or excuses behaviors. If addiction is an illness or disease of the brain, then blame for poor behavior can be shifted to the disease and away from the individual. Moreover, if drug addiction is incurable, can people ever be held responsible for their behavior?

The National Institute on Drug Abuse contends that addiction is caused by heredity, biochemistry, and environment influences. If drug addiction is the result of factors beyond the individual's control, then one should not be held responsible for one's behavior and that loss of control is not inevitable. Critics assert that many individuals have the same ability of alcoholics to stop their abuse of drugs. For example, it has been shown that many cocaine and heroin users do not lose control while using these drugs. In their study of U.S. service personnel in Vietnam, epidemiologist Lee N. Robins and colleagues showed that most of the soldiers who used narcotics regularly during the war did not continue using them once they returned home. Many service personnel in Vietnam reportedly used drugs because they were in a situation they did not want to be in. Additionally, without the support of loved ones and society's constraints, they were freer to gravitate to behaviors that would not be tolerated by their families and friends.

Attitudes toward treating drug abuse are affected by whether it is perceived as a brain disease or as an act of free will. The disease concept implies that one needs help in overcoming addiction. By calling drug addiction a medical condition, the body is viewed as a machine that needs fixing; character and free will become secondary. Also, by calling addiction a disease, the role of society in causing drug addiction is left unexplored. What roles do poverty, crime, unemployment, inadequate health care, and poor education have in drug addiction?

Opponents to the disease concept argue that the addictive qualities of drugs, especially heroin, are exaggerated. By claiming that certain drugs are highly addictive, it is easier to demonize those drugs and people who use them. It has been demonstrated that more people are dependent on legal drugs such as alcohol and tobacco. Some studies show that a number of heroin users are weekend users. This dispels the notion that heroin use always causes addiction.

According to the disease perspective, an important step for addicts to take in order to benefit from treatment is to admit that they are powerless against their addiction. They need to acknowledge that their drug addiction controls them and that it is a lifelong problem. The implication of this view is that addicts are never cured. Addicts must therefore abstain from drugs for their entire lives.

Is addiction caused by psychological or biological factors? Can drugs produce changes in the brain that result in drug addiction? How much control do drug addicts have over their use of drugs? In the Yes and No selections, the position of the National Institute on Drug Abuse is that addiction is a disease of the brain, whereas Gene Heyman contends that drug use, and consequently drug addiction, is based on one's behavior.

The Science of Addiction

Drug Abuse and Addiction

What Is Drug Addiction?

Addiction is defined as a chronic, relapsing brain disease that is character-ized by compulsive drug seeking and use, despite harmful consequences. It is considered a brain disease because drugs change the brain—they change its structure and how it works. These brain changes can be long lasting, and can lead to the harmful behaviors seen in people who abuse drugs.

Is Continued Drug Abuse a Voluntary Behavior?

The initial decision to take drugs is mostly voluntary. However, when drug abuse takes over, a person's ability to exert self control can become seriously impaired. Brain imaging studies from drug-addicted individuals show physi-cal changes in areas of the brain that are critical to judgment, decisionmak-ing, learning and memory, and behavior control. Scientists believe that these changes alter the way the brain works, and may help explain the compulsive and destructive behaviors of addiction.

Why Do Some People Become Addicted to Drugs, While Others Do Not?

As with any other disease, vulnerability to addiction differs from person to per-son. In general, the more risk factors an individual has, the greater the chance that taking drugs will lead to abuse and addiction. "Protective" factors reduce a person's risk of developing addiction.

What Factors Determine If a Person Will Become Addicted?

No single factor determines whether a person will become addicted to drugs. The overall risk for addiction is impacted by the biological makeup of the individual—it can even be influenced by gender or ethnicity, his or her devel-opmental stage, and the surrounding social environment (e.g., conditions at home, at school, and in the neighborhood).

Published by National Institutes of Health, NIH Pub. no. 07-5605, April 2007, pp. 5, 7–8, 10, 15–20.

Which Biological Factors Increase Risk of Addiction?

Scientists estimate that genetic factors account for between 40 and 60 percent of a person's vulnerability to addiction, including the effects of environment on gene expression and function. Adolescents and individuals with mental disorders are at greater risk of drug abuse and addiction than the general population.

The Brain Continues to Develop into Adulthood and Undergoes Dramatic Changes During Adolescence

One of the brain areas still maturing during adolescence is the prefrontal cortex—the part of the brain that enables us to assess situations, make sound decisions, and keep our emotions and desires under control. The fact that this critical part of an adolescent's brain is still a work-in-progress puts them at increased risk for poor decisions (such as trying drugs or continued abuse). Thus, introducing drugs while the brain is still developing may have profound and long-lasting consequences.

Drugs and the Brain

Introducing the Human Brain

The human brain is the most complex organ in the body. This three-pound mass of gray and white matter sits at the center of all human activity—you need it to drive a car, to enjoy a meal, to breathe, to create an artistic master-piece, and to enjoy everyday activities. In brief, the brain regulates your basic body functions; enables you to interpret and respond to everything you experience, and shapes your thoughts, emotions, and behavior.

The brain is made up of many parts that all work together as a team. Different parts of the brain are responsible for coordinating and performing specific functions. Drugs can alter important brain areas that are necessary for life-sustaining functions and can drive the compulsive drug abuse that marks addiction. Brain areas affected by drug abuse—

- *The brain stem* controls basic functions critical to life, such as heart rate, breathing, and sleeping.
- *The limbic system* contains the brain's reward circuit—it links together a number of brain structures that control and regulate our ability to feel pleasure. Feeling pleasure motivates us to repeat behaviors such as eating—actions that are critical to our existence. The limbic system is activated when we perform these activities—and also by drugs of abuse. In addition, the limbic system is responsible for our perception of other emotions, both positive and negative, which explains the mood-altering properties of many drugs.
- *The cerebral cortex* is divided into areas that control specific functions. Different areas process information from our senses, enabling us to see, feel, hear, and taste. The front part of the cortex, the frontal cortex or forebrain, is the thinking center of the brain; it powers our ability to think, plan, solve problems, and make decisions.

How Does the Brain Communicate?

The brain is a communications center consisting of billions of neurons, or nerve cells. Networks of neurons pass messages back and forth to different structures within the brain, the spinal column, and the peripheral nervous system. These nerve networks coordinate and regulate everything we feel, think, and do.

- *Neuron to Neuron*
  Each nerve cell in the brain sends and receives messages in the form of electrical impulses. Once a cell receives and processes a message, it sends it on to other neurons.
- *Neurotransmitters—The Brain's Chemical Messengers*
  The messages are carried between neurons by chemicals called neurotransmitters. (They transmit messages between neurons.)
- *Receptors—The Brain's Chemical Receivers*
  The neurotransmitter attaches to a specialized site on the receiving cell called a receptor. A neurotransmitter and its receptor operate like a "key and lock," an exquisitely specific mechanism that ensures that each receptor will forward the appropriate message only after interacting with the right kind of neurotransmitter.
- *Transporters—The Brain's Chemical Recyclers*
  Located on the cell that releases the neurotransmitter, transporters recycle these neurotransmitters (i.e., bring them back into the cell that released them), thereby shutting off the signal between neurons.

How Do Drugs Work in the Brain?

Drugs are chemicals. They work in the brain by tapping into the brain's communication system and interfering with the way nerve cells normally send, receive, and process information. Some drugs, such as marijuana and heroin, can activate neurons because their chemical structure mimics that of a natural neurotransmitter. This similarity in structure "fools" receptors and allows the drugs to lock onto and activate the nerve cells. Although these drugs mimic brain chemicals, they don't activate nerve cells in the same way as a natural neurotransmitter, and they lead to abnormal messages being transmitted through the network.

Other drugs, such as amphetamine or cocaine, can cause the nerve cells to release abnormally large amounts of natural neurotransmitters or prevent the normal recycling of these brain chemicals. This disruption produces a greatly amplified message, ultimately disrupting communication channels. The difference in effect can be described as the difference between someone whispering into your ear and someone shouting into a microphone.

How Do Drugs Work in the Brain to Produce Pleasure?

All drugs of abuse directly or indirectly target the brain's reward system by flooding the circuit with dopamine. Dopamine is a neurotransmitter present in regions of the brain that regulate movement, emotion, cognition, motivation, and feelings of pleasure. The overstimulation of this system, which rewards our natural behaviors, produces the euphoric effects sought by people who abuse drugs and teaches them to repeat the behavior.

How Does Stimulation of the Brain's Pleasure Circuit Teach Us to Keep Taking Drugs?

Our brains are wired to ensure that we will repeat life-sustaining activities by associating those activities with pleasure or reward. Whenever this reward circuit is activated, the brain notes that something important is happening that needs to be remembered, and teaches us to do it again and again, without thinking about it. Because drugs of abuse stimulate the same circuit, we learn to abuse drugs in the same way.

Why Are Drugs More Addictive Than Natural Rewards?

When some drugs of abuse are taken, they can release 2 to 10 times the amount of dopamine that natural rewards do. In some cases, this occurs almost immediately (as when drugs are smoked or injected), and the effects can last much longer than those produced by natural rewards. The resulting effects on the brain's pleasure circuit dwarfs those produced by naturally rewarding behaviors such as eating and sex. The effect of such a powerful reward strongly motivates people to take drugs again and again. This is why scientists sometimes say that drug abuse is something we learn to do very, very well.

What Happens to Your Brain If You Keep Taking Drugs?

Just as we turn down the volume on a radio that is too loud, the brain adjusts to the overwhelming surges in dopamine (and other neurotransmitters) by producing less dopamine or by reducing the number of receptors that can receive and transmit signals. As a result, dopamine's impact on the reward circuit of a drug abuser's brain can become abnormally low, and the ability to experience any pleasure is reduced. This is why the abuser eventually feels flat, lifeless, and depressed, and is unable to enjoy things that previously brought them pleasure. Now, they need to take drugs just to bring their dopamine function back up to normal. And, they must take larger amounts of the drug than they first did to create the dopamine high—an effect known as tolerance.

How Does Long-Term Drug Taking Affect Brain Circuits?

We know that the same sort of mechanisms involved in the development of tolerance can eventually lead to profound changes in neurons and brain circuits, with the potential to severely compromise the long-term health of the brain. For example, glutamate is another neurotransmitter that influences the reward circuit and the ability to learn. When the optimal concentration of glutamate is altered by drug abuse, the brain attempts to compensate for this change, which can cause impairment in cognitive function. Similarly, long-term drug abuse can trigger adaptations in habit or nonconscious memory systems. Conditioning is one example of this type of learning, whereby environmental cues become associated with the drug experience and can trigger uncontrollable cravings if the individual is later exposed to these cues, even without the drug itself being available. This learned "reflex" is extremely robust and can emerge even after many years of abstinence.

What Other Brain Changes Occur with Abuse?

Chronic exposure to drugs of abuse disrupts the way critical brain structures interact to control behavior—behavior specifically related to drug abuse. Just as continued abuse may lead to tolerance or the need for higher drug dosages to produce an effect, it may also lead to addiction, which can drive an abuser to seek out and take drugs compulsively. Drug addiction erodes a person's self-control and ability to make sound decisions, while sending intense impulses to take drugs.

Gene M. Heyman  **NO**

Addiction: A Disorder of Choice

Voluntary Behavior, Disease, and Addiction

In 1818 Samuel Judd, a New York whale-oil merchant, was summoned to court for refusing to pay the city fish-oil tax (Burnett, 2007). Judd refused on the grounds that a whale is not a fish. Experts testified on the anatomy of whale sexual organs, their mating behavior, parenting, how they breathe, and skeletal structure. According to these behavioral, physiological, and anatomical features, whales were more like dogs and even humans than tuna and sardines. But the jury understood that fish were animals that lived in the sea and mammals were animals that lived on land. Since whales lived in the sea, a whale was a fish. Indeed, unless Mr. Judd could show that whales lived on land, he had to pay the fish-oil tax. The jury was aware that mother whales nursed baby whales, but this did not count as much as the long-held classification schemes that fish were water animals, mammals were land animals, and birds flew in the air.

The story is instructive. It shows that arguments about how to classify a phenomenon can reflect different understandings of the basic terms as much as the particular features of the phenomenon in question. No one mentioned that a fish has a two-chambered heart, whereas a whale has a four-chambered heart with two ventricles, just like cows and other mammals. Rather the differences in opinion concerned the criteria for distinguishing mammals and fish. One school of thought based the distinction on habitat, the other based the distinction on physiological characteristics. This chapter makes a similar point regarding the classification of addiction. It shows that scientific explanations for why addiction should be considered a disease depend on assumptions regarding the relevant categories, which in this case are involuntary and voluntary behaviors. For example, one of the mainstays of the claim that addiction is a disease is evidence that it has a genetic basis. The idea is that if genes influence an activity, then it can't be voluntary. There are, however, everyday experiences which suggest that even clearly voluntary activities have a genetic basis. As children get older, they often find themselves adopting attitudes that are more and more like those of their parents, even when they have moved far away and don't particularly appreciate the similarities. Attitudes are learned, but aspects of this common experience suggest that genes are also at play. Thus, we need to check if genetic differences play an important role in voluntary activities. If so, then a genetic basis for addiction does not automatically mean that addicts are "compulsive, involuntary" drug users. Put more generally, if a key feature of a disease state is that the symptoms are involuntary, then we need to know how to distinguish between voluntary and involuntary behavior.

What Sort of Disease Is Addiction?

In the preface to *Alcoholics Anonymous* (1939), Dr. W. D. Silkworth suggests that alcoholics have an "allergy." The allergen is alcohol, and the allergic reaction is loss of control over drinking. One drink leads to another drink, which leads to another, just as ragweed pollen initiates a fit of sneezing. In recent years the allergy model of addiction has expanded to include many other involuntary medical states. In clinical texts and scientific journals, researchers say that addiction should be grouped with such diseases as Alzheimer's, hypertension, Type 2 diabetes, schizophrenia, asthma, arthritis, and even cancer and heart disease (e.g., Leshner, 1997; McLellan et al., 2000; O'Brien & McLellan, 1996; USDHHS, 2007). If these comparisons are apt, then it is cruel and unjust to subject those who meet the criteria for dependence to criminal charges or even criticism. This would be like scolding someone with Alzheimer's for getting lost or reprimanding a Tourette's syndrome patient for gesticulating wildly. In this vein, Dr. Enoch Gordis (1995), a champion of science-based alcoholism treatment and previous head of NIAAA, writes: "the disease concept . . . has helped remove the stigma from a chronic disorder [alcoholism] that is no more inherently immoral than diabetes or heart disease." Taking this argument to its logical conclusion, a group of leading addiction researchers argued (in the pages of the *Journal of the American Medical Association*) that insurance plans should provide the same coverage for heroin addiction, crack addiction, and alcoholism as they do for traditional chronic diseases such as cancer, arthritis, and high blood pressure (McLellan et al., 2000). Although this may seem a radical (and expensive) proposal, if addiction is a disease, it is not unreasonable.

Why Addiction Is a Disease

Although it will be shown that intuitions regarding the nature of voluntary behavior prove to be the foundation for the disease interpretation of addiction, there are also important empirical arguments to consider. These have appeared in scholarly and scientific venues, such as psychiatric handbooks, journal articles, and clinic mission statements. They typically focus on three lines of evidence and reasoning: (1) addiction has a biological basis; (2) addictive drugs have the capacity to transform a voluntary user into an involuntary one; and (3) the disease interpretation leads to better treatment for addicts. These views will be discussed in turn.

Is There a Genetic Predisposition for Addiction?
At the NIDA-sponsored College on Problems of Drug Dependence meetings in 2003, which is the major conference for addiction researchers, there was a symposium on the disease interpretation of addiction. At the end of the talks, someone in the audience stated that addiction was a disease "because it has a genetic basis, and we do not choose our genes." This is a succinct summary of

an idea that is broadly endorsed by scientists and nonscientists alike. In discussions of addiction, the claim that addicts choose to get high is often countered with the point, "But there is a genetic predisposition for alcoholism." This response encompasses two important ideas. The first is that addiction has a genetic basis; the second is that if an activity is influenced by genes, it is not correct to say that it is voluntary. Let's first check if it is really true that genes can influence whether someone becomes an addict.

Genetics and Addiction.   Most of the research on the role of genetics in drug use has focused on alcoholics. This is because it is easier to conduct multi-generational research on legal drugs than on illegal ones. The basic finding is that alcoholism runs in families, and this is true even when the family members did not live together. Dr. Robert Cloninger (1987) led a project that nicely illustrates the genetic approach to the study of alcoholism. The research was carried out in Sweden, a country in which adoption was not uncommon, and in which the biological and nonbiological parents' drinking histories were on record.

The subjects were men who had been given up for adoption at an average age of 4 months. This population was of special interest to researchers, because the Swedish social service agencies had detailed records of not only the boys, but their biological parents and their adoptive parents. In particular much was known about the drinking histories of all parties. According to the agency records, there were about 1,700 adoptees that had developed drinking problems, with about half meeting the criteria for "severe" alcohol abuse and half meeting the criteria for "less severe" alcohol abuse.

The major finding was that the biological father's drinking pattern was a better predictor of alcohol abuse in the adopted son than the father by adoption's drinking pattern. For instance, the rates of alcoholism for boys whose biological fathers were severe alcoholics were nearly identical regardless of whether their adoptive father was an alcoholic or teetotaler. For those who grew up in a home with an alcoholic (adoptive) father, the rate of alcoholism was 18 percent; for those who grew up in a home free of parental alcoholism, the rate was 17 percent. That is, given that the biological father was a severe alcoholic, parental drinking patterns did not matter.

Studies of the genetics of illicit drug use yield similar findings. The researchers, though, typically compared twins rather than following adoptees. In a representative example of the twin approach, Dr. Kenneth Kendler and his colleagues at the Medical College of Virginia and Virginia Commonwealth University (2000) tabulated the correlations in illegal drug use and illegal drug addiction for fraternal and identical twins. Their hypothesis was that if there was a genetic basis for addiction, then the correlations among identical twins would be significantly greater than those for fraternal twins. The results for addiction supported the genetic hypothesis but not the results for use, which includes experimentation that did not proceed to addiction. For identical and fraternal twins, the correlations were nearly identical for simple use. If one twin had experimented with an illicit drug, then there was about a 75 percent chance that the other had as well. That is, number of shared genes did not influence the correlations for experimenting with illegal drugs. In contrast, the correlations for drug addiction varied as a function of the percentage of shared genes. If one member of a fraternal twin pair had been dependent, then there was about a 25 percent chance that his co-twin was also dependent; whereas if one member of an identical twin pair was dependent, then there was a 40 percent chance that his identical brother was also dependent. When the number of shared genes was doubled, there was more than a 50 percent increase in between-twin similarity for addiction. Dr. Ming Tsuang and his colleagues at Harvard Medical School have conducted similar studies with twins who were in the military during the Vietnam War (1998). Their results are similar to those of the Virginia study.

There can be little doubt that genes can play an important role in the etiology of addiction. But does this mean in these cases, drug use has become involuntary? We can answer this question by asking whether genes also play a role in activities that are voluntary. If they do, then genetic influences do not preclude choice. But before I present some relevant data on this topic, notice that the correlation for addiction among identical twins was far less than 100 percent and that fewer than 20 percent of the biological sons of serious alcoholics became alcoholics themselves, even when their adoptive fathers were alcoholics. These facts say that the pathway from DNA to addiction is indirect, with genes programming proteins that affect the probability of addiction rather than insuring that it does or does not occur. The same point is made by a more general consideration.

We inherit genes; we do not inherit behaviors. As a function of a variety of factors that come under the term "gene expression" and which include behavioral and environmental influences, genes make proteins. Differences in the proteins lead to differences in behavior, but since the genes make proteins not behaviors, the genetic influences are indirect. In the case of alcohol, the following pathways are well documented: metabolism (e.g., Luczak et al., 2001), antisocial behavior (Haber et al., 2005), and tolerance (Schuckit, 1994). Presumably, there are other pathways as well. But none include DNA-programmed behavioral modules for shooting up or going to the store to buy a six-pack. Rather, genes are one of the various factors that exercise some influence over drug-seeking and drug self-administration. Indeed what they do, albeit indirectly, is affect the relative value of alcohol. If a genetic difference makes alcohol toxic, then you are less likely to prefer alcohol.

Do Genes Also Influence Voluntary Activities?   The famous Charles Addams cartoon of the separated-at-birth Mallifert twins showing up at the same time in the same patent attorney's office hoping to get a patent for the identical gizmos sitting on their respective laps suggests that everyday life offers plenty of evidence that voluntary activities are influenced by genes. In recent years, researchers have caught up with intuition. They have examined the role of heredity in social attitudes, such as support for the death penalty and whether women should have nondomestic professions (Bouchard et al., 2003; Tesser & Crelia, 1994). One of the most interesting studies evaluated the role of genes in religious beliefs. Religious beliefs are learned and voluntary. In early adulthood, many people question their faith, sometimes discarding the beliefs they grew up with and replacing them with new ones. Conversely, those who keep their faith often reaffirm it after encountering situations that question the ideas they learned as children. Thus, religious beliefs provide a powerful test of the role of genes in voluntary behavior. If heredity influences beliefs about a deity, then it is hard to imagine voluntary actions that are not to some degree influenced by heredity.

The next graph reports the results of a study on religious beliefs in twins (Waller et al., 1990). The twins grew up in different families and were separated before the age of one year. Religious beliefs and behavior were assessed by questionnaires that identified the informants' thoughts about the nature of God, the role of prayer in their lives, and the literal accuracy of Bible stories. The results are summarized in Figure 1. The black bars show the level of agreement between identical twins; the grey bars show the level of agreement between fraternal twins. Identical twins often agreed with each other; fraternal twins agreed at about a chance level. But neither the identical nor the fraternal twins grew up together. They grew up in different families. These results do not stand alone. There are now many studies on the heritability of attitudes and beliefs, and they typically show that beliefs reflect genetic as well as familial and cultural influences (e.g., Olson et al., 2001; Rutherford et al., 1993). Religious beliefs are voluntary; genes affect religious beliefs; genes affect voluntary behavior. . . .

Figure 1

The Correlation Between Religious Values and Heredity in Fraternal and Identical Twins Who Were Raised Apart. Data Are from Waller et al., 1990.

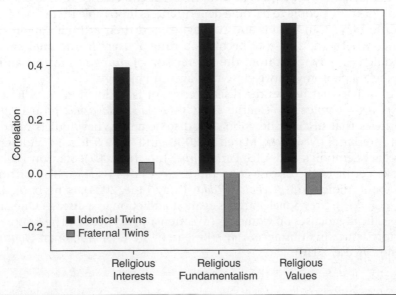

POSTSCRIPT

Is Drug Addiction a Brain Disease?

There is little debate that drug addiction is a major problem. Drug addiction wreaks havoc for society and ruins the lives of numerous individuals and people who care for them. Addressing the causes of drug addiction and what to do about people who become addicted is especially relevant. Views on whether or not drug addiction is a brain disease diverge. Because drug abuse can be viewed as a matter of free will or as a brain disorder, there are also different views on how society should deal with drug abusers. Should drug addicts be incarcerated or treated? Does it matter whether one is responsible for one's drug addiction?

One could argue that free will and the concept of a brain disorder both apply to drug addiction. What may start out as a matter of free will may turn into an illness. Likewise, drug use may start out as an occasional behavior that may become abusive. To illustrate this point, many people may use alcohol for recreational or social purposes, but their alcohol use may develop into a chronic, abusive pattern—one that the person cannot easily overcome. Initially, one can stop using alcohol without too much discomfort. As time passes, however, and alcohol consumption becomes more frequent and the amounts increase, stopping for many people becomes difficult. By its very definition, social drinkers can stop drinking at will. Alcoholics drink out of necessity.

Many people who use addictive drugs do not become dependent on them. Perhaps there are factors beyond free will and changes in the brain that account for these people to become dependent. Is it possible that social factors come into play? Can friends and colleagues and their attitudes about drugs influence whether a drug user becomes a drug abuser? In the final analysis, drug addiction may result from the interaction of numerous factors and not simply be a dichotomy between psychology and biology.

An article that refutes the disease concept is "Addiction: New Research Suggests It's a Choice" by Charlie Gillis (*Maclean's Magazine*, June 1, 2009). Two articles that discuss addiction as a disease are "What Addicts Need" by Jeneen Interlandi (*Newsweek*, March 3, 2008) and "The Science of Addiction" by Michael Lemonick and Alice Park (*Time*, July 16, 2007). Stanton Peele, an outspoken critic of the disease concept, discusses this issue in "The Surprising Truth About Addiction," *Psychology Today* (May/June, 2004). In his book *Addiction Is a Choice*, Jeffrey Schaler argues against addiction as a disease. One article that specifically focuses on women is "Women and Addiction: The Importance of Gender Issues in Substance Abuse Research" by Ellen Tuchman (*Journal of Addictive Disease*, 2010).

ISSUE 7

Should There Be More Regulation of Performance-Enhancing Drugs?

YES: Jan Todd and Terry Todd, from "Scenes from the Front Lines," *Hastings Center Report* (March–April 2010)

NO: Laura K. Egendorf, from *Performance Enhancing Drugs* (Reference Point Press, 2007)

ISSUE SUMMARY

YES: University of Texas kinesiology professors Jan Todd and Terry Todd, who were competitive powerlifters, are concerned about the impact of performance-enhancing drugs. One of their biggest concerns is that competitors who do not use performance-enhancing drugs will feel compelled to use them to keep up with other competitors. They advocate for more drug testing because of the safety issues related to performance-enhancing drugs and to ensure that competition is fair.

NO: In her book, author Laura Egendorf cites individuals who feel that athletes are aware of the risks of taking steroids and other performance-enhancing drugs. Competition and the desire to succeed drive individuals to improve their athletic performance. Allowing steroid use would essentially level the playing field for all athletes. In addition, some experts believe that the negative consequences are exaggerated.

Performance-enhancing drugs cover numerous drugs. One type that is especially popular is anabolic steroids. Anabolic steroids are synthetic derivatives of the male hormone testosterone. Although they have legitimate medical uses, steroids are used increasingly by individuals to build up muscle quickly and to increase personal strength. Concerns over the potential negative effects of performance-enhancing drugs like steroids seem to be justified: an estimated 1 million Americans, including 2 out of every 100 high school seniors, use steroids. Users of anabolic steroids and other performance-enhancing drugs span all ethnic groups, nationalities, and socioeconomic groups. The emphasis on winning has led many athletes to take risks that are potentially destructive. Despite the widespread belief that anabolic steroids are used primarily by athletes, up to one-third of users are nonathletes who use these drugs to improve their physiques and self-images.

Society places much emphasis on winning, and to come out on top, many individuals are willing to make sacrifices—sacrifices that might compromise their health. Some people will do anything for the sake of winning. The sports headlines in many newspapers mention how various professional and Olympic athletes have used drugs to improve performance. Drug testing is a major issue every time the Olympic competition is held. Besides the adverse physical consequences of performance-enhancing drugs, there is the ethical question regarding fair play. Do these drugs give competitors an unfair advantage? Should they be banned even if the side effects are not harmful? Do nonusers feel pressured to use these drugs to keep up with the competition? Would there be better regulation of performance-enhancing drugs if their use was permitted?

The short-term consequences of performance-enhancing drugs are well documented. For example, possible short-term effects of anabolic steroids among men include testicular atrophy, sperm count reduction, impotency, baldness, difficulty urinating, and breast enlargement. Among women, some potential effects are deepening of the voice, breast reduction, menstrual irregularities, the growth of body hair, and clitoral enlargement. Both sexes may develop acne, swelling in the feet, reduced levels of high-density lipoproteins (the type of cholesterol that is good for the body), hypertension, and liver damage. Taking steroids as an adolescent will stunt one's growth. Also related to steroid use are psychological changes, including mood swings, paranoia, and violent behavior.

The long-term effects of performance-enhancing drugs have not been researched thoroughly. The problem with identifying the long-term effects of performance-enhancing drugs is the lack of systematic, long-term studies. Much of the information regarding the long-term effects of these drugs comes from personal reports, not well conducted, controlled studies. However, personal stories and anecdotal evidence are often accepted as fact.

In regards to anabolic steroids, the American Medical Association opposes stricter regulation on two grounds. First, anabolic steroids have been used medically to improve growth and development and for certain types of anemia, breast cancer, endometriosis, and osteoporosis. If stricter regulations are imposed, people who may benefit medically from these drugs will have more difficulty acquiring them. Second, it is highly unlikely that illicit use of these drugs will cease if they are banned. By maintaining legal access to these drugs, more studies regarding their long-term consequences can be conducted.

In the YES selection, Jan Todd and Terry Todd feel that there should be greater regulation of performance-enhancing drugs because nonusers may feel pressured to use these drugs. Moreover, competition would be fairer. In the NO selection, Laura Egendorf argues that athletes level the playing field when they use performance-enhancing drugs. Furthermore, states Egendorf, some of the harmful psychological and physical effects of performance-enhancing drugs may be exaggerated.

YES

Jan Todd and Terry Todd

Scenes from the Front Lines

For several intertwined reasons, our lives have spread across the sport of powerlifting—a type of competitive weightlifting that includes the squat, the bench press, and the dead lift—for the past half century. One of us, Terry, won the superheavyweight class in the first national championships. The other one, Jan, set a national record at the first women's championships and went on to set world records over five bodyweight divisions. Both of us have coached national and world record holders, coached national teams in world championships, written many dozens of articles on the sport for the popular press, done color commentary for national television networks, and been elected to halls of fame in the sport.

During our time in powerlifting we've seen the coming of anabolic steroids and related substances, the entry of women into the sport, its gradual outward movement into countries around the world, and its unprecedented fractionalization into a Babel of federations riven by rancor regarding standards of performance, costumes, and—above all else—drugs. Our unique vantage point, located sometimes inside and sometimes just outside the belly of the beast, has allowed us to be there, like Forrest Gump, when things happened that were wonderful, horrible, or both at the same time. Below, each in his or her own voice, we've tried to share a bit of what we've seen.

Terry: *Ironbound*

In 1996, the American weightlifter Mark Henry trained with us at our summer home on Ironbound, a remote island off the coast of Nova Scotia. We invited him to come so he could escape the media drawn to his four-hundred-pound body, his equally outsized personality, and his outspoken criticism of the lack of effective drug testing in a sport which had sustained more positive tests than any other Olympic event. Not unexpectedly, however, a few well-heeled TV people persisted, making the effort to reach our retreat.

The "talent" for one media contingent, after the usual song and dance, approached the drug issue via a different path, asking, "Mark, do you ever wonder how much you could lift if you took the same drugs as the other top men?" Mark hesitated for just a moment, and then said in a wistful voice something I'd never heard him say: "No. But I do wonder about one thing. I wonder how much they could lift if they didn't."

From *Hastings Center Report*, March/April 2010, pp. 15–18. Copyright © 2010 by The Hastings Center. Reprinted by permission of the publisher and the authors.

Jan: *Lamar*

In the early 1980s, we helped the powerlifter Lamar Gant find a job at a local equipment manufacturer near us, and Terry began to coach him. "Coaching Lamar was easy," Terry has often said, "since he was already the greatest lifter the sport has ever seen." A diminutive man with a giant's strength, Lamar trained with the powerlifting team at Auburn University, a team we coached. We believed, for reasons too complicated to address here, that Lamar was life-time drug-free and, as such, an ideal role model for our young lifters, one of whom was Terry Ptomey, a uniquely talented undergraduate.

She and Lamar became friends, and he helped me as I worked with her during the run-up to the national women's championships I was promoting. His help was important because Ptomey's opponent was one of the first women in the sport who used anabolic steroids and made little attempt to hide either her drug use or her disdain for those who chose to remain drug-free.

The meet had no drug testing because the men who then governed pow-erlifting wouldn't allow it, even though almost all of the women in the sport wanted it. The men—most active lifters who used drugs banned by the Inter-national Olympic Committee—feared that if the women were tested, the pres-sure would mount for the men to be tested. In any event, Ptomey was her usual jolly self at the meet site, whereas her rival acted as if her job was to hype the gate for a professional boxing match, shouting loudly to her follow-ers in a deep voice and almost flaunting her male pattern baldness and thickly muscled body.

The contest was fairly (or unfairly) even, but as it drew to a close it looked as if Ptomey was too far behind. Her only chance was to lift a record weight she had never made before. As she approached the bar, loaded to more than three times her own bodyweight, Lamar walked beside her, whispering cour-age in his improbable *basso profundo*. The hall grew silent as everyone stopped to see this clash of personalities and perspective. When Ptomey began to pull the bar, it didn't move at first, but then it bent and, very slowly, came off the platform, then to her knees, and then, majestically, to the tops of her thighs as she finally stood straight up and the judge shouted "Down!"—a shout lost among the screams and roars of the crowd. But Lamar's deep voice stood out above all the rest, announcing again and again, "Don't need no drugs to be a champion."

The following morning, the second place trophy won by the woman Ptomey overcame was found broken at the bottom of the motel's swimming pool. And, as women's use of banned drugs became more prevalent, it was the last national championship Ptomey ever won.

Terry: *Mariusz*

In 2004, the organizers of the forthcoming annual World's Strongest Man con-test conducted drug testing because of pressure from the British Broadcasting Corporation, which was reportedly urged by its sponsors to do so. The decision to test had been announced several months before the competition, and when the athletes arrived in the Bahamas for the contest, they were told that they would draw straws and that the men who drew the two short straws would be tested.

As it happened, both of the men who drew short straws were former winners of the event—Svend Karlsen of Norway, who won in 2001, and the then-current champion, Mariusz Pudzianowski of Poland, who had won in 2002 and 2003, and who went on to win in 2005, 2007, and 2008. Just after the drawing of straws, one of the people involved in the World's Strongest Man event asked both men when they had last taken any anabolic steroids. Karlsen reported that he stopped all use shortly after getting the news that there would be drug testing, but Pudzianowski smiled and asked, "What time is it now?"

Terry: *Salesmanship*

In 1979, the Men's World Powerlifting Championships were held in Dayton, Ohio. The promoter of the meet was Larry Pacifico, probably the most dominant powerlifter in the world at that time with eight consecutive world titles. The manager of a chain of health clubs, the personable Pacifico supplemented his income by selling training gear and muscle-building drugs, and the world championships were always a busy time for him. He was held in very high regard by many foreign lifters, who hung on his every word regarding training, gear, diet, or anabolic supplementation. One day, as he drove along in his van with several members of the Japanese national team, they asked him about drugs and what they should take. "Dianbol," he said, naming the first anabolic steroid ever developed. "It's still the best." They nodded respectfully and then asked him how much to take. At that point he smiled, took from a small sack a bottle containing one hundred five-milligram tablets, unscrewed the cap, tossed them all into his mouth, and washed them down with a Coke.

Might have been a Pepsi.

Jan: *Burger King*

Back in the early 1980s I attended most of the major contests of the newly created American Drug-Free Powerlifting Association, a sports federation started by men and women who believed they could never convince the major powerlifting federation to follow international rules and institute Olympic-level drug testing. I recall many moments from those days—most of them good because drug-free lifters were so happy to finally have a federation they could call their own.

One moment I'll never forget came in 1983 at the ADFPA National Championships when Maurice Peak, a short but massive lifter, approached the platform with the rolling gait characteristic of superheavies. The crowd, seeing Peak for the first time, gasped at his depth of muscle and his sheer size. After Peak made a national record, I heard a man behind me whisper, "Could this guy be drug-free?" Later, accepting his trophy, Peak put his hands on his hips, scowled, and somberly surveyed the audience from left to right. Then, all at once, he broke into a commercial-worthy smile, slapped his keg-like abdomen with both hands, and shouted, "Ain't no steroids here! This all Burger King!" (The moment was mimicked two years later when Gerald Welch, a lifter from south Louisiana who had just broken a national ADFPA record, rubbed his wide, hard belly and shouted, "No steroids! Boudin!")

Jan: *Calls and Letters*

In the early years of women's powerlifting, back in the late 1970s and early 1980s, I set many official and unofficial national and world records. Therefore—because the media are all too often attracted, not to all things bright and beautiful, but to all things strange and different—I received a great deal of publicity, most of it favorable. Appearing on television shows such as *I've Got a Secret, To Tell the Truth*, and *The Tonight Show with Johnny Carson* and being the subject of profiles in *People, Sports Illustrated,* and the *Guinness Book of World Records* made me, for a time, the face of my emerging sport.

I was also elected to chair the women's subcommittee of the United States Powerlifting Federation, and the combination of the publicity I received and my executive position in the sport meant that most of the phone calls and letters from girls and young women who wanted to get stronger and to compete in powerlifting came to me. The saddest aspect of this often rewarding position was how many of these girls and young women, as we talked on the phone, would begin to cry when they told me how were being pushed by their boyfriends, husbands, fathers, or brothers to take anabolic steroids as a shortcut to strength, even though they didn't want to do so. The most frustrating aspect of these conversations was that quite a few of the lifters told me that the person who was pushing them toward anabolic drugs would say something like, "If you really want to be strong you've got to take steroids like Jan Todd does. You don't think she squatted five hundred pounds on her own, do you?"

Looking back, I feel sure that some of my efforts to implement "appropriate" drug testing for women were driven by my belief that I had no other argument against the boyfriends, husbands, fathers, and brothers who championed drug use. The only other thing I could do was to tell these women as earnestly as I could that I did not use such drugs and never had. But that was weak. "What else could she say? Don't be naive," is what many of the women were told by their steroid "enablers." I realized, of course, that passing a drug test didn't prove that I was "clean," but I also knew that a negative test would lend weight to my argument. In fact, at the height of this struggle, as my women's committee's pleas for drug testing were rebuffed again and again by the male-dominated executive committee of the powerlifting federation, I went to a clinic in Atlanta right after a contest and paid to have a urinalysis done just so I could use the results of the test in my campaign to counter the self-serving men who wanted to live through the accomplishments of a particular woman in their lives. Sometimes the drug test was helpful when I spoke to these women; sometimes it wasn't. But it was something.

Terry and Jan: *The Takeaway*

During our tenure, strength sports have been born, overtaken, dominated, and shattered by strength-building substances to a degree possibly exceeded only by competitive bodybuilding and professional bicycle racing. We continue to direct an annual "strongman" competition at the Arnold Sports Festival that attracts the strongest men in the world, most but not all of whom almost certainly use ergogenic substances. The Arnold Strongman Classic has never tested for such substances, but our aspiration is to craft a way to diminish their use. Many of the men who use these drugs have told us they'd be happy to compete clean if they believed their competitors would. We believe them. They don't want to take a knife to a gunfight.

Finding a way to level the lifting platform in a small yet geographically widespread sport will be very difficult, but we remain hopeful. Here are several things that we want to do to make it easier to compete clean. First of all, we'd like to convince a sponsor to fund a testing program for our contest. We would also like to affiliate with a reputable testing organization (perhaps the World Anti-Doping Agency, although it sometimes comes across as overly zealous in its "detect and punish" stance) that would help us design a transparent, sport-specific testing protocol. Finally, we intend to continue to give the best prize package in the world at our annual contest, which would help to convince the top athletes to take part in a drug-tested competition. Would such a test make the contest drug-free? Of course not. Would it mean that the athletes would use fewer drugs in the run-up to our particular event? Almost certainly. Would this be worth doing? We think so.

Should we be successful in this initial effort, we'd try to convince promoters of the few other major strongman contests to work with us to create a year-long series of tested events. We've seen enough early deaths, altered personalities, and relatively undeserving champions to convince us that science and artful politics could improve the lot of strongmen. And as Tip O'Neill so famously said, "All politics is local."

Is the Use of Performance Enhancing Drugs Cheating?

"Athletes chemically propelled to victory do not merely overvalue winning, they misunderstand why winning is properly valued."

—George F. Will, "Steroids Scandal Is Damaging to Baseball,"
Conservative Chronicle, December 2005.

Although modern-day athletes have used performance-enhancing drugs for decades, it was not until the 1960s that the leaders of the international and professional sports communities began to view the use of these drugs as cheating. The general disgust toward steroids and other performance-enhancing drugs has been especially strong since the late 1980s, following the discovery that Canadian sprinter Ben Johnson's world-record-setting victory in the 100-meter race in the 1988 Summer Olympics was fueled by his use of the steroid stanozolol. Before then, explains John Hoberman, a professor at the University of Texas and the author of several books on sports, "[the] use of performance enhancing substances was not viewed as cheating. It was simply a way of life for athletes of the times."

Athletes in the past did not deny their use of performance-enhancing drugs; for example, in the 1970s, Olympic weightlifters openly declared their use of steroids. Howard Bryant, in his book *Juicing the Game*, writes: "Drugs were part of the weightlifting world. . . . Gyms across America provided the conduits to information about which substances worked best and where illegal drugs could be obtained." The International Olympics Committee instituted drug testing in 1968 for narcotics and amphetamines, but steroids were not added to the list until 1975. Until then, Olympians were free to add muscle to their body through chemical means, and athletes with access to the best performance-enhancing drugs could continue to use them without fear of punishment.

Reasons for Using Performance-Enhancing Drugs

Athletes use performance-enhancing drugs for a variety of reasons. Steroids increase strength and reduce the time it takes to recover from injury. As a result, athletes who use them are able to push themselves harder and further than a clean athlete. Increased strength allows them to record more tackles, hit a ball farther, and grab more rebounds. Other drugs increase the red blood cell count, allowing the blood to carry more oxygen and thus enabling the athlete to run or bike over long distances without tiring.

Yet no matter what sport they play, athletes know that their salaries are dependent on their statistics. It is therefore not surprising that so many would choose to artificially enhance their talents with performance-enhancing drugs. Few baseball fans can remember who hit the most singles in any given year, but almost all of them know that Barry Bonds set the MLB single-season home-run record with 73 home runs in 2001. Olympic medalists are famous for life; the athlete who finishes in fourth place in the 100-meter dash is soon forgotten, even if he or she was only a few hundredths of a second behind the gold medalist.

Changing Views Toward Performance-Enhancing Drugs

Prior to the 1980s the lack of testing, other than in the Olympic Games, gave tacit approval to performance-enhancing drugs. The stories of rampant drug use in various professional sports leagues reveal a lackadaisical response that created a culture of acceptance and led to more and more athletes experimenting with drugs because they knew they could use whatever substances they wished without suffering any consequences. For example, Major League Baseball did not ban steroids until 2003, and once it did so, the penalty for failing a drug test was only a 10-game suspension.

However, the indifference toward performance-enhancing drugs that marked the 1960s through the middle of the 1980s began to be replaced by greater concerns as people became more aware of the health effects of these substances. Although the National Football League started testing for steroids in 1987, followers of the game likely did not recognize the dangerous effects of steroids until Lyle Alzado, a fearsome defensive end best know for his years with the Los Angeles Raiders, revealed in 1991 that he had brain cancer; he died the following year. Bryant writes, "Though many team doctors in the NFL doubted Lyle Alzado's claim that there was a direct connection between his steroid use and his brain cancer, his death in 1991 served as a sobering reminder of the influence of steroids in their sport."

People also began to consider the use of performance-enhancing drugs to be cheating, because athletes were using the drugs to enhance their abilities unnaturally. Such usage thus distorts the notion of a level playing field and misinterprets the importance of sports, many people argue. President George W. Bush has stated, "The use of performance-enhancing drugs . . . sends the wrong message . . . that there are shortcuts to accomplishment, and that performance is more important than character." Syndicated political columnist George Will suggests that the power of sports is diluted when winning becomes dependent on chemistry and not hard work.

Claims That Performance-Enhancing Drugs Have Limited Effects

One of the counterarguments to the idea that steroids cause a significant increase in athletic ability is that athletes still rely heavily on their natural ability; most people, no matter how hard they try, will never become professional or Olympic athletes. While performance-enhancing drugs can improve endurance and strength and speed up recovery, they cannot make a curve ball easier to hit or take seconds off of a sprinter's 100-meter time. As radio talk show host Steve Yuhas explains, "Popping a pill or injecting yourself with steroids, although harmful to the individual in the long run, does not make a person more athletically talented than anyone else."

Some people even argue that natural ability is as unfair an advantage as performance-enhancing drugs—perhaps even more so, because while the drugs are available to anyone, athletes cannot change the genes with which they were born. In fact, many people contend that the use of performance-enhancing drugs is simply a way to level the playing field. They argue that it is genetics, not drugs, that make a competition unfair; some people are simply better equipped to compete. One example is Finnish cross-country skier Eero Maentyranta, who won three gold medals in the 1964 Winter Olympics. Later tests revealed his blood naturally contained 40 to 50 percent more red blood cells than average. This gave him a significant advantage over his competitors because long-distance performance relies on delivery of oxygen to muscles, which is the job of red blood cells. His natural ability outmatched any benefit someone with an average level of red blood cells would receive from using drugs.

Similarly, one theory states that European distance runners lag behind their African counterparts because African runners, such as those from Kenya and Ethiopia, can resist fatigue longer and go farther on the same amount of oxygen. Studies also show that Kenyan runners tend to have slimmer legs than European runners, which means they do not need as much energy to run. Examination of this subject can be difficult, as it can lead to controversial conclusions on racial differences; however, physical evidence does suggest that body types are not universal—after all, no one would deny that the average man is too short to succeed in the National Basketball Association. As Julian Savulescu, Bennett Foddy, and Megan Clayton argue, "Sport discriminates against the genetically unfit. Sport is the province of the genetic elite."

At the same time, note people who disagree with that argument, performance-enhancing drugs can make a significant difference if taken by an elite athlete. If taking a steroid will enable a hitter to develop the arm strength needed to drive a baseball 15 feet farther, that could be the difference between a fly ball to the warning track and a home run. Using EPO might enable a world-class sprinter to shave enough time off his or her 100-meter dash to win an Olympic medal. Talent is essential for athletic success, but performance-enhancing drugs can provide a small but critical boost. At the topmost levels of sports, differences between athletic ability are minimal, save for a few exceptional athletes—the Michael Jordans and Wayne Gretzkys of the world.

Legalizing Performance-Enhancing Drugs

Some argue that the best way to even the playing field is by legalizing performance-enhancing drugs. Proponents of this view contend that legalization would eliminate any genetic advantages some athletes may possess. One writer even suggests that athletes who do not use steroids should be banned from competition. In the view of Sidney Gendin, "For all the money they have to lay out, fans are entitled to the best possible performances. Why, then, should they have to put up with the inferior performances of non-drug users?"

Legalizing drugs would bring with it a host of new complications. First, each major sports organization would have to decide which performance-enhancing drugs its athletes would be permitted to use. The drugs would have to be strictly regulated to ensure that they were not laced with banned substances. Athletes would need to be recompensed if they developed health problems as a result of using steroids or other drugs. Society would also need to decide whether performance-enhancing drugs should be legalized at the high school or college level. In addition, as Charles E. Yesalis, an expert on the history of drugs in sports, states, "Legalization of steroids in sport might lessen hypocrisy, but it would place an extremely heavy burden on individual athletes who then would be forced either to take drugs known to be harmful or compete at a disadvantage."

Whether using performance-enhancing drugs is a type of cheating or merely a way for athletes to create level playing fields is a matter of perspective. What is clear is that use of these drugs leads to considerable controversy and pointed debate. And as long as athletes come from different social and economic backgrounds and are of different shapes and sizes, athletic competitions can never take place between true equals.

How Dangerous Are Performance-Enhancing Drugs?

"The price of steroid abuse is high."

—Doug West, "Steroid Abuse—Getting Bigger,"
Youthculture@today, Fall 2002.

Steroids and other performance-enhancing drugs do more than improve athletic performance. They can also shorten or worsen the lives of the athletes who use them. The physical effects of performance-enhancing drugs have been well documented. Steroid users run the risk of heart attacks, liver cancer, and strokes. Less fatal but still troubling consequences include impotence and breast development for male users and breast reduction and facial hair for women. These gender-specific effects occur because steroids contain testosterone; too much testosterone gives women male characteristics, but it also changes the secondary sexual characteristics of men. Excessive levels of testosterone have also been found to kill brain cells, a discovery that researchers believe may be linked to behavior changes such as suicidal tendencies and hyperaggressiveness.

Consequences of Steroid Use

The fate of East German women athletes who were given steroids to improve their chances in the Olympic games shows that using these drugs can have unintended consequences. Howard Bryant writes, "In thousands of cases, the East German government had injected so much testosterone into its female athletes that some had essentially turned into men. Breast size shrank, facial hair grew, male pattern baldness developed, and the clitoris grew enlarged and deformed. A few, their bodies ravaged by years' worth of male hormones, would undergo sex-change operations."

Steroid users may also be more prone to injuries, in particular, tendon damage, because of their increased muscle mass. Some doctors believe this may be why Mark McGwire's home-run totals fell off rapidly after his record-setting season in 1998 and why injuries forced him to retire in 2001. Bryant suggests, "[Doctors] were . . . convinced that the types of injuries McGwire suffered were typical of a body affected by steroids, a by-product of overdevelopment, of joints weakened by anabolic substances, making his body far too powerful for his frame. McGwire grew so big his joints gave in."

Steroids and Organ Damage

Steroids can cause serious harm to the heart, liver, and kidneys. People who use steroids have an increased chance of blood clots and of enlargement and weakening of the heart. Androgen use has also been associated with heart attacks. Because the liver filters blood before it reaches the kidneys, it must constantly work to remove traces of drugs, such as steroids, from the blood. If too large an amount of drugs reaches the liver, the organ releases bile into the bloodstream. Bile causes the eyes and skin to turn yellow, a condition known as jaundice. Steroid use can also result in liver tumors and the condition peliosis hepatitis, in which blood-filled cysts form in the liver. These can rupture and lead to internal bleeding. Extensive steroid use can also cause kidney failure because every drug a person takes also has to be processed through the kidneys.

Performance-enhancing drugs also affect athletes emotionally and psychologically. The hyperaggressiveness associated with steroid use is known colloquially as "roid rage." Paranoia and antisocial behavior can also occur. Steroids can also be addictive, according to the Drug Enforcement Administration (DEA). The DEA explains, "An undetermined percentage of steroid abusers may become addicted to the drug, as evidenced by their continuing to take steroids in spite of physical problems, negative effects on social relations, or nervousness and irritability. Steroid users can experience withdrawal symptoms such as mood swings, fatigue, restlessness, and depression."

Have the Dangers of Performance-Enhancing Drugs Been Exaggerated?

Despite these effects, many people maintain that performance-enhancing drugs are not terribly dangerous. One person who has argued that the health risks of steroid use have been overstated is Rick Collins, a bodybuilder and attorney who has written extensively about steroids. He asserts, "A flawed 1988 study suggested that psychiatric disorders occur with unusual frequency among athletes using anabolics. But the conclusions of these researchers have been regarded with skepticism from other experts."

Furthermore, some performance-enhancing drugs have legitimate medical uses and thus, proponents say, should not be considered as wholly dangerous. Steroids speed the healing of injured muscles, help aging men build muscle mass, and increase libido. Human growth hormone has helped increase the height of thousands of children.

Would Legalization Reduce the Health Risks of Performance-Enhancing Drugs?

Some contend that one way to make sure that athletes do not experience health problems when they take performance-enhancing drugs is to legalize these drugs. If steroids and similar substances were legalized, athletes could take them under the supervision of doctors. Michael Le Page, writing for *New Scientist,* argues, "Allow the use of drugs, and have sports authorities focus on testing the health of athletes rather than their use of drugs. This is the suggestion of ethicists Julian Savulescu at the University of Oxford and Bennett Foddy at the University of Melbourne, Australia. They argue that any drugs that are safe should be permitted, whatever their effect on performance."

POSTSCRIPT

Should There Be More Regulation of Performance-Enhancing Drugs?

There are several reasons why long-term research into the effects of performance-enhancing drugs is lacking. First, it is unethical to give drugs to people that may prove harmful, even lethal. Also, the amount of drugs given to subjects in a laboratory setting may not replicate what illegal users actually take. Users who take performance-enhancing drugs illegally may take substantially more than that which subjects are given in a clinical trial. For example, it is not uncommon for steroid users to "stack" their drugs, meaning they take several different steroids.

Second, to determine the true effects of drugs, double-blind studies need to be conducted. This means that neither the researcher nor the people receiving the drugs know whether the subjects are receiving the steroids or the placebos (inert substances). This approach is not practical with performance-enhancing drugs because subjects can tell if they received the drugs or the placebos. The effects of performance-enhancing drugs could be determined by following up with people who are known users. However, this method lacks proper controls. If physical or psychological problems appear in a subject, for example, it cannot be determined whether the problems are due to performance-enhancing drugs or other drugs the person may have been taking. Also, the type of person who uses performance-enhancing drugs may be the type of person who has emotional problems in the first place.

In regard to anabolic steroids, the Drug Enforcement Administration estimates the black-market trade in anabolic steroids to be several hundred million dollars a year. One could argue that steroids and other performance-enhancing drugs are symptomatic of a much larger social problem. Society places much emphasis on appearance and performance. From the time we are children, we are bombarded with constant reminders that we must do better than the next person. If you want to make the varsity team, if you want that scholarship, or if you want to be a professional athlete, then you need to do whatever it takes to get there. We are also constantly reminded of the importance of appearance—to either starve ourselves or pump ourselves up (or both) in order to satisfy the cultural ideal of beauty. If we cannot achieve these cultural standards through exercising, dieting, or drug use, then we can turn to surgery. Many males growing up are given the message that they should be "big and strong." One shortcut to achieving that look is through the use of drugs. Using performance-enhancing drugs fit into the larger social problem of people not accepting themselves and their limitations.

A good review of who is using anabolic steroids and the effects of these drugs are described in "Anabolic Steroids," by Matthew Rhea and others, *Clinician Reviews* (2010). The widespread use of performance-enhancing drugs in various sports is described in "The Doping Dilemma: Game Theory to Explain the Pervasive Abuse of Drugs in Cycling, Baseball and Other Sports" by Michael Shermer, *Scientific American* (April 2008). In "Enhanced Athletes? It's Only Natural," *Washington Post* (August 3, 2008), Andy Miah examines the use of technology, including steroids, in the development of the modern-day athlete. Testing for steroid use is discussed in Scott Laffe's article "Steroids: To Test or to Educate? Several School Districts Find a Will and a Way to Examine Their Athletes for Illegal Substance Use," *School Administrator* (June 2006). The use of steroids in sports is dealt with in "Chemical Edge: The Risks of Performance-Enhancing Drug," by Marissa Saltzman, *Odyssey* (May 1, 2006) and "Drugs and the Olympics," *The Economist* (August 7, 2004).

Internet References . . .

National Institute on Alcohol Abuse and Alcoholism (NIAAA)

This site provides research on the causes, consequences, treatment and prevention of alcoholism and alcohol-related problems.

http://www.niaaa.nih.gov

American Medical Association (AMA)

Information regarding the development and promotion of standards in medical practice, research and education are included through this website.

http://www.ama-assn.org

Columbia University College of Physicians and Surgeons Complete Home Medical Guide

This site provides information about health and medicine, including information dealing with psychotherapeutic drugs.

http://cpmcnet.columbia.edu/texts/guide/hmg06_005.html

American Psychological Association (APA)

Research concerning different psychological disorders and the various types of treatments, including drug treatments that are available, can be accessed through this site.

http://www.apa.org

CDC's Tobacco Information and Prevention Source

This location contains current information on smoking prevention programs. Much data regarding teen smoking can be found at this site.

http://www.cdc.gov/tobacco

Drugs and Social Policy

*E*xcept *for the debates over whether laws prohibiting marijuana use should be relaxed and whether drug addicts should be provided clean needles, each debate in this section focuses on drugs that are already legal. Despite concerns over the effects of illegal drugs, the most frequently used drugs in society are legal drugs. Because of their prevalence and legal status, the social, psychological, and physical impact of drugs like tobacco, caffeine, alcohol, and prescription drugs are often minimized or negated. However, tobacco and alcohol cause far more death and disability than all illegal drugs combined.*

The recent trend toward medical self-help raises questions of how much control one should have over one's health. The current tendency to identify secondhand smoke and caffeine consumption as harmful to one's health has generated much controversy. Is the demand by consumers for prescription drugs resulting from television and print advertisements a good thing? Lastly, the proliferation of Ritalin and other stimulants for children with ADHD has created much concern.

- Are the Risks of Secondhand Smoke Overstated?

- Should Laws Prohibiting Marijuana Use Be Relaxed?

- Should Drug Addicts Be Given Access to Free Needles?

- Is Caffeine a Health Risk?

- Should School-Age Children with Attention Deficit/Hyperactivity Disorder (ADHD) Be Treated with Ritalin and Other Stimulants?

- Do Consumers Benefit When Prescription Drugs Are Advertised?

ISSUE 8

Are the Risks of Secondhand Smoke Overstated?

YES: Robert A. Levy and Rosalind B. Marimont, from "Lies, Damned Lies, and 400,000 Smoking-Related Deaths," *Regulation* (vol. 21, no. 4, 1998)

NO: Lissy C. Friedman, from "Tobacco Industry Use of Corporate Social Responsibility Tactics as a Sword and a Shield on Secondhand Smoke Issues," *Journal of Law, Medicine & Ethics* (Winter 2009)

ISSUE SUMMARY

YES: Robert Levy and Rosalind Marimont claim that the government distorts and exaggerates the dangers associated with cigarette smoking. They state that factors like poor nutrition and obesity are overlooked as causes of death among smokers. They note that cigarette smoking is harmful, but the misapplication of statistics should be regarded as "junk science."

NO: Lissy C. Friedman claims that the tobacco industry uses the mantle of corporate responsibility as a ruse to alter its public perception. Friedman argues that the tobacco industry was aware of the deleterious effects of secondhand smoke but tried to minimize or negate that information.

Most people, including those who smoke, recognize that cigarette smoking is harmful. However, are nonsmokers in jeopardy due to secondhand smoke? Because of tobacco's reputation as a substance that jeopardizes people's health, many activists are requesting that more stringent restrictions be placed on it, including secondhand smoke. Currently, cigarette packages are required to carry warnings describing the dangers of tobacco products but they do not mention the effects of secondhand smoke. In many countries tobacco products cannot be advertised on television or billboards. Laws that prevent minors from purchasing tobacco products are being more vigorously enforced. The World Health Organization feels that global leadership for curtailing the proliferation of cigarette smoking is lacking. Should not there be greater regulation regarding secondhand smoke?

Defenders of the tobacco industry point to benefits associated with nicotine, the mild stimulant that is the chief active chemical in tobacco. In previous centuries, for example, tobacco was used to help people with a variety of ailments including skin diseases, internal and external disorders, and diseases of the eyes, ears, mouth, and nose. Tobacco and its smoke were employed often by Native Americans for sacramental purposes. For users, smoking provides a sense of euphoria, and is a source of gratification that does not impair thinking or performance. One can drive a car, socialize, study for a test, and engage in a variety of activities while smoking. Nicotine can relieve anxiety and stress, and it can reduce weight by lessening one's appetite and by increasing metabolic activity. Many smokers assert that smoking cigarettes enables them to concentrate better and that abstaining from smoking impairs their concentration. One could ask the question as to how much secondhand smoke impairs others and whether smokers should be deprived of smoking.

Critics paint a very different picture of tobacco products, citing some of the following statistics: Tobacco is responsible for about 30 percent of deaths among people between ages 35 and 69, making it the single most prominent cause of premature death in the developed world. The relationship between cigarette smoking and cardiovascular disease, including heart attack, stroke, sudden death, peripheral vascular disease, and aortic aneurysm, is well documented. Even as few as one to four cigarettes daily can increase the risk of fatal coronary heart disease. Cigarettes have also been shown to reduce blood flow and the level of high-density lipoprotein cholesterol, which is the beneficial type of cholesterol.

According to the United States Surgeon General, exposure to secondhand smoke causes lung cancer, cardiovascular disease, damage to the respiratory tract, middle-ear disease, exacerbation of asthma in children, and sudden infant death syndrome (SIDS). Secondhand smoke contains more than 50 carcinogens.

According to smokers' rights advocates, the majority of smokers are already aware of the potential harm of tobacco products; in fact, most smokers tend to overestimate the dangers of smoking. Adults should therefore be allowed to smoke if that is their wish. Many promote the idea that the Food and Drug Administration (FDA) and a number of politicians are attempting to deny smokers the right to engage in a behavior that they freely choose. Balancing the rights of smokers and nonsmokers is difficult. The question remains as to whether employers should limit the exposure of secondhand smoke to nonsmokers. What would be the impact of limiting smoking on the morale of smokers and nonsmokers?

In the YES selection, Robert Levy and Rosalind Marimont argue that the scientific evidence demonstrating that tobacco use is harmful to smokers is disputable. They state that smoking has been demonized unfairly. Cigarette smoking is not illegal and does not cause intoxication, violent behavior, or unemployment. In the NO selection, Lissy Friedman argues that secondhand smoke is harmful and that large corporations have purposely misguided people regarding the dangers of secondhand smoke.

YES

Robert A. Levy and
Rosalind B. Marimont

Lies, Damned Lies, and 400,000 Smoking-Related Deaths

T ruth was an early victim in the battle against tobacco. The big lie, repeated ad nauseam in anti-tobacco circles, is that smoking causes more than 400,000 premature deaths each year in the United States. That mantra is the principal justification for all manner of tobacco regulations and legislation, not to mention lawsuits by dozens of states for Medicaid recovery, class actions by seventy-five to eighty union health funds, similar litigation by thirty-five Blue Cross plans, twenty-four class suits by smokers who are not yet ill, sixty class actions by allegedly ill smokers, five hundred suits for damages from secondhand smoke, and health-related litigation by twelve cities and counties—an explosion of adjudication never before experienced in this country or elsewhere.

The war on smoking started with a kernel of truth—that cigarettes are a high risk factor for lung cancer—but has grown into a monster of deceit and greed, eroding the credibility of government and subverting the rule of law. Junk science has replaced honest science and propaganda parades as fact. Our legislators and judges, in need of dispassionate analysis, are instead smothered by an avalanche of statistics—tendentious, inadequately documented, and unchecked by even rudimentary notions of objectivity. Meanwhile, Americans are indoctrinated by health "professionals" bent on imposing their lifestyle choices on the rest of us and brainwashed by politicians eager to tap the deep pockets of a pariah industry.

The aim of this paper is to dissect the granddaddy of all tobacco lies—that smoking causes 400,000 deaths each year. To set the stage, let's look at two of the many exaggerations, misstatements, and outright fabrications that have dominated the tobacco debate from the outset.

Third-Rate Thinking About Secondhand Smoke

"Passive Smoking Does Cause Lung Cancer, Do Not Let Them Fool You," states the headline of a March 1998 press release from the World Health Organization. The release begins by noting that WHO had been accused of suppressing

From *Regulation*, vol. 21, no. 4, 1998. Copyright © 1998 by Cato Institute. Reprinted by permission via Copyright Clearance Center.

its own study because it "failed to scientifically prove that there is an association between passive smoking . . . and a number of diseases, lung cancer in particular." Not true, insisted WHO. Smokers themselves are not the only ones who suffer health problems because of their habit; secondhand smoke can be fatal as well.

The press release went on to report that WHO researchers found "an estimated 16 percent increased risk of lung cancer among nonsmoking spouses of smokers. For workplace exposure the estimated increase in risk was 17 percent." Remarkably, the very next line warned: "Due to small sample size, neither increased risk was statistically significant." Contrast that conclusion with the hype in the headline: "Passive Smoking Does Cause Lung Cancer." Spoken often enough, the lie becomes its own evidence.

The full study would not see the light of day for seven more months, until October 1998, when it was finally published in the *Journal of the National Cancer Institute*. News reports omitted any mention of statistical insignificance. Instead, they again trumpeted relative risks of 1.16 and 1.17, corresponding to 16 and 17 percent increases, as if those ratios were meaningful. Somehow lost in WHO's media blitz was the National Cancer Institute's own guideline: "Relative risks of less than 2 [that is, a 100 percent increase] are considered small. . . . Such increases may be due to chance, statistical bias, or effects of confounding factors that are sometimes not evident." To put the WHO results in their proper perspective, note that the relative risk of lung cancer for persons who drink whole milk is 2.4. That is, the increased risk of contracting lung cancer from whole milk is 140 percent—more than eight times the 17 percent increase from secondhand smoke.

What should have mattered most to government officials, the health community and concerned parents is the following pronouncement from the WHO study: After examining 650 lung cancer patients and 1,500 healthy adults in seven European countries, WHO concluded that the "results indicate no association between childhood exposure to environmental tobacco smoke and lung cancer risk."

EPA's Junk Science

Another example of anti-tobacco misinformation is the landmark 1993 report in which the Environmental Protection Agency declared that environmental tobacco smoke (ETS) is a dangerous carcinogen that kills three thousand Americans yearly. Five years later, in July 1998, federal judge William L. Osteen lambasted the EPA for "cherry picking" the data, excluding studies that "demonstrated no association between ETS and cancer," and withholding "significant portions of its findings and reasoning in striving to confirm its *a priori* hypothesis." Both "the record and EPA's explanation," concluded the court, "make it clear that using standard methodology, EPA could not produce statistically significant results." A more damning assessment is difficult to imagine, but here are the court's conclusions at greater length, in its own words.

EPA publicly committed to a conclusion before research had begun; excluded industry [input thereby] violating the [Radon Research] Act's procedural requirements; adjusted established procedure and scientific norms to validate the Agency's public conclusion, and aggressively utilized the Act's authority to disseminate findings to establish a de facto regulatory scheme intended to restrict Plaintiff's products and to influence public opinion. In conducting the ETS Risk Assessment, EPA disregarded information and made findings on selective information; did not disseminate significant epidemiologic information; deviated from its Risk Assessment Guidelines; failed to disclose important findings and reasoning; and left significant questions without answers. EPA's conduct left substantial holes in the administrative record. While so doing, EPA produced limited evidence, then claimed the weight of the Agency's research evidence demonstrated ETS causes cancer.

—*Flue-Cured Tobacco Coop. Stabilization Corp. v. United States Environmental Protection Agency,* 4 F. Supp. 2d 435, 465–66 (M.D.N.C. 1998)

Hundreds of states, cities, and counties have banned indoor smoking—many in reaction to the EPA report. California even prohibits smoking in bars. According to Matthew L. Myers, general counsel of the Campaign for Tobacco-Free Kids, "the release of the original risk assessment gave an enormous boost to efforts to restrict smoking." Now that the study has been thoroughly debunked, one would think that many of the bans would be lifted. Don't hold your breath. When science is adulterated and debased for political ends, the culprits are unlikely to reverse course merely because they have been unmasked.

In reaction to the federal court's criticism EPA administrator Carol M. Browner said, "It's so widely accepted that secondhand smoke causes very real problems for kids and adults. Protecting people from the health hazards of secondhand smoke should be a national imperative." Like *Alice in Wonderland,* sentence first, evidence afterward. Browner reiterates: "We believe the health threats . . . from breathing secondhand smoke are very real." Never mind science; it is Browner's beliefs that control. The research can be suitably tailored.

For the EPA to alter results, disregard evidence, and adjust its procedures and standards to satisfy agency prejudices is unacceptable behavior, even to a first-year science student. Those criticisms are about honesty, carefulness, and rigor—the very essence of science.

Classifying Diseases as Smoking-Related

With that record of distortion, it should come as no surprise that anti-tobacco crusaders misrepresent the number of deaths due to smoking. Start by considering the diseases that are incorrectly classified as smoking-related. The Centers for Disease Control and Prevention (CDC) prepares and distributes information on smoking-attributable mortality, morbidity and economic costs (SAMMEC). In its *Morbidity and Mortality Weekly Report* for 27 August 1993, the CDC states that 418,690 Americans died in 1990 of various diseases that they contracted because, according to the government, they smoked.

Diseases are categorized as smoking-related if the risk of death for smokers exceeds that for nonsmokers. In the jargon of epidemiology, a relative risk that is greater than 1 indicates a connection between exposure (smoking) and effect (death). Recall, however, the National Cancer Institute's guideline: "Relative risks of less than two are considered small. . . . Such increases may be due to chance, statistical bias, or effects of confounding factors that are sometimes not evident." And the *Federal Reference Manual on Scientific Evidence* confirms that the threshold test for legal significance is a relative risk of two or higher. At any ratio below two, the results are insufficiently reliable to conclude that a particular agent (e.g., tobacco) caused a particular disease.

What would happen if the SAMMEC data were to exclude deaths from those diseases that had a relative risk of less than two for current or former smokers? Table 1 shows that 163,071 deaths reported by CDC were from diseases that

Table 1

Disease Category	Relative Risk	Deaths From Smoking
Cancer of pancreas	1.1–1.8	2,931*
Cancer of cervix	1.9	647*
Cancer of bladder	1.9	2,348*
Cancer of kidney, other urinary	1.2–1.4	353
Hypertension	1.2–1.9	5,450
Ischemic heart disease (age 35–64)	1.4–1.8	15,535*
Ischemic heart disease (age 65+)	1.3–1.6	64,789
Other heart disease	1.2–1.9	35,314
Cerebrovascular disease (age 35–64)	1.4	2,681*
Cerebrovascular disease (age 65+)	1.0–1.9	14,610
Atherosclerosis	1.3	1,267*
Aortic aneurysm	1.3	448*
Other arterial disease	1.3	372*
Pneumonia and influenza	1.4–1.6	10,552*
Other respiratory diseases	1.4–1.6	1,063*
Pediatric diseases	1.5–1.8	1,711
Sub-total		160,071
Environmental tobacco smoke	1.2	3,000
Total		163,071

* Number of deaths for this category assumes population deaths distributed between current and former smokers in same proportion as in Cancer Prevention Survey CPS-II, provided by the American Cancer Society.

should not have been included in the report. Add to that another 1,362 deaths from burn injuries—unless one believes that Philip Morris is responsible when a smoker falls asleep with a lit cigarette. That is a total of 164,433 misreported deaths out of 418,690. When the report is properly limited to diseases that have a significant relationship with smoking, the death total declines to 254,257. Thus, on this count alone, SAMMEC overstates the number of deaths by 65 percent.

Calculating Excess Deaths

But there is more. Writing on "Risk Attribution and Tobacco-Related Deaths" in the 1993 *American Journal of Epidemiology,* T. D. Sterling, W. L. Rosenbaum, and J. J. Weinkam expose another overstatement—exceeding 65 percent—that flows from using the American Cancer Society's Cancer Prevention Survey (CPS) as a baseline against which excess deaths are computed. Here is how one government agency, the Office of Technology Assessment (OTA), calculates the number of deaths caused by smoking:

The OTA first determines the death rate for persons who were part of the CPS sample and never smoked. Next, that rate is applied to the total U.S. population in order to estimate the number of Americans who would have died if no one ever smoked. Finally, the hypothetical number of deaths for assumed never-smokers is subtracted from the actual number of U.S. deaths, and the difference is ascribed to smoking. That approach seems reasonable if one important condition is satisfied: The CPS sample must be roughly the same as the overall U.S. population with respect to those factors, other than smoking, that could be associated with the death rate. But as Sterling, Rosenbaum, and Weinkam point out, nothing could be further from the truth.

The American Cancer Society bases its CPS study on a million men and women volunteers, drawn from the ranks of the Society's members, friends, and acquaintances. The persons who participate are more affluent than average, overwhelmingly white, married, college graduates, who generally do not have hazardous jobs. Each of those characteristics tends to reduce the death rate of the CPS sample which, as a result, enjoys an average life expectancy that is substantially longer than the typical American enjoys.

Because OTA starts with an atypically low death rate for never-smokers in the CPS sample, then applies that rate to the whole population, its baseline for determining excess deaths is grossly underestimated. By comparing actual deaths with a baseline that is far too low, OTA creates the illusion that a large number of deaths are due to smoking.

That same illusion pervades the statistics released by the U.S. Surgeon General, who in his 1989 report estimated that 335,600 deaths were caused by smoking. When Sterling, Rosenbaum, and Weinkam recalculated the Surgeon General's numbers, replacing the distorted CPS sample with a more representative baseline from large surveys conducted by the National Center for Health Statistics, they found that the number of smoking-related deaths declined to 203,200. Thus, the Surgeon General's report overstated the number of deaths by more than 65 percent simply by choosing the wrong standard of comparison.

Sterling and his coauthors report that not only is the death rate considerably lower for the CPS sample than for the entire U.S. but, astonishingly, even smokers in the CPS sample have a lower death rate than the national average for both smokers and nonsmokers. As a result, if OTA were to have used the CPS death rate for smokers, applied that rate to the total population, then subtracted the actual number of deaths for all Americans, it would have found that smoking saves 277,621 lives each year. The authors caution, of course, that their calculation is sheer nonsense, not a medical miracle. Those "lives would be saved only if the U.S. population would die with the death rate of smokers in the affluent CPS sample."

Unhappily, the death rate for Americans is considerably higher than that for the CPS sample. Nearly as disturbing, researchers like Sterling, Rosenbaum, and Weinkam identified that statistical predicament many years ago; yet the government persists in publishing data on smoking-related deaths that are known to be greatly inflated.

Controlling for Confounding Variables

Even if actual deaths were compared against an appropriate baseline for non-smokers, the excess deaths could not properly be attributed to smoking alone. It cannot be assumed that the only difference between smokers and nonsmokers is that the former smoke. The two groups are dissimilar in many other respects, some of which affect their propensity to contract diseases that have been identified as smoking-related. For instance, smokers have higher rates of alcoholism, exercise less on average, eat fewer green vegetables, are more likely to be exposed to workplace carcinogens, and are poorer than nonsmokers. Each of those factors can be a "cause" of death from a so-called smoking-related disease; and each must be statistically controlled for if the impact of a single factor, like smoking, is to be reliably determined.

Sterling, Rosenbaum, and Weinkam found that adjusting their calculations for just two lifestyle differences—in income and alcohol consumption—between smokers and nonsmokers had the effect of reducing the Surgeon General's smoking-related death count still further, from 203,200 to 150,000. That means the combined effect of using a proper standard of comparison coupled with controls for income and alcohol was to lower the Surgeon General's estimate 55 percent—from 335,600 to 150,000. Thus, the original estimate was a disquieting 124 percent too high, even without adjustments for important variables like occupation, exercise, and nutritional habits.

What if smokers got plenty of exercise and had healthy diets while non-smokers were couch potatoes who consumed buckets of fast food? Naturally, there are some smokers and nonsmokers who satisfy those criteria. Dr. William E. Wecker, a consulting statistician who has testified for the tobacco industry, scanned the CPS database and found thousands of smokers with relatively low risk factors and thousands of never-smokers with high risk factors. Comparing the mortality rates of the two groups, Dr. Wecker discovered that the smokers were "healthier and die less often by a factor of three than the never-smokers."

Obviously, other risk factors matter, and any study that ignores them is utterly worthless.

Yet, if a smoker who is obese; has a family history of high cholesterol, diabetes, and heart problems; and never exercises dies of a heart attack, the government attributes his death to smoking alone. That procedure, if applied to the other causal factors identified in the CPS study, would produce more than twice as many "attributed" deaths as there are actual deaths, according to Dr. Wecker. For example, the same calculations that yield 400,000 smoking-related deaths suggest that 504,000 people die each year because they engage in little or no exercise. Employing an identical formula, bad nutritional habits can be shown to account for 649,000 excess deaths annually. That is nearly 1.6 million deaths from only three causes—without considering alcoholism, accidents, poverty, etc.—out of 2.3 million deaths in 1995 from all causes combined. And on it goes—computer-generated phantom deaths, not real deaths—constrained neither by accepted statistical methods, by common sense, nor by the number of people who die each year.

Adjusting for Age at Death

Next and last, we turn to a different sort of deceit—one pertaining not to the number of smoking-related deaths but rather to the misperception that those deaths are somehow associated with kids and young adults. For purposes of this discussion, we will work with the far-fetched statistics published by CDC—an annual average from 1990 through 1994 of 427,743 deaths attributable to tobacco. Is the problem as serious as it sounds?

At first blush, it would seem that more than 400,000 annual deaths is an extremely serious problem. But suppose that all of the people died at age ninety-nine. Surely then, the seriousness of the problem would be tempered by the fact that the decedents would have died soon from some other cause in any event. That is not far from the truth: while tobacco does not kill people at an average age of ninety-nine, it does kill people at an average age of roughly seventy-two—far closer to ninety-nine than to childhood or even young adulthood. Indeed, according to a 1991 RAND study, smoking "reduces the life expectancy of a twenty-year-old by about 4.3 years"—not a trivial concern to be sure, but not the horror that is sometimes portrayed.

Consider Table 2, which shows the number of deaths and age at death for various causes of death: The three nonsmoking categories total nearly 97,000 deaths—probably not much different than the correctly calculated number of smoking-related deaths—but the average age at death is only thirty-nine. As contrasted with a seventy-two-year life expectancy for smokers, each of those nonsmoking deaths snuffs out thirty-three years of life—our most productive years, from both an economic and child-rearing perspective.

Perhaps that is why the Carter Center's "Closing the Gap" project at Emory University examined "years of potential life lost" (YPLL) for selected diseases, to identify those causes of death that were of greatest severity and consequence. The results were reported by R.W. Amler and D.L. Eddins,

Table 2

Cause of Death	Number of Deaths per Year	Mean Age at Death
Smoking-attributed	427,743	72
Motor vehicle accidents	40,982	39
Suicide	30,484	45
Homicide	25,488	32

Source: Centers for Disease Control and Prevention

Table 3

Cause	Deaths	YPLL
Alcohol-related	99,247	1,795,458
Gaps in primary care*	132,593	1,771,133
Injuries (excluding alcohol-related)	64,169	1,755,720
Tobacco-related	338,022	1,497,161

* Inadequate access, screening and preventive interventions.

"Cross-Sectional Analysis: Precursors of Premature Death in the United States," in the 1987 *American Journal of Preventive Medicine*. First, the authors determined for each disease the annual number of deaths by age group. Second, they multiplied for each age group the number of deaths times the average number of years remaining before customary retirement at age sixty-five. Then they computed YPLL by summing the products for each disease across age groups.

Thus, if smoking were deemed to have killed, say, fifty thousand people from age sixty through sixty-four, a total of 150,000 years of life were lost in that age group—i.e., fifty thousand lives times an average of three years remaining to age sixty-five. YPLL for smoking would be the accumulation of lost years for all age groups up to sixty-five.

Amler and Eddins identified nine major precursors of preventable deaths. Measured by YPLL, tobacco was about halfway down the list—ranked four out of nine in terms of years lost—not "the number one killer in America" as alarmists have exclaimed. Table 3 shows the four most destructive causes of death, based on 1980 YPLL statistics. Bear in mind that the starting point for the YPLL calculation is the number of deaths, which for tobacco is grossly magnified for all of the reasons discussed above.

According to Amler and Eddins, even if we were to look at medical treatment—measured by days of hospital care—nonalcohol-related injuries impose a 58 percent greater burden than tobacco, and nutrition-related diseases are more burdensome as well.

Table 4

U.S. Smoking-Attributable Mortality by Cause and Age of Death
1990–1994 Annual Average

Age at Death	Pediatric Diseases	Burn Victims	All Other Diseases	Total
Under 1	1,591	19	0	1,610
1–34	0	300	0	300
35–49	0	221	21,773	21,994
50–69	0	286	148,936	149,222
70–74	0	96	62,154	62,250
75–84	0	133	120,537	120,670
85+	0	45	71,652	71,697
Totals	1,591	1,100	425,052	427,743

Source: Private communication from the Centers for Disease Control and Prevention

Another statistic that more accurately reflects the real health repercussions of smoking is the age distribution of the 427,743 deaths that CDC mistakenly traces to tobacco. No doubt most readers will be surprised to learn that—aside from burn victims and pediatric diseases—*tobacco does not kill a single person below the age of 35.*

Each year from 1990 through 1994, as shown in Table 4, only 1,910 tobacco-related deaths—less than half of 1 percent of the total—were persons below age thirty-five. Of those, 319 were burn victims and the rest were infants whose parents smoked. But the relationship between parental smoking and pediatric diseases carries a risk ratio of less than 2, and thus is statistically insignificant. Unless better evidence is produced, those deaths should not be associated with smoking.

On the other hand, the National Center for Health Statistics reports that more than twenty-one thousand persons below age thirty-five died from motor vehicle accidents in 1992, more than eleven thousand died from suicide, and nearly seventeen thousand died from homicide. Over half of those deaths were connected with alcohol or drug abuse. That should put smoking-related deaths in a somewhat different light.

Most revealing of all, almost 255,000 of the smoking-related deaths— nearly 60 percent of the total—occurred at age seventy or above. More than 192,000 deaths—nearly 45 percent of the total—occurred at age seventy-five or higher. And roughly 72,000 deaths—almost 17 percent of the total—occurred at the age of 85 or above. Still, the public health community disingenuously refers to "premature" deaths from smoking, as if there is no upper age limit to the computation.

The vast overestimate of the dangers of smoking has had disastrous results for the health of young people. Risky behavior does not exist in a vacuum; people compare uncertainties and apportion their time, effort, and money according to the perceived severity of the risk. Each year, alcohol and drug abuse kills tens of thousands of people under the age of thirty-five. Yet according to a 1995 survey by the U.S. Department of Health and Human Services, high school seniors thought smoking a pack a day was more dangerous than daily consumption of four to five alcoholic beverages or using barbiturates. And the CDC reports that the number of pregnant women who drank frequently quadrupled between 1991 and 1995—notwithstanding that fetal alcohol syndrome is the largest cause of preventable mental retardation, occurring in one out of every one thousand births.

Can anyone doubt that the drumbeat of antismoking propaganda from the White House and the health establishment has deluded Americans into thinking that tobacco is the real danger to our children? In truth, alcohol and drug abuse poses an immensely greater risk and antismoking zealots bear a heavy burden for their duplicity.

Conclusion

The unvarnished fact is that children do not die of tobacco-related diseases, correctly determined. If they smoke heavily during their teens, they may die of lung cancer in their old age, fifty or sixty years later, assuming lung cancer is still a threat then.

Meanwhile, do not expect consistency or even common sense from public officials. Alcoholism contributes to crime, violence, spousal abuse, and child neglect. Children are dying by the thousands in accidents, suicides, and homicides. But states go to war against nicotine—which is not an intoxicant, has no causal connection with crime, and poses little danger to young adults or family members.

The campaign against cigarettes is not entirely dishonest. After all, a seasoning of truth makes the lie more digestible. Evidence does suggest that cigarettes substantially increase the risk of lung cancer, bronchitis, and emphysema. The relationship between smoking and other diseases is not nearly so clear, however; and the scare-mongering that has passed for science is appalling. Not only is tobacco far less pernicious than Americans are led to believe, but its destructive effect is amplified by all manner of statistical legerdemain—counting diseases that should not be counted, using the wrong sample as a standard of comparison, and failing to control for obvious confounding variables.

To be blunt, there is no credible evidence that 400,000 deaths per year—or any number remotely close to 400,000—are caused by tobacco. Nor has that estimate been adjusted for the positive effects of smoking—less obesity, colitis, depression, Alzheimer's disease, Parkinson's disease and, for some women, a lower incidence of breast cancer. The actual damage from smoking is neither known nor knowable with precision. Responsible statisticians agree that it is impossible to attribute causation to a single variable, like tobacco, when there are multiple causal factors that are correlated with one another. The damage from cigarettes is far less than it is made out to be.

Most important, the government should stop lying and stop pretending that smoking-related deaths are anything but a statistical artifact. The unifying bond of all science is that truth is its aim. When that goal yields to politics, tainting science in order to advance predetermined ends, we are all at risk. Sadly, that is exactly what has transpired as our public officials fabricate evidence to promote their crusade against big tobacco.

Lissy C. Friedman  **NO**

Tobacco Industry Use of Corporate Social Responsibility Tactics as a Sword and a Shield on Secondhand Smoke Issues

I. Introduction

A. Corporate Social Responsibility

Corporate social responsibility has become a potential path to legitimacy and improved public relations for both companies that produce mainstream products and those that sell vice, such as the tobacco industry. Since the early 1990s, the tobacco industry has sought to bridge the gap between the public perception it has earned as a merchant of death and its goal of gaining corporate legitimacy and normality by promoting programs, positions, and policies it hopes the general public will believe are aimed at preventing or mitigating some of the societal ills that smoking causes, such as youth smoking. There is, however, an intractable problem that corporate social responsibility efforts can mask but not resolve: the tobacco industry's products are lethal when used as directed, and no amount of public relations or funding of ineffective youth smoking prevention programs can reconcile that fundamental contradiction with ethical corporate citizenship. The focus of this study is to better understand the tobacco industry's corporate social responsibility efforts and to assess whether there has been any substantive change in the way it does business with regard to the issue of exposure to secondhand smoke.

The tobacco industry has used its corporate social responsibility activities as a tool to transform its defensive position on issues such as causation, youth smoking, and secondhand smoke into an offensive campaign of persuasion and public relations. The tobacco companies, like many other corporations, have used corporate social responsibility activities not only as a shield when publicly attacked but as a sword to try to change the perception of its very nature in order to hold on to its customer base and stave off litigation and regulation. Only in an actual litigation setting or before a regulatory body does the industry drop the pretense that it has changed its views and practices.

From *Journal of Law, Medicine and Ethics*, Winter 2009, pp. 819–827. Copyright © 2009 by American Society of Law, Medicine & Ethics. Reprinted by permission of Wiley-Blackwell via Rightslink.

At least one tobacco company has employed a strategy it calls "societal align-ment" not only to convince the public it has changed its business model, but to try to proactively shape society's expectations of the type of change that is acceptable.

B. Tobacco Industry Denormalization

There have been calls for a countervailing effort on the part of state tobacco control programs and other public health advocates to expose the disingenu-ous nature of the tobacco industry's corporate social responsibility efforts, and to defuse any benefits it may be gaining as a result of such activity. Tobacco industry denormalization prevents the tobacco industry from arguing that it's just like any other legitimate industry. Tobacco industry denormalization shifts the focus from individual smokers' judgment to corporate misbehav-ior, showing how the industry has "operated outside the boundaries of civi-lized corporate behavior" by marketing a deadly product. The main purpose of tobacco industry denormalization is to inform the public of the tobacco industry's role as a disease vector.

Using tobacco industry denormalization counter-marketing messages that include information about the tobacco industry's deceptive marketing, manipulation of science, and the dangers of secondhand smoke can help crys-tallize negative attitudes about the tobacco industry. For instance, debunk-ing the industry's use of "junk science" can incite indignation among those targeted by the tobacco industry. Another important goal of tobacco industry denormalization is to educate the public about the dangers of secondhand smoke. Making it clear to the public that they are involuntarily breathing the dangerous and deadly smoke of others counters the "personal choice" argu-ment from the tobacco industry's public relations arsenal. This argument is effective for use with both smokers and nonsmokers. Research shows that cul-tivating an anti-industry attitude helps deter and reduce adolescent, young adult, and adult smoking. A further benefit of tobacco industry denormaliza-tion is that it garners support for the advancement of a strong legislative or regulatory reform agenda. One study has found that tobacco industry denor-malization efforts ultimately could so marginalize the tobacco industry as to "destabilize, reduce or even eventually eliminate the industrial production of tobacco."

C. Focus of This Study

This study focuses on a new collection of tobacco industry documents that emerged from the United States Department of Justice's ground-breaking rack-eteering litigation against the tobacco industry, deepens our understanding of the tobacco industry's corporate social responsibility activities and motives, and shows the contradiction between the tobacco companies' attempts to bur-nish their image while changing virtually nothing about the way they do busi-ness. Documents from the collection highlighted in this study touch on the subjects of corporate social responsibility efforts, manipulation of science con-cerning secondhand smoke, and public relations efforts to subvert support for further secondhand smoke regulations. This study exposes the industry's corporate social responsibility strategy as insincere and without substance, and presents more useful evidence for state tobacco control programs and public health advocates to publicize in seeking to further denormalize and regulate the tobacco industry. Moreover, the results show that in addition to trying to appear to meet society's expectations, the tobacco industry seems intent on using offensive measures to shape and lower those expectations.

On October 10, 2007, 8, 862 documents discovered in the Department of Justice's racketeering suit became available online at the Legacy Tobacco Documents Library. Using the search term "speccoll:justice" to isolate documents in this collection, the author searched for documents pertaining to tobacco industry corporate social responsibility activities and the topic of secondhand smoke. Search terms pertaining to corporate social responsibility included various permutations of the phrase "corporate social responsibility," as well as terms such as "credibility," "values," "ethics," "mission," "public relations," and "image". The document research dealing with secondhand smoke used terms such as "secondhand smoke" and "environmental tobacco smoke," as well as scientific project names and the names of specific scientists, lawyers, and public relations spokespeople. The snowball method led to additional documents within the collection. Strategies and programs discussed in documents were then coded as either offensive (intended to proactively shape and change the public's and regulators' perceptions), defensive (intended to stave off litigation, regulation, or bad press), or a mixture of both.

Wherever possible, the veracity and outcome of the plans and strategies discussed in the documents were triangulated with news accounts, trial testimony and litigation documents, published studies, tobacco company websites, and other information available in the public record. Documents were selected for this study using criteria based on whether they had yet been discussed in other published studies, and whether their substance was addressed in the Department of Justice lawsuit. After weeding out duplicates, an analysis was conducted on 88 documents that pertained to the study's topic, and then honed for relevance. The final tally of documents used for this study included 15 documents pertaining to corporate social responsibility and 17 documents pertaining to secondhand smoke policy, all of which came from the Department of Justice collection. Limitations of this study are that it was confined to one specific document collection and constrained by the litigation discovery process.

II. The Tobacco Industry Uses Corporate Social Responsibility Tactics to Mask the Contradictory Way It Still Does Business

On September 22, 1999, the Department of Justice brought suit for racketeering, conspiracy, and fraud against the major transnational tobacco companies and their trade organizations. On August 17, 2006, United States District Court Judge Gladys Kessler issued a lengthy opinion finding the tobacco defendants guilty.

The court found that the defendants had formed and carried out a corrupt enterprise which conspired to defraud consumers and the public. The tobacco companies' transgressions included the following: (1) falsely denying the adverse health effects of cigarettes and their addictive properties; (2) manipulating nicotine levels in cigarettes and then denying that they were doing it; (3) falsely marketing their "light" cigarettes as less harmful; (4) intentionally marketing their products to underage smokers and viewing them as "replacement smokers"; (5) publicly denying what they internally acknowledged to be true: that secondhand smoke is hazardous to non-smokers; and (6) destroying documents and suppressing scientific evidence. The D.C. Circuit Court of Appeals affirmed the District Court's judgment on May 22, 2009.

Despite the tobacco defendants using their traditional scorched earth legal tactics to prevent discovery of internal documents in the Department of Justice case, which included document destruction and specious and overbroad claims of attorney/client privilege, the judge denied their motions to suppress and eventually the documents became available online. These documents show that while the tobacco companies were interested in rehabilitating their corporate image through corporate social responsibility activities, they also were continuing to maintain their traditional business practices of fighting litigation and regulation through manipulating scientific studies, trying to influence press coverage and attempting to convince the public and regulators that further regulation of their products is not warranted, particularly on the issue of secondhand smoke. They used a mixture of offensive and defensive strategies not only to prevent further erosion of their corporate image, but to change how the public, the press, and regulators expect them to behave.

A. Societal Alignment to Cultivate Credibility

A key reality of corporate social responsibility, which is reflected in the tobacco industry's internal documents, is that companies generally only change their positions and practices when public opinion and subsequent political pressure forces such changes. A 1999 memo written for Philip Morris's Worldwide Scientific Affairs division frankly acknowledged that "[a] real 'Company Position' is only needed when warranted by outside influential factors that demand a clear statement, to prevent the business from suffering." The memo cautioned against reacting too abruptly for fear of losing credibility and being seen as flip-flopping or admitting guilt.

Although there is evidence that British American Tobacco was concerned with appearing to be "a socially responsible company" as far back as 1982, the watershed event in tobacco industry corporate social responsibility activities appears to have been its 1998 settlement of a lawsuit with 46 of the United States' attorneys general and four other states individually, reimbursing the states for Medicaid payments for smoking-related illnesses. The tobacco companies started to realize that they had to at least appear that they were changing the way they did business, even if in reality they changed nothing substantively. In an effort to be more proactive in creating a favorable company image, in 1999 Philip Morris launched a major offensive communications

program that included a website and an accompanying public relations campaign which proclaimed that Philip Morris would no longer dispute public
health officials' stance that smoking causes disease and is addictive. Instead,
Philip Morris employed a strategy of "societal alignment" to rebuild credibility
with its customers, potential regulators, and society at large. In a 1999 memo
discussing the rationale for its new positions enunciated on its website, Philip
Morris admitted, "We have not done a good job of effectively communicating our positions regarding key tobacco issues, either to the general public or
to our own employees." Philip Morris's new policy was "to align our public
communications regarding this issue with conclusions of the public health
authorities." The company believed that "defining and improving [Philip
Morris's] corporate image will have a positive, long-term impact on the Philip
Morris family of companies." Philip Morris would still maintain that its scientific views were correct internally and when faced with litigation or regulation, but conceded that it was losing the public relations war by continuing to
voice those views, and instead opted for a message it felt was more consistent
with what society expected it to say. Despite making some apparent conces-
sions on causation and addiction, Philip Morris hedged on this strategy when
discussing the particularly thorny issue of secondhand smoke, an area fraught
with peril if smoking becomes socially unacceptable and harder to practice
due to the creation of smokefree zones through regulation. The memo stated
that Philip Morris's website message on secondhand smoke did not represent
an abdication of its position that there is no scientific proof that exposure to
secondhand smoke is harmful.

Previous research shows that tobacco companies seem much more concerned about the public's attitude towards them and their perceived credibility
than establishing truly ethical business practices, and the documents in the
Department of Justice collection further that finding. The tobacco industry
has realized it has a lack of credibility on all fronts, including its scientific
studies, litigation, legislative strategies, and how it is perceived by the press.
An undated Lorillard Corporate Communication Project presentation noted
that the industry has "no credibility" and described as its long-term objective to "begin to establish some credibility with the general public," a fairly
weak offensive goal. The presentation admitted that "smoking and health
[are] important, but credibility depends on admissions," which the document's author warned might harm them in litigation. A 1994 Philip Morris
Strategic Alternatives memo recommended a stronger offensive approach,
suggesting that acting in a "dramatic" fashion to quell "the current hysteria
swirling around the tobacco industry" could help stave off unfavorable regulation. Foreshadowing tactics Philip Morris used a decade later to support legislation allowing the Food and Drug Administration to regulate cigarettes, the
memo stated "it will be important to seek support for the program from prominent individuals and organizations, including perhaps those who are current
critics." The next section of this study will show that this cooperative and con-
ciliatory attitude did not extend to regulating secondhand smoke, which all
of the tobacco companies sought to forestall in spite of their corporate social
responsibility activities.

B. Manipulating Science and the Press to Change Public Opinion about Secondhand Smoke and Avoid Regulation

1. Manipulating Science

Despite the tobacco industry's use of corporate social responsibility initiatives to lend the impression it is presenting a more forthright face to the public, internal documents show that the companies appear to have tried to improperly influence the scientific studies they commissioned. A 1995 email written by R.J. Reynolds Associate General Counsel Mary Ward asserted frankly that John Rupp, an attorney representing the Tobacco Institute (a trade organization for the tobacco industry), steered scientists of his choosing to draw apparently pre-ordained conclusions in secondhand smoke studies. About a secondhand smoke study for which the scientists did not feel the protocol was sufficiently sound, Ward stated:

> [R.J. Reynolds and the Tobacco Institute] has been trying to rein John in, especially in Asia. Some of the Rupp-planned studies over there have not turned out so well. [R.J. Reynolds and the Tobacco Institute] and [Philip Morris International] have come to realize that the projects come out better when they are scientist-planned, and when the scientists choose the investigators on meritorious grounds, not when John chooses his scientist friends with the aim of trying to teach them something. Also, John has shown an amazing insensitivity in the way he continually proposes using [the Center for Indoor Air Research] as a money conduit for things that are purely and simply Rupp projects, and not properly funded by the Center.

When he testified in the Department of Justice trial, Rupp denied interfering with scientists carrying out research projects for the Tobacco Institute.

There's evidence the companies also tried to aggressively suppress their own scientists' reaction to outside studies. A letter written in 1981 to Brown & Williamson Senior Vice President and General Counsel, Ernest Pepples, by the head of British American Tobacco's Public Affairs, Robert Ely, discussed the problem presented when Peter Lee (a scientist working for the Tobacco Institute's British equivalent, the Tobacco Advisory Council) took issue with the Tobacco Institute's position disputing the validity of a groundbreaking study by Takeshi Hirayama showing that the spouses of smokers suffered adverse health consequences from their exposure to secondhand smoke. Because this schism led to "diplomatic difficulties between [the Tobacco Institute] and [the Tobacco Advisory Council]," the decision was made to direct Lee not to talk to outsiders about his opinion. Despite a denial by Rupp in his Department of Justice testimony that the Tobacco Institute had never tried to silence its scientists, the judge's final ruling in the case found that the Tobacco Institute knew that the study's data was correct and that Lee's conclusion was valid, and noted that an internal company memo called Lee's insistence on validating Hirayama's findings an "act of extreme disloyalty." This supported the judge's conclusion that the tobacco defendants publicly denied what they internally acknowledged: that secondhand smoke is hazardous to nonsmokers.

2. Influencing the Press

In addition to manipulating scientific research, the tobacco companies tried various offensive corporate social responsibility tactics to influence the press's interpretation of their scientific positions. R.J. Reynolds apparently had a practice of ghostwriting articles for its scientists. A 1989 memo regarding the Tobacco Institute's secondhand smoke activities recommended new strategies that included trying to "make the media more skeptical" and "hammer[ ] away at the inconclusiveness of the studies" through the dissemination of a briefing book to "targeted" journalists. The Tobacco Institute also realized that non-American scientists were more favorably received by American journalists and planned to make them more available for interviews on secondhand smoke.

R.J. Reynolds employees strategized in 1997 about how best to influence reporters and editorial boards on the topic of secondhand smoke. It was suggested that they proactively organize one-on-one meetings with reporters with only one scientist and a public relations person in the hopes that such an approach "might garner more credibility with the press." The theory was that journalists would be less apt to feel like they were being given a sales pitch if they were approached individually. The company hoped to avoid creating a group dynamic in which the journalists would feel pressured to write a story adverse to the tobacco industry's interests because they got the impression that the "[t]obacco industry meets with journalists because industry is running scared." In 1999, when the press took notice of a whistleblower's allegations that Philip Morris's new website was designed to "attempt to present a 'friendlier' face" on its position on secondhand smoke, Philip Morris coupled a defensive denial with an offensive diversionary tactic, showing selected reporters a presentation about its PM21 charitable giving program and its website.

3. Changing the Public's and Regulators' Opinions on Secondhand Smoke Regulation

The tobacco industry considered and employed corporate social responsibility strategies to change its image with both the general public and regulators, particularly on the issue of secondhand smoke. In the minutes of a 1988 Tobacco Institute committee meeting, attendees deemed previous messaging campaigns emphasizing "courtesy" and "freedom of choice" to be "unsuccessful" and praised an alternative, aggressive approach of "focusing on the extremism of anti-smokers." Some attendees felt that the companies must take the initiative and change public opinion as the key to winning the battle on secondhand smoke, including Tobacco Institute lawyer John Rupp, who reportedly stated that "the greatest threat to public smoking is not legislation, but rather social attitude." An internal debate emerged as to the efficacy of using scientific studies to create a more favorable public attitude. Philip Morris attorney Don Hoel, advocating a more offensive strategy, asserted that "the scientific and public affairs elements of the industry must work together if the [secondhand smoke] issue is to be successfully addressed." But one of the scientists present, Dr. Franz Adlkofer, stated that he "refused to endorse a situation in which scientific research is guided by public relations needs."

Recognizing that the public and regulators were increasingly embracing the creation of smokefree zones which could seriously harm its profits, Philip Morris considered changing its traditional stance on objecting to all restrictions on public smoking as a way of avoiding the most draconian forms of regulation. An undated report proposed agreeing to voluntarily and proactively "embrace designated smoking areas," with the caveat that Philip Morris would not concede that it had changed its opinion that the underlying science did not support such a policy. One of the company's main concerns in changing this policy was whether it could adversely impact its defensive position in products liability litigation, and therefore the policy was not adopted. A 1988 Brown & Williamson proposal to endorse a "threshold" level of safe exposure to secondhand smoke was similarly rejected because it could be viewed as an admission of causation in a lawsuit if it could be proved that the plaintiff's exposure was higher than the threshold. A 2001 Philip Morris email laid out three options for a new offensive secondhand smoke policy that might possibly thread the needle between courting public and governmental opinion while avoiding overly burdensome regulation or legal liability. The three options included:

> [1] deference to the government, coupled with agreement that public policy should be based on the government view; [2] agreement with the government as a matter of corporate policy, not science (except with respect to litigation); [and [3]] a science-based position, still coupled with agreement that public policy should be based on the government view.

The company appears to have adopted option one, stating on its website that the public should rely on public health officials' opinions about secondhand smoke and that the government has the authority to regulate it, with no mention of the company's scientific position that secondhand smoke does not cause harm.

In 1991, the Tobacco Institute launched a media tour called the "truth squad" featuring Gray Robertson, the president of Healthy Buildings International, an indoor air quality management company, the purpose of which was to persuade regulators that smoking bans were not necessary and that proper ventilation could adequately address the problem of secondhand smoke exposure. Robertson testified in the Department of Justice case that he had formed these opinions prior to contracting to testify before regulatory bodies on the Tobacco Institute's behalf, and that it was well known that Healthy Buildings International represented the Tobacco Institute. But in a 1987 letter to a Philip Morris executive in which he declined an offer to work specifically for Philip Morris, Robertson asserted that his testimony before regulators would be much more effective if he was not aligned with any one tobacco company but rather was seen as an impartial witness whose positions "occasionally and coincidentally coincide[d]" with the tobacco industry, and asserted that it would be a disadvantage for him to be seen as a tobacco industry spokesperson. In his letter, he boasted that "despite massive media attention, to date no one has identified such a link" between Healthy Buildings International and the tobacco companies, and claimed that his success as a witness for the Tobacco Institute lay in maintaining the "invisible bond" between them. In his Department of Justice testimony, Robertson tried to neutralize this letter's potency as a prosecution exhibit by claiming he really had wanted to avoid working for Philip Morris because he felt his "personal business would be damaged far too much."

III. Conclusion

Although many of the tobacco companies' tactics traditionally had been defensive, they strove for a way to change to a more offensive strategy. The industry's societal alignment concept, enunciated through websites, speeches, and television commercials, was created to recalibrate regulators' and the public's expectations of what change should look like for the tobacco industry. The companies' strategy sessions recognized that insisting their scientific positions were correct was no longer an effective way of staving off regulation because it was too easy to accuse them of manipulating their scientific studies. Instead, they turned to public relations to create support for their position and deny regulators any traction and public support for further legal strictures on smoking. Offensive tactics to aid the overall corporate social responsibility strategy of appearing to have improved their corporate practices included the following: courting journalists; putting forth purportedly independent experts to tout the companies' secondhand smoke positions; creating the impression of a "dramatic" new strategy to change the momentum towards increased regulation and litigation; forcefully attacking legitimate scientific studies on secondhand smoke; creating websites and public relations campaigns to enunciate company positions on causation, addiction, and secondhand smoke; focusing on changing social attitude towards public smoking; and even contemplating making some compromises on the issue of secondhand smoke. Almost without exception, however, their purported desire to appear to be good corporate citizens was at odds with their aversion to further regulation and compromising their legal position, which may be an irreconcilable conflict.

Despite the attention and resources that the tobacco companies have devoted to corporate social responsibility, they did not change fundamentally, as evidenced by their improperly influencing the scientific studies they commissioned, silencing scientists who disagreed with them, and continuing to deny the truth that secondhand smoke is harmful. The judge in the Department of Justice case found that the tobacco defendants did not change the way they do business in any substantive way, carrying on a racketeering enterprise designed to put the profits of their corporate interests above the public's health. The judge held that despite a consensus among public health officials that secondhand smoke is harmful, which the tobacco industry internally acknowledged, and despite public statements that they supported such a position, the industry worked to undermine efforts to regulate secondhand smoke, and she adjudicated them racketeers.

The information contained in this study can aid tobacco industry denormalization efforts by exposing the cynical machinations of the tobacco industry's corporate social responsibility efforts and the secondhand smoke strategy it pursued that contradicts any illusion of improved corporate behavior. Showing that the industry's corporate social responsibility efforts are insincere, coupled with a focus on the topic of secondhand smoke, can provide persuasive material for an effective counter-marketing campaign aimed at showing the public and regulators that, once again, the tobacco companies have tried to deceive and manipulate them into believing the companies had changed. A strong pushback against the industry's offensive drive for legitimacy would make it harder for the tobacco companies to apply corporate social responsibility tactics in the future to the topic of secondhand smoke by helping to de-legitimize the concept of a company whose product is deadly to both those who use it and to bystanders exposed to it having a voice in a moral and ethical dialogue.

POSTSCRIPT

Are the Risks of Secondhand Smoke Overstated?

Much data indicate that smoking cigarettes and secondhand smoke are injurious to human health. For example, more than 400,000 people die from tobacco-related illnesses each year in the United States, costing the United States health care system billions of dollars annually. Exposure to secondhand smoke is estimated to increase the risk of heart disease by 25 to 30 percent and lung cancer by 20 to 30 percent for nonsmokers. The cost of tobacco-related illnesses is borne by smokers and non-smokers alike.

Thousands of people develop debilitating conditions such as chronic bronchitis and emphysema from cigarette smoking. Levy and Marimont, however, question the accuracy of the data. How the data are presented and interpreted may affect how one feels about the issue of placing more restrictions on tobacco products and secondhand smoke. If cigarette smoking is demonized, as Levy and Marimont suggest, it is not difficult to influence people's positions on regulating tobacco. There is currently a great deal of antismoking sentiment in society because of how the statistics are presented. Levy and Marimont do not recommend that people use tobacco products; however, they state only that the consequences linked to it are exaggerated. If the health effects of cigarette smoking were not deemed as hazardous as they are, would people feel differently about smoking as well as secondhand smoke?

Despite the hazards of tobacco smoking and secondhand smoke, should companies be responsible for the effects of secondhand smoke on its employees? What responsibility does a company have toward its smokers who claim that they are dependent on tobacco? One could contend that the decision to start smoking is a matter of choice, but once tobacco dependency occurs, most smokers are in effect deprived of the choice to stop smoking. Many companies are faced with an ethical dilemma in that they may alienate workers who smoke by restricting their freedom to smoke. On the other hand, companies may alienate workers who do not want to be exposed to secondhand smoke.

Despite the reported hazards of tobacco smoking, numerous proponents of smokers' rights assert that cigarette smoking is a matter of choice. However, many people could argue that smoking is not a matter of choice because smokers become addicted to nicotine. Others contend that the decision to start smoking is a matter of choice, but once tobacco dependency occurs, most smokers are in effect deprived of the choice to stop smoking. Yet, it has been shown that millions of smokers have been able to quit smoking. Contributing to the tobacco dilemma is the expansion of tobacco manufacturers into many developing countries and the proliferation of advertising despite its ban from television and radio. Print advertisements and billboards are popular tools for advertising tobacco products.

Tobacco proponents maintain that people make all types of choices, and if the choices that people make are ultimately harmful, then that is their responsibility. A basic question is "do people have the right to engage in self-destructive behavior?" Does one have the right to expose others, such as co-workers, to their self-destructive behavior? If people are looked down upon because they smoke cigarettes, then should people be looked down upon if they eat too much or exercise too little? Does one have the right to eat a half dozen double cheese burgers, to be a couch potato, or to drink until one passes out? At what point does one lose the right to engage in deleterious behaviors—assuming that the rights of others are not adversely affected?

Changes in exposure to secondhand smoke are described in "Disparities in Secondhand Smoke Exposure—United States, 1988–1994 and 1999–2004," by S. E. Schober, C. Zhang, D. J. Brody, and C. Marano (*MMWR: Morbidity and Mortality Weekly Report*, July 11, 2008). Exposure of children to secondhand smoke is discussed in "Children's Secondhand Smoke Exposure in Private Homes and Cars: An Ethical Analysis," by Jill Jarvie and Ruth Malone (*American Journal of Public Health*, December 2008). An article that researches women in developing nations who are exposed to secondhand smoke is "Tobacco Use and Secondhand Smoke Exposure During Pregnancy: An Investigative Survey of Women in 9 Developing Nations," by Michele Bloch and associates (*American Journal of Public Health*, October 2008).

ISSUE 9

Should Laws Prohibiting Marijuana Use Be Relaxed?

YES: **Kevin Drum**, from "The Patriot's Guide to Legalization," *Mother Jones* (July/August 2009)

NO: **National Institute on Drug Abuse**, from *Marijuana Abuse* (National Institute on Drug Abuse Research Report Series, September 2010)

ISSUE SUMMARY

YES: Writer Kevin Drum argues that many assumptions about marijuana are questionable and says marijuana is not likely to become rampant if it was legal, nor would legalization necessarily lead to the use of other, more dangerous drugs.

NO: The research report from the National Institute on Drug Abuse identifies various deleterious effects associated with marijuana. For example, marijuana alters perception and time, conditions that interfere with driving ability, impairs memory and learning, and academic performance is compromised. This report also notes that long-term marijuana use can lead to addiction and negatively affect the fetuses of women who used marijuana while pregnant.

Despite the fact that marijuana is the most commonly used illegal drug in the United States, the federal government maintains that it is a potentially dangerous substance. Also, its use represents a danger, not just to the user, but to others. The government claims that marijuana can be addictive and that more young people are in treatment for marijuana than for other illegal drugs. Thus, the federal government does not advocate relaxing laws regarding marijuana.

The federal government argues that relaxing laws against marijuana use, even for medical purposes, is unwarranted. However, since the mid-1990s voters in California, Arizona, Oregon, Colorado, and other states have passed referenda to legalize marijuana for medical purposes. Despite the position of these voters, however, the federal government does not support the medical use of marijuana, and federal laws take precedence over state laws. A major concern of opponents of these referenda is that legalization of marijuana for medicinal purposes will lead to its use for recreational purposes.

The use of marijuana dates at least 5000 years ago. It was utilized medically as far back as 2737 B.C., when Chinese emperor Shen Nung recommended marijuana, or cannabis, for medical use. By the 1890s some medical reports had stated that cannabis was useful as a pain reliever. However, despite its historical significance, the use of marijuana for medical treatment is still a widely debated and controversial topic. The easing of marijuana laws, despite the drug's possible medical benefits, is viewed as a slippery slope. If marijuana is used medically, then its nonmedical use may increase. Opponents argue that there has not been an increase in recreational marijuana use in those states where marijuana has been legalized for medical purposes.

Many of the concerns about the effects of marijuana date back to the 1930s when movies such as *Reefer Madness* were produced. Marijuana was painted as a drug that caused sexual perversions and violent behavior. In the absence of research, many people believed that marijuana was an evil drug that resulted in these horrendous acts. When the Marijuana Tax Act was enacted in 1937, there was only small opposition to the law.

In more current times, marijuana is purported to cause mental illness and addiction. It is believed that marijuana affects academic achievement. Moreover, it is considered a gateway drug leading to other and more dangerous drugs. Kevin Drum argues that these assumptions are untrue. He maintains that the federal government has not scientifically proven these assumptions to be valid. Proponents of marijuana claim that the research is lacking. Moreover, proponents for relaxing marijuana laws indicate that marijuana does not cause significant problems for individuals in European countries where marijuana is used.

Advocates for relaxing marijuana laws feel that the drug is unfairly labeled as a dangerous drug. For example, many more people throughout the world die from tobacco smoking and alcohol than from marijuana. Yet, adults using those products do not go to jail or are deprived of rights that other citizens enjoy. There are as many people in jail today for marijuana offenses as from cocaine, heroin, methamphetamine, Ecstasy, and all other illegal drugs combined.

Another point raised by those people in favor of relaxing marijuana laws is that it would be easier to educate young people about marijuana's effects if it was legal. By simply keeping the drug illegal, the message is "Don't use marijuana," rather than how to reduce harms associated with it. Marijuana proponents do not advocate the unregulated use of marijuana. They favor a more reasoned, controlled approach. They feel governmental resources could be better used on stopping serious criminal activity.

In the YES selection, Kevin Drum asserts that the federal government is overzealous in its enforcement of marijuana laws. The federal government, according to Drum, continues to perpetuate myths regarding the dangers of marijuana use such as marijuana leading to other, more dangerous drugs. In the NO selection, the National Institute of Drug Abuse (NIDA) argues that marijuana is far more dangerous than many young people realize. NIDA tries to dispel many of the myths associated with marijuana and maintains that marijuana can lead to physical and mental problems, and birth defects.

YES

Kevin Drum

The Patriot's Guide to Legalization

Have you ever looked at our marijuana policy? I mean, *really* looked at it?

When we think of the drug war, it's the heavy-duty narcotics like heroin and cocaine that get most of the attention. And why not? That's where the action is. It's not marijuana that is sustaining the Taliban in Afghanistan, after all. When Crips and Bloods descend into gun battles in the streets of Los Angeles, they're not usually fighting over pot. The junkie who breaks into your house and steals your Blu-ray player isn't doing it so he can score a couple of spliffs.

No, the marijuana trade is more genteel than that. At least, I used to think it was. Then, like a lot of people, I started reading about the open warfare that has erupted among the narcotraffickers in Mexico and is now spilling across the American border. Stories of drugs coming north and arsenals of guns going south. Thousands of people brutally murdered. Entire towns terrorized. And this was a war not just over cocaine and meth, but marijuana as well.

And I began to wonder: Maybe the war against pot is about to get a lot uglier. After all, in the 1920s, Prohibition gave us Al Capone and the St. Valentine's Day Massacre, and that was over plain old whiskey and rum. Are we about to start paying the same price for marijuana?

If so, it might eventually start to affect me, too. Indirectly, sure, but that's more than it ever has before. I've never smoked a joint in my life. I've only seen one once, and that was 30 years ago. I barely drink, I don't smoke, and I don't like coffee. When it comes to mood altering substances, I live the life of a monk. I never really cared much if marijuana was legal or not.

But if a war is breaking out over the stuff, I figured maybe I should start looking at the evidence on whether marijuana prohibition is worth it. Not the spin from the drug czar at one end or the hemp hucksters at the other. Just the facts, as best as I could figure them out. So I did. Here's what I found.

In 1972, the report of the National Commission on Marihuana and Drug Abuse urged that possession of marijuana for personal use be decriminalized. A small wave of states followed this recommendation, but most refused; in Washington, President Carter called for eliminating penalties for small-time possession, but Congress stonewalled. And that's the way things have stayed since the late '70s. Some states have decriminalized, most haven't, and possession is still a criminal offense under federal law. So how has that worked out?

I won't give away the ending just yet, but one thing to know is this: On virtually every subject related to cannabis (an inclusive term that refers to both the sativa and indica varieties of the marijuana plant, as well as hashish, bhang, and other derivatives), the evidence is ambiguous. Sometimes even mysterious. So let's start with the obvious question.

Does Decriminalizing Cannabis Have Any Effect at All?

It's remarkably hard to tell—in part because drug use is faddish. Cannabis use among teens in the United States, for example, went down sharply in the '80s, bounced back in the early '90s, and has declined moderately since. Nobody really knows why.

We do, however, have studies that compare rates of cannabis use in states that have decriminalized vs. states that haven't. And the somewhat surprising conclusion, in the words of Robert MacCoun, a professor of law and public policy at the University of California-Berkeley, is simple: "Most of the evidence suggests that decriminalization has no effect."

But decriminalization is not legalization. In places that have decriminalized, simple possession is still illegal; it's just treated as an administrative offense, like a traffic ticket. And production and distribution remain felonies. What would happen if cannabis use were fully legalized?

No country has ever done this, so we don't know. The closest example is the Netherlands, where possession and sale of small amounts of marijuana is de facto legal in the famous coffeehouses. MacCoun and a colleague, Peter Reuter of the University of Maryland, have studied the Dutch experience and concluded that while legalization at first had little effect, once the coffeehouses began advertising and promoting themselves more aggressively in the 1980s, cannabis use more than doubled in a decade. Then again, cannabis use in Europe has gone up and down in waves, and some of the Dutch increase (as well as a later decrease, which followed a tightening of the coffeehouse laws in the mid-'90s) may have simply been part of those larger waves.

The most likely conclusion from the overall data is that if you fully legalized cannabis, use would almost certainly go up, but probably not enormously. MacCoun guesses that it might rise by half—say, from around 15 percent of the population to a little more than 20 percent. "It's not going to triple," he says. "Most people who want to use marijuana are already finding a way to use marijuana."

Still, there would be a cost. For one thing, a much higher increase isn't out of the question if companies like Philip Morris or R.J. Reynolds set their finest minds on the promotion of dope. And much of the increase would likely come among the heaviest users. "One person smoking eight joints a day is worth more to the industry than fifty people each smoking a joint a week," says Mark Kleiman, a drug policy expert at UCLA. "If the cannabis industry were to expand greatly, it couldn't do so by increasing the number of casual users. It would have to create and maintain more chronic zonkers." And that's a problem. Chronic use can lead to dependence and even long-term cognitive impairment. Heavy cannabis users are more likely to be in auto accidents. There have been scattered reports of respiratory and fetal development problems. Still, sensible regulation can limit the commercialization of pot, and compared to other illicit drugs (and alcohol), its health effects are fairly mild. Even a 50 percent increase in cannabis use might be a net benefit if it led to lower rates of use of other drugs.

So Would People Just Smoke More and Drink Less?

Maybe. The generic term for this effect in the economics literature is "substitute goods," and it simply means that some things replace other things. If the total demand for transportation is generally steady, an increase in sales of SUVs will lead to a decrease in the sales of sedans. Likewise, if the total demand for intoxicants is steady, an increase in the use of one drug should lead to a decrease in others.

Several years ago, John DiNardo, an economist now at the University of Michigan, found a clever way to test this via a natural experiment. Back in the 1980s, the Reagan administration pushed states to raise the drinking age to 21. Some states did this early in the decade, some later, and this gave DiNardo the idea of comparing data from the various states to see if the Reagan policy worked.

He found that raising the drinking age did lead to lower alcohol consumption; the effect was modest but real. But then DiNardo hit on another analysis—comparing cannabis use in states that raised the drinking age early with those that did it later. And he found that indeed, there seemed to be a substitution effect. On average, among high school seniors, a 4.5 percent decrease in drinking produced a 2.4 percent increase in getting high.

But what we really want to know is whether the effect works in the other direction: Would increased marijuana use lead to less drinking? "What goes up should go down," DiNardo told me cheerfully, but he admits that in the absence of empirical evidence this hypothesis depends on your faith in basic economic models.

Some other studies are less encouraging than DiNardo's, but even if the substitute goods effect is smaller than his research suggests—if, say, a 30 percent increase in cannabis use led to a 5 or 10 percent drop in drinking—it would still be a strong argument in favor of legalization. After all, excessive drinking causes nearly 80,000 deaths per year in the United States, compared to virtually none for pot. Trading alcohol consumption for cannabis use might be a pretty attractive deal.

But What About the Gateway Effect?

This has been a perennial bogeyman of the drug warriors. Kids who use pot, the TV ads tell us, will graduate to ecstasy, then coke, then meth, and then—who knows? Maybe even talk radio.

Is there anything to this? There are two plausible pathways for the gateway theory. The first is that drug use of any kind creates an affinity for increasingly intense narcotic experiences. The second is that when cannabis is illegal, the only place to get it is from dealers who also sell other stuff.

The evidence for the first pathway is mixed. Research in New Zealand, for example, suggests that regular cannabis use is correlated with higher rates of other illicit drug use, especially in teenagers. A Norwegian study comes to similar conclusions, but only for a small segment of "troubled" teenagers. Other research, however, suggests that these correlations aren't caused by gateway effects at all, but by the simple fact that kids who like drugs do drugs. All kinds of drugs.

The second pathway was deliberately targeted by the Dutch when they began their coffeehouse experiment in the '70s in part to sever the connection of cannabis with the illicit drug market. The evidence suggests that it worked: Even with cannabis freely available, Dutch cannabis use is currently about average among developed countries and use of other illicit drugs is about average, too. Easy access to marijuana, outside the dealer network for harder drugs, doesn't seem to have led to greater use of cocaine or heroin.

So, to recap: Decriminalization of simple possession appears to have little effect on cannabis consumption. Full legalization would likely increase use only moderately as long as heavy commercialization is prohibited, although the effect on chronic users might be more substantial. It would increase heroin and cocaine use only slightly if at all, and it might decrease alcohol consumption by a small amount. Which leads to the question:

HIGH SIERRAS

The woods are lovely dark, and . . . full of gun-toting narcofarmers.

Early one morning in August 2005, a small team of game wardens and deputies climbed through coyote brush and manzanita in the Sierra Azul Open Space Preserve outside San Jose, California, searching for an illegal pot farm. As they crested a ridge, they discovered densely planted rows of cannabis stalks. Suddenly, a high-powered rifle cracked and an officer fell to the ground, shot through both legs. Seconds later, another deputy shot and killed a man wielding a sawed-off shotgun. "It was literally like a jungle firefight," recalls warden John Nores, who fired at the other shooter before he escaped into the woods. Left behind in a meadow just minutes from the heart of Silicon Valley were 22,000 marijuana plants worth some $88 million.

Over the past decade, marijuana patches known as "grows" or "gardens" have sprung up on public lands across the West, including a third of California's national parks and nearly 40 percent of all national forests. Where hippies once grew just enough weed to peace out, traffickers now cultivate more than 100,000 plants at a time on 30-acre terraces irrigated by plastic pipe, laced with illegal pesticides, and guarded by men with MAC-10S and Uzis. Grows have turned up everywhere from the deepest backcountry to the edges of suburban subdivisions. Farming pot on public land can be more profitable than smuggling it across the increasingly militarized border. The 3.1 million pot plants seized in national forests in the year prior to last September had an estimated street value of $12.4 billion.

Rangers and game wardens say pot growers are a major threat to California's 23,500 square miles of wilderness (which doesn't include state or regional lands). "These guys literally create cities within your national forests," says Laura Mark, a special agent with the US Forest Service. Growers clear land year-round, plant crops in the spring, and haul out the harvest in the fall, often leaving behind mounds of trash and dead animals, denuded hillsides, and streams full of sediment and human waste. Last year, the community of Snow Creek, California, traced feces in its water treatment plant to a grow in the nearby San Bernardino National Forest. Restoring the 10,000 acres of national forest fouled by pot farms could cost more than $30 million.

Pot farmers who till public lands avoid the risk of forfeiting their property if they're busted, but they must also ward off competitors. "They are going to point guns at you first and ask questions later," says Troy Bolen, the Bureau of Land Management's head of law enforcement in California. In the past decade, growers have killed two people who have stumbled upon their fields, held nature lovers at gunpoint, and had numerous shoot-outs with cops. Last year, in California's national forests the state's anti-grow task force killed one grower and arrested 177, 80 percent of whom were Mexican citizens.

Officials believe that Mexican drug cartels control the grows, but proving that is tough. Last year, Nores caught a pot grower who revealed almost everything about his operation but said he didn't know whom he worked for. "They're kind of set up like terrorist cells," he observes. After the bloody 2005 ambush, he says, his team now treats raids like potential battles, bringing along medics and keeping air support on standby—just in case.

—Josh Harkinsor

Can We Still Afford Prohibition?

The consequences of legalization, after all, must be compared to the cost of the status quo. Unsurprisingly, this too is hard to quantify. The worst effects of the drug war, including property crime and gang warfare, are mostly associated with cocaine, heroin, and meth. Likewise, most drug-law enforcement is aimed at harder drugs, not cannabis; contrary to conventional wisdom, only about 44,000 people are currently serving prison time on cannabis charges—and most of those are there for dealing and distribution, not possession.

Still, the University of Maryland's Reuter points out that about 800,000 people are arrested for cannabis possession every year in the United States. And even though very few end up being sentenced to prison, a study of three counties in Maryland following a recent marijuana crackdown suggests that a third spend at least one pretrial night in jail and a sixth spend more than ten days. That takes a substantial human toll. Overall, Harvard economist Jeffrey Miron estimates the cost of cannabis prohibition in the United States at $13 billion annually and the lost tax revenue at nearly $7 billion.

So What Are the Odds of Legalization?

Slim. For starters, the United States, along with virtually every other country in the world, is a signatory to the 1961 Single Convention on Narcotic Drugs (and its 1988 successor), which flatly prohibits legalization of cannabis. The only way around this is to unilaterally withdraw from the treaties or to withdraw and then reenter with reservations. That's not going to happen.

At the federal level, there's virtually no appetite for legalizing cannabis either. Though public opinion has made steady strides, increasing from around 20 percent favoring marijuana legalization in the Reagan era to nearly 40 percent favoring it today, the only policy change in Washington has been Attorney General Eric Holder's announcement in March that the Obama administration planned to end raids on distributors of medical marijuana. (Applications for pot dispensaries promptly surged in Los Angeles County.)

The real action in cannabis legalization is at the state level. More than a dozen states now have effective medical marijuana laws, most notably California. Medical marijuana dispensaries are dotted all over the state, and it's common knowledge that the "medical" part is in many cases a thin fiction. Like the Dutch coffeehouses, California's dispensaries are now a de facto legal distribution network that severs the link between cannabis and other illicit drugs for a significant number of adults (albeit still only a fraction of total users). And the result? Nothing. "We've had this experiment for a decade and the sky hasn't fallen," says Paul Armentano, deputy director of the National Organization for the Reform of Marijuana Laws. California Assemblyman Tom Ammiano has even introduced a bill that would legalize, tax, and regulate marijuana; it has gained the endorsement of the head of the state's tax collection agency, which informally estimates it could collect $1.3 billion a year from cannabis sales. Still, the legislation hasn't found a single cosponsor, and isn't scheduled for so much as a hearing.

Which is too bad. Going into this assignment, I didn't care much personally about cannabis legalization. I just had a vague sense that if other people wanted to do it, why not let them? But the evidence suggests pretty clearly that we ought to significantly soften our laws on marijuana. Too many lives have been ruined and too much money spent for a social benefit that, if not zero, certainly isn't very high.

And it may actually happen. If attitudes continue to soften; if the Obama administration turns down the volume on anti-pot propaganda; if medical dispensaries avoid heavy commercialization; if drug use remains stable; and if emergency rooms don't start filling up with drug-related traumas while all this is happening, California's experience could go a long way toward destigmatizing cannabis use. That's a lot of ifs.

Still, things are changing. Even GOP icon Arnold Schwarzenegger now says, "I think it's time for a debate." That doesn't mean he's in favor of legalizing pot right this minute, but it might mean we're getting close to a tipping point. Ten years from now, as the flower power generation enters its 70s, you might finally be able to smoke a fully legal, taxed, and regulated joint.

JUST SAY KNOW

Dust off your short-term memory and test your drug war knowledge, with a quiz based on Ryan Grim's new book, *This Is Your Country on Drugs: The Secret History of Getting High in America.*

1. A 1918 *New York Times* article suggested Germany was trying to make Americans "cokeys" and "hop fiends" with . . .
   A. Drugs mixed into sausage
   B. Drugs in toothpaste and teething syrup
   C. Narco-polkas

2. How much "ditchweed"—wild hemp with no psychoactive properties—did the DEA destroy in 2005?
   A. 219 plants
   B. 219,000 plants
   C. 219 million plants

3. During the late 19th century, most opium addicts were first turned on to the drug by . . .
   A. Doctors
   B. Hobos
   C. Chinese opium dens

4. Which of the following did *not* support efforts to criminalize marijuana in the 1930s?
   A. Pharmaceutical industry
   B. American Medical Association
   C. Liquor industry

5. Which president first declared cocaine "the most dangerous drug problem that the US ever faced"?
   A. William Taft
   B. Ronald Reagan
   C. George W. Bush

6. In 2004, the White House buried a study that found that a $1.4 billion anti-pot ad campaign had . . .
   A. Increased first-time pot use among 14- to 16-year-olds
   B. Increased first-time pot use among whites
   C. Both A and B

(Answers: 1-B, 2-C, 3-A, 4-B, 5-A, 6-C)

Marijuana Abuse

. . .

How Does Marijuana Use Affect Your Brain and Body?

Effects on the Brain

As THC enters the brain, it causes the user to feel euphoric—or high—by acting on the brain's reward system, which is made up of regions that govern the response to pleasurable things like sex and chocolate, as well as to most drugs of abuse. THC activates the reward system in the same way that nearly all drugs of abuse do: by stimulating brain cells to release the chemical dopamine.

Along with euphoria, relaxation is another frequently reported effect in human studies. Other effects, which vary dramatically among different users, include heightened sensory perception (e.g., brighter colors), laughter, altered perception of time, and increased appetite. After a while, the euphoria subsides, and the user may feel sleepy or depressed. Occasionally, marijuana use may produce anxiety, fear, distrust, or panic.

Marijuana use impairs a person's ability to form new memories and to shift focus. THC also disrupts coordination and balance by binding to receptors in the cerebellum and basal ganglia—parts of the brain that regulate balance, posture, coordination, and reaction time. Therefore, learning, doing complicated tasks, participating in athletics, and driving are also affected.

Marijuana users who have taken large doses of the drug may experience an acute psychosis, which includes hallucinations, delusions, and a loss of the sense of personal identity. Although the specific causes of these symptoms remain unknown, they appear to occur more frequently when a high dose of cannabis is consumed in food or drink rather than smoked. Such short-term psychotic reactions to high concentrations of THC are distinct from longer-lasting, schizophrenia-like disorders that have been associated with the use of cannabis in vulnerable individuals. (See section on the link between marijuana use and mental illness.)

Our understanding of marijuana's long-term brain effects is limited. Research findings on how chronic cannabis use affects brain *structure*, for example, have been inconsistent. It may be that the effects are too subtle for reliable detection by current techniques. A similar challenge arises in studies

From *National Institute on Drug Abuse Research Report*, September 2010, pp. 3–9, U.S. Department of Health and Human Services.

of the effects of chronic marijuana use on brain *function*. Although imaging studies (functional MRI; fMRI) in chronic users do show some consistent alterations, the relation of these changes to cognitive functioning is less clear. This uncertainty may stem from confounding factors such as other drug use, residual drug effects (which can occur for at least 24 hours in chronic users), or withdrawal symptoms in long-term chronic users.

An enduring question in the field is whether individuals who quit marijuana, even after long-term, heavy use, can recover some of their cognitive abilities. One study reports that the ability of long-term heavy marijuana users to recall words from a list was still impaired 1 week after they quit using, but returned to normal by 4 weeks. However, another study found that marijuana's effects on the brain can build up and deteriorate critical life skills over time. Such effects may be worse in those with other mental disorders, or simply by virtue of the normal aging process.

Effects on General Physical Health

Within a few minutes after inhaling marijuana smoke, an individual's heart rate speeds up, the bronchial passages relax and become enlarged, and blood vessels in the eyes expand, making the eyes look red. The heart rate—normally 70 to 80 beats per minute—may increase by 20 to 50 beats per minute, or may even double in some cases. Taking other drugs with marijuana can amplify this effect.

Limited evidence suggests that a person's risk of heart attack during the first hour after smoking marijuana is four times his or her usual risk. This observation could be partly explained by marijuana raising blood pressure (in some cases) and heart rate and reducing the blood's capacity to carry oxygen. Such possibilities need to be examined more closely, particularly since current marijuana users include adults from the baby boomer generation, who may have other cardiovascular risks that may increase their vulnerability.

The smoke of marijuana, like that of tobacco, consists of a toxic mixture of gases and particulates, many of which are known to be harmful to the lungs. Someone who smokes marijuana regularly may have many of the same respiratory problems that tobacco smokers do, such as daily cough and phlegm production, more frequent acute chest illnesses, and a greater risk of lung infections. Even infrequent marijuana use can cause burning and stinging of the mouth and throat, often accompanied by a heavy cough. One study found that extra sick days used by frequent marijuana smokers were often because of respiratory illnesses.

In addition, marijuana has the *potential* to promote cancer of the lungs and other parts of the respiratory tract because it contains irritants and carcinogens—up to 70 percent more than tobacco smoke. It also induces high levels of an enzyme that converts certain hydrocarbons into their cancer-causing form, which could accelerate the changes that ultimately produce malignant cells. And since marijuana smokers generally inhale more deeply and hold their breath longer than tobacco smokers, the lungs are exposed longer to carcinogenic smoke. However, while several lines of evidence have suggested that

CONSEQUENCES OF MARIJUANA ABUSE

Acute (present during intoxication)

- Impairs short-term memory
- Impairs attention, judgment, and other congnitive functions
- Impairs coordination and balance
- Increases heart rate
- Psychotic episodes

Persistent (lasting longer than intoxication, but may not be permanent)

- Impairs memory and learning skills
- Sleep impairment

Long-term (cumulative effects of chronic abuse)

- Can lead to addiction
- Increases risk of chronic cough, bronchitis
- Increases risk of schizophrenia in vulnerable individuals
- May increase risk of anxiety, depression, and amotivational syndrome*

*These are often reported co-occurring symptoms/disorders with chronic marijuana use. However, research has not yet determined whether marijuana is causal or just associated with these mental problems.

---

marijuana use may lead to lung cancer, the supporting evidence is inconclusive. The presence of an unidentified active ingredient in cannabis smoke having protective properties—if corroborated and properly characterized—could help explain the inconsistencies and modest findings.

A significant body of research demonstrates negative effects of THC on the function of various immune cells, both in vitro in cells and in vivo with test animals. However, no studies to date connect marijuana's suspected immune system suppression with greater incidence of infections or immune disorders in humans. One short (3-week) study found marijuana smoking to be associated with a few statistically significant negative effects on the immune function of AIDS patients; a second small study of college students also suggested the possibility of marijuana having adverse effects on immune system functioning. Thus, the combined evidence from animal studies plus the limited human data available, seem to warrant additional research on the impact of marijuana on the immune system.

Is There a Link Between Marijuana Use and Mental Illness?

Research in the past decade has focused on whether marijuana use actually causes other mental illnesses. The strongest evidence to date suggests a link between cannabis use and psychosis. For example, a series of large prospective studies that followed a group of people over time showed a relationship between marijuana use and later development of psychosis. Marijuana use also worsens the course of illness in patients with schizophrenia and can produce a brief psychotic reaction in some users that fades as the drug wears off. The amount of drug used, the age at first use, and genetic vulnerability can all influence this relationship. One example is a study that found an increased risk of psychosis among adults who had used marijuana in adolescence *and* who also carried a specific variant of the gene for catechol-O-methyltransferase (COMT), an enzyme that degrades neurotransmitters such as dopamine and norepinephrine.

In addition to the observed links between marijuana use and schizophrenia, other less consistent associations have been reported between marijuana use and depression, anxiety, suicidal thoughts among adolescents, and personality disturbances. One of the most frequently cited, albeit still controversial, is an amotivational syndrome, defined as a diminished or absent drive to engage in typically rewarding activities. Because of the role of the endocannabinoid system in regulating mood, these associations make a certain amount of sense; however, more research is needed to confirm and better understand these linkages.

Is Marijuana Addictive?

Long-term marijuana use can lead to addiction; that is, people have difficulty controlling their drug use and cannot stop even though it interferes with many aspects of their lives. It is estimated that 9 percent of people who use marijuana will become dependent on it. The number goes up to about 1 in 6 in those who start using young (in their teens) and to 25–50 percent among daily users. Moreover, a study of over 300 fraternal and identical twin pairs found that the twin who had used marijuana before the age of 17 had elevated rates of other drug use and drug problems later on, compared with their twin who did not use before age 17.

According to the 2008 NSDUH, marijuana accounted for 4.2 million of the estimated 7 million Americans dependent on or abusing illicit drugs. In 2008, approximately 15 percent of people entering drug abuse treatment programs reported marijuana as their primary drug of abuse; 61 percent of persons under 15 reported marijuana as their primary drug of abuse, as did 56 percent of those 15 to 19 years old.

Marijuana addiction is also linked to a withdrawal syndrome similar to that of nicotine withdrawal, which can make it hard to quit. People trying to quit report irritability, sleeping difficulties, craving, and anxiety. They also show increased aggression on psychological tests, peaking approximately 1 week after they last used the drug.

How Does Marijuana Use Affect School, Work, and Social Life?

Research has shown that marijuana's negative effects on attention, memory, and learning can last for days or weeks after the acute effects of the drug wear off. Consequently, someone who smokes marijuana daily may be functioning at a reduced intellectual level most or all of the time. Not surprisingly, evidence suggests that, compared with their nonsmoking peers, students who smoke marijuana tend to get lower grades and are more likely to drop out of high school. A meta-analysis of 48 relevant studies—one of the most thorough performed to date—found cannabis use to be associated consistently with reduced educational attainment (e.g., grades and chances of graduating). However, a *causal* relationship is not yet proven between cannabis use by young people and psychosocial harm.

That said, marijuana users themselves report poor outcomes on a variety of life satisfaction and achievement measures. One study compared current and former long-term heavy users of marijuana with a control group who reported smoking cannabis at least once in their lives but not more than 50 times. Despite similar education and income backgrounds, significant differences were found in educational attainment: fewer of the heavy users of cannabis completed college, and more had yearly household incomes of less than $30,000. When asked how marijuana affected their cognitive abilities, career achievements, social lives, and physical and mental health, the majority of heavy cannabis users reported the drug's negative effects on all of these measures. In addition, several studies have linked workers' marijuana smoking with increased absences, tardiness, accidents, workers' compensation claims, and job turnover. For example, a study among postal workers found that employees who tested positive for marijuana on a pre-employment urine drug test had 55 percent more industrial accidents, 85 percent more injuries, and a 75-percent increase in absenteeism compared with those who tested negative for marijuana use.

Does Marijuana Use Affect Driving?

Because marijuana impairs judgment and motor coordination and slows reaction time, an intoxicated person has an increased chance of being involved in and being responsible for an accident. According to the National Highway Traffic Safety Administration, drugs other than alcohol (e.g., marijuana and cocaine) are involved in about 18 percent of motor vehicle driver deaths. A recent survey found that 6.8 percent of drivers, mostly under 35, who were involved in accidents tested positive for THC; alcohol levels above the legal limit were found in 21 percent of such drivers.

Can Marijuana Use During Pregnancy Harm the Baby?

Animal research suggests that the body's endocannabinoid system plays a role in the control of brain maturation, particularly in the development of emotional responses. It is conceivable that even low concentrations of THC, when administered during the perinatal period, could have profound and long-lasting consequences for both brain and behavior. Research has shown that some babies born to women who used marijuana during their pregnancies display altered responses to visual stimuli, increased tremulousness, and a high-pitched cry, which could indicate problems with neurological development. In school, marijuana-exposed children are more likely to show gaps in problem-solving skills, memory, and the ability to remain attentive. More research is needed, however, to disentangle the drug-specific factors from the environmental ones.

Available Treatments for Marijuana Use Disorders

Marijuana dependence appears to be very similar to other substance dependence disorders, although the long-term clinical outcomes may be less severe. On average, adults seeking treatment for marijuana abuse or dependence have used marijuana nearly every day for more than 10 years and have attempted to quit more than six times. It is important to note that marijuana dependence is most prevalent among patients suffering from other psychiatric disorders, particularly among adolescent and young adult populations. Also, marijuana abuse or dependence typically co-occurs with use of other drugs, such as cocaine and alcohol. Available studies indicate that effectively treating the mental health disorder with standard treatments involving medications and behavioral therapies may help reduce cannabis use, particularly among heavy users and those with more chronic mental disorders. Behavioral treatments, such as motivational enhancement therapy (MET), group or individual cognitive-behavioral therapy (CBT), and contingency management (CM), as well as family-based treatments, have shown promise.

Unfortunately, the success rates of treatment are rather modest. Even with the most effective treatment for adults, only about 50 percent of enrollees achieve an initial 2-week period of abstinence, and among those who do, approximately half will resume use within a year. Across studies, 1-year abstinence rates have ranged between 10 and 30 percent for the various behavioral approaches. As with other addictions, these data suggest that a chronic care model should be considered for marijuana addiction, with treatment intensity stepped up or down based on need, comorbid addictions or other mental disorders, and the availability of family and other supports.

Currently, no medications are available to treat marijuana abuse, but research is active in this area. Most of the studies to date have targeted the marijuana withdrawal syndrome. For example, a recent human laboratory study showed that a combination of a cannabinoid agonist medication with lofexidine (a medication approved in the United Kingdom for the treatment of opioid withdrawal) produced more robust improvements in sleep and decreased marijuana withdrawal, craving, and relapse in daily marijuana smokers relative to either medication alone. Recent discoveries about the inner workings of the endogenous cannabinoid system raise the future possibility of a medication able to block THC's intoxicating effects, which could help prevent relapse by reducing or eliminating marijuana's appeal.

POSTSCRIPT

Should Laws Prohibiting
Marijuana Use Be Relaxed?

The restrictive laws against marijuana have resulted in a burgeoning number of people in prison for marijuana offenses. Drum maintains that the scientific proof demonstrating that marijuana is harmful is lacking. Nonetheless, politicians have shown little interest in overturning the laws banning marijuana. Drum does not contend that marijuana is a safe drug, but that legalizing it would enable officials to have better control over its use. The government's objection to marijuana, says Drum, is based more on politics than scientific evidence.

Relaxing marijuana laws would raise a number of questions. If an easing of the laws resulted in much abuse and physical or psychological problems, how easy would it be to return to more restrictive marijuana laws? For example, if there is a significant increase in the number of people using marijuana, could the law be made more restrictive and how would users react? Also, would limitations be placed on marijuana use if laws were less restrictive? Would there be a limit on how much one could possess? Would the age of consent be 18, 21, or some other age? Would there be restrictions on the secondhand effects of marijuana smoke? What kind of penalties would apply to adults supplying marijuana to a minor?

Despite its popularity, the federal government notes that parents should and can assert more influence on their children's desire to use marijuana. The government claims that marijuana is not the harmless drug that many proponents believe. Marijuana can have adverse effects, on mental health, physical well-being, and academic performance. In addition, thousands of young people enter substance abuse treatment for their addiction to marijuana. It is important, states the National Institute on Drug Abuse, to counteract how culture trivializes the dangers of marijuana use.

Many marijuana proponents contend that the effort to prevent the legalization of marijuana for medical use and nonmedical use is purely a political battle. Detractors maintain that the issue is purely scientific—that the data supporting marijuana's medical usefulness are inconclusive and scientifically unsubstantiated. And although the chief administrative law judge of the Drug Enforcement Administration (DEA) made a recommendation to change the status of marijuana from Schedule I to Schedule II, the DEA and other federal agencies are not compelled to do so and they have resisted any change in the law.

Concerns about the impact of marijuana on educational achievement is discussed in "Why Parents Worry: Initiation into Cannabis Use by Youth and

Their Educational Attainment" by Jan van Ours and Jenny Williams, *Journal of Health Economics* (2008). Whether marijuana should be legalized is debated by John Walters, the previous director of the Office of National Drug Control Policy, and Ethan Nadelmann, founder and director of the Drug Policy Alliance, in *National Review* (September 27, 2004). An extensive review of marijuana usage and effects is discussed in *Non-Medical Marijuana: Rite of Passage or Russian Roulette?* (The National Center on Addiction and Substance Abuse at Columbia University, June 2008). Two papers that examine the effects of marijuana are *Teen Marijuana Use Worsens Depression: An Analysis of Recent Data Shows "Self-Medicating" Could Actually Make Things Worse* (Office of National Drug Control Policy, May 2008) and "Prospective Associations Between Cannabis Use, Abuse, and Dependence and Panic Attacks and Disorder," by Michael Zvolensky and associates, *Journal of Psychiatric Research* (2007).

Should Drug Addicts Be Given Access to Free Needles?

YES: Don C. Des Jarlais, Courtney McKnight, Cullen Goldblatt, and David Purchase, from "Doing Harm Reduction Better: Syringe Exchange in the United States," *Addiction* (2009)

NO: Drug Free Australia, from *The Kings Cross Injecting Room: The Case for Closure* (Drug Free Australia, 2010)

ISSUE SUMMARY

YES: Don Des Jarlais and his colleagues argue that the free exchange of syringes is an effective way to reduce the harm, especially HIV (human immunodeficiency virus), associated with injecting drugs. Moreover, syringe exchange programs provide an arena in which drug abusers can obtain health and social services. Des Jarlais and his associates believe that the number of syringe exchange programs will continue to proliferate.

NO: The group Drug Free Australia, which opposes syringe exchange programs, believes that providing free syringes gives the wrong message. Drugs like heroin and cocaine are illegal and drug abusers should not be allowed to continue their abuse by being provided with free syringes. Drug Free Australia also questions the validity of those statements supporting the value of syringe exchange programs.

$\mathbf{A}$cquired immunodeficiency syndrome (AIDS) can be transmitted through the use of unclean hypodermic syringes. Any type of drug injection, whether it is intravenous (mainlining), intramuscular, or just below the surface of the skin (skin-popping), can result in the transmission of AIDS. Technically, what is transmitted is not AIDS but the human immunodeficiency virus (HIV), which ultimately leads to the development of AIDS.

Until a cure for AIDS is found or a vaccine against HIV is developed, the relationship between AIDS and injecting drugs will remain a cause of great concern. On a worldwide basis, there are nearly 16 million people who inject themselves with drugs, many of whom share their needles/syringes. In a number of countries, 20 percent of those injection drug users are infected with HIV. Of course, another major concern is that those who contract HIV through drugs can pass the disease to their sexual partners. A significant number of pediatric AIDS cases are related to drug injection.

No one disagrees that the spread of AIDS is a problem and that the number of people who inject drugs is a problem. The issue that needs to be addressed is what is the best course of action to take to reduce drug injection and the transmission of AIDS? Is it better to set up more drug treatment facilities or to allow people who inject drugs access to clean needles? Another option, as proposed by Drug Free Australia, is to simply close places where people have access to clean needles because these programs are ineffective.

One concern of needle exchange opponents is that endorsement of these programs conveys the wrong message concerning drug use. Instead of discouraging drug use, they feel that such programs merely teach people how to use drugs or encourage drug use. Needle exchange advocates point to studies showing that these programs have not resulted in an increase of intravenous drug users. Other studies indicate that many drug users involved in needle exchange programs drop out and that drug users who remain in the programs are not as likely to share needles in the first place.

Proponents of needle exchange programs argue that HIV is easily transmitted when needles are shared and that something needs to be done to stem the practice. Opponents argue that whether or not needle exchange programs are available, needles will be shared. Three reasons cited by drug users for sharing needles are as follows: (1) they do not have access to clean needles, (2) they do not own their own needles, and (3) they cannot afford to buy needles. If clean needles were readily available, would addicts necessarily use them? Some studies show that people who inject drugs are concerned about contracting AIDS and will alter their drug-taking behavior.

Although needle exchange programs may result in the use of clean needles and encourage people to obtain treatment, they do not get at the root cause of drug addiction. Drug abuse and many of its concomitant problems stem from inadequate or nonexistent employment opportunities, unsafe neighborhoods, underfunded schools, and insufficient health care. Some argue that until these underlying problems are addressed, stopgap measures like needle exchange programs should be implemented.

Needle exchange programs generate a number of legal and social questions. Since heroin and cocaine are illegal, giving needles to people for the purpose of injecting these drugs contribute to illegal behavior. Should people who are addicted to drugs be seen as criminals or as victims who need compassion? Should drug users, especially drug addicts, be incarcerated or treated? The majority of drug users involved with needle exchange programs are members of minorities. Could it be that needle exchange programs promote the continuation of drug use and, hence, the enslavement of minorities rather than a turn to healthier alternatives?

In the YES selection, Don Des Jarlais and his colleagues assert that needle exchange programs represent a way to reduce harm associated with drug injection. Drug abusers can be offered other services when they go to needle exchange programs. In the NO selection, Drug Free Australia contends that needle exchange programs are ineffective and should be closed. Promoting drug abuse with a place to inject drugs sends a wrong message according to Drug Free Australia.

YES

Don C. Des Jarlais et al.

Doing Harm Reduction Better: Syringe Exchange in the United States

Introduction

The concept of 'harm reduction' for psychoactive drug use clearly predates the discovery of acquired immune deficiency syndrome (AIDS) among injecting drug users. The physician prescription of heroin for maintenance treatment of opiate addiction in the United Kingdom and the development of methadone maintenance treatment are two important examples of pre-AIDS harm reduction. The discovery of AIDS among injecting drug users (IDUs), however, has focused attention on the harm reduction perspective. As an almost uniformly fatal disease, AIDS increased dramatically the harm associated with injecting drug use. Human immunodeficiency virus (HIV) can also be transmitted to sexual partners and newborn children of infected IDUs, so this new harm was not confined to the drug users themselves. Finally, because HIV is transmitted through the multi-person use ('sharing') of drug injection equipment rather than through drug use itself, it is quite possible to prevent HIV transmission among people who continue to inject drugs.

Syringe exchange programs (SEPs)—in which sterile needles and syringes are exchanged for used, potentially HIV-contaminated needles and syringes—have come to symbolize harm reduction programming for drug users. Models of how this exchange occurs vary (i.e. one-for-one versus unlimited supply) and have different goals and outcomes. It has now been more than 25 years since the discovery of AIDS among injecting drug users and more than 20 years since the first implementation of SEPs. Syringe exchange has been particularly controversial in the United States, with determined proponents clashing with entrenched opponents. There has been a consistent lack of federal government support for syringe exchange, but also growing support from state and local governments, foundations and from individuals. This paper will examine the growth and current state of syringe exchange/harm reduction in the United States, while companion papers will examine syringe exchange/harm reduction in selected other countries. The overall purpose of the papers is to examine what has been learned over the last two decades and how syringe exchange/harm reduction programming might be improved over the coming years.

Methods

The primary data presented here were collected through surveys of SEP directors in the United States. These surveys have been conducted since 1996 by
the staff from Beth Israel Medical Center (BIMC) and the North American
Syringe Exchange Network (NASEN). In the spring of each year, a survey form
is mailed to the directors of all US SEPs known to NASEN. The survey includes
questions on syringes exchanged, services provided, program characteristics,
community relationships, budgets and funding for the previous calendar year.
Follow-up telephone interviews are conducted to obtain missing data and to
clarify responses.

NASEN provides multiple services to its member programs, including
technical assistance, 'start-up kits,' and large volume–low price purchasing of
sterile syringes, with no membership fee. Thus it is highly likely that the great
majority of programs in the United States belong to NASEN.

Results

Basic Syringe Exchange Services in the United States

Table 1 shows the numbers of programs known to NASEN, the numbers of
programs participating in the surveys and the numbers of syringes exchanged
and budget information for the participating programs that participated in
the surveys from 1994–95 to 2007. There was a period of very rapid growth
in numbers of programs, cities and states with programs, syringes exchanged
and budgets during the mid- to late-1990s. More recently, there has been stabilization of the numbers of programs, although with continued increases in
budgets and syringes exchanged.

Table 2 presents the distribution of programs by program size in 2007.
The greatest amount of exchanging is clearly carried out by the very large and
large programs. Only 10% of the programs are 'very large', but these programs
exchanged more than half of all syringes for 2007. The very large and large
programs together comprise 46% of the programs, but exchanged more than
95% of the syringes.

Most (66%) US programs do not adhere to a 'one-for-one' policy (in
which a participant is to obtain only the same number of new syringes as he or
she brought to the program at that visit). Forty-nine per cent of the programs
provided 'start-up packs' (syringes and other materials given to participants
at their first visit). Thirty-three per cent provide a minimum number of new
syringes regardless of the number of used syringes returned to the program at
that visit. Seven per cent of the programs operate on a 'distribution' model in
which the participant receives the number of syringes requested, regardless of
the number of syringes being returned.

A very large majority of US SEPs (89%) permit 'secondary exchange' in
which an individual participant is permitted to exchange for peers (who do
not necessarily attend the exchange). Table 3 shows the percentages of programs that permit secondary exchange, encourage secondary exchange and
utilize different specific strategies to encourage secondary exchange.

Table 1

Characteristics of Syringe Exchange Programs (SEPs) Participating in Beth Israel Medical Center (BIMC)/North American Syringe Exchange Network (NASEN) Surveys—United States, 1994–2007

Numbers of . . .	1994–95	1996	1997	1998	2000	2002	2004	2005	2006	2007
SEPs known to NASEN	68	101	113	131	154	148	174	166	188	186
SEPs Participating in survey (%)	60 (88%)	87 (86%)	100 (88%)	110 (84%)	127 (82%)	126 (85%)	109 (63%)	118 (71%)	150 (80%)	131 (70%)
Cities with SEPs participating	44	69	78	77	98	97	88	90	113	100
States with SEPs participating*	21	29	33	33	36	32	32	29	32	31
Syringes exchanged (millions)	8	13.9	17.5	19.4	22.6	24.9	24	22.5	27.6	29.5
Total of SEP budgets ($, millions)	6.3	7.3	8.4	8.6	12	13	11.6	14.5	17.4	19.6
Total of SEP public funding ($, millions)	3.9	4.5	5.6	5.9	8.9	8.7	8.8	10.7	13.8	14.4

*This category includes the District of Columbia and/or Puerto Rico.

Table 2

Number of Syringes Exchanged by Syringe Exchange Programs (SEPs), by Program Size: United States, 2007

SEP size	Syringes exchanged, 2007	No. of SEPs, 2007	Total, syringes exchanged, 2007	% of total syringes exchanged, 2007
Small	<10 000	23	80 402	0.30%
Medium	10 000–55 000	37	1 162 722	4.40%
Large	55 001–499 999	57	10 727 292	40.60%
Very large	<500 000	13	14 472 373	54.70%
Total		130	29 500 000	100

Table 3

Secondary (Satellite) Exchange and Methods of Encouraging it, by Syringe Exchange Programs (SEPs) in 2007

Secondary exchange	
SEPs allowing secondary exchange	116 (89%)
SEPs encouraging secondary exchange	99 (76%)
Methods of encouragement	
Talked about it	93 (71%)
Had no limit on syringes exchanged	78 (60%)
Gave extra supplies	91 (69%)
Provided sharps containers	86 (66%)
Enrolled people receiving syringes from secondary exchange	29 (22%)
Peer education	62 (47%)

Other Services Provided by US SEPs

Table 4 shows the percentages of US programs that provided various prevention supplies, on-site services and referrals to off-site services in 2007. Almost all programs provided condoms, alcohol pads and HIV counseling and testing, referrals to substance abuse treatment and education about HIV, hepatitis A virus (HAV), hepatitis B virus (HBV) and hepatitis C virus (HCV), condom use, vein care and abscess prevention. More than half provided HCV counseling and testing. Slightly fewer than half of the programs provided HAV and HBV vaccination and sexually transmitted disease (STD) screening. Forty per cent provided naloxone for reversing opiate overdoses, 33% provided on-site medical care and 7% provided buprenorphine treatment. A majority of programs provide food, clothing and personal hygiene products (soap, shampoo, etc.).

Table 4

Number and Percentage of Syringe Exchange Programs (SEPs) by Selected Types of Services and Supplies Provided: United States, 2007

	2007: no. (%)
Prevention supplies	
Condoms	130 (99.2%)
Receptive condoms	112 (86%)
Alcohol pads	131 (100%)
Bleach	77 (59%)
Narcan (naloxone)	52 (40%)
Buprenorphine	9 (7%)
Clothes	83 (63%)
Food	89 (68%)
Hygiene items	107 (79%)
Referrals	
Substance abuse treatment	120 (92%)
Screening and services	
HIV counseling and testing	115 (88%)
HAV testing	22 (17%)
HCV testing	72 (55%)
HBV vaccine	58 (44%)
HAV vaccine	59 (45%)
STD screening	64 (49%)
TB screening	31 (24%)
On-site medical care	43 (33%)
Delivery service	59 (45%)
Education	
HIV/AIDS prevention	124 (95%)
HAV, HBV and HCV prevention	127 (97%)
Safer injection	126 (96%)
Vein care	123 (94%)
STD prevention	
Abscess prevention	123 (94%)
Condom use	124 (95%)
Receptive condom use	104 (79%)

AIDS: acquired immune deficiency virus; HIV: human immunodeficiency virus; HAV: hepatitis A virus; HBV: hepatitis B virus; HCV: hepatitis C virus; STD: sexually transmitted disease; TB: tuberculosis.

Table 5

Problems Encountered by Syringe Exchange Programs (SEPs) in 2007

Lack of resources/lack of funding	74 (56%)
Staff shortage	62 (47%)
Staff burnout	43 (33%)
Lack of political support	27 (21%)
Lack of community support	24 (18%)
Lack of outreach	28 (21%)
Legal status	15 (11%)
Police harassment of participants (at/near site)	38 (29%)
Police harassment of staff/program	10 (8%)
Reaching or recruiting participants	46 (35%)
Retaining participants	20 (15%)
Any type of problem due to gentrification	24 (18%)
Other	23 (18%)

Operational Issues

US SEPs encountered a variety of operational problems in 2007. Table 5 presents various problems reported by US exchanges in 2007. The most common problem was 'lack of funding/lack of resources', reported by 56% of the programs. Staff shortages (47%), reaching participants (35%), staff burnout (33%) and police harassment of participants (29%) were the other commonly reported problems.

Discussion

Syringe exchange began rather late in the United States. First, HIV prevalence among IDUs in New York City had already reached 50% before AIDS was discovered among IDUs. Secondly, the United States experienced a crack cocaine epidemic during the middle and late 1980s. The crack epidemic was associated with dramatic increases in violent street crime that led to strong antidrug sentiments and intense opposition to syringe exchange among racial/ethnic minority groups in the United States. The combined opposition from social conservatives, law enforcement and racial/ethnic minority groups delayed official support for syringe exchange by many years. That many drug users were members of ethnic minority groups both increased stigmatization of drug users and made opposition to syringe exchange by minority community leaders more intense.

Two other factors were important in the initial development of syringe exchange in the United States. The United States has a federal governmental system, with individual states having great authority in matters of public health. Thus, while the US federal government has refused to provide any federal funding for syringe exchange, state and local government have often provided such funding. (Approximately half of all US exchanges currently receive state or local funding, and almost all the very large programs receive such funding.) The federal system and the lack of any national plan for syringe exchange has also led to great diversity in programs across the country.

Large numbers of AIDS cases occurred in the United States shortly after AIDS was first identified. The number of AIDS cases doubled approximately every 6 months in the initial years. This led to great public fears about AIDS and discrimination against people with AIDS. It also led to grass-roots activism to establish prevention and care services, which included the development of SEPs in many areas. Because these programs were started without official government sponsorship, they were often more free to adopt organizational tactics that might have been precluded had they been part of a more regulated public health system.

Syringe exchange programming in the United States expanded rapidly in the early and mid-1990s and has grown and evolved within two guiding principles: providing large numbers of sterile syringes to the IDU community through secondary exchange and using the exchange as a platform for providing many other health and social services to IDUs.

While it is difficult to draw precise causal inferences, the expansion of syringe exchange in the United States has been followed by substantial reductions in HIV prevalence and incidence among IDUs in the country. In the 33 US states with consistent reporting, new HIV diagnoses declined by approximately 10% per year during 2001–05. Injecting drug use was the only transmission category that declined over this time-period. Cohort studies and serial cross-sectional studies indicate that HIV incidence among IDUs has declined from approximately 4/100 person-years at risk to under 1/100 person-years in US cities with initially high HIV prevalence. Interestingly, these same studies indicate that the majority of new HIV infections among IDUs in these cities are due to unsafe sexual behavior rather than unsafe injecting behavior.

'Coverage' by syringe exchanges refers to the numbers of syringes exchanged/distributed per year divided by the number of injections by IDUs per year. (Syringes obtained from other 'guaranteed sterile' sources such as pharmacies can also be included in estimating coverage.) One hundred per cent coverage would be ideal for preventing transmission of blood-borne viruses and reducing skin infections, but clearly is not required for preventing HIV transmission. IDUs can re-use their own syringes, HIV seronegatives can share among themselves and HIV seropositives can share among themselves without transmitting the virus. Templaski and colleagues conducted a national study of syringe exchange coverage using 1996 estimates of the numbers of IDUs and 2000 data on the numbers of syringes exchanged. They found extreme variation in the extent of coverage—from two syringes exchanged per 10 injection events to three syringes per 10 000 injection events, with a mean of three syringes per 100 injection events. Higher coverage was associated with the number of males-who-have-sex with-males (MSM) per 1000 population in the MSA (Metropolitan Statistical Area) (a proxy for political activism), longer length of exchange program operation, and the exchange receiving public funding. (Note, however, that US exchanges have increased the numbers of syringes exchanged since 2000; see Table 1.) Bluthenthal and colleagues, conducted studies of coverage in California exchanges, and found higher coverage was associated with less restrictive exchange policies and lower rates of risk behavior. Given the complexities in attempting to assess 'adequate' coverage and the great variation among programs in the United States, it is not possible to make an overall assessment. The reductions in HIV incidence and prevalence noted above are clearly an optimistic sign, but it is also certain that there are many areas of the country with less than adequate coverage.

The increasing relative importance of sexual transmission of HIV among IDUs in the United States is consistent with increasing HIV prevalence among non-injecting drug users in the country. HIV prevalence among non-injecting drug users in New York City is now equal to HIV prevalence among injecting drug users. Reducing sexual transmission of HIV among both injecting and non-injecting drug users and MSM drug users is the next major challenge for harm reduction HIV prevention in the United States.

HCV is also transmitted through the sharing of drug injection equipment, including filters, cookers and rinse water. Because HCV is transmitted much more efficiently than HIV, the extent to which syringe exchange and other types of harm reduction programs can reduce HCV transmission among IDUs is still an open question. HCV prevalence has clearly declined among IDUs in New York City since the expansion of the SEPs in the mid-1990s. It fell from 80% prevalence in 1990–91 to 63% prevalence in 2000–01 among the population of IDUs, and from 80% to 38% among HIV seronegative new injectors (people injecting for 6 years or less). Among the new injectors, however, the 38% prevalence corresponds to an average incidence of 18/100 person-years. We suspect that it will be necessary to reduce incidence among new injectors to 5/100 person-years or less before the majority of IDUs will be able to avoid becoming infected with HCV during their injection careers. This clearly would require a massive expansion of 'safer injection' programs.

The great majority of US SEPs have encouraged secondary exchange in order to reach IDUs who do or do not personally attend the programs. Sales of sterile needles and syringes through pharmacies have complemented the SEPs. As discussed above, the available epidemiological data indicate that this strategy appears to have been very successful in reducing injecting-related HIV transmission in the country. Incidence of HIV has declined to under 1/100 person-years and the majority of new HIV infections among IDUs appear to be sexually transmitted. This strategy has also led to a reduction in HCV prevalence among IDUs, although HCV infection among IDUs in the United States is still a major public health problem.

The second major strategy utilized by US SEPs have been to use the programs as a platform for providing multiple health and social services to IDUs (and to a limited extent to other community members). As shown in Table 4, the programs are providing a wide variety of services. The provision of naloxone to drug users themselves to reverse opiate overdoses among their peers is a notable example of a service that was not provided to IDUs until SEPs adopted it. A cost-effectiveness analysis would probably be the most relevant method for assessing the provision of these additional services to IDUs through SEPs. Given the very modest budgets of US SEPs (see Table 1), it is almost certain that utilizing SEPs is cost-effective providing these services.

Doing Syringe Exchange/Harm Reduction Better, in the United States and Globally

SEPs in the United States started well after HIV had already infected large numbers of IDUs in the country. The programs have faced intense political opposition, although this has declined over time at the state and local level. Important operational concerns also exist, most related to lack of resources (Table 5). Despite these problems, the two guiding principles of utilizing secondary exchange to increase the diffusion of sterile syringes in the IDU population and utilizing the programs to provide multiple other health and social services have provided an excellent basis for the development of SEPs in the country. No one, however, would argue that the present system in the United States is optimal for continued provision of services to drug users.

The obvious areas for improvement are: (i) an increased and stable source of funding for the programs; and (ii) a national plan for addressing HIV and other health problems among injecting and non-injecting drug users.

The third issue is much more debatable. SEPs in the United States have developed separately from mainstream health-care services. Indeed, SEPs are largely independent of drug abuse treatment programs in the United States. Among the programs with relatively good funding, syringe exchange has been moving towards becoming an alternative health-care system for injecting drug users, with many services provided on site.

Should the programs continue in this direction of becoming an alternative health-care platform for drug users? The advantages of being an independent, alternative system include responsiveness to the needs of the participants, organizational flexibility, increased innovation, relatively low cost and, most importantly, providing services within a harm reduction framework—treating IDUs with dignity and respect. There are many practical problems in attempting to provide a wide variety of health and social services to drug users through syringe exchanges, but the primary disadvantage of an alternative system is simple. In the words of the US Supreme Court, 'separate . . . facilities are inherently unequal'. In the absence of an AIDS crisis mentality, it may be very difficult to maintain even the present level of services for drug users within a separate delivery system. Integrating the services currently provided at syringe exchanges into the regular health-care system, however, would require the system to adopt a harm reduction perspective—including treating drug users with dignity and respect. While there are many individuals and organizations in the current US health-care system who treat drug users with dignity and respect, this attitude certainly does not pervade the system as a whole.

Whether HIV prevention and other services to drug users should be provided primarily within an alternative system or whether these services should be provided primarily within the regular health-care system is not simply a matter of cost-efficient service delivery. Rather, it reflects the stigmatization of drug users in society. The issue is certainly not relevant only to the United States.

NO

The Kings Cross Injecting Room: The Case for Closure

Was the Public Misled?

The injecting room's own public relations unit continually stated that each overdose intervention in the injecting room was a life saved. This resulted in increased public support which went from 68% in 2000 to 78% in 2002. The fact is that their own advisors found that just one in 25 overdoses is ever fatal yet the following was reported:

> "Four overdoses have been recorded on site. In each case the user had arrived at the centre alone, which is a known risk factor in drug overdose death," Dr van Beek said. "Potentially we've **saved four lives** in the first month." Kelly Burke—SMH 22/6/2001
>
> "In the first month of operation, **four lives were saved** . . ." John Della Bosca, NSW Special Minister of State, NSW Legislative Council Hansard 4 July 2001 based on Dr van Beek's claims
>
> "Since its controversial opening three months ago, the Sydney Kings Cross centre . . . says its staff has **saved more than a dozen lives** from overdoses." Reporter Joe O'Brien The World Today Archive—Wednesday, 15 August , 2001
>
> "The visit concluded with a public forum. . . . Careful not to promote the centre at this stage as anything other than a solution to a local problem (i.e., preventing fatal drug overdoses in Kings Cross), Dr Van Beek presented compelling evidence that in its first nine months, the centre has **saved more than 100 lives**." http//www.hepatitisc.org.au/resources/documents/36_01.pdf
>
> "To date, the trial injecting room has reported that there were 2,729 registered clients and 250 overdoses. Therefore, because of the available trained medical staff **250 lives were saved**." The Hon Bryce Gaudry MP, NSW Legislative Assembly Hansard 29 May 2002 based on claims by Dr van Beek
>
> "A final report on the controversial Kings cross injecting centre is expected to declare it a resounding success that has **saved hundreds of lives**." Steve Dow & Frank Walker—Sun-Herald June 15 2003

10 Crucial Things You Need to Know

1. Only 38% of injections in the injecting room in 2006 were heroin injections. Substances such as cocaine and 'ice,' highly destructive in the longer term but not presenting high risk of immediate overdose, are commonly injected, as is prescription morphine.

From *The Kings Cross Injecting Room: The Case for Closure*, Drug Free Australia, 2010.

2. The International Narcotics Control Board (INCB) specifically singled out the Kings Cross injecting room trial as being in breach of the International Conventions against illicit drug use. This trial does not utilise legal heroin but rather depends on clients illegally procuring heroin, illegally transporting heroin, and illegally using heroin. Furthermore, if the injecting room trial had been valid, the 2003 evaluation should have marked the end of the trial. Results should have been forwarded to the INCB and the injecting room closed.

3. On average one out of every 35 injections per user was in the injecting room, despite the public being told that every heroin injection is potentially fatal. So under-utilised is the injecting room that it has averaged just 200 injections per day despite having the capacity to host 330 per day.

4. Based on the overdose figures published by the Medically Supervised Injecting Centre (MSIC) the overdose rate in the injecting room was 36 times higher than on the streets of Kings Cross.

5. The high overdose rate was attributed by the MSIC's own evaluation report to clients taking more risk with higher doses of heroin in the injecting room. More injected heroin means more heroin sold by Kings Cross drug dealers.

6. Currently a disturbing 1.6% of Australians have used heroin. However surveys show that 3.6% of NSW respondents say they would use heroin if an injecting room was available to them, most for the first time, potentially doubling the number who would use the drug.

7. The government-funded estimate of 4 lives saved per year failed to take the enormously increased overdose rate into consideration. Adjusted for the high rates of overdose, the injecting room saved statistically 0.18 lives in its 18 month evaluation period.

8. Only 11% of injecting room clients were referred to maintenance treatment, detox or rehab. 3.5% of clients were referred to detox and only 1% referred to rehabilitation. None of Sydney's major rehabs such as Odyssey House, WHOS or the Salvation Army ever sighted one of the referrals.

9. The injecting room did not improve public amenity. The injecting room quite evidently drew drug dealers to its doors. Reductions in the number of public injections and discarded needles in Kings Cross decreased only in line with reduced distributions of needles due to the heroin drought. Recent reports indicate increases in publicly discarded needles.

10. The independent government-funded evaluation of the injecting room, released July 9, 2003 and from which much of the data in this report is drawn, was done by a research team of five, three of whom were colleagues in the same NSW University medical faculty as the Medical Director of the injecting room. A fourth researcher was one of those who, during the 1999 NSW Drug Summit, shaped the proposed injecting room trial. Drug Free Australia has questioned the independence of this evaluation team.

Statistically Impossible to Save Even One Life Per Year (Cost: $2.5 Million Per Annum)

Only two statistics need be known to demonstrate that the injecting room cannot possibly save even one life statistically per year.

Statistc 1

Less than 1% of dependent heroin users die from overdose each year in Australia

Statistic 2

A dependent heroin user averages at least three heroin injections per day. Taking these two statistics together, it is clear that the injecting room would need to host 300 injections per day (ie enough injections for 100 heroin addicts injecting 3 times per day) before they could claim they had saved the life of the one (1%) of those 100 who would have died.

But the injecting room has only averaged 156 heroin injections per day since its evaluation period ended.

High Cost for Little Benefit

The injecting room costs $2.5 million a year to operare. That is enough money for the NSW government to fund 109 drug rehabilitation beds or supply more than 700 dependent heroin users with life-saving Naltrexone implants for an entire year.

Injector Safety Not Enhanced

Heroin addicts inject at least three times a day, or around 1,100 times in a year. If a heroin user wanted to avoid a fatal overdose she would have every injection inside the injecting room. But clients average just 2-3 visits per month, leaving themselves open to a fatal overdose for 34 out of 35 of their heroin injections.

Increased the Use of Heroin

[Table 1] reproduces the results from two surveys commissioned by the injecting room evaluators, one in 2000 with 1018 respondents and the other in 2002 with 1070 respondents.[1]

In each case respondents were asked whether they would use an injecting room if made available. 3.6% replied they would. Yet only 1.6% in the 2001 National Drug Strategy Household Survey indicated prior use of heroin. Alarmingly, 26 of the 28 who replied affirmatively in the 2002 survey had never tried heroin before. If more injecting rooms were opened this could lead to much higher heroin use.

Inject Anything You Want in an Under-Used Facility
Only 38% of Injections Are Heroin

In 2006 only 38% of injections in the injecting room were for heroin. Yet the dangers of heroin overdose were the clear rationale given by its supporters for opening such a facility.

Reports from the injecting room in 2006 show that 'ice,' a highly destructive substance in the longer term but with much lower risks of overdose, is

Table 1

Number (Percentage) of Kings Cross and NSW Residents Reporting That They Would Use the MSIC and the Reason for Use

Characteristics	Kings Cross		NSW	
	2000 n = 515	2002 n = 540	2000 n = 1018	2002 n = 1070
Would use a SIC	19 (4%)	0 (0%)	47 (5%)	28 (3%)
Reason for MSIC use		–		
Safety	12 (2%)	–	19 (2%)	18 (2%)
Hypothetical	5 (1%)	–	2 (<1%)	8 (1%)
Not IDU	2 (1%)	–	0 (0%)	1 (<1%)
Anti-drugs	0 (0%)	–	1(<1%)	1 (<1%)
Not asked the reason[1]		–	25 (3%)	

1 = Most of the first 25 NSW resident respondents who reported that they would be more likely to inject heroin if they had access to a SIC were aged over 50 years, therefore a question was added to determine whether people responding in the affirmative would actually commence drug injection.

being consumed in the room. This drug is responsible for increasing numbers of violent attacks in the community.

Attendees use the following:

Heroin: 38%

Ice: 6%

Cocaine: 21%

Prescription Morphine: 31%[1]

The injecting room is clearly a facility that doesn't meet its own publicised reason for being. It supports the use of any drug as often as you like. That just doesn't make sense.

Running at 2/3rds Capacity

Despite almost 900 injecting room clients living within walking distance of the facility[2], the injecting room has averaged just 200 injections per day[3], despite a capacity for 330 injections per day[4].

The high overdose rates and the low utilisation rates might suggest that clients are not using the injecting room for day-to-day safety, as per the injecting room's originating rationale. Rather, clients may be infrequently using the safety of the room for a different purpose—experimentation with high doses of heroin.

An Evident Honey-Pot Effect?

The injecting room is 25 metres opposite the entrance to the Kings Cross train station on Darlinghurst Road.

The following was stated in the injecting room's own government-funded evaluation of 2003.

"We've got problems at the entrance [of the train station] with people just hanging around. We've got members of the public complaining about drug users, homeless and drunks hanging around the entrance on Darlinghurst Road." (City Rail worker, 12 months interview—p 146)"

"The police who participated in the twelve-month discussion group commented that they had received complaints from the public and the City Rail staff about the increase in the number of people loitering at the train station. They noted that, while other factors, such as police operations, would have contributed to the increase in loitering outside the train station, there was **a notable correlation between the loitering and the MSIC opening times.**" (MSIC Evaluation p 146)

"The increase in loitering was considered to be a displacement of existing **users and dealers** from other locations." (MSIC Evaluation p 146)

"**The train station never featured as a meeting place before.** It used to be springfield Mall and Roslyn street." (Police 12 month interview—p 147)

Andrew Strauss, owner of Blinky's Photos next door to the injecting room, said: "You see drug dealers at the front of the injecting room every day."

"It hasn't reduced illegal drug taking, it has encouraged it. And the police walk up and down the footpath doing nothing."

Drought Reduced Needles, Not the Injecting Room

In the 'Interim Evaluation Report No. 2' for the Sydney Medically supervised Injecting Centre, released in 2006, the conclusion of the report stated:

"Residents and business operators in the Kings Cross area perceived a decrease in the level of public drug use and publicly disposed syringes seen in the last month."

The conclusion was based on the finding that:

"58% of residents and 60% of business operators reported that they had ever seen public injecting in 2005. In both groups, the overall proportions were similar to 2000 but there were significant decreases in the proportions of residents who had seen public injecting or a discarded syringe in the past month."

However, data reproduced in the adjacent column from pages 116–122 of the injecting room's own government-funded evaluation of 2003 clearly shows a direct correlation between the decreases in needle distributions from needle exchanges and pharmacies in Kings Cross and decreases in sightings of public injection and discarded needle/syringe counts.

Surveys by the injecting room's evaluators were in July 2000 and July 2002, and shows a decrease from roughly 108,000 needles in the year 2000 to roughly 88,000 needles distributed in 2002, a decrease in distribution of 19%.

Surveys and syringe counts recorded in the injecting room's evaluation appear in the left hand table below. Surveyed reductions in discarded needles and sightings of public injecting before and after the injecting room opened are in line with the 19% reduction in distributions. Clearly the heroin drought is responsible for these reductions, not the injecting room as its staff have so often inferred.

In 2005, discarded syringes still rated as one of the top three annoyances for residents and businesses surveyed in the Kings Cross area.

KINGS CROSS	July'00	July'02	Change
Local Residents			
Observed discarded syringes	38%	35%	−8%
Observed public injecting	10%	8%	−20%
Local Business			
Observed discarded syringes	35%	31%	−11%
Observed public injecting	9%	9%	−9%
Needle/Syringe Counts			
KRC Needle Exchange clean-up team	60%	55%	−8%
Injecting room staff research team	7	3	−57%
South Sydney Council clean-up	284	240	−15%

Injecting Room Scorecard—No Demonstrated Success

The injecting room's 2003 evaluation demonstrated a litany of failure. Various justifications for the introduction of an injecting room in Sydney were proposed which are assessed in the scorecard below.

Number of overdose deaths in the area	no evidence of any impact p 62
Ambulance overdose attendances in the area	no evidence of any impact p 61
Ambulance overdose attendance during hours the injecting room was open	no evidence of any impact p 60
Overdose presentations at hospital emergency wards	no evidence of any impact p 60
HIV infections amongst injecting drug users	worsened p 71
Hep B infections	no improvement p 71

Notifications of newly-diagnosed Hep C	worsened p 71
Frequency of public injection injection	on the street—57% (2001) to 46% (2002) in a public toilet—40% (2001) to 33% (2002); use of commercial shooting galleries—16% (2001) to 14% (2002) p 94
New needle and syringe use	no advantage by injecting room over the nearby needle-exchange p 92
Re-use of someone else's syringe	no improvement p 93
Re-use of injecting equipment other than syringes	no improvement p 93
Tests taken for HIV and Hep C	no Improvement p 96
Tests taken for Hep B	improved in 2001, worsened in 2002 p 98
Referrals to drug rehab and treatment	extremely poor—8% of clients referred to methadone or buprenorphine maintenance. Only 4.7% referred to abstinence-based detox or residential rehab pp 98–99
Publicly discarded syringes	declined and increased in line with the number of distributed needles during heroin drought pp 116–122
Perception of public nuisance caused by drug use	decreased only in line with heroin drought impact p 113
Public injections sighted	mixed—residents reported less in line with heroin drought impact, businesses reported no improvement p 116
Acquisitive crime (break & enter etc)	no improvement p 147
Drug dealing at rear door of MSIC	continual p 148
Drug dealing at Kings Cross station	worsened p 149
Injecting related health/vein care	improved, but can be viewed as teaching people how to be better junkies

** These results recorded in the government-funded evaluation of the injecting room

Massive Rates of Overdose . . . Why?

The injecting room had an extraordinary rate of overdose—9.6 overdoses for every 1,000 injections. But its evaluation report curiously failed to compare these injecting room overdose rates with other known rates of overdose.

There are three other known overdose rates that can be compared:

1. Comparison with overdose rates in the rest of Kings Cross
2. Comparison with injecting room client overdose rates before they entered the injecting room
3. Comparison with Australian national estimates of rates of overdose

1. 36 Times Higher than Streets of Kings Cross

The government-funded evaluation recorded 329 heroin overdoses in the first eighteen months of injecting room operation. There were roughly 35,000 heroin injections in the room during that period, resulting in an overdose for every **106** heroin injections in the room.

The same evaluation estimated that there were 6,000 heroin injections happening every day in Kings Cross (or 3.2 million injections during the evaluation period of eighteen months). Using Kings Cross ambulance call-out rates for heroin overdose during that same period, there were an estimated 845 overdoses outside the injecting room for all those millions of injections. The rate of overdose for Kings Cross was one overdose for every **3,820** injections.

The injecting room had 36 times more overdoses than on the streets outside in Kings cross—a staggering rate of overdose.

2. At Least 40 Times Higher than MSIC Client's Previous History

Registration questionnaires, which all clients completed upon first entering the injecting room, indicated an average 3 overdoses per client over an average 12 years of illicit drug abuse (Table 2.1). This averages one non-fatal overdose for every 4 years of drug abuse.

Yet inside the injecting room these very same heroin addicts averaged an overdose rate of 10 per year per client. This is more than 40 times higher than their recorded previous rate of overdose before entering the injecting room.

3. 49 Times Higher than Estimated National Overdose Averages

The last official estimate of 74,000 dependent heroin users within Australia was for 1997.

In that same year there was an estimated 15,600 overdoses, of which exactly 600 were fatal.

At a conservative 3 injections per day, 74,000 heroin users would inject 81,030,000 times per year with an overdose for every **5,200** injections. Yet the injecting room had an overdose for every **106** injections in its facility—49 times higher.

Why So Many Overdose?

The injecting room's own evaluation on page 62 stated that:

> "In this study of the Sydney MSIC there were 9.2 (sic) heroin overdoses per 1000 heroin injections in the MSIC, and this rate of overdose is likely to be higher than among heroin injectors generally. The MSIC clients seem to have been a high-risk group with a higher rate of heroin injections than heroin injectors who did not use the MSIC, they were often injecting on the streets, and they may have taken more risks and used more heroin in the MSIC."

The explanation of higher-risk clients does not accord with the facts but the alternate explanation of clients using higher doses of heroin means that the injecting room is significantly adding to the profits of the local drug dealers. This should be a major concern for NSW residents.

Exposing the Myths About Overdose & the Injecting Room

Myth 1—All heroin overdoses are fatal *(used by the injecting room to get public support for its introduction)*

"Darke et al. (1996) showed that an ambulance attends in 51% of non-fatal overdose events and Darke et al. (in press) reported an estimate of **4.1 fatal overdoses for every 100 non-fatal overdoses** in the community, . . ."[6]

Myth 2—Most heroin overdoses are in public places *(used by the drug legalisation lobby to justify the existence of injecting rooms)*

"**The majority of deaths occur in a private home.** Studies typically report that approximately half of all overdose fatalities occur in the victim's own home, while one-quarter occur in the home of a friend or relative."[7]

Myth 3—Heroin overdoses are caused by street heroin being cut with toxic contaminants *(used by drug legalisation lobby to justify a heroin prescription triol)*

"Two popular misconceptions, among both heroin users and the wider community, are that the major causes of opioid overdose are either unexpectedly high potency of heroin or the presence of toxic contaminants in heroin. The evidence supporting these notions is, at best, sparse."[8]

Myth 4—The MSIC ensures no first time users or pregnant women use the facility

The injecting room uses a 20 minute interview at registration that relies on the self-reported disclosure of age, pregnancy or user status. If you are a good liar you could probably get in.

Myth 5—The only way high-risk drug users can be reached by health professionals is via the injecting room

Extensive needle exchange services have operated for years in Kings Cross to provide non-judgmental access to needles and syringes and a chance for health workers to build relationships which will encourage users towards treatment.

Major Causes of Heroin Overdose

"The evidence of polydrug use in fatal overdose is consistent with the experience of non-fatal overdose victims, particularly in terms of alcohol and benzodiazepine use. Overall, overdoses involving heroin use alone are in the minority. Alcohol appears to be especially implicated, with the frequency of alcohol consumption being a significant predictor of overdose."

"A recent decrease in tolerance to opioids has been proposed as a possible explanation for the low blood morphine levels typically seen in overdose victims."

ANCD Research Paper No 1 'Heroin Overdose' pp. xi, xii

Frequently Asked Questions

1. Doesn't the injecting room have high overdoses because it helps a high-risk sub-group?

This claim does not stand up to scrutiny as can be seen from other previous surveys of heroin user groups.[9] **The fact is that injecting room clients had 34 in every 35 of their injections outside the injecting room**, where their high overdose rates should reasonably have been expected to be replicated. They weren't.

Study	Ever Overdosed	Overdosed Last l2mths
Injecting Room 2002	44%	12%
Aust. IDRS study 1999	51%	29%
Sydney study 1996	68%	20%
British study 1999	58%	30%

2. Is it true the injecting room had higher overdose numbers than the above-mentioned surveys because heroin users don't remember the majority of their previous overdoses?

This explanation for the high number of overdoses was first offered by the Medical Director for the injecting room, Dr Ingrid van Beek.

This line of argument posits that heroin users are actually having far more overdoses than they report and that most of their overdoses are unrecognised or forgotten. But a 1996 review by Shane Darke[10] of studies on the circumstances of fatal heroin overdoses found that **between 58% and 79% of fatal overdoses are in the company of other people.**

Another study[11] by Shane Darke estimated that **49% of overdoses in the community are not attended by paramedics.** Drug Free Australia has already calculated this percentage into its comparisons of injecting room overdoses with those in the community.

3. Why do I read that there is high public acceptance of the injecting room?

Nationally, acceptance of the injecting room is not that high. However it may be that those in favour have believed it is saving hundreds of lives, as promoted, when this is clearly not the case of this document.

4. I have heard that 12% of clients were referred to treatment or rehab. Is that a good or bad referral rate?

Drug Free Australia Fellow, Dr Stuart Reece, a doctor working in addiction medicine in Brisbane reports that he refers 91% of his drug-dependent patients to treatment or rehab. Referral can of course be accomplished by any health worker service, even a soup kitchen.

5. Weren't all 1,385 injecting room referrals to assistance that would help them stop using drugs?

Only 134 referrals were to detox and another 56% rehab. Much higher was the number of referrals (227) for social welfare assistance, which might well be assumed to be predominantly Centrelink benefits. Other referrals were for legal matters (51), counselling for issues other than drugs (63), legal and advocacy issues (51), medical/dental (313), health education (86) and testing for blood-borne viruses and sexually transmitted diseases (40). There were 304 referrals to drug maintenance, and another 107 to drug and alcohol counselling. There is no record of follow-up of any referral.

Prevention/Early Intervention or Harm-minimisation: What's Best?

The $2.5 million per year currently being spent on the injecting room would fund 109 drug rehabilitation beds or supply more than 700 dependent heroin users with life-saving Naltrexone implants. This would represent many lives saved from heroin and heroin overdose. If Australia has successfully reduced its tobacco addiction problem via anti-smoking campaigns, it can also reduce its drug addiction problem via clear anti-drug messages on TV, radio and through Public Health.

The United Nations View

In the 2004 Report of the United Nations Office of Drug Control & Crime Prevention (ODCCP), **Australia's statistics indicated the highest levels of illicit drug abuse amongst OECD countries**, which may well be due to its long history of allowing harm minimisation policies to predominate over prevention policies. It had the highest levels of cannabis and amphetamine use, with the fifth highest use of cocaine. Australia's more recent prevention messages and excellent work by the Federal police have seen solid reductions in illicit drug use in Australia, despite harm minimisation still predominating. It is certain that these decreases have not been produced by harm minimisation but by prevention strategies.

Australia from 1985 to Now

Australia is considered to be one of the world's most advanced harm-minimisation countries. Adopted in 1985, harm minimisation pragmatically accepts that people will use illicit drugs and seeks to minimise the harms of doing so. Consequently, harm minimisation characteristically places little emphasis on the prevention of drug use.

Sweden from 1967 to Now

Sweden, a previously drug-liberal country with the highest European drug use levels, now has the lowest levels of drug use amongst OECD countries. Sweden's highly successful restrictive drug policy, unlike a zero tolerance approach which just pushes people into jails, puts a heavy emphasis on prevention of drug use with a minimal harm minimisation program. It has the support of 95% of its citizens.

Rehabilitation Successful

A key to the success of the Swedish model is mandatory drug rehabilitation for those found addicted to drugs. Swedish school education does not assume, as does Australian school education material produced by the Australian Drug Foundation, that illicit drug use is normal or should be socially accepted.

Prevention and early intervention programs send a clear message that the harms of illicit drug use are too great to be socially acceptable and that Australians adhere to the aim of a drug-free society.

Naltrexone Implants

So what about helping those stuck using heroin now? Studies show that up to 45% of methadone patients still use illegal heroin, and many stay on methadone for decades. Naltrexone, though, is a substance similar to Narcan in that it blocks the opioid receptors from responding to opiates. Implants, which last up to 6 months each, feed Naltrexone into the blood, reducing cravings for opiates and preventing any chance of overdose. Trials with more than 2000 Naltrexone implants have thus far had excellent success.

Recommendations

1. That the injecting room be closed and the funding redirected to establishment of more beds in rehabilitation centres which focus on ultimate abstinence from use of illicit drugs.
2. That the NSW Government follow the lead of the WA Government and significantly fund Naltrexone implants for those wishing to become abstinent (including drug-dependent prisoners).
3. That the NSW Government examine the Swedish model and its restrictive drug policies. This includes the adoption of strong policing of street selling and a replication of the Cabramatta model which resulted in a significantly lowered overdose rate (policing of supply and demand).
4. That the NSW Government examine abstinence-based rehabilitation programs which have shown considerable success, including Australian programs such as the Salvation Army and Drugbeat (South Australia), as well as international programs such as Hassela (Sweden), San Patrignano (Italy; and Daytop International or phoenix House (United States).

Notes

1. MSIC Evaluation; p 158
2. Report from Dr A. Byrne, Update, 21/7/2006
3. MSIC Evaluation, p 17
4. Report from Dr A. Byrne, Update, 21/2006
5. MSIC Evaluation p 38

6. MSIC Evaluation p 59

7. ANCD Research Paper No 1 'Heroin Overdose—Prevalence, Correlates, Consequences and Interventions, p xi

8. ANCD Research Paper No 1 'Heroin Overdose, p xiii

9. ANCD Research Paper No 1 'Heroin Overdose, p 10

10. Darke, Shone and Zador, Deborah, "Fatal Heroin 'Overdose': A Review." Addiction. 1996; 91(12): pp. 1765–1772.

11. See Final Report of the Evaluation of the Sydney Medically Supervised Injecting Centre p 59.

POSTSCRIPT

Should Drug Addicts Be Given Access to Free Needles?

Whether or not providing free needles to drug abusers will help slow the spread of AIDS is extremely relevant. Not only does the drug user but also that person's sexual partner risk infection. People who inject drugs are a primary source for heterosexual transmission of AIDS to sexual partners. Also, the immune systems of drug abusers are impaired by their drug abuse and typically poor environment as well. With a weakened immune system, one can contract HIV more easily.

One potential advantage of giving drug abusers free access to needles is that needles may be safely discarded after they have been used. Unsafely discarded needles may accidentally prick someone and lead to HIV transmission. A second potential benefit is that when people come to needle exchange sites, they can be encouraged to enter drug treatment programs. It is not always easy to locate the drug-injecting population; one place to reach these individuals is where they exchange needles.

Despite the difficulties of studying people who inject drugs, long-term studies are needed to determine the impact of needle exchange programs on (1) the incidence of AIDS, (2) the continuation or reduction of drug use, (3) whether or not these programs attract new users to the drug culture, (4) the likelihood of program participants entering drug treatment programs, and (5) the impact on other high-risk behaviors. Research on whether supplying free needles is effective is contradictory. A program in Tacoma, Washington, demonstrated that needle sharing declined by 30 percent. However, in a study in Louisville, Kentucky, nearly two-thirds of drug-injecting individuals continued to share needles. It should be noted in the Louisville study that needles were obtained through a prescription and that may account for a difference in the results.

An article that researched the effectiveness of syringe exchange programs on the incidence of HIV is "Syringe Sharing and HIV Incidence Among Injection Drug Users and Increased Access to Sterile Syringes" by Thomas Kerr and associates (*American Journal of Public Health*, August 2010). Norah Palmateer and colleagues reviewed a number of studies addressing the effectiveness of needle exchange programs in "Evidence for the Effectiveness of Sterile Injecting Equipment Provision in Preventing Hepatitis C and Human Immunodeficiency Virus Transmission Among Injecting Drug Users: A Review of Reviews" (*Addiction*, 2010). A critique of providing a safe place for drug abusers to inject drugs was described in "Road to Recovery" by the Australian House of Representatives Standing Committee on Family and Community Affairs (2010).

Is Caffeine a Health Risk?

YES: Carrie Ruxton, from "Health Aspects of Caffeine: Benefits and Risks," *Nursing Standard* (November 4, 2009)

NO: Peter J. Rogers, from "Caffeine—Our Favourite Drug," *Biologist* (August 2009)

ISSUE SUMMARY

YES: Carrie Ruxton, a dietician in Scotland, maintains that certain sources of caffeine and the extent of caffeine intake have been linked to health-related problems. For example, tea has been linked to reduced iron absorption, high levels of coffee have been associated with hypertension; cola has been shown to increase the likelihood of dental cavities and dental erosion; and chocolate has high amounts of calories, sugar, and fat. Carrie Ruxton states that caffeinated products should be used carefully.

NO: Peter Rogers, a professor of biological psychology at Bristol University, acknowledges that caffeine is a stimulant but that it offers some positive effects. Caffeine, says Rogers, which is the most popular drug worldwide, increases alertness and mental performance. Rogers believes that claims regarding caffeine's negative effects on hypertension and cardiovascular disease are overstated. Moreover, its potential for addiction is low.

Caffeine is one of the most widely consumed legal drugs in the world. In the United States, more than 9 out of every 10 people drink some type of caffeinated beverage, mostly for its stimulating effects. Caffeine elevates mood, reduces fatigue, increases work capacity, and stimulates respiration. Caffeine often provides the lift people need to start the day. Although many people associate caffeine primarily with coffee, caffeine is also found in numerous soft drinks, over-the-counter medications, chocolate, and tea. Because caffeinated drinks are common in society and there are very few legal controls regarding the use of caffeine, its physical and psychological effects frequently are overlooked, ignored, or minimized.

In recent years, coffee consumption has declined; however, the amount of caffeine being consumed has not declined appreciably because of the increase in caffeinated soft drink consumption. To reduce their levels of caffeine intake, many people have switched to decaffeinated drinks and coffee. Although this results in less caffeine intake, decaffeinated coffee still contains small amounts of caffeine.

Research studies evaluating the effects of caffeine consumption on personal health date back to the 1960s. In particular, the medical community has conducted numerous studies to determine whether or not there is a relationship between caffeine consumption and cardiovascular disease, because heart disease is the leading cause of death in many countries, including the United States. In spite of the many studies on this subject, a clear relationship between heart disease and caffeine is not yet apparent. Studies have yielded conflicting results. Rather than clarifying the debate regarding the consequences of caffeine, the research only adds to the confusion. As a result, studies suggesting that there is a connection between caffeine consumption and adverse physical and psychological effects have come under scrutiny by both the general public and health professions.

One serious limitation of previous research indicating that caffeine does have deleterious effects is that the research focused primarily on coffee use. There may be other ingredients in coffee besides caffeine that produce harmful effects. Moreover, an increasing percentage of the caffeine being consumed comes from other sources, such as soft drinks, tea, chocolate, antihistamines, and diet pills. Therefore, caffeine studies involving only coffee are not truly representative of the amount of caffeine that people ingest.

Another important criticism of caffeine research, especially studies linking caffeine use and heart disease, is gender bias. Until recently, research has focused primarily on the caffeine consumption of men. The bias in medical research is not limited to caffeine studies; men have traditionally been the primary group studied regarding many facets of health. This situation is changing. There is increasing research into the potential consequences of caffeine use on the fetus and nursing mother.

People who believe that drinking caffeine in moderation does not pose a significant health threat are critical of previous and current studies. This is particularly true of those studies that demonstrate a relationship between caffeine and heart disease. Critics contend that it is difficult to establish a definitive relationship between caffeine and heart disease due to a myriad of confounding variables. For example, cardiovascular disease has been linked to family history, a sedentary lifestyle, cigarette smoking, obesity, fat intake, and stress. Many individuals who consume large amounts of coffee also smoke cigarettes, drink alcohol, and are hard-driven. Several factors also affect caffeine's excretion from the body. Cigarette smoking increases caffeine metabolization, while the use of oral contraceptives and pregnancy slow down metabolization. Therefore, determining the extent to which caffeine use causes heart disease while adjusting for the influence of these other factors is difficult.

In the YES selection, Carrie Ruxton cautions readers about the extensive use of caffeine and indicates that the evidence demonstrates that caffeine is linked to hypertension and dental problems. In contrast, in the NO selection, Peter Rogers casts doubt on the negative effects associated with caffeine intake and that the effects of caffeine may not be as harmful as many people speculate. He also states that caffeine improves alertness and mental performance.

YES

Carrie Ruxton

Health Aspects of Caffeine: Benefits and Risks

Aims and Intended Learning Outcomes

The aim of this article is to enhance your understanding of the potential benefits and risks of foods and drinks that contain caffeine. After reading this article and completing the time out activities you should be able to:

- Identify sources of caffeine in the diet.
- Understand the evidence linking caffeine consumption with health, cognitive function, hydration and performance.
- Appreciate the role of polyphenol compounds in health, and how tea contributes to antioxidant intake.
- Advise different patient groups on appropriate intake of caffeinated beverages.

Background

Caffeinated foods and beverages are consumed on a regular basis by a large proportion of the population in the UK. However, the media and nurses sometimes view caffeine as undesirable, giving rise to advice for people to avoid or reduce their intake of caffeinated products. In contrast, research suggests that caffeinated beverages, such as tea, coffee and cocoa, may offer health benefits, in part, because of the presence of polyphenol compounds (natural plant antioxidants that display anti-inflammatory and anti-cancer properties). Studies have also found that a moderate intake of caffeine may have a positive effect on mood, alertness and mental performance.

This article discusses the risks and benefits of regular consumption of caffeinated products. The implications for different population groups are also considered, including healthy individuals, people at risk of cardiovascular disease (CVD), those with existing hypertension and pregnant women.

Caffeine

Caffeine (1,3,7-trimethylxanthine) is a natural component of certain plants. It is used in traditional south American and African communities as a stimulant in the form of cola nut or maté, while in Western countries it is a popular ingredient of medications, supplements, energy drinks and weight management products.

From *Nursing Standard*, November 4, 2009, pp. 41–48. Copyright © 2009 by RCN Publishing Company Ltd. Reprinted by permission.

Caffeine is rapidly absorbed from the gastrointestinal tract, with plasma levels peaking at 60–90 minutes post-ingestion. The average half-life of caffeine is 2.5 to 4.5 hours, but this can vary from one to ten hours in certain individuals. Children are believed to excrete caffeine faster than adult.

Daily caffeine intakes in the UK are approximately 4 mg/kg body weight, for example 280 mg for a 70 kg individual. The main dietary sources are tea, coffee, cocoa products, cola and chocolate. Table 1 shows the average caffeine content of standard portions of these products. So-called decaffeinated drinks still contain a few milligrams of caffeine. Herbal infusions, which are often described inaccurately as 'tea', do not generally contain caffeine.

Caffeinated beverages have been consumed in the UK for nearly 400 years. The UK National Diet and Nutrition Survey of nearly 2,000 adults revealed that 77% of people drank tea, while 71% drank coffee. According to the most recent National Drinks Survey, the average adult consumer drinks 2.1 cups of tea and 1.1 cups of coffee a day.

TIME OUT 1

Identify sources of caffeine in your diet or a patient's diet. Using Table 1 estimate the overall caffeine intake for one day.

Table 1

Caffeine Content (mg/Portion) of Foods and Drinks Commonly Consumed in the UK

Beverage (Portion Size)	Range (mg/Portion)	Average (mg/Portion)
Tea (190 ml)	1–90	50
Instant coffee (190 ml)	21–120	75
Ground coffee (190 ml)	15–254	100
Espresso coffee (40 ml)	No data	140
Hot chocolate (150 ml)	1–6	No data
Dark chocolate (bar)	No data	50*
Cola (330 ml)	11–70	40
Energy drink (250 ml)	27–87	80

* Milk chocolate contains about half as much caffeine as dark chocolate.

Adapted from the Food Standards Agency (2008). Pregnant Women Advised to Limit Caffeine Consumption. www.food.gov.uk/news/newsarchive/2008/nov/caffeinenov08 (Last accessed: October 22, 2009.)

Caffeine and Health

The evidence base on caffeine and health is vast, covers a number of topics and uses various research methods and dietary sources. Observational studies, which consider associations between diet and health, tend to focus on consumption of tea and coffee as markers of caffeine consumption. Intervention or clinical studies tend to compare caffeine pills with placebos to investigate how caffeine affects specific health outcomes, for example blood pressure (BP) and mental alertness.

The non-uniformity of caffeine sources in these studies makes interpretation of results difficult because most caffeinated products contain other compounds that can influence disease risk. For example, tea is rich in the polyphenols—quercetin, catechin and epigallocatechin gallate—which have been linked with reduced CVD risk. Coffee is a source of the antioxidant, chlorogenic acid, while chocolate is a source of saturated fat. An overview of the benefits and risks associated with caffeinated products is given in Table 2.

Heart and Vascular Health

Research on caffeinated products has included analysis of overall CVD risk, myocardial infarction (MI) risk, blood lipids, metabolic syndrome, inflammation and BP. In observational studies, it is impossible to separate the effects of caffeine and polyphenols since coffee and tea contain both. Polyphenols are believed to have a positive influence on heart and vascular health because of their antioxidant properties, which inhibit the oxidation of cholesterol. Polyphenols may also help normalise vascular tone by promoting the relaxation of endothelial cells in the walls of blood vessels.

Studies on CVD risk are mainly observational. A review by Gardner *et al* described 20 studies published from 1990 to 2004, which found significant associations between regular tea drinking (at around four cups per day) and heart health, for example reduced mortality, lower risk of MI or lower plasma cholesterol. Three cohort studies, representing more than 90,000 patients, reported a link between four cups per day of caffeinated beverages and a lower risk of CVD. In a long-term study of 26,500 middle-aged smokers, men who drank more than two cups of tea per day had a 21% lower risk of having a stroke. In contrast, two observational studies, representing more than 200,000 subjects, found no association between coffee or caffeine intake and risk of CVD.

TIME OUT 2

Write down the benefits and risks associated with caffeine and compare your list with the text beiow. How would this influence the advice you might give to someone who wishes to consume caffeinated drinks and foods?

Table 2

Benefits and Risks of Caffeine-Containing Foods and Drinks

	Benefits	Risks
Tea	Polyphenol content linked with heart health, improved vascular and less cognitive decline in older adults. Contributes to hydration. Caffeine content is much lower than other caffeinated beverages.	Phenolic compounds can reduce non-haem iron absorption, potentially affecting iron status. Therefore vegetarians and others with low intakes of haem iron (from red meat) should avoid drinking tea at mealtimes.
Ground coffee	Polyphenol content linked with heart health. Contributes to hydration when drunk in moderation.	See comments for tea. Caffeine level can exceed 200 mg in one serving. High coffee intakes are associated with increased risk of hypertension in some studies.
Instant coffee	Polyphenol content linked with heart health. Contributes to hydration.	See comments for tea. The potassium level can make instant coffee unsuitable for patients with renal disease.
Cola	Contributes to hydration.	Versions containing sugar pose a risk for dental caries and are a source of calories. The acidity can pose a risk for dental erosion.
Cocoa	Represents a healthy source of calcium if made with low-fat milk. Contributes to hydration.	See comments for tea. Fat and sugar content can be high.
Chocolate	Polyphenol content of dark chocolate linked with heart health and improved blood flow.	Fat, sugar and calorie content can be high.

Negative studies on MI risk have focused on coffee drinking, although the studies have been observational and need verification from randomised controlled trials (RCTs) to establish cause and effect. Three studies reported an increased risk of MI with 'heavy' coffee consumption. This was defined as about five cups a day, which could equate to 400–500 mg of caffeine. Other studies have found no effect of caffeine on MI risk.

Most of the concern around caffeine and heart health has focused on BP and the risk of hypertension. Caffeine can raise systolic and diastolic BP, but this seems to depend on the study population, the source of caffeine and whether consumption is acute (large intake during one day) or chronic (moderate habitual intake). Two large observational studies, representing more than 155,000 healthy individuals, found no association between caffeine intake and BP. In contrast, a small observational study noted a link between caffeine consumption and higher systolic BP in adolescents.

Intervention studies have reported that exposure to caffeine (via pills or coffee) can raise systolic and diastolic BP in the short and long term. The effect was seen at a daily caffeine intake of 250–300 mg. However, a meta-analysis (a statistical analysis of similar high-quality studies) of 16 RCTs suggested that coffee had less of an effect on BP than caffeine alone. Exposure to caffeine pills increased systolic BP and diastolic BP by 4.16 mmHg and 2.41 mmHg, respectively, while exposure to coffee increased systolic BP and diastolic BP by 1.22 mmHg and 0.49 mmHg, respectively.

In one acute study, participants with pre-existing hypertension, or BP at the high end of normal, exhibited a greater response to caffeine pills over 45 minutes than those with normal or optimal BP. This suggests that caffeine restriction may benefit patients at risk of hypertension as well as those who have the condition. A study comparing caffeine powder with green or black tea (all matched for caffeine level) found that tea had less of an effect on blood pressure than caffeine powder over seven days. This may have been because of tea polyphenols minimising the effect of caffeine.

The evidence linking caffeinated products with other CVD risk factors is contradictory. Some studies have found reductions in cholesterol, triglycerides and metabolic syndrome, but others have reported increases.

There is no official recommendation for people with CVD or hypertension to restrict caffeine. The available evidence suggests that a moderate consumption of tea and coffee may offer heart health benefits, perhaps as a result of the polyphenol and chlorogenic acid content. However, as a precautionary measure, those at risk of hypertension should consider limiting caffeine consumption. As the available evidence suggests that effects on BP are seen above 250 mg per day, this may represent a sensible limit.

Mental Health and Mood

Caffeine is believed to affect mood and performance by inhibiting the actions of two neurotransmitters, adenosine and benzodiazepine, which slow down brain activity. Caffeine intake also causes changes to other neurotransmitters, such as noradrenaline (norepinephrine), dopamine, serotonin, acetylcholine and glutamate.

A recent review of caffeine examined the evidence linking caffeine consumption with mood and mental health. A total of 23 RCTs were examined, many of which used caffeine pills. The majority of these reported benefits of a caffeine intake in the region of 37.5–450 mg, improved alertness, short-term recall and reaction time, positive reported mood and lower perceived fatigue. Some sleep disturbances were observed once intakes exceeded 400 mg/day.

Although most of the studies were short-term, the half-life of caffeine is 60–90 minutes and any cognitive effects would be expected to occur during this time. This is supported by the finding that the caffeine contained in a second cup of tea or coffee, for example, does not induce additional cognitive or mood benefits.

Tea and coffee appear to have similar effects on mental health and mood, but differ when compared with caffeine pills. This is probably because of the presence of other compounds in caffeinated drinks, such as theophylline, theanine or theobromine, which may affect cognitive function and mood independently of caffeine.

The evidence for mental health and mood indicates benefit at around 38–450 mg/day of caffeine. However, taking into account the potential for disrupting sleep, 400 mg per day would seem to be a safer upper limit of benefit in the author's opinion.

Physical Performance

Caffeine is believed to have ergogenic (performance enhancing) properties; for example, it may enhance exercise performance. Until 2004, the International Olympic Committee restricted caffeine use during sports competition to remove any unfair advantage. Caffeine is thought to affect physical performance by stimulating fat oxidation, which, in turn, spares muscle glycogen stores. It may also enhance muscle contractions, and increase tolerance to fatigue through the production of plasma catecholamines or the inhibition of adenosine receptors.

Ruxton reviewed the evidence for caffeine and physical performance finding 11 RCTs, most of which were based on young, fit individuals. Only two RCTs found no effect, while the majority reported short-term improvements in running or cycling endurance and perception of fatigue. Intakes of caffeine were in the range of 2.5–6.0 mg/kg body weight (175–420 mg per day for an average male). Of relevance to nurses is the study Norager *et al*, which found that a caffeine intake of 6 mg/kg body weight improved physical endurance and walking speed in 30 healthy older people. This suggests that active older adults may benefit from a moderate consumption of caffeinated beverages.

The findings of Ruxton are supported by two meta-analyses. Doherty and Smith examined the evidence from 40 double-blind studies on exercise performance, and found that caffeine improved physical endurance by 12%. In the second analysis, Doherty and Smith considered 21 studies and found that 30% of the improvement in exercise performance was the result of caffeine's beneficial effect on perceived exertion.

Pregnancy

In response to new evidence and recommendations from the Committee on Toxicology, the Food Standards Agency amended its advice to pregnant women to recommend a reduction in the previous caffeine limit from 300 mg per day to 200 mg per day. The underlying concern was that higher intakes of caffeine may increase the risk of low birthweight.

Studies examining the potential effect of caffeine during pregnancy have been mainly observational, which makes it difficult to ascertain cause and effect. The study that prompted the FSA to alter its advice involved more than 2,600 pregnant women, recruited at eight to 12 weeks' gestation and followed until birth. Caffeine intake was assessed by a salivary marker. It was found that intakes in excess of 100 mg/day were associated with a progressively increased risk of low birthweight, with the greatest effect evident at intakes greater than 300 mg/day. Three other studies observed correlations between caffeine consumption and the risk of low birthweight, although two of these considered smokers only.

Table 3

General Advice on Caffeine and Dietary Sources for Different Patient Groups

Patient Group	Suggested Caffeine Limit	General Patient Advice
Healthy adults	No official UK guideline. Around 400 mg/day* would be a reasonable limit.	Polyphenol compounds in tea may offer heart health benefits at intakes greater than four cups per day. Coffee is also a source of polyphenols, but is higher in caffeine. Tea and coffee can make a positive contribution to hydration when caffeine intakes remain below 400 mg/day*. This equates to eight cups of tea or five cups of instant coffee if no other dietary sources of caffeine are consumed. Avoid adding sugar to beverages. Limit soft drinks, caffeinated or otherwise, to one per day.
Healthy children	No official UK guideline. Health and Welfare Canada suggests 45 mg/day for four to six year olds; 62.5 mg/day for seven to nine year olds and 85 mg/day for ten to 12 year olds. Expert group reports increased anxiety levels above 95 mg/day or 3 mg/ kg body weight/day.	There is no need for school-aged children to avoid tea and coffee if overall caffeine levels remain below 95 mg/day. This equates to one to two small cups of tea or one small cup of weak instant coffee if no other dietary sources of caffeine are consumed. Adding plenty of milk to unsweetened tea or coffee provides a source of calcium and is healthier for teeth than acidic fruit juices or sugar-containing soft drinks. Limit soft drinks, caffeinated or otherwise, to one per day.
Athletes	No official UK guideline. Around 400 mg/day* would be a reasonable limit.	A moderate amount of caffeine may help support exercise training. Intakes of 3–6 mg caffeine per kg body weight (210–420 mg for an average male) can improve endurance and lessen perceived fatigue. Caffeine pills are sometimes used by athletes and would not be harmful as long as daily caffeine intakes remained below 400 mg.

(Continued)

Table 3

General Advice on Caffeine and Dietary Sources for Different Patient Groups (*continued*)

Patient Group	Suggested Caffeine Limit	General Patient Advice
Vegetarians	No official UK guideline. Around 400 mg/day* would be a reasonable limit.	Same as for healthy adults. To maximise absorption of iron, drink fruit juice rather than tea at mealtimes.
Pregnant women	Food Standards Agency advises limiting caffeine to 200 mg/day.	Tea and coffee are not harmful during pregnancy if daily caffeine remains below 200 mg. This equates to three to four cups of tea or two cups of instant coffee if no other dietary sources of caffeine are consumed. Obese pregnant women should limit consumption of chocolate and sugar-containing soft drinks because of the calorie level.
Lactating women	No official UK guideline. No evidence of adverse effects in the breast-fed infant when mothers consumed 500 mg/day. However, 400 mg/day* would be a reasonable limit.	A moderate intake of caffeine, for example from tea and coffee, is not harmful to breastfeeding mothers or their babies. Same as for healthy adults.
Patients with hypertension	No official UK guideline. Evidence from studies on hypertensive patients suggests increased risk above 250 mg/day.†	Polyphenol compounds in tea have been associated with improved vascular function. Tea and coffee can raise systolic and diastolic blood pressure when daily caffeine intakes exceed 250 mg. This equates to five cups of tea or two to three cups of weak coffee per day if no other dietary sources of caffeine are consumed.
Normotensive patients with coronary heart disease	No official UK guideline. Around 400 mg/day* would be a reasonable limit.	Polyphenol compounds in tea have been associated with improved vascular function. There is no consistent evidence that tea, coffee or caffeine have adverse effects on blood cholesterol, triglycerides or glucose tolerance.
Patients with renal failure	No official UK guideline. Around 400 mg/day* would be a reasonable limit.	Polyphenol compounds in tea have been associated with improved vascular function. There is no need for patients with renal failure or impaired renal function to avoid caffeinated drinks. Instant coffee contains potassium and would be unsuitable for patients on a restricted potassium intake.

Table 3

General Advice on Caffeine and Dietary Sources for Different Patient Groups (*continued*)

Patient Group	Suggested Caffeine Limit	General Patient Advice
Older individuals and inpatients where maintaining good hydration is an issue	No official guideline. Around 400 mg/day* would be a reasonable limit.	Tea and coffee make a positive contribution to hydration when caffeine intake remains below 400 mg/day. This equates to eight cups of tea or four cups of instant coffee if no other dietary sources of caffeine are consumed. Milk in tea and coffee contributes to calcium intake. There is good evidence that caffeine improves alertness while tea drinking may improve mood and mental performance.

* This figure is based on literature reviews conducted by the author for this article and for Ruxton CH (2008). The impact of caffeine on mood, cognitive function, performance and hydration: a review of benefits and risks. Nutrition Bulletin. 33, 15–25.

† This figure is based on the minimum level of caffeine to affect blood pressure adversely as reported by Rakic V, Burke V, Beilin LJ (1999). Effects of coffee on ambulatory blood pressure in older men and women: a randomized controlled trial. *Hypertension*. 33, 3, 869–873 and Lovallo WR, Wilson MF, Vincent AS, et al (2004). Blood pressure response to caffeine shows incomplete tolerance after short-term regular consumption. *Hypertension*. 43, 4, 760–765.

In contrast, no significant benefits were seen during a clinical trial that aimed to reduce caffeine intake during pregnancy. Half of the 1,200 women recruited to the trial reduced their daily caffeine consumption by 180 mg on average by switching to decaffeinated coffee. Yet it was found at the end of the study that birthweight and gestational length were similar between the decaffeinated and caffeinated coffee groups. Other aspects of fetal health have been examined in relation to maternal caffeine, for example the risk of a Down syndrome conception, spontaneous abortion and fetal death, but a clear link with caffeine was not found.

Hydration

It is a common perception that caffeinated drinks cause a net loss in fluid and may lead to dehydration. In theory, caffeine could have an adverse effect on

TIME OUT 3

Create an advice sheet for a non-pregnant inpatient to maintain hydration. Show how he or she can safely consume caffeinated beverages as part of his or her daily fluid consumption.

hydration as it increases blood flow to the kidneys and inhibits the reabsorption of sodium, calcium and magnesium, thus expelling more water. Caffeine may also induce a need to urinate by stimulating the bladder's detrusor muscles, although this was not confirmed by a RCT involving 69 women with detrusor overactivity.

Despite the theory, consumption of caffeine in practice does not ppear to be dehydrating. Ruxton reviewed the evidence linking caffeine intake and hydration, finding only eight RCTs on people. Of these, five found no significant effect of a daily caffeine intake of 1.4–6.0 mg/kg body weight (98–420 mg/day for an average 70 kg person). In two studies, urine output increased significantly when caffeine intakes were in the region of 600 mg per day. This suggests that caffeine only presents a risk to hydration at higher intakes equating to around 12 cups of tea or six strong cups of coffee per day.

Discussion

Just as vitamins and minerals need to be consumed within an optimal range to maximise benefit and minimise the risk of toxicity, the published evidence suggests that it is sensible to consume caffeinated beverages within certain limits to deliver benefits to cognitive function and heart health without compromising other areas of health. Such limits differ depending on the patient group.

While it may be tempting for nurses to advise patients simply to cut out caffeine, it is worth bearing in mind the widespread consumption of tea, coffee, chocolate and cola, indicating the enjoyment associated with these products. In addition, the contribution of regular tea, for example to polyphenol intakes, cannot be ignored. Therefore, a more balanced approach is needed to guide patients towards a safer pattern of consumption, using daily caffeine limits as a starting point.

The only UK guideline restricting caffeine intake refers to pregnancy, where the FSA has identified a daily limit of 200 mg. However, there is sufficient evidence to provide at least some practical guidance to nurses. The available evidence suggests the safe range of caffeine consumption to be 38–400 mg/day for healthy adults and certain patient groups (Table 3), which equates to a daily maximum of eight cups of tea, five cups of instant coffee, four cups of brewed coffee or five cans of energy drinks (although this level of energy drinks could not be recommended because of the calorie content). Other dietary considerations, for example potassium restriction or low-fat diets, should be taken into account when advising on the appropriateness of specific caffeinated foods and drinks.

For other groups, such as children, people with hypertension and pregnant women, it is advisable to limit caffeine further. In the absence of UK guidelines for children, official Canadian opinion provides a useful steer. Research on the impact of caffeine on BP, while not offering a consensus, indicates a caffeine level (250 mg/day) that appears to minimise risk, although the response of individual patients to regular caffeine intake should be considered when offering advice.

TIME OUT 4

Work out how much tea, coffee, cola or chocolate could be consumed by a person wishing to limit his or her daily caffeine intake to 200 mg. Use Tables 2 and 3 to plan what written advice about the caffeinated products you might give to the patient groups in your clinical area.

Conclusion

According to the literature reviewed by the author, caffeine and certain caffeinated drinks appear to offer heath benefits in a range of 38–400 mg of caffeine per day. Patients can continue to enjoy caffeinated products if advised correctly about specific daily caffeine limits. Nurses have an important role in delivering evidence-based advice about caffeine.

TIME OUT 5

Now that you have completed the article you might like to write a practice profile. . . .

Peter J. Rogers

Caffeine—Our Favourite Drug

Caffeine is the most popular drug in the world. Per capita consumption is particularly high in Europe where, despite the popularity of cola and 'energy' drinks, tea and coffee remain the predominant sources—over 90% of the caffeine currently consumed in the UK comes from tea and coffee. But are its claimed benefits being oversold?

Tea and coffee are enjoyed in a variety of contexts, but caffeine is valued mainly for its alerting effects. Officially, sleepy drivers and even troops in combat have been encouraged to use caffeine to counteract tiredness and mental fatigue. However, while many studies apparently confirm a psychostimulant effect of caffeine in regular caffeine consumers, there is doubt as to whether this represents a net benefit for alertness and mental performance. In addition, caffeine raises blood pressure, increases anxiety and decreases hand steadiness. This begins to look not so good for our favourite drug.

After drinking tea, coffee, or other caffeine-containing drink, caffeine is distributed rapidly throughout the body, reaching its highest concentration in blood and brain within 30–40 minutes. Caffeine and its metabolites are then gradually eliminated from the body, mainly in the urine. For adults, the elimination half-life of caffeine (i.e. the time it takes for half of the caffeine consumed to be eliminated from the body) is around 3 to 6 hours, although this is longer during pregnancy and shorter in smokers.

The average cup of tea drunk in the UK contains about 40 mg of caffeine, whereas instant coffee contains about 55 mg and filter coffee about 105 mg of caffeine. In these amounts, the physiological and behavioural effects of caffeine occur primarily via antagonism of the neuromodulator adenosine at adenosine A_1 and A_{2A} receptors. These cell-surface receptors are distributed throughout the body, and by blocking the action of endogenous adenosine, caffeine has significant cardiovascular, cerebrovascular, renal, gastrointestinal and metabolic effects. Adenosine is also involved in the regulation of sleep, wakefulness and arousal—hence caffeine's potential to affect alertness and mental performance, and especially performance on tasks requiring sustained attention.

In response to regular caffeine consumption, however, there are changes in adenosine signalling that serve to counter the effects of caffeine and, at least in part, maintain normal functioning. For example, caffeine causes vasoconstriction, and following caffeine withdrawal there is vasodilation leading to increased cerebral blood flow which increases vulnerability to headache. Cessation of caffeine consumption also causes tiredness and fatigue. Headache, reduced alertness and associated decrements in performance generally peak after 24–36 hours without consuming caffeine, but these effects are also detectable after overnight caffeine abstinence. For example, it has been found that morning alertness in caffeine consumers before they have had their first cup of tea or coffee of the day is lower (and drowsiness and tiredness are higher) than that rated at the same time in the morning by non-consumers of caffeine (Figure 1).

More surprisingly, consumption of caffeine increases alertness in caffeine consumers, but it has little or no effect on alertness in non-consumers. Mental performance, especially performance on simple tasks where continuous monitoring is required, is affected in a similar way (unpublished). This,

Figure 1

Drowsiness mid-morning in caffeine consumers who abstained from caffeine overnight but were given caffeine 90 minutes before testing (1.5 h group), in caffeine consumers who had abstained from caffeine overnight but were not given caffeine (13 h group), in caffeine consumers who had abstained from caffeine for at least 7 days, and in caffeine non-consumers. Mean daily caffeine intakes of the caffeine consumers and the non-consumers before the experiment were 250 and 3 mg respectively. These participants rated their drowsiness on a 100 mm line-scale labelled 'not at all' (=0) at the left-hand end and 'extremely' (=100) at the right hand end.

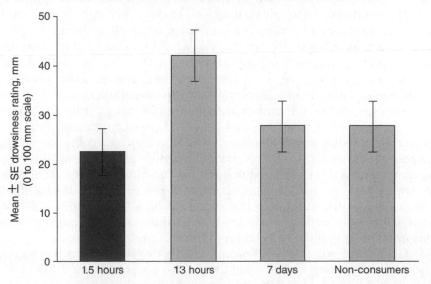

and the further finding that levels of alertness and performance in consumers after caffeine do not exceed those experienced by non-consumers without caffeine (Figure 1), form the basis for the so-called withdrawal reversal hypothesis, which states that acute caffeine withdrawal lowers alertness and degrades performance, and caffeine restores alertness and performance to, but not above, normal levels.

In relation to morning alertness, the implication is that the common feeling of drowsiness on waking is actually a symptom of caffeine withdrawal (a large majority of adults in the UK consume significant amounts of caffeine— around four in five consume 120 mg caffeine or more per day), rather than this being normal after a night's sleep.

The claim that no acute benefit is gained for alertness and mental performance from caffeine consumption has been variously disputed, but evidence in its favour is accumulating steadily. Perhaps most importantly, after a week (or a bit less) of caffeine abstinence, former caffeine consumers come to resemble non-consumers (or 'never consumers') in their waking and daytime levels of alertness (Figure 1) and performance, and also in their lack of responsiveness to caffeine on these tests. Such findings make a strong case for caffeine dependence in regular caffeine consumers; that is, they require caffeine to function normally. On the other hand, caffeine use poses a low risk of addiction, perhaps mainly because its psychoactive effects are not experienced as particularly pleasurable.

Why Are Caffeine Drinks So Popular?

After water, tea is the most commonly consumed drink worldwide, while the higher concentration of caffeine in coffee makes it the major source of caffeine in many countries. These drinks, therefore, make a very significant contribution to fluid intake, and clearly one motive for consuming them is to quench thirst. This may be especially true for tea, which is rated as more 'refreshing' than coffee. Contrary to some popular opinion the net effect of these drinks on fluid balance is positive, notwithstanding the diuretic effect of caffeine (to which regular caffeine consumers may develop partial tolerance).

Another motive for consuming caffeine-containing drinks is the conscious recognition of their potential beneficial psychostimulant properties— "I can't start the day without a coffee", "caffeine keeps me going when I begin to flag". Of course, withdrawal reversal (as described above) means that regular caffeine intake is merely maintaining normal functioning; however, individually we are not able to distinguish between a net stimulant effect and withdrawal relief, as the experience of a change from a less to a more alert state is the same. Additionally, it appears that withdrawal relief indirectly affects consumption by increasing liking for caffeine-containing drinks.

Liking here refers to our hedonic or affective response to the taste and flavour of tea or coffee, and it is clear that we are not born liking the taste of, for example, black coffee. In part this is because it contains bitter-tasting compounds, including caffeine, and humans have an inborn dislike of bitter tastes (most likely because bitterness signals the presence of possibly harmful constituents in the potential food or drink—caffeine may function as a pesticide in the plants that produce it. Liking, however, can be modified through association of the taste and flavour of the drink (or food) with the after-effects of its ingestion.

The most dramatic example of this is the strong and specific aversion (dislike) that can develop when consumption of a drink or food is followed by nausea and vomiting. Such aversions are especially likely to develop if the food or drink is relatively novel for the individual. Similarly, association of a taste or flavour paired with positive consequences can result in increased liking for that specific taste or flavour. In other words, there is a change in how good the food or drink tastes to the individual corresponding to the benefit or harm resulting from an earlier experience of that food or drink. As with aversion to bitter tastes, learned aversions and preferences help guide adaptive dietary choices. In relation to tea and coffee, it may be that liking for their taste is reinforced by the associated psychostimulant after-effects.

This hypothesis has been tested in experiments in which volunteers were given a novel-flavoured, and initially only moderately pleasant, fruit juice to drink either with or without caffeine (in one experiment the caffeine and placebo, starch, were given in capsules swallowed with the drink). Even though there was generally equal liking for the two drinks on the first occasion they were tasted, there was, as predicted, a greater increase in preference for the caffeine-containing drink on re-exposure. This learning was found to occur rather quickly; for example, marked differences in favour of liking a caffeine-containing drink have been observed after just a very few exposures to the drink. Other results from this research are that the presence or absence of caffeine in the drink only had a clear effect on preference if the volunteers usually included caffeine in their diet and if they were acutely deprived of caffeine (overnight caffeine abstinence) before taking the experimental drink. These regular caffeine consumers developed an aversion for the drink if it did not contain caffeine, and an increase in preference if it did. This is as predicted by the withdrawal reversal hypothesis—aversion developed for the drink without caffeine because its consumption was associated with the negative effects of caffeine withdrawal, and increased liking occurred because the caffeine-containing drink removed these effects. Psychologically speaking, this is negative reinforcement.

Negative reinforcement of liking helps to explain how caffeine consumption is maintained (we consume coffee, at least in part because we like it, and not just as an unpleasant tasting medicine for combating fatigue), but what gets us started on caffeine? If there really is no psychostimulant benefit for caffeine non-consumers, what reinforces initial consumption? One possibility, as mentioned above, is reduction in thirst, and the sociability and perhaps peer-pressure associated with drinking tea and coffee will also encourage consumption. Additionally, these drinks can be made more acceptable by adding milk and/or sugar, and consuming weaker (more dilute) tea or coffee may also improve initial acceptability. Then with daily intake of even moderate amounts of caffeine, psychostimulant effects will play an important role in (negatively) reinforcing consumption, paving the way for some of us to acquire a regular habit of double espressos.

Individual Differences in Consumption and Effects

Although caffeine is consumed very widely, amounts and sources of caffeine intake differ greatly between and within countries. Undoubtedly, the origin of much of this variation is historical and cultural. Within population groups, family tradition, current fashion, lifestyle, etc, are likely to affect whether, for example, an individual mainly drinks tea or coffee or cola, or avoids caffeine altogether. It has also been suggested that biology may account partly for individual differences in intake. Specifically, a variant of the gene that codes for the adenosine A_{2A} receptor confers susceptibility to caffeine-induced anxiety, and people with this gene variant (TT genotype of the ADORA2A rs5751876 SNP) have been found, at least in one study, to consume less caffeine. This is a nice example of a link between genetics and human behaviour. The same genotype is also associated with increased risk of panic disorder.

It would seem, on the other hand, unlikely that caffeine's anxiogenic effect has a major impact on caffeine use. This is because caffeine consumers develop at least partial tolerance to this adverse effect (unpublished), and even susceptible non-consumers do not experience a very marked increase in anxiety after caffeine. Furthermore, we found in a survey of nearly 6,000 people living in and around Bristol (UK) that only around 5% of non-coffee and/or non-tea consumers gave anxiety or related effects as a reason for avoiding these drinks (unpublished). Most of these people had tried tea and coffee, but reported not liking their taste. Perhaps they did not persist with trying these drinks often or regularly enough to acquire a liking for them especially if, as described above, this depends on negative reinforcement founded on caffeine dependence. Despite the inherent limitations of such surveys, these results do appear to accord with the conclusions arising from rigorously controlled, laboratory studies.

Another possibility we have investigated is that non-consumers of caffeine are more sensitive to bitterness than regular consumers. While we did find this to be the case, the difference in sensitivity was rather small (unpublished), so this may not have much effect on the likelihood of becoming a caffeine consumer. In any case, as mentioned above, the negative effect of bitterness on taste can be offset by addition of sugar or other sweetener to the drink.

Individual differences in the effects of caffeine are partly rooted in inherited characteristics; however, tolerance related to individuals' recent level of caffeine exposure is particularly important in determining responses to this drug, including its effects on alertness, mental performance, anxiety and blood pressure.

More to Tea and Coffee Than Caffeine

Caffeine is only one of thousands of compounds present in tea and coffee, which include nearly a thousand aromatic compounds found in coffee alone. While no single constituent matches caffeine in terms of impact on human physiology and behaviour, there is increasing evidence that other compounds do contribute significantly to the health effects of these drinks. Theanine, for example, which occurs in tea, has been found to lower blood pressure, and in particular to antagonise the blood-pressure raising effect of caffeine. It has also been suggested that theanine is anxiolytic (i.e. that it can reduce anxiety and/ or induce a relaxed state), an effect which might help account for perceived differences in the psychoactive effects of tea and coffee, as coffee does not contain theanine. Indeed, it is tempting to claim that the combination of theanine and caffeine in tea can bring about a state of 'calm energy'. Unfortunately, this may be too good to be true—evidence concerning the calming effects of theanine is by no means clear cut and, as described above, it seems that caffeine does not enhance alertness beyond reversing the fatiguing effects of withdrawal.

Blood pressure effects are potentially very important for health. For example, it has been argued that, by increasing blood pressure (owing to its vasoconstrictive effects), caffeine consumption may contribute substantially to the prevalence of cardiovascular disease and stroke and by implication to an increased risk of cognitive decline in older age. It is reassuring therefore that tea consumption has not generally been found to be associated with these effects. Indeed, some studies even suggest that consumption of tea may reduce the risk of cardiovascular and cerebrovascular disease. It is plausible that polyphenols present in tea, including catechin, might be at least partly responsible for this, possibly via vasorelaxant effects and effects on blood cholesterol, blood coagulation and inflammatory processes. The blood-pressure lowering effect of theanine may contribute as well, perhaps along with partial tolerance to the hypertensive effect of caffeine.

The risks of hypertension and cardiovascular disease associated with coffee consumption are also less than might be expected from its caffeine content. Again, the presence of other physiologically active compounds is likely to be important. Certain compounds such as cafestol (the concentration of which is affected by brewing method) may increase risk, but chlorogenic acid and other phenols are thought to have beneficial effects.

Finally, caffeine itself may reduce the risk of cognitive decline via enhancement of the neuroprotective effects of adenosine. A significant cause of cognitive decline in older age is transient ischaemic episodes linked to underlying vascular disease. Brain ischaemia is the loss of glucose and oxygen supply to the brain, and can lead to cell death. During ischaemia there is a large increase in extracellular adenosine which, acting via adenosine A_1 and A_{2A} receptors, helps to counter some of the key pathophysiological processes that lead to ischaemic cell death. Studies using animal models show that a one-off dose of caffeine increases ischaemic brain damage, but chronic pre-treatment with caffeine (more akin to the habits of regular tea and coffee consumers) reduces it. This suggests that a protective effect is gained through up-regulation of adenosine receptors, perhaps, ironically, in combination with caffeine withdrawal.

Pain and Physical Performance

Caffeine is combined with aspirin, paracetamol, ibuprofen and codeine in a variety of widely available analgesic products, and evidence shows that caffeine does add to their efficacy, especially in treating headache. The vasocontrictive action of caffeine is likely to be important here, although often a significant cause of the headache may be withdrawal from caffeine itself. Headache associated with colds and flu, for example, may well be exacerbated by cessation of caffeine consumption owing to loss of appetite for caffeine-containing drinks.

Headache and fatigue are the most common symptoms of caffeine withdrawal, and 'flu-like' symptoms have also been described. Similarly, caffeine withdrawal has been implicated as a potentially important factor contributing to headache following general anaesthesia. Fasting prior to anaesthesia and other medical procedures includes avoidance of all dietary sources of caffeine. The most effective immediate remedy for caffeine withdrawal is, of course, caffeine; in the long term, though, complete caffeine abstinence should reduce vulnerability to headache and fatigue.

Among athletes, caffeine has a reputation as an 'ergogenic aid', and there is indeed good evidence that caffeine can enhance physical performance, mainly by increasing endurance. Studies in this field have tended to test the effects of fairly high doses of caffeine (usually equivalent to several cups of filter coffee), but within the acceptable limit set by the International Olympic Committee. Most significantly, it seems that in contrast to its effects on mental performance, caffeine use in this context does provide a means to gain a real advantage. This is based on the observation that caffeine enhances physical performance to a similar extent in caffeine consumers and non-consumers, indicating that withdrawal reversal is not the mechanism. The physiological basis of caffeine's effects on athletic performance has not been indentified conclusively, but this probably involves fundamental aspects of muscle contractility.

Conclusion

Caffeine-containing products are important commercially and, given their widespread consumption and caffeine's varied physiological and psychoactive effects, they potentially have a significant impact on population health and well-being. However, despite extensive research, not enough is currently known to do a full risk assessment of the impact of lifelong consumption of coffee or tea or other caffeine-containing drinks (some effects are positive, others less desirable). Unfortunately, as far as caffeine itself is concerned, it appears that its alerting effects are largely illusionary, as frequent consumption merely maintains normal levels of functioning.

POSTSCRIPT

Is Caffeine a Health Risk?

Although caffeine is commonly consumed by millions of people without much regard to its physical and psychological effects, many studies have questioned its safety. However, other studies have reported very few hazards. The basic question is whether or not people who drink several cups of coffee or other caffeinated beverages daily should be more concerned than they are. Are the claims of caffeine's benefits or hazards exaggerated?

Determining if certain foods or beverages promote disease or have health benefits can be trying because the research is unclear. Sometimes the research is contradictory. Many people become frustrated because quite a few of the things that we eat or drink are suspected of being unhealthy. For example, various reports indicate that the fat in beef can lead to various forms of cancer and heart disease; that we should consume less salt and sugar; that processed foods should be avoided; and that whole milk, butter, and margarine should be reduced or eliminated from our diets. If people paid attention to every report about the harmful effects of the foods and beverages they consumed, then they would not be able to eat much at all. What is the average consumer supposed to do?

A legitimate question is whether or not food studies are worth pursuing because so many of the products that are reportedly bad are enjoyed by millions of people. Some people claim they cannot start their day without caffeine. Caffeine is simply one more example of a commonly used product that has come under scrutiny. In addition, although the research is vast, it is inconclusive. One study, for instance, linked caffeine to pancreatic cancer, only to find later that the culprit was not caffeine but cigarette smoking. Research on caffeine's effects on cancers of the bladder, urinary tract, and kidney has also proven to be inconsistent and inconclusive. Because caffeinated products are consumed by millions of people, it is important to know if its dangers are significant or exaggerated. However, if professional researchers cannot agree as to whether a product is safe or harmful, how can the average person know what to believe?

Critics of caffeine claim that caffeine may cause dependence because it shares some of the same characteristics of cocaine, alcohol, and nicotine. They state that too much caffeine causes tolerance as well as withdrawal symptoms. Despite their concern, there are not support groups for people addicted to caffeine. Peter Rogers counters that caffeine's adverse effects are overstated and in some instances it is beneficial. Carrie Ruxton indicates that caffeine is a stimulant and that it has proven adverse effects.

The effects of caffeine during pregnancy are addressed in "Maternal Caffeine Intake during Pregnancy and Risk of Fetal Growth Restriction: A Large

Prospective Observational Study," by Justin Konje and others, *BMJ* (November 3, 2008) and "Does Caffeine in Pregnancy Cause Birth Defects?" *Child Health Alert* (June 2006). Jackie Berning looks at the implications for athletes using caffeinated products in "Caffeine and Athletic Performance," *Clinical Reference Systems* (May 24, 2006). Other articles that examine caffeine's psychological and physical effects are "Caffeine: The Good, the Bad, and the Maybe," in *Nutrition Action* (March 2008) and "Night-time Thoughts in High and Low Worriers: Reaction to Caffeine-induced Sleeplessness," by Siri Omvik, Stale Pallesen and Bjorn Bjorvatn, *Behaviour Research and Therapy* (April 2007). To find out how much caffeine is found in various products, one should access the Web site MayoClinic.com.

ISSUE 12

Should School-Age Children with Attention Deficit/Hyperactivity Disorder (ADHD) Be Treated with Ritalin and Other Stimulants?

YES: **Michael Fumento**, from "Trick Question," *The New Republic* (February 3, 2003)

NO: **Lawrence H. Diller**, from *The Last Normal Child: Essays on the Intersection of Kids, Culture and Psychiatric Drugs* (Prager, 2006)

ISSUE SUMMARY

YES: Writer Michael Fumento disputes the idea that Ritalin is over-prescribed and contends that despite myths associated with Ritalin, it does not lead to abuse and addiction. Fumento believes Ritalin is an excellent medication for ADHD, may be under-utilized, and that more students would benefit from Ritalin and other stimulants.

NO: Behavioral pediatrician Lawrence Diller contends that Ritalin is overused and that, while Ritalin can moderate behavior, many school districts advocate the use of Ritalin and other stimulants so that they do not have to provide other services, and does not over-come learning disabilities.

$\mathbf{T}$he number one childhood psychiatric disorder in the United States is attention deficit/hyperactivity disorder (ADHD), which affects approximately 3–5 percent of American school children. ADHD is characterized by inattentiveness, hyperactivity, and impulsivity. Many children are diagnosed as having only attention deficit disorder (ADD), which is ADHD without the hyperactivity. One commonly prescribed drug for ADHD is the stimulant Ritalin (generic name methylphenidate). American children consume 90 percent of all Ritalin produced worldwide. Only a very small percentage of European children are diagnosed with ADHD. Ritalin is therefore much less likely to be prescribed in Europe.

The use of stimulants to treat such behavioral disorders dates back to 1937. The practice of prescribing stimulants for behavioral problems increased dramatically beginning in 1970, when it was estimated that 150,000 American children were taking stimulant medications. It seems paradoxical for physicians to be prescribing a stimulant such as Ritalin for a behavioral disorder that already involves hyperactivity. However, Ritalin appears to be effective with many children, as well as with many adults, who suffer from this condition. Looking at this issue from a broader perspective, one needs to ask whether behavioral problems should be treated as a disease. Also, do Ritalin and other stimulants really address the problem? Or could it be covering up other maladies that otherwise should be treated?

Ritalin enhances the functioning of the brain's reticular activating system, which helps one to focus attention and to filter out extraneous stimuli. The drug has been shown to improve short-term learning. Ritalin also produces adverse effects such as insomnia, headaches, irritability, nausea, dizziness, weight loss, and growth retardation. Psychological dependence may develop, but physical dependence is unlikely. The long-term effects of Ritalin and other stimulants' use are unknown.

Since 1990, the number of children receiving Ritalin and other stimulants has increased 500 percent. This large increase in the number of children diagnosed with ADHD may be attributed to a broader application of the criteria for diagnosing ADHD, heightened public awareness, and changes in American educational policy regarding schools' identifying children with the disorder. Some people feel that the increase in prescriptions for Ritalin and other stimulants reflects an increased effort to satisfy the needs of parents whose children exhibit behavioral problems. Ritalin has been referred to as "mother's little helper." Regardless of the reasons for the increase, many people question whether Ritalin and other stimulants are overprescribed.

One problem with the increased prevalence of Ritalin prescriptions is that illegal use of the drug has also risen. There are accounts of some parents getting prescriptions for their children and then selling the drugs illegally. On a number of college campuses, there are reports of students using Ritalin to get high or to stay awake in order to study. Historically, illegal use of Ritalin has been minimal, although officials of the Drug Enforcement Administration (DEA) are now concerned that its illegal use is proliferating. Problems with its use are unlikely to rival those of cocaine because the effects of Ritalin and other stimulants are more moderate than those of cocaine or amphetamines.

The fact is that children now receive prescriptions for Ritalin and other stimulants rather readily. Frequently, parents will pressure their pediatricians for prescriptions. One survey found that almost one-half of all pediatricians spent less than an hour assessing children before prescribing Ritalin. On the other hand, if there is a medication available that would remedy a problem and improve academic performance, should it not be prescribed?

In the YES selection, Michael Fumento maintains that ADHD is underdiagnosed in many instances. He asserts that Ritalin's bad reputation arises from many misconceptions regarding the drug. In the NO selection, Lawrence Diller questions the use and effectiveness of Ritalin. He contends that it is overprescribed because of the way the drug is marketed and that Ritalin does not improve learning.

YES

Michael Fumento

Trick Question

It's both right-wing and vast, but it's not a conspiracy. Actually, it's more of an anti-conspiracy. The subject is Attention Deficit Disorder (ADD) and Attention Deficit Hyperactivity Disorder (ADHD), closely related ailments (henceforth referred to in this article simply as ADHD). Rush Limbaugh declares it "may all be a hoax." Francis Fukuyama devotes much of one chapter in his latest book, *Our Posthuman Future,* to attacking Ritalin, the top-selling drug used to treat ADHD. Columnist Thomas Sowell writes, "The motto used to be: 'Boys will be boys.' Today, the motto seems to be: 'Boys will be medicated." And Phyllis Schlafly explains, "The old excuse of 'my dog ate my homework' has been replaced by 'I got an ADHD diagnosis.'" A March 2002 article in *The Weekly Standard* summed up the conservative line on ADHD with this rhetorical question: "Are we really prepared to redefine childhood as an ailment, and medicate it until it goes away?"

Many conservative writers, myself included, have criticized the growing tendency to pathologize every undesirable behavior—especially where children are concerned. But, when it comes to ADHD, this skepticism is misplaced. As even a cursory examination of the existing literature or, for that matter, simply talking to the parents and teachers of children with ADHD reveals, the condition is real, and it is treatable. And, if you don't believe me, you can ask conservatives who've come face to face with it themselves.

Myth: ADHD Isn't a Real Disorder

The most common argument against ADHD on the right is also the simplest: It doesn't exist. Conservative columnist Jonah Goldberg thus reduces ADHD to "ants in the pants." Sowell equates it with "being bored and restless." Fukuyama protests, "No one has been able to identify a cause of ADD/ADHD. It is a pathology recognized only by its symptoms." And a conservative columnist approvingly quotes Thomas Armstrong, Ritalin opponent and author, when he declares, "ADD is a disorder that cannot be authoritatively identified in the same way as polio, heart disease or other legitimate illnesses."

The Armstrong and Fukuyama observations are as correct as they are worthless. "Half of all medical disorders are diagnosed without benefit of a lab procedure," notes Dr. Russell Barkley, professor of psychology at the

From *The New Republic,* Vol. 228, no. 4, February 3, 2003, pp. 18–21. Copyright © 2003 by New Republic. Reprinted by permission.

College of Health Professionals at the Medical University of South Carolina. "Where are the lab tests for headaches and multiple sclerosis and Alzheimer's?" he asks. "Such a standard would virtually eliminate all mental disorders."

Often the best diagnostic test for an ailment is how it responds to treatment. And, by that standard, it doesn't get much more real than ADHD. The beneficial effects of administering stimulants to treat the disorder were first reported in 1937. And today medication for the disorder is reported to be 75 to 90 percent successful. "In our trials it was close to ninety percent," says Dr. Judith Rapoport, director of the National Institute of Mental Health's Child Psychiatry Branch, who has published about 100 papers on ADHD. "This means there was a significant difference in the children's ability to function in the classroom or at home."

Additionally, epidemiological evidence indicates that ADHD has a powerful genetic component. University of Colorado researchers have found that a child whose identical twin has the disorder is between eleven and 18 times more likely to also have it than is a non-twin sibling. For these reasons, the American Psychiatric Association (APA), American Medical Association, American Academy of Pediatrics, American Academy of Child Adolescent Psychiatry, the surgeon general's office, and other major medical bodies all acknowledge ADHD as both real and treatable.

Myth: ADHD Is Part of a Feminist Conspiracy to Make Little Boys More Like Little Girls

Many conservatives observe that boys receive ADHD diagnoses in much higher numbers than girls and find in this evidence of a feminist conspiracy. (This, despite the fact that genetic diseases are often heavily weighted more toward one gender or the other.) Sowell refers to "a growing tendency to treat boyhood as a pathological condition that requires a new three R's—repression, re-education and Ritalin." Fukuyama claims Prozac is being used to give women "more of the alpha-male feeling," while Ritalin is making boys act more like girls. "Together, the two sexes are gently nudged toward that androgynous median personality . . . that is the current politically correct outcome in American society." George Will, while acknowledging that Ritalin can be helpful, nonetheless writes of the "androgyny agenda" of "drugging children because they are behaving like children, especially boy children." Anti-Ritalin conservatives frequently invoke Christina Hoff Sommers's best-selling 2000 book, *The War Against Boys*. You'd never know that the drug isn't mentioned in her book—or why.

"Originally I was going to have a chapter on it," Sommers tells me. "It seemed to fit the thesis." What stopped her was both her survey of the medical literature and her own empirical findings. Of one child she personally came to know she says, "He was utterly miserable, as was everybody around him. The drugs saved his life."

Myth: ADHD Is Part of the Public School System's Efforts to Warehouse Kids Rather Than to Discipline and Teach Them

"No doubt life is easier for teachers when everyone sits around quietly," writes Sowell. Use of ADHD drugs is "in the school's interest to deal with behavioral and discipline problems [because] it's so easy to use Ritalin to make kids compliant: to get them to sit down, shut up, and do what they're told," declares Schlafly. The word "zombies" to describe children under the effects of Ritalin is tossed around more than in a B-grade voodoo movie.

Kerri Houston, national field director for the American Conservative Union and the mother of two ADHD children on medication, agrees with much of the criticism of public schools. "But don't blame ADHD on crummy curricula and lazy teachers," she says. "If you've worked with these children, you know they have a serious neurological problem." In any case, Ritalin, when taken as prescribed, hardly stupefies children. To the extent the medicine works, it simply turns ADHD children into normal children. "ADHD is like having thirty televisions on at one time, and the medicine turns off twenty-nine so you can concentrate on the one," Houston describes. "This zombie stuff drives me nuts! My kids are both as lively and as fun as can be."

Myth: Parents Who Give Their Kids Anti-ADHD Drugs Are Merely Doping Up Problem Children

Limbaugh calls ADHD "the perfect way to explain the inattention, incompetence, and inability of adults to control their kids." Addressing parents directly, he lectures, "It helped you mask your own failings by doping up your children to calm them down."

Such charges blast the parents of ADHD kids into high orbit. That includes my Hudson Institute colleague (and fellow conservative) Mona Charen, the mother of an eleven-year-old with the disorder. "I have two non-ADHD children, so it's not a matter of parenting technique," says Charen. "People without such children have no idea what it's like. I can tell the difference between boyish high spirits and pathological hyperactivity. . . . These kids bounce off the walls. Their lives are chaos; their rooms are chaos. And nothing replaces the drugs."

Barkley and Rapoport say research backs her up. Randomized, controlled studies in both the United States and Sweden have tried combining medication with behavioral interventions and then dropped either one or the other. For those trying to go on without medicine, "the behavioral interventions maintained nothing," Barkley says. Rapoport concurs: "Unfortunately, behavior modification doesn't seem to help with ADHD." (Both doctors are quick to add that ADHD is often accompanied by other disorders that are treatable through behavior modification in tandem with medicine.)

Myth: Ritalin Is "Kiddie Cocaine"

One of the paradoxes of conservative attacks on Ritalin is that the drug is alternately accused of turning children into brain-dead zombies and of making them Mach-speed cocaine junkies. Indeed, Ritalin is widely disparaged as "kiddie cocaine." Writers who have sought to lump the two drugs together include Schlafly, talk-show host and columnist Armstrong Williams, and others whom I hesitate to name because of my long-standing personal relationships with them.

Mary Eberstadt wrote the "authoritative" Ritalin-cocaine piece for the April 1999 issue of *Policy Review,* then owned by the Heritage Foundation. The article, "Why Ritalin Rules," employs the word "cocaine" no fewer than twelve times. Eberstadt quotes from a 1995 Drug Enforcement Agency (DEA) background paper declaring methylphenidate, the active ingredient in Ritalin, "a central nervous system (CNS) stimulant [that] shares many of the pharmacological effects of amphetamine, methamphetamine, and cocaine." Further, it "produces behavioral, psychological, subjective, and reinforcing effects similar to those of d-amphetamine including increases in rating of euphoria, drug liking and activity, and decreases in sedation." Add to this the fact that the Controlled Substances Act lists it as a Schedule II drug, imposing on it the same tight prescription controls as morphine, and Ritalin starts to sound spooky indeed.

What Eberstadt fails to tell readers is that the DEA description concerns methylphenidate *abuse.* It's tautological to say abuse is harmful. According to the DEA, the drugs in question are comparable when "administered the same way at comparable doses." But ADHD stimulants, when taken as prescribed, are neither administered in the same way as cocaine nor at comparable doses. "What really counts," says Barkley "is the speed with which the drugs enter and clear the brain. With cocaine, because it's snorted, this happens tremendously quickly, giving users the characteristic addictive high." (Ever seen anyone pop a cocaine tablet?) Further, he says, "There's no evidence anywhere in literature of [Ritalin's] addictiveness when taken as prescribed." As to the Schedule II listing, again this is because of the potential for it to fall into the hands of abusers, not because of its effects on persons for whom it is prescribed. Ritalin and the other anti-ADHD drugs, says Barkley, "are the safest drugs in all of psychiatry." (And they may be getting even safer: A new medicine just released called Strattera represents the first true non-stimulant ADHD treatment.)

Indeed, a study just released in the journal *Pediatrics* found that children who take Ritalin or other stimulants to control ADHD cut their risk of future substance abuse by 50 percent compared with untreated ADHD children. The lead author speculated that "by treating ADHD you're reducing the demoralization that accompanies this disorder, and you're improving the academic functioning and well-being of adolescents and young adults during the critical times when substance abuse starts."

Myth: Ritalin Is Overprescribed Across the Country

Some call it "the Ritalin craze." In *The Weekly Standard,* Melana Zyla Vickers informs us that "Ritalin use has exploded," while Eberstadt writes that "Ritalin use more than doubled in the first half of the decade alone, [and] the number of schoolchildren taking the drug may now, by some estimates, be approaching the *4 million mark.*"

A report in the January 2003 issue of *Archives of Pediatrics and Adolescent Medicine* did find a large increase in the use of ADHD medicines from 1987 to 1996, an increase that doesn't appear to be slowing. Yet nobody thinks it's a problem that routine screening for high blood pressure has produced a big increase in the use of hypertension medicine. "Today, children suffering from ADHD are simply less likely to slip through the cracks," says Dr. Sally Satel, a psychiatrist, AEI fellow, and author of *PC, M.D.: How Political Correctness Is Corrupting Medicine.*

Satel agrees that some community studies, by the standards laid down in the APA's *Diagnostic and Statistical Manual of Mental Disorders (DSM),* indicate that ADHD may often be over-diagnosed. On the other hand, she says, additional evidence shows that in some communities ADHD is *under*-diagnosed and *under*-treated. "I'm quite concerned with children who need the medication and aren't getting it," she says.

There *are* tremendous disparities in the percentage of children taking ADHD drugs when comparing small geographical areas. Psychologist Gretchen LeFever, for example, has compared the number of prescriptions in mostly white Virginia Beach, Virginia, with other, more heavily African American areas in the southeastern part of the state. Conservatives have latched onto her higher numbers—20 percent of white fifth-grade boys in Virginia Beach are being treated for ADHD—as evidence that something is horribly wrong. But others, such as Barkley, worry about the lower numbers. According to LeFever's study, black children are only half as likely to get medication as white children. "Black people don't get the care of white people; children of well-off parents get far better care than those of poorer parents," says Barkley.

Myth: States Should Pass Laws That Restrict Schools From Recommending Ritalin

Conservative writers have expressed delight that several states, led by Connecticut, have passed or are considering laws ostensibly protecting students from schools that allegedly pass out Ritalin like candy. Representative Lenny Winkler, lead sponsor of the Connecticut measure, told *Reuters Health,* "If the diagnosis is made, and it's an appropriate diagnosis that Ritalin be used, that's fine. But I have also heard of many families approached by the school system [who are told] that their child cannot attend school if they're not put on Ritalin."

Two attorneys I interviewed who specialize in child-disability issues, including one from the liberal Bazelon Center for Mental Health Law in Washington, D.C., acknowledge that school personnel have in some cases stepped over the line. But legislation can go too far in the other direction by declaring, as Connecticut's law does, that "any school personnel [shall be prohibited] from recommending the use of psychotropic drugs for any child." The law appears to offer an exemption by declaring, "The provisions of this section shall not prohibit *school medical staff* from recommending that a child be evaluated by an appropriate medical practitioner, or prohibit school personnel from consulting with such practitioner, with the consent of the parent or guardian of such child." [Emphasis added.] But of course many, if not most, schools have perhaps one nurse on regular "staff." That nurse will have limited contact with children in the classroom situations where ADHD is likely to be most evident. And, given the wording of the statute, a teacher who believed a student was suffering from ADHD would arguably be prohibited from referring that student to the nurse. Such ambiguity is sure to have a chilling effect on any form of intervention or recommendation by school personnel. Moreover, 20-year special-education veteran Sandra Rief said in an interview with the National Education Association that "recommending medical intervention for a student's behavior could lead to personal liability issues." Teachers, in other words, could be forced to choose between what they think is best for the health of their students and the possible risk of losing not only their jobs but their personal assets as well.

"Certainly it's not within the purview of a school to say kids can't attend if they don't take drugs," says Houston. "On the other hand, certainly teachers should be able to advise parents as to problems and potential solutions. . . . [T]hey may see things parents don't. My own son is an angel at home but was a demon at school."

If the real worry is "take the medicine or take a hike" ultimatums, legislation can be narrowly tailored to prevent them; broad-based gag orders, such as Connecticut's, are a solution that's worse than the problem.

The Conservative Case for ADHD Drugs

There are kernels of truth to every conservative suspicion about ADHD. Who among us has not had lapses of attention? And isn't hyperactivity a normal condition of childhood when compared with deskbound adults? Certainly there are lazy teachers, warehousing schools, androgyny-pushing feminists, and far too many parents unwilling or unable to expend the time and effort to raise their children properly, even by their own standards. Where conservatives go wrong is in making ADHD a scapegoat for frustration over what we perceive as a breakdown in the order of society and family. In a column in *The Boston Herald*, Boston University Chancellor John Silber rails that Ritalin is "a classic example of a cheap fix: low-cost, simple and purely superficial."

Exactly. Like most headaches, ADHD is a neurological problem that can usually be successfully treated with a chemical. Those who recommend or prescribe ADHD medicines do not, as *The Weekly Standard* put it, see them as "discipline in pill-form." They see them as pills.

In fact, it can be argued that the use of those pills, far from being liable for or symptomatic of the Decline of the West, reflects and reinforces conservative values. For one thing, they increase personal responsibility by removing an excuse that children (and their parents) can fall back on to explain misbehavior and poor performance. "Too many psychologists and psychiatrists focus on allowing patients to justify to themselves their troubling behavior," says Satel. "But something like Ritalin actually encourages greater autonomy because you're treating a compulsion to behave in a certain way. Also, by treating ADHD, you remove an opportunity to explain away bad behavior"

Moreover, unlike liberals, who tend to downplay differences between the sexes, conservatives are inclined to believe that there are substantial physiological differences—differences such as boys' greater tendency to suffer ADHD. "Conservatives celebrate the physiological differences between boys and girls and eschew the radical-feminist notion that gender differences are created by societal pressures," says Houston regarding the fuss over the boy-girl disparity among ADHD diagnoses. "ADHD is no exception."

But, however compatible conservatism may be with taking ADHD seriously, the truth is that most conservatives remain skeptics. "I'm sure I would have been one of those smug conservatives saying it's a made-up disease," admits Charen, "if I hadn't found out the hard way." Here's hoping other conservatives find an easier route to accepting the truth.

The Last Normal Child: Essays on the Intersection of Kids, Culture, and Psychiatric Drugs

Ritalin Works! Great?

"Annie's grades and behavior have improved so much that she no longer qualifies for special education," the school psychologist announced decisively. I was attending nine-year-old Annie's annual Individualized Educational Plan (IEP) review at her school as her behavioral pediatrician. The school psychologist sounded congratulatory almost triumphant. Wasn't Annie an example of the goal of special education—to return a child to as normal a class setting as possible? Why then was I so uneasy about the school's decision to no longer provide services to this girl? As I left the school grounds, I shuddered while pondering the national implications of little Annie's "triumph."

As recently as three months ago, third-grader Annie was struggling with distractibility and inattention in her classroom. Getting her homework done and turned in on time was a nightly two-hour monumental effort on the part of her single-parent mother, Gail. Daily temper tantrums over rules and chores were also part of Annie's behavioral repertoire. Before coming to see me, Annie had been identified as learning disabled by the school in the first grade and had been enrolled in a special education program. Annie's pediatrician started her on Concerta, a long-acting version of the better-known stimulant drug Ritalin, for attention-deficit/hyperactivity disorder (ADHD), inattentive type.

Despite the confusion caused by its name, this kind of ADHD does not include hyperactivity or even much impulsivity, two of the three cardinal symptoms of ADHD. Simply the child must appear inattentive, distractible, and disorganized with poor task completion. Virtually all children with inattentive ADHD have learning or processing problems, and their cognition has been described as "sluggish."

I coached Gail to respond to Annie much more quickly at home with rewards and punishments. I suggested to Annie's teacher that she handle Annie in a similar fashion. I also doubled Annie's medication dose for school. Annie responded beautifully, and within three months the school was ready to eliminate her tutoring and behavioral plan. So why was I unhappy?

Everyone in the room, including Annie's mother and me, believed increasing Annie's medication was the single intervention that was making the difference so quickly. Study after study has demonstrated that stimulants such as Ritalin, Concerta, and Adderall improve, on the short term, the performance and behavior of ADHD children. I was certain that if Annie stopped the medication, most of her problems would return—I doubted she could have changed that quickly solely with the behavioral program.

But with the medication improving Annie's performance, the school was no longer obligated to provide services to Annie, as the law was interpreted by school district's attorneys. In 1999, in *Sutton v. United Airlines*, the U.S. Supreme Court ruled that when persons with the use of mitigating measures are no longer functionally disabled, they then no longer qualify for services under the American with Disabilities Act. Thus, for example, if glasses can correct a visual impairment, then the individual no longer is eligible for services.

John N. Hartson, a pediatric psychologist, is the national consultant to the American College of Testing Program for students with ADHD requesting accommodations or services for disabilities. His interpretation of the law goes beyond even this school district's policies. If Dr. Hartson's suggestions were followed, Annie might never have received any special education from her school in the first place.

Dr. Hartson believes, under his interpretation of federal guidelines coming from these court decisions, that if a school psychologist diagnoses ADHD along with co-occurring problems (such as a learning disability or processing disorder), the child should first be given a trial of Ritalin or its equivalent before any services for that child are proposed by the school. Hartson expands on the Ritalin-glasses analogy with the following straw man case report to illustrate the question "Why offer services when glasses will correct all the problems?":

> A child presents at an optometrists' office and is evaluated for visual problems. The child is diagnosed with a problem with visual acuity and the doctor suggests that the child be prescribed glasses. The optometrist then sends the child to an educational specialist who evaluates the child. The educational specialist sees the child without glasses and notes that the child has a great deal of difficulty with reading and with correctly seeing items on a page. A number of recommendations are then offered including the need for preferential seating, larger print books . . . and additional time to complete reading and other visual tasks.

Following Dr. Hartson's analogy, if a child like Annie with learning problems and ADHD demonstrates few or no problems in the classroom while on medication, then she should receive no services from the school. Only if she continued to have problems while on medication should she then be retested and offered appropriate educational services and accommodations. To offer services first or even simultaneously with medication is not consistent with federal guidelines according to Dr. Hartson.

But if we consider *all* federal guidelines, I'm confused. It would appear, given the interpretation of Annie's school district and Dr. Hartson, that a school could deny services and accommodations to a child with ADHD if the child was not first medicated. Yet Congress, reacting to perceived school pressure on families to medicate their children, added an amendment to the most recent authorization of the Individuals with Disability Education Act (IDEA) of 2004 that specifically prohibits schools from insisting that a child be medicated in order to attend classes in that district.

I'm not sure in the end how the government and the courts will reconcile what appears to be a conflict in "federal guidelines." In the short run, though, I suspect more and more school districts will try the medication-first approach and reconsider only if there is resistance from the family.

Dr. Hartson and others make an analogy between glasses for visual acuity and medication for ADHD. But is Ritalin the same as glasses? Apparently school districts continually looking to save money think so. Therefore, even inexpensive behavioral interventions, such as preferential seating in the front of the class, use of contingency rewards (e.g., stars, stickers, M&M's), and discipline contracts that have been shown to improve ADHD children's behavior and reduce the necessary dosage and frequency of medication, will not be offered if the medication alone "works."

In many children with the symptoms of ADHD (especially the inattentive type) who also have learning problems, who's to say which problem came first or what is causing what? In other words, might the learning or processing problems be contributing to the child's inattention and distractibility? Could addressing the educational needs of the child first without medication reduce or eliminate the need for drugs?

Furthermore, there's no evidence that just medication makes a difference in the *long-term* outcome of ADHD or learning problems. Ritalin teaches a child nothing. ADHD children "learn" to improve their behavior with appropriate behavioral and educational interventions. Yet the pressure on parents coming from schools to medicate their children will only grow when school districts look for legal ways to save money.

Dr. Hartson, like many other ADHD experts, considers two different types of interventions, medical interventions and nondrug interventions, equivalent if they both "work." However, the two types of interventions are not *morally* equivalent. The best way to make clear this error, called a "logical fallacy of the means," is to also use an analogy, this one, literary. In the eighteenth century, the famous satirist Jonathan Swift wrote an essay entitled "A Modest Proposal." In it he offers a "solution" to the Irish potato famine crisis by suggesting Irish children be fed to their parents, providing nutrition while simultaneously decreasing the number of mouths to feed in one stroke.

My "modest proposal" goes as follows. Currently about four million children take Ritalin or its equivalent, and classroom size averages about twenty-nine children per class. It is well know that Ritalin improves the performance of children with ADHD, with borderline ADHD, or even without ADHD. I propose we increase the number of children taking Ritalin to seven million. We could do this by continuing to broaden the criteria for ADHD (a process that's already been going on for fifteen years). Perhaps any child who performs below the median in a class might be referred for an ADHD evaluation and medication?

In any case, by increasing the number of children taking medication to seven million, we could enlarge class size to forty children, hire fewer teachers, and save school districts and tax payers a bundle of money. If, indeed, the medication–glasses analogy is valid and medication is the same as addressing the individual educational needs of children, there should be many educators and politicians ready to support my "modest proposal."

No takers? I wonder why not—because in a way we already substitute medication for nondrug services at school (in the cases of Annie and thousands of children like her). Until we are clear that a child's success while on Ritalin is not morally equivalent to a child's success with educational support, my proposal has a chance. But in all seriousness, we need to take a closer look at our priorities, the moral implications of our policies, and the way we determine which children get what help at school and at home.

Getting Up to Speed for the SAT

American children are taking stimulants and other psychiatric drugs at an unprecedented rate. The reasons for this phenomenon are complex and widespread. But stories that I've been hearing for years and that are now confirmed by research data illuminate at least one part of the answer. My first clue came in 2002, when a television news producer called me about a Manhattan doctor who was giving her high school son Ritalin before important exams. She asked me if I had ever heard of such a practice. I had not, but I wasn't shocked. It seemed, rather inevitable that parents would use Ritalin that way to boost their kids' performance.

Indeed, about six months later, I too directly received a telephone call from a psychiatrist parent who asked me if I would consider medicating her teenager son just for exam taking. He had previously tried Concerta and found that it cut down on his "sociability" and wanted to take it just for exams. She could write the prescriptions herself, but she thought it would be better if her son was managed by someone other than his mother. I knew I would never agree to such a plan, but I was intrigued. I suggested that she, her husband, and her son come in, but I never heard back from them.

People are still surprised to learn that Ritalin, Adderall, and Concerta, along with all the other new stimulant drug formulations prescribed ostensibly to treat ADHD, also work in "normal" children and adults. A myth continues, which began with the very first case reports in the 1930s, that stimulants work "paradoxically" to calm hyperactive children. In reality, stimulant drugs have the same effect on everybody—low doses (such as those for ADHD) improve everyone's concentration and get people to be more methodical. The hyperactivity of ADHD decreases because the kids stick longer with tasks that used to bore them quickly.

Experts have known about the universal enhancing effects of the stimulants for years. The army explored the routine use of stimulants on GIs in the 1950s. (The Allies widely distributed amphetamine to soldiers in World War II after learning that the German general Rommel was giving stimulants to his famed Afrika Corps.) Although stimulants regularly improved the soldiers' alertness and performance on boring tasks, there were enough episodes of "erratic" behavior that the generals decided that giving amphetamine routinely to guys with guns was not a good idea.

In the late 1970s, the National Institute of Mental Health (NIMH) proved irrefutably that stimulants improve the performance of normal men and boys as much as they do for those with ADHD. College students have also known about the performance-enhancing effects of Ritalin, and since the 1990s boom in ADHD diagnosis, prescription stimulants have been freely traded or sold on campus, often crushed and snorted, for "power" studying or to get high. Recent reports have up to one in four students on some college campuses using prescription stimulants illegally. A specter of misuse of, tolerance of, and addiction to prescription stimulants hangs over such use.

But I was not especially surprised by these stories I'd heard or by the call I received about Ritalin being considered for children just to improve performance on tests. Of course, that mother-physician was acting unethically when prescribing the drug to her own son. Regardless of the ethics of performance enhancement, treating members of your own family for any reason is considered a "no-no" in all of medicine.

But what is disturbing is that many kids are probably getting stimulants from their doctors for alleged ADHD (or are taking them on their own) and using them just "as needed." This isn't necessarily because doctors are bad or lousy diagnosticians. Teenage and adult ADHD, except in extreme cases, is actually difficult to delineate. The line between the unmotivated or learning impaired and those with ADHD is very much in the eye of the beholder. Doctors already routinely prescribe stimulants like Ritalin or Adderall "just for school." Several of my college-age patients take Concerta only three days a week—on the days they have classes. They say they don't need the drug otherwise.

I draw the line though with people who want the drug only for occasional use—even if they meet my criteria for ADHD. Such intermittent use enables the procrastination and last minute panic typical of an ADHD lifestyle. But Ritalin for the ADHD diagnosis is a slippery slope, and many of the kids getting Ritalin from their doctors look pretty normal to me. Still they will do "better than normal" on Ritalin.

Unlike young children who never become addicted, teens and adults do run the risk of abuse, tolerance, and addiction with prescription stimulants. Just recently, in February of 2006, I received phone calls within two weeks of each other from parents who had discovered that their teenagers were abusing Adderall. (I predict we will ultimately learn that Adderall and Adderall XR are the prescription stimulant drugs most abused by teens and young adults in comparison with Ritalin or Concerta. That's because Adderall is amphetamine, and the other two are methylphenidate-based. And although the two chemicals are very similar, I feel that amphetamine is the more intense experience, even when used therapeutically, and therefore it will attract the greater number of abusers.)

One of these kids, a seventeen-year-old senior at the local high school told his mother that he had taken "a hit" of Adderall just before taking the SAT exam. He thought it was very helpful, and indeed he received a perfect 800 in the verbal part of the three-part exam. He had always "underperformed" in school according to his mother, and now both she and her son were interested in his trying the drug on a more regular basis. Unfortunately, as I learned more about this boy—his daily marijuana use, his selling it at school, and the general chaos of his home life—I knew that neither he nor his mother had the organizational responsibility necessary to safely handle a drug with the abuse potential of Adderall (or Concerta for that matter).

These individual stories of illegal use and abuse of prescription stimulants and the many more anecdotes reported nationally were finally confirmed by a statistical study of misuse of these drugs that appeared in the journal *Drug and Alcohol Dependence* in early 2006. The authors analyzed government-collected data of face-to-face interviews with 54,000 people in 2002. Taking into account U.S. 2000 census data, the researchers estimated that over seven million people have misused prescription stimulants. Of children between twelve and seventeen years old, 2.6 percent reported misusing stimulants, and in the age group of eighteen to twenty-five, 5.9 percent admitted to illegal prescription stimulant use.

More sobering are the stories of those younger kids who acknowledged use of these drugs and who met *DSM-IV* criteria for drug dependency or drug abuse. A little more than one in ten children who begin with casual use of these drugs go on to become stimulant addicts. This translates to about 75,000 teens and young adults in 2002 addicted to prescription stimulants. And annual production quota rates from the Drug Enforcement Administration (DEA) indicate that more legal speed has been produced in our country since that time.

A couple of doctors like me and officials from the Chemical Diversion Division of the DEA have fretted for years about the likelihood of a fourth wave of doctor-prescribed stimulant abuse. I earlier mentioned the Allies' use of these drugs with American GIs during World War II. Many of these soldiers came back to the States addicted to amphetamine. The early 1960s were marked by an era of "Dr. Feelgoods" who went so far as to inject amphetamine intravenously into their patients for a variety of ill-defined medical and emotional problems. The last wave of doctor-prescribed stimulant abuse (until this current one) took place in the 1970s and only ended when Congress and the states set limits and penalties on the use of prescription amphetamine for weight loss and control.

Repeatedly, American doctors and American society seem to lose their collective memory over these drugs and find another reason to prescribe them. "America Taking 'Uppers'," legal or illegal, ran a headline of a UN Narcotic Control Report in 1999. These drugs "work," no doubt, but at least in adults, whether they are used for losing weight or concentrating better, the evidence is only for short-term benefits. When the long-term data on weight loss and stimulants was examined by doctors and public officials in the 1970s, it was clear that in the long term, the medications were ineffective, and development of tolerance (needing increasing doses for the same effect) was common.

The longest study on the effects of prescription stimulants among teens and adults ran only two to three months. There are no long-term studies of, say, five years. In my experience of treating about fifteen older teens and adults for over five years, I'd estimate that in only three or four cases has the drug really made a difference in the quality of their lives (e.g., improved their employment status or family life). Ominously, tolerance has developed in four of these patients (my limit with them is 90 mg of Adderall XR daily).

The downside of prescription stimulants has been well known to researchers for decades, but for example, as of early 2006, I had still not found one research article on the development of tolerance with the use of prescription stimulants in adults. To some extent, doctors and the public have been misled by the excellent safety record of the use of these drugs in the preteen population. No child under thirteen has ever been reported to be addicted to Ritalin. Children don't have access to the medication and interestingly don't like higher doses ("I feel nervous. I feel weird" is what they tell their parents when the dose gets too high for them.). But access to the medication and response to higher doses ("I feel powerful. I feel grand.") are different in older teens and adults.

Ironically, the first study that analyzed the government data on prescription stimulant abuse was funded by Eli Lilly, the makers of Strattera, the only nonstimulant, non-abusable drug approved for the treatment of ADHD. Lilly's strategy is obvious. Lilly hopes this study will raise further concerns about drugs such as Adderall and Concerta that clearly work better than Strattera for ADHD but that have abuse potential. It seems in America that if there isn't money to be made, no one will do the work necessary to find out if any drug is safe or works long-term.

But in fact, most people can use prescription stimulants occasionally without much trouble. As word of the "benefits" of these drugs continues to spread, we will hear more about the use of Ritalin (and the other prescription stimulants) in questionable situations. In sports competition, the use of performance enhancing drugs is banned. In athletics we value not just the performance itself but also the effort involved in the achievement. Taking a drug somehow cheapens that performance.

These drugs are also banned because if we permit one athlete to take performance drugs, then we actually put pressure on all the other competing athletes to take the drug too, just in order to stay even. My seventeen-year-old son, a junior in high school, tells me about rampant Adderall use at his school during exam time for studying or test taking. We've talked about it at home and agree that improved performance by taking a drug isn't worth the improvement or the risk, but I still wonder if he isn't feeling some pressure to take these drugs too.

But isn't school different from sports anyway? Well, yes and no, yet there's certainly a competitive element to academics, especially with exams like the SAX GREs, MCATs, and LSATs. Without a clear line for diagnosis, how do we really know who legitimately "has or doesn't have" ADHD and who can benefit from Ritalin? And with so much available prescription stimulant medication out there anyway, you don't really need to go to a doctor to get your pills for the test.

It sounds incredible at this moment to consider, but will we in the near future need to require students to submit to random drug urine testing before they take important exams? Our national obsession with performance continues, and Ritalin will only complicate the race. But ultimately, a society that chooses to cope with life's challenges by turning to drugs does so at its own peril.

POSTSCRIPT

Should School-Age Children with Attention Deficit/Hyperactivity Disorder (ADHD) Be Treated with Ritalin and Other Stimulants?

To satisfy their own emotional needs, many parents push their physicians into diagnosing their children with attention-deficit/hyperactivity disorder (ADHD). Some of these parents believe that their children will benefit if they are labeled with ADHD. The pressure for children to do well academically in order to get into the right college and graduate school is intense. Some parents feel that if their children are diagnosed with ADHD, then they may be provided special circumstances or allowances such as additional time when taking college entrance examinations. Some parents also realize that if their children are identified as having ADHD, then their children will be eligible for extra services in school. In some instances, the only way to receive such extra help is to be labeled with a disorder. Also, some teachers favor the use of Ritalin and other stimulants to control students' behavior. During the last few years, there has been increasing emphasis on controlling school budgets. The result is larger class sizes and higher student-to-teacher ratios. Thus, it should not be surprising that many teachers welcome the calming effect of Ritalin and other stimulants on students whose hyperactivity is disruptive to the class.

Whether or not drug therapy should be applied to behavioral problems raises another concern. What is the message that children are receiving about the role of drugs in society? Perhaps children will generalize the benefits of using legal drugs like Ritalin to remedy life's problems to using alcohol or illegal drugs to deal with other problems that they may be experiencing. Children may find that it is easier to drink alcohol or ingest a pill rather than to put the time and effort into resolving personal problems. For many adults, drugs seem to represent a shortcut to correcting life's difficulties. Through its reliance on drugs, is American society creating a wrong impression for its children, an illusion of believing that there is a pill for every ill?

When to prescribe Ritalin and other stimulants for children also places physicians in a quandary. They may see the benefit of helping students function more effectively in school. However, are physicians who readily prescribe Ritalin and other stimulants unintentionally promoting an antihumanistic, competitive environment in which performance matters regardless of cost? On the other hand, is it the place of physicians to dictate to parents what is best for their children? Should physicians acquiesce to the desires of parents who want to place their children on these drugs? In the final analysis, will the increase in prescriptions for Ritalin and other stimulants result in benefits for the child, for the parents, and for society?

The benefits and adverse effects of treating ADHD with drugs are discussed in Sharon Wigal's "Efficacy and Safety Limitations of Attention-Deficit Hyperactivity Disorder Pharmacotherapy in Children and Adults," *CNS Drugs* (2009). Two articles that question the validity of ADHD are "The Myth of ADHD and the Scandal of Ritalin: Helping John Dewey Students Succeed in Medicine-Free College Preparatory and Therapeutic High School" by Thomas Bratter, *International Journal of Reality Therapy* (Fall 2007) and Rachel Ragg's "School Uniformity," in *The Ecologist* (November 2006). An article that addresses how individuals with attention deficit disorder are portrayed in popular culture is "Media Representations of Attention Deficit Disorder: Portrayals of Cultural Skepticism in Popular Media" by Elizabeth Kennedy, *The Journal of Popular Culture* (2008). The use of Ritalin and Adderall on college campuses are discussed in "High and Mighty" by Abigail Rasminsky, *Dance Spirit* (September 2008). The proliferation of stimulant use for ADHD is described in "ADHD and the Rise in Stimulant Use Among Children" by Rick Mayes, Catherine Bagwell, and Jennifer Erkulwater, *Harvard Review of Psychiatry* (2008).

ISSUE 13

Do Consumers Benefit When Prescription Drugs Are Advertised?

YES: Paul Antony, from "Testimony Before the Senate Special Committee on Aging," Congressional Testimony to the U.S. Senate Special Committee on Aging (September 29, 2005)

NO: Peter Lurie, from "DTC Advertising Harms Patients and Should Be Tightly Regulated," *Journal of Law, Medicine & Ethics* (Fall 2009)

ISSUE SUMMARY

YES: Paul Antony, the chief medical officer for the Pharmaceutical Research and Manufacturers of America (PhRMA) contends that the direct advertising of prescription drugs to consumers results in better communication between patients and their doctors. Furthermore, patients take a more proactive role in their own health care. Advertising prescription drugs fills an educational purpose, says Paul Antony.

NO: Peter Lurie, a physician who is the deputy director of the Health Research Group at Public Citizen in Washington, D.C., argues that the direct advertising of prescription drugs leads to more patients asking for drugs that are unnecessary or inappropriate. In addition, many prescription drug advertisements are misleading and a means for drug manufacturers to encourage and pressure physicians to prescribe drugs.

One of the most lucrative businesses in the world today is the prescription drug business. Billions of dollars are spent every year for prescription drugs in the United States alone. But, the *only* way for consumers to obtain a prescribed drug is through a physician. In the early 1980s, drug companies in the United States began to advertise directly to the consumer. It is logical for drug companies to advertise to physicians because they are responsible for writing prescriptions. However, is it logical for pharmaceutical manufacturers to advertise their drugs directly to consumers? Are consumers capable of making informed, rational decisions regarding their pharmaceutical needs? Do consumers derive any benefits when prescription drugs are advertised?

An increasing number of individuals are assuming more responsibility for their own health care. In the United States, more than one-third of all prescriptions are written at the request of patients. Also, many patients do not take their doctors' prescriptions to pharmacies to be filled. Both of these scenarios raise the question of whether consumers are adequately educated to make decisions pertaining to their pharmaceutical needs or to assess risks associated with prescription drugs. Evidence suggests that many are not. Prescription drugs, for example, cause more worksite accidents than illegal drugs do.

Some commentators, however, argue that there are several advantages to directly advertising drugs to consumers. One advantage is that direct advertisements make consumers better informed about the benefits and risks of certain drugs. For example, it is not unusual for a person to experience side effects from a drug without knowing that the drug was responsible for the side effects. Advertisements can provide this information. Another advantage for consumers is that they may learn about medications that they might not have known existed. Furthermore, advertising lowers the cost of prescription drugs because consumers are able to ask their physicians to prescribe less expensive drugs than the physician might be inclined to recommend. Finally, prescription drug advertising allows consumers to become more involved in choosing the medications that they need or want.

Critics argue that there are a number of risks associated with the direct advertising of prescription drugs. One concern is with the content of drug advertisements. Consumers may not pay enough attention to information detailing a drug's adverse effects. Also, sometimes a drug's benefits are exaggerated. Another problem is that there are many instances in which drugs that have been approved by the Food and Drug Administration (FDA) for one purpose have been promoted for other purposes. Is the average consumer capable of understanding the purposes of the drugs that are being advertised?

Opponents of direct-to-consumer drug advertisements express concern with the way in which the information in the advertisements is presented. Promotions for drugs that appear as objective reports are often actually slick publicity material. In such promotions, medical experts are shown providing testimony regarding a particular drug. Many consumers may not be aware that these physicians have financial ties to the pharmaceutical companies. Celebrities—in whom the public often places its trust despite their lack of medical expertise—are used to promote drugs also. Finally, the cost of the drugs advertised, a major concern to most consumers, is seldom mentioned in the advertisements.

Two benefits of advertising drugs directly to patients, according to Paul Antony, is that communication between doctors and patients is vastly improved and it allows consumers more input into their own health care. Peter Lurie contends that the direct advertising of prescription drugs results in more patients requesting unnecessary or inappropriate drugs.

YES

Paul Antony

Testimony Before the Senate
Special Committee on Aging

Mr. Chairman, Ranking Member Kohl and Members of the Committee, on behalf of the Pharmaceutical Research and Manufacturers of America (PhRMA), I am pleased to appear at this hearing today on direct-to-consumer (DTC) advertising. I am Paul Antony, M.D., Chief Medical Officer at PhRMA.

DTC advertising has been proven to be beneficial to American patients. And, continuing regulatory oversight by the FDA helps ensure that the content of DTC advertising informs and educates consumers about medical conditions and treatment options. PhRMA and its member companies have a responsibility to ensure that ads comply with FDA regulations. We take that job seriously. We want to continue to be a valuable contributor to improving public health.

DTC advertising can be a powerful tool in educating millions of people and improving health. Because of DTC advertising, large numbers of Americans are prompted to discuss illnesses with their doctors for the first time. Because of DTC advertising, patients become more involved in their own health care decisions, and are proactive in their patient–doctor dialogue. Because of DTC advertising, patients are more likely to take their prescribed medicines.

PhRMA's Guiding Principles on
Direct-to-Consumer Advertisements
about Prescription Medicines

PhRMA and its member companies have long understood the special relationship we have with the patients that use our innovative medicines. Despite the very positive role DTC advertising plays in educating patients about health issues and options, over the years, we have heard the concerns expressed about DTC advertising—that some ads may oversell benefits and undersell risks; that some ads may lead to inappropriate prescribing; that some patients may not be able to afford the advertised medicines; and that some ads may not be appropriate for some audiences. Some doctors have also complained that drug companies launch advertising campaigns without helping to educate doctors in advance. Although actual practice and data on the effects of DTC advertising differ from these concerns, PhRMA recognized our obligation to act. On July 29, 2005, PhRMA's Board of Directors unanimously approved Guiding Principles

U.S. Senate, September 29, 2005.

on Direct-to-Consumer Advertisements About Prescription Medicine. These principles help ensure that DTC advertising remains an important and powerful tool to educate patients while at the same time addressing many of the concerns expressed about DTC advertising over the past few years.

First, PhRMA member companies take their responsibility to fully comply with FDA advertising regulations very seriously. Our advertising is already required to be accurate and not misleading; it can only make claims supported by substantial evidence; it must reflect the balance between risks and benefits; and it must be consistent with FDA-approved labeling. However, patients, health care providers and the general public expect us to do more than just meet our exacting legal obligations, and our Guiding Principles do go further.

Our principles recognize that at the heart of our companies' DTC communications efforts is patient education. This means that DTC communications designed to market a medicine should responsibly educate patients about a medicine, including the conditions for which it may be prescribed. DTC advertising should also foster responsible communications between patients and health care professionals to help the patient achieve better health and a better appreciation of a medicine's known benefits and risks. Specifically, the Principles state that risk and safety information should be designed to achieve a balanced presentation of both risks and benefits associated with the advertised medicines.

Our Guiding Principles recognize that companies should spend appropriate time educating health care professionals about a new medicine before it is advertised to patients. That way, providers will be prepared to discuss the appropriateness of a given medication with a patient.

Current law provides that companies must submit their DTC television advertisements to FDA upon first use for FDA's review at its discretion. Companies that sign onto these Guiding Principles agree to submit all new DTC television ads to the FDA before releasing these ads for broadcast, giving the agency an opportunity to review consistent with its priorities and resources. Companies also commit to informing FDA of the earliest date the advertisement is set to air. Should new information concerning a previously unknown safety risk be discovered, companies commit to work with FDA to "responsibly alter or discontinue a DTC advertising campaign."

In addition, the Principles encourage companies to include, where feasible, information about help for the uninsured and underinsured in their DTC communications. Our member companies offer a host of programs that can assist needy patients with their medicines.

The Principles also recognize that ads should respect the seriousness of the health condition and medicine being advertised and that ads employing humor or entertainment may not be appropriate in all instances.

As a result of concerns that certain prescription drug ads may not be suitable for all viewing audiences, the Guiding Principles state that, "DTC television and print advertisements should be targeted to avoid audiences that are not age appropriate for the messages involved."

Signatory companies are committed to establishing their own internal processes to ensure compliance with the Guiding Principles and to broadly disseminate them internally and to advertisers. In addition, PhRMA's Board unanimously approved the creation of an office of accountability to ensure the public has an opportunity to comment on companies' compliance with these Principles. The office of accountability will be responsible for receiving comments from the general public and from health care professionals regarding DTC ads by any company that publicly states it will follow the principles. The PhRMA office of accountability will provide to these companies any comment that is reasonably related to compliance with the Principles. Periodic reports will be issued by the PhRMA office of accountability to the public regarding the nature of the comments. Each report will also be submitted to the FDA.

PhRMA's Board also agreed to select an independent panel of outside experts and individuals to review reports from the office of accountability after one year and evaluate overall trends in the industry as they relate to the Principles. The panel will be empowered to make recommendations in accordance with the Principles. The Principles will go into effect in January 2006.

We believe these Principles will help patients and health care professionals get the information they need to make informed health care decisions.

The Value of DTC Advertising

Informing and Empowering Consumers

Surveys indicate that DTC advertising makes consumers aware of new drugs and their benefits, as well as risks and side effects with the drugs advertised. They help consumers recognize symptoms and seek appropriate care. According to an article in *The New England Journal of Medicine,* DTC advertising is concentrated among a few therapeutic categories. These are therapeutic categories in which consumers can recognize their own symptoms, such as arthritis, seasonal allergies, and obesity; or for pharmaceuticals that treat chronic diseases with many undiagnosed sufferers, such as high cholesterol, osteoporosis, and depression.

DTC advertising gets patients talking to their doctors about conditions that may otherwise have gone undiagnosed or undertreated. For example, a study conducted by RAND Health and published in *The New England Journal of Medicine* found that nearly half of all adults in the United States fail to receive recommended health care. According to researchers on the RAND study, "the deficiencies in care . . . pose serious threats to the health of the American public that could contribute to thousands of preventable deaths in the United States each year." The study found underuse of prescription medications in seven of the nine conditions for which prescription medicines were the recommended treatment. Conditions for which underuse was found include asthma, cerebrovascular disease, congestive heart failure, diabetes, hip fracture, hyperlipidemia and hypertension. Of those seven conditions for which RAND found underuse of recommended prescription medicines, five are DTC advertised.

The Rand Study, as well as other studies, highlight the underuse of needed medications and other healthcare services in the U.S.

- According to a nationally representative study of 9,090 people aged 18 and up, published in *JAMA*, about 43 percent of participants with recent major depression are getting inadequate therapy.
- A 2004 study published in the *Archives of Internal Medicine*, found that, "In older patients, failures to prescribe indicated medications, monitor medications appropriately, document necessary information, educate patients, and maintain continuity are more common prescribing problems than is use of inappropriate drugs."
- A May/June 2003 study published in the *Journal of Managed Care Pharmacy*, which examined claims data from 3 of the 10 largest health plans in California to determine the appropriateness of prescription medication use based upon widely accepted treatment guidelines, found that "effective medication appears to be underused." Of the four therapeutic areas of study—asthma, CHF, depression, and common cold or upper respiratory tract infections—asthma, CHF, and depression were undertreated. The researchers concluded that "the results are particularly surprising and disturbing when we take into account the fact that three of the conditions studied (asthma, CHF, and depression) are known to produce high costs to the healthcare system."
- According to a study released in May 2005 by the Stanford University School of Medicine, among patients with high cholesterol in moderate and high-risk groups, researchers found fewer than half of patient visits ended with a statin recommendation. Based on the findings, the researchers say physicians should be more aggressive in investigating statin therapy for patients with a high or moderate risk of heart disease, and that patients should ask for their cholesterol levels to be checked regularly.

Increasing Communication between the Doctor and Patient

A vast majority of patients (93 percent) who asked about a drug reported that their doctor "welcomed the questions." Of patients who asked about a drug, 77 percent reported that their relationship with their doctor remained unchanged as a result of the office visit, and 20 percent reported that their relationship improved. In addition, both an FDA survey of physicians (from a random sample of 500 physicians from the American Medical Association's database) and a survey by the nation's oldest and largest African-American medical association, found that DTC advertisements raise disease awareness and bolster doctor–patient ties.

The doctor–patient relationship is enhanced if DTC advertising prompts a patient to talk to his doctor for the first time about a previously undiscussed condition, to comply with a prescribed treatment regimen, or to become aware of a risk or side effect that was otherwise unknown. A 2002 *Prevention Magazine* survey found that 24.8 million Americans spoke with their doctor about a medical condition for the first time as a result of seeing a DTC advertisement. Similarly, the FDA patient survey on DTC advertising found that nearly one in five patients reported speaking to a physician about a condition for the first time because of a DTC ad.

PhRMA and its member companies believe it is vital that patients, in consultation with their doctors, make decisions about treatments and medicines. Prescribing decisions should be dominated by the doctor's advice. While our member companies direct a large majority of their promotional activities toward physicians, such promotion in no way guarantees medicines will be prescribed.

According to a General Accounting Office report, of the 61.1 million people (33 percent of adults) who had discussions with their physician as a result of a DTC advertisement in 2001, only 8.5 million (5 percent of adults) actually received a prescription for the product, a small percentage of the total volume of prescriptions dispensed. Indeed, an FDA survey of physicians revealed that the vast majority of physicians do not feel pressure to prescribe. According to the survey, 91 percent of physicians said that their patients did not try to influence treatment courses in a way that would have been harmful and 72 percent of physicians, when asked for prescription for a specific brand name drug, felt little or no pressure to prescribe a medicine.

De-stigmatizing Disease

DTC advertising also encourages patients to discuss medical problems that otherwise may not have been discussed because it was either thought to be too personal or that there was a stigma attached to the disease. For example, a Health Affairs article examined the value of innovation and noted that depression medications, known as selective serotonin reuptake inhibitors (SSRIs), that have been DTC advertised, have led to significant treatment expansion. Prior to the 1990s, it was estimated that about half of those persons who met a clinical definition of depression were not appropriately diagnosed, and many of those diagnosed did not receive clinically appropriate treatment. However, in the 1990s with the advent of SSRIs, treatment has been expanded. According to the article, "Manufacturers of SSRIs encouraged doctors to watch for depression and the reduced stigma afforded by the new medications induced patients to seek help." As a result, diagnosis and treatment for depression doubled over the 1990s.

Utilization and DTC Advertising

According to reports and studies, there is no direct relationship between DTC advertising and the price growth of drugs. For example, in comments to the FDA in December 2003, the FTC stated, "[DTC advertising] can empower consumers to manage their own health care by providing information that will help them, with the assistance of their doctors, to make better informed decisions about their treatment options. . . . Consumer receive these benefits from DTC advertising with little, if any, evidence that such advertising increases prescription drug prices." Notably, since January 2000, the CPI component that tracks prescription medicines have been in line with overall medical inflation.

The FTC comments referenced above also note, "DTC advertising accounts for a relatively small proportion of the total cost of drugs, which reinforces the view that such advertising would have a limited, if any, effect on price." Likewise, a study by Harvard University and the Massachusetts Institute of Technology and published by the Kaiser Family Foundation found that DTC advertising accounts for less than 2 percent of the total U.S. spending for prescription medicines.

One study in *The American Journal of Managed Care* looked at whether pharmaceutical marketing has led to an increase in the use of medications by patients with marginal indications. The study found that high-risk individuals were receiving lipid-lowering treatment "consistent with evidence-based practice guidelines" despite the fact that "a substantial portion of patients continue to remain untreated and undertreated. . . ." The study concluded that "greater overall use did not appear to be associated with a shift towards patients with less CV [cardiovascular] risk."

Pharmaceutical utilization is increasing for reasons other than DTC advertising. As the June 2003 study of DTC advertising commissioned by the Kaiser Family Foundation found, "[O]ur estimates indicate that DTCA is important, but not the primary driver of recent growth [in prescription drug spending]."

Other reasons pharmaceutical utilization is increasing, include:

- Improved Medicines—Many new medicines replace higher-cost surgeries and hospital care. In 2004 alone, pharmaceutical companies added 38 new medicines and over the last decade, over 300 new medicines have become available for treating patients. These include important new medicines for some of the most devastating and costly diseases, including: AIDS, cancer, heart disease, Alzheimer's, and diabetes. According to a study prepared for the Department of Health and Human Services, "[n]ew medications are not simply more costly than older ones. They may be more effective or have fewer side effects; some may treat conditions for which no treatment was available."
- New Standards of Medical Practice Encouraging Greater Use of Pharmaceuticals—Clinical standards are changing to emphasize earlier and tighter control of a range of conditions, such as diabetes, hypertension and cardiovascular disease. For example, new recommendations from the two provider groups suggest that early treatment, including lifestyle changes and treatment with two or more types of medications, can significantly reduce the risk of later complications and improve the quality of life for people with type 2 diabetes.
- Greater Treatment of Previously Undiagnosed and Untreated Conditions—According to guidelines developed by the National Heart, Lung, and Blood Institute's National Cholesterol Education Program (NCEP) Adult Treatment Panel (ATP), approximately 36 million adults should be taking medicines to lower their cholesterol, a number that has grown from 13 million just 8 years ago.

- Aging of America—The aging of American translates into greater reliance on pharmaceuticals. For example, congestive heart failure affects an estimated 2 percent of Americans age 40 to 59, more than 5 percent of those aged 60 to 69, and 10 percent of those 70 or more.

While some assume that DTC advertising leads to increased use of newer medicines rather than generic medicines, generics represent just over 50 percent of all prescriptions (generics are historically not DTC advertised). In contrast, in Europe, where DTC advertising is prohibited, the percentage of prescriptions that are generic is significantly lower. Likewise, it is worth noting that while broadcast DTC has been in place since 1997, the rate of growth in drug cost increases has declined in each of the last 5 years and in 2004 was below the rate of growth in overall health care costs.

Economic Value of DTC Advertising

Increased spending on pharmaceuticals often leads to lower spending on other forms of more costly health care. New drugs are the most heavily advertised drugs, a point critics often emphasize. However, the use of newer drugs tends to lower all types of non-drug medical spending, resulting in a net reduction in the total cost of treating a condition. For example, on average replacing an older drug with a drug 15 years newer increases spending on drugs by $18, but reduces overall costs by $111.

The Tufts Center for the Study of Drug Development reports that disease management organizations surveyed believe that increased spending on prescription drugs reduces hospital inpatient costs. "Since prescription drugs account for less than 10 percent of total current U.S. health care spending, while inpatient care accounts for 32 percent, the increased use of appropriate pharmaceutical therapies may help moderate or reduce growth in the costliest component of the U.S. health care system," according to Tufts Center Director Kenneth I. Kaitin.

Opponents also compare the amount of money spent by drug companies on marketing and advertising to the amount they spend on research and development of new drugs. However, in 2004, pharmaceutical manufacturers spent an estimated $4.15 billion on DTC advertising, according to IMS Health, compared to $49.3 billion in total R&D spending by the biopharmaceutical industry, according to Burrill & Company. PhRMA members alone spent $38.8 billion on R&D in 2004.

Conclusion

DTC advertising provides value to patients by making them aware of risks and benefits of new drugs; it empowers patients and enhances the public health; it plays a vital role in addressing a major problem in this country of undertreatment and underdiagnosis of disease; it encourages patients to discuss medical problems with their health care provider that may otherwise not be discussed due to a stigma being attached to the disease; and it encourages patient compliance with physician-directed treatment regimens.

Given the progress that continues to be made in society's battle against disease, patients are seeking more information about medical problems and potential treatments. The purpose of DTC advertising is to foster an informed conversation about health, disease and treatments between patients and their health care practitioners. Our Guiding Principles are an important step in ensuring patients and health care professionals get the information they need to make informed health care decisions.

This concludes my written testimony. I would be happy to answer any questions or to supply any additional material by Members or Committee Staff on this or any other issue.

Peter Lurie  **NO**

DTC Advertising Harms Patients and Should Be Tightly Regulated

Like all interventions in health care, direct-to-consumer (DTC) advertising should be evaluated by comparing its risks to its benefits, in the context of the available or potentially available alternatives. The objective, of course, is to realize any unique benefits while minimizing the risks. On balance, the adverse effects of DTC advertising outweigh the still-undemonstrated benefits of the advertising.

Historical Background

DTC advertising must be seen in the context of overall pharmaceutical company expenditures on advertising. In 2005, the industry spent $29.9 billion dollars on promotions (up from $11.4 billion in 1996), of which a relatively small fraction, $4.2 billion (14.2%), was spent on DTC advertising. The percentage spent on DTC advertising has been relatively constant this decade. Promotions to professionals (24.2%) and samples (61.8%) accounted for far larger percentages of total promotional spending in 2005.

Nonetheless, the advent of television DTC advertisements in particular has made a big impact upon public consciousness. Most viewers have little idea how this came to be. In general, there are three kinds of DTC advertisements. In the first ("reminder" advertisements), the name of the drug and its manufacturer are mentioned, but not the disease. In the second ("help-seeking" advertisements), the disease is mentioned along with the manufacturer, but the drug name is not. Presumably it is the third category that would be most likely to be influential: those that link the disease in question with a drug that can treat it. Until 1997, however, all DTC broadcast advertisements in this third category had to provide the so-called Brief Summary, an often-extensive review of the actions, indications, and potential adverse effects of the drug being advertised. The result was very little broadcast DTC advertising, and most of that produced was in the first two categories, which require no Brief Summary. In 1997, the Food and Drug Administration (FDA) reversed course and permitted companies airing broadcast DTC advertisements to refer consumers to websites, print advertisements, or toll-free telephone numbers to obtain the Brief Summary information. It is this regulatory change that produced the growth in DTC advertising we have since experienced.

In fact, the United States is unique in its embrace of DTC advertising. Only New Zealand has ever permitted DTC advertising, and even there professional

From *Journal of Law, Medicine and Ethics,* Fall 2009, pp. 444–450. Copyright © 2009 by American Society of Law, Medicine & Ethics. Reprinted by permission of Wiley-Blackwell via Rightslink.

opposition to the advertising has grown and the government is considering abolishing it. The European Union debated but rejected the idea early this decade, but there are now pharmaceutical company efforts afoot to permit DTC advertisements by recasting them as the provision of objective information.

For a decade, the United States Congress watched these developments. But early versions of the Food and Drug Administration Amendments Act of 2007 contained a number of measures seeking to curb DTC advertising. Most of these were either weakened or never adopted. A plan to require an immediate postapproval moratorium before DTC advertisements could run was rejected amid claims that commercial speech was being restricted. A measure to permit voluntary submission of television advertisements passed but was never implemented when Congress failed to appropriate the necessary funding. However, the FDA was for the first time granted the power to levy civil monetary penalties for violative advertisements.

Potential Risks of DTC Advertising

Examples of Problematic DTC Advertisements

In the decade since the FDA deregulated broadcast DTC advertising, numerous inappropriate advertisements have appeared. The most widely discussed have been the DTC campaigns waged by the manufacturers of the Cox-2 inhibitors. Importantly, these drugs were never proved to be more effective pain relievers than other non-steroidal anti-inflammatory drugs. For most patients the purported stomach protection offered by these drugs (a claim that the FDA permitted only for the now-withdrawn Vioxx [rofecoxib], but through industry promotional efforts came to be associated with the other Cox-2 inhibitors as well) was irrelevant as those patients tolerated conventional pain relievers without stomach upset. Nonetheless, an estimated two-thirds of the growth in Cox-2 use between 1999 and 2000 was among such patients. In 2000, Vioxx was the number one DTC-advertised drug—at $160 million, larger than the campaigns that year for both Pepsi and Budweiser—and retail sales quadrupled. With as many as 140,000 serious cardiovascular events attributed to Vioxx alone, the dangers of such promotions are now evident. Other drugs that have been transformed from pedestrian to blockbuster by marketing campaigns that included DTC advertising are Claritin (loratadine) for allergies and Singulair (montelukast) for asthma.

Empirical studies document the impact of the DTC campaign on the prescribing of Vioxx. In one, using conservative assessments for which patients should be prescribed a Cox-2 inhibitor, there was a 21% rate of appropriate prescribing of non-steroidal anti-inflammatory drugs (NSAIDs) among patients who were exposed to a DTC advertisement and asked their physician about the drug compared to 55% among those without such exposure. Most of the inappropriate prescribing took the form of substituting a Cox-2 inhibitor for a conventional NSAID. In another study, television DTC advertising of Vioxx was associated with increased physician visits for osteoarthritis as well as higher prescribing rates for Vioxx.

Three additional examples convey the broad scope of DTC advertisements, although none has been evaluated for its effect on prescribing. In one less-publicized case, Galderma Laboratories, the makers of the prescription acne medication Differin (adapalene), created an advertisement for both the Internet and MTV. The advertisements steered teenage viewers to a portion of the Differin website to receive free music downloads. The advertisements were clearly directed at teenagers: the viewer was exhorted to obtain a Teen Survival Handbook and to take a self-test on acne called Zit 101, a course offered at "Acne High." The advertisement played to teenage fears ("Remember: There are thousands of pores on your face, which means your skin has the potential to 'give birth to' thousands of microcomedones.") and notions of empowerment ("Fight Acne with Free Music. How Cool is That?"). Realizing that many teens would visit physicians only with their parents, the website had an entire section on "Talking to Parents About Acne." The website offered "3 levels of cool"; Level 1: sign up (two free music downloads); Level 2: get and fill Differin prescription (seven free downloads); and Level 3: refill Differin prescription (ten free downloads). Bribing physicians to prescribe medications has long been held to be illegal. This advertisement essentially paid teenagers to convince adults to procure this drug for them.

A November 2004 advertisement by AstraZeneca on its website and in print actually misled the public by misrepresenting the FDA. In an advertisement for the cholesterol-lowering drug Crestor (rosuvastatin), a drug associated with muscle and kidney damage, AstraZeneca claimed that "[w]e have been assured today at senior levels in the FDA that there is no concern in relation to CRESTOR's safety." In fact, the agency was on record stating that "[the Agency] has been very concerned about Crestor since the day it was approved, and we've been watching it very carefully." The agency forced the company to terminate its campaign.

More recently, Pfizer was forced to end a DTC advertising campaign that featured the artificial heart pioneer Robert Jarvik endorsing the company's drug Lipitor (atorvastatin). However, Dr. Jarvik turned out not to have a medical license, and video of him rowing required the hiring of a body double as he did not engage in the sport.

DTC advertisements have now started to surface in a new area: genetic testing. This is an even greater concern than drug DTC advertisements as the vast majority of genetic tests have not been approved by the FDA, the information is more complex than many non-genetic tests, and the tests must be interpreted in a particular social context. Because pharmaceuticals have been marketed for longer than genetic tests, consumers have more realistic expectations and physicians are better informed about pharmaceuticals than genetic tests. Moreover, the number of new genetic tests that becomes available per year greatly exceeds the number of new drugs approved by the FDA and there is no compendium of standard information on genetic tests akin to the *Physicians' Desk Reference* for drugs. Finally, whatever its limitations (see the Discussion section below), the pharmaceutical industry does have an ethical code for advertising; there is nothing comparable for genetic testing. Together, these factors argue for a still more cautious approach to DTC advertising for genetic tests.

Some claims made on genetic test websites stretch the bounds of credulity. One company claims its test can "not only help determine if you have the potential for Olympic size success but also tell you if you are more susceptible to sports related injury." Another conducts genetic testing and sells dietary supplements as part of a program that "works with your body's own natural repair mechanisms which promote repair of DNA damage caused by the stress of life in the 21st century." Clearly, this area will need ongoing monitoring by the Federal Trade Commission (FTC) which has jurisdiction over these advertisements.

Do DTC Advertisements Bear a Significant Relationship to Public Health Needs?

As these examples illustrate, DTC advertising has been concentrated on new, expensive drugs for conditions that are bothersome and incurable. Thus, according to the Government Accountability Office (GAO), the top 15 DTC-advertised drugs in 2000 accounted for 54% of all DTC advertising expenditures. Only one of the top 50 DTC-advertised drugs was an antibiotic, presumably because patients are generally cured and have no need for refills. Because patient entreaties are unlikely to induce a physician to initiate or change a prescription for a cancer drug, these are also less likely to be advertised. DTC advertising shoulders aside nondrug interventions such as behavioral smoking cessation, weight-loss, or exercise programs, which can be less costly, safer, or more effective. Strikingly, one never encounters advertisements for generic drugs. By promoting newer drugs at the expense of drugs that have longer safety records, DTC promotion has the potential to lead to increases in adverse drug reactions that may take place before the dangers are recognized by medical authorities (see Vioxx, above). In sum, there is little relationship between our true public health needs and the subjects of DTC advertising.

Are Consumers Being Misled?

Consumers have many misconceptions about DTC advertising. In one survey, 50% believed that DTC advertisements had to be pre-approved by the government, and 43% thought that only "completely safe" drugs were allowed to be advertised (neither is true). Studies conducted by the FDA itself suggest the potential dangers of DTC advertising. The agency's 2002 survey found that 60% of patients thought that the advertisements provide insufficient information about drug risks and 44% felt similarly about benefits. Fifty-eight percent believed the advertisements made the drugs appear better than they are, and 42% said the advertisements made it seem as if the drug would work for everyone.

Consumer support for these advertisements is actually declining. Compared to a similar FDA survey in 1999, fewer patients responding to the FDA's 2002 survey said that the advertisements had prompted them to talk to a doctor (27% in 1999 vs. 18% in 2002); fewer said that the advertisements provide enough information even to decide whether to consult a physician (70% vs. 58%); fewer felt that the advertisements helped them make better decisions about their own health (47% vs. 32%); and fewer "liked seeing" the advertisements (52% vs. 32%).

Are Doctors Being Pressured to Prescribe?

Early defenses of DTC advertising asserted that physicians would not be manipulated by patient demands based on DTC advertisements, an ironic assertion given that the very purpose of the advertisement is to alter physician behavior. Unfortunately, this assertion has proved to be wrong. In a classic study published in the *Journal of the Amrican Medical Association*, Kravitz and colleagues sent "standardized patients" with either major depression or adjustment disorder into doctors' offices. The patients either (1) described their symptoms and made no specific request for medication; (2) said they had seen a program on television and wondered about drug treatment; or (3) said they had seen a DTC advertisement for the antidepressant Paxil (paroxetine). For standardized patients with adjustment disorder, a condition not generally requiring drug treatment, 10% of those making no specific request received a prescription for an antidepressant (none of those for Paxil), compared with 39% of those making a general request (26% of those for Paxil) and 55% of those saying they had seen a Paxil advertisement (67% of those for Paxil). DTC adverlisements can therefore spur unnecessary drug prescribing, and drug-specific advertisements are more likely to do so.

Of course, in principle, doctors could be grateful for patients' prompting. But empirical research suggests otherwise. In one study, doctors were asked whether they considered drugs they had just prescribed to be only "possible" or "unlikely" choices. Fifty percent answered affirmatively for DTC-advertised drugs that were prescribed at the patient's request, compared to only 12% of new prescriptions not requested by patients. Thus, physicians often accede to patients' DTC-driven requests, but are left feeling uneasy.

What Is the Impact on the Cost of Health Care?

Predictably, the cost of health care is being driven up, as patients are induced to request newer, more expensive medications instead of equally effective, older, generic alternatives. One report indicated that the top 25 DTC-advertised drugs accounted for 41% of the growth in retail drug spending in 1999. The report did not separate the effects of DTC advertising from those of advertising to physicians; the two often go hand-in-hand. In a study that did separate out the various forms of advertising, the growth in DTC advertisements for the 25 largest therapeutic classes accounted for 12% of drug sales growth from 1999 to 2000 and resulted in an additional $2.6 billion in pharmaceutical expenditures in 2000. The GAO agreed that "DTC advertising appears to increase prescription drug spending," primarily because of increased utilization, not increased prices. That report estimated that a 10% increase in DTC advertising translates into a 1% increase in sales for that class of drugs, an enormous increase given that many drug classes sell in the billions of dollars. One way or another—through insurance premiums, co-payments, or taxes—consumers foot the bill.

Potential Benefits of DTC Advertising

The principal benefit asserted by supporters of DTC advertising is that patients with undertreated conditions might receive treatment they otherwise would not have received. While 18% of patients in the FDA's most recent survey report that they consulted a physician as a result of a DTC advertisement, this would have to lead to a prescription that was more likely to be efficacious than the patient's current care for any health benefit to be realized. To date, this chain of causation remains theoretical. The only comprehensive review of studies on DTC advertising concluded that "[n]o empirical research has demonstrated better communication [between patients and physicians] and improved health outcomes." The authors, approaching this issue from a public health perspective, continue: "The onus is on those who might support [DTC advertising] to produce evidence of benefit and, in the absence of this evidence, we must assume that the likely disbenefits (clinical and economic) outweigh the as yet unproven benefits."

Can Any Benefits of DTC Advertising Be Otherwise Obtained?

The review just cited excluded the Kravitz study. While it is true that, in that study, DTC advertisements led to more prescribing of antidepressants for those standardized patients presenting with depression, general entreaties to physicians (the second arm in the Kravitz study) were actually more effective than those based on DTC advertisements (76% prescribing rate vs. 53%). (This assumes that prescribing an antidepressant to a depressed patient at his or her first visit is good medicine.) The study leaves unanswered which of the particular forms of advertising studied is more likely to induce patients to approach their doctors.

If the industry truly wished to exhort patients to seek care for undertreated medical conditions, it would instead avail itself only of the apparently more effective "help-seeking" advertisements, which inform patients of the existence of particular diseases without naming a treatment. Such advertisements are regulated by the FTC instead of the FDA, presumably because they have less capacity to mislead. The purported benefits of DTC advertising can thus be secured more effectively through non-commercial public-service announcements (or pharmaceutical company-funded "help-seeking" advertisements), without the risk of misleading the public or driving up health-care costs unnecessarily.

Recommendations

Two contextual matters merit consideration. First, the growth of broadcast DTC advertising did not arise magically. Rather, it was the predictable result of the FDA's 1997 deregulatory efforts. It follows that the genie can, to a large extent, be put back in the bottle. Second, at least under prevailing legal interpretations, DTC advertising is unlikely to be prohibited in the United States as it is considered protected commercial speech.

The industry however, has demonstrated a marked inability to police itself. It was only the public-relations disaster of Vioxx that has roused the

Pharmaceutical Research and Manufacturers of America (PhRMA) to develop DTC advertising guidelines. These guidelines are voluntary, and designed primarily to stave off more aggressive legislation or regulation. The guidelines recommend that companies should wait "an appropriate amount of time" after launching a new drug before initiating a DTC campaign.

How, then, is the public to be protected from this misleading information? First and foremost, FDA-approved patient information for all prescription drugs is necessary. In 1979, the FDA proposed just this, but opposition from organized medicine, which feared the erosion of its authority, and the pharmaceutical industry ensured that the proposal was withdrawn early in the Reagan administration. In the 1990s, the idea was revisited in the form of FDA-approved Medication Guides, but fewer than 200 drugs of the thousands on the market have such Guides. Instead, the market has been left to the makers of Patient Information Leaflets, which are not FDA-approved and which, as we have shown in three studies, often omit important safety information. FDA-approved information for patients, rather than self-serving advertising, is the appropriate response to the dearth of patient-appropriate drug information. Other federal agencies such as the National Institutes of Health and the Agency for Healthcare Research and Quality could supplement the FDA's efforts. The failure of these agencies to step into the information gap and fulfill their educational missions allows the industry to cloak its advertising in the mantle of education. As Franz Ingelfinger, the former editor of the *New England Journal of Medicine* once argued, "advertisements should be overtly recognized for what they are—an unabashed attempt to get someone to buy something, although some useful information may be provided in the process."

The FDA, which has sole authority over prescription drug advertising, has never released a comprehensive regulation on DTC advertising. Some guidances on particular topics have been promulgated, but these are voluntary and the agency has little ability to enforce them. At a minimum, regulations should provide for pre-review of television advertising, moratoria on the advertising of new drugs and prohibitions on celebrity endorsements. The advertising division remains severely understaffed and, while it can now levy civil monetary penalties, negotiations in Congress reduced these to $250,000 to $500,000 over three years, a cost that many multinationals will regard as a cost of doing business.

For years, Public Citizen has tracked the FDA's drug advertising enforcement. . . . Much of this decrease predates the current administration, but there was an added drop in 2002. This drop was due to the policy of then-Chief Counsel Daniel Troy to require all regulatory letters to pass through his office, a departure from previous practice and a change that, according to the GAO, "adversely affected" the FDA's oversight. The GAO concluded that "[s]ince the policy change, [the Office of the Chief Counsel's] reviews of draft regulatory letters from the FDA, have taken so long that misleading advertisements may have completed their broadcast life cycle before the FDA issued the letters." According to a report by the Minority staff of the Committee on Government Reform, in 2003 the average time from initial placement of a prescription drug advertisement and an enforcement action (if any) was 177 days. These letters may arrive after the advertisement has completed its run, by which time millions of people will have already been exposed to their misleading messages. Recidivism is common; the companies with the largest numbers of advertising-related regulatory letters between 2002 and 2005 were Pfizer (11); Roche, Boehringer Ingelheim and Novartis (five each); and Glaxo (four).

Health-care observers have long noted that health care is unlike other markets in that patients typically do not purchase services directly. Rather, due to the complexity of the decisions involved and the potentially life-threatening nature of poor choices, the physician acts as a "learned intermediary" on the patient's behalf. DTC advertising is nothing less than an end-run around the doctor-patient relationship—an attempt to turn patients into the agents of pharmaceutical companies as they pressure physicians for medications they may not need.

POSTSCRIPT

Do Consumers Benefit When Prescription Drugs Are Advertised?

Opponents of prescription drug advertising contend that drug companies' promotions are frequently inaccurate or deceptive. Furthermore, they maintain that drug companies are more interested in increasing their profits, not in truly providing additional medical benefit to the average consumer. Drug companies do not deny that they seek to make profits from their drugs, but they argue that they are offering an important public service by educating the public about new drugs through their advertisements. Also, after investing millions of dollars into developing and testing new drugs, should not pharmaceutical companies profit from the sale of these drugs?

An important issue is whether or not the average consumer is capable of discerning information distributed by pharmaceutical companies. Are people without a background in medicine, medical terminology, or research methods sufficiently knowledgeable to understand literature disseminated by drug companies? With the help of the Internet and other media, prescription drug advertising proponents maintain that the average consumer is capable of understanding information about various drugs. On the other hand, will most people take the time to follow up on drugs that are advertised? And, if people do not take the time to read about drugs they see advertised in the media, is that the fault of the drug companies?

Some critics argue that restricting drug advertisements is a moot point because consumers cannot obtain prescriptions without the approval of their physicians. Yet, in numerous instances physicians acquiesce to the wishes of their patients and write prescriptions upon the request of the patient. If in this way patients receive prescriptions that are not appropriate for their needs, who is responsible: the patient, the physician, or the drug manufacturer and advertiser? Is the role of the physician to dictate to the patient what drugs are appropriate or is it the role of the physician to explain to the patient the various options and then let the patient decide what to do?

When drug manufacturers introduce a new drug, they get a patent on the drug to protect their investment. Drug companies, therefore, receive financial rewards for introducing new drugs. Of course, drug companies also take financial risks when developing new drugs. One could argue that drug companies should be awarded for the financial risks they take. However, some critics maintain that many of these new drugs are merely "me-too" drugs that are similar to existing drugs and that they do not provide any additional benefit. Are consumers being fooled into requesting more expensive drugs that are no better than drugs already on the market?

Whether consumers benefit for the advertising if prescription drugs is discussed in "Consumer Response to Drug Risk Information: The Role of Positive Affect" by Anthony Cox, Dena Cox, and Susan Mantel, *Journal of Marketing* (2010). Whether or not advertising prescription drugs is a matter of free speech is discussed in "Drug Risks and Free Speech—Can Congress Ban Consumer Drug Ads?" by Miriam Shuchman, *The New England Journal of Medicine* (May 31, 2007). Other articles that address this issue are "Hidden in Plain Sight Marketing Prescription Drugs to Consumers in the Twentieth Century" by Jeremy Greene and David Helzberg, *American Journal of Public Health* (May, 2010) and "A Decade of Controversy: Balancing Policy with Evidence in the Regulation of Prescription Drug Advertising" by Dominick Frosch and others, *American Journal of Public Health* (January, 2010).

Internet References . . .

National Clearinghouse for Alcohol and Drug Information (NCADI)

Information regarding a variety of drugs and research published by the federal government is available through this site. Up-to-date developments in drug use are available through NCADI.

http://www.health.org

American Council for Drug Education

The American Council for Drug Education is a substance abuse prevention and education agency that develops programs and materials based on the most current practices.

http://www.acde.org

D.A.R.E. (Drug Abuse Resistance Education)

The D.A.R.E. is a drug prevention and education program that involves police officers teaching children about the hazards of drugs.

http:// www.dare.com

Partnership for a Drug-Free America

Extensive information on the effects of drugs and the extent of drug use by young people are discussed at this Web site.

http://www.drugfreeamerica.org

National Council on Alcoholism and Drug Dependence

This site contains objective information and referral for individuals, families, and others seeking intervention and treatment.

http://www.ncadd.org

Drug Prevention and Treatment

*I*n spite of their legal consequences and the government's interdiction efforts, drugs are widely available and used. Two common ways of dealing with drug abuse is to incarcerate drug users and to intercept drugs before they enter the country. However, many drug experts believe that more energy should be put into preventing and treating drug abuse. An important step toward prevention and treatment is to find out what contributes to drug abuse and how to nullify these factors.

By educating young people about the potential hazards of drugs and by developing an awareness of social influences that contribute to drug use, many drug-related problems may be averted. The debates in this section focus on different prevention and treatment issues such as promoting smokeless tobacco for cigarette smoking, the benefits and risks of legalizing marijuana for medical purposes, the effectiveness of drug abuse treatment, whether alcoholism is hereditary, drug testing students and whether schools should adopt a zero tolerance drug policy.

- Should Smokeless Tobacco Be Promoted as an Alternative to Cigarette Smoking?

- Is Alcoholism Hereditary?

- Should Marijuana Be Approved for Medical Use?

- Should Schools Drug Test Students?

- Does Drug Abuse Treatment Work?

- Should Schools Enforce a Zero Tolerance Drug Policy?

ISSUE 14

Should Smokeless Tobacco Be Promoted as an Alternative to Cigarette Smoking?

YES: **John Britton and Richard Edwards**, from "Tobacco Smoking, Harm Reduction, and Nicotine Product Regulation," *The Lancet* (February 2, 2008)

NO: **Adrienne B. Mejia and Pamela M. Ling**, from "Tobacco Industry Consumer Research on Smokeless Tobacco Users and Product Development," *American Journal of Public Health* (January 2010)

ISSUE SUMMARY

YES: Professors John Britton and Richard Edwards advocate the use of smokeless tobacco as an alternative to tobacco smoking because the harm from tobacco is rooted more in the act of smoking than from nicotine. They recognize that smokeless tobacco carries certain risks, although they note that nicotine is neither a known carcinogen nor does it reduce birthweight as much as tobacco smoking.

NO: Adrienne Mejia and Pamela Ling maintain that tobacco manufacturers are marketing smokeless tobacco products as a way to counter smoke-free laws at the workplace and in bars and restaurants. They feel that smokeless products are especially targeted toward younger smokers. Mejia and Ling argue that smokeless tobacco is not a healthy alternative to smoked tobacco.

$\mathbf{T}$here is no debate as to whether cigarette smoking is deadly. On a worldwide basis, it is estimated that 100 million people die annually from this addiction. In the United States, over 400,000 die each year from cigarette smoking. Besides causing premature death, millions more people are afflicted with diseases such as bronchitis, lung cancer, and emphysema. Cigarette tobacco emits secondhand smoke that has an impact on coworkers as well as spouses and children living with smokers. Health care professionals are adamant about the need to reduce cigarette smoking. Clearly, cigarette smoking interferes with one's quality of life. The issue being debated is not whether smokeless tobacco is beneficial, but whether or not it should be promoted as an alternative to cigarette smoking.

There are a number of adverse health effects associated with smokeless tobacco. Because there is more nicotine in smokeless tobacco than in cigarettes, the potential for addiction is high. Conversely, frequent use of smokeless tobacco greatly hinders one's ability to stop its use. According to its detractors, smokeless tobacco can be carcinogenic. Although, oral cancer has been associated with its use, the risk of lung cancer from cigarette smoking is greater. Other oral health effects include dental cavities, gingivitis, and periodontitis.

Proponents of smokeless tobacco as an alternative to cigarette smoking agree that it is best for smokers to stop smoking altogether. However, in light of the fact that many people cannot quit smoking, despite numerous attempts, they maintain that smokeless tobacco is less harmful. In essence, the use of smokeless tobacco is a harm reduction strategy. Cigarette smoking is simply more deleterious than using smokeless tobacco. Smokeless tobacco is the lesser of two evils.

Those individuals who support smokeless tobacco as an alternative to cigarette smoking note that nicotine is not a recognized carcinogen and that it does not impair lung functioning. As noted previously, opponents of smokeless tobacco claim that smokeless tobacco may cause cancer. Currently, many people use nicotine patches and gums to reduce cigarette smoking. One could argue that smokeless tobacco is another example of nicotine replacement.

Opponents of the harm reduction strategy argue that smokeless tobacco use discourages individuals from stopping all tobacco use. Their position is that although smokeless tobacco may be less harmful than cigarette smoking, all tobacco use should be discouraged. Opponents dispel the notion of "harmful but safer" when discussing the use of smokeless tobacco. Any tobacco use is a public health problem. To stop or reduce the level of cigarette smoking, opponents would rather increase the tax on cigarettes or place other restrictions on its use.

It is believed that young people who start out using smokeless tobacco may eventually smoke cigarettes. Also, one could question whether young people get the wrong message if smokeless tobacco was advocated in lieu of cigarette smoking? Teenagers are influenced by the media. It has been shown that movies portraying cigarette smoking result in an increase in adolescents smoking. Perhaps young people may get the impression that it is okay to use smokeless tobacco if it is advocated as an alternative to cigarette smoking.

In the YES selection, John Britton and Richard Edwards advocate the use of smokeless tobacco as a safer alternative to cigarette smoking. They maintain that the hazards associated with smokeless tobacco may be exaggerated. In the NO selection, Adrienne Mejia and Pamela Ling argue that smokeless tobacco should not be promoted as a safer alternative to cigarette smoking. They believe that smokeless tobacco is promoted by tobacco companies as a way to circumvent anti-tobacco forces.

YES

John Britton and
Richard Edwards

Tobacco Smoking, Harm Reduction, and Nicotine Product Regulation

Cigarette smoking is highly addictive, widely prevalent, and very hazardous. Smoking killed 100 million people in the 20th century, and is predicted to kill 1 billion in the 21st century. Worldwide, there are about 1.1 billion smokers, and there are expected to be 1·6 billion by 2025. Half of all smokers will die prematurely, unless they stop smoking.

In the 50 years since the health risks of smoking first became widely recognised, the political and public health responses to smoking at national and international levels have been grossly inadequate. Although the main components of current recommended tobacco control policy (panel 1) have changed little from those first proposed in 1962, they have still not been widely applied and, in any case, achieve a reduction in smoking prevalence of typically about 0·5, and at best 1·0, percentage point per year. Full implementation of these policies might be sufficient to prevent smoking in countries in which the smoking epidemic has yet to take hold, but this is only part of the necessary solution for countries with an established smoking population. In the UK, for example, where 24% of adults still smoke, at a reduction rate of 0·5 percentage point per year it would take more than 20 years to reduce the prevalence of smoking by half. Even then, there will be more than 5 million smokers in the UK alone, predominantly from the most socioeconomically disadvantaged sectors of society, bearing a vast burden of avoidable morbidity and mortality. In fact most of the 150 million deaths from smoking that are expected over the next 20 years will occur in current smokers who are alive today. Since millions of these are unlikely to stop smoking in the near future, we argue, on the basis of a new report from the Royal College of Physicians, that in addition to conventional tobacco control policies, the application of harm reduction principles to nicotine and tobacco use could deliver substantial reductions in the morbidity and mortality currently caused by tobacco consumption. However, achievement of these reductions will require radical structural reform of the way in which nicotine and tobacco products are regulated and used.

Panel 1: Essential components of tobacco control policy

- Use of price, tax increases, or both to reduce consumption
- Prevent smoking in public places and in workplaces
- Health warnings on packets of tobacco products
- Health promotion and public information campaigns
- Prohibition of advertising and other promotion
- Provision of smoking cessation services
- Prevention of smuggling
- Prohibition of sales and reduction of availability to people under age 18 years

Most people continue to smoke because they are addicted to nicotine. Inhaled tobacco smoke is especially addictive because it delivers high doses of nicotine to the brain very rapidly, and because nicotine confers rewarding properties on other stimuli associated with smoking. Exposure to high nicotine concentrations at an early age might also determine the intensity of addiction through effects on nicotinic receptor numbers in the brain.

Nicotine is available from a wide range of products: smoked tobacco, of which the cigarette is pre-eminent; medicinal nicotine, currently available as nicotine replacement therapy; and smokeless tobacco products, of which oral tobacco is the most widely used. Cigarettes and other smoked tobacco products, such as cigars and pipes, are by far the most harmful because they deliver nicotine in conjunction with hundreds of other toxins and carcinogens. It is these toxins and carcinogens that are mainly responsible for the major adverse health effects of smoking—particularly lung cancer, chronic obstructive pulmonary disease (COPD), heart disease, and stroke. By contrast, the safety record of medicinal nicotine products is very good.

Nicotine is not a recognised carcinogen and does not cause COPD. It has effects on blood pressure and heart rate that might be expected to increase risk of cardiovascular disease, but these effects are not seen in practice. Nicotine reduces placental blood flow, but medicinal nicotine does not reduce birthweight as much as smoking does. Therefore, although medicinal nicotine is not wholly safe, for practical purposes, and certainly when compared with smoking, the hazard associated with medicinal nicotine use is very low.

The risk profile of smokeless tobacco products is more wide ranging and includes oral cancer, other gastrointestinal cancers, and heart disease. These risks vary substantially between different smokeless products, but are low for products low in nitrosamine, such as Swedish snus. Snus use increases the risk of pancreatic cancer, but not of lung and oral cancers, or COPD. Use of other smokeless products has been linked to an increased risk of cardiovascular disease, but snus has little, if any, effect. The risk of adverse effects associated with snus use is lower than that associated with smoking, overall by an estimated 90%. Whatever the true overall hazard, use of low nitrosamine smokeless products is clearly substantially less harmful than tobacco smoking.

The rationale behind harm reduction is that although the best option would be to avoid the harmful behaviour completely, the next best option, if the behaviour is likely to continue, is to ensure that the harm caused is kept to a minimum. A logical harm reduction approach for the millions of smokers who are unlikely to achieve complete abstinence in the short-term or medium-term future is to promote the substitution of tobacco smoking with an alternative, less hazardous means of obtaining nicotine.

The least hazardous alternative is medicinal nicotine. Since their development around 20 years ago, medicinal nicotine products have been promoted as cessation therapies, for use as short-term substitutes for smoking in the context of attempts to stop smoking. In clinical trials, use of medicinal nicotine increases the likelihood of stopping smoking by around 80%, but the absolute increase in quit rates is modest because the baseline success rates are low. Thus, in a quit attempt using medicinal nicotine in conjunction with best-practice behavioural support, only about one in five smokers succeed in stopping for 6 months. These products are not strongly effective or competitive substitutes for smoking because they deliver nicotine in lower doses and more slowly than do cigarettes. Medicinal nicotine products are also much less available than cigarettes in most countries; are marketed and advertised as smoking cessation therapies (rather than long-term smoking substitutes); are expensive to buy; and are widely perceived as harmful by smokers.

Anecdotally, smokeless tobacco products have a history of use as temporary substitutes for smoking by occupational groups, such as coal miners, who cannot smoke while at work. In Sweden at least some of the substantial reduction in daily smoking prevalence in the past 20 years or so seems attributable to substitution of smoking by snus use, especially by men. Although there has been uptake of regular smoking by smokeless users who might not otherwise have smoked (gateway progression), the extent to which this progression has happened is much less than that from regular smoking to snus. However, this pattern of use has not been replicated elsewhere. In the USA, where other forms of smokeless tobacco have also been available for some time, the prevalence of smokeless tobacco use has fallen progressively in conjunction with that of smoking—to below 5% in men and 1% in women by 2000. In Norway, snus use has increased recently to about 11% of all men, and 18% of men aged 16–24 years, with no evidence yet of effect on the rate of decline in smoking prevalence [Erik Dybing, personal communication].

The effectiveness of smokeless tobacco as a substitute for smoking, and the relative extent to which wider availability and promotion of smokeless products would result in gateway progression into or out of smoking, are controversial topics. Some argue that health professionals should not condone any use of nicotine, and also that encouraging use of alternative nicotine products, particularly smokeless tobacco, would invite abuse of the market by their commercial producers. Others argue that if smokeless products are an effective and less hazardous substitute for smoking it would be in the public interest to harness that potential to public health benefit, particularly if the Swedish pattern of predominant gateway progression from smoking to smokeless use could be realised in other countries.

The arguments are finely balanced. However, on the basis of the Swedish data we believe that the potential role of smokeless products at least merits further consideration and investigation to find out whether and to what extent these products can act as substitutes for smoking; whether tobacco products are more effective smoking substitutes than medicinal nicotine; and, if so, whether the product characteristics responsible can be identified and used to develop more acceptable low-risk medicinal products. We also believe that the development of such products should happen only within an overall strategy of radical reform of the regulatory systems that apply to nicotine products, including much stronger regulation of smoked tobacco, to ensure that the harm caused by all nicotine use is kept to a minimum.

Effective harm reduction strategies, and particularly the option of providing nicotine without smoke as an acceptable long-term or even lifelong substitute for smoking, have not been widely applied to tobacco smoking. The pharmaceutical companies have not evidently engaged in the development of medicinal devices that are strongly competitive with cigarettes. Use of smokeless tobacco is actively discouraged by many health professionals and by WHO. This opposition to smokeless products is despite predicted benefits from modelling studies. If a product such as snus were marketed in the USA with a health warning stating that it is addictive and might increase risk of disease, but that it is substantially less harmful than cigarettes, the prevalence of smoking in the USA would be reduced by an estimated additional 1·3% to 3·1% over 5 years (ie, by about 0·44% per year). In a study modelling the effect of the introduction of snus as an alternative to smoking in Australia, the investigators concluded that the overall net effect would be beneficial to public health.

We believe that the absence of effective harm reduction options for smokers is perverse, unjust, and acts against the rights and best interests of smokers and the public health. Addicted smokers have a right to choose from a range of safer nicotine products, as well as accurate and unbiased information to guide that choice. There are, however, several obstacles to the development of an effective harm reduction strategy for tobacco smoking in the UK and many other countries, and particularly to the development and marketing of more effective medicinal products. Paramount among these is the current system of regulations that apply to different nicotine products in most countries.

A major reason why tobacco products have remained exempt from consumer protection regulation in most countries is that the logical and proportionate application of existing regulations would result in their immediate withdrawal from sale. Thus, the most dangerous and addictive nicotine products remain only slightly regulated, in great disproportion to their hazard, and are freely available and widely used. Tobacco companies are also free to develop or modify, and bring to market, new smoked tobacco products and other tobacco derivatives with little regulatory control.

By contrast, medicinal nicotine products, which are the safest source of nicotine, are generally subject to the highest levels of regulation since they are generally classified as drugs. This is almost certainly a major disincentive to new product development and innovation, and to market competition to create better and more effective cigarette substitutes. The present regulatory system also discourages innovation through the real or perceived likelihood that most effective smoking substitutes, which would almost certainly be more addictive than the present range of medicinal products, would be subject to even stricter controls on marketing and supply, or perhaps even prevented from coming to market.

Current regulation of smokeless tobacco products is also inconsistent, since most products are subject to minimal regulatory controls, whereas the supply of snus, which is one of the least hazardous of such products, is prohibited in most European countries. Extention of that prohibition across the range of smokeless products would resolve this inconsistency, but at the expense of the loss of a potentially effective alternative to smoking. On the other hand, removing the prohibition on snus would deal the tobacco industry a free hand to exploit the smokeless tobacco market with apparent endorsement by legislators. Neither of these options is ideal; hence, an alternative approach, designed to benefit public health rather than industry profit, is needed.

Our argument is that nicotine products should all be regulated rationally in relation to each other, in proportion to their level of hazard, in a system designed to reduce the overall harm caused by nicotine dependence and use. The regulatory framework should promote complete cessation of nicotine product use as the preferred option, but also encourage existing smokers who are unable to stop smoking to adopt a less hazardous source of the drug. An obvious prerequisite of this change would be an acceptance by society in general, and particularly by health professionals, that use of low-hazard nicotine products might be prevalent for many years.

Achievement of a rational nicotine regulatory framework needs a radical overhaul of existing systems to encourage the innovation, development, and use of new medicinal nicotine products at the least hazardous end of the spectrum, and to achieve the fastest possible reductions in use of products at the smoked tobacco extreme. The regulatory framework should therefore apply the levers of affordability, promotion, and availability in direct inverse relation to the hazard of the product, thus creating the most favourable market environment for the least hazardous products while also strongly discouraging the use of smoked tobacco. The anomalies that inhibit market competition to develop new and better rapid delivery, user-friendly medicinal nicotine products (eg, inhaled nicotine) that can compete with cigarettes for long-term use need to be removed; and there needs to be more widespread promotion and sale of existing or new lower-hazard products. The regulatory system should include a robust surveillance function so that potentially counterproductive trends in marketing or use of all nicotine products—particularly those that are tobacco-based—are promptly detected and resolved. The regulatory system should ensure that alternative nicotine products, medicinal or tobacco-based, are marketed with appropriate health information and, where appropriate, professional endorsement. Nicotine product regulation should also be applied over time to ensure that smoked tobacco products are subject to progressively increased restrictions—on availability and marketing, with the long-term objective of reducing and, in due course, eradicating all smoked tobacco use.

The options for rationalising nicotine regulation include making all nicotine product regulation the responsibility of an existing agency, such as a food or drug regulation agency, or by coordination and rationalisation of the activities of the different agencies that regulate nicotine products. We conclude, however, that meeting the challenges of implementing effective tobacco control and nicotine harm reduction policies (panel 2), both nationally and internationally, needs the creation of dedicated, autonomous, and fully resourced national (and where appropriate international) nicotine and tobacco product regulatory authorities. This approach might be unrealistic in many resource-poor countries, and less of a priority in those at the earliest stages of the smoking epidemic, but that is certainly not the case in those that already have a substantial population of established smokers, and hence the most to gain from this strategy.

Panel 2: Suggested roles and functions of a national nicotine regulatory authority

Functions at initiation

- Baseline measurement of all current nicotine product use
- Ensure full implementation of conventional tobacco control policies (panel 1)
- Permissive licensing of medicinal nicotine products for use as smoking substitutes
- Substantial relaxation of restrictions on marketing and sale of medicinal nicotine products
- Removal of tax on medicinal nicotine products
- Communication of objective health risk information for nicotine products and promotion of harm reduction principles to smokers and the public
- Establishment of ground rules for monitoring the use of health messages in promoting the use of lower hazard nicotine products as substitutes for smoking
- Imposition of generic packaging for all tobacco products
- Prohibition of retail display of smoked tobacco products
- Strong graphic health warnings on smoked tobacco products
- Setting of tax and consequently retail price of all nicotine products in relation to their probable relative risk to health
- Prohibition of all sale of nicotine products to individuals under age 18 years
- Introduce licensing of retailers of all smoked tobacco products
- Assume responsibility for overseeing nicotine product delivery and toxicity monitoring
- Mandate the introduction of reduced ignition propensity cigarettes
- Take expert advice on how current restrictions on smokeless nicotine products could be reformed to public health benefit

Continuing functions

- Regular monitoring of trends in nicotine product use, promotion, and availability
- Monitoring of effect of licensing and marketing relaxation on medicinal nicotine use, and revision as necessary to promote public health
- Progressive increases in tax on the most hazardous products
- Continued promotion of health information on different nicotine products and development and monitoring of mass communication strategies to prevent uptake, promote cessation, and reduce harm
- Progressive reduction in retail licences for smoked tobacco products
- Monitoring and policing of illicit and underage tobacco and nicotine trade
- Work with the commercial sector to promote competition and innovation in the medicinal nicotine market
- Monitoring and prevention of smoked product placement and new methods of marketing (eg internet, viral marketing)
- Act on expert advice to set framework for licensing of low-hazard smokeless products and possible test marketing
- Progressively incentivise minority, high risk smokeless tobacco users to quit or else migrate to safer products
- Identify and respond to new developments or threats to health from new or existing product development or promotion
- Control of expenditure on tobacco control interventions to ensure evidence-based and cost-effective interventions are used
- Support nicotine regulation and tobacco control approaches in resource-poor countries

The consequence of failing to intensify tobacco control efforts, and to address the current imbalance in nicotine product regulation, will be the unnecessary perpetuation of current smoking by millions of people, especially in disadvantaged communities, and a continued epidemic of avoidable death and disability. Specifically, cigarettes and other smoked tobacco products will continue to be freely available with few restrictions on their safety or content; the medicinal nicotine market will continue to focus on low-addiction, low-dose, low-effectiveness products while also stifling competition and innovation; and the current irrational regulation of smokeless products will continue. Most of the millions of smokers alive today will therefore continue to smoke tobacco, and half will die as a result.

Adrienne B. Mejia and
Pamela M. Ling

Tobacco Industry Consumer Research on Smokeless Tobacco Users and Product Development

Since 2006, RJ Reynolds (RJR) and Philip Morris have both introduced new smokeless "snus" tobacco products. We analyzed previously secret tobacco industry documents describing the history of RJR and Philip Morris's consumer research, smokeless product development, and marketing strategies. We found that RJR had invested in smokeless research, development, and marketing since 1968. RJR first targeted low-income males through sampling and sponsorship at fishing, rodeo, and baseball events, and through advertising portraying the user as "hard working." In the early 1990s, Philip Morris and RJR hoped to attract more urban, female smokeless users. The current "snus" campaigns appear to appeal to these targeted consumers and smokers in smoke-free environments. These efforts may expand the tobacco market and undermine smoking cessation. (*Am J Public Health.* 2010;100:78–87, doi:10.2105/ AJPH.2008.152603)

The debate over the health community and tobacco companies promoting tobacco "harm reduction" by encouraging smokers to switch to smokeless tobacco products has primarily centered on a product resembling a Swedish smokeless tobacco called "snus," which is finely ground oral tobacco (moist snuff) packaged in small porous pouches. In 1982, RJ Reynolds (RJR) recognized moist snuff as the "most profitable and fastest growing segment of the non-cigarette tobacco industry," and from 1982 to 2008, moist snuff remained the only growing segment of the smokeless tobacco market. Smokeless tobacco products are addictive, and their use has been linked to oral cancer, oropharyngeal cancer, heart disease, and pancreatic cancer. Dual use of cigarettes and smokeless tobacco, given that their associated health effects are different and may be additive, may increase the risk of tobacco-related diseases and mortality above single-product use. Through increased dual use and new uptake, smokeless tobacco promotion may actually lead to an increase in tobacco-related harm at the population level (A.M. Mejia, MPH; P.M. Ling, MD; and S.A. Glantz, PhD, unpublished data, 2009).

Leading cigarette companies are entering the smokeless tobacco market, perhaps because of continuing declines in US cigarette consumption and increases in smoke-free ordinances. Between 2006 and 2007, both RJR and

From *American Journal of Public Health,* January 2010, pp. 78–87. Copyright © 2010 by American Public Health Association. Reprinted by permission via Sheridan Reprints.

Philip Morris leveraged their strongest cigarette brands to promote new moist snuff products, such as Camel Snus, Marlboro Snus, and Marlboro Moist Snuff, in test markets around the United States. The new products are line extensions of well-known cigarette brands, giving them a sense of familiarity that may increase their appeal to smokers, and they may promote the dual use of both cigarettes and smokeless tobacco products that share the same brand name.

In March 2008, RJR announced plans to expand Camel Snus into 10 additional major US metropolitan areas. In the second quarter of 2008, the Liggett Group began test marketing Grand Prix Snus, an addition to the Grand Prix cigarette brand, in 7 of the 8 test markets where Camel Snus was available. Most of the cities where snus was introduced have 100% smoke-free laws in workplaces, bars, or restaurants. Advertisements for Camel and Marlboro Snus tout it as a temporary way to deal with smoke-free policies in public places, bars, workplaces, and airplanes. Such messages may undermine the effectiveness of smoke-free environments in motivating smoking cessation. The style and content of the advertising also appears designed to attract young people and other new users. There is concern that promotion of smokeless tobacco could lead to (1) previous nontobacco users becoming users of smokeless products, (2) smokeless tobacco serving as a potential gateway product to smoking, and (3) smokers who would have quit using tobacco entirely instead becoming dual users of cigarettes and smokeless tobacco.

Understanding how tobacco companies have profiled, targeted, and marketed to smokeless tobacco users in the past provides a valuable context for understanding current marketing activities. Although tobacco industry documents may not contain direct information about marketing the newest products, many current efforts resulted from years of past research. Cigarette companies conducted consumer research on the demographic and psychological characteristics of smokeless tobacco users, what factors motivated them to use smokeless products, their beliefs about smokeless tobacco and its harms or benefits, and what product characteristics (such as flavoring or nicotine levels) or advertising messages appeared to motivate purchase or use behaviors. Industry documents also show how consumer research was applied to develop new products and marketing strategies.

We analyzed previously secret documents from Philip Morris and RJR to better understand their current marketing activities, asking the following research questions: How have tobacco companies characterized and understood smokeless tobacco users? How have target user profiles been developed and matched to advertising appeals? What have been the main "selling" messages for smokeless products over time? How do these profiles and message strategies compare with current marketing activities?

Methods

We searched tobacco industry document archives from the University of California, San Francisco Legacy Tobacco Documents Library (http://legacy.library. ucsf.edu) between June 2007 and August 2008. Initial search terms included the following: smokeless tobacco, chewing tobacco, snus, specialty tobacco products, marketing development, smoke-free, R&D, moist snuff, Skoal, Copenhagen, and US Tobacco. Initial searches yielded thousands of documents; we reviewed documents relevant to chewing tobacco, moist snuff, and related consumer research or marketing activities. We repeated and focused searches using standard techniques. In addition, we conducted "snowball" searches for contextual information on relevant documents using names, project titles, brand names, document locations, dates, and reference (Bates) numbers.

This analysis was based on a final collection of 234 research reports, presentations, marketing development proposals, and project status reports. We reviewed the documents, organized them thematically, and wrote summary memoranda. Common themes were identified and discussed. Information found in industry documents was triangulated with data from searches of the tobacco company annual and quarterly reports and investor webcasts, online search engines, and official company Web sites (US Smokeless Tobacco, RJ Reynolds, Conwood, and Philip Morris), brand Web sites (Camel Snus, Marlboro Snus), news stories, and promotional materials such as print and Internet advertisements.

Results

RJR has manufactured smokeless tobacco products since the early 1900s and has invested in chewing tobacco consumer research, marketing, and advertising since at least 1968.

Traditional Smokeless Tobacco Users

The 1968 National Tobacco Chewing Survey (a section of a tobacco usage survey mailed to National Family Opinion Inc panels), as reported by William Esty Company to RJR, reported that (1) the heaviest concentrations of chewers were in the lowest income groups, (2) chewing tobacco use was higher among farmers and unskilled blue-collar workers than among white-collar and professional men, and (3) chewing tobacco use was highest in rural areas and lowest in the largest cities.

In January 1970, Edward Simon, a qualitative researcher, conducted focus groups of chewers in Charleston, West Virginia, for RJR to provide "in-depth background information on consumer experience with and attitudes toward [the product]." Simon found that most participants had taken up chewing because they worked in factories or mines that prohibited smoking, although some used chewing tobacco in dusty environments to keep their mouths and throats moist. Chewing tobacco was thought to be a calming, relaxing, and tension-reducing experience, pleasantly associated with outdoor activities.

A 1978 Philip Morris smokeless consumer profile described the typical consumer as a male farmer, athlete, or factory worker whose average age was between 40 and 50; the Philip Morris document stated that this profile was supported by a series of interviews conducted by the Department of Health, Education, and Welfare in 1970, which found that twice as many men used smokeless tobacco as did women. A 1983 Philip Morris memo stated that although traditional smokeless users were primarily older farmers and factory workers in the Midwest and Northwest, market growth throughout the early 1980s was among those aged 18 to 35 years:

> Recent evidence indicates that almost 60% of consumers are below the age of 24 and . . . the product is used by growing numbers of women. In addition many users are first-time tobacco users. A 1981 study by Simmons Market Research Bureau indicated that . . . the typical user was a married 18–34 year old male, had an annual income of less than $25,000 and had no more than a high school education.

Philip Morris collected data from Simmons Market Research Bureau on smokeless tobacco from 1980 to 1984; a report for J.E. Lincoln (vice president for planning at Philip Morris International) included profiles of dual users of chewing tobacco, snuff, and cigarettes. The 1983 Simmons data were cited in a 1984 Philip Morris memo to Hugh Cullman, vice chairman of the board of directors, for him to weigh when considering entering the smokeless market. The attached data described the majority of chewing tobacco users as White, from the South, non–high school graduates, and with a household income under $25000.

Potential New Smokeless Tobacco Users

As early as 1968, a report prepared by William Esty for RJR noted that "scrap tobacco" (loose leaf) was more popular among the highest income group and those in white-collar occupations. A report by David E. Rawson of Rawson Associates (a marketing firm) summarizing qualitative research for RJR emphasized the increasing popularity of moist snuff in urban settings: "[T]here seems to be a growing desire among city folks to emulate cowboys, freedom, the wild west." Although tobacco users participating in the research associated moist snuff with outdoor men, with rugged, individualistic people who worked in places where they could not smoke, and with farm or rural backgrounds, they did not perceive moist snuff to be as "low class" as other chewing tobacco. They considered moist snuff to be the only form of tobacco that could be used discreetly, as it reportedly did not interfere with speech, hands, or other activities, and did not require spitting.

In late 1971, Claude E. Teague Jr, assistant chief in research and development at RJR, wrote a confidential research-planning memorandum on modified chewing tobacco–like products. Teague proposed solutions to the problems with chewing tobacco that he saw as barriers to making chewing and snuff tobacco "a potentially large, profitable market." The major problems with spit tobacco products were as follows: they required saliva flow and expectoration, they contained high amounts of nicotine (which may be "undesirable to the general public"), and they were messy and bulky in the mouth. The modified products Teague proposed were based on controlled nicotine levels, so that "juices can be swallowed and not spit out," and would be packaged in small units that were not "messy or unsightly to dispose of."

RJR's 1970 consumer research revealed that many chewers did not perceive chewing tobacco as harmful to their health. In 1971, Teague asserted that chewing tobacco was the "most free of alleged health hazards" of all tobacco products and cited surveys indicating that chewing tobacco provided most of smoking's "physiological satisfactions." Teague also recommended that any modified smokeless tobacco be advertised as though it was an existing chewing tobacco or snuff product, which should "minimize legal or regulatory problems, and should avoid scrutiny by the Food and Drug Administration." By 1978, Rawson's report summarizing RJR's qualitative consumer research noted that with heightened health concerns about smoking, snuff was perceived as a good, safer alternative. Rawson also suggested that RJR promote the "safety and smokeless feature, but stress the less macho, more sophisticated upscale image more compatible with newer types of users for the milder versions."

Early Product Development and Testing

In 1978, RJR established a Specialty Tobacco Products division that included little cigars, pipe tobacco, roll-your-own (loose) tobacco, wet snuff, and chewing tobacco. In 1980, the total approved Specialty Tobacco Products budget was $8222000 for advertising, promotion, and marketing development; in 1981, total Specialty Tobacco Products spending on marketing was $13.5 million. Specialty Tobacco Products marketing activities emphasized "primary product and psychological benefits" and focused on consumer research and competitive product testing with other brands. New brand families were planned to compete directly with established brands in the market (Table 1).

RJR's 1982 marketing plans emphasized that the "highest Specialty Tobacco Products priority [would be] to position RJR as a major competitor in the moist snuff category, the most profitable and fastest growing segment of the non-cigarette industry." For example, RJR's consumer research with users of flavored moist snuff who were aged 18 to 34 years led to a highly wintergreen flavored, fine-cut prototype (internally called "Project WSH" by RJR) to compete with Hawken moist snuff. In January 1982, WSH was introduced as Timberline to test markets; it targeted young males at "country and western night clubs, [and] sports arenas." Additional qualitative research conducted for RJR found that fancy packaging appealed more to new users: "the association of colorful package graphics to the newer, milder and 'candy-like' brands, suggests that new moist snuff packaging should be basic with sharp and simple graphics if it is to appeal to experienced Skoal and Copenhagen users."

The Assessor Testing System was a laboratory test market simulation procedure that RJR used to evaluate new brands; it included a laboratory phase (simulated shopping situation) in a shopping mall and 3 telephone callbacks. Demographic data were collected along with brand preference, brand awareness, and product attributes. Advertising recall, like-ability, believability, and meaningfulness were assessed through exposure to a portfolio of television commercials.

In March 1982, an assessor experiment on Timberline was conducted with 445 males aged 18 years and older who used flavored moist snuff. The main conclusions were as follows: (1) most smokeless tobacco users participating in the research were young (aged 18–24 years) single men, with at least

Table 1

RJ Reynolds Specialty Tobacco Products Projects, With Positioning Concepts and Summaries: 1985

Project	Product Name	Key Competitor Products	Positioning Concept	Prime Prospect Demographics	Prime Prospect Psychographics
WSS ("Wet Snuff-Skoal" type); solo entry	High Country	Skoal (US Tobacco), Kodiak (Conwood)	"[A] new wintergreen flavor snuff that refreshes you. Whether you're working or playing, you want to get the most out of each day. This snuff provides tobacco satisfaction, with a refreshing wintergreen flavor that keeps you going all day long . . . satisfies the active man—a user perceived as out-going, energetic."	Males aged 18–34 y / Middle income / Blue-collar occupation / High school education / Rural residence / West Central, Southwest, Southeast regions	Outgoing, fun loving, makes friends easily / Susceptible to peer influence / Leisure activity centers around outdoor sports
WSC ("Wet Snuff-Copenhagen" type); solo entry	Caliber	Copenhagen (US Tobacco)	"[A] new natural flavor snuff for the man who thinks for himself. Unlike those who follow the crowd, he is known by his friends as one who thinks things through, and then does what's right for him. Knowing he is true to himself gives him a lot of satisfaction."	Males aged 18–34 y / Middle income / Blue-collar occupation / High school education / Rural residence / West Central, Southwest, Pacific regions	Confident, goal-driven, self-reliant, proud of individuality / Selective at establishing close friendships / Leisure time centers on outdoor sports
WSS and WSC Brand Family	High Country	Hawken (Conwood) Gold River (General Cigar) Skoal and Copenhagen (US Tobacco) Kodiak (Conwood)	"[H]elps keep the active man going—user perceived as outgoing, energetic and striving to get the most out of each day."	Males aged 18–34 y (particularly 18–24 y) / Middle income / Blue-collar occupation / High school education / Residence in West Central, Southeast, Southwest, and Pacific regions	Traditional family values / Strong family ties / Considerate of others / Leisure time interests center around outdoor sporting activities
GC ("Good Chew")	Woodsman	Redman (Conwood)	"[U]ser to be perceived as self-confident, masculine individual who as an avid sportsman enjoys an active, participative outdoors life-style."	Males aged 18–49 y / Midscale or above income and education / Blue-collar occupation / Residence in East Central, Southeast, and Southwest	Self-confident / Leisure time interests center around sporting activities

Note. Data are from an RJ Reynolds 1985 marketing plan review for Specialty Tobacco products and brand positioning statement documents.

some college education and incomes of at least $15000 per year, and (2) participants rated product attributes (e.g., the product being "fresh," "moist," or "satisfying") more important than how they perceived the users of smokeless products (e.g., users being "experienced" or "outdoorsmen," having a "physical job" or being "action oriented"). Positive Timberline product attributes were its moistness, wintergreen flavor, and plastic pack; repeat buyers were somewhat older and more affluent than nonrepeaters. The test predicted an 11.6% market share projection; shortly thereafter, RJR made plans for "Timberline Natural" prototype blends.

Consumer Profiles, Brand Positioning, and Communications

RJR Research on Smokeless Consumers' Wants and Motivations

Throughout the 1970s, RJR conducted and commissioned qualitative research on the moist snuff market. In 1978, David E. Rawson reviewed the results of various focus groups and one-on-one interviews among men with varying levels of chewing tobacco experience and use patterns to understand consumer segments and wants (Table 2). Although Rawson observed that some smokeless tobacco users were cigarette smokers who were trying to reduce or quit smoking, this was clearly not the only motivation to use

Table 2

Different Types of Smokeless Tobacco Users, as Described in a 1978 Qualitative Analysis for RJ Reynolds

	Substitutors	Variety People	Role Players	Sensors
Needs and values	Wish to reduce cigarette consumption or quit altogether	Need variety in their tobacco usage, either for the sake of variety or due to situations	Wish to fulfill or project a specific image that is associated with the use of moist snuff	Desire the unique taste, oral, or physiological experience they believe moist snuff provides
Possible hierarchy of wants	Freshness, satisfaction, taste or flavor, ease of control, low price	Freshness, taste or flavor, satisfaction, ease of control, low price	Freshness, image, taste or flavor, ease of control, low price	Freshness, taste or flavor, ease of control, satisfaction, low price
Subdivisions	Triers or beginners, occasional users, heavy users	Triers or beginners, occasional users	Triers or beginners, occasional users	Triers or beginners, occasional users, heavy users

Note. The column headings and content in table fields are original terms from the report.

Source. RJ Reynolds.

smokeless tobacco. Those trying to substitute smokeless tobacco for cigarettes were not motivated by image and were less motivated by taste or flavor than by "satisfaction" (a common tobacco industry euphemism for the physiological effects of nicotine).

Brand Positioning

RJR defined "positioning" as the basic selling concept used to motivate consumers to select a given product over that of the competition. Results from qualitative studies were used to create brand positioning statements. For example, a 1985 internal strategic document stated that Work Horse would be positioned as the "loose-leaf chewing tobacco that provides longer lasting flavor for the working man." The Timberline target was males 18 to 34 years old, and positioning aimed to have the product "perceived as a wintergreen flavored smokeless tobacco . . . unsurpassed in delivering consistently good taste for masculine, self-reliant moist snuff users."

Twenty consumer-oriented positioning concepts were developed and tested in focus groups for moist snuff projects WSS, WSC, and GC, which would later become the products High Country, Caliber, and Woodsman (Table 1). The positioning with the strongest purchase intent was "satisfaction," which promoted WSC as the snuff that "provides you with the real tobacco taste that keeps you going all day."

Philip Morris In-store Market Research

Philip Morris conducted 3 consumer research studies in collaboration with Marketing Information Systems Inc, a market research company, to determine the incidence of smokeless tobacco use among males and to profile the users. Interview questions included the length of time the interviewee had used smokeless tobacco, his regular brand of smokeless tobacco, terminology for the amount of smokeless tobacco placed in the mouth (such as "dip" or "pinch"), how the user was first introduced to smokeless tobacco, cigarette usage, and occasions when cigarettes were used in place of smokeless tobacco and vice versa.

Philip Morris found that fine-cut moist snuff appeared to be the most popular type of smokeless tobacco and that "45 percent of smokeless tobacco users had never smoked, 26 percent were current smokers and 29 percent former smokers. Within the former smokers group, almost 60 percent stated that smokeless tobacco was a replacement for cigarettes." Philip Morris continued to request market research on smokeless tobacco over time. Results of 272 interviews with male smokeless tobacco users in Atlanta, Georgia; Tallahassee, Florida; and Jacksonville, Florida, found age and regional preferences for different types of smokeless tobacco. They also found significant rates of dual smokeless and cigarette use: in addition to using smokeless tobacco, more than half of the men interviewed in each market had experience with cigarettes, and among dual users in Atlanta, Georgia, a higher proportion claimed that smokeless was more enjoyable than cigarettes.

Early Marketing Activities

The marketing activities that RJR pursued for its smokeless products appeared to target men of lower socioeconomic status, rural backgrounds, and young age; they included sampling, television commercials, and sports sponsorship. For example, in 1981 and 1982, the Work Horse brand was promoted with sampling at "opportunistic events" such as tractor pull contests, spitting contests, and fishing tournaments. The 1981 RJR public relations strategy included plans to write a feature article about supplying free chewing tobacco products to "college baseball teams" and about how there were now "a larger number of young people chewing." Other promotional items and contests included R.J. Gold (a brand of smokeless tobacco) banners, logo-bearing hats and shirts, and cash giveaways. Sporting events provided a fun, exciting atmosphere that built positive associations with tobacco products and encouraged trial of free samples. An RJR special events document from 1989 noted that although sampling was becoming less acceptable to the general public, attendees of special events "actively seek out the samplers . . . and the surroundings provide an attractive trial-inducing climate."

In 1982, RJR advertised Work Horse and R.J. Gold on the radio and on television and made plans for Timberline television advertising. A 1982 Marketing Development Department document written to J. W. Johnston, a one-time RJR president, chairman, and chief executive officer (CEO), reported that WSH [Timberline] commercials under development were tested for their "ability to attract attention to and communicate the desired user image attributes of masculinity and self-reliance." A 1982 weekly status report written to Johnston confirmed that R.J. Gold marketing plans included fishing tournament sponsorship and associated television coverage on ESPN.

Despite the marketing, RJR's product test results revealed that regular users rated all of the Specialty Tobacco Products products inferior to competitors' products in terms of tobacco taste or flavor. In 1983, following a 2-year period of stagnation and decline, RJR reduced support for Work Horse and R.J. Gold. RJR failed to develop a moist snuff-product that competed successfully with existing smokeless products at the time, and the Specialty Tobacco Products Brands Division was dissolved in February 1985.

Renewed Interest in the Smokeless Tobacco Market

The cigarette companies' interests in expanding the smokeless tobacco market that were first expressed in the 1980s were revisited a decade later. During the 1990s, RJR assigned a task force to conduct surveys and interviews to explore the appeal of RJR's cigarette trademarks among moist snuff users who smoked and moist snuff users who did not smoke, to explore consumer expectations of a moist snuff product, and to understand the purchase behavior of current users. In the early 1990s, the consumer profile of smokeless tobacco users as reported by RJR continued to center on White males with low education and low socioeconomic status.

Philip Morris also monitored and collected data from industry analysts' reports on the demographic profile associated with smokeless tobacco use, with an interest in acquiring new users. In 1989, a Philip Morris historical review of the US Tobacco Company asked, "Will women or professionals provide viable markets for expansion?" and "Is there room for international expansion?" A 1993 document written for William Campbell (Philip Morris president and CEO) stated that "the three primary groups driving current growth [of the moist snuff category] are young adult males who choose moist snuff over loose leaf, college males who choose snuff over cigarettes, and converted or dual usage smokers." Although the heaviest smokeless tobacco users were adult males and blue-collar workers, a 1992 planning document written by Philip Morris manager Louis Lembo noted

> [R]ecent studies cited by industry analysts indicate that smokeless tobacco is expanding its base to include active outdoor oriented adult males and more college educated white collar workers. UST [US Tobacco Company] feels the increase in smoking restrictions and the health controversy surrounding cigarettes is a major factor in improving smokeless tobacco's demographics. UST estimates that at least 25% of their customers also smoke cigarettes, and might be using moist snuff when smoking is inconvenient or prohibited.

A 1993 smokeless tobacco industry analysis written by Lembo for Campbell stated, "UST claims its moist snuff consumers are younger, better educated, less rural and have a higher income than traditional smokeless tobacco users." Furthermore, Lembo cited data from a 1990 study by the National Collegiate Athletic Association (NCAA), which showed that the percentage of athletes using smokeless tobacco "rose dramatically" in all sports surveyed from 1985 to 1988, as an "indicator of smokeless tobacco's improving image among young, educated adult males." Throughout the 1990s, industry analysts noted that increasing "smoking restrictions in the workplace and cultural changes" worked to expand the consumer base for smokeless tobacco.

In 2006, RJR saw the moist snuff category as representing an "increasingly acceptable alternative to cigarettes" because of perceptions of less risk, fewer regulations, and lower price than for cigarettes, and "an expanding customer base, many of whom are 'dual-users' of moist snuff and cigarettes."

New Smokeless Tobacco Product Marketing

In May 2006, RJR began test marketing Camel Snus in Portland, Oregon, and Austin, Texas, presenting it as a smoke-free, spit-free product in small pouches that originated in Sweden. A Camel Snus fact sheet said that as part of "direct-to-consumers (one-on-one)" marketing for Camel Snus at bars and nightclubs, those who wished "to participate in the promotion and receive communications from a tobacco company, will be given two tins of Camel Snus." At these marketing events, participants provided proof of age (most often a driver's license), which was scanned and used to generate mailing lists for Camel promotions, coupons, and other direct mail marketing.

The Camel Snus promotions appear to have shifted in focus from the traditional rural, blue-collar target markets to a more sophisticated, urban, professional market. Although the basic marketing strategies employed (giveaways, free samples, promotions, free tickets, etc.) have stayed fairly constant, the venues for these strategies have changed from rodeos, sports events, and car races to concerts and urban nightclubs.

Tobacco Company Webcasts and Conference Calls for Investors
In the 2007 annual analysts' day presentation for Reynolds American Inc (the parent company for RJR), Susan Ivey, chairman and CEO, stated that their strategic vision included positioning themselves as a "total tobacco company." Daan Delen, CEO of RJR Tobacco Co, stated, "Camel isn't just for smokers anymore," and explained that "consumer experience marketing"—in the form of one-on-one dialogue with consumers at retail outlets, bars, nightclubs, and Camel promotional events—was a focus for Camel Snus. "Consumer experience marketing" was described as "word of mouth marketing in retail, in bars, and in night clubs," which also allowed the company to respond to consumer feedback. Delen stated that RJR's snus product appealed mostly to smokers ("really, the adult smoker under thirty"), and that the product had some appeal to women, as about 15% of Camel Snus users in 2006 were women, whereas historically fewer than 10% of smokeless tobacco users were women. The 2007 presentation also included plans to improve Camel and other RJR brands' visibility at the retail level, with vertical and electronic displays, new Camel Snus packaging, and plans to use refrigerated display cases to help differentiate Camel Snus from moist snuff.

In concluding remarks, it was also stated that "RJR feels they are best in position to deal with the migration trends around smokers switching to alternative means in the face of indoor smoking restrictions, [and] a 3.5% decline in cigarette consumption." In a Reynolds American Inc third-quarter-earnings conference call on October 25, 2007, it was reported that RJR was pleased with responses from Camel Snus test markets, with "good repeat business," and that RJR planned to expand test marketing.

Discussion

Since the 1980s, cigarette companies have spent millions of dollars annually on consumer research for smokeless tobacco product development, marketing, and advertising. RJR and Philip Morris developed profiles of the demographics, lifestyles, attitudes, behavior patterns, and preferences of smokeless tobacco consumers; produced tailored product positioning statements, advertising copy, and message tone for these audiences; and took into account the media channel preferences of each group. They found that, historically, the heaviest use of smokeless tobacco products has been concentrated among low-income, blue-collar, less-educated, White adult males, with an increase in usage among active, outdoor-oriented males occurring in the 1990s.

RJR and Philip Morris also observed consumption pattern shifts in the 1990s, during changing social and legislative attitudes toward cigarettes and smokeless tobacco. Both companies have attempted to expand beyond the traditional user groups, and are currently test marketing cigarette-branded "smokeless, spitless" snus tobacco products that employ their most popular brand names (Camel and Marlboro) and appeal more to upscale, urban, and female users. The appearance and packaging of Camel Snus are unique: the product comes in an "oblong tin" (resembling a package of pocket mints) and is sold in refrigerated cases, whereas chewing tobacco has long been sold in round cans on convenience store shelves. Camel Snus is also sold in bars and clubs in most of the largest US metropolitan areas, including New York City, New York; Los Angeles, California; Miami, Florida; Washington, District of Columbia; Chicago, Illinois; Atlanta, Georgia and San Francisco, California.

In general, smokeless tobacco advertising has focused either on product characteristics or on establishing the image of the user. Although the primary venues for the new cigarette-branded smokeless tobacco advertising campaigns have changed from fishing tournaments and rodeos to urban bars and nightclubs, the core promotional elements are similar: event promotions and sponsorships, colorful packaging and free samples to promote trial by new users and to "teach" people how to use the product, coupons or "buy one, get one free" promotional offers at the point of sale, and hired spokespeople to "educate" consumers about the product one-on-one.

The new Camel Snus advertising emphasizes the novelty of snus and its Swedish origins; the Web site features a Swedish model who demonstrates how to translate Swedish phrases and "how to snus" "on the plane from Miami to L.A." or how to "snus while doing the samba." The Marlboro Snus Web site, on the other hand, mentions that snus was "invented in Sweden, perfected in Marlboro Country." The Camel Snus images appear to be more unisex and upscale, with a tone of glamour and sophistication (featuring scenes from Sweden, nightclubs, business meetings, and airplanes) than Marlboro Snus advertising. The Marlboro Snus marketing has a more masculine edge and highlights how one can use snus on "an adventure," on a road trip, or while fishing. Both the Camel and Marlboro Snus Web sites provide educational, step-by-step guides on "how to snus." [A] direct-mail piece . . . reads, "you can Snus virtually anywhere, from work to bars to trains to your fussy friend's party," and it emphasizes that "snus is NOT dip," suggesting that the targeted users are not already using spit tobacco.

With increasing denormalization of smoking and smoke-free policies, smokeless tobacco marketing messages have also shifted. The current focus for smokeless tobacco markets is on settings with clean indoor air laws. Throughout the 1980s, RJR's Specialty Tobacco Products advertising campaigns centered around messages that their moist snuff products provided a user with "the satisfaction that keeps you going while working hard," or "a way to enjoy outdoor activities for young energetic independent masculine men." The newest marketing messages promote new moist smokeless products as follows: as a way to enjoy indoor, social activities where one cannot smoke; as a product for smokers to use temporarily; as a trendy, popular, urban, sophisticated activity; and as a product for adventurous women and young men highly concerned with their image. Camel Snus is advertised as "pleasure for wherever" and Marlboro Snus is advertised as "flavor anytime." Both messages center on the promotion of tobacco use without restrictions.

Tobacco companies have a long history of developing initiation or "starter" products. Flavored smokeless tobacco products have consistently been perceived by current smokeless tobacco users as "for beginners" or a way to recruit younger men to try the product (e.g., Wintergreen refreshment positioning). RJR focus group research showed that flavored products were not popular among older or more experienced users, who saw them as being for beginners. In 2009, Camel Snus was available in Original, Frost, and Spice varieties, while Marlboro Snus was sold in Mild, Mint, Spice, and Rich flavors. Similarly, nicotine content was tailored to the user, with lower nicotine content continuing to be typically for starters or new users. Marlboro Snus is reported to contain very low levels of nicotine.

Current smokeless marketing strategies may undermine effective public health practice such as taxation, smoke-free policies, and the denormalization of tobacco use. The audience for the advertising and promotional activity of new snus products appears not to be inveterate smokers; instead, these messages are likely to encourage new users to try the products, and may lead smokers who would have quit tobacco use to defer quitting. Camel and Marlboro Snus advertisements may promote dual use of cigarettes and smokeless tobacco, with snus used as a temporary aid only where smoking is not permitted or acceptable. Dual use is a problem largely ignored by pro-snus advocates, but it leads to maintenance of smoking behavior and increased exposure to toxicants.

Cigarette advertising is associated with increased use, especially among youth. Results from a 2008 study indicate that youths' exposure to smokeless tobacco advertisements, through popular magazines with significant adolescent readership, has increased since 1998. A 1982 RJR marketing intelligence report includes quotes from articles relating to smokeless tobacco and states, "Rising popularity of smokeless tobacco can also be attributed to better advertising and new packaging," both of which are a major focus of the Camel Snus campaign today. Our study suggests that marketing activities appealing to new users or encouraging dual use, including distribution of free samples, "teaching" new consumers how to use the product, messages suggesting temporary smokeless product use, new flavors and low nicotine levels, and advertising that appeals to teens, such as sports sponsorship, should be curtailed to prevent increases in overall harm from tobacco use in the population. If public health researchers can gain understanding of snus marketing strategies and identify effective countermarketing messages soon, there is an opportunity to avoid a major expansion in smokeless tobacco use and avert a potential increase in dual use. The medical and public health communities need to be proactive to prevent this next phase of the tobacco epidemic.

POSTSCRIPT

Should Smokeless Tobacco Be Promoted as an Alternative to Cigarette Smoking?

To address the problem of cigarette smoking and the numerous health consequences associated with it, some people advocate that smokeless tobacco be promoted as an alternative. Britton and Edwards believe that smokeless tobacco causes less harm and should be explored as a means to get people from continuing their addiction to cigarettes. They maintain that cigarette smoking represents an economic burden to society and that everyone would benefit from a reduction in cigarette smoking. They believe that smokers are deprived of the right to choose safer alternatives if that information is withheld. In addition, smokers who switch to smokeless tobacco may eventually cease use of all tobacco products.

From the perspective of Mejia and Ling, promoting smokeless tobacco as an alternative to cigarette smoking would be a mistake because any tobacco use is harmful. They maintain that the risks of smokeless tobacco outweigh its benefits. Critics of smokeless tobacco believe that all tobacco use should be eliminated. Moreover, they see an ethical dilemma in promoting smokeless tobacco. Although the health dangers of smokeless tobacco may be less significant as compared with cigarette smoking, they feel that it is not a good alternative because it is addicting and carries health risks. Opponents to smokeless tobacco question whether the average person can distinguish between "safe" and "safer."

One concern of promoting smokeless tobacco is that some people may misinterpret its promotion as being a safe product. Marketing smokeless tobacco as a desirable alternative to cigarette smoking may give one the impression that it is safe. An additional concern is that the use of smokeless tobacco may lead to the use of other forms of tobacco. The use of any tobacco products, opponents argue, is antithetical to good health.

The concept of harm reduction is not new. For example, methadone has been given to heroin addicts as a way to wean them off heroin. Given drug addicts clean hypodermic needles as a way of preventing the spread of HIV/AIDS is another harm reduction strategy. Parents who agree to drive their children home after drinking alcohol, without interrogating their children, is a harm reduction strategy. Parents do not want their teenage children drinking alcohol, but they are also worried about their safety. When one balances out the pros and cons of giving children rides home after drinking, many parents opt for their children's safe return home. One weighs the relative harm of smokeless tobacco against that of cigarette smoking. Again, one is not in favor of a potentially unhealthy behavior, but one may be in favor of a less unhealthy behavior.

The extent of smokeless tobacco use is described in "Smokeless Tobacco Use, Initiation, and Relationship to Cigarette Smoking: 2002 to 2007" (*The NSDUH Report*, May 5, 2009). The merits of promoting smokeless tobacco as an alternative to cigarette smoking are discussed in "You Don't Smoke It, But It's Still Tobacco" (*Harvard Health Letter*, November 2007). Research regarding the switch from cigarettes to smokeless tobacco in the military was conducted by Robert C. Klesges and others in "Tobacco Use Harm Reduction, Elimination, and Escalation in a Large Military Cohort" (*American Journal of Public Health*, December 2010). The advertising of smokeless tobacco is the focus of "Under the Radar: Smokeless Tobacco Advertising in Magazine with Substantial Youth Readership," by Margaret Morrison, Dean Krugman, and Pumsoon Park (*American Journal of Public Health*, 2008).

ISSUE 15

Is Alcoholism Hereditary?

YES: Markus Heilig, from "Triggering Addiction," *The Scientist* (December 2008)

NO: Grazyna Zajdow, from "Alcoholism's Unnatural History: Alcoholism Is Not a Health Issue, But One of Personal and Existential Pain. Recognising This Would Force Us to Acknowledge One of the Most Successful Methods of Dealing With Alcohol Addiction," *Arena Magazine* (April–May 2004)

ISSUE SUMMARY

YES: Markus Heilig, Clinical Director of the National Institute on Alcohol Abuse and Alcoholism, argues that molecular changes in the brain result in positive reinforcement from alcohol. Heilig notes that alcoholism has a behavioral component, but certain genes may be responsible for individuals who abuse alcohol despite its adverse consequences.

NO: Grazyna Zajdow, a lecturer in sociology at Deakin University, maintains that the concept of alcoholism results from a social construct of what it means to be alcoholic. Because alcoholism is a social stigma, it is viewed as a disease rather than as a condition caused by personal and existential pain. Environmental conditions, especially consumerism, says Zajdow, are the root cause of alcoholism.

Alcoholism is a serious health problem throughout the world. The number of people with an addiction to alcohol surpasses the number of addicts of any other drug. Estimates from the National Institute on Alcohol Abuse and Alcoholism indicate that there are approximately 10 to 20 million alcoholics in the United States and millions more that are problem drinkers. Yet, it is not fully understood what determines a person's disposition to alcoholism. For years scientists have been reporting that there is a genetic tendency towards alcoholism. Research shows that there may exist specific biochemical and behavioral differences in the way sons and daughters of alcoholics respond to alcohol that may be a key to why these children are more prone to becoming addicted to or abusive of the drug.

Children of alcoholics have been consistently shown to have higher rates of alcoholism than children of nonalcoholics. Children of alcoholics are two to four times more likely to become alcoholic than children of nonalcoholic parents, according to the National Council on Alcoholism. Thus, alcoholism has been called a "family disease" because it tends to run in families.

The degree to which hereditary and biological risk factors make some individuals more likely candidates for addiction once they begin drinking is unknown. Psychological forces and environmental influences may also play a major role in predisposing one to alcoholism. Certainly, there is agreement among experts that a combination and interplay of all three of these factors—biological, psychological, and environmental—are responsible for alcoholic behaviors.

In one of the largest studies ever conducted on females and alcoholism, the *Journal of the American Medical Association* reports that heredity plays a major role in determining whether a woman becomes an alcoholic. Researchers found that genes do not automatically cause alcoholism, but they do account for 50 to 61 percent of a woman's risk of becoming an alcoholic. The report mirrors the results for men. Another research group found that college-aged sons of alcoholics tend to have a lower hormonal response to alcohol and feel less drunk when they drink too much when compared to young men whose parents are not alcoholic. And, many adoption and twin studies indicate a genetic predisposition to alcoholism among children of alcoholic parents.

Although many scientists and psychologists believe that there is a genetic component of alcoholism for many people, genetic theories are still inconclusive. Researchers have not identified a single gene that carries a predisposition to alcohol abuse. Some argue that risk factors for alcoholism cannot be translated directly into genetic and biological terms and that factors such as personality traits, values, individual needs, attitudes, family upbringing, peers, and other sociocultural influences in a person's life affect one's use or abuse of alcohol.

Studies of family members show (1) common causal factors that are shared among relatives and (2) risk factors that are unique to an individual family member's life experiences and environment. In addition to sharing genes, many family members share similar environments, customs, culture, diet, and patterns of behavior. The interaction of these factors may be the foundation for a pattern of alcoholism in the family or individual family member. Thus, the conclusion that the sole cause of alcoholism is genetic is viewed skeptically because there are too many other psychological and environmental factors that play a key role in the onset of alcoholism.

Markus Heilig argues that alcoholism has a genetic component and is not the result of family environment. He maintains that changes within the brain reinforce the overuse of alcohol that may lead to alcoholism. Grazyna Zajdow contends that alcoholism is not based on genetics but on society's view of what constitutes alcoholism. Zajdow argues that addictive drinking is a choice.

YES

Markus Heilig

Triggering Addiction

Alcohol abuse is the third leading preventable cause of death (defined as death due to lifestyle choice or modifiable behavior). In the United States alone it accounts for more than 75,000 deaths annually. To put it another way, if all cancers were miraculously cured tomorrow, those lives and the life years saved would be a drop in the bucket compared to what would be achieved by eliminating alcohol-related death and morbidity. In contrast to many other common conditions, alcohol abuse affects people whose life expectancy would otherwise be considerable, robbing them of an average 30 potential life years. The unmet medical needs are enormous.

And yet, as striking as these numbers are, they don't begin to capture the despair and sorrow of alcohol problems. I had been teaching students about the pharmacology of addictive drugs for several years before I met my first patient as a clinician. Knowing alcoholic patients, and understanding their day to day struggle has shaped my thinking about the problem and informed the questions I have asked in the laboratory.

Beyond the tragedy of this disease, there is also a fascination. What makes people set aside their most obvious needs and continue to abuse alcohol? Why do they do this despite knowing that it will kill them, harm them, or destroy the lives of those they love? This puzzle offers a window on what makes us humans tick, whether addicted or not.

Fermented beverages have been used since the Neolithic period, through ancient Egypt and China down to the present. Alcohol is the one drug that remains socially and legally acceptable in most of the Western world. I, along with more than half of the adult population, drink—personally I enjoy a good wine. Even though alcohol use disorders are among the most common serious medical conditions, they still only affect about 10% of those who use alcohol.

The disease is not just about drinking too much. Nor is it just about physical dependence characterized by an increased tolerance over time and severe withdrawal when use is stopped. Neither of these phenomena are necessary or sufficient to capture the disease.

At its core, alcoholism is a behavioral disorder. Cravings lead to a narrowed behavioral repertoire, so that seeking and consuming the drug crowds out other normal behaviors. Then there is the loss of control that results in someone planning on having one glass of wine, but ending up passed out on the couch. The combination of craving, loss of control and impaired judgment results in compulsive use, despite an intimate knowledge of the harmful effects. For most—but not all—who reach this state, a return to moderation seems difficult if not impossible.

Modern approaches to treating this disease have focused on the behaviors associated with alcoholism. They help patients develop a set of skills to recognize and avoid situations carrying a high risk of relapse. Such situations involve stressors, primarily of a social nature, and exposure to alcohol-associated cues, such as environments and people. Although treatments based on these principles are clearly documented to provide some benefit, two-thirds of patients still relapse within a one-year period. So, while good behavioral methods should be available to patients, it is also painfully clear that we need something beyond that.

Thankfully, we are finally learning something about the molecular basis of the behavior and compulsion of alcoholism.

In the early 1990s, Charles O'Brien at the University of Pennsylvania, and later Stephanie O'Malley at Yale University, made a breakthrough. They showed that the opioid receptor blocker, naltrexone, could help prevent relapse to heavy drinking in alcohol-dependent patients. The logic, which has gathered considerable support since, goes like this: When you drink, your brain releases endogenous opioid-like substances, called endorphins. These act on opioid receptors and give the sensation of pleasure or, in psychological lingo, "positive reinforcement" of the effects of alcohol. The enjoyment of alcohol has long been thought important in driving excessive drinking. Naltrexone blocks the opioid signaling chain, helping make drinking less pleasant.

There had been some controversy regarding the efficacy of naltrexone, and not every study had replicated its beneficial actions. But 15 years and some 30 controlled studies later, there could be no question: Once all the data were put into a meta-analysis, it was clear that naltrexone could provide a benefit. However, the magnitude of the effect was not very impressive, leading some to dismiss the value of naltrexone as a treatment.

I always looked at opioid-mediated stimulation by alcohol with some degree of skepticism. Remember your high school or college class? There were always two or three guys who danced on the table, and did crazy things when they drank alcohol. Look closer and you'll find that many of them have a family history of alcoholism, and got in trouble themselves down the line. But the rest of us were more likely to experience a welcome relief of tension, followed, at higher doses, by an irresistible desire to fall asleep on the couch. Among that majority, quite a few still developed alcohol use disorders. And even among the people who started out by getting the characteristic kick out of alcohol, 10 years into alcoholism there is little if any pleasure or stimulation left. Clearly, there had to be other mechanisms at play in the development and maintenance of alcoholism besides chasing the buzz.

Clinicians began to notice that naltrexone had certain limitations, and that these matched broad behavior categories. In some patients, the treatment turns their lives around. For the majority, however, you'd have to work hard to convince yourself there was any effect at all.

These days, whenever a basic researcher sees these kinds of individual differences, we think "genetics." In this case, there was a particular reason to do so. Ten years ago, Mary-Jeanne Kreek at the Rockefeller University found genetic variation at the locus encoding the μ-opioid receptor, or OPRM1—the target for naltrexone's therapeutic action. Among Caucasians, about 15% carry at least one copy of a variant that might change the function of the receptor to make carriers more susceptible to both alcoholism and naltrexone therapy.

While researchers still debate what the variant does on the molecular level, carriers of the variant allele consistently experience more of a subjective high in response to alcohol. Human laboratory studies in which the effects of alcohol intake can be directly assessed are limited in the amount of alcohol that can be given to subjects. However, a functionally equivalent variant of OPRM1 has been found in rhesus macaques. Studies in our own program at the National Institute on Alcohol Abuse and Alcoholism (NIAAA) spearheaded by Christina Barr showed that carriers of the rhesus ORPM1 allele variant were much more stimulated by high doses of alcohol, and that these carriers—but not other monkeys—voluntarily consumed alcohol to intoxication when given the opportunity. This work suggests that pleasure-mediated reward from alcohol plays a particularly important role in carriers of the OPRM1 variant. A recent NIAAA sponsored COMBINE trial led by Raymond Anton, confirmed what had been suggested a few years ago by David Oslin and Charles O'Brien at the University of Pennsylvania. It showed that only carriers of the variant receptor benefit from naltrexone treatment. And that minority benefits quite a bit: Twice as many in that group achieved a good clinical outcome when treated with naltrexone compared to placebo.

We had a gene that contributed to differences in alcohol responses, and a drug that could treat the disease pharmacologically. But we had only scratched the surface. What happens in the brains of alcoholics in whom this mechanism is not driving the process?

In the last five years or so, research in experimental animals has shown that the brain undergoes long-term changes as a result of repeated exposure to cycles of pronounced intoxication and withdrawal. Data are consistent between our own laboratory, and those of George Koob at the Scripps Research Institute in La Jolla, Calif., George Breese at the University of North Carolina, Chapel Hill, and Howard Becker at the Medical University of South Carolina in Charleston.

The brain pathology induced by a history of dependence has three key features. One, a history of dependence established through repeated cycles of excessive alcohol intake and withdrawal leads to a long lasting, perhaps lifelong pattern of excessive alcohol intake. Two, there is an equally persistent increase in responses to fear and stress. Three, while stress doesn't affect voluntary alcohol intake in non-dependent animals, it does so potently in animals with a history of dependence.

These findings are closely in line with patient reports and clinical experience. Some of them have already been translated into human studies. For instance, exaggerated responsiveness of brain stress and fear systems in human alcoholics has been shown by Dan Hommer's group in our program.

This suggests that long-term neuro-adaptations occur in the alcohol-addicted brain which provide a very different motivation for relapse than the pleasure-seeking response of those who have that genetic susceptibility. In the absence of alcohol, the individual will now find himself in a negative emotional state, which in the short term can be relieved by renewed intake of alcohol. The big question is what underlying biology is driving this shift into what George Koob has labeled "the dark side of addiction."

Since stress and fear are at the core of this new model of alcoholism, we started to look for molecular targets within the neural circuitry of stress. Our best bet was corticotropin releasing hormone (CRH). Discovered in 1982 by Wylie Vale, CRH is now in every medical textbook as the top-level control signal for the hormonal stress response. Much less recognized was the fact that extensive CRH systems within the brain mediate behavioral stress responses that are in concert with, but distinct from the physiological stress effects. A key target for this extrahypothalamic CRH is the amygdala complex, and studies from many laboratories have shown that CRH acting on CRH1 receptors within this structure mediate many behavioral stress responses.

Our recent work has shown that a history of alcohol dependence leads to a persistent up-regulation of CRH1 receptor gene expression and binding within the amygdala. This is exactly the type of molecular plasticity we would expect to see in response to stress and stress-driven excessive alcohol intake. But of course the gene expression data are only correlative. The only way to demonstrate causality is by pharmacology: Only if a CRH1 antagonist rescues the behavioral phenotype of post-dependent animals, that is, makes them normal again, would causality be demonstrated. Working with colleagues at Eli Lilly, we were able to show just that. George Koob's group verified the finding using several other antagonists for the CRH1 receptor. All these molecules have the same signature: They don't do anything to non-dependent animals with low alcohol intake levels, but totally eliminate the excessive drinking that occurs in the post-dependent state.

Based on these observations, the CRH1 receptor appeared to be a very promising target for treatment of the "dark," relief-driven alcoholism. Human trials are now in the planning stages to test this prediction, but continue to face extensive obstacles with regard to the chemistry and toxicology. For instance, making molecules that will dissolve and enter the brain after having been taken as a pill, has turned out to be hard nut to crack.

While investigating the properties of CRH, we badly wanted to find some tool that would allow us to test these ideas in humans sooner. The answer came in the form of a category of compounds that had been collecting dust on many pharmaceutical companies' shelves for years. Substance P (SP), an 11 amino acid peptide discovered by Nobel Prize winner Ulf von Euler back in the 1930s, had for many years been implicated in pain and inflammation. In 1991 researchers at Pfizer developed a small molecule that blocked the main human SP receptor for the transmission of pain, called the neurokinin 1 receptor (NK1R). This was followed by the discovery of several other chemical series that successfully targeted this receptor. But to the disappointment of many, these turned out to be ineffective in treating any pain or inflammation-related clinical condition you can imagine.

Several research groups showed that SP is released in both rat and human amygdala upon exposure to stress, and mediates at least some behavioral effects of the stressor. In fact, several of the effects were identical to those induced by CRH, although its actions were not as general as those of CRH, and less pronounced. It was clear that these were converging systems that generated the same functional outcomes. Jokingly, we started calling SP "CRH light." We realized that an NK1R antagonist might allow us to assess some of our ideas and experimental approaches in humans.

What followed was a rare experience. By any measure we applied, the predictions held up. Mouse mutants that lacked the NK1R drank markedly lower amounts of alcohol, and didn't seem to obtain any reward from this drug. Moving into humans, we treated a group of recently detoxified alcoholics with an orally available, brain penetrating NK1R antagonist for three weeks. Treated subjects had fewer alcohol cravings, and reported markedly improved overall well-being when evaluated weekly by a blinded physician who followed a standard assessment questionnaire. During a challenge session, we mimicked a real-life situation with a high relapse risk: A social stressor, followed by exposure to handling and smelling a preferred alcoholic beverage. This procedure induces powerful craving in placebo-treated subjects, but those responses were markedly suppressed in patients given the NK1R blocker. In parallel with the suppressed cravings, we also found a marked suppression of the hormonal stress-response.

Surprisingly, we could see some of the most striking effects using functional magnetic resonance imaging (fMRI). By looking at the degree of oxygen use, fMRI can visualize activity of neurons in response to various stimuli. As expected based on prior work, placebo-treated alcoholics had exaggerated activation of brain circuits that process negative emotions when presented with unpleasant or scary pictures. This was particularly pronounced in the insula, a region of the brain that has been associated both with perception of aversive experience and with drug cravings. These negative responses were almost eliminated by the treatment. Conversely, placebo treated subjects had all but absent brain responses to pleasant pictures, which otherwise typically activate brain reward circuitry. Remarkably, when treated with the NK1R blocker, the patients could once again respond to pleasant stimuli.

That brain responses to aversive stimuli were dampened by an anti-stress treatment was according to our hypothesis. But the ability of the anti-stress treatment to restore reward responses was an interesting surprise. It is typically thought that stress and reward are mediated through distinct systems. Based on our findings, it would appear that there is cross-talk between the two.

NK1R antagonists are now heading into full-scale outpatient treatment trials. As promising as the early data appear, one should remember that drug development is a high stakes game. Even having reached this stage, only about 10–20% of candidates succeed. With very few exceptions, medical progress is incremental. There is no single achievement one could say has cured childhood cancer. Yet when the outcomes of 20 years ago are compared with those of today, survival has improved dramatically. The same will happen with alcoholism, and we are only in the early days of improving outcomes.

Once the new treatments are developed, a key challenge remains. Alcoholism is a chronic relapsing disease, not unlike asthma, diabetes or hypertension. None of these conditions may be possible to cure, but they can all be successfully managed. Our ability to do so will improve as the range of therapeutics expands, and knowledge about mechanisms allows us to tailor treatment to the specific characteristics of the individual patient. But for all of this to succeed, the naïve notion that alcoholism can be cured in a 28-day rehab session has to give way to a realization that our brains undergo complex and long-lasting changes in addiction.

Grazyna Zajdow  **NO**

Alcoholism's Unnatural History: Alcoholism Is Not a "Health" Issue, But One of Personal and Existential Pain. Recognising This Would Force Us to Acknowledge One of the Most Successful Methods of Dealing With Alcohol Addiction

Watching former Tasmanian premier Jim Bacon on TV, resigning himself to continuing a course of palliative care for lung cancer and urging young Australians not to be "idiots" and smoke, reminds one that there is such a thing as addiction. Bacon prefers to say he was stupid rather than addicted. And this is to a substance that is not mind-altering!

This example gives us an interesting view of how we deal with addictive substances on a social and personal level. Addiction is a problem for the late modern world because it questions the very basis of consumption and choice. In a wider social world, choice is everything; for the addict, choice can be death. Yet the Australian response to addiction is marked by ambivalence, particularly in the case of addiction to alcohol. Despite the widespread acknowledgement of the serious nature of this social problem, the attitude to one of the most successful ways of dealing with alcoholism—through Alcoholics Anonymous—is often one of downright antagonism. As a sociologist who reads the literature on addictions and problematic drug use, I often wonder why—and here I will try to unravel the mystery.

The most prominent narrative of addiction in the last few years in Australia and other places is the narrative of social construction. This narrative presents drug use as an integral part of the social world and cuts it loose from biology and physiology. Addiction only exists if there is a stigmatised role of "addict." Without this deviant category there would not be a notion of addiction. Thomas de Quincey wrote about his seventeen-year addiction to opium and even lengthier time with laudanum. He could write so openly because

From *Arena* Magazine, issue 70, April/May 2004, pp. 41–43. Copyright © 2004 by Arena Magazine.

there was no notion of addiction as a stigmatised social category at the time, but what he described was addiction nonetheless.

There is also the postmodern, discursive view of addiction as an extension of social constructionism. Discourses of addiction, in this view, are part of the Foucauldian notion of disciplinary power and knowledge. The addict is part of the "web of power" that plugs him/her into a network that constrains and limits the individual. This is a particularly abstract notion of addiction that rarely admits to material reality of the individual body, or even the social body. This narrative comes not from the sociological study of the experience of addiction, but cultural studies research on written texts such as the book *What's Wrong with Addiction* by Helen Keane.

These narratives of addiction often merge and become entangled in academic discussions. Combine these with the antagonism-towards-the-disease model of addiction that is sometimes—erroneously in my view—linked to Temperance and Prohibition and we might get an idea of why AA and its models have had such bad press, particularly on the social welfare Left. Take a typical example from a major textbook called *Drug Use in Australia,* in which one chapter refers to the AA model of addiction as the grand narrative of the "alcoholic as sinner." The evidence the authors present is one person's reported statements in an AA meeting from another academic text! Another chapter presents it as a disease model of addiction—but nowhere in the text is any of the large-scale and in-depth studies of AA referred to.

I would argue that the fundamental fact about alcoholism must be that this problem lies in the individual body as much as the social body and it is experienced as a highly individual pain. This pain is materially real and cannot be explained away as a form of discourse, amenable to the linguistic contortions of postmodernity or dismissed as simply a social construction. Alcoholics are different from non-alcoholics. The difference is not easy to distinguish— it only really becomes apparent in its most extreme manifestations—but it is there. I cannot say that my first drink of alcohol changed my life—I cannot even remember it—but I know plenty of alcoholics who say just that. They remember their first drink and how it made them feel. For some who always believed they were different or outsiders, their first drink made them feel part of humanity. For others, their natural shyness disappeared and they became loquacious and humorous. Again others just drank themselves into a stupor from the first moment because they hated the world so much and never seemed to leave this state, at least not until the pain became too great and they permanently left this world.

The sociologist Norman Denzin, in his opus *The Alcoholic Society,* wrote that every alcoholic he talked to drank "to escape an inner emptiness of self." Of course, many of us experience an inner emptiness at many times of our lives, but what Denzin talks about is an emptiness which is a constant. For Denzin, the "alcoholic self" is constantly in search of fulfilment through alcohol, but alcohol just pushes the alcoholic further away from him/herself and all others. No drug or cognitive therapy produces permanent fulfilment—only sobriety through the experience of likeminded others. One could suggest that the divided self produced by alcoholism precedes the first drink, and an existential pain must exist which is married to some physiological and biochemical response to alcohol. There is some genetic component, but what it is and how it works is not understood, and it is unlikely that any pharmaceutical therapy can ever offer a solution—though medical experts, along with pharmaceutical companies are always hinting at the possibility. For Denzin, the answer to the individual alcoholic's pain is the community of others, specifically the community of alcoholics. He is talking, of course, about Alcoholics Anonymous.

A Parallel World

Many years ago, I worked as a youth worker in what was known as the Community Youth Support Scheme. We worked out of an old house, but there was one room that we did not use and which was generally locked. One day I had to go in to do something and I felt that I had stumbled on the meeting room of a secret order, like the Masons. What struck me at first was the terrible odour of tobacco (this was in the days when we could smoke absolutely anywhere) and then I noticed the banners on the wall. They were full of strange language which included the terms God, higher power and surrender. It looked to me as if I had fallen through a hole in the floor and found myself in a parallel world. My stoned friends and I lived off jokes about it for years.

Thus, as a sociologist and a materialist, feminist and atheist, my first AA meeting—which I attended as a non-alcoholic—came as a shock to me. I imagined it had to be a cult, that it produced automatons who were close to born-again Christians. For me, the answer to alcohol and drug problems was to sweep away poverty and inequality; the social and personal body were indistinguishable—what was good for one was equally good for the other. After listening to the unmediated stories of pain, anguish and redemption, I came to believe that I was wrong. Not that poverty and inequality should not be swept away, but that alcoholism would be swept away with them. However, I did meet many stalwarts of the Left in those AA meetings and stalwarts they stayed. I know academics, unionists, politicians, writers, folk singers, musos from the 1970s who regularly maintain their sober conditions through AA. To get to this position and stay in AA, these people had to cross a line that would have been unimaginable, and the only explanation can be the intense, existential pain they experienced when they drank.

Many, whatever the drug of choice had originally been, ended up drinking themselves into oblivion. It may only have been because alcohol was the cheapest and most freely available. There are many paths into addiction and many different categories of addicts. In the end, I never truly understood what they were doing or what they were feeling. I could not understand, ever. I am not like them. I do not feel their pain, I could never cause pain to people the way they did, and nothing I do could ease their suffering. I suspect this is one of the reasons there is such a distrust of AA and its notion of alcoholism—that alcoholism produces a different category of individual, one not amenable to the niceties of living in the world as nonaddicts might do.

But I do know people who are like them. They come together in rooms (no longer smoke-ridden) and recite a prayer at the end of their meetings. Most of them have found some kind of religious understanding; many are still atheists; but all have some form of spiritual fulfilment. Those meetings are more egalitarian than almost any other community they may belong to, although sexism and racism still exist to some extent.

Here people seek to change the way they live in the world and it is a change in morality, as much as in alcohol consumption. We may find the way that television has taken up this public confession distasteful, but the AA meeting is not an episode of Oprah—it is not a mediated televisual experience. To the same extent as any conversation, it is unmediated. It also demands an ethical understanding of individual experience. Obviously some people are better at it than others. An old AA saying is that a sober horse-thief is still a horse-thief.

There are many well-known people who admit to membership of AA. Even in death, however, many people's friends and relatives often refuse to acknowledge the importance of AA in their lives. It is as if acknowledging AA is a recognition that some things (like sobriety) are more important than motherhood or friendship or other social roles.

Why are we so reluctant to recognise this state of addiction that some people find themselves in? There are strong cultural and economic forces that make alcoholism almost impossible to speak about. To recognise it would mean having to do something about it. In Australia at the moment, it would mean having to deal with the availability of help to overcome the problems of drunkenness, and it would mean facing up to the key issue of whether it should be portrayed to any degree as a "health" issue. While it has health consequences, it is not a health issue; it is an issue of personal and existential pain. Even after his public humiliation, Democrats leader Andrew Bartlett would not admit to an alcohol problem. He called it instead a "health" problem. More people are now willing to admit to problems with depression but few mention that they have been compulsively drinking a depressant for most of their adult lives. They are happy to admit to Prozac but not the sobriety (or lack of).

It is more than likely that it is a cultural distrust of AA, its religiosity and its American influence, that keeps many antagonistic to it. Ultimately, one of the most powerful arguments in AA's favour is that it works. A sixty-year follow-up by the writer George Vaillant—carried out fifteen years after the release of his *The Natural History of Alcoholism,* which looked at American men with clear alcohol problems in the 1940s—found that those who were still alive were most likely to be abstinent.

Beyond that, most alcohol-related problems in Australia are not connected to alcoholism or addiction, but to drunkenness and its consequences. Indeed, alcoholics or chronic heavy drinkers make up between 5 and 15 percent of the drinking population. Mixed with aggressive forms of masculinity, drunkenness contributes to all forms of violent crime, from the minor altercation in the pub between drunken bulls, to domestic assault and then to deaths of all sorts. It does not matter whether it is used as a form of excuse or "time-out"—without the intoxicating effects of alcohol, violent crime would be much reduced.

Large and small epidemiological studies show quite clearly that the cheaper and more readily available the alcohol is, and the greater the number of alcohol outlets, the greater the problems that exist. Some cultural factors may ameliorate or enhance its worst effects, but the reality is that humans, especially those in societies which are based on endless consumerism, will endlessly consume alcohol and other intoxicating substances. Attempting to minimise its most harmful effects without dealing with supply is to park an ambulance at the bottom of the cliff. I am not saying we should not provide the ambulance, but we cannot pretend that it is anything more than that. It is here that the abstract nature of academic discussions combines with libertarian constructions of personal choice. Resistance, then, to the restriction of the supply of alcohol means that we are really unable to effectively deal with the worst aspects of alcohol consumption.

POSTSCRIPT

Is Alcoholism Hereditary?

Is there a significant, substantiated relationship between heredity and alcoholism? The National Institute on Alcohol Abuse and Alcoholism (NIAAA) notes that numerous studies demonstrate a high probability of biological vulnerability to alcohol addiction. The NIAAA claims that there are differences in the brains of alcoholics compared to others. Critics agree that alcoholism runs in families, but they argue that there are critical environmental and psychological risk factors for alcoholism that cannot be overlooked. In the final analysis, this issue comes down to which research one chooses to accept.

Some experts have expressed concern for certain people who feel that alcoholism is a family legacy. An individual who believes that he or she is destined to become an alcoholic because his or her mother, father, aunt, uncle, or grandparent has suffered from alcoholism may become alcoholic to satisfy a self-fulfilling prophecy. Some psychologists believe this may have lamentable consequences for such individuals who feel that alcoholism is their destiny anyway. Although it is true that alcoholism tends to run in families, most children of alcoholics do not become alcoholics. A person whose parent or parents were alcoholic should be more wary of the possibility of becoming an alcoholic, but becoming an alcoholic is not a foregone conclusion for children of alcoholics.

Whether or not alcoholism is genetic or environmental has serious implications. For example, if a genetic predisposition to alcoholism was conclusively proven, then medical therapies could be designed to help those who had the hereditary risk. Second, if a person was diagnosed as having a genetic predisposition, then he or she could adopt behaviors that would help avoid problem drinking. That is, they would become aware of the hereditary factor and adjust their attitudes and actions accordingly. If alcoholism is environmental, then one's environment could be altered to influence drinking behavior.

Because of the lack of conclusive evidence identifying heredity as the primary cause for alcoholism, it may be wise to err on the side of caution with regard to consigning children of alcoholics to a fate of alcoholism. On the other hand, research that consistently finds higher rates of alcoholism and alcohol abuse among children of alcoholics cannot be dismissed. This link alone provides ample support for additional funding of research studies that may delineate the exact nature of and risk factors of alcoholism. Still, efforts against the perils of alcoholism via progressive alcohol prevention and education programs to meet the needs of children of alcoholics as well as the general public need to be strengthened.

Two technical publications from the National Institute on Alcohol Abuse and Alcoholism (NIAAA) that discuss the hereditary viability of alcoholism are "The Genetics of Alcohol and Other Drug Dependence" by Danielle Dick and Arpana Agrawal (2008) and "Systems Genetics of Alcoholism" by Chantel Sloan, Vicki Sayarath, and Jason Moore (2008). A less technical article that reviews the hereditary basis of alcoholism is "Unraveling the Genetics of Alcoholism" by Patrick Perry (*The Saturday Evening Post*, 2007). The psychosocial effects of alcoholism are examined in "Alcohol and the Burden of Disease" by Walter Gubinat (*Addiction Research and Theory*, December 2008).

ISSUE 16

Should Marijuana Be Approved for Medical Use?

YES: Peter J. Cohen, from "Medical Marijuana 2010: It's Time to Fix the Regulatory Vacuum," *Journal of Law, Medicine & Ethics* (Fall 2010)

NO: Drug Enforcement Administration, from *The DEA Position on Marijuana* (July 2010)

ISSUE SUMMARY

YES: Peter Cohen argues that the federal argument has thwarted attempts to study the medicinal benefits of marijuana. Cohen refers to scientific studies in which marijuana has shown to be safe and effective in controlling nausea, relieving spasticity caused by multiple sclerosis, ameliorating certain types of pain, and reducing weight loss associated with AIDS.

NO: The Drug Enforcement Administration (DEA) states that marijuana has not been proven to have medical utility. The DEA cites the positions of the American Medical Association, the American Cancer Society, the American Academy of Pediatrics, and the National Multiple Sclerosis Society to support its position. The DEA feels that any benefits of medicinal marijuana are outweighed by its drawbacks.

Numerous states have passed referenda to legalize marijuana for medical purposes. Despite the position of these voters, however, the federal government does not support the medical use of marijuana, and federal laws take precedence over state laws. A major concern of opponents of these referenda is that legalization of marijuana for medicinal purposes will lead to its use for recreational purposes.

Marijuana's medicinal qualities have been recognized for centuries. Marijuana was utilized medically as far back as 2737 B.C., when Chinese emperor Shen Nung recommended marijuana, or cannabis, for medical use. By the 1890s some medical reports had stated that cannabis was useful as a pain reliever. However, despite its historical significance, the use of marijuana for medical treatment is still a widely debated and controversial topic.

Marijuana has been tested in the treatment of glaucoma, asthma, convulsions, epilepsy, and migraine headaches, and in the reduction of nausea, vomiting, and loss of appetite associated with chemotherapy treatments. Many medical professionals and patients believe that marijuana shows promise in the treatment of these disorders and others, including spasticity in amputees and multiple sclerosis. Yet others argue that there are alternative drugs and treatments available that are more specific and effective in treating these disorders than marijuana and that marijuana cannot be considered a medical replacement.

Because of the conflicting viewpoints and what many people argue is an absence of reliable, scientific research supporting the medicinal value of marijuana, the drug and its plant materials remain in Schedule I of the Controlled Substances Act of 1970. This act established five categories, or schedules, under which drugs are classified according to their potential for abuse and their medical usefulness, which in turn determines their availability. Drugs classified under Schedule I are those that have a high potential for abuse and no scientifically proven medical use. Many marijuana proponents have called for the Drug Enforcement Administration (DEA) to move marijuana from Schedule I to Schedule II, which classifies drugs as having a high potential for abuse but also having an established medical use. A switch to Schedule II would legally allow physicians to utilize marijuana and its components in certain treatment programs. To date, however, the DEA has refused.

Currently, marijuana is used medically but not legally. Most of the controversy surrounds whether marijuana and its plant properties are indeed of medical value and whether the risks associated with its use outweigh its proposed medical benefits. Research reports and scientific studies have been inconclusive. Some physicians and many cancer patients say that marijuana greatly reduces the side effects of chemotherapy. Many glaucoma patients believe that marijuana use has greatly improved their condition. In view of these reports by patients and the recommendations by some physicians to allow inclusion of marijuana in treatment, expectations have been raised with regard to marijuana's worth as a medical treatment.

Marijuana opponents argue that the evidence in support of marijuana as medically useful suffers from far too many deficiencies. The DEA, for example, believes that studies supporting the medical value of marijuana are scientifically limited, based on biased testimonies of ill individuals who have used marijuana and their families and friends, and grounded in the unscientific opinions of certain physicians, nurses, and other hospital personnel. Furthermore, marijuana opponents feel that the safety of marijuana has not been established by reliable scientific data weighing marijuana's possible therapeutic benefits against its known negative effects.

In the following selections, Peter J. Cohen notes that marijuana has a long history of medicinal use. He asserts that the federal government is unfairly putting up roadblocks which would validate marijuana's medicinal value. The Drug Enforcement Agency (DEA) argues that marijuana should not be used for legal medical purposes because the current research on marijuana's medicinal benefits is inconclusive. Other drugs are available that preclude the need to use marijuana.

YES

Peter J. Cohen

Medical Marijuana 2010: It's Time to Fix the Regulatory Vacuum

Washington, D.C.'s City Council has recently taken the first step towards legalizing the use of "medical marijuana" in accordance with the provisions of the *Legalization of Marijuana for Medical Treatment Initiative of 1998* (*Initiative 59*). This action was not overruled by the United States Congress within the 30–day deadline imposed by the District of Columbia's Home Rule Statute. The Council is now crafting regulations that will govern the therapeutic and palliative use of this drug with the goal of avoiding some of the problems faced by the other states that have legalized medical marijuana; however, the proposed rules do not establish criteria for legitimate medical practice when medical marijuana is recommended (discussed *infra*). If the enabling regulations are passed by the D.C. Council and not rejected by the Congress, the District of Columbia will join over one-quarter of the states in legalizing medical marijuana (Table 1). On the other hand, if the D.C. Council fails to act favorably on the final regulations (or if Congress nullifies the Council's approval), then the effective legalization of medical marijuana will die and not be reconsidered until next year.

In either case, the fact that legalizing medical marijuana in the nation's capital has moved so far has great symbolic weight. Thus, it is appropriate at this time to take stock of the scientific value of marijuana for medical use, the reluctance of several federal agencies to evaluate its safety and efficacy in treating (curing, ameliorating, or palliating) certain illness, and the significant policy issues raised by state legalization of medical marijuana—legalization to date unaccompanied, for the most part, by appropriate regulations based on sound science and careful policy development. This state statutory and regulatory vacuum needs to be addressed if marijuana is to become a safe and efficacious component of the medical armamentarium of the United States in the coming years.

Congress Has Declared Marijuana to Be an Unsafe and Ineffective Drug

Marijuana is currently classified by the federal government as a Schedule I controlled substance with no value as a therapeutic agent, a designation that normally requires scientific evaluation and input before being imposed.

From *Journal of Law, Medicine and Ethics*, Fall 2010, pp. 654–666. Copyright © 2010 by American Society of Law, Medicine & Ethics. Reprinted by permission of Wiley-Blackwell via Rightslink.

Table 1[A]

Jurisdictions Legalizing Marijuana for Medical Purposes

Adopted	Year Statute	Jurisdiction
Alaska[B]	1998	Stat. §11.71.090
Arizona[B]	1996	Ariz.Rev.Stat.Ann. §13-3412.01 [A]—Not implementedC
California[B]	1996	Cal. Health & Safety Code Ann. §11362.5
Colorado[B]	2000	Colo. Const. Art. XVIII §4
District of Columbia[E]	2009	Initiative 59 (pending implementing legislation)
Hawaii[B]	2000	Rev. Stat. §§329-121 to 329-128
Maine[B]	1999	Me.Rev.Stat.Ann. tit.22 §1102 or 2382-B[5]
Michigan[D]	2008	Comp. Law §333.26421-Comp. Law §333.26430 (2008)
Montana[B]	2004	Mont.Code Ann. §§50-46-101 to 50-46-210
Nevada[B]	2000	Nev.Rev.Stat.Ann.§§453A.010 to 453A.400
New Jersey[E]	2010	Compassionate Use Medical Marijuana Act (S119;A804)
New Mexico[D]	2007	N.M.Stat.Ann. §30-3IC-I (2007)
Oregon[B]	1998	Ore.Rev.Stat. §§475.300 to 475.346
Rhode Island[D]	2006	R.I. Gen. Laws §1-21-28.6 (2006)
Vermont[B]	2004	VtStat.Ann.tit. 18.§§4472-4474d
Washington State[B]	1998	Wash.Rev.Code Ann. §§69.51 A.005-69.51 A.902

References to Table 1

[A] "Medical Marijuana: ProCon. Org," *available at* <http://medicalmarijuana.procon.org/view.resource.php?resourceID=000881> (last visited July 30, 2010). See also D.E. Hoffmann and E. Weber, "Medical Marijuana and the Law," *New England Journal of Medicine* 362 (2010): 1453-1457, at 1455-1456.

[B] Cong. Research Serv., 109th Cong: Review and Analysis of Federal and State Policies 12-13 & n.44 (2005), *available at* <http://digital.library.unt.edu/govdocs/crs/permalink/meta-crs-8244:1>.

[C] A. Riley and A. Crawford, "Voters Might Get Another Shot at Medical Marijuana," *available at* <http://stoparrestingpatients.org/home/news/5/voters-might-get-another-shot-medical-marijuana> (last visited August 3, 2010). Although the 1996 measure passed with approximately 65 percent of the vote, it does not have the force of law since the initiative allowed patients to use marijuana only if they had a *prescription* from a doctor, not just a *recommendation*. However, marijuana's classification as a schedule 1 controlled substance precludes physicians from *prescribing* it since this classification designates marijuana to be a harmful drug without medical value.

[D] Active State Medical Marijuana Programs, *available at* <http://norml.org/index.cfm?Group_ID=3391> (last visited August 3, 2010).

[E] Marijuana Policy Project *available at* <http://www.mpp.org/states/district-of-columbia/> (last visited August 3, 2010).

[F] State of New Jersey, 213th Legislature, *available at* <http://www.njleg.state.nj.us/2008/bills/a 1000/804_il.pdf> (last visited August 3, 2010). An excellent overview of requirements for patient registration is provided by D. E. Hoffmann and E. Weber, "Medical Marijuana and the Law," *New England Journal of Medicine* 362 (2010): 1453-1457, at 1454:

The laws vary in terms of whether they establish a registry and issue identification cards for qualifying patients. Eleven of the 14 states have a registry, and Maine and New Jersey will soon. In most states where patients have identification cards, they are protected from arrest and prosecution. In some states, however, registered patients with identification cars may be arrested but can use the defense that they have demonstrated medical need for marijuana.

However, the usual review process under the Controlled Substances Act was bypassed when Congress itself assigned this status to marijuana. In addition to declaring that marijuana has no value as a therapeutic agent, this designation significantly impeded research into the therapeutic and palliative uses of the drug, since this requires investigators to obtain a special license from the Drug Enforcement Agency (DEA) before they may undertake any clinical investigations of marijuana and indirectly calls upon the National Institutes of Drug Abuse (NIDA) to provide marijuana for such studies. These requirements, as well as financial and political considerations, have proven to be major roadblocks to investigators' ability to conduct scientific studies of the potential medical utility of *Cannabis*.

Federal agencies have been loathe to allow well-qualified scientists to evaluate the medical uses of marijuana. For example, in the 1990s, Dr. Donald Abrams, a physician and professor of medicine at the University of California, San Francisco, made numerous attempts to study the efficacy of smoked marijuana in treating weight loss associated with the AIDS-wasting syndrome. His research protocol (Investigational New Drug No. 43,542) was fully funded by the University of California; and had been approved by the FDA; the University of California, San Francisco's, Institutional Review Board; the California Research Advisory Panel; and the scientific advisory committee of the San Francisco Community Consortium. Nonetheless, the DEA refused to permit Dr. Abrams to import marijuana from the Netherlands and the NIDA rejected his request for access to its own supply of *Cannabis* that was grown specifically for research purposes. In view of Abrams' desire to conduct *bona fide* scientific research, rather than rely on anecdotal reports, a far more appropriate federal response would have been to facilitate his investigation. As a group of commentators has stated:

> Given the limited sources of support for research on marijuana (pharmaceutical companies, for example, are not interested in supporting such research), the U.S. government by now should have taken note of the increasingly persuasive therapeutic claims and sponsored its own clinical trials through the National Institutes of Health. Instead, as . . . the handling of Dr. Abram's protocol indicate[s], the government has responded by . . . creating obstacles that make the research impossible to pursue.

These actions by federal agencies effectively blocked Abrams' investigation for many years. NIDA finally relented in 1998—perhaps as a result of recommendations made by an earlier NIH Consensus Conference (discussed *infra*)—and provided the marijuana necessary for Abrams' study (NIH Grant 5-MO1-RR00083).

The federal government's refusal to allow Dr. Abrams' study to proceed was not an isolated event. In another instance, in 2005, the DEA denied the application of Lyle E. Craker, Ph.D., a professor in the Department of Plant and Soil Sciences at the University of Massachusetts, Amherst, for a schedule I license to grow research-grade *Cannabis* for medical studies. He appealed this decision and, in response, DEA Administrative Law Judge Mary Ellen Bittner recommended that his application be granted on the grounds that the existing supply of marijuana available outside the purview of federal agencies was inadequate. She stated that as a schedule I controlled substance, *Cannabis* can be researched only with federal approval and that with NIDA in control of the supply for U.S. studies, the government's tight grip was stifling the kind of research used to test other drugs with therapeutic possibilities. In her non-binding opinion, Judge Bittner went on to observe:

> NIDA's system for evaluating requests for marijuana for research has resulted in some researchers who hold DEA registrations and requisite approval from the Department of Health and Human Services being unable to conduct their research because NIDA has refused to provide them with marijuana.

The DEA, however, did not accept her ruling. These examples suggest that political considerations rather than a desire to guarantee *bona fide* scientific research impeded these studies. There have been no recent indications that the FDA plans to reverse its current policy and conduct a scientific evaluation of the medical use of marijuana, although NIDA appears to have developed a greater willingness to supply marijuana for such studies (discussed *infra*). Moreover, there have been no signs that Congress is either prepared to acknowledge scientific investigations suggesting that marijuana may have legitimate medical uses or to recommend that the drug be rescheduled.

"Science, Not Ideology" Should Be Dispositive

In spite of the impediments that federal agencies had erected to the conduct of scientific evaluations of the medical use of marijuana, several scientific bodies have suggested that the FDA allow such studies to proceed. They have proposed that its formal evaluation as a legitimate medical therapy was warranted, and that either the DEA should grant investigators a schedule I license or else Congress should reschedule the drug.

This was recommended as early as 1997 when a Consensus Conference sponsored by the National Institutes of Health concluded that:

> For at least some potential indications, marijuana looks promising enough to recommend that there be new controlled studies done. The indications in which varying levels of interest were expressed are the following: appetite stimulation and cachexia; nausea and vomiting following anticancer therapy; neurological and movement disorders; analgesia; glaucoma.

This view was also advocated by a group charged with evaluating the therapeutic and palliative utility of marijuana that met in February, 1998 under the aegis of the National Academies of Sciences-Institute of Medicine (NAS-IOM). Proceedings of the Conference (*Workshop on Prospects for Cannabinoid Drug Development, National Academies of Sciences-Institute of Medicine*) were published in 1999. Scientific contributors indicated that smoked marijuana could be a valuable agent in the treatment of chemotherapy-induced nausea and vomiting, HIV-related gastrointestinal disorders, AIDS wasting, severe pain, and some forms of spasticity.

Some participants stressed—as had those at the preceding year's NIH Consensus Conference—that since the whole marijuana plant contains many possibly active cannabinoids besides fig-tetrahydrocannabinol (THC), its medical efficacy might not be replicated by medications containing only THC such as oral THC (Marinol™), an FDA-approved medication.

Nonetheless, the suggestion by an impartial conference of experts that marijuana might have some medical utility and that its properties should be subjected to scientific investigation was dismissed by the FDA and other federal agencies. An inter-agency advisory stated:

> A past evaluation by several Department of Health and Human Services (HHS) agencies, including the Food and Drug Administration (FDA), Substance Abuse and Mental Health Services Administration (SAMHSA) and National Institute for Drug Abuse (NIDA), concluded that no sound scientific studies supported medical use of marijuana for treatment in the United States, and no animal or human data supported the safety or efficacy of marijuana for general medical use.

The advisory did not go unnoticed. Dr. John Benson, co-chair of the IOM committee and professor of internal medicine at the University of Nebraska Medical Center, strongly disputed the FDA's stance. Dr. Jerry Avorn, professor of medicine at the Harvard Medical School (Chief of the Division of Pharma-coepidemiology and Pharmacoeconomics at Brigham and Women's Hospital) declared, "Unfortunately, this is yet another example of the F.D.A. making pronouncements that seem to be driven more by ideology than by science."

In 2001, the Council on Scientific Affairs of the American Medical Association (AMA) acknowledged that *Cannabis* might have medical utility and recommended that medical marijuana be subject to scientific review. Report 6 of the Council on Scientific Affairs (A-01, Medical Marijuana) of the American Medical Association stated:

> The AMA calls for further adequate and well-controlled studies of marijuana and related cannabinoids in patients who have serious conditions for which preclinical, anecdotal, or controlled evidence suggests possible efficacy and the application of such results to the understanding and treatment of disease. . . . The AMA urges the National Institutes of Health (NIH) to implement administrative procedures to facilitate grant applications and the conduct of well-designed clinical research into the medical utility of marijuana. This effort should include . . . confirming that marijuana of various and consistent strengths and/or placebo will be supplied by the National Institute on Drug Abuse to investigators registered with the Drug Enforcement Agency who are conducting bona fide clinical research studies that receive Food and Drug Administration approval, regardless of whether or not the NIH is the primary source of grant support. . . . The AMA believes that effective patient care requires the free and unfettered exchange of information on treatment alternatives and that discussion of these alternatives between physicians and patients should not subject either party to criminal sanctions.

Eight years later, the AMA's House of Delegates recommended that marijuana's schedule I status was no longer appropriate and interfered with legitimate medical research. A newspaper account of the meeting summarized the Delegates' action:

> **Houston**—It is time to re-examine whether marijuana should be legally categorized as a schedule I drug, the AMA House of Delegates said at its Interim Meeting.

The goal of such a review is to facilitate "the conduct of clinical research and development of cannabinoid-based medicines and alternate [sic] delivery methods," says the newly adopted house policy.

The current scheduling "limits the access to cannabinols for even research—it is very difficult," said AMA Board of Trustees member Edward L. Langston, M.D., a Lafayette, Ind., family physician. "We believe there should be a scientific review of cannabinols in the treatment of pain and other issues. . . . We support research on the use of cannabinols for medical use."

Scientists researching marijuana's medical properties must get the Drug Enforcement Administration's approval every step of the way, and the sole legal national source of cannabis for scientific purposes is the National Institute on Drug Abuse. A number of bureaucratic hurdles apply to cannabis research that do not impede other drug investigations, said a report from the AMA Council on Science and Public Health.

In 2008, the American College of Physicians (ACP) joined these groups in urging "an evidence-based review of marijuana's status as a Schedule I controlled substance to determine whether it should be reclassified to a different schedule. . . . [This review] should consider the scientific findings regarding marijuana's safety and efficacy in some clinical conditions."

Thus, consistent and strong recommendations by four separately sponsored committees (NIH, AMA, NAS-IOM, ACP), with input from well-regarded scientific and medical authorities, were ignored by the very federal authorities that were in a position to aid studies of medical marijuana's potential utility as a therapeutic agent.

Scientists and Clinicians Suggest Marijuana Might Be a Safe and Effective Medication

There is now considerable evidence in the peer-reviewed scientific literature that smoked marijuana has legitimate therapeutic and palliative uses that are not accompanied by dangerous side effects. Several studies published *after dissemination* of the recommendations of four national scientific committees mentioned above have demonstrated that the drug is safe and effective in controlling nausea and other adverse effects of chemotherapy, relieving multiple sclerosis-induced spasticity, easing certain types of pain, and ameliorating weight loss accompanying AIDS (Table 2). These data summarize the results of five scientifically based studies (randomized, blinded, and placebo-controlled as appropriate) that have been published in peer-reviewed journals.

Table 2

Some Beneficial Effects of Smoked Marijuana Reported in Several Peer-Reviewed Scientific Journals

Authors	Results
Abrams et al.[G]	In this randomized, placebo-controlled investigation, smoked marijuana produced significant improvement in patients with chronic HIV-induced neuropathic pain. Over twice as many of the subjects who smoked marijuana reported a significant reduction in pain compared with the placebo group. Pain relief was rapid; the first marijuana cigarette reduced chronic pain by 72 percent while only 15 percent of the placebo group reported immediate relief. No serious adverse events occurred during the study.
Ellis et al.[H]	A double-blind placebo-controlled randomized study demonstrating that smoked marijuana produced a statistically significant decrement in the pain score of subjects with medically refractory pain due to HIV while their mood and daily functioning improved.
Sylvestre et al.[I]	This prospective observation study demonstrated that *cannabis* use relieves "side-effects associated with HCV [hepatitis C] treatment, including nausea, anorexia, weight loss, musculoskeletal pain, insomnia, anxiety, and mood instability."
Wallace et al.[J]	Smoked marijuana in appropriate doses relieved capsaicin-induced pain in healthy volunteers and did not produce significant decrements in mental performance.
Wilsey et al.[K]	This randomized placebo-controlled study "adds to a growing body of evidence that cannabis may be effective at ameliorating neuropathic pain, and may be an alternative for patients who do not respond to, or cannot tolerate, other drugs."

References to Table 2

[G] D.I. Abrams, C.A. Jay, and S.B. Shade et al.,"Cannabis in Painful HIV-Associated Sensory Neuropathy: A Randomized Placebo-Controlled Trial," *Neurology* 68 (2007): 515–521.
[H] R.J. Ellis, W. Toperoff, and F. Vaida et al., "Smoked Medicinal Cannabis for Neuropathic Pain in HIV: A Randomized, Crossover Clinical Trial," *Neuropsychopharmacology* 25 (2009): 672–680.
[I] D.L. Sylvestre, B.J. Clements, and Y. Malibu "Cannabis Use Improves Retention and Virological Outcomes in Patients Treated for Hepatitis C," *European Journal of Gastroenterology & Hepatology* 18 (2006): 1057–1063.
[J] M. Wallace, G. Schulteis, and J. H. Atkinson et al.,"Dose-Dependent Effects of Smoked Cannabis on Capsaicin-Induced Pain and Hyperalgesia in Healthy Volunteers," *Anesthesiology* 107 (2007): 785–796.
[K] B. Wilsey, T. Marcotte, and A. Tsodikov et al., "A Randomized, Placebo-Controlled, Crossover Trial of Cannabis Cigarettes in Neuropathic Pain," *Journal of Pain* 9 (2008): 506–521.

While marijuana is not necessarily superior to currently used drugs for achieving these benefits, the Food and Drug Administration (FDA) does not require demonstration that a new drug be *more effective than* already approved medications before it will approve the drug for use in patients. It requires only proof of a drug's safety and efficacy for the condition under review. However, for some patients marijuana may actually be more effective than currently approved drugs. For instance, the noted biologist Stephen Jay Gould found that only smoked marijuana could alleviate the pain and nausea produced by treatments given him for the deadly form of cancer that eventually killed him. He wrote:

Absolutely nothing in the available arsenal of antiemetics worked at all. I was miserable and came to dread the frequent treatments with an almost perverse intensity. . . . Marijuana worked like a charm. . . . The sheer bliss of not experiencing nausea—and not having to fear it for all the days intervening between treatments—was the greatest boost I received in all my year of treatment.

Some claim that marijuana, even when used for legitimate medical purposes, might be unsafe because of its alleged properties as a "gateway drug" leading to the illegal use of other controlled substances. They therefore maintain that it should not be approved for medical use. The "gateway hypothesis" proposes that:

> Associations between early cannabis use and later drug use and abuse/ dependence cannot solely be explained by common predisposing genetic or shared environmental factors. The association may arise from the effects of the peer and social context within which cannabis is used and obtained. In particular, early access to and use of cannabis may reduce perceived barriers against the use of other illegal drugs and provide access to these drugs.

However, there is little evidence that marijuana is a gateway drug when specifically used for medical purposes under a physician's supervision. As with the appropriate medical use of morphine, studies indicate that *when marijuana is properly administered* to treat pain, nausea, spasticity, and other conditions for which it has been found effective, patients can achieve relief without experiencing addiction or other untoward side-effects (Table 2). Whether marijuana becomes a gateway drug when used for recreational purposes is a different question that has not yet been definitely answered, since it has proven difficult to demonstrate whether such use of marijuana *causes* the use of other drugs or is only *associated* with other drug use.

Inadequate State Attempts to Regulate the Use of Medical Marijuana

Whether the federal intransigence detailed above and pressure exerted by advocates for both sides of the "medical marijuana debate" are responsible for the failure to craft appropriate state regulations designed to exert meaningful control over the distribution and use of medical marijuana remains an interesting, but unproven, hypothesis. In any case, in the absence of federal evaluation and regulation, individual states have taken the initiative in legalizing the medical use of marijuana. In doing so, however, they have created what is essentially a regulatory vacuum.

Is there a basic structure to the state laws that legalize medical marijuana? Robert Mikos, a professor of law at Vanderbilt University Law School, has summarized common factors in this legislation:

> I focus on five common state medical marijuana provisions [which are] (1) exemptions from state legal sanctions [for those recommending, supplying, and using marijuana for medical purposes]; (2) state registration/ID

programs; (3) laws shielding users, suppliers, and physicians from private sanctions [such as when hospitals deny privileges to physicians recommending marijuana in accordance with state law, or when landlords terminate the leases of patients using marijuana as allowed by their state]; (4) state operated marijuana cultivation/distribution programs; and (5) laws requiring state agents to return marijuana to patients.

Unfortunately, these statutes are currently loosely worded, quite permissive, and require minimal scientific data in order to demonstrate that marijuana might be effective in treating *every condition* for which it may be recommended by a willing physician. For example, California's *Compassionate Use Act of 1996* (Cal. Health & Safety Code Ann. §11362.5) states that "the people of the State of California hereby find and declare that the purposes of the [Act] are as follows:

(A) To ensure that seriously ill Californians have the right to obtain and use marijuana for medical purposes where that medical use is deemed appropriate and has been recommended by a physician who has determined that the person's health would benefit from the use of marijuana in the treatment of cancer, anorexia, AIDS, chronic pain, spasticity, glaucoma, arthritis, migraine, or any other illness for which marijuana provides relief.
(B) To ensure that patients and their primary caregivers who obtain and use marijuana for medical purposes upon the recommendation of a physician are not subject to criminal prosecution or sanction.
(C) Notwithstanding any other provision of law, no physician in this state shall be punished, or denied any right or privilege, for having recommended marijuana to a patient for medical purposes.

It is noteworthy that (1) the number of marijuana dispensaries is not limited by statute; (2) the criteria by which *Cannabis* is to be "deemed appropriate" are not mentioned in the Act legalizing its use; and (3) that the presence of a *bona fide* doctor/patient relationship is not addressed.

In view of California's loosely worded legislation, it is not surprising that a recent *New York Times* article profiled one California town in which abuses appear to be widespread as a result of this lax policy. It alleged that that:

> [O]ne in five homes are "indoor grows," with rooms or even entire structures converted into marijuana greenhouses.
> That shift in cultivation [from outdoors to indoors] has been blamed for a housing shortage for Humboldt students, residential fires, and the powerful—and distracting—smell of the plant in some neighborhoods during harvest.
> "There were a handful initially and then all of a sudden, they started to sprout all over," said . . . a member of the Los Angeles City Council. We had marijuana facilities next to high schools and there were high school kids going over there and there was a lot of abuse taking place."

Colorado's medical marijuana statute is similar to that adopted in California. The legislation allows the medical use of marijuana to treat or palliate any "debilitating medical condition":

1. (a) "Debilitating medical condition" means:

   (I) Cancer, glaucoma, positive status for human immunodeficiency virus, or acquired immune deficiency syndrome, or treatment for such conditions;
   (II) A chronic or debilitating disease or medical condition, or treatment for such conditions, which produces, for a specific patient, one or more of the following, and for which, in the professional opinion of the patient's physician, such condition or conditions reasonably may be alleviated by the medical use of marijuana: cachexia; severe pain; severe nausea; seizures, including those that are characteristic of epilepsy; or persistent muscle spasms, including those that are characteristic of multiple sclerosis; or
   (III) Any other medical condition, or treatment for such condition, approved by the state health agency, pursuant to its rule making authority or its approval of any petition submitted by a patient or physician as provided in this section.
   (b) "Medical use" means the acquisition, possession, production, use, or transportation of marijuana or paraphernalia related to the administration of such marijuana to address the symptoms or effects of a patient's debilitating medical condition, which may be authorized only after a diagnosis of the patient's debilitating medical condition by a physician or physicians, as provided by this section.

However, while Colorado's statute also mentions a *bona fide* doctor-patient relationship, it does not strictly define what this entails (discussed *infra* [such a relationship is unlikely when a Colorado physician is reported to have issued such recommendations more than 700 times in one month]):

   (c) It shall be an exception from the state's criminal laws for any physician to:

   (I) Advise a patient whom the physician has diagnosed as having a debilitating medical condition, about the risks and benefits of medical use of marijuana or that he or she might benefit from the medical use of marijuana, provided that such advice is based upon the physician's contemporaneous assessment of the patient's medical history and current medical condition and a *bona fide physician-patient relationship*; or
   (II) Provide a patient with written documentation, based upon the physician's contemporaneous assessment of the patient's medical history and current medical condition and a *bona fide physician-patient relationship*, stating that the patient has a debilitating medical condition and might benefit from the medical use of marijuana. [Emphasis added.]

As a result of Colorado's medical marijuana statute which allows practitioners to recommend. *Cannabis* for any "medical condition, or treatment for such condition, approved by the state health agency . . . or . . . [any approved request] submitted by a patient or physician," without critically defining the requirements for a genuine physician-patient relationship, what is said to be "medical" marijuana has become the bedrock of a major industry in Colorado where there are now innovations such as a 5,000-square foot dispensary, dispensaries with hair stylists on site, and even one dispensary that claims to have the country's only medical-marijuana restaurant. This regulatory vacuum in Colorado and California, similar to that in many of the other states that have legalized the use of medical marijuana, has opened the door to a scenario out of the Wild West with the volume of marijuana dispensaries exceeding the number of Starbucks.

Of even more importance, however, is the failure of enabling legislation to recognize the need to establish and verify the existence of a *bona fide* doctor/patient relationship when marijuana is recommended for therapy or palliation (see next section's discussion, *infra*). As a result of this omission of physicians' ethical and fiduciary responsibilities to their patients, current medical marijuana legislation requires little or no oversight of the distribution and recommendation of *Cannabis* by qualified physicians. It should be obvious that unless physicians adhere to their ethical and fiduciary responsibilities to patients, controlling the number of dispensaries or limiting the areas allowed for cultivation will not suffice to allow marijuana to be treated as a genuine medication recommended in good faith as part of the legitimate practice of medicine. Consequently, entrepreneurs, physicians, and "patients/customers" in many of these states are "gaming" the system and may very well be involved in the sale and use of marijuana for purposes that have nothing to do with the legitimate practice of medicine.

Some Proposed Revisions in State Regulations Governing the Medical Use of Marjuana

Inadequately crafted and enforced regulations should not allow misguided and inappropriate claims of medical necessity to act as a subterfuge for the *de facto* legalization of "recreational marijuana." It is time to stop playing games with medical marijuana and to regulate it in the same way that we do any other FDA-approved controlled substance, such as morphine, Demerol®, or Valium®. This would be neither difficult nor unprecedented. However, it would require that physicians actively participate as "therapeutic gatekeepers" in the process of recommending and distributing medical marijuana in fulfillment of their ethical responsibility and fiduciary duty to seek the well-being of their patients.

State boards of medicine have the power to inspect the medical records of their licensed physicians to make sure they are engaged in the legitimate practice of medicine. If a physician's practice strays outside the realm of legitimacy, then a state board of medicine may suspend or revoke his or her license to practice. This was done in Virginia, for example, in 1998, when the Virginia Board of Medicine revoked the medical license of a physician who had routinely prescribed excessive amounts of narcotics to patients without appropriate screening and monitoring. This action was upheld by a Virginia court.

Therefore, states that have passed medical marijuana laws can and should establish a mechanism to allow their boards of medicine or a delegated authority to rigorously supervise the recommendations made by physicians for medical marijuana. This board or agency should require evidence that physicians making such recommendations have established a *bona fide* doctor-patient relationship with those seeking access to marijuana for medical use. This requires, at a minimum, that they have taken a medical history, performed a physical examination, and can demonstrate that a logical connection exists between the medical complaint, the medical history, the physical examination, and the drug prescribed. Moreover, state regulations should follow the federal rules mandating that prescriptions for controlled substances "must be issued for a legitimate medical purpose by an individual practitioner acting in the usual course of his [sic] professional practice."

The specific requirements for recommending medical marijuana should not differ from those already imposed on physicians who prescribe FDA-approved Schedule II controlled substances (this is the most likely classification were the federal government to reschedule medical marijuana). For example, according to these requirements, a practitioner must write and sign the order (which can only be telephoned into the pharmacy in an emergency), and refills are not available unless the patient has seen the practitioner again in order to obtain an appropriate re-supply of the medication. Obviously, "completing a questionnaire that is then reviewed by a doctor hired by the [dispensary], could not be considered the basis for a doctor/patient relationship" or legitimate medical practice. State regulations could be written to follow these reasonable and cautious federal requirements.

The absence of proper documentation for the use of marijuana by a physician would constitute *prima facie* evidence to a medical board that he or she had failed to enter into a *bona fide* doctor-patient relationship and to fulfill the requirements of legitimate medical practice. If medical records were to reveal obvious subterfuges for the use of marijuana for non-medical purposes, complicit physicians would be disciplined by a regulatory medical board in the same way they would be by the DEA or their state Board of Medicine had they prescribed other controlled substances such as morphine, Oxycontin, or Demerol outside the bounds of legitimate medical practice.

Strict state regulation of the medical use of marijuana according to these standards *is* possible. This may eventually be demonstrated by recent actions of the legislatures of New Jersey and Colorado, whose proposed legislation seeks to parallel federal rules governing the prescription of FDA-approved controlled substances.

New Jersey recently passed the *Compassionate Use Medical Marijuana Act* which would regulate the drug under the same strict conditions used to track the distribution of medically prescribed opiates like Oxycontin and morphine. It permits doctors to prescribe it only for a list of serious chronic illnesses. Moreover, it strictly defines a *bona fide* physician-patient relationship to require that the "physician has completed a full assessment of the patient's medical history and current medical condition, including a personal physical examination." The legislation also forbids patients from both growing their own marijuana (they must obtain it from state-monitored dispensaries) and using it in public; it would regulate the drug under the strict conditions used to track the distribution of medically prescribed opiates like Oxycontin and morphine. In crafting the bill, the New Jersey legislature "wanted to make sure that New Jersey did not follow the path of other states that have legalized the medical use of marijuana." Its sponsor has claimed that it is "the most restrictive medical marijuana law in the nation." Although these provisions appear consistent with the recommendations for the control of medical marijuana made above, the act was only signed into law in January 2010; how it will be implemented remains to be seen.

The Colorado Senate, perhaps motivated by bad publicity, recently voted overwhelmingly in favor of more stringent regulation of medical marijuana than had previously been in effect. The terms of this more rigorous new bill would require residents to have an established relationship with a doctor in order to obtain a recommendation to use marijuana for medical reasons. Furthermore, the proposed statute would ban doctors from issuing recommendations at marijuana dispensaries (thus avoiding the conflict of interest inherent when the "recommender" and "seller" are identical), require that a recommendation for marijuana be made by two physicians, and impose penalties for doctors who violate the law. Of importance to a major thrust of this paper, Colorado's proposed legislation clearly sets forth the requirements for a *bona fide* doctor-patient relationship when medical marijuana is recommended:

> "Bona fide physician-patient relationship" means: A physician and a patient have a treatment or counseling relationship, in the course of which the physician has completed a full assessment of the patient's medical history and current medical condition, including a personal physical examination; the physician has consulted with the patient with respect to the patient's debilitating medical condition before the patient applies for a registry identification card; and the physician provides follow-up care and treatment to the patient including but not limited to patient examinations, to determine the efficacy of the use of medical marijuana as a treatment of the patient's debilitating medical condition.

However, this bill has not yet been acted upon by the Colorado Assembly or signed by the Governor. Unfortunately, this bill has been strongly opposed by medical-marijuana advocates who insist that the rules will be costly and burdensome to patients, some of whom are indigent or disabled. Therefore, at this time its prospects are unclear.

These legislative actions in New Jersey and Colorado suggest that *Cannabis can be regulated* without impeding its legitimate medical use. However, since "the devil is in the details," it is far too early to reach a definite conclusion regarding the effectiveness of the actions taken by these two states.

Conclusion

Approval of any drug for medical use should be based on scientific evidence rather than political considerations. Such evidence should be dispositive in deciding whether the risk-benefit profile of marijuana justifies its approval by the FDA for specific medical uses. There is now sufficient evidence for the safety and efficacy of smoked marijuana administered for certain medical purposes to justify its evaluation and, if the evidence continues to support its safety and efficacy for these uses, its eventual approval by the FDA as a *bona fide* therapeutic agent. However, as matters currently stand, formal FDA evaluation of smoked marijuana seems unlikely to be conducted in the near future. In the meanwhile, 14 states and possibly the District of Columbia have elected to legalize medical marijuana through the political process. Yet most of them have neglected to develop appropriate regulations. The result, by and large, has been medical and legal chaos (New Jersey and Colorado may prove to be exceptions). However, the significant and possibly dangerous problems regarding patient safety and abuse that now exist in many states due to inadequate regulation of the medical use of this drug are not inevitable. They can be overcome by instituting regulations that treat marijuana as a legitimate therapeutic agent and supervising its use to ensure that it is being distributed in a way that is safe and justified by scientific evidence, medical ethics, and patient need.

The DEA Position on Marijuana

The campaign to legitimize what is called "medical" marijuana is based on two propositions: first, that science views marijuana as medicine; and second, that the DEA targets sick and dying people using the drug. Neither proposition is true. Specifically, smoked marijuana has not withstood the rigors of science—it is not medicine, and it is not safe. Moreover, the DEA targets criminals engaged in the cultivation and trafficking of marijuana, not the sick and dying. This is true even in the 14 states that have approved the use of "medical" marijuana.

On October 19, 2009 Attorney General Eric Holder announced formal guidelines for federal prosecutors in states that have enacted laws authorizing the use of marijuana for medical purposes. The guidelines, as set forth in a memorandum from Deputy Attorney General David W. Ogden, makes clear that the focus of federal resources should not be on individuals whose actions are in compliance with existing state laws, and underscores that the Department will continue to prosecute people whose claims of compliance with state and local law conceal operations inconsistent with the terms, conditions, or purposes of the law. He also reiterated that the Department of Justice is committed to the enforcement of the Controlled Substances Act in all states and that this guidance does not "legalize" marijuana or provide for legal defense to a violation of federal law. While some people have interpreted these guidelines to mean that the federal government has relaxed its policy on "medical" marijuana, this in fact is not the case. Investigations and prosecutions of violations of state and federal law will continue. These are the guidelines DEA has and will continue to follow.

The Fallacy of Marijuana for Medicinal Use

Smoked Marijuana Is Not Medicine

There is no sound scientific evidence that smoked marijuana can be used safely and effectively as medicine. Congress enacted laws against marijuana in 1970 based in part on its conclusion that-marijuana has no scientifically proven medical value. The Food and Drug Administration (FDA) is the federal agency responsible for approving drugs as safe and effective medicine based on valid scientific data. The FDA has not approved smoked marijuana for any condition or disease. The FDA noted that "there is currently sound evidence that smoked marijuana is harmful," and "that no sound scientific studies supported medical use of marijuana for treatment in the United States, and no

From a report issued by The Justice Department, July 2010.

animal or human data supported the safety or efficacy of marijuana for general medical use."

In 2001, the Supreme Court affirmed Congress's 1970 judgment about marijuana in *United States v. Oakland Cannabis Buyers' Cooperative et al.*, 532 U.S. 438 (2001), which held that, given the absence of medical usefulness, medical necessity is not a defense to marijuana prosecution. Furthermore, in *Gonzales v. Raich*, 545 U.S. 1 (2005), the Supreme Court reaffirmed that the authority of Congress to regulate the use of potentially harmful substances through the federal Controlled Substances Act (CSA) includes the authority to regulate marijuana of a purely intrastate character, regardless of a state law purporting to authorize "medical" use of marijuana.

On March 27, 2006, Raich submitted an appeal to the United States Court of Appeals for the Ninth Circuit seeking declaratory and injunctive relief based on the alleged unconstitutionality of the CSA, and a declaration that medical necessity precludes enforcement of the CSA against her. The court heard this matter on remand following the Supreme Court's decision in *Gonzales v. Raich*, 545 U.S. 1 (2005). On March 14, 2007, the Ninth Circuit ruled that a terminally ill woman (Angel Raich) using marijuana was not immune to federal prosecution because of her condition. This decision reaffirms that medical marijuana users and their suppliers could be prosecuted for breaching federal drug laws even if the state they live in has made it legal to do so.

In a show of international support for the U.S. Supreme Court's Raich decision, the International Narcotics Control Board (INCB) issued a statement urging other countries to consider the real dangers of cannabis. ". . . Cannabis is classified under international conventions as a drug with a number of personal and public health problems. It is not a 'soft' drug as some people would have you believe. There is new evidence confirming well-known mental health problems, and some countries with a more liberal policy towards cannabis are reviewing their position. Countries need to take a strong stance towards cannabis abuse."

The DEA and the federal government are not alone in viewing smoked marijuana as having no documented medical value. Voices in the medical community likewise do not accept smoked marijuana as medicine:

- The **American Medical Association (AMA)** has always endorsed "well-controlled studies of marijuana and related cannabinoids in patients with serious conditions for which preclinical, anecdotal, or controlled evidence suggests possible efficacy and the application of such results to the understanding and treatment of disease." In November 2009, the AMA amended its policy, urging that marijuana's status as a Schedule I controlled substance be reviewed "with the goal of facilitating the conduct of clinical research and development of cannabinoid-based medicines, and alternate delivery methods." The AMA also stated that "this should not be viewed as an endorsement of state-based medical cannabis programs, the legalization of marijuana, or that scientific evidence on the therapeutic use of cannabis meets the current standards for prescription drug product."

- The **American Society of Addiction Medicine's (ASAM)** public policy statement on "Medical Marijuana," clearly rejects smoking as a means of drug delivery. ASAM further recommends that "all cannabis, cannabis-based products and cannabis delivery devices should be subject to the same standards applicable to all other prescription medication and medical devices, and should not be distributed or otherwise provided to patients . . ." without FDA approval. ASAM also "discourages state interference in the federal medication approval process."
- The **American Cancer Society (ACS)** "does not advocate inhaling smoke, nor the legalization of marijuana," although the organization does support carefully controlled clinical studies for alternative delivery methods, specifically a tetrahydrocannabinol (THC) skin patch.
- The **American Glaucoma Society (AGS)** has stated that "although marijuana can lower the intraocular pressure, the side effects and short duration of action, coupled with the lack of evidence that its use alters the course of glaucoma, preclude recommending this drug in any form for the treatment of glaucoma at the present time."
- The **American Academy of Pediatrics (AAP)** believes that "[a]ny change in the legal status of marijuana, even if limited to adults, could affect the prevalence of use among adolescents." While it supports scientific research on the possible medical use of cannabinoids as opposed to smoked marijuana, it opposes the legalization of marijuana.
- The **National Multiple Sclerosis Society (NMSS)** has stated that it could not recommend medical marijuana be made widely available for people with multiple sclerosis for symptom management, explaining: "This decision was not only based on existing legal barriers to its use but, even more importantly, because studies to date do not demonstrate a clear benefit compared to existing symptomatic therapies and because side effects, systemic effects, and long-term effects are not yet clear."
- The **British Medical Association (BMA)** voiced extreme concern that downgrading the criminal status of marijuana would "mislead" the public into believing that the drug is safe. The BMA maintains that marijuana "has been linked to greater risk of heart disease, lung cancer, bronchitis and emphysema." The 2004 Deputy Chairman of the BMA's Board of Science said that "[t]he public must be made aware of the harmful effects we know result from smoking this drug."

In 1999, **The Institute of Medicine (IOM)** released a landmark study reviewing the supposed medical properties of marijuana. The study is frequently cited by "medical" marijuana advocates, but in fact severely undermines their arguments.

- After release of the IOM study, the principal investigators cautioned that the active compounds in marijuana may have medicinal potential and therefore should be researched further. However, the study concluded that "there is little future in smoked marijuana as a medically approved medication."
- For some ailments, the IOM found ". . . potential therapeutic value of cannabinoid drugs, primarily THC, for pain relief, control of nausea and vomiting, and appetite stimulation." However, it pointed out that

"[t]he effects of cannabinoids on the symptoms studied are generally modest, and in most cases there are more effective medications [than smoked marijuana]."

- The study concluded that, at best, there is only anecdotal information on the medical benefits of smoked marijuana for some ailments, such as muscle spasticity. For other ailments, such as epilepsy and glaucoma, the study found no evidence of medical value and did not endorse further research.

- The IOM study explained that "smoked marijuana . . . is a crude THC delivery system that also delivers harmful substances." In addition, "plants contain a variable mixture of biologically active compounds and cannot be expected to provide a precisely defined drug effect." Therefore, the study concluded that "there is little future in smoked marijuana as a medically approved medication."

- The principal investigators explicitly stated that using smoked marijuana in clinical trials "should not be designed to develop it as a licensed drug, but should be a stepping stone to the development of new, safe delivery systems of cannabinoids."

Thus, even scientists and researchers who believe that certain active ingredients in marijuana may have potential medicinal value openly *discount the notion that smoked marijuana is or can become "medicine."*

The Drug Enforcement Administration supports ongoing research into potential medicinal uses of marijuana's active ingredients. As of May 2010:

- There are 119 researchers registered with DEA to perform studies with marijuana, marijuana extracts, and non-tetrahydrocannabinol marijuana derivatives that exist in the plant, such as cannabidiol and cannabinol.

- Studies include evaluation of abuse potential, physical/psychological effects, adverse effects, therapeutic potential, and detection.

- Eighteen of the researchers are approved to conduct research with smoked marijuana on human subjects.

At present, however, *the clear weight of the evidence is that smoked marijuana is harmful.* No matter what medical condition has been studied, other drugs already approved by the FDA have been proven to be safer than smoked marijuana.

The only drug currently approved by the FDA that contains the synthetic form of THC is Marinol®. Available through prescription, Marinol® comes in pill form, and is used to relieve nausea and vomiting associated with chemotherapy for cancer patients and to assist with loss of appetite with AIDS patients.

Sativex®, an oromucosal spray for the treatment of spasticity due to Multiple Sclerosis is already approved for use in Canada and was approved in June 2010 for use in the United Kingdom. The oral liquid spray contains two of the cannabinoids found in marijuana—THC and cannabidiol (CBD)—but unlike smoked marijuana, removes contaminants, reduces the intoxicating effects, is grown in a structured and scientific environment, administers a set dosage and meets criteria for pharmaceutical products.

The legalization movement is not simply a harmless academic exercise. The mortal danger of thinking that marijuana is "medicine" was graphically illustrated by a story from California. In the spring of 2004, Irma Perez was "in the throes of her first experience with the drug Ecstasy . . . when, after taking one Ecstasy tablet, she became ill and told friends that she felt like she was . . . 'going to die' . . . Two teenage acquaintances did not seek medical care and instead tried to get Perez to smoke marijuana. When that failed due to her seizures, the friends tried to force-feed marijuana leaves to her, "apparently because [they] knew that drug is sometimes used to treat cancer patients." Irma Perez lost consciousness and died a few days later when she was taken off life support. She was 14 years old.

Organizers behind the "medical" marijuana movement have not dealt with ensuring that the product meets the standards of modern medicine: quality, safety and efficacy. There is no standardized composition or dosage; no appropriate prescribing information; no quality control; no accountability for the product; no safety regulation; no way to measure its effectiveness (besides anecdotal stories); and no insurance coverage. Science, not popular vote, should determine what medicine is.

The Legalization Lobby

The proposition that smoked marijuana is "medicine" is, in sum, false–trickery used by those promoting wholesale legalization.

- The Marijuana Policy Project (MPP) provides funding and assistance to states and localities to promote "marijuana as medicine" initiatives and legislation. Yet their vision statement clearly indicates that they have a much broader goal of decriminalizing marijuana. At the same time the marijuana legalization proponents are soliciting support for laws allowing marijuana to be used as medicine, they are working to *modify policies to regulate marijuana similarly to alcohol.*
- Ed Rosenthal, senior editor of *High Times,* a pro-drug magazine, once revealed the legalization strategy behind the "medical" marijuana movement. While addressing an effort to seek public sympathy for glaucoma patients, he said, "I have to tell you that I also use marijuana medically. I have a latent glaucoma which has never been diagnosed. The reason why it's never been diagnosed is because I've been treating it." He continued, "I have to be honest, there is another reason why I do use marijuana . . . and that is because I like to get high. Marijuana is fun."
- A few billionaires—not broad grassroots support—started and sustain the "medical" marijuana and drug legalization movements in the United States. Without their money and influence, the drug legalization movement would shrivel. According to National Families in Action, four individuals—George Soros, Peter Lewis, George Zimmer, and John Sperling—contributed $1,510,000 to the effort to pass a

"medical" marijuana law in California in 1996, a sum representing nearly 60 percent of the total contributions.

- In 2000, *The New York Times* interviewed Ethan Nadelmann, Director of the Lindesmith Center. Responding to criticism that the medical marijuana issue is a stalking horse for drug legalization, Mr. Nadelmann stated: "Will it help lead toward marijuana legalization? . . . I hope so. . . ."

The Failure of Legalized Marijuana Efforts

The argument that "caregivers" who participate in legalized marijuana efforts are "compassionate" is contradicted by revelations that all too often cannabis clubs are fronts for drug dealers, not health facilities. Even the author of Proposition 215 believes the program is "a joke."

- Reverend Scott T. Imler, co-author of Proposition 215, the 1996 ballot initiative that legalized medical marijuana in California, expressed his disappointment with the way the program has been implemented in a series of interviews in late 2006.

  - "We created Prop. 215 so patients would not have to deal with black market profiteers. But today it is all about the money. Most of the dispensaries operating in California are a little more than dope dealers with store fronts."
  - "When we wrote 215, we were selling it to the public as something for seriously ill people. . . . It's turned into a joke. I think a lot of people have medicalized their recreational use."
  - "What we set out to do was put something in the statutes that said medicine was a defense in case they got arrested using marijuana for medical reasons," Imler says. "What we got was a whole different thing, a big new industry."

- In an interview with National Public Radio in August 2009, Reverend Imler stated that he believes that the law has been subverted. "What we have is de-facto legalization." The article continues, "He never envisioned that medicinal pot would turn into a business, open to virtually anyone."

In Oregon, where voters legalized, "medical" marijuana for qualifying patients in November 1998, patients must grow their own marijuana or have a licensed grower provide it for them through an unpaid arrangement. While the initiative had good intentions, numerous problems exist.

- According to Lt. Michael Dingeman, Director of the Oregon State Police Drug Enforcement Section, many calls from cardholders are about never receiving the marijuana from their designated growers. The "growers are simply using the cardholders for cover, and selling their crops on the black market. In fact, some county sheriffs estimate that as much as one half of the illegal street marijuana they're seeing is being grown under the protection of the state's medical marijuana program."
- Deputy Chief Tim George of the Medford Police Department says that the region is "swimming in weed," and the problem keeps getting

worse. "People are traveling with large sums of money to buy marijuana. Weed is being shipped out of Oregon at record levels. Medical marijuana has made it easier for criminals to grow it."

- Sergeant Erik Fisher of the Drug Enforcement Section of the Oregon State Police says that the perception of the marijuana drug trade is mellower than other drug operations is wrong." He notes that almost all the distributors and growers carry firearms. "The other striking trend has been the increase in home invasion robberies of medical marijuana folks, and how absolutely violent they can be. We have more home invasions going on with medical marijuana people than any other drug dealer I can think of."

Neighborhood residents, doctors and other professionals associated with marijuana dispensaries admit there have been problems.

- In a letter to the Editor of the Denver Post, Dr. Christian Thurstone, Medical Director of an Adolescent Substance Abuse Treatment Program in Denver, has seen what impact Colorado's policies regarding "medical" marijuana has had on young adults.

  - "About 95 percent of the hundreds of young people referred to my clinic each year have problems with marijuana. I see teenagers who choose pot over family, school, friends and health every day. When they're high, these young people make poor choices that lead to unplanned pregnancies, sexually transmitted diseases, school dropouts and car accidents that harm people. When teenagers are withdrawing from marijuana, they can be aggressive and get into fights or instigate conflicts that lead to more trouble."
  - Dr. Thurstone talks about a 19-year-old who he was treating for severe addiction for several months. "He recently showed up at my clinic with a medical marijuana license. How did he get it? He paid $300 for a brief visit with another doctor to discuss his "depression." The doctor took a cursory medical history that certainly didn't involve contacting me. The teenager walked out with the paperwork needed not only for a license to smoke it, but also for a license permitting a "caregiver" to grow up to six marijuana plants for him. My patient, who had quit using addictive substances after a near-death experience, is back to smoking marijuana daily, along with his caregiver."
  - In a three month period, Dr. Thurstone saw over a dozen patients between 18 and 25 with histories of substance abuse who had received a recommendation from other doctors to smoke marijuana.
  - "Kids without licenses tell me about potent pot they buy from caregivers whose plants yield enough supply to support sales on the side."

- In a professional pharmacology journal, a doctor of pharmacology wrote, "The ethical quandary that I have as a pharmacist is allowing lay people to open dispensaries for profit and supply marijuana to people without any quality control over what's dispensed or accountability to those being dispensed this potent drug. . . ."

POSTSCRIPT

Should Marijuana Be Approved for Medical Use?

The delay in the medicalization of marijuana stems from arduous and restrictive procedures of the federal government according to many people who support marijuana's medical use. They argue that the federal government prevents research from being conducted that would validate the medical benefits of marijuana. Thus, they argue that the government blocks people in need from receiving medication that is both therapeutic and benign. The government's objection to marijuana, according to these supporters, is based more on politics than scientific evidence.

From the federal government's perspective, promoting marijuana as a medicinal agent would be a mistake because it has not been proven medically useful or safe. Moreover, it feels that the availability of marijuana should not be predicated on personal accounts of its benefits or whether the public supports its use. Also, the Drug Enforcement Agency (DEA) disputes that although those studies show that marijuana may have medical value, much of that research has been based on bad scientific methodology and other deficiencies. The results of previous research, the DEA contends, do not lend strong credence to marijuana's medicinal value.

Some people have expressed concern about what will happen if marijuana is approved for medicinal use. Would it then become more acceptable for nonmedical, recreational use? Would it not be easy for people to get prescriptions for marijuana even though they may not have a medical need for the drug? There is also a possibility that some people would misinterpret the government's message and think that marijuana cures cancer when, in fact, it would only be used to treat the side effects of the chemotherapy.

A central question is if physicians feel that marijuana use is justified to properly care for seriously ill patients, should they promote this form of medical treatment even though it falls outside the law? Does the relief of pain and suffering for patients warrant going beyond what federal legislation says is acceptable? Also, should physicians be prosecuted if they recommend marijuana to their patients? What about the unknown risks of using an illegal drug? Is it worthwhile to ignore the possibility that marijuana may produce harmful side effects in order to alleviate pain or to treat other ailments?

Many marijuana proponents contend that the effort to prevent the legalization of marijuana for medical use is purely a political battle. Detractors maintain that the issue is purely scientific—that the data supporting marijuana's medical usefulness are inconclusive and scientifically unsubstantiated. And although the chief administrative law judge of the Drug Enforcement Administration (DEA) made a recommendation to change the status of marijuana from Schedule I to Schedule II, the DEA and other federal agencies are not compelled to do so, and they have resisted any change in the law.

Dispensing of medical marijuana is described in "Don't Call It Pot; It's Medicine Now. Dealers Are Caregivers, and Buyers Are Patients. . . . How Marijuana Got Mainstreamed," by Andrew Ferguson (*Time*, November 22, 2010). Other articles that discuss whether marijuana should be legalized as a medication include "Smoked Marijuana as Medicine: Not Much Future," by Harold Kalant (*Clinical Pharmacology and Therapeutics*, 2008); and, "Medical Marijuana," in *The Economist* (April 27, 2006). Two additional articles that deal with specific medical uses of marijuana are "Cannabis Has Potential as a Drug to Relieve the Side Effects of Cancer and Its Treatment," by Donald Abrams in *Oncology News International* (March 1, 2006) and "Cannabis and AIDS," by Jule Klotter in *Townsend Letter for Doctors and Patients* (June 2006).

ISSUE 17

Should Schools Drug Test Students?

YES: Susanne James-Burdumy, Brian Goesling, John Deke, Eric Einspruch, and Marsha Silverberg, from *The Effectiveness of Mandatory-Random Student Drug Testing: Executive Summary* (National Center for Education Evaluation and Regional Assistance, Institute of Education Services, U.S. Department of Education, 2010)

NO: Jennifer Kern, Fatema Gunja, Alexandra Cox, Marsha Rosenbaum, Judith Appel, and Anjuli Verma, from *Making Sense of Student Drug Testing: Why Educators Are Saying No* (January 2006)

ISSUE SUMMARY

YES: Susanne James-Burdumy of Mathematica Policy Research and her colleagues report that schools which implemented mandatory random drug testing had less substance use. Moreover, random drug testing did not have a negative impact on the number of students engaging in school activities. Likewise, drug testing did not affect how students feel about their schools.

NO: Jennifer Kern and associates maintain that drug testing is ineffective and that the threat of drug testing may dissuade students from participating in extracurricular activities. Moreover, drug testing is costly, it may make schools susceptible to litigation, and it undermines relationships of trust between students and teachers. Drug testing, according to Jennifer Kern, does not effectively identify students who may have serious drug problems.

Attempting to reduce drug use by students is a desirable goal. Whether or not drug testing students is a means to achieve this goal is the subject of this debate. If it can be shown that drug testing results in less student drug use, then it is worthwhile. However, people on both sides of this issue do not agree on whether drug use is curtailed by drug testing.

According to Susanne James-Burdumy and her colleagues, drug testing acts as a deterrent to drug use. Additionally, the threat of drug testing has been shown to be extremely effective in reducing drug use by students in schools who participate in extracurricular activities as well as by individuals in the workplace. On the other hand, Jennifer Karn and associates believe that drug testing does not have an impact on drug use. They indicate that drug testing is counterproductive in that the threat of drug testing will cause many students to avoid extracurricular activities. Moreover, drug testing may lead to false positives in which students may be erroneously accused of using drugs.

Should the expense of drug testing be a factor in whether schools test students? Very few students are detected as having used illegal drugs. When school districts are strapped for funds, is drug testing a good use of funds? Critics maintain that a more effective strategy for reducing drug use would be better drug education programs that are geared to having students understand the hazards associated with drugs. Drug testing is geared to preventing drug use, not to reducing the harms that come from drug use.

An important question revolves around the legality of drug testing. Does drug testing unfairly discriminate against student athletes? In June 2002, the Supreme Court, in a 5 to 4 decision, ruled that random drug testing for all middle and high school students participating in extracurricular activities is allowable. Prior to 2002, only student athletes could be tested. Should students who participate in school government, band, plays, or other school-related activities undergo drug testing?

One reason why the federal government supports drug testing is that students who use drugs do not perform as well academically as those students who do not use drugs. The point of drug testing, states the federal government, is to help students, not to punish them. One criticism of drug testing is that it focuses on illegal drugs. Teenagers are far more likely to use tobacco and alcohol than illegal drugs. Drug testing does not address the problem of tobacco and alcohol use. Tobacco and alcohol cause far more harm than illegal drugs. Drug testing proponents agree that tobacco and alcohol are not adequately addressed, but that does not mean that students should not be tested for illegal drugs.

In the YES selection, Susanne James-Burdumy and her colleagues advocate drug testing as a means of reducing illegal drug use by students. They claim that the threat of drug testing is sufficient for stopping drug use or preventing drug use from occurring in the first place. In the NO selection, Jennifer Karn and her associates question the effectiveness of drug testing. They maintain that drug testing has the opposite effect in that many students will choose not to participate in extracurricular activities for fear of testing positive for illegal drugs.

YES  Susanne James-Burdumy et al.

The Effectiveness of Mandatory-Random Student Drug Testing: Executive Summary

Executive Summary

Despite a decline in adolescent substance use over the past 10 years, the prevalence of illicit substance use among youth remains high and a cause of concern. Recent national estimates indicate that 47 percent of students report having ever used illicit drugs and 72 percent report having ever drunk alcohol before leaving high school. The negative consequences associated with substance use in adolescence include low academic outcomes, delinquency, and risky sexual behaviors.

One approach to addressing student substance use is school-based mandatory-random student drug testing (MRSDT). Under MRSDT, students and their parents sign consent forms agreeing to the students' random drug testing as a condition of participation in athletics and other school-sponsored competitive extracurricular activities. The programs are designed to supplement existing school-based substance use prevention strategies and have the twin goals of (1) identifying students with substance use problems for referral to appropriate counseling or treatment services and (2) deterring student substance use. Recent national estimates indicate that 14 percent of U.S. public school districts conducted random drug testing in at least one of their high schools during the 2004–2005 school year; since 2003, the U.S. Department of Education's Office of Safe and Drug-Free Schools (OSDFS) has operated a grant program to support MRSDT programs in schools.

To help assess the effects of school-based random drug testing programs, the U.S. Department of Education's Institute of Education Sciences (IES) contracted with RMC Research Corporation and Mathematica Policy Research to conduct an experimental evaluation of the MRSDT programs in 36 high schools within seven districts that received OSDFS grants in 2006. This report describes the implementation of the MRSDT programs and their impacts on students—focusing primarily on student-reported substance use but also examining other outcomes.

The study's key findings indicate that:

1. Consistent with the goals of the program, students subject to MRSDT reported less substance use than comparable students in high schools

From *Mandatory-Random Student Drug Testing: Executive Summary*, 2010.

without MRSDT. Specifically, student-reported past-30-day use of substances tested under their districts' MRSDT policies was lower in schools implementing MRSDT than in schools without such policies. A similar, though not statistically significant, pattern was observed on other student-reported substance use measures.
2. However, the MRSDT program had no "spillover effects" on the substance use reported by students who were not subject to testing and had no effect on any group of students' reported intentions to use substances in the future.
3. Contrary to concerns raised about the possible unintentional negative consequences of random drug testing, the MRSDT program had no effect on the proportion of students participating in activities subject to drug testing or on students' attitudes toward school and perceived consequences of substance use.
4. There was some evidence that impacts of the MRSDT program were related to the ways in which the programs were implemented. Both testing for a larger number of substances and testing for alcohol and tobacco were significantly correlated with lower substance use in the treatment schools relative to the control schools. However, it was not possible to distinguish between these two factors due to the fact that districts that tested for a larger number of substances were also those districts that tested for alcohol or tobacco. Impacts were not significantly related to other implementation characteristics examined.

Background on MRSDT Programs and Evaluation

In 2003, the MRSDT grant program sponsored by OSDFS began supporting MRSDT in schools. The goal of the MRSDT grants is to reduce substance use among students enrolled in high schools whose districts apply for and receive funding to implement MRSDT programs. The programs are meant to supplement—not replace—other school-based prevention strategies, so in order to receive grant funding, districts must document the other policies and programs that they already have in place to prevent substance use.

The OSDFS grant program leaves a number of implementation decisions to the discretion of individual grantees. All districts are required to follow a basic set of testing procedures, including administering tests to a minimum of 50 percent of eligible students; testing for a minimum of five substances (marijuana, amphetamines, cocaine, methamphetamines, and opiates); and establishing procedures to maintain the confidentiality of test results. However, within these basic requirements, individual districts determine the following four criteria: (1) the list of competitive extracurricular activities that will be covered by their drug testing policies, (2) the frequency of testing and proportion of eligible (covered) students to be tested during each testing event, (3) any additional substances for which testing will be conducted beyond those required by the grant, and (4) the period of the school year during which eligible students may be subject to testing. The study examined whether and how these various implementation decisions relate to the effectiveness of the MRSDT programs.

OVERVIEW OF EVALUATION

Intervention: MRSDT, funded by OSDFS grants, requires that students consent to random drug testing as a condition of participating in covered activities. A parent or guardian must also consent to the student's testing.

Study sample: 7 grantees, 36 high schools, and 4,723 9th through 12th grade students. Participating districts and their schools received MRSDT grants from OSDFS in fall 2006.

Research design: After baseline data collection, about half the schools within each grantee district were randomly assigned either to the treatment group that was permitted to begin implementing MRSDT immediately (and during the 2007–2008 school year) or to the control group that was not permitted to begin implementing MRSDT until after the follow-up student survey was conducted in spring 2008.

Key outcomes: Students' self-reported substance use, perceptions of the consequences of substance use, connectedness with school, intentions to use substances in the future, and participation in activities covered by MRSDT; number of disciplinary incidents reported by school officials.

The evaluation of these programs is guided by a logic model predicting that MRSDT may reduce student substance use in three ways:

1. *By Deterring Substance Use.* If students are sufficiently aware of the possibility of drug testing, the threat of testing may cause students to stop using substances or give them a reason to refuse offers from peers to use substances.
2. *By Detecting Substance Use.* Students who test positive for drugs can be identified by school staff and referred to appropriate drug treatment or counseling services.
3. *By Having Spillover Effects on Nonparticipants.* Although MRSDT is most likely to affect the substance use of students who participate in activities subject to drug testing, it may also have spillover effects to other students in the school, as they observe and are influenced by the behavior of their peers.

Study Design

The study was designed as a rigorous program evaluation focused on assessing the effectiveness of MRSDT programs implemented in real-world settings. Schools were randomly assigned within districts either to a treatment group that was permitted to begin implementing MRSDT immediately after random assignment was conducted in spring 2007 (and to continue implementation during the 2007–2008 school year) or to a control group that was not permitted to implement MRSDT until after the study's spring 2008 follow-up survey was administered. Thus, impacts for this study are calculated over a one-year period (spring 2007–2008) and do not represent longer-term effects.

Within the treatment and control schools, students in grades 9–12 were randomly sampled to participate in data collection. As shown in Table 1, the evaluation is based on data collected from six sources: (1) student rosters provided by each district, (2) student surveys administered at baseline (spring 2007) and follow up (spring 2008), (3) school-records information collected from each study school, (4) forms documenting the drug testing procedures used in the study's treatment schools, (5) structured interviews with a key staff member at each study school, and (6) structured interviews with a staff member from each district. Active parental consent, which was required for study participation, was not obtained for all students sampled for the surveys, and thus the study's results are not necessarily generalizable to the schools as a whole.

Table 1

Data Collection Instruments

Data Source	Time Collected	Description of Data
Student rosters	January 2007 (baseline sampling), August 2007 (second sampling), March 2008 (follow up)	These rosters provided personal identifying information used to sample students and track the study sample, such as the student's name, gender, grade level, date of birth, and home address.
Student survey	April–May 2007 (baseline), March–April 2008 (follow up)	This survey included questions about student demographics, participation in school activities, retrospective substance use (lifetime, 6-month, and 30-day), attitudes toward substance use, attitudes toward school, and awareness of school policies.
Schoolwide records rollection form	April–November 2007 (baseline), March–May 2008 (follow up)	This form gathered data on student demographics, school policies, substance use incidents, prevention programs, teacher training, and student mobility.
Drug testing collection form	September 2007–July 2008	This form collected data on the demographics of tested students, testing procedures, substances for which tests were conducted, and aggregated test results.
School staff interviews	May 2008	These interviews gathered two types of data. In both treatment and control schools, the interviews collected information on substance abuse prevention strategies, school policies regarding suspicion of student drug use, and student awareness of drug testing. In treatment schools, the interviews also collected information on the procedures used for mandatory random-student drug testing.
District staff interviews	March 2009	These interviews collected data on the period in which students were subject to drug testing and the information students received about the substances covered by the tests.

The study's impact analysis focuses on comparing rates of self-reported substance use among students in the treatment and control schools based on data from the spring 2008 follow-up survey. Results of the drug tests conducted in the treatment schools are described in aggregate as a part of the study's implementation analysis, but do not factor into the study's impact analysis as the drug tests were not administered to students in control schools.

To determine whether MRSDT affects the substance use and attitudes reported by students who are subject to testing, we compared students in the treatment and control schools who participated in activities covered under their districts' MRSDT policies. For example, if football and soccer were covered activities, we compared rates of substance use reported by football and soccer players in the treatment and control schools. Due to the experimental design used in this study, differences in outcomes of students in the treatment and control groups are attributable to the effect of the MRSDT program (not other factors). To determine whether MRSDT has spillover effects to other students in the school, we estimated impacts for students who did *not* participate in covered activities.

Findings from the Study's Primary Impact Questions

The study's primary research questions were shaped by two factors. First, because the MRSDT programs are intended to affect most directly students who are subject to drug testing, the primary research questions focus on students who participate in athletics or other extracurricular activities covered under their district's testing policy. Second, although the study is primarily concerned with impacts on student substance use, to capture the full range of effects of MRSDT programs the study also examines impacts on other student outcomes, such as participation in activities subject to drug testing and attitudes toward school. Accordingly, the study's five main research questions and the study's findings on each question are:

1. **Do students who are subject to MRSDT report less use of alcohol, tobacco, and other illicit substances than comparable students in high schools without MRSDT?**
   Sixteen percent of students subject to MRSDT reported using substances covered by their district's MRSDT policy in the past 30 days, compared with 22 percent of comparable students in schools without MRSDT (see Figure 1). Similar patterns were observed on other student-reported substance use measures (see Figure 1), but those differences were not statistically significant.
2. **Are students who are subject to MRSDT less likely to report that they will use illicit substances in the future than comparable students in high schools without MRSDT?**
   No, 34 percent of students subject to MRSDT reported that they "definitely will" or "probably will" use substances in the next 12 months, compared with 33 percent of comparable students in schools without MRSDT.

Figure 1

Impacts of MRSDT on Retrospective Substance Use for Participants in Covered Activities

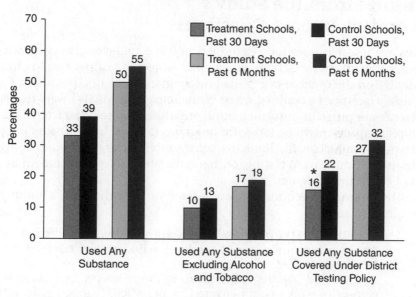

Statistically different from the control group at the .05 level.

3. **Do students who are subject to MRSDT report different perceptions of the consequences of substance use than comparable students in high schools without MRSDT?**
   No , on two measures of students' perceptions of the positive and negative consequences of using substances, students subject to MRSDT did not report having different perceptions of the consequences of substance use relative to comparable students in high schools without MRSDT. The lack of statistically significant impacts on students' perceived consequences of substance use in this study differs from prior research suggesting that MRSDT may have unintended negative consequences on these outcomes.
4. **Do students in high schools with MRSDT have different participation rates in extracurricular activities than comparable students in high schools without MRSDT?**
   No, 53 percent of students in treatment schools reported participating in an activity covered by MRSDT, relative to 54 percent of comparable students in high schools without MRSDT.
5. **Do students who are subject to MRSDT report different attitudes toward school than comparable students in high schools without MRSDT?**
   No, there was no impact on the extent to which students reported feeling connected to their schools. The lack of statistically significant

impacts on students' attitudes toward school in this study differs from prior research suggesting that MRSDT may have unintended negative consequences on these outcomes.

Findings from the Study's Secondary Impact Questions

Secondary research questions examined possible spillover effects of MRSDT to other students in the school who are *not* subject to testing, and the impact of MRSDT on the number of reported disciplinary incidents in schools. Other secondary questions examined whether the impacts of MRSDT were related to differences in program implementation and other grantee characteristics. For example, impacts might be larger for programs that test for a broader range of substances, conduct testing more frequently, subject a larger number or higher proportion of students to testing, or that have a higher level of student awareness of the testing program.

The three main secondary research questions and the study's findings on each question are:

1. **Does the MRSDT program have spillover effects on the substance use or other outcomes of students who are not covered by the MRSDT policies?**
   No, the MRSDT program had no spillover effects. For example, 36 percent of students not covered by the MRSDT policy in treatment schools and 36 percent of comparable students in control schools reported using a substance in the past 30 days (see Figure 2).

Figure 2

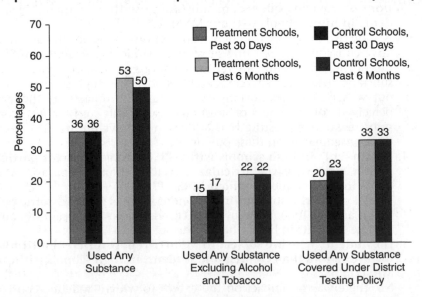

Impacts of MRSDT on Retrospective Substance User for Nonparticipants

2. **Does the MRSDT program affect the number of disciplinary incidents reported by schools?**
   No, the MRSDT program had no impact on school-reported disciplinary incidents. For example, treatment schools reported an average of five instances per 1,000 students of distribution, possession, or use of illegal drugs compared with four such instances in control schools.
3. **Are the impacts of the MRSDT program associated with the way in which the program was implemented?**
   There was some evidence that impacts of the MRSDT program were related to implementation characteristics. Both testing for a larger number of substances and testing for alcohol and tobacco were significantly correlated with lower substance use in the treatment schools relative to the control schools. However, it was not possible to distinguish between these two factors due to the fact that districts that tested for a larger number of substances were also those districts that tested for alcohol or tobacco. Impacts were not significantly related to testing frequency, number of drug tests conducted, or level of student awareness of MRSDT.

Description of the MRSDT Program

The study examined the characteristics of the MRSDT programs being implemented by participating schools. One purpose of the implementation analysis was to describe the key features of the drug testing programs implemented by treatment schools. Understanding how the programs were implemented is important for two reasons: (1) this study is an evaluation of MRSDT programs as they were carried out in real-world conditions, rather than an efficacy study carried out in more tightly controlled conditions; and (2) variation in program implementation may be correlated with the impacts of the program (as noted earlier).

The key characteristics of the MRSDT programs implemented by the participating treatment schools include:

- Five of the seven study districts chose to cover both sports and other competitive extracurricular activities in their MRSDT policies. Two districts limited MRSDT to student athletes.
- The frequency with which treatment schools conducted drug testing through their MRSDT grants ranged from four times per year to five or six times per month.
- Six of the seven districts tested for the five substances required by their grant award (marijuana, amphetamines, methamphetamines, opiates, and cocaine). The remaining district tested for three of the five required substances.
- Across the study's 20 treatment schools, a total of 3,476 drug tests were conducted during 324 testing events.
- The rate of positive drug tests—38 of 3,476 tests—was lower than the rate at which students reported using substances, a finding that is consistent with prior research.

Because MRSDT is thought to deter substance use through the threat of testing, the implementation analysis examined the extent to which students were aware of the MRSDT program. At follow up, students' awareness of the presence of MRSDT was higher in treatment schools than in control schools. In particular, 84 percent of treatment school students reported that students in their schools who participated in sports or other activities could be randomly tested for drugs, compared with 50 percent of students in the control schools.[1]

Other Substance Use Prevention Activities in Study Schools

The analysis also examined the other substance use prevention strategies that were used in treatment and control schools—information that is important for understanding the context within which the MRSDT programs operated and for assessing whether control schools attempted to compensate for their control group assignment through the implementation of other substance use prevention programs or policies during the evaluation period. There was no evidence that control schools attempted to compensate for their assignment to the control group through the implementation of other substance use prevention strategies. At follow up, the implementation of other substance use prevention strategies—for example, policies for students suspected of being under the influence of drugs or for students found in the possession of drugs—was no higher in control schools than in treatment schools. In addition, there was no evidence that the implementation of MRSDT in the treatment schools influenced the substance use of students in the control schools. In particular, over the one-year evaluation period (spring 2007–2008), trends in student substance use were no different in control schools than in a similar set of schools outside the study districts recruited by the study team to serve as a nonexperimental comparison group.

Note

1. The study team expected some reported awareness of MRSDT in the control schools, for two reasons. First, as part of the OSDFS grant requirements, schools assigned to the control group were instructed not to announce, promote, or implement MRSDT until after the study's spring 2008 follow-up survey was administered. However, it is possible that, through school board or community meetings, the grant application process, or the implementation of MRSDT in the districts' treatment schools, students in control schools became aware of the testing program. Second, the study team also found evidence that even in schools *without* MRSDT programs, some students mistakenly believe that extracurricular activity participants can be randomly tested for drugs. In particular, in data the study team collected from a nonexperimental sample of seven high schools outside the study districts, 32 percent of students reported that students in their schools could be randomly tested for drugs, even though none of the seven schools had MRSDT programs.

Jennifer Kern et al.  **NO**

Making Sense of Student Drug Testing: Why Educators Are Saying No

Executive Summary

Comprehensive, rigorous and respected research shows there are many reasons why random student drug testing is not good policy:

- Drug testing is not effective in deterring drug use among young people;
- Drug testing is expensive, taking away scarce dollars from other, more effective programs that keep young people out of trouble with drugs;
- Drug testing can be legally risky, exposing schools to potentially costly litigation;
- Drug testing may drive students away from extracurricular activities, which are a proven means of helping students stay out of trouble with drugs;
- Drug testing can undermine trust between students and teachers, and between parents and children;
- Drug testing can result in false positives, leading to the punishment of innocent students;
- Drug testing does not effectively identify students who have serious problems with drugs; and
- Drug testing may lead to unintended consequences, such as students using drugs (like alcohol) that are more dangerous but less detectable by a drug test.

There *are* alternatives to drug testing that emphasize education, discussion, counseling and extracurricular activities, and that build trust between students and adults.

Random Drug Testing Does Not Deter Drug Use

Proponents assert the success of random student drug testing by citing a handful of reports from schools that anecdotally claim drug testing reduced drug use. The only formal study to claim a reduction in drug use was based on a snapshot of two schools and was suspended by the federal government for lack of sound methodology.[1,2]

In a 2005 report evaluating the available evidence, Professor Neil McKeganey critiqued the methodology and biases of the studies repeatedly presented in support of random student drug testing, saying, "It is a matter of concern that student drug testing has been widely developed within the USA . . . on the basis of the slimmest available research evidence."[3]

Largest National Study Shows Drug Testing Fails

The first large-scale national study on student drug testing found virtually no difference in rates of drug use between schools that have drug testing programs and those that do not.[4] Based on data collected between 1998 and 2001 from 76,000 students nationwide in 8th, 10th and 12th grades, the study found that drug testing did not have an impact on illicit drug use among students, including athletes.

Dr. Lloyd D. Johnston, an author of the study, directs *Monitoring the Future*, the leading survey by the federal government of trends in student drug use and attitudes about drugs. According to Dr. Johnston, "**[The study] suggests that there really isn't an impact from drug testing as practiced . . . I don't think it brings about any constructive changes in their attitudes about drugs or their belief in the dangers associated with using them.**"[5] Published in the April 2003 *Journal of School Health*, the study was conducted by researchers at the University of Michigan and funded in part by the National Institute on Drug Abuse (NIDA).

Follow-Up Study Confirms Results: Drug Testing Fails

The researchers at the University of Michigan conducted a more extensive study later that year with an enlarged sample of schools, an additional year of data and an increased focus on random testing programs.[6] The updated results reinforced their previous conclusions:

> **So, does drug testing prevent or inhibit student drug use? Our data suggest that, as practiced in recent years in American secondary schools, it does not . . . The two forms of drug testing that are generally assumed to be most promising for reducing student drug use—random testing applied to all students . . . and testing of athletes—did not produce encouraging results.**[7]

The follow-up study was published in 2003 as part of the Youth, Education and Society (YES) Occasional Papers Series sponsored by the Robert Wood Johnson Foundation.

The strongest predictor of student drug use, the studies' authors note, is students' attitudes toward drug use and their perceptions of peer use. The authors recommend policies that address "these key values, attitudes and perceptions" as effective alternatives to drug testing.[8] The results of these national studies are supported by numerous other surveys and studies that examine the effectiveness of various options for the prevention of student drug misuse.[9]

Who Says No to Random Drug Testing?

A groundswell of opposition has emerged to random drug testing among school officials, experts, parents and state legislatures.

School Officials and Parents Say No to Drug Testing

We stopped testing because "we didn't think it was the deterrent that we thought it would be . . . we didn't think it was as effective with the money we spent on it."

—Scot Dahl, President at school board in Guymon, Oklahoma[10]

We decided not to drug test because "it really is a parental responsibility . . . it is not our job to actually test [students]."

—Harry M. Ward, Superintendent in Mathews County, Virginia[11]

"The concerns of parents [in opposing a student drug testing proposal] have ranged from the budgetary issues to losing our focus on education to creating a threatening environment."

—Laura Rowe, President of Band Aids, a parent association of the high school band program in Oconomowoc, Wisconsin[12]

"We object to the urine-testing policy as an unwarranted invasion of privacy. We want school to teach our children to think critically, not to police them."

—Hans York, parent and Deputy Sheriff in Wahkiakum, Washington[13]

"I would have liked to see healthy community participation that stimulates thoughtful interaction among us. Instead, this [drug testing] policy was steamrolled into place, powered by mob thinking."

—Jackie Puccetti, parent in El Paso, Texas[14]

Educators and School Officials

The majority of school officials—including administrators, teachers, coaches, school counselors and school board members—have chosen not to implement drug testing programs. With their concerns rooted in knowledge and practical experience, school officials object to drug testing for a variety of reasons, including the cost of testing, the invasion of privacy and the unfair burden that student drug testing places on schools. For many educators and school officials, drug testing simply fails to reflect the reality of what works to establish safe school environments.

Experts

Physicians, social workers, substance abuse treatment providers and child advocates agree that student drug testing cannot replace pragmatic drug prevention measures, such as after-school activities. Many prominent national organizations representing these groups have come forward in court to oppose drug testing programs. These groups include the American Academy of Pediatrics, the National Education Association, the American Public Health Association, the National Association of Social Workers, and the National Council on Alcoholism and Drug Dependence. These experts have stated: **"Our experience— and a broad body of relevant research—convinces us that a policy [of random student drug testing]** *cannot* **work in the way it is hoped to and will, for many adolescents, interfere with more sound prevention and treatment processes."**[15]

Experts Say No to Drug Testing

"Social workers, concerned with a child's well-being, question whether [drug testing] will do more harm than good . . . What is most effective in keeping kids away from drugs and alcohol are substance abuse prevention programs based on scientific research."

—Elizabeth J. Clark, Ph.D., A.C.S.W., M.P.H., Executive Director of the National Association of Social Workers[16]

"Protecting America's youth from alcohol and drugs requires more than a simple drug test. We need a greater commitment to prevention and treatment . . . At-risk and marginal students need the support systems and mentoring relationships that extracurricular activities provide. Excluding students who test positive for drugs will likely exacerbate their problems."

—Bill Burnett, President, the Association for Addiction Professionals[17]

"Let us not rush to accept the illusory view that drug testing in schools is the silver bullet for the prevention of youth substance abuse . . . While [drug tests] are increasing in popularity, their efficacy is unproven and they are associated with significant technical concerns."

—Dr. John R. Knight, Director of the Center for Adolescent Substance Abuse Research at Children's Hospital in Boston and Dr. Sharon Levy, Director of Pediatrics for the Adolescent Substance Abuse Program at Children's Hospital in Boston[18]

The Oklahoma policy **"falls short doubly if deterrence is its aim: It invades the privacy of students who need deterrence least, and risks steering students at greatest risk for substance abuse away from extracurricular involvement that potentially may palliate drug problems."**

—U.S. Supreme Court Justice Ruth Bader Ginsburg's Dissenting Opinion in Board of Education of Pottawatomie v. Earls[19]

Parents

Many parents oppose drug testing for the same reasons as school staff and administrators. In addition, some parents believe that schools are misappropriating their roles when they initiate drug testing programs. They believe that it is the role of parents, not schools, to make decisions about their children's health.

State Governments

Since the U.S. Supreme Court's 2002 decision that schools may randomly drug test students participating in competitive extracurricular activities, several state legislatures have opposed student drug testing after hearing community and expert concerns about privacy, confidentiality, potential liability and overall effectiveness. For example, the Hawaii legislature tabled a bill that would have established a drug testing pilot program at several public high schools.[20] In Louisiana, a bill was defeated that would have mandated drug testing state scholarship recipients.[21]

Drug Testing Has a Negative Impact on the Classroom

Drug testing can undermine student-teacher relationships by pitting students against the teachers and coaches who test them, eroding trust and leaving students ashamed and resentful.

As educators know, student-teacher trust is critical to creating an atmosphere in which students can address their fears and concerns about drug use

---

THE HUMAN COSTS OF DRUG TESTING: A CASE IN POINT

Lori Brown of Texas felt her son was wronged by his school's random drug testing program. Seventeen-year-old Mike, an upstanding senior at Shallowater High School near Lubbock, Texas, was taking a number of medications for allergies, as well as some antibiotics, when his school randomly tested him. One of these antibiotics, his doctor later confirmed, can cause a false positive for cocaine. The school failed to properly follow their own policies by neglecting to ask Mike to list the medications he was taking. To make matters worse, South Plains Compliance, the drug testing company hired by the school to administer the tests, maintained that their procedures were 100 percent accurate despite the extenuating circumstances.

After the test came up positive for cocaine, Lori had Mike tested several times by their own physician for her own peace of mind. Each test confirmed what she already knew: Mike was not using cocaine. Lori defended her son, explaining to school authorities what she learned from Mike's doctor. But they refused to listen. Over the next six months, he was "randomly" picked for testing several more times and began to feel harassed and stigmatized as a result.

(Continued)

"In my opinion, schools are using the [drug] testing program as a tool to police students, when they should be concentrating on education," Lori says.

Finally, Lori and Mike had reached their emotional limit when a South Plains Compliance representative yelled at Mike for not producing enough urine for his sixth test. Together they decide to remove him from the drug testing program. As a result, Mike could no longer participate in extracurricular activities.

PROBLEMS WITH DIFFERENT TYPES OF TESTS[24]

School officials lack the expertise to determine which type of testing is more reliable.

Urine	Marijuana Cocaine Opiates Amphetamine PCP	$10–$50 per test	• Tests commonly used in schools often do not detect alcohol or tobacco • Since marijuana stays in the body longer than other drugs, drugs like cocaine, heroin and methamphetamine often go undetected • Test is invasive and embarrassing • Specimen can be adulterated
Hair	Marijuana Cocaine Opiates Amphetamine PCP MDMA/ [Ecstasy]	$60–$75 per test	• Expensive • Cannot detect alcohol use • Will not detect very recent drug use • The test is discriminatory: dark-haired people are more likely to test positive than blondes, and African Americans are more likely to test positive than Caucasians • Passive exposure to drugs in the environment, especially those that are smoked, may lead to false positive results
Sweat Patch	Marijuana Cocaine Opiates Amphetamine PCP	$20–$50 per test	• Limited number of labs able to process results • Passive exposure to drugs may contaminate patch and result in false-positives • People with skin eruptions, excessive hair, or cuts and abrasions cannot wear the patch
Saliva	Marijuana Cocaine Opiates Amphetamine PCP	$10–$50 per test	• Detects only very recent use and limited number of drugs • New technology; accuracy rates and testing guidelines not established

itself, as well as the issues that can lead to drug use, including depression, anxiety, peer pressure and unstable family life.[22] Trust is jeopardized if teachers act as confidants in some circumstances but as police in others.

Drug testing also results in missed classroom instruction. Officials at some schools with testing programs reported that many students would flagrantly ridicule the testing process by stalling for hours to produce a urine sample—during which time they remained absent from class.[23]

Drug Testing Is Expensive and a Waste of School Resources

Drug testing costs schools an average of $42 per student tested, which amounts to $21,000 for a high school testing 500 students.[25] This figure is for the initial test alone and does not include the costs of other routine components of drug testing, such as additional tests throughout the year or follow-up testing.

The cost of drug testing often exceeds the total a school district spends on existing drug education, prevention and counseling programs combined. In fact, drug testing may actually take scarce resources away from the very health and treatment services needed by students who are misusing drugs.

The process for dealing with a positive test is usually long and involved; not only must a second test be done to rule out a false positive result, but treatment referral and follow-up systems must also be in place. In one school district, the cost of detecting the 11 students who tested positive amounted to $35,000.[26]

Beyond the initial costs, there are long-term operational and administrative expenses associated with student drug testing, including:

COST-BENEFIT ANALYSIS IN DUBLIN, OHIO[27]

In Dublin, Ohio, school administrators ended their drug testing program and hired two full time substance abuse counselors instead, concluding that drug testing reduces resources for more effective drug prevention programs.

	Drug Testing	Substance Abuse Counselor
Cost of program	$35,000 per school year	$32,000 annual starting salary per counselor
Number of students	Out of 1,473 students tested, 11 tested positive	Prevention programs for all 3,581 high school students incorporated in a weekly class curriculum
Cost per student	$24 per student for drug test $3,200 per student who tested positive	$18 per student for drug prevention, education and intervention Intervention programs for all targeted students who need help

---

U.S. SUPREME COURT DID NOT SAY . . .

- The Court DID NOT say that schools are required to test students involved in competitive extracurricular activities.
- The Court DID NOT say drug testing of all students or specific groups of students outside of those participating in competitive extracurricular activities (i.e. student drivers) is constitutional.
- The court DID NOT say it is constitutional to drug test elementary school children.
- The Court DID NOT say that it is constitutional to test by means other than urinalysis.
- The Court DID NOT say that schools are protected from lawsuits under their respective state laws.

- Monitoring students' urination to collect accurate samples;
- Documentation, bookkeeping and compliance with confidentiality requirements; and
- Tort or other insurance to safeguard against potential lawsuits.

Not All Drug Testing Is Protected Under the Law

In 2002, by a margin of five to four, the U.S. Supreme Court in *Board of Education of Pottawatomie v. Earls* permitted public school districts to drug test students participating in competitive extracurricular activities. In its ruling, however, the Court only interpreted *federal* law. Schools are also subject to *state* law, which may provide greater protections for students' privacy rights. These laws vary greatly from state to state and, in many states, the law may not yet be well-defined by the courts.

Since the 2002 *Earls* decision, lawsuits have been filed in many states, including Indiana, New Jersey, Oregon, Pennsylvania, Texas and Washington, challenging school districts' drug testing policies.[28] Most of these school districts will spend thousands of taxpayer dollars battling these lawsuits with no guarantee of success.

What National Experts Said to the U.S. Supreme Court[29]

A mandatory drug testing policy "injects the school and its personnel, unnecessarily, into a realm where parental and medical judgment should be preeminent."

—American Academy of Pediatrics, et al.

School drug testing policies often operate "in disregard for prevention and treatment principles that doctors and substance abuse experts view as fundamental . . ."

—American Public Health Association, et al.

"There is growing recognition that extracurricular involvement plays a role in protecting students from substance abuse and other dangerous health behaviors."

—National Education Association, et al.

The risk that testing students for illicit drugs "will be understood to signal that alcohol and tobacco are of lesser danger is not an idle concern."

—National Council on Alcoholism and Drug Dependence, et al.

Random Drug Testing Is a Barrier to Joining Extracurricular Activities

Random drug testing is typically directed at students who want to participate in extracurricular activities, including athletics, which have proven among the most effective pathways to preventing adolescent drug use. However, all too often drug testing policies actually prevent students from engaging in these activities.

Research shows a vastly disproportionate incidence of adolescent drug use and other dangerous behavior occurs during the unsupervised hours between the end of classes and parents' arrival home in the evening.[30]

Research also shows that students who participate in extracurricular activities are:

- Less likely to develop substance abuse problems;
- Less likely to engage in other dangerous behavior such as violent crime; and
- More likely to stay in school, earn higher grades, and set and achieve more ambitious educational goals.[31]

In addition, after-school programs offer students who are experimenting with or misusing drugs productive activities as well as contact with teachers, coaches and peers, who can help them identify and address problematic drug use.

The Tulia Independent School District, one of the many districts facing heightened public concerns about privacy and confidentiality, has seen a dramatic reduction in student participation in extracurricular activities since implementing drug testing.[32] . . .

Drug Testing Results in False Positives That Punish Innocent Students

A positive drug test can be a devastating accusation for an innocent student. The most widely used drug screening method, urinalysis, will falsely identify some students as illicit drug users when they are not actually using illicit drugs,

VIOLATING CONFIDENTIALITY

When Tecumseh High School in Oklahoma enacted its random drug testing program, the school failed to ensure the protection of private information concerning prescription drug use submitted under the testing policy. The choir teacher, for instance, looked at students' prescription drug lists and inadvertently left them where other students could see them. The result of a positive test, too, were disseminated to as many as 13 faculty members at a time. Other students figured out the results when a student was abruptly suspended from his/her activity shortly after the administration of a drug test.[36] This not only violates students' privacy rights, but can also lead to costly litigation.

because drug testing does not necessarily distinguish between drug metabolites with similar structures. For example:

- Over-the-counter decongestants may produce a positive result for amphetamine.[33]
- Codeine can produce a positive result for heroin.[34]
- Food products with poppy seeds can produce a positive result for opiates.[35]

Out of a desire to eliminate the possibility for false positives, schools often ask students to identify their prescription medications before taking a drug test. This both compromises students' privacy rights and creates an added burden for schools to ensure that students' private information is safely guarded.

Drug Testing Is Not the Best Way to Identify Students with a Drug Problem

Drug testing says very little about who is misusing or abusing drugs. Thousands of students might be tested in order to detect a tiny fraction of those who may have used the drugs covered by the test. Additionally, students misusing other harmful substances not detected by drug tests will not be identified. If schools rely on drug testing, they may undervalue better ways of detecting young people who are having problems with drugs. Most often, problematic drug use is discovered by learning to recognize its common symptoms. Properly trained teachers, coaches and other school officials can identify symptoms of a potential drug problem by paying attention to such signs as student absences, erratic behavior, changes in grades and withdrawal from peers.

FIRST, ASK THESE HARD QUESTIONS

- Has the drug test been proven to identify students likely to have future problems and to clear those who will not?
- Have schools been proven to be more appropriate or cost-effective places to perform these tests than a doctor's office?
- Are resources in place to assist students who fail the test, regardless of health insurance status or parental income?
- Is the financial interest of a proprietary firm behind the test's promotion?
- Is the school staff using precious time to elicit parental permission, explain the test, make the referrals and assure follow-up?

Adapted from the American Association of School Administrators' website[37]

Drug Testing Has Unintended Consequences

Students may turn to more dangerous drugs or binge drinking Because marijuana is the most detectable drug, with traces of THC remaining in the body for weeks, students may simply take drugs that exit the body quickly, like methamphetamine, MDMA (Ecstasy) or inhalants.[38] Knowing alcohol is less detectable, they may also engage in binge drinking, creating health and safety risks for students and the community as a whole.

Students can outsmart the drug test Students who fear being caught by a drug test may find ways to cheat the test, often by purchasing products on the Internet. A quick Internet search for "pass drug test" yields nearly four million hits, linking students to websites selling drug-free replacement urine, herbal detoxifiers, hair follicle shampoo and other products designed to beat drug tests. Students may also try dangerous home remedies. The president of the school board for Guymon, Oklahoma, described a frantic parent who had caught her daughter drinking bleach;[39] the district's drug testing program was subsequently abandoned. In one Louisiana school district, students who were facing a hair test shaved their heads and body hair, making a mockery of the drug testing program.[40]

Students learn that they are guilty until proven innocent Students are taught that under the U.S. Constitution people are presumed innocent until proven guilty and have a reasonable expectation of privacy. Random drug testing undermines both lessons; students are assumed guilty until they can produce a clean urine sample with no regard for their privacy rights.

Alternatives to Student Drug Testing

The current push to increase drug testing comes from the drug testing industry as well as well-intentioned educators and parents frustrated by the lack of success of drug prevention programs such as Drug Abuse Resistance Education (DARE).[41] However, there are more effective ways to keep teens out of trouble with drugs.

Engage Students in After-School Programs

Schools and local communities should help engage students in extracurricular activities and athletics, as these are among the best deterrents to drug misuse.

Incorporate Reality-Based Drug Education into the School Curriculum

Drugs of all sorts abound in our society. We are constantly confronted by a wide variety of substances with recreational and medicinal uses that can be purchased over-the-counter, by prescription and illegally. Since our decisions about drugs of all kinds should be based on complete, accurate information, quality drug education should be incorporated into a broad range of science disciplines, including physiology, chemistry and biology as well as psychology, history and sociology. Drug education should avoid dishonest scare tactics and should also recognize the wide spectrum of drug use and misuse, and the reasons why young people might choose to use (or not use) drugs.

Provide Counseling

Schools should provide counseling for students who are using drugs in a way that is causing harm to themselves or others. An emerging model that stresses relationships between students and counselors is that of a comprehensive Student Assistance Program (SAP).[42] Such a program advocates a mix of prevention, education and intervention. Counselors who teach about drugs can remain an important resource for students after the formal session ends, while trained student counselors can engage those students who feel more comfortable talking about their problems with peers.[43]

Allow Students to Be Assessed and Treated by Healthcare Professionals

Schools can refer students to healthcare professionals who can play a role in screening, intervening and referring adolescents to treatment. Several screening tools other than urinalysis, such as questionnaires, are available to healthcare professionals in diagnosing drug abuse among adolescents.[44]

Encourage Parents to Become Better Informed

Informed parents play a key role in preventing and detecting student drug misuse, so they should learn as much as they can. Schools can encourage parents to open a dialogue when adolescents are first confronted with alcohol and other intoxicating drugs, usually in middle school. At this point, "drug talks" should be two-way conversations. It is important for parents to teach, as well as learn from, their children.[45]

Cultivate Trust and Respect Among Students and Adults

Trust and respect are perhaps the most important elements of relationships with teens. Young people who enjoy the confidence of their parents and teachers, and who are expected to assume responsibility for their actions, are the most likely to act responsibly. They need to practice responsibility while in high school, where they have a crucial parental and school safety net.

The combination of these methods will help ensure that students:

- **Receive comprehensive, science-based information;**
- **Receive help when they need it; and**
- **Stay busy and involved in productive activities when the school day ends.**

Resources

Studies on Students, Drug Testing and/or After-School Activities

Neil McKeganey, *Random Drug Testing of Schoolchildren: A Shot in the Arm or a Shot in the Foot for Drug Prevention?* (York, UK: Joseph Rowntree Foundation, 2005). . . .

Ryoko Yamaguchi, Lloyd D. Johnston, and Patrick M. O'Malley, *Drug Testing in Schools: Policies, Practices, and Association With Student Drug Use,* Youth, Education, and Society (YES) Occasional Papers Series (Ann Arbor, MI: The Robert Wood Johnson Foundation, 2003). . . .

Ryoko Yamaguchi, Lloyd D. Johnston, and Patrick M. O'Malley, "Relationship Between Student Illicit Drug Use and School Drug-Testing Policies," *Journal of School Health* 73, no. 4 (2003): pp. 159–164. . . .

William J. Bailey, "Suspicionless Drug Testing in Schools," Indiana Prevention Resource Center (1998). . . .

Julie Pederson and others, "The Potential of After-School Programs" in *Safe and Smart: Making After-School Hours Work for Kids* (Washington, D.C.: U.S. Department of Education and U.S. Department of Justice, 1998). . . .

Nicholas Zill, Christine Winquist Nord, and Laura Spencer Loomis, "Adolescent Time Use, Risky Behavior and Outcomes: An Analysis of National Data," U.S. Department of Health and Human Services (1995). . . .

Recommended Reading and Viewing

Rodney Skager, Ph.D., *Beyond Zero Tolerance: A Reality-Based Approach to Drug Education and Student Assistance* (San Francisco, CA: Drug Policy Alliance, 2005). This 23-page booklet offers educators an approach to secondary school drug education that is honest, interactive and cost-effective. The booklet also addresses student assistance and restorative practices as an alternative to punitive zero tolerance policies. . . .

Brave New Films, *The ACLU Freedom Files: The Supreme Court* (2005) is a television show featuring the story of Lindsay Earls, the high school sophomore who opposed her school's drug testing policy for violating her privacy. Screen the half-hour program online and see how she stood up for her beliefs in front of the U.S. Supreme Court. Lindsay Earls was a student at Tecumseh High School, a member of the debate team and a performer in the choir, when a mandatory drug testing policy was instituted for anyone participating in extracurricular activities. She opposed the order as an unconstitutional invasion of her privacy in *Board of Education of Pottawatomie v. Earls.* The show traces the Earls' family experience and gives an insider's view of the high court and the justices who serve on it. . . .

Andrew Weil, M.D. and Winifred Rosen, *From Chocolate to Morphine: Everything You Need to Know About Mind-Altering Drugs* (Boston, MA: Houghton Mifflin, 2004).

Marsha Rosenbaum, Ph.D., *Safety First: A Reality-Based Approach to Teens, Drugs and Drug Education* (San Francisco, CA: Drug Policy Alliance, 2004). This 20-page booklet provides parents and educators with pragmatic ways to address teenage drug use. . . . The Safety First website also contains "fact sheets" about drugs, strategies for talking with teens, news about teen drug use and drug education, an "Ask the Experts" column containing questions submitted by parents and educators, links to relevant sites, ordering information and more.

Mark Birnbaum and Jim Schermbeck, *Larry v. Lockney* (Dallas, TX: Independent Television Service, KERA Unlimited and Public Broadcasting Service, 2003). This documentary follows a parent's fight against a student drug testing program in his son's school. The film's website includes lesson plans and other related resources. . . .

Friend-of-the-Court brief of the American Academy of Pediatrics, et al. in Support of Lindsay Earls, in *Earls,* 536 U.S. 822 (2002). . . .

American Bar Association, *Teaching about Drug Testing in Schools* adapted from Street Law, Inc. (1999). This lesson plan educates students about drug testing in schools and allows them to consider and discuss the consequences of a student drug testing policy. . . .

Recommended Websites

"Drug Testing Fails" provides resources for parents, educators, coaches, and other interested and concerned adults, who believe that safe and trusting learning environments are critical to our young people's health and safety, and that student drug testing programs get in the way of creating that kind of environment. . . .

"A Test You Can't Study For" is a special ACLU web feature on student drug testing that includes a guide for students, fact sheets, reports and other materials. . . .

Student for Sensible Drug Policy (SSDP), an organization with more than 115 college and high school chapters nationwide, is committed to providing education on harms caused by the war on drugs, working to involve youth in the political process, and promoting an open, honest and rational discussion of alternative solutions to our nation's drug problems. SSDP offers talking points, background materials and organizational assistance to students and families working to counteract drug testing programs in their school districts. . . .

Endnotes

1. Office for Human Research Protections to Peter O. Kohler, M.D., president, Oregon Health and Science University, determination letter, October 24, 2002; Adil E. Shamoo and Jonathan D. Moreno, "Ethics of Research Involving Mandatory Drug Testing of High School Athletes in Oregon," *The American Journal of Bioethics* 4, no. 1 (2004): pp. 25–31.

2. Linn Goldberg, the author of the study suspended by federal authorities, now agrees that "even his study did not prove that testing limits consumption. 'Schools should not implement a drug testing program until they're proven to work,' he added. 'They're too expensive. It's like having experimental surgery that's never been shown to work.'" Greg Winter, "Study Finds No Sign That Testing Deters Students' Drug Use," *New York Times,* May 17, 2003.

3. Neil McKeganey, *Random Drug Testing of Schoolchildren: A Shot in the Arm or a Shot in the Foot for Drug Prevention?* (York, UK: Joseph Rowntree Foundation, 2005), p. 12. . . .

4. Ryoko Yamaguchi, Lloyd D. Johnston, and Patrick M. O'Malley, "Relationship Between Student Illicit Drug Use and School Drug–Testing Policies," *Journal of School Health* 73, no. 4 (2003): pp. 159–164. . . .

5. Greg Winter, "Study Finds No Sign That Testing Deters Students' Drug Use," *New York Times,* May 17, 2003.

6. Ryoko Yamaguchi, Lloyd D. Johnston, and Patrick M. O'Malley, *Drug Testing in Schools, Policies, Practices, and Association With Student Drug Use,* Youth, Education, and Society (YES) Occasional Papers Series (Ann Arbor, MI: The Robert Wood Johnson Foundation, 2003). . . .

7. Ibid., p. 16.

8. Ryoko Yamaguchi, Lloyd D. Johnston, and Patrick M. O'Malley, "Relationship Between Student Illicit Drug Use and School Drug-Testing Policies," *Journal of School Health* 73, no. 4 (2003): p. 164.

9. See, for example: Nicholas Zill, Christine Winquist Nord, and Laura Spencer Loomis, "Adolescent Time Use, Risky Behavior and Outcomes: An Analysis of National Data," U.S. Department of Health and Human Services (1995). . . . Lee Shilts, "The Relationship of Early Adolescent Substance Use to Extracurricular Activities, Peer Influence, and Personal Attitudes," *Adolescence* 26, no. 103 (1991): pp. 613, 615; William J. Bailey, "Suspicionless Drug Testing in Schools," Indiana Prevention Resource Center (1998). . . . Robert Taylor, "Compensating Behavior and the Drug Testing of High School Athletes," *The Cato Journal* 16, No. 3 (1997). . . . and Rodney Skager, *Beyond Zero Tolerance: A Reality-Based Approach to Drug Education and Student Assistance* (San Francisco, CA: Drug Policy Alliance, 2005).

10. Jessica Raynor, "Guymon to Eliminate Drug Program," *Amarillo Globe-News Online,* August 15, 2002. . . .

11. Andrew Petkofsky, "School Scraps Drug Testing; but Mathews Will Make Kits Available," *Richmond Times Dispatch,* July 27, 2002.

12. Kay Nolan, "District Drops Random Drug Testing Plan; Proposal for Oconomowoc Schools Lacks Parents' Support," *Milwaukee Journal Sentinel,* October 22, 2003.

13. ACLU of Washington, "First Lawsuit Filed Challenging Suspicionless Student Urine-Testing in Washington," press release, December 17, 1999. . . .

14. Jackie Puccetti to Cathedral High School Community, February 28, 2003. . . .

15. Brief of Amici Curiae American Academy of Pediatrics, et al. at 1, *Board of Education of Independent School District No. 92 of Pottawatomie County, et al. v. Lindsay Earls, et al.,* 536 U.S. 822 (2002) (No. 01-332). . . .

16. National Association of Social Workers, "Social Workers Disagree with Supreme Court Decision to Test Students for Drug Use," press release, June 27, 2002. . . .

17. The Association for Addiction Professionals, "Supreme Court Ruling on Student Drug Testing Misguided: NAADAC Speaks Out Against Court's Approval of Random Drug Tests for Public School Students," press release, June 27, 2002. . . .

18. John R. Knight and Sharon Levy, "An F for School Drug Tests," *Boston Globe,* June 13, 2005.

19. *Board of Education of Independent School District No. 92 of Pottawatomie County, et al. v. Lindsay Earls, et al.,* 536 U.S. 822 (2002) (Ginsburg, R., dissenting).

20. Hawaii State Legislature, HB 273 "Relating to Education: Drug Testing Public School Students," Introduced January 21, 2005. . . .

21. Louisiana State Legislature, SB117 "Tuition Opportunity Program for Students," Considered April 24, 2003. . . .

22. See, for example: Clea A. McNeely, James M. Nonnemaker, and Robert W. Blum, "Promoting School Connectedness: Evidence from the National Longitudinal Study of Adolescent Health," *Journal of School Health* 72, no. 4 (2002): pp. 138–46; Rodney Skager, *Beyond Zero Tolerance: A Reality-Based Approach to Drug Education and Student Assistance* (San Francisco: Drug Policy Alliance, 2005).

23. "Proposed Random Drug Testing Plan Expected to Pass with Minor Changes," *Drug Detection Report,* 15 no. 10 (2005): p. 77.

24. "Student Drug Testing: An Investment in Fear," Drug Policy Alliance. . . .

25. Robert L. DuPont. Teresa G. Campbell and Jacqueline J. Mazza, *Report of a Preliminary Study: Elements of a Successful School-Based Student Drug Testing Program* (Rockville, MD: United States Department of Education, 2002), p. 8.

26. Mary Bridgman and Dean Narciso, "Dublin Halts Drug Tests; School District Stops Screening Athletes," *Columbus Dispatch,* June 26, 2002.

27. Mary Bridgman and Dean Narciso, "Dublin Halts Drug Tests; School District Stops Screening Athletes," *Columbus Dispatch,* June 26, 2002; Dublin Coffman High School Guidance Department, personal communication., July 2003; Richard Caster, Executive Director of Administration at the Dublin Schools, personal communication, April 2005; "Student Drug Testing: An Investment in Fear," Drug Policy Alliance. . . .

28. "ACLU Drug Testing Cases Across the Nation," ACLU. . . .

29. Statements come from the Brief of Amici Curiae of the American Academy of Pediatrics, et al., *Board of Education of Independent School District No. 92 of Pottawatomie County, et al. v. Lindsay Earls,* 536 U.S. 822 (2002) (No. 01-332). . . .

30. Julie Pederson and others, "The Potential of After-School Programs" in *Safe and Smart: Making After-School Hours Work for Kids* (Washington, D.C.: U.S. Department of Education and U.S. Department of Justice, 1998). . . .

31. Maureen Glancy, F. K. Willits and Patricia Farrell, "Adolescent Activities and Adult Success and Happiness: Twenty-four years later," *Sociology and Social Research* 70, no. 3 (1986): p. 242.

32. Plaintiffs in the lawsuit *Bean v. Tulia Independent School District,* claim that, "In 1990-1991 participation of black seniors was 100% in extracurricular clubs and activities and 100% in sports; while the 2000–2001 participation rates [after student drug testing] of black seniors fell to 0% within both." Affidavit of Nancy Cozette Bean, p. 3, *Bean v. Tulia Independent School District,* 2003 WL 22004511 (N.D. Tex. Feb. 18, 2003).

33. American Civil Liberties Union, *Drug Testing: A Bad Investment* (New York: ACLU, 1999), p. 18. . . .

34. Ibid.

35. C. Meadway, S. George, and R. Braithwaite, "Opiate Concentrations Following the Ingestion of Poppy Seed Product: Evidence for 'The Poppy Seed Defense,'" *Forensic Science International* 96, no. 1 (1998): pp. 29–38; American Civil Liberties Union, *Drug Testing: A Bad Investment* (New York: ACLU, 1999), p. 18. . . .

36. Respondents' Brief at 3, *Board of Education of Independent School District No. 92 of Pottawatomie County, et al. v. Lindsay Earls, et al.,* 536 U.S. 822 (2002) (No. 01-332).

37. Howard Taras, "Maximizing Student Health Resources," American Association of School Administrators (2003). . . .

38. American Civil Liberties Union, *Drug Testing: A Bad Investment* (New York: ACLU, 1999), p. 13. . . .

39. Annette Fuentes, "Student Drug Tests Aren't the Answer" *USA Today,* June 10, 2005.

40. Rob Nelson, "Jeff Schools Trim Drug Test Loophole; Hair Samples Will be Required by Policy," *Times Picayune,* July 11, 2003.

41. U.S. General Accounting Office, *Youth Illicit Drug Use Prevention: DARE Long-Term Evaluations and Federal Efforts to Identify Effective Programs* (Washington, D.C.: January 15, 2003).

42. Student Assistance Programs (SAPs) are comprehensive models for the delivery of K-12 prevention, intervention and support services. SAPs are designed to reduce student risk factors, promote protective factors, and increase personal development and decision-making skills by students. For information about developing SAPs, see the National Student Assistance Association. . . .

43. See: Rodney Skager, *Beyond Zero Tolerance: A Reality-Based Approach to Drug Education and Student Assistance* (San Francisco, CA: Drug Policy Alliance, 2005). . . .

44. Physician Leadership on National Drug Policy, *Adolescent Substance Abuse: A Public Health Priority; An Evidence-Based. Comprehensive and Integrative*

Approach (Providence, RI: Physician Leadership on National Drug Policy, 2002), pp. 23–31. . . . These tools include the Personal Experience Inventory (PEI), Drug Abuse Screening Test for Adolescents (DAST-A), and Adolescent Drug Involvement Scale (ADIS), among others.

45. See: Marsha Rosenbaum, *Safety First: A Reality-Based Approach to Teen, Drugs, and Drug Education* (San Francisco, CA: Drug Policy Alliance, 2004). . . .

POSTSCRIPT

Should Schools Drug Test Students?

Advocates for random drug testing and people opposed to drug testing do not agree on whether such programs reduce illegal drug use. Regardless of whether drug testing curtails the use of drugs, some critics are concerned that drug testing programs undermine relationships of trust between students and teachers. Teachers are often put in the position of enforcers.

An important question revolves around the role of parents regarding their children. Is it the responsibility of schools to test students for drug use? Should parents be responsible for their children's behavior? In addition, if students test positive for drugs, is it the schools or the parents' responsibility to deal with this problem?

Another concern regarding drug testing is that some schools may be susceptible to litigation. What is the school's role if a student is falsely identified as having used drugs? The federal government recognizes this risk and strongly supports that school districts that randomly drug test students have safeguards in the event that students test positive. Moreover, what actions should schools take if students test positive for drugs? Is the purpose to punish or help students who test positive? Lastly, which school personnel should have access to the results of drug tests? Generally, it is recommended that only school administrators and parents have access to this confidential information.

Some school administrators oppose drug testing on the grounds that such programs create a threatening environment. In addition, some administrators feel that drug testing represents an unwarranted invasion of privacy. Others maintain that whether or not students use drugs is the responsibility of parents, not schools. Proponents of drug testing point out that many parents abdicate their parental responsibilities. They claim that schools are the logical place to implement drug testing.

One concern is that students will try to outsmart the drug test. Whether or not one can fool a drug test is not the point. The point is that students may engage in unhealthy practices to avoid detection. One only has to surf the Internet to find hundreds of advertisements discussing ways to beat drug tests. One can purchase herbal detoxifiers, hair follicle shampoo, or drug-free replacement urine.

According to Supreme Court Justice Ruth Bader Ginsburg, drug testing "risks steering students at greater risk for substance abuse away from extracurricular involvement that potentially may palliate drug problems." At the present time, the vast majority of schools do not randomly drug test student athletes.

The federal government does not support that all schools drug test students. Its position is that schools should drug test if it or the community feels that there is a drug problem among its students. Without community support, drug testing is not advocated. Because the federal government recognizes that some students may test falsely positive, it recommends that reputable drug testing laboratories be used.

The legality of random drug testing is reviewed in "Drug Testing of Students," by David Evans, *Journal of Global Drug Policy and Practice* (2010) and in "Respect Versus Surveillance: Drug Testing Our Students," by Larry Brendtro and Gordon Martin in *Reclaiming Children and Youth* (Summer 2006). Two articles that point to the effectiveness of drug testing programs to reduce drug use are "High School Drug Testing Program Dramatically Reduces Drug Use" in *Medical Letter on the CDC and FDA* (February 2, 2003) and Norm Brodsky's article "Street Smarts," in *INC Magazine* (November 2004). The issue of drug testing teachers was discussed in "To Test or Not to Test? Drug Testing Teachers: The View of the Superintendent," by Todd DeMitchell, Stephen Kossakoski, and Tony Baldasaro, *Teachers College Record* (2008).

ISSUE 18

Does Drug Abuse Treatment Work?

YES: National Institute on Drug Abuse, from *Principles of Drug Addiction Treatment: A Research-Based Guide* (April 2009)

NO: Robert Hubbard, D. Dwayne Simpson, and George Woody, from "Treatment Research: Accomplishments and Challenges," *Journal of Drug Issues* (2009)

ISSUE SUMMARY

YES: The National Institute on Drug Abuse report acknowledges that drug addiction is difficult to overcome but that treatment can be effective and works best when individuals are committed to remain in treatment for an extended time.

NO: Drug treatment experts Robert Hubbard, D. Dwayne Simpson, and George Woody indicate that there is a need to establish scientific evidence for treatment to achieve desirable outcomes, and there is no clear consensus on what constitutes substance abuse treatment.

Numerous drug experts feel that more funding should go toward preventing drug use from starting or escalating and toward treating individuals who are dependent on drugs. Today, when taxpayers dispute how their tax monies are spent, the question of whether government funds should be used to treat people who abuse drugs is especially relevant. Questions surrounding this debate include: Does drug abuse treatment reduce criminal activities associated with drugs? Will drug addicts stop their abusive behavior if they enter treatment? Will more drug addicts receive treatment than currently do if services are expanded? Will the availability and demand for illegal drugs decline?

The research on the effectiveness of drug treatment is mixed. In *The Effectiveness of Treatment for Drug Abusers Under Criminal Justice Supervision* (National Institute of Justice, 1995), Douglas S. Lipton states that drug abuse treatment not only reduces the rate of arrests but also reduces crime and lowers the cost to taxpayers over the long run. Also, it has been shown that illicit drug use is curtailed by drug abuse treatment and that treated drug addicts are better able to function in society and maintain employment. Perhaps most important, drug treatment may prove beneficial in curbing the escalation of HIV (human immunodeficiency virus), the virus that causes AIDS. During treatment they can be advised about behaviors that lead to HIV transmission.

Some experts contend that reports regarding the effectiveness of drug treatment are not always accurate and that research on drug abuse has not been subjected to rigorous standards. Some question how effectiveness should be determined. If a person relapses after one year, should the treatment be considered ineffective? Would a reduction in an individual's illegal drug use indicate that the treatment was effective, or would an addict have to maintain complete abstinence? Also, if illegal drug use and criminal activity decline after treatment, it is possible that these results would have occurred anyway, regardless of whether the individual had been treated.

There are a variety of drug treatment programs. One type of treatment program developed in the 1960s is *therapeutic communities*. Therapeutic communities are usually residential facilities staffed by former drug addicts. Although there is no standard definition of what constitutes a therapeutic community, the program generally involves task assignments for residents (the addicts undergoing treatment), group intervention techniques, vocational and educational counseling, and personal skill development. Inpatient treatment facilities, such as the Betty Ford Center, are the most expensive type of treatment and are often based on a hospital model. These programs are very structured and include highly regimented schedules, demanding rules of conduct, and individual and group counseling.

Outpatient treatment, the most common type of drug treatment, is less expensive, less stigmatizing, and less disruptive to the abuser's family than other forms of treatment. Vocational, educational, and social counseling is provided. Outpatient treatment is often used after an addict leaves an inpatient program. One type of treatment that has proliferated in recent years is the self-help group. Members of self-help groups are bound by a common denominator, whether it is alcohol, cocaine, or narcotics. Due to the anonymous and confidential nature of self-help groups, however, it is difficult to conduct follow-up research to determine their effectiveness.

Individuals addicted to narcotics are often referred to methadone maintenance programs. Methadone is a synthetic narcotic that prevents narcotic addicts from getting high and eliminates withdrawal symptoms. Because methadone's effects last about 24 hours, addicts need to receive treatment frequently. Unfortunately, the relapse rate is high once addicts stop treatment. Because there is much demand for methadone maintenance in some areas, there are lengthy waiting lists. A newer, more effective drug for treating narcotic addiction is buprenorphine.

In the YES selection, the National Institute on Drug Abuse report maintains that treatment can be effective. However, it is necessary for the individual to be committed and to remain in treatment for an extensive time. Drug treatment results in lesser drug use and lower health and social costs. In the NO selection, Hubbard, et al., contend there needs to be a better way to determine the effectiveness of drug treatment. They also feel that there is a lack of consensus on what successful drug treatment entails.

Principles of Drug Addiction Treatment: A Research-Based Guide

1. Why Do Drug-Addicted Persons Keep Using Drugs?

Nearly all addicted individuals believe at the outset that they can stop using drugs on their own, and most try to stop without treatment. Although some people are successful, many attempts result in failure to achieve long-term abstinence. Research has shown that long-term drug abuse results in changes in the brain that persist long after a person stops using drugs. These drug-induced changes in brain function can have many behavioral consequences, including an inability to exert control over the impulse to use drugs despite adverse consequences—the defining characteristic of addiction.

Long-term drug use results in significant changes in brain function that can persist long after the individual stops using drugs.

Understanding that addiction has such a fundamental biological component may help explain the difficulty of achieving and maintaining abstinence without treatment. Psychological stress from work, family problems, psychiatric illness, pain associated with medical problems, social cues (such as meeting individuals from one's drug-using past), or environmental cues (such as encountering streets, objects, or even smells associated with drug abuse) can trigger intense cravings without the individual even being consciously aware of the triggering event. Any one of these factors can hinder attainment of sustained abstinence and make relapse more likely. Nevertheless, research indicates that active participation in treatment is an essential component for good outcomes and can benefit even the most severely addicted individuals.

2. What Is Drug Addiction Treatment?

Drug treatment is intended to help addicted individuals stop compulsive drug seeking and use. Treatment can occur in a variety of settings, in many different forms, and for different lengths of time. Because drug addiction is typically a

From *Principles of Drug Addiction Treatment: A Research-Based Guide*, April 2009, National Institute on Drug Abuse.

chronic disorder characterized by occasional relapses, a short-term, one-time treatment is usually not sufficient. For many, treatment is a long-term process that involves multiple interventions and regular monitoring.

There are a variety of evidence-based approaches to treating addiction. Drug treatment can include behavioral therapy (such as individual or group counseling, cognitive therapy, or contingency management), medications, or their combination. The specific type of treatment or combination of treatments will vary depending on the patient's individual needs and, often, on the types of drugs they use. The severity of addiction and previous efforts to stop using drugs can also influence a treatment approach. Finally, people who are addicted to drugs often suffer from other health (including other mental health), occupational, legal, familial, and social problems that should be addressed concurrently.

The best programs provide a combination of therapies and other services to meet an individual patient's needs. Specific needs may relate to age, race, culture, sexual orientation, gender, pregnancy, other drug use, comorbid conditions (e.g., depression, HIV), parenting, housing, and employment, as well as physical and sexual abuse history.

Drug addiction treatment can include medications, behavioral therapies, or their combination.

Treatment medications, such as methadone, buprenorphine, and naltrexone, are available for individuals addicted to opioids, while nicotine preparations (patches, gum, lozenges, and nasal spray) and the medications varenicline and bupropion are available for individuals addicted to tobacco. Disulfiram, acamprosate, naltrexone, and topiramate are medications used for treating alcohol dependence, which commonly co-occurs with other drug addictions. In fact, most people with severe addiction are polydrug users and require treatment for all substances abused. Even combined alcohol and tobacco use has proven amenable to concurrent treatment for both substances.

Psychoactive medications, such as antidepressants, antianxiety agents, mood stabilizers, and antipsychotic medications, may be critical for treatment success when patients have co-occurring mental disorders, such as depression, anxiety disorders (including post-traumatic stress disorder), bipolar disorder, or schizophrenia.

Behavioral therapies can help motivate people to participate in drug treatment; offer strategies for coping with drug cravings; teach ways to avoid drugs and prevent relapse; and help individuals deal with relapse if it occurs. Behavioral therapies can also help people improve communication, relationship, and parenting skills, as well as family dynamics.

Many treatment programs employ both individual and group therapies. Group therapy can provide social reinforcement and help enforce behavioral contingencies that promote abstinence and a non-drug-using lifestyle. Some of the more established behavioral treatments, such as contingency management and cognitive-behavioral therapy, are also being adapted for group settings to improve efficiency and cost-effectiveness. However, particularly in adolescents, there can also be a danger of iatrogenic, or inadvertent, effects of group treatment; thus, trained counselors should be aware and monitor for such effects.

Because they work on different aspects of addiction, combinations of behavioral therapies and medications (when available) generally appear to be more effective than either approach used alone.

Treatment for drug abuse and addiction is delivered in many different settings using a variety of behavioral and pharmacological approaches.

3. How Effective Is Drug Addiction Treatment?

In addition to stopping drug abuse, the goal of treatment is to return people to productive functioning in the family, workplace, and community. According to research that tracks individuals in treatment over extended periods, most people who get into and remain in treatment stop using drugs, decrease their criminal activity, and improve their occupational, social, and psychological functioning. For example, methadone treatment has been shown to increase participation in behavioral therapy and decrease both drug use and criminal behavior. However, individual treatment outcomes depend on the extent and nature of the patient's problems, the appropriateness of treatment and related services used to address those problems, and the quality of interaction between the patient and his or her treatment providers.

Relapse rates for addiction resemble those of other chronic diseases such as diabetes, hypertension, and asthma.

Like other chronic diseases, addiction can be managed successfully. Treatment enables people to counteract addiction's powerful disruptive effects on the brain and behavior and to regain control of their lives. The chronic nature of the disease means that relapsing to drug abuse is not only possible but also likely, with relapse rates similar to those for other well-characterized chronic medical illnesses—such as diabetes, hypertension, and asthma (see figure, "Comparison of Relapse Rates Between Drug Addiction and Other Chronic Illnesses")—that also have both physiological and behavioral components.

Unfortunately, when relapse occurs many deem treatment a failure. This is not the case: successful treatment for addiction typically requires continual evaluation and modification as appropriate, similar to the approach taken for other chronic diseases. For example, when a patient is receiving active treatment for hypertension and symptoms decrease, treatment is deemed successful, even though symptoms may recur when treatment is discontinued. For the addicted patient, lapses to drug abuse do not indicate failure—rather, they signify that treatment needs to be reinstated or adjusted, or that alternate treatment is needed.

4. Is Drug Addiction Treatment Worth Its Cost?

Substance abuse costs our Nation over one half-trillion dollars annually, and treatment can help reduce these costs. Drug addiction treatment has been shown to reduce associated health and social costs by far more than the cost

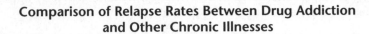

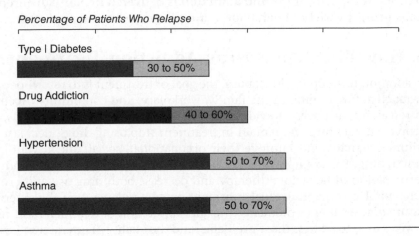

Comparison of Relapse Rates Between Drug Addiction and Other Chronic Illnesses

Percentage of Patients Who Relapse

Type I Diabetes — 30 to 50%

Drug Addiction — 40 to 60%

Hypertension — 50 to 70%

Asthma — 50 to 70%

of the treatment itself. Treatment is also much less expensive than its alternatives, such as incarcerating addicted persons. For example, the average cost for 1 full year of methadone maintenance treatment is approximately $4,700 per patient, whereas 1 full year of imprisonment costs approximately $24,000 per person.

Drug addiction treatment reduces drug use and its associated health and social costs.

According to several conservative estimates, every $1 invested in addiction treatment programs yields a return of between $4 and $7 in reduced drug-related crime, criminal justice costs, and theft. When savings related to health care are included, total savings can exceed costs by a ratio of 12 to 1. Major savings to the individual and to society also stem from fewer interpersonal conflicts; greater workplace productivity; and fewer drug-related accidents, including overdoses and deaths.

5. How Long Does Drug Addiction Treatment Usually Last?

Individuals progress through drug addiction treatment at various rates, so there is no predetermined length of treatment. However, research has shown unequivocally that good outcomes are contingent on adequate treatment length. Generally, for residential or outpatient treatment, participation for less than 90 days is of limited effectiveness, and treatment lasting significantly longer is recommended for maintaining positive outcomes. For methadone maintenance, 12 months is considered the minimum, and some opioid-addicted individuals continue to benefit from methadone mainte-nance for many years.

Good outcomes are contingent on adequate treatment length.

Treatment dropout is one of the major problems encountered by treatment programs; therefore, motivational techniques that can keep patients engaged will also improve outcomes. By viewing addiction as a chronic disease and offering continuing care and monitoring, programs can succeed, but this will often require multiple episodes of treatment and readily re-admitting patients that have relapsed.

6. What Helps People Stay in Treatment?

Because successful outcomes often depend on a person's staying in treat-ment long enough to reap its full benefits, strategies for keeping people in treatment are critical. Whether a patient stays in treatment depends on fac-tors associated with both the individual and the program. Individual factors related to engagement and retention typically include motivation to change drug-using behavior; degree of support from family and friends; and, fre-quently, pressure from the criminal justice system, child protection services, employers, or the family. Within a treatment program, successful clinicians can establish a positive, therapeutic relationship with their patients. The cli-nician should ensure that a treatment plan is developed cooperatively with the person seeking treatment, that the plan is followed, and that treatment epectations are clearly understood. Medical, psychiatric, and social services should also be available.

Whether a patient stays in treatment depends on factors associated with both the individual and the program.

Because some problems (such as serious medical or mental illness or crim-inal involvement) increase the likelihood of patients dropping out of treatment, intensive interventions may be required to retain them. After a course of intensive treatment, the provider should ensure a transition to less intensive continuing care to support and monitor individuals in their ongo-ing recovery. . . .

Reducing this gap requires a multipronged approach. Strategies include increasing access to effective treatment, achieving insurance parity (now in its earliest phase of implementation), reducing stigma, and raising awareness among both patients and health care professionals of the value of addiction treatment. To assist physicians in identifying treatment need in their patients and making appropriate referrals, NIDA is encouraging widespread use of screening, brief intervention, and referral to treatment (SBIRT) tools for use in primary care settings. SBIRT—which has proven effective against tobacco and alcohol use—has the potential not only to catch people before serious drug problems develop but also to connect them with appropriate treatment providers.

7. How Can Families and Friends Make a Difference in the Life of Someone Needing Treatment?

Family and friends can play critical roles in motivating individuals with drug problems to enter and stay in treatment. Family therapy can also be important, especially for adolescents. Involvement of a family member or significant other in an individual's treatment program can strengthen and extend treatment benefits. . . .

Robert Hubbard, D. Dwayne
Simpson, and George Woody

 **NO**

Treatment Research: Accomplishments and Challenges

Introduction

The social and political history of drug abuse in the United States has helped set the stage for current public policy regarding drug addiction. The modern history of treatment research on substance use disorders can be traced to the residential programs that were established at the federal facilities at Lexington, Kentucky and Fort Worth, Texas in the 1930s. Research then focused on the pharmacological and psychiatric effects of abused substances, detoxification regimens, psychopathology, and follow-up studies of patients after they had been discharged and returned to their home environments.

[T]he 1960s were pivotal years. The Narcotic Addict Rehabilitation Act of 1966 initiated historical shifts from a limited institution-based approach to a national community-based treatment system for dealing with drug problems. By introducing a civil commitment (mandatory treatment) alternative to prison incarceration for addicted persons charged with certain types of crime, this legislation helped declare drug addiction a "health" problem. Some of the first outpatient studies were begun in the 1960s . . . with methadone maintenance. In 1972, President Richard Nixon declared the first "War on Drugs." With the establishment of the National Institute on Drug Abuse (NIDA) in the 1974, the scope of treatment research expanded, and through an unprecedented infusion of funding for community-based treatment programs, the modern era of drug abuse treatment and evaluation research was created. This work was further expanded when NIDA received substantial funding increases in the late 1980s after it became clear that HIV was being transmitted through substance-related behaviors, such as needle sharing. The expanding research scope at NIDA is reflected in the expanding scope and number of attendees at the annual meeting of the Committee on Problems of Drug Dependence, which increased from several hundred attendees in the 1980s to more than 1,200 by the year 2000.

The actions during this period of expansion put treatment services and research on the map, establishing programs in hundreds of communities. Four fundamental treatment modalities (mainly for addressing heroin addiction) were established, including methadone maintenance treatment, drug-free outpatient treatment, drug-free residential treatment, and opioid detoxification programs of varying lengths. Implementation and funding of these treatment approaches raised questions of effectiveness that carried implications for both science and policy.

Evaluation research has been crucial in establishing the credibility of a national network of drug treatment programs and in obtaining public funds for their support. It has led to new avenues of study involving modification and improvement of assessment and intervention strategies, and in the case of AIDS outreach initiatives, helped the field move beyond traditional treatment approaches to establish additional behavior change initiatives in the community. Many findings of evaluation studies have been translated into public policy and program development, in accord with the visibility given to those findings and their urgency. The following comments provide different research perspectives on the results of this work over the past 40 years.

Advancements in Treatment

Importance of Research in Treatment: Dwayne Simpson

Questions asked of addiction scientists during the past 40 years have moved beyond "does treatment work?" to "how and when is it effective?" Long-standing findings from large-scale national evaluations and clinical trials show that more time in treatment is related to better outcomes. Outcome research indicates that therapeutic benefits tend to begin showing up behaviorally (and reliably) after about three months of treatment. For agonist treatment, this retention threshold for posttreatment improvements is closer to a year. To explain this relationship, evaluation efforts have increasingly focused on the interactions between client attributes and clinical dynamics, and how they relate to retention and recovery indicators.

The results have addressed the needs for establishing scientific evidence for treatment process as well as for practical applications for improving delivery of services. Longitudinal designs have been used to explain the sequential relationships between needs and motivation for treatment, early engagement, early recovery, length of stay in treatment, and post-treatment outcomes as elements of a stage-based process. Findings show that higher pretreatment levels of client motivation and readiness for treatment are related to better treatment engagement, and that general indicators of treatment progress can be represented in three stages. First, clients entering treatment must participate and begin forming positive therapeutic relationships with the counseling team. Favorable indicators of early engagement are especially important in the first two months after treatment admission, and they are positively related with client motivation and treatment readiness. Second, indicators of early recovery by month three are directly related to the level of early engagement shown by clients. Third, favorable evidence on early recovery indicators predicts better retention in treatment. Identifying some of these critical elements and how they are linked to treatment effectiveness helps service providers make more informed choices about improving services.

Several reliable assessments of client functioning and treatment engagement have been developed for clinical applications. One option for monitoring client needs and progress is the *Client Evaluation of Self and Treatment* (CEST) assessment, which includes brief scales for motivation, psychological and social functioning, therapeutic engagement, and social support. Repeating such assessments over time can also be used to evaluate the progress of individual clients or the overall program.

By establishing measurable stages of treatment process, interventions can be strategically planned and evaluated based on their efficacy for addressing specific needs. Treatment effectiveness literature generally supports the value of motivational enhancement techniques, cognitive strengths-based counseling, behavioral reinforcement therapy, and social support networking. To enhance clinical practice, however, treatment strategies and interventions need to be adapted logically to define the optimal client treatment sequence. Client needs and progress at each stage of care therefore should guide the flow of services. Furthermore, the collective use of manual-guided interventions contributed proportionally to improvements in post-treatment outcome performance. Effective treatment process is defined by deliberate integration of client needs and progress assessments with a specialized series of interventions. It is the goal of treatment care planning to monitor and manage these issues.

Changing Treatment Options: George Woody

Options for the treatment of substance abuse have advanced significantly in the past 40 years from the days of self-help groups, limited slots in residential programs, and few referrals. The number of residential programs and therapeutic communities has increased, and intensive outpatient treatments have been developed. The 1989 Medications Development Program at NIDA facilitated a variety of advances. Benzodiazepines had been shown to be effective detoxification agents for alcohol dependence in earlier studies, and key elements of methadone maintenance programs, such as using adequate doses, were established. Although still not widely used, naltrexone has been approved for opioid dependence and more recently found helpful for preventing relapse to alcohol dependence. The use of buprenorphine, although off to a slow start, has been attracting those with opioid dependence who did not do well on existing treatment options. Nicotine replacement and buproprion therapies were developed for nicotine dependence.

Studies showing that psychosocial treatments are helpful broke new ground, moving research beyond its primarily pharmacological basis. The most widely studied psychosocial treatment has been contingency management followed by drug counseling. A range of psychotherapies have been used, including cognitive-behavioral, supportive-expressive, interpersonal, motivational enhancement and motivational interviewing, and self-help groups.

Most individuals with substance use disorders have psychiatric and medical problems that complicate the course of their recovery, and research has demonstrated that addressing these problems improves the overall prognosis. The emergence of HIV and hepatitis C added new challenges, any studies show that HIV risk can be prevented by substance abuse treatment and risk reduction counseling. Prevention efforts have also been focused on the risky sexual behaviors associated with cocaine and amphetamine addictions.

Although NIDA research has uncovered many ways to help persons with substance use disorders, no medication or combination of pharmacotherapy and psychotherapy has yet been developed that cures addiction. The fact that treatment can help but not cure the phenomenon of relapse even after extended periods of remission have led to addiction being viewed more as a chronic relapsing disorder rather than an acute problem that can be corrected with a single treatment.

Although self-help groups, addiction researchers, and clinicians have recognized that substance use disorders often require years or even a lifetime of sustained treatment, politicians and the general public do not share this view. This has created ambivalence about the degree to which treatment should be supported and presents barriers to the full application of research findings, including sufficient funding to meet treatment demand.

The Importance of Research: Robert Hubbard

Over 40 years of research, fundamental facts have been observed, including the positive effects of duration of treatment, as well as the positive benefit-cost ratios of treatment and the cost-effectiveness of treatment when compared to other options, such as prison. Major national studies, as well as individual studies, replicated these findings: Drug Abuse Reporting Program (DARP) 1969–1973, Treatment Outcome Prospective Study (TOPS) 1979–1981, and Drug Abuse Treatment Outcome Study (DATOS) 1991–1993. This occurred despite major changes in the client populations, the treatment programs, and the funding context. We have also made great strides in more complete and comprehensive descriptions of the clients entering treatment, the treatment they receive and the environments in which programs function.

Barriers to Organizational Change: Dwayne Simpson

As treatment programs are being pressed to adopt evidence-based innovations for improving therapeutic effectiveness and efficiency, questions about organizational structure and functioning are beginning to receive greater attention. Relying on dissemination of innovation has proven to be ineffective, and evidence is mounting that organizational functioning is directly related to quality of care. Therefore, some treatment systems are becoming increasingly interested in how to conduct an organizational assessment that is related to "readiness for change" by staff members.

Treatment programs trying to implement innovations progress through systematic steps before new ways of doing things become accepted as practice. To adopt new ideas, decisions must be made based on the support solicited from both staff and leadership, the adequacy of resources committed to the change, and how well the change fits with prevailing values about treatment process and recovery. The next step involves implementation, which is guided according to the feasibility of innovations as well as staff and client perceptions about effectiveness. The ultimate step of new interventions from trial to routine practice depends largely on benefits (compared to costs), as well as having an effective monitoring and rewards system for sustaining progress. At each step of the way, however, barriers are present.

Bringing together clearly integrated assessment and intervention resources that are relevant to client needs and that can be implemented with the modest resources typically available is required for making meaningful changes in clinical care for drug-related problems. A crucial overarching dynamic in this change process involves institutional "atmosphere" and leadership, staff skills and interrelationships, resources, and motivational pressures. Implementation efforts require that appropriate staff skills be available, and a climate of vision, tolerance, and commitment is necessary to make them permanent. Resolving these barriers to widespread use of "evidence-based treatment" carries a high priority.

Ambivalence Toward Addiction and Treatment: George Woody

One of the greatest barriers to implementing research findings seems related to unresolved ambivalence about whether addiction is a moral/self-control problem or a medical disorder. This ambivalence has a long history that has alternated between these two positions both in the U.S. and other countries and has important treatment implications. If addiction were a medical disorder, then use of medications and other biologically-based therapies would seem appropriate. However, if addiction is a failure of morality or self-control, then psychosocial, religious, or criminal interventions seem more appropriate.

Throughout most of the 20th century, the prevailing view in the U.S. has been that addiction is a moral or self-control problem. This view is reflected in the proportion of funds spent for law enforcement as compared to treatment, the strict anti-drug laws and liberal use of prison as opposed to treatment for drug offenders, and in the reductions in money spent on substance abuse treatment over the past ten years.

The increased use of mandated treatment rather than incarceration for nonviolent drug offenders and the rapid expansion of drug courts can be seen as an attempt to find a middle ground between the moral or self-control view and medical view. A study done in Delaware demonstrated benefits from a combination of legal pressure and treatment. Addicted individuals who received psychosocial treatment modeled after methods used in therapeutic communities while in prison had improved outcomes, with even better outcomes if treatment was continued following release. Unfortunately, few insurance plans pay for opioid maintenance treatment although many studies have consistently shown that it is safe and effective when administered according to standard guidelines. Along the same lines, courts rarely refer opioid-dependent patients to methadone maintenance, which, paradoxically, is the single treatment with the greatest level of empirical support.

Treating addicted Vietnam veterans has been the only wide-scale program to receive unambivalent political support. As a result of widespread concern about returning veterans with heroin addictions, special funding was allocated for addiction treatment programs in the Department of Veterans Affairs in the early 1970s, toward the end of the Vietnam war. These programs grew with strong administrative support but began to slow in the mid 1980s and then declined sharply in 1995 when funds were reallocated to primary care.

Treatment advocacy has been very helpful in getting popular support for many medical disorders, but advocacy for addiction treatment suffers for many reasons. Many who have recovered or are doing well in treatment are reluctant to speak because they fear adverse social consequences, especially those who have been addicted to illegal drugs. In addition, many addicted persons have serious behavioral problems that generate negative responses from neighbors, the general public, and even their own families, making it difficult to obtain support for anything other than an expansion of criminal justice responses.

The founders of Alcoholics Anonymous (AA) believed that collaboration between 12-Step programs and the medical profession could provide benefits, but somehow that message found in the early writings became modified so that many 12-Step programs developed a philosophy that opposed the use of medications. The result was, in many cases, a peer-based opposition to the use of medication unless it was for detoxification. Compounding the problem of organized opposition to using medications was the fact that much addiction treatment in the U.S. developed outside the medical system. The result was that for many years AA was the only place to turn for help, and treatment became dominated by a non-medical approach. This problem has lessened with the development of methadone maintenance, along with studies showing that medications to treat associated psychiatric problems, such as depression, are helpful.

Relapse is a common problem even among patients who have been abstinent over long periods of time, and relapses lead to the perception that treatment does not work. This view is not applied to other chronic, relapsing disorders where improvement in the absence of cure is valued and it seems related to the idea that addiction is a moral rather than a medical problem. Addressing comorbidities and using medication require medical personnel, who are the most expensive treatment staff. Administrators trying to reduce health care costs have strong incentives to minimize the amount of medical services, which can result in barriers to treatments that use medications or that address comorbidity. Other barriers have been the regulatory structures under which methadone maintenance programs have been required to operate.

The Institute of Medicine published a comprehensive report on the effect of regulations on access to methadone. This report concluded that although regulations were necessary, the current structure was overly restrictive. It led to a shift for monitoring methadone programs from the regulatory approach of the Food and Drug Administration (FDA) to accreditation involving Joint Commission on Accreditation of Healthcare Organizations (JCAHO), Commission on Accreditation of Rehabilitation Facilities (CARF), or state agencies and provided the basis for the Addiction Treatment Act of 2000. This act permits agonist and other medications classified as Schedule III or below and approved for addiction treatment to be used under less restrictive circumstances than has been the case with methadone. Related to this legislation was the approval of buprenorphine/naloxone (Suboxone®) as a Schedule III medication for maintenance treatment of opioid dependence. The increasing use of buprenorphine for detoxification and maintenance demonstrates how this Congressional action helped reduce barriers to agonist treatment.

Perspectives on Research: Robert Hubbard

The field has made great strides to develop professional competence, use evidence-based practice, and integrate with the general health care system. The benefits of this movement should be weighed against the possible unanticipated negative effects, such as managed care, shortages and turnover of credentialed staff, evidence-based practices incompatible with many treatment contexts, and the stigma attached to the field within the general health care system. The attempt to develop scientific credibility for the field has resulted in an emphasis on clinical trials of specific interventions at the expense of critically needed research on the complex issues of organizational structure, treatment process, and recovery dynamics impossible to address within a clinical trial paradigm. Narrow perspectives on the broad array of core and comprehensive components of treatment and a myopic vision of the field may hinder future advances as well as place effective programs and approaches at risk. The arbitrary constriction of "28-day" short-term inpatient programs and the shift to group therapy are two major changes in the treatment system undertaken without empirical basis.

Future

Research and Application: Dwayne Simpson

In 1968, Texas Christian University (TCU) launched the first national evaluation of community-based treatment effectiveness (DARP). The late Saul B. Sells assembled a small team of researchers to address the "question of the day" on whether a new national system for delivering treatment for substance abuse through existing community health agencies was feasible and effective. This created a "niche" of applied evaluators, and several original members of this team are still together at TCU and still working on the answers for treatments being provided in community and correctional settings. After several hundred publications, however, it seems the questions have grown more complicated over time. The attributes, needs, and situations of clients; the attributes, counseling styles, and cognitions about clients and colleagues of counselors; and program settings all represent dynamic forces that preclude stable or simplistic conclusions about effectiveness. The applications of randomized clinical trial designs for clinical efficacy studies and natural (longitudinal) designs for field effectiveness studies still seek peaceful coexistence in their mutual pursuit of evidence, but a balance between these perspectives is necessary to sustain progress in addiction treatment. In the end, it is important to hear from real-world service providers who can apply the findings (and related resources) and say thanks for helping to make them better. Most scientists staring at their "40-year reflection" in the mirror will likely admit that such feedback from the front-lines is the most powerful motivator for what they do.

Progress and Improvements: George Woody

Over the last 40 years, the range and availability of addiction treatments have improved substantially. NIDA funding and the many dedicated professionals working in the field have greatly facilitated progress despite the many barriers to the implementation of evidence-based treatments. The NIDA Clinical Trials Network (CTN) is a recent effort to overcome some of the barriers and seems to be making progress as judged by its success in conducting treatment outcome studies in a wide range of community-based programs.

Persistence in working to improve treatment and reduce barriers so that treatment benefits can be more fully realized is essential. In looking back, the patients I saw on the medical and surgical units during medical school rounds in the early 1960s would now have a much better chance of finding a treatment that helped, it seems important to keep a longer-term perspective in mind and to be thankful for what we have achieved, while at the same time trying to do better.

Coping with Complexity: Robert Hubbard

Despite the major advances in knowledge and practice over the past 40 years, the system is still marginalized, stigmatized, and fractionated. It is under pressure and at risk of failure in many areas, particularly for rural, uninsured, and underserved populations. Improved effectiveness must be the goal for both knowledge and practice. This can only be achieved through research, political support for treatment development, and practice that takes into account how clients and programs function in complex and changing real-world contexts.

POSTSCRIPT

Does Drug Abuse Treatment Work?

Much of the research on drug abuse treatment effectiveness is inconclusive; furthermore, researchers do not agree on what the best way is to measure effectiveness. Determining the effectiveness of drug abuse treatment is extremely important because the federal government and a number of state governments debate how much fund should be allocated for drug treatment. Many experts in the drug field agree that much of the money that has been used to deal with problems related to drugs has not been wisely spent. To prevent further wastage of taxpayer funds, it is essential to find out if drug abuse treatment works before funding for it is increased.

Another concern related to this issue is that addicts who wish to receive treatment often face many barriers. One of the most serious barriers is that there is a lack of available treatment facilities. Compounding the problem is the fact that many communities resist the idea of having a drug treatment center in the neighborhoods, even though there is little research on the effects of treatment facilities on property values and neighborhood crime rates. Another barrier to treatment is cost, which, with the exception of self-help groups, is expensive. Furthermore, some addicts avoid organized treatment altogether for fear that if they go for treatment, they will be identified as drug abusers by law enforcement agencies. Likewise, many female drug addicts avoid drug treatment because they fear they will lose custody of their children.

Many addicts in treatment are there because they are given a choice of entering either prison or treatment. Are people who are required to enter treatment more or less likely to succeed than people who enter treatment voluntarily? Early studies showed that treatment was more effective for voluntary clients. However, a study conducted by the U.S. federal government on 12,000 clients enrolled in 41 publicly funded treatment centers found that clients referred by the criminal justice system fared as well as if not better than voluntary clients in terms of reduced criminal activity and drug use. People who enter treatment voluntarily have an easier time walking away from treatment. Typically, the longer one stays in treatment, the more likely the treatment will be effective.

One emerging trend is to provide drug treatment to people in prison. Prison-based drug treatment has increased in recent years. Drug abuse treatment to prison inmates has been shown to reduce recidivism.

All age groups are affected by drug abuse as noted in "Sociodemographic Characteristics of Substance Abuse Treatment Admissions Aged 50 or Older: 1992 to 2008" (*The TEDS Report*, Substance Abuse and Mental Health Services

Administration, August 5, 2010) and "Primary and Secondary/Tertiary Marijuana Use Among Substance Abuse Treatment Admissions" (*The TEDS Report*, Substance Abuse and Mental Health Services Administration, December 16, 2010). The impact of drug treatment on criminality is discussed in "Criminality and Addiction: Selected Issues for Future Policies, Practice, & Research" by M. Douglas Anglin, Barry Brown, Richard Dembo, and Carl Leukefeld (*Journal of Drug Issues*, 2009).

ISSUE 19

Should Schools Enforce a Zero Tolerance Drug Policy?

YES: Tracy J. Evans-Whipp, Lyndal Bond, John W. Toumbourou, and Richard F. Catalano, from "School, Parent, and Student Perspectives of School Drug Policies," *Journal of School Health* (March 2007)

NO: Rodney Skager, from "Beyond Zero Tolerance: A Reality-Based Approach to Drug Education and School Discipline" (*Drug Policy Alliance,* 2007)

ISSUE SUMMARY

YES: Tracy J. Evans-Whipp, of the Murdoch Children's Research Institute in Melbourne, Australia, and her colleagues maintain that an abstinence message coupled with harsh penalties is more effective at reducing drug use than a message aimed at minimizing the harms of drugs. They contend that an abstinence message is clear and that a harm reduction message may give a mixed message.

NO: Rodney Skager, formerly a professor at UCLA, argues that a zero tolerance drug policy does not change drug-taking behavior among young people. Instead of merely punishing drug offenders, Skager suggests that effective drug education is needed. Instances in which drug use presents a significant problem for the user may require intervention and treatment. Again, zero tolerance does very little to rectify behavior.

Drug education is arguably one of the most logical ways of dealing with the problems of drugs in American society. Drug-taking behavior has not been significantly affected by attempts to reduce the demand for drugs, and drug prohibition has not been successful either. One remaining option to explore is drug education. Drug education is not a panacea for eliminating drug problems. Rates of cigarette smoking are much lower today than they were thirty and forty years ago, but it took several decades of public health efforts to achieve this decline. If drug education is to ultimately prove successful, it too will take years. However, will a zero tolerance policy reduce drug use? Will students heed the message that they should abstain from drug use?

Many early drug education programs were misguided. One emphasis was on scare tactics. Experts erroneously believed that if young people saw the horrible consequences of drug use, then they would certainly abstain from drugs. Another faulty assumption was that drug use would be affected by knowledge about drugs, but knowledge is not enough. Over 400,000 people die each year from tobacco use, but many adults and teenagers continue to smoke even though most know the grim statistics about tobacco. Young people have a hard time relating to the potential problems like cancer and cirrhosis of the liver (which is caused by long-term alcohol abuse) because these problems take years to manifest themselves. Another problem with early drug education is that much of the information that teachers relayed concerning drugs was either incorrect or exaggerated. Teachers were therefore not seen as credible.

One could argue that a zero tolerance policy does not ultimately change behavior. Many people who go to prison for drug use return to using drugs after their release. A zero tolerance approach, according to some people, is a Band-Aid on a larger problem. One's unhealthy behavior, drug use, is not exchanged for a healthy behavior. Moreover, even if drug use is prevented in a school environment, drug use can occur outside of school. The zero tolerance approach overlooks the possibility that young people may turn to drugs because they want to be accepted by their peers, because drugs are forbidden, or simply because they enjoy the high that comes from drug use. Acceptance and euphoria provide more reward for some young people than abstinence.

The current emphasis in drug education is on primary prevention. It is easier to have young people not use drugs in the first place than to get them to stop after they have already started using drugs. One popular drug prevention program, Drug Abuse Resistance Education (DARE), attempts to get upper-elementary students to pledge not to use drugs. The rationale is that putting energy into teaching elementary students about drugs rather than high school students will be more likely to reduce drug use because the latter are more likely to have already begun using drugs. The program focuses mainly on tobacco, alcohol, and marijuana. These are considered gateway drugs, which means that students who use other drugs are most likely to have used these first. The longer students delay using tobacco, alcohol, and marijuana, the less likely they will be to use other drugs.

In the following selections, Tracy J. Evans-Whipp and her colleagues feel that the most effective message for reducing drug use is abstinence coupled with harsh punishment. Rodney Skager believes that an abstinence-only message is ineffective and that a zero tolerance policy is merely punitive. He advocates promoting drug education to reduce the harms associated with drug use.

YES

Tracy J. Evans-Whipp et al.

School, Parent, and Student Perspectives of School Drug Policies

Introduction

Schools are now recognized as much more than centers for academic instruction, with their role in contributing to the health and social well-being of students and staff now widely accepted.(1–5) Schools acknowledge their important influence on preventing youth tobacco, alcohol, and illicit-drug use (and their associated harms) and implement a range of education programs and policy directives to this end.

School drug policies form an important component of school-wide drug prevention, acting to set normative values and expectancies for student behavior as well as documenting procedures for dealing with drug-related incidents. (6) However, it is not clear to what degree, if any, school drug policies influence student behavior and the mechanism by which any such influence occurs. (7,8) Thus, policy makers are provided with little empirical guidance for developing and implementing effective school drug policy. It is likely that schools develop drug policies that reflect the values of the community, state, and country in which they reside, and a recent cross-country comparison of school policies in the United States and Australia(9) indeed found this to be the case.

In working toward an understanding of what constitutes effective school policy, it is important to establish an effective method for collecting information about schools' current policies. Most descriptive accounts of school policies have used school personnel and/or higher level bodies (such as school districts or local education authorities) as informants.(10,11) However, implementation of school drug policy is likely to be a key determinant of policy impact, and investigation of student and parent perspectives of policy provides a broader insight into how policy is carried out in practice. Few studies of school drug policies and student substance-use behaviors have collected information from multiple school policy stakeholders. Where data have been collected from students, the focus has mostly been on student substance-use behaviors rather than on students' understanding of policy content and implementation. (7,12–14) One notable exception is a study by Griesbach et al (15) in which the impact of school drug policy components on student smoking at school was measured. This study found that student perceptions of smoking at school were significantly lower in schools where pupil smoking restrictions were consistently enforced, thereby highlighting the importance of measuring policy implementation in addition to documentation. It appears that no other studies have collected information on school drug policy from parents.

We have recently developed and tested a school drug policy survey questionnaire on schools in Victoria, Australia, and Washington State, USA. (9) These 2 states share many sociodemographic characteristics(16) but differ in their approach to drugs, alcohol, and illicit drugs. US drug policies tend to reflect an abstinence-only orientation, (17) whereas Australian policies are based on a combination of abstinence and harm-minimization principles. (17,18) In measuring school policies in states in 2 countries with contrasting policy approaches, a wide variety of policy descriptions and implementation procedures were observed. The survey collected responses from school personnel, usually school principals, who are considered to be knowledgeable about the policy content. The current paper extends the observations collected from school administrators by examining parent and student reports of school drug policy gathered in parallel surveys. Thus, it is possible to compare responses between the 3 groups of respondents to gain a more comprehensive picture of how school policy operates. In particular, cross-comparison of responses will enable us to (1) determine how effectively schools are communicating school drug policy information to parents and students, (2) gain insight into how school policies are implemented, and (3) investigate what policy variables impact students' drug use at school and their perceptions of other students' drug use at school.

Methods

Participants and Procedures

The surveys were conducted in 2003 as part of the International Youth Development Study (IYDS), a longitudinal research study of adolescent substance use and its predictors in Washington State and Victoria. Samples of public and private schools in both states were drawn to constitute representative samples of students at seventh and ninth grade. Procedures for the IYDS sampling, school administrator survey, and student survey have been described previously. (9,19)

This study used data collected from secondary schools and the grade 7 and 9 students (and their parents) attending them.

School administrator survey. The 205 schools (104 from Washington and 101 from Victoria) represent 97.6% of participating secondary (grade 7 through to highest) and mixed (combination of pre- and postgrade 7) schools. The majority of respondents were principals or heads of school (72.1% in Washington and 46% in Victoria), or assistant/vice principals (13.5% in Washington and 22% in Victoria).

Student survey. Students in grade 7 and grade 9 classes yielded a total of 5085 eligible students, of whom 3899 (76.7%) consented to and participated in the survey (1942 in Washington and 1957 in Victoria). Honesty criteria, which included student reports of being "not honest at all" when completing the survey, using a fictional drug, or using illicit drugs more than 120 times in the past 30 days, were used to remove surveys of 23 students from the sample (8 from Washington and 15 from Victoria).

Parent survey.   Concurrent with the student survey, a 15-minute telephone interview was administered to a parent/guardian of each participating student, using computer-assisted telephone interviewing technology. A total of 1886 Washington parents, representing 98% of the valid student sample, and 1858 Victorian parents (95% of the student sample) were successfully contacted and interviewed. The survey was administered in English for most respondents but also conducted in Vietnamese and Cantonese in Victoria and in Spanish, Korean, Vietnamese, and Russian in Washington. The majority of parents interviewed were biological parents (94% in Washington and 98% in Victoria) and female (74% in Washington and 81% in Victoria).

Measures

Parent awareness of policy and involvement.   School administrators were asked to report how aware they thought parents were of existing substance-use policies and how involved parents were in making decisions and setting substance-use policies at their school.

Awareness of school drug policies was assessed in the parent interview by asking to what degree parents were aware of what happened to a student caught smoking, drinking alcohol, or possessing or using illicit drugs at their child's school. A single construct for parental awareness of school drug policy was generated from the mean of the responses to all 3 items.

Communication methods.   School administrators were asked to indicate which of the following methods they use to communicate policy to parents: parent handbook, structured meetings with school staff (conferences), newsletters/bulletins, letters home to parents, orientation/parent night, or other.

Parents were asked in the interview whether or not details of school drug policies were communicated by their child's school via newsletters or bulletins, parent/teacher meetings, parent handbooks, or student diaries/handbooks, indirectly through their child, or through verbal communication with school staff.

Policy philosophy/orientation.   To index policy orientation toward abstinence-only and harm-minimization principles, administrators were asked to indicate the degree to which the following 2 statements described their school: "School policies emphasize total abstinence from drug use" and "School policies are based on the assumption that most youth will experiment with drugs." For school drug education orientation, administrators were asked to what degree they agreed with these statements: "Drug education programs emphasize total abstinence from drug use" and "Drug education programs emphasize safe drug use rather than no drug use."

To index policy and drug education orientation toward abstinence and harm minimization, respectively, students were asked to indicate the degree to which they agreed with the following two statements: "We are taught to say no to alcohol" and "We are taught to use alcohol safely."

Policy enforcement.   Policy enforcement was measured in the school administrator survey by a series of items asking the likelihood of specific consequences for students caught using tobacco, alcohol, and illicit drugs on school grounds or at school events. These included referral to a school counselor or nurse, in-school or out-of-school suspension, expulsion from school, and referral to legal authorities (police).

In the student survey, policy enforcement was assessed by a series of items asking which consequences are used for students caught using tobacco, alcohol, and illicit drugs at school. The consequences given were: he or she would be talked to by a teacher about the dangers of smoking cigarettes/drinking alcohol/using drugs, he or she would be suspended, he or she would be expelled, or the police would be called.

Student drug use on school grounds.   Two items in the student survey measured students' perceptions about tobacco and alcohol use at school: "Many students smoke on school grounds without getting caught" and "Many students drink alcohol on school grounds without getting caught."

Students were asked to report their own drug taking on school grounds with the following item: "How many times in the past year (12 months) have you been drunk or high at school?" Responses were dichotomized into "never" and "one or more times" categories.

Results

Parental Awareness of Policy

The percentage of parents aware of specific drug policies at their child's school was higher in Washington than in Victoria (81.6% aware of smoking policies, 86.7% aware of alcohol policies, and 88.8% aware of illicit-drug policies vs 72.1%, 70.3%, and 71.9%, respectively, for Victoria). . . . There was no significant difference between the 2 states in terms of school perceptions of parent awareness (82.5% in Washington vs 80.2% in Victoria), . . . but Victorian schools perceived greater parent awareness than was actually reported by parents.

It was hypothesized that schools that involved their parent body in the policy setting process would report higher levels of parental policy awareness. Less than 10% of schools in both states reported that parents were "very involved" in the policy setting process, and there was no significant difference in the levels of parental policy awareness between schools that did or did not involve parents in policy setting (89% vs 80%). . . .

Methods Used to Communicate Policy

. . . Schools in both states reported that the most commonly used method for communicating school drug policy information to parents was via newsletters/ bulletins and then orientation/parent night. Parents also rated newsletters/ bulletins as the most commonly used method, but in both states, it was reported that parent handbooks and student diaries/handbooks were other commonly used methods. Parent/teacher meetings were not as frequently used.

Washington parents reported the use of each of the communication methods more frequently than Victorian parents, whereas school administrators reported that only one of the communication methods (parent handbook) was used more frequently by Washington schools. . . .

Abstinence and Harm-Minimization Messages

Washington school administrators reported that their school policies placed more emphasis on total abstinence from drug use than policies of Victorian school administrators. . . . Washington school drug education programs also emphasized total abstinence from drug use, whereas Victorian administrators reported that school policies had a stronger abstinence message than did drug education curricula.

More Victorian than Washington school administrators (18% vs 5%) reported that their school drug policies were based on the assumption that most youth will experiment with drugs. Similarly, the harm-minimization concept was adopted within drug education curricula to a much greater extent by Victorian schools than by Washington schools (33% vs 2%) (table not shown). . . .

As with school administrator reports, an emphasis on abstinence was reported by more Washington students and an emphasis on harm minimization by Victorian students. . . .

Policy Enforcement

The most common consequences for all drug policy violations reported by school administrators in both states were referral of the student to a counselor/ nurse or suspension. . . . Highly punitive measures such as expulsion and contacting the police were more commonly used for illicit-drug offences than for tobacco and alcohol policy violations. Washington school administrators were more likely than Victorian administrators to use highly punitive measures.

More Washington than Victorian students reported that highly punitive measures were used for all drug-type violations. Students in both states agreed with school administrators that highly punitive measures were used for illicit-drug offences than for tobacco and alcohol policy violations. Students did not report that referral to a teacher was a common consequence, with only around 50% or less of students reporting use of this method. Victorian students were more likely than Washington students to report this consequence for all drug-type violations.

Policy and Student Drug Use on School Grounds

Students in Victoria were twice as likely to report that students smoke on school grounds without getting caught as students in Washington (61% vs

30%). . . . Perceptions of alcohol use on school grounds were lower than for smoking and similar in both states (12% in Victoria and 14% in Washington) . . . , as was student self-reported drug and/or alcohol use at school in the past year (5% in Victoria and 7% in Washington). . . .

Characteristics of students, including their being in ninth grade and recent use in the past month, increased their perceptions of smoking on school grounds, and living in Washington reduced the likelihood of perceptions of smoking on school grounds. Student perceptions of smoking on school grounds were lower where students reported having received a strong abstinence drug education message . . . or perceiving harsh penalties if caught smoking at school. . . , parents reported awareness of school drug policy. . . , and if the school reported using an abstinence-based policy . . . or strict policy enforcement. . . . Monitoring of school grounds and bathrooms was significantly associated with higher student perceptions of smoking on school grounds. . . .

Characteristics of students, including being in ninth grade and smoking in the last 30 days, increased the perceptions of drinking on school grounds. Student perceptions of drinking on school grounds were lower when students perceived harsh penalties if caught drinking at school . . . , and were higher if the school reported monitoring of bathrooms. . . .

Ninth grade students and those who used tobacco in the last 30 days reported more drinking or drug taking on school grounds. Student self-reported drinking or drug taking on school grounds was lower where students reported having received a strong abstinence drug education message or a strong harm-minimization drug education message. . . .

Adjusting for state, cohort, and recent (past 30 days) self-reported tobacco use, student perception of harsh penalties for drug policy violations continued to be statistically significantly associated with lower student perceptions of smoking . . . and drinking . . . at school. . . . Student perceptions of a strong abstinence drug education message continued to be statistically significantly associated with lower drug use at school. . . . Harm-minimization drug education continued to be statistically significantly associated with lower perceptions of smoking at school . . . , and marginally significant with self-report of being drunk or high at school. . . . The relationship between school report of monitoring bathrooms and school grounds and high levels of drinking at school also continued to be significant after adjusting for state, cohort, and recent tobacco use. . . . School reports for expulsion for alcohol violations continued to be associated with lower numbers of students reporting being drunk or high at school. . . .

Discussion

This study collected information on school drug policy from 3 different sources and provides detailed insight into policy implementation in schools from 2 countries that have different drug policy environments. Collecting parent reports on policy was important since schools are encouraged to involve their parent body in policy development and ensure that all relevant parties, including parents, are aware of the policy. The considerable investment on the part of schools to achieve this is considered acceptable, as parent involvement is expected to facilitate the school's ability to handle drug incidents in a manner consistent with community expectations, and parental involvement enables parents to enforce similar restrictions outside of school.(22-24) Parents' self-reported awareness of school drug policy in this study indicated that schools in Victoria tend to overestimate slightly how well they are communicating school drug policy information to parents. Interestingly, about 30% fewer Victorian parents reported receiving drug policy information via school newsletters, the most commonly used method, than schools reported using them. It is possible that schools are producing these materials, but that parents do not always receive or remember receiving them. In Washington, about 10% more parents recall receiving drug policy information via school newsletters than schools reported using them.

It is difficult to determine from this study any potential benefits from parent involvement in policy setting since less than 10% of schools reported high levels of parental involvement. This finding is in accordance with other studies in the United States and England that also found low levels of parent involvement in policy setting.(25,26)

How and if student drug use is influenced by school drug policy will be related to students' understanding of policy and their perceptions of its enforcement. This study assessed how well schools communicate their drug policy messages to their students. It appears that schools in both states are successfully communicating their stance on at least alcohol use since the observed differences in policy orientation between schools in the 2 states was also reported by students. By adopting an abstinence-based policy stance to drug issues, Washington schools are able to provide a more consistent message to their students with strong abstinence messages in both drug policy and drug education messages. The harm-minimization concept adopted by most Victorian schools takes a broader view, encouraging abstinence as a key method of reducing harms, but accepting some degree of experimentation and attempting to equip students with knowledge on safe levels of use. As a consequence, Victorian schools report that their policies place strong emphasis on abstinence (the use of drugs being inappropriate at school), while their drug education programs have a greater harm-minimization focus.

Students in both states were generally knowledgeable about the likely consequences for drug policy violations in their school. Students confirmed school reports that Washington schools were more likely than Victorian schools to use highly punitive measures such as expulsion and referral to the police. Students in both states believed that remedial consequences such as counseling were less likely to be used, especially for illicit-drug use, than was indicated by the schools. This disparity in responses might reflect a genuine difference between policy documentation and implementation (ie, schools overreport the use of counseling) or might result from students not being well informed about the remedial consequences of policy violations. It is possible that when communicating school drug policy, schools place more emphasis on the highly punitive consequences to enhance the deterrent effect. The impact of the perception of punitive measures for smoking and drinking is also associated with lower perceptions of smoking and drinking at school, but interestingly, it is less strongly associated with student reports of being drunk or high at school. This area warrants further investigation as there is emerging evidence that the use of education and counseling along with disciplinary sanctions is associated with lower student smoking rates than the use of punitive measures alone.(14,27) The finding that students are generally well aware of their school's policy implementation is an important one as there is strong evidence that school drug policy will only impact student behavior if it is perceived to be well enforced.(15,28,29)

Measuring the impact of school drug policies on student behaviors is a difficult task given the number of known influences on students' decisions to use tobacco, alcohol, and other drugs.(30) It was hypothesized that school policy would be expected to have the greatest effect on student drug use on school grounds. In this study, self-reported drug use on school grounds was measured as well as perceptions of smoking and drinking by other students at school without getting caught. Importantly, reductions in the ORs for these behaviors were observed in schools where students reported receiving an abstinence drug education message and perceived harsh penalties if caught using drugs at school, even when controlling for known influences (cohort, state, and recent tobacco use). Strong harm-minimization messages were also associated with lower levels of self-reported use, indicating that clearly delivered policy messages of either orientation can be effective in lowering levels of drug use at school.

Interestingly, monitoring drug use on school grounds or in bathrooms was associated with increases in perceptions of student smoking and alcohol use but not self-reports of being drunk or high at school. This suggests that monitoring may increase perceptions of student drug use whilst not serving to reduce actual use levels. This may be worrisome since perceptions of drug use are associated with higher levels of drug initiation. (31)

The current study has a number of limitations that should be noted. Only one school informant completed the School Administrator Survey, and it is possible that the responses might more accurately depict school policy if additional school respondents were surveyed. The wording of questions was not always consistent across student, parent, or administrator surveys. For example, when asking about the consequences for policy violations, schools were asked about student referral to a counselor or nurse, whereas students were asked about referral to a teacher. However, there are a number of key strengths to the study, namely its very large representative sample from 2 states with different national drug policy backgrounds, collection of data from 3 key school groups, and measures of actual and perceived student drug use on school grounds.

The implications of this study for school policy makers are preliminary but encouraging. Schools in the 2 study states generally have some impact in educating their students about drug policy. When delivered effectively, policy messages are associated with reduced student drug use at school. Abstinence messages and harsh penalties convey a coherent message to students associated with reduced student drug use at school. Strong harm-minimization messages delivered within a "no drugs at school" context are also associated with reduced drug use at school, but effects are weaker than those for abstinence messages. It is possible that the smaller impact of harm-minimization messages is a result of conflicting messages between policy (abstinence) and drug education (acceptance of experimentation). Harm-minimization advocates would argue that this smaller effect is acceptable given the anticipated reduction in the levels of current and future harmful use and school drop out within the student population. Given that nearly all schools invest substantial time and money developing and implementing policies for tobacco, alcohol, and illicit drugs and drug education, it is imperative that further research is conducted to evaluate which aspects of policy are important in reducing student drug use.

References

1. Commonwealth Department of Health and Family Services. A National Framework for Health Promoting Schools (2000–2003). Canberra Australia: Commonwealth Department of Health and Family Services and Australian Health Promoting Schools Association; 2001.

2. Rutter M, Maughan B, Mortimore P, Ouston J, Smith A. fifteen thousand hours: secondary schools and their effects on children. London: Open Books; 1979.

3. Resnick MD, Bearman PS, Blum RW, et al. Protecting adolescents from harm: findings from the National Longitudinal Study on Adolescent Health. JAMA. 1997;278(10):823–832.

4. Bond L, Patton G, Glover S, et al. The Gatehouse Project: can a multilevel school intervention affect emotional well-being and health risk behaviours? J Epidemiol Community Health. 2004;58(12):997–1003.

5. Patton G, Bond L, Butler H, Glover S. Changing schools, changing health? Design and implementation of the Gatehouse Project. J Adolesc Health. 2003;33(4):231–239.

6. Goodstadt MS. Substance abuse curricula vs. school drug policies. J Sch Health. 1989;59(6):246–250.

7. Evans-Whipp T, Beyers JM, Lloyd S, et al. A review of school drug policies and their impact on youth substance use. Health Promot Int. 2004; 19(2):227–234.

8. Flay BR. Approaches to substance use prevention utilizing school curriculum plus social environment change. Addict Behav 2000;25(6):861–885.

9. Beyers JM, Evans-Whipp T, Mathers M, Toumbourou JW, Catalano RF. A cross-national comparison of school drug policies in Washington State, United States, and Victoria, Australia. J Sch Health. 2005;75(4): 134–140.

10. Small ML, Jones SE, Barrios LC, et al. School policy and environment: results from the School Health Policies and Programs Study 2000. J Sch Health. 2001;71(7):325–334.

11. Ross JG, Einhaus KB, Hohenemser LK, Greene BZ, Kann L, Gold RS. School health policies prohibiting tobacco use, alcohol and other drug use, and violence. J Sch Health. 1995;65(8):333–338.

12. Pentz MA, Brannon BR, Charlin VL, Barrett EJ, MacKinnon DP, Flay BR. The power of policy: the relationship of smoking policy to adolescent smoking. Am J Public Health. 1989;79(7):857–862.

13. Charlton A, While D. Smoking prevalence among 16–19-year-olds related to staff and student smoking policies in sixth forms and further education. Health Educ J. 1994;53:28–39.

14. Hamilton G, Cross D, Lower T, Resnicow K, Williams P. School policy: what helps to reduce teenage smoking? Nicotine Tob Res. 2003;5(4):507–513.

15. Griesbach D, Inchley J, Currie C. More than words? The status and impact of smoking policies in Scottish schools. Health Promot Int. 2002;17(1):31–41.

16. McMorris BJ, Hemphill SA, Toumbourou JW, Catalano RF, Patton GC. Prevalence of substance use and delinquent behavior in adolescents from Victoria, Australia and Washington State, USA. Health Educ Behav. 2006.

17. Caulkins JP, Reuter P. Setting goals for drug policy: harm reduction or use reduction? Addiction. 1997;92(9):1143–1150.

18. Munro G, Midford R. "Zero tolerance" and drug education in Australian schools. Drug Alcohol Rev. 2001;20(1):105–109.

19. Patton GC, McMorris BJ, Toumbourou JW, Hemphill SA, Donath S, Catalano RF. Puberty and the onset of substance use and abuse. Pediatrics. 2004;114(3):e300–e306.

20. Stata statistical software: Release 8. College Station, TX: StataCorp; 2001.

21. Carlin JB, Wolfe R, Coffey C, Patton GC. Tutorial in biostatistics: analysis of binary outcomes in longitudinal studies using weighted estimating equations and discrete-time survival methods: prevalence and incidence of smoking in an adolescent cohort. Stat Med. 1999;18(19):2655–2679.

22. Peck DD, Acott C, Richard P, Hill S, Schuster C. The Colorado Tobacco-Free Schools and Communities Project. J Sch Health. 1993;63(5):214–217.

23. Commonwealth Department of Education Training and Youth Affairs. National School Drug Education Strategy, May 1999. . . .

24. Commonwealth Department of Education Science and Training. Innovation and Good Practice in Drug Education. Effective Communication. Canberra: Commonwealth of Australia; 2003: 10.

25. Brener ND, Dittus PJ, Hayes G. Family and community involvement in schools: results from the School Health Policies and Programs Study 2000. J Sch Health. 2001;71(7):340–344.

26. Denman S, Pearson J, Hopkins D, Wallbanks C, Skuriat V. The management and organisation of health promotion: a survey of school policies in Nottinghamshire. Health Educ J. 1999;58:165–176.

27. Hamilton G, Cross D, Resnicow K, Hall M. A school-based harm minimization smoking intervention trial: outcome results. Addiction. 2005; 100(5):689–700.

28. Moore L, Roberts C, Tudor-Smith C. School smoking policies and smoking prevalence among adolescents: multilevel analysis of cross-sectional data from Wales. Tob Control. 2001;10(2):117–123.

29. Wakefield MA, Chaloupka FJ, Kaufman NJ, Orleans CT, Barker DC, Ruel BE. Effect of restrictions on smoking at home, at school, and in public places on teenage smoking: cross sectional study. BMJ. 2000;321(7257):333–337.

30. Hawkins JD, Catalano RF, Miller JY. Risk and protective factors for alcohol and other drug problems in adolescence and early adulthood: implications for substance abuse prevention. Psychol Bull. 1992;112(1):64–105.

31. Hansen WB, Graham JW. Preventing alcohol, marijuana, and cigarette use among adolescents: peer pressure resistance training versus establishing conservative norms. Prey Med. 1991;20(3):414–430.

Rodney Skager

Beyond Zero Tolerance: A Reality-Based Approach to Drug Education & School Discipline

Beyond Zero Tolerance: A Reality-Based Model

Where We Are Today

Most American high schools do not offer effective drug education, nor do they provide interventions to assist students struggling with abuse of alcohol and other drugs. Instead, they rely primarily on deterrent punishment for students who are caught violating the rules. Proponents of the "big four" consequences—exclusion from extracurricular activities, transfer to another school, suspension, and expulsion—believe that harsh consequences for those who are caught will deter other students from committing similar offenses, and too often constitute the whole of prevention.

But research has shown that these punishments are not likely to change students' behavior. Ironically, rather than serving as an effective deterrent, drug education that lacks credibility and is backed by punitive measures often fosters resentment and oppositional behavior. The few secondary schools that offer drug education often repeat messages that may have had some credence for elementary school students but lack credibility for older, more experienced teenagers. Current "science-based" programs are more sophisticated than earlier "just say no" programs, but are still based on questionable assumptions about the reasons so many teens experiment with drugs.

Empowering Tomorrow: A Comprehensive Approach

A reality-based model incorporates three mutually reinforcing elements: *education, intervention/assistance,* and *restorative consequences.* The basic tenets, which are described later in more detail, are as follows:

- Drug education should be honest, balanced, interactive, and delivered in a way that involves full participation of students.
- Intervention for students who need assistance should be an integral part of drug education.
- A restorative process, in which offenders identify harms they have caused and then make amends, should replace most suspensions and expulsions.

From *Beyond Zero Tolerance: A Reality-Based Approach to Drug Education & School Discipline* (SafetyFirst.org, 2007), pp. 3–10, 13–14. Copyright © 2007 by Drug Policy Alliance. Reprinted by permission. www.safetyfirst.org

Guiding Realities

The use of alcohol and marijuana is common among high school students, and most young people accept it as part of teenage social life.

For decades, alcohol and other drug use has been widely accepted among older teens. A majority of them, including those who choose abstinence, view the use of alcohol and marijuana as a common social activity rather than abhorrent behavior practiced only by outcasts and deviants. In the California Student Survey, most older teens consistently report that their peers try alcohol or marijuana because they are curious about the effects and that "having fun" is the main reason to continue. This social climate tolerates drug experimentation and occasional use, though not necessarily use that causes problems.

Throughout the '90s, my students at UCLA joined in lively class discussions and wrote reports based on anonymous interviews with other college students about the use of alcohol and other drugs in their high school communities. Findings from over 300 interviews included the following:

- Alcohol and other drugs were readily available to students in their high schools and most students, whether they used them or not, were tolerant of friends who did. Those who abstained did not condemn the user as a person even though they disapproved of the behavior.
- The interviewees did not remember much about prevention education in their elementary schools ("they just told us drugs were bad").
- Most denied that teenagers try drugs because of direct peer pressure.
- All were aware that use of alcohol or other drugs caused problems for some of their peers, but many also cited benefits associated with moderate use and others made it clear that they did not view users as immoral.

"Smoking pot for my friends was like watching TV for me. It was just normal."

"It's possible for someone to think that drug use is immoral, but to also not have a biased opinion of the user. I have friends who do it, but I'm still friends with them."

"Among my friends some people choose not to do it and others do. And nobody thinks less of any other person."

"The D.A.R.E. program made it seem like smoking bud was a horrible thing to do, but when I saw my friends do it they were having a blast, so I joined in."

"The people I knew were well informed on the consequences of drugs, but they didn't care. When they did drugs they were bonding with friends."

Over the last 30 years the national Monitoring the Future survey (. . .) has consistently shown that marijuana accounts for the lion's share of illegal drug use among teenagers. The results since 1991 continue to confirm its popularity.

- 42% of current high school seniors have smoked marijuana in their lifetime compared to a peak of 50% in 1999 and a 33% low in 1992.

- 27% used an illegal drug other than marijuana at least once compared to a peak of 31% in 2001 and a low of 25% in 1992.

Although underage drinking is at its lowest level in recent history (unlike use of illegal drugs), the great majority of older teens have tried alcohol at least once in their lives and substantial numbers drink heavily and frequently.

- 73% of high school seniors tried alcohol compared to a peak of 88% in 1991.
- 56% have been drunk at least once compared to a peak of 65% in 1991.

Use of pharmaceutical drugs without a doctor's prescription is on the increase, possibly explaining the decline for alcohol.

- 10% of high school seniors used pain-killers, such as Vicodin, in the last year, and 4% used OxyContin.
- 7% used tranquilizers, such as Xanax, and 7% used sedative barbiturates in the last year.

Use rates fluctuate from year to year, but they never come close to reflecting universal abstinence. Perhaps this is because young people live in a society where a range of legal substances, including alcohol, over-the-counter drugs, and pharmaceuticals are not only tolerated, but promoted through popular culture and the media.

As a result, drug prevention programs for preteens, instituted nationwide in the mid-80s, have not reduced widespread acceptance and use of alcohol and marijuana among contemporary high school populations. These savvy teens have easy access to these substances, and are skeptical of "just say no" messages.

Drug prevention programs designed to "inoculate" children against later alcohol and other drug experimentation have failed.

Most existing drug education programs are delivered with the assumption that elementary school students can be *inoculated* against later temptation. While a few of these programs offer secondary school "booster sessions," the curricula mainly recap the same messages heard in elementary school, even though little evidence supports the theory that early prevention education has been successful in reducing use of alcohol and other drugs by the mid-teen years.

Older teens become skeptical about the warning messages heard in elementary school prevention programs and can identify little or nothing of what they learned in their pre-teen years. Independent scientists have identified serious flaws in research ostensibly supporting even "science-based" elementary school programs. Given students' limited retention of the information taught in these programs, it seems the best time to *start* school-based drug education is at the beginning of the teenage years, immediately before experimentation escalates.

Those who have reared or taught children know they become adolescents rather suddenly at 11 or 12 years old, when physical and motivational changes are obvious. The equally important leap forward in mental capacity that occurs at this age is usually less apparent. "Formal reasoning" ability, as psychologists call it, enables teenagers to arrive at answers to problems in the same way as adults, by thinking of possible explanations and testing them out. However, in modern developed societies young people have been prevented from assuming responsibilities commensurate with their capabilities. The response to this "infantilizing" is often oppositional, with substance use an "in your face" example.

An adolescent's ability to reason helps to explain why early one-sided or factually inaccurate drug prevention messages are rejected by the mid-teen years. The information conveyed by adults often conflicts with knowledge teens have acquired on their own, through observation or personal experience. In a social climate of widespread acceptance of the use of alcohol and other drugs, underestimating teens' mental agility and delivering simplistic "drugs are bad" messages results in cynicism rather than obedience.

Given today's climate of government-sanctioned fear, I appreciate the difficulty adults may have delivering a balanced message. It can be professionally dangerous for teachers to acknowledge benign use and/or the positive aspects of alcohol and other drugs. By omitting these realities, we seriously compromise our ability to establish and maintain credibility. To go a step further and admit that most young people who do try alcohol or other drugs do not get into lifelong patterns of abuse provokes the accusation that, "you are sending the wrong message!" and thereby granting permission to use.

Teenagers do not ask adults whether they can drink alcohol, smoke cigarettes, or try marijuana. Instead, most young people respond to the norms of their own social world, just as they do for modes of talk, dress, sexual behavior, or music.

"Nothing about us without us!"—Drug education that ignores the views of young people is bound to fail.
Historically, drug prevention education has been a top-down enterprise that has ignored the experience and opinions of young people, resulting in cynicism.

Our society relies heavily on polling and other tools to gauge customer opinions. Drug prevention programs would benefit from the application of similar techniques: What do teenagers remember from the drug education they experienced as children? Do they later see inaccuracies or lack of balance in the information and messages? What about the information and images they have been bombarded with since then—do they ring true? Do young people view the programs as effective, or are they perceived as just more hypocritical indoctrination?

Students should also be involved in setting school policies regarding consequences for violating rules. The battle cry of the disability rights movement, "nothing about us without us!" applies with equal force to working with teenagers.

Severe punishment of those caught with alcohol and other drugs has not affected use rates among other high school students.

Most Americans believe education is the primary tool for preventing substance use among young people. However, in practice, *deterrent punishment* is the key component in prevention. Deterrent punishment refers generally to punitive measures such as expulsion, suspension, or exclusion from participation in student government, sports, and other extracurricular activities. These "consequences" are thought to insure abstinence among teens.

Yet, defying adults through oppositional behavior is a tactic frequently used in striking back at what many young people perceive as unreasonable and arbitrary rules and decisions. When it comes to the use of alcohol and other drugs, we have no proof that punishing the few who are caught actually deters others from predictable experimentation. Additionally, deterrent punishment undermines a sense of connection—among those caught and observers alike— leaving young people feeling isolated and believing that "the system" is uneven, unfair, and cruel.

Moreover, draconian punishments largely ignore the welfare of the students who are cast out of the school community.

Research has shown that young people who feel connected to family and school are more likely to make positive health choices, including abstinence. That's why the California State Parent Teacher Association passed an "Alternatives to Zero Tolerance" resolution at its annual convention in 2003.

Most high school students report that friends troubled by their use of alcohol or other drugs are not likely to find help at their schools. They are aware that these offenders are instead "disappeared" through suspension, expulsion, or transfer to another school where the process starts all over again. To most of them, this seems both callous and unwise.

From the UCLA interviewees:

"Expulsion just encourages the negative behavior. It leaves no alternative open to the kid."

"Expelling a student is getting rid of problem kids and not getting rid of the problem in those kids."

"You are continuing the problem with expulsion. A kid who comes to school high is obviously in need of some attention and guidance. By kicking him or her out of school, you may eliminate the only stability that he or she has in life."

"Kicking kids out of school is the dumbest thing ever. Then what are they going to do? Just sit home and smoke pot all the time?"

"If the school expels the student, he or she is just going to be transferred to another school . . . (and) repeat the same behaviors. The rest of the students don't care . . . because they think that they won't get caught and they're right, most students don't get caught."

The 2006 California Student Survey found that in any 30-day period almost 12% of 11th graders admit to having used alcohol or other drugs at least once on campus. A much smaller minority are actually caught selling drugs at school, with wide variability in administrative responses to such violations, although suspension or expulsion tends to be the norm.

REALITY: 12% The 2006 CALIFORNIA STUDENT SURVEY found that in any 30-day period almost 12% of 11th graders admit to having used alcohol or other drugs at least once on campus; that is one out of every eight students.

When dealing with offenders, I believe that consequences likely to *reform rather than disadvantage* the student will significantly reduce oppositional behavior, including drug possession and use on campus, while increasing the likelihood of ultimate success in school and work. "Restorative practices," alternative methods for dealing with offenders, are discussed beginning on page 13 of this booklet.

Some students are so seriously involved with alcohol and/or other drugs that they would benefit from *professional* intervention and treatment in lieu of expulsion. In one UCLA interview, a severely drug-involved student at a Catholic girls preparatory school told a story with a happy ending. She had been coming to school intoxicated on a daily basis. Eventually she was caught and suspended. Fortunately, teachers and counselors begged her to get help and managed to get her the resources to do just that.

This student desperately needed direct intervention and compassionate assistance, and was helped as a result.

As she said:
"Some days it would be vodka in my water bottle, other days I would pop speed in the girl's bathroom before class. If I were expelled, I never would have gotten a chance at life. I would have dropped out of high school, not gotten into rehab, and not been in college right now. Thank God for them (the counselors and teachers) and thank goodness for my friends."

Education or Surveillance?

In light of the deficiencies in current prevention approaches, the federal government advocates widespread implementation of random student drug testing. Unfortunately, this policy perpetuates many of the problematic aspects of zero tolerance strategies:

- Random drug testing erodes relationship of trust between students and adults at school, hindering open communication and damaging an essential component of a safe and rewarding learning environment.
- Drug testing programs are counter-productive, erecting barriers to participation in extracurricular activities—the very activities likely to increase students' connection to caring adults at school, and provide structure and supervision during the peak hours of adolescent drug use, from 3–6 pm.
- Drug testing programs do not effectively identify students who have serious problems with drugs and further marginalize at-risk students.

- Testing may trigger oppositional behavior by inadvertently encouraging more students to abuse alcohol—not included in many standard testing panels—or by motivating some drug-involved adolescents to switch to harder drugs that leave the system more quickly.
- Specimen collection is invasive and humiliating.
- Drug testing can result in false positives, leading to the punishment of innocent students.
- Drug testing is expensive, wasting scarce dollars that could be better spent on other, more effective programs that keep young people out of trouble with drugs.
- The scientific literature does not support the safety or effectiveness of random student drug testing. The only national peer-reviewed study conducted on the topic to date compared 94,000 students in almost 900 American schools with and without a drug testing program, and found virtually no difference in illegal drug use.
- Prominent national organizations representing experts on adolescent health oppose student drug testing, including the American Academy of Pediatrics, the Association for Addiction Professionals, the National Education Association, the American Public Health Association, the National Association of Social Workers and the National Council on Alcoholism and Drug Dependence, among others.
- Drug testing fails to reach students' key attitudes and beliefs. Instead, we should spend our scarce resources educating students through comprehensive, interactive and honest drug education with identification of, and assistance for, students whose lives are disrupted by substance use.

Schools should implement a policy of restorative practices in lieu of expulsion or suspension

The majority of youth who violate school rules involving drugs do not need formal treatment, suspension, or expulsion. Instead, they should be involved in a process likely to replace alienation with changed attitudes.

Restorative practices, as described by Dr. Francis Barnes, former school superintendent and current Pennsylvania Secretary of Education, are "a set of practical responses to student behavior and proactive strategies that strengthen accountability and improve school culture."

Young people are often unaware of the harmful impact of their behavior on themselves or others. A restorative experience, which is an interactive process rather than a punitive sentence, begins with awareness. The individual then finds ways to repair the damage, including service activities and making personal amends.

In the case of substance use, amends can include apologies to teachers disturbed and frustrated by disruptive or insultingly inattentive behavior, as well as to fellow students who want a serious and productive experience in their classrooms.

It is up to the offender to decide how he or she will make things right with others and the institution. This teaches accountability while repairing damage.

There is nothing new about restorative practices, which have a long history of effectiveness. Alcoholics Anonymous's ninth step, "making amends," provides an example. For young people, actively making amends rather than passively enduring punishment is likely to promote positive feelings, rather than resentment and alienation toward school, the adults who work there, and the community.

POSTSCRIPT

Should Schools Enforce a Zero Tolerance Drug Policy?

Is it more desirable to promote an abstinence and zero tolerance approach or to promote drug education as a means of addressing drug use? Before the effectiveness of drug education programs can be determined, it is necessary to define the goals of drug education. Are the goals of drug education to prevent drug use from starting? To prevent drug abuse? To prevent drug dependency? Perhaps the goal of drug education is to teach young people how to protect themselves and others from harm *if* they are going to use drugs. Should the messages about drugs be tailored to different audiences? Without a clear understanding of the goals one wants to achieve in teaching about drugs, it is impossible to determine the effectiveness of drug education and whether it is better than an abstinence approach.

Before a drug education program can be designed, questions regarding what to include in the drug education curriculum needs to be addressed. Should the primary focus be on teaching abstinence or responsible use? Is it feasible to teach abstinence from some drugs and responsible use of other drugs? The vast majority of high school students have drunk alcohol; should they be taught that they should not drink at all, or should they be taught how to use alcohol responsibly? Is it ethical to teach responsible use of a substance that is illegal? Does the age of the children make a difference in what is taught? Do elementary students have the reasoning skills of high school students? Should the goal be for students to engage in a decision-making process or simply to adopt certain behaviors?

Surveys of drug use by secondary students over the past thirty years show that the rate of drug use is cyclical. Periods of high drug use are followed by periods of lower drug use. This fact could lead one to conclude that drug education has little bearing on whether drugs are used and that other factors contribute to the use, or nonuse, of drugs. It is possible that the availability of drugs is a factor in their use as well as stories in the media.

If drug prevention programs are going to be effective in reducing drug use, schools and other institutions will need to work together. Many young people drop out of school or simply do not attend, so community agencies and faith-based institutions need to become involved. The media have a large impact on young people. What is the best way to incorporate the media in the effort to reduce drug use? Are antidrug commercial spots shown during programs aimed at teenage audiences effective? Do movies and music videos in which drug use is depicted contribute to whether drugs are used?

The effect of three different drug education programs is reviewed in "Drug Prevention in Elementary Schools: An Introduction to the Special Issue," by Chris Ringwalt, Michael Hecht, and Suellen Hopfer (*Journal of Drug Education*, 2010). Drug education in British schools is discussed in "We Don't Have No Drugs Education: The Myth of Universal Drugs Education in English Secondary Schools?" by Adam Fletcher, Chris Bonell, and Annik Sorhaindo (*International Journal of Drug Policy*, November 2010). The role of teachers in drug education is discussed in "Teaching Teachers to Just Say 'Know': Reflections on Drug Education" by Kenneth Tupper (*Teaching and Teacher Education*, February 2008). Lastly, Marsha Rosenbaum of the Drug Policy Alliance addresses the importance of effective drug education in *Safety First: A Reality-Based Approach to Teens and Drugs* (2007).

Contributors to This Volume

EDITOR

RAYMOND GOLDBERG is the dean for health sciences for Vance-Granville Community College in Henderson, North Carolina. Previously, he served as the associate dean for the School of Professional Studies for the State University of New York at Cortland. In addition, he was the graduate coordinator for its graduate programs and a professor in its health department. He received his Ph.D. in health education from the University of Toledo, his master's degree from the University of South Carolina, and his bachelor's degree from the University of North Carolina at Pembroke. He is the author of *Drugs Across the Spectrum,* 6th edition (Cengage Publishers, Inc.). He has received more than $750,000 in grants for his research in health and drug education.

AUTHORS

JUDITH APPEL is the executive director of Our Family Coalition. Appel has more than 15 years of experience as a public interest lawyer involved in policy-based work. Appel previously was director of legal affairs for the Drug Policy Alliance, a national nonprofit organization dedicated to reducing harm caused by drugs and drug policies.

ILENE B. ANDERSON is a clinical professor of pharmacy at the University of California in San Francisco. She is a senior toxicology management specialist with the San Francisco Division of the California Poison Control System and has served as the co-chair of the California Poison Control System Research Committee since 2002.

PAUL ANTONY is executive director of Global Health Progress and the chief medical officer for the Pharmaceutical Research and Manufacturers of America (PhRMA). He advocates on health care and medical policy issues on behalf of the PhRMA. Dr. Antony is board-certified in preventive medicine and public health as well as in aerospace medicine. He earned his medical degree from the George Washington University School of Medicine and serves on its faculty in the Department of Microbiology, Immunology and Tropical Medicine.

SHANNON A. BIGLETE is a staff pharmacist with the CVS Pharmacy in San Diego, California. Ms. Biglete has been recognized for her work in counseling people on over-the-counter herbal supplements.

LYNDAL BOND is the associate director at the Medical Research Council, located at the University of Glasgow. Bond was awarded her Ph.D. at the University of Glasgow. Previously, Bond was a senior research fellow with the University of Melbourne based at the Centre for Adolescent Health, Royal Children's Hospital, Australia. She conducted a study which focused on understanding the effects of social and school environments on adolescent health and investigated how these environments can be successfully modified to promote health and learning outcomes.

JOHN BRITTON is a professor of epidemiology at the University of Nottingham School of Community Health where he directs the UK Centre for Tobacco Control Studies. The Centre researches policies and practices to reduce the prevalence of smoking and the harm it causes through prevention of uptake of smoking, promotion of smoking cessation, and development of more effective harm reduction strategies for those currently unable to stop smoking.

JOSEPH A. CALIFANO JR. is the Chairman of the National Center on Addiction and Substance Abuse at Columbia University. Califano has written several books, including *High Society—How Substance Abuse Ravages America and What to Do About It.*

RICHARD F. CATALANO is professor and the associate director of the Social Development Research Group at the University of Washington's School of Social Work in Seattle, Washington. For more than 25 years, he has led research and program development to promote positive youth development and prevent problem behavior. His work has focused on discovering risk and protective factors for positive and problem behavior, and designing and evaluating programs to address these factors.

PETER J. COHEN was a physician and attorney. He had published more than 100 scientific papers, several books, article reviews, book chapters, and law reviews. Dr. Cohen was a professor and Chair of Anesthesiology at the Universities of Michigan and Colorado. He also taught as an adjunct professor at Georgetown University Law Center.

ALEXANDRA COX works for the Office of Legal Affairs for Drug Policy Alliance, which promotes alternatives to the war on drugs.

JOHN DEKE, a senior researcher with Mathematica Policy Research, has extensive experience in the design and analysis of data from rigorous evaluations based on diverse designs, including random assignment, regression discontinuity, and propensity score matching. Mathematica Policy Research conducts research dealing with disability, early childhood, education, family support, health care, labor, and nutrition policy. Deke's research focuses on evaluating reading comprehension curricula and supplemental educational services.

DON C. DES JARLAIS is director of research for The Baron Edmond de Rothschild Chemical Dependency Institute at Beth Israel Medical Center, a research fellow with the National Development and Research Institutes, Inc., and professor of epidemiology and social medicine at Albert Einstein College of Medicine in New York. He is one of the leading authorities on AIDS and intravenous drug use, and has published extensively on these related topics.

LAWRENCE DILLER practices behavioral-developmental pediatrics and family therapy in Walnut Creek, California. He is the author of *Running on Ritalin: A Physician Reflects on Children, Society, and Performance in a Pill.*

DRUG ENFORCEMENT ADMINISTRATION (DEA) has a mission to enforce the controlled substances laws and regulations of the United States and bring to the criminal and civil justice systems of the United States, or other competent jurisdiction, those organizations and principal members of organizations involved in the growing, manufacture, or distribution of controlled substances appearing in or destined for illicit traffic in the United States; and to recommend and support nonenforcement programs aimed at reducing the availability of illicit controlled substances on the domestic and international markets.

DRUG FREE AUSTRALIA strives to deal with drug-related problems by focusing on drug prevention rather than drug treatment, which receives a disproportionate amount of funding to address problems associated with drugs. Drug Free Australia advocates for more drug education in schools. It maintains schools play a crucial role in preventing drug problems.

KEVIN DRUM is a graduate of California State University at Long Beach. Besides writing for *Mother Jones,* Mr. Drum has published with the *Washington Monthly.* He frequently blogs about the oil crisis.

RICHARD EDWARDS is trained as a public health physician in the United Kingdom. Dr. Edwards is a senior lecturer in epidemiology at New Zealand's University of Otago Wellington School of Medicine and Health Science. His research deals with tobacco use epidemiology and control, secondhand smoke, and smoke-free policies and legislation , smoking and eye disease, and noncommunicable diseases in sub-Saharan Africa.

LAURA K. EGENDORF is a prolific author who has published numerous books on topics ranging from drug testing to smoking, terrorism, social networking, organ donation, mental health, heroin, and Iraq. In addition, she has written about sexually transmitted diseases, illegal immigration, energy alternatives, and students' rights.

ERIC EINSPRUCH is a senior research associate and project director at RMC Research Corporation in Portland, Oregon. He received his bachelor's degree from The Evergreen State College in Olympia, Washington, and his master's and doctoral degrees from the University of Miami. His current research involves evaluating school-based and community-based social service programs.

TRACY J. EVANS-WHIPP is a research manager for the Centre for Adolescent Health, Murdoch Children's Research Institute, Melbourne, Australia.

JEANNE FLAVIN is a professor at Fordham University whose research involves how the state enforces gendered social arrangements through its criminal justice and other formal policies and practices. She focuses on battered women, incarcerated women, and women who are addicted to drugs. She chairs the board of directors for National Advocates for Pregnant Women, advocating for the social and civil rights of all women, but especially low-income women who are pregnant and parenting. Professor Jeanne received a Fulbright Award in 2009 to study women's pathways to prison in South Africa.

LISSY C. FRIEDMAN is a senior staff attorney with the Public Health Advocacy Institute at Northeastern University. Her research examines how the tobacco industry strives to improve its perception through the use of corporate social responsibility rhetoric and tactics. Besides her numerous publications, Ms. Friedman frequently presents at national tobacco control and public health conferences.

MICHAEL FUMENTO is an author, journalist, and attorney specializing in science and health issues. He is a science columnist for Scripps-Howard and a senior fellow of the Hudson Institute in Washington, D.C. He has also been a legal writer for the *Washington Times* and an editorial writer for the *Rocky Mountain News* in Denver, and he was the first "National Issues" reporter for *Investor's Business Daily*. He has lectured on science and health issues throughout the world, including Great Britain, France, the Czech Republic, Greece, Austria, China, and South America. His publications include *BioEvolution: How Biotechnology Is Changing Our World* (Encounter Books, 2003).

BRIAN GOESLING, a senior researcher with Mathematica Policy Research, has expertise in social programs and trends affecting families and youth. Mathematica Policy Research conducts research dealing with disability, early childhood, education, family support, health care, labor, and nutrition policy. Goesling currently serves as deputy project director for the Evaluation of Adolescent Pregnancy Prevention Approaches. He also reviews programs to reduce teen pregnancy, sexually transmitted infections, and associated sexual risk behaviors for U.S. Department of Health and Human Services.

CULLEN GOLDBLATT is a researcher with the Baron Edmond de Rothschild Chemical Dependency Institute located at the Beth Israel Medical Center (New York).

FATEMA GUNJA has worked on drug policy issues, initially as a communications coordinator at the American Civil Liberties Union and then as the first director of the Drug Policy Forum in Massachusetts. During her drug policy days, she became a passionate spokesperson and writer on racial justice and students' rights in the context of the war on drugs.

MARKUS HEILIG is the chief of the Laboratory of Clinical Studies (LCS), and clinical director in the National Institute on Alcohol Abuse and Alcoholism's Division of Intramural Clinical and Biological Research. Dr. Heilig received the M.D. degree from Sweden's Lund University and a Ph.D. in psychiatric neurochemistry from the same institution. He has been a leader in addiction research in the European Community, having organized a trans-European initiative in drug dependence as well as a number of conferences and other meetings.

GENE M. HEYMAN has a Ph.D. in experimental psychology from Harvard University. He has taught at a number of universities including Brandeis University, Boston College, and Harvard University where he received teaching awards. Dr. Heyman was awarded research grants from the National Science Foundation, the National Institute on Alcohol Abuse and Alcoholism, and the National Institute on Drug Abuse.

ROBERT HUBBARD is director of the North Carolina office of NDRI, the Institute for Community-Based Research (NDRI-NC). The Institute for Community-Based Research focuses exclusively on drug abuse treatment research. He is the principal investigator on the Clinical Trials Network (CTN), and has been principal investigator on the Drug Abuse Treatment Outcome Study (DATOS), an ongoing national study of drug abuse treatment and the Treatment Outcome Prospective Study (TOPS), an earlier study initiated in 1976.

SUSANNE JAMES-BURDUMY, an associate director of research with Mathematica Policy Research, is an expert in the design and conduct of rigorous evaluations of educational programs and interventions. Mathematica Policy Research conducts research dealing with disability, early childhood, education, family support, health care, labor, and nutrition policy. In addition to her research into student drug testing, she is evaluating reading comprehension programs for fifth-grade students. She is also evaluating Playworks, a program that provides elementary school students with opportunities for physical activity and play during the school day.

JENNIFER KERN is a research associate at the Drug Policy Alliance's Office of Legal Affairs in Berkeley. Ms. Kern serves as the national campaign coordinator for DPA's "Drug Testing Fails Our Youth," a public education project. She has been interviewed by a wide range of national print and broadcast media, including *Newsweek, Reuters, The Associated Press, The Washington Post, Christian Science Monitor, Houston Chronicle*, and *Milwaukee Journal Sentinel* among others.

HERBERT KLEBER founded at Columbia University the Division on Substance Abuse, now one of the leading centers in the country. Dr. Kleber is the author of more than 200 papers, and the co-editor of the *American Psychiatric Press Textbook of Substance Abuse Treatment*.

EMILY P. LAI is a staff pharmacist with the San Ramon, California, Walgreen's Pharmacy.

DIANA Y. LEE is a staff pharmacist with the Safeway Pharmacy in San Francisco, California.

ROBERT A. LEVY, a senior fellow in constitutional studies, joined the Cato Institute in 1997 after 25 years in business. He is director of the Institute for Justice and a member of the board of visitors of the Federalist Society. Levy received his Ph.D. in business from American University in 1996.

PAMELA M. LING is a physician in Internal Medicine. She earned her medical degree at the University of California at San Francisco where she is currently on its faculty. Dr. Ling has published more than 30 articles dealing with a wide range of tobacco-related topics.

PETER LURIE is a physician with the Food and Drug Administration's Office of Policy, where he will help develop strategies to facilitate medical product availability to meet critical public health needs. Previously, Dr. Lurie was Deputy Director of Public Citizen's Health Research Group in Washington, DC. He is an adjunct faculty member at Johns Hopkins Bloomberg School of Public Health and the George Washington University School of Public Health and Life Sciences.

CARLA T. MAIN practiced law in New York City and litigated commercial cases involving real-estate-related disputes, the First Amendment, fraud, art law, and civil rights. She was the associate editor of *The National Law Journal* and has published articles in *The Wall Street Journal, Policy Review, National Review, The American Lawyer*, and *The New York Sun*, as well as other publications.

ROSALIND B. MARIMONT is a retired mathematician and scientist, having done research and development for the National Institute of Standards and Technology for 18 years and for the National Institute of Health (NIH) for another 19. She started in electronics defense work during World War II, then went into the logical design of the early digital computers during the 1950s. At the NIH, she published papers on human vision, speech, and biomathematical subjects. Since her retirement, she has been active in health policy issues, particularly the war on smoking.

COURTNEY McKNIGHT is the assistant director of Research for the Baron Edmond de Rothschild Chemical Dependency Institute located at the Beth Israel Medical Center (New York). Mr. McKnight has written extensively about harm reduction and has given numerous presentations dealing with this topic.

JUDITH G. MCMULLEN is a graduate of Yale Law School, who joined the faculty in 1987 and teaches in the areas of family law, trusts and estates, and property. Her articles on family and children's issues have appeared in the *University of Michigan Journal of Law Reform*, the *Indiana Law Review*, and other publications.

ADRIENNE B. MEJIA is affiliated with the Center for Tobacco Control Research and Education at the University of California, San Francisco. Ms. Mejia writes extensively about the promotion and potential problems associated with smokeless tobacco.

ETHAN NADELMANN is the founder and executive director of the Drug Policy Alliance, the leading organization in the United States promoting alternatives to the war on drugs. Nadelmann received his B.A., J.D., and Ph.D. from Harvard, and a master's degree in international relations from the London School of Economics. In 1994, Nadelmann founded the Lindesmith Center, a drug policy institute created with the philanthropic support of George Soros. In 2000, the growing center merged with another organization to form the Drug Policy Alliance, which advocates for drug policies grounded in science, compassion, health, and human rights.

NATIONAL INSTITUTE ON DRUG ABUSE (NIDA) has at its mission led our nation in bringing the power of science to bear on drug abuse and addiction.

PEARL P. NYI is a clinical pharmacist with Long Beach (California) Memorial Medical Center. In addition to writing about *Salvia divinorum*, Ms. Nyi has also published in the *American Journal of Health-Systems Pharmacy*.

LYNN M. PALTROW is the founder and executive director of National Advocates for Pregnant Women. A graduate of New York University School of Law, Ms. Paltrow has worked for leading reproductive rights organizations including the ACLU's Reproductive Freedom Project and the Center for Reproductive Law and Policy. In her current position, she works to secure the human and civil rights, health, and welfare of all women, focusing particularly on pregnant and parenting women and those who are most vulnerable—low-income women, women of color, and drug-using women.

DAVID PURCHASE is an advocate for syringe exchange programs. He is affiliated with the North American Syringe Exchange Network in Tacoma, Washington.

PETER J. ROGERS is a professor of Biological Psychology at Bristol University. He has degrees in biology (B.Sc.) and experimental psychology (M.Sc.) from the University of Sussex (1972–1976) and a Ph.D. on eating behavior from the University of Leeds. Rogers is a Chartered Psychologist, a Fellow of the British Psychological Society, and a Registered Nutritionist.

MARSHA ROSENBAUM is director of the Safety First Project and director of the San Francisco office of the Drug Policy Alliance. She received her doctorate in medical sociology from the University of California at San Francisco in 1979. From 1977 to 1995, Rosenbaum was the principal investigator on National Institute on Drug Abuse–funded studies of heroin addiction, methadone maintenance treatment, MDMA (Ecstasy), cocaine, and drug use during pregnancy. She is the author of three books: *Women on Heroin*, *Pursuit of Ecstasy: The MDMA Experience* (with Jerome E. Beck), and *Pregnant Women on Drugs: Combating Stereotypes and Stigma* (with Sheigla Murphy).

CARRIE RUXTON is a dietitian with a Ph.D. in child nutrition. She heads her own nutritional consulting firm called Nutrition Communications. She has helped companies develop healthy, innovative food and beverage products. Dr. Ruxton has written for numerous magazines and newspapers, and appeared on a number of radio and television programs. She consults with the Scottish National Health Service and is on the Scottish Food Advisory Committee, which advises the Scottish Food Standards Agency.

MARSHA SILVERBERG is an economist with the Institute of Education Services, located in Washington, D.C. In addition to studying mandatory random drug testing of students, Silverberg has studied the impact of charter schools and the District of Columbia Opportunity Scholarship program.

D. DWAYNE SIMPSON is the emeritus director Institute of Behavioral Research at Texas Christian University. Simpson has more than 300 publications and his research focused on drug addiction and treatment. He has also researched client functioning and service delivery process, and how these factors influence treatment engagement and retention rates, stages of recovery, and long-term outcomes. Simpson has been an advisor to national and international research centers and government organizations that address drug treatment and related policy issues and a fellow in the American Psychological Association and American Psychological Society.

RODNEY SKAGER retired as a professor of education psychology from UCLA. He also served as the director of the California Attorney General's annual Survey of Student Substance Use in California Public Schools. Professor Skager published extensively on prevention policy, comparative studies of national drug policies, and treatment and recovery from alcohol and illicit drug abuse and was a member of the Board of Directors for the national therapeutic community Phoenix House in California. Professor Skager earned his graduate degrees at the University of California at Los Angeles.

BRENDA SMITH is a professor of social work at the University of Alabama at Tuscaloosa. She received her Ph.D. from the University of Chicago. Professor Smith's research interests include child welfare services and policy, frontline practice in human service organizations, service delivery in substance abuse treatment, and women and social policy.

JACOB SULLUM is a senior editor for *Reason* magazine. He writes on public policy issues, including freedom of speech, criminal justice, and education. His work has appeared in *The Wall Street Journal*, *The New York Times*, and the *Los Angeles Times*. In 1988, he won the Keystone Award for investigative reporting. He has been a fellow of the Knight Center for Specialized Journalism.

MARK F. TESTA is a professor at the University of North Carolina (Chapel Hill) School of Social Work. He is the first Sandra Reeves Spears and John B. Turner Distinguished Professor. Professor Testa is a nationally recognized child welfare expert and the architect of innovative reforms in the fields of child protection and foster care.

JAN TODD is a professor in the Department of Kinesiology and Health Education at The University of Texas at Austin. She and her husband, Terry Todd, are the founders and codirectors of the H. J. Lutcher Stark Center for Physical Culture and Sports, which contains the largest archive in the world devoted to the study of physical fitness, resistance training, and alternative medicine. She set world records in five bodyweight classes during her 12-year powerlifting career and was the first woman inducted into the International Powerlifting Hall of Fame.

TERRY TODD authored five books and more than 400 articles in both popular and academic publications, including *Sports Illustrated*, *Readers' Digest*, the *Journal of Sport History*, *Men's Journal*, and the *National Strength and Conditioning Association Journal*. He has appeared many times on such shows as the McNeil/Lehrer News Hour, the Today Show, Good Morning America, Nightline, ABC Nightly News, CBS Evening News, NBC Nightly News, and CNN News. He regularly serves as a consultant on sport and performance-enhancing drugs.

GILSKY I. TORRECER is the pharmacy manager with Dominick's Pharmacy in Chicago, Illinois.

JOHN W. TOUMBOUROU is associate professor at the Department of Paediatrics, University of Melbourne, and a senior researcher at the Center for Adolescent Health. He is a founding member and outgoing Chair of the College of Health Psychologists within the Australian Psychological Society. Professor Toumbourou is a principal investigator on a number of studies investigating healthy youth development including the Australian Temperament Project (investigating the role of childhood temperament and behavior in the prediction of adolescent substance use, delinquency, and depression), and the International Youth Development study (a collaborative longitudinal study with the University of Washington).

U.S. DEPARTMENT OF HEALTH AND HUMAN SERVICES is the U.S. government's principal agency for protecting the health of all Americans and providing essential human services, especially for those who are least able to help themselves.

ANJULI VERMA is the Public Education Coordinator at the ACLU Drug Law Reform Project (DLRP), located in Santa Cruz, California. She creates and executes public education campaigns around the DLRP's litigation and is active in national ACLU campaigns to defend and disband regional narcotics task forces, expose drug laws' disproportionate impact on women and families, especially in communities of color, and educate the rave and other music communities about their rights.

GEORGE WOODY is a professor in the Department of Psychiatry at the University of Pennsylvania School of Medicine. He received his medical degree from Temple University. Dr. Woody has worked on the DSM-IV Work Group on Substance Use Disorders and the Drug Abuse Advisory Committee for the U.S. Food and Drug Administration. He was a founding member of the Board of Addiction Psychiatry of the American Psychiatric Association and a member of the Institute of Medicine (IOM) committees on future directions for alcohol research and future directions for drug abuse research. He has studied the efficacy of psychosocial and pharmacological treatments for addiction, the relationship between drugs of abuse, psychiatric symptoms, and treatment outcome and risk factors for HIV infection among persons who abuse drugs.

GRAZYNA ZAJDOW is a senior lecturer at Deakin University. Dr. Zajdow's expertise is in sociology of alcohol and drug use and women's experiences with alcoholic families.